Pre-Calculus
Mathematics

The Addison-Wesley Mathematics Series

Pre-Calculus Mathematics

Merrill E. Shanks

Charles R. Fleenor

Charles F. Brumfiel

Addison-Wesley Publishing Company

Menlo Park, California   •   Reading, Massachusetts
London • Amsterdam • Don Mills, Ontario • Sydney

To E. and to V.

Books in the *Addison-Wesley Mathematics Series*

ALGEBRA
R. Johnson, L. Lendsey, W. Slesnick

GEOMETRY
E. Moise, F. Downs

ALGEBRA AND TRIGONOMETRY
R. Johnson, L. Lendsey, W. Slesnick, G. Bates

PRE-CALCULUS MATHEMATICS
M. Shanks, C. Fleenor, C. Brumfiel

**ELEMENTS OF CALCULUS AND
ANALYTIC GEOMETRY**
G. Thomas, R. Finney

Photo Credits

The Bettmann Archive Inc.: 15, 127, 155, 183, 229, 263L, 335, 355, 389, 505
Culver Pictures: 95, 263R, 437
Historical Pictures Service Inc.: 525
Wayland Lee*/Addison-Wesley Publishing Company: 473

*Photographs provided expressly for the publisher.

Cover Photo: © Manfred P. Kage/Peter Arnold, Inc.

Copyright © 1981 by Addison-Wesley Publishing Company, Inc. All rights reserved. No part of this publication may be reproduced, stored in a retrieval system, or transmitted, in any form or by any means, electronic, mechanical, photocopying, recording, or otherwise, without the prior written permission of the publisher. Printed in the United States of America. Published simultaneously in Canada.

ISBN 0-201-07684-5
   BCDEFGHIJKL-VH-887654321

PREFACE

Pre-Calculus Mathematics covers topics which traditionally follow an intermediate algebra course. The topics in this text are arranged in two broad parts.

Part I covers the elementary functions. These include polynomial, exponential, logarithmic and trigonometric (or circular) functions and their combinations. A chapter on functions on the natural numbers covers sequences, series, and combinatorial problems. The final chapter of Part I gives a brief but valuable introduction to differential and integral calculus.

Part II contains a full treatment of plane and space analytic geometry including vectors. The usual work with lines and planes is presented as well as material dealing with conic sections, other coordinate systems, and parametric representation of curves and surfaces.

Teachers familiar with previous editions of *Pre-Calculus Mathematics* will note many significant changes in this revision. Among these changes is a revision of the problem sets, which now include many new exercises. The problems are grouped into three sets.

Set A problems are relatively easy or demand little more than straightforward computation but cover most of the basic material.

Set B problems are somewhat more difficult than Set A. Average students should be assigned these exercises.

Set C problems are usually more difficult and often call for proofs. Better students should be assigned selected problems in this set.

A new feature of this edition is Calculator Problems at the end of every problem set. These problems provide an opportunity for the student to work with equations and interesting applications that would be numerically cumbersome without the calculator.

In this revision of Pre-Calculus Mathematics we have assumed that students will have access to hand-held calculators with trigonometric, exponential and logarithmic functions. As a consequence, material on computation with logarithms and interpolation of tables appears only in the Appendix.

As before, features of the book are clear definitions, logical development, chapter summaries and chapter tests. Historical notes are given that illuminate the development of mathematical concepts. Because progress in mathematics is highly dependent on ability to read, we have promoted this skill. The text is meant to be *read*. Attention is given to proofs, since this text is more than a source of formulas to be applied to problems.

We are greatly indebted to our friends and colleagues at Ball State University where the original material was extensively tested. Finally we owe much to many teachers and students who, by their insistence on clarity of concept, have guided our exposition.

M.E.S., C.R.F., C.F.B
January 2, 1980

TO THE STUDENT

With this book you are beginning a study of mathematics that thoroughly combines algebra and geometry. Since functions are the foundations of calculus, this text has been specifically designed to give you an understanding of the so-called elementary functions. Thus polynomial, rational, exponential, logarithmic, and trigonometric (or circular) functions, as well as some of their properties and graphs, are discussed in detail.

Since many of the important properties of functions have a strong geometric flavor, we have included the geometric interpretation of ideas that actually involve only numbers and their relations. This interplay between number and geometry, frequently called "analytic geometry," has many different aspects and ramifications. In this text we combine the properties of numbers and number systems with the properties of lines, triangles, circles, etc. which were deduced from a few postulated proper-

ties. In spite of this step, no new postulates are needed, since the development of each topic is based on the known properties of numbers and the known theorems of geometry. Thus proofs will rest, as always, on postulates, previous theorems, definitions, and logic. However, quite a few proofs will be given in sketchy form, and you will be asked to supply most of the missing details.

Each dot pattern design used on the chapter opening pages and on the cover is based on a simple modular design generated by computer. Sometimes the overall pattern is created by altering this design with reflections or turns of the module. For other patterns the basic module is set in different positions, reflected, distorted, etc. according to a random number program in the computer. All designs are the work of James R. Warner and Richard J. Yuskaitis of Precision Visuals, Boulder, Colorado.

Good luck!
The Authors

CONTENTS

Part I Functions

Chapter 1 Real Numbers and Coordinates

Chapter 2 Functions and Their Graphs

Chapter 3 Polynomials

Chapter 4 Exponential and Logarithmic Functions

Part I
Functions

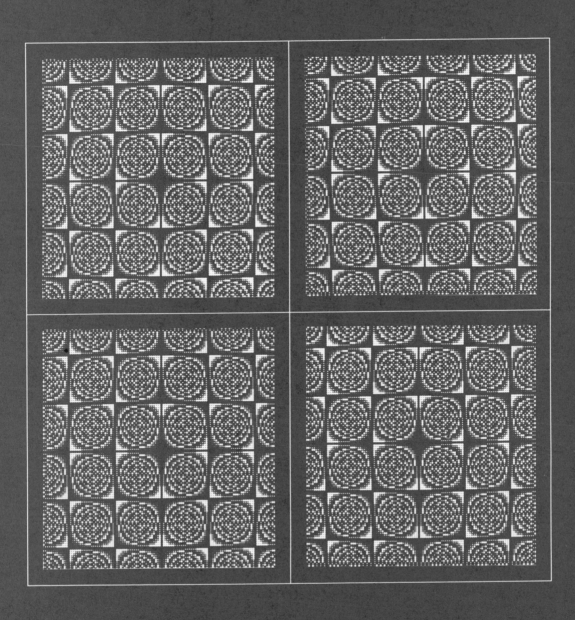

Chapter 1
Real Numbers and Coordinates

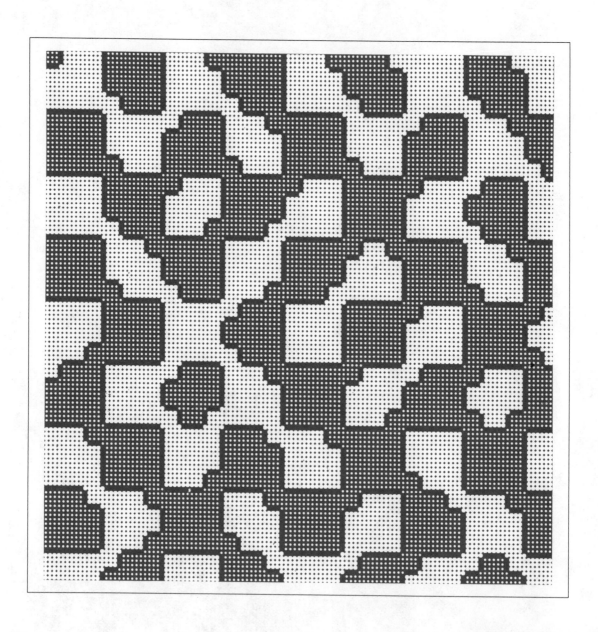

1–1   Introduction

Most of your work in previous courses in mathematics has been concerned with the structure and properties of the *real number system*. You will recall that real numbers are numbers that can be represented by decimals which may be terminating, repeating, or nonrepeating. Some examples of real numbers are given below.

$$1 = 1.0 \qquad\qquad \tfrac{1}{3} = 0.333\ldots \qquad\qquad \sqrt{3} = 1.73205\ldots$$

$$\pi = 3.141592\ldots \qquad\qquad -2\tfrac{1}{4} = -2.25 \qquad\qquad 10^{100}$$

$$\sqrt[3]{51} = 3.7084\ldots \qquad\qquad \sqrt[7]{-100} = -1.93069\ldots$$

In this chapter we shall be primarily concerned with the relationship between the set of real numbers and the points on a line. The fact that there is a one-to-one correspondence between the set of real numbers and the points on a line enables us to establish a coordinate system on a line. We can then extend this idea to establish a coordinate system in the plane and, eventually, use a coordinate system to describe any point in space.

1–2   The Real Number Field

The basic axioms for the real number system come in three parts. First are the *field* axioms, for the real numbers are an example of a field. Second are the *order* axioms, for the real numbers are ordered. And finally there is the *completeness* axiom which ensures that we have all the numbers we need.

The Field Axioms

EXISTENCE AND UNIQUENESS OF SUMS AND PRODUCTS (CLOSURE)

> *For all real numbers a and b, $a + b$ and ab are unique real numbers.*

COMMUTATIVE PRINCIPLES

> *For all real numbers a and b,*

$$a + b = b + a \qquad \text{and} \qquad ab = ba.$$

ASSOCIATIVE PRINCIPLES

For all real numbers, a, b, and c,

$$(a + b) + c = a + (b + c)$$

and

$$(ab)c = a(bc).$$

IDENTITY ELEMENTS

The numbers 0 and 1 are the additive and multiplicative identity elements, respectively; that is, for all real numbers a,

$$a + 0 = a \quad \text{and} \quad a \cdot 1 = a.$$

INVERSE ELEMENTS

Each real number a has an additive inverse, $-a$, such that

$$a + (-a) = 0.$$

Each real number a, except 0, has a multiplicative inverse, a^{-1}, such that

$$a \cdot a^{-1} = 1.$$

DISTRIBUTIVE PRINCIPLE

For all real numbers, a, b, and c,

$$a(b + c) = (ab) + (ac).$$

Remarks

1. The multiplicative inverse of the non-zero real number a may be written $1/a$.

2. The computational rules for addition, subtraction, multiplication, and division of real numbers can be justified by means of the axioms given, and we assume that the reader is familiar with these algebraic matters.

Any set of objects for which these axioms hold is called a *field,* and there are many different fields. What characterizes the real number field **R** are the order and completeness axioms.

R is an ordered field. This means there are the relations *is less than, is equal to,* and *is greater than* $(<, =, >)$ between pairs of real numbers such that the following properties hold.

The Order Axioms

TRICHOTOMY PROPERTY

For all real numbers a and b, exactly one of the following relations is true:

$$a < b, \quad a = b, \quad a > b.$$

That is, a is less than b, a is equal to b, or a is greater than b.

TRANSITIVE PROPERTY

For all real numbers a, b, and c,

$$\text{if } a < b \quad \text{and} \quad b < c, \qquad \text{then} \quad a < c.$$

ADDITIVE PROPERTY

For all real numbers a, b, and c,

$$\text{if } a < b, \qquad \text{then} \quad a + c < b + c.$$

MULTIPLICATIVE PROPERTY

For all real numbers a, b, and for all real numbers c > 0,

$$\text{if } a < b, \qquad \text{then} \quad ac < bc.$$

Remark

3. The positive numbers are the numbers that are greater than 0. That is, x is *positive* if and only if $x > 0$, and x is *negative* if and only if $x < 0$. Then if x is not 0, either x is positive or $-x$ is positive.

The Completeness Axiom

The ordered field R is complete. This means that if S is a non-empty set of real numbers such that, for some number M,

$$x \leq M \qquad \text{for all } x \text{ in } S,$$

then there is a least real number L such that

$$x \leq L \qquad \text{for all } x \text{ in } S.$$

The number M is called an *upper bound* of S. The number L is called the *least upper bound* of the set S. We write

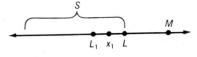

FIGURE 1

$$L = \text{lub } S.$$

That L is as small as possible means that if $L_1 < L$, then there is at least one number, say x_1, in S such that $L_1 < x_1 \leq L$, as shown in Fig. 1.

Remarks

4. For sets bounded below, one has lower bounds and a *greatest lower bound* abbreviated "glb."

5. The order axioms and the completeness axiom, which are expressed in a purely algebraic, or arithmetic, manner, permit one to assign coordinates to lines, where the order relation is a purely geometric concept. The completeness property ensures that there are no "gaps" in the real numbers; or, speaking geometrically, that there are no "holes" in the line.

It is the completeness property which supplies a basis for proving that certain real numbers exist. For illustration, consider the following example.

Example 1 Let S be the set of all real numbers x such that $x^3 < 2$. Then S is bounded above, for certainly 2 itself is an upper bound of S. (There are other upper bounds; for example, 5, 10,000, 1.5, etc.) From the completeness property, there is a *least* real number L such that if x is in S, then $x \leq L$. Furthermore, there are numbers in S arbitrarily close to L but less than L.

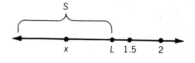

FIGURE 2

It should be clear that $L^3 = 2$, although a proof is not so easy as might be expected. In other words $L = \sqrt[3]{2}$.

Definition 1-1 If x is a non-zero real number, then the *absolute value* of x, denoted by $|x|$, is the positive number of the pair x and $-x$. The absolute value of 0 is simply 0; that is, $|0| = 0$.

Example 2 $|-5| = 5$, $|2.7| = 2.7$, $|4 - 9| = 5$

   3 If $|x| = 6$, then either $x = 6$ or $-x = 6$. Hence $x = 6$ or $x = -6$.

   4 If $|x| \leq 2$, then $x \leq 2$ and $-x \leq 2$. Multiplying each side of the latter inequality by -1 we have $x \geq -2$. Therefore $-2 \leq x \leq 2$.

Problems

Set A

Which of the field axioms is illustrated by each statement?

1. $129 \cdot 37 = 37 \cdot 129$

2. $\sqrt{2} + \sqrt{3}$ is a real number

3. $3(x + 4) = 3x + 12$

4. $(\frac{1}{2} + \frac{1}{4}) + \frac{1}{3} = \frac{1}{2} + (\frac{1}{4} + \frac{1}{3})$

5. There is a real number x such that $1.8397x = 1$.

Use the distributive principle to multiply the following.

6. $x(x + 1)$

7. $3x(2x - 5)$

8. $(x + 2)(x - 2)$

9. $(2x + 1)(3x + 5)$

Give the multiplicative inverse of the following.

10. 5 **11.** $\frac{1}{3}$ **12.** -0.7 **13.** $\sqrt{3}$

14. Consider the set of all real numbers x such that $x < 7$.

    (a) Is 10 an upper bound of the set?
    (b) Is 6.999 an upper bound of the set?
    (c) What is the least upper bound of the set?

Express the following without absolute value signs.

15. $|-9|$ **16.** $|-\sqrt{5}|$ **17.** $|0.3|$

18. $|x|$ if $x > 0$ **19.** $|x|$ if $x < 0$ **20.** $|x^2|$

Set B

Solve the following inequalities.

21. $x + 6 < 1$

22. $3x + 2 < 5$

23. $2y + 21 < y - 4 - 4y$

24. $x \leq -2x$

25. $(x - 1)(x - 3) > 0$

26. $(x - 1)(x - 3) \leq 0$

Solve.

27. $|x| = 5$

28. $|x| \leq 4$

29. $|x - 1| < 10$

30. $|x| > 2.5$

31. $|x - 2| \leq 1$

32. $|x| \leq 0$

33. Find lub S for the set of numbers S, where $n = 1, 2, \ldots$, if

$$S = \left\{ 1 - \frac{1}{1}, 1 - \frac{1}{2}, \ldots, 1 - \frac{1}{n}, \ldots \right\},$$

$$n = 1, 2, \ldots$$

Set C

34. Show that if $x + z < y + z$, then $x < y$.
[*Hint:* Use the additive property with $-z$.]

35. Show that if $x < y$ and $z < 0$ then $xz > yz$.
[*Hint:* If $z < 0$, $-z > 0$. Use the multiplicative property with $-z$.]

36. Show that $|x|^2 = x^2$ for all real numbers.

37. Is $|xy| = |x| \cdot |y|$ for all real numbers? Explain.

Calculator Problem

Let S be the set of all real numbers x such that $x^2 < 7$. Show by computing that each number below is in S.

(a) 2.6

(b) 2.64

(c) 2.645

(d) 2.6457

(e) 2.64575

(f) 2.645751

(g) Show that 2.65 is an upper bound of S.

(h) Find a smaller upper bound of S than 2.65.

(i) What is lub S?

1-3   The Real Number Line

The basic relation between the field of real numbers and geometry is that given by a coordinate system on a line. You are familiar with this idea from working with "number lines" in previous math courses. For each number x there corresponds a unique point P_x on the line. Figure 3 shows some points corresponding to the rational numbers $-2, -1, -\frac{1}{3}, 0, 1, \frac{3}{2}, 2, \frac{11}{4}$.

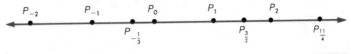

FIGURE 3

It is natural to suppose that the points corresponding to the rational numbers comprise *all* points on the line. However, even after all rational numbers have been assigned points on the number line, there are still points left over that correspond to the irrational numbers.

We will accept as a fundamental postulate of geometry the idea that there is a one-to-one correspondence of the real numbers onto all points of the line. This correspondence pairs each real number x with a unique point P_x on the line—on the positive side of P_0 if $x > 0$, and on the negative side if $x < 0$, such that

$$\text{distance } P_x P_{x'} = |P_x P_{x'}| = |x - x'|. \tag{1}$$

Furthermore, the order of the points P_x, P_y, P_z on the line is the same as the order of the real numbers x, y, z. That is, if $x < y < z$, then P_y is between P_x and P_z.

Definition 1-2 A *coordinatization* of (or a *coordinate system* on) a line is a one-to-one correspondence between the real numbers and the points of the line with the property described in equation (1). A line with such a correspondence is called a *coordinate line*.

Remark There are many coordinate systems on a line because several choices are available, and a decision must be made about (a) an origin P_0, (b) a unit of length, (c) one side of P_0 as the positive side.

To *graph a real number* x on a coordinate line is to mark on the line, as closely as you can, the point P_x corresponding to x. We say that x is the coordinate of P_x. For brevity we shall often refer simply to "the point x" when we mean the point P_x.

Usually, instead of indicating the point corresponding to x by P, it is simpler just to write the numeral next to the point to which P corresponds, as in Fig. 4.

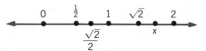

FIGURE 4

Example 1 If $x = -5$ and $x' = 6$, then distance $P_x P_{x'} = |-5 - 6| = 11$.

2 The solution of the inequality $|x - 1| < \frac{1}{2}$ is the set of real numbers x satisfying $\frac{1}{2} < x < \frac{3}{2}$. The graph of this set on a coordinate line is an interval that can be shown as in Fig. 5.

FIGURE 5

FIGURE 6

If the inequality were $|x - 1| \leq \frac{1}{2}$ instead of $|x - 1| < \frac{1}{2}$, the graph of the solution could be indicated by using solid dots at the ends of the interval (Fig. 6).

Often it is useful to be able to speak of the directed distance from a first point to a second on a coordinate line. All we need do is use the difference of the coordinates.

Definition 1-3 The *directed distance* from P_x to $P_{x'}$ is denoted by $P_x P_{x'}$, and is given by $P_x P_{x'} = x' - x$.

The directed distance is a positive number if $P_{x'} \neq P_x$ and if $P_{x'}$ is on the positive ray from P_x; otherwise it is negative or 0. Observe that it is the first coordinate that is subtracted from the second.

Example 3 The directed distance from P_9 to P_2 is $2 - 9 = -7$.

4 The directed distance from P_2 to P_9 is $9 - 2 = 7$.

Problems

Set A

Find $|P_x P_{x'}|$ for each pair of numbers.

1. $x = 6$, $x' = 10$

2. $x = -1$, $x' = 3$

3. $x = 4.9$, $x' = -3.1$

4. $x = \frac{1}{2}$, $x' = -\frac{1}{2}$

5. $x = 0$, $x' = -10$

6. $x = -20$, $x' = -19$

Find the directed distance from P_x to $P_{x'}$.

7. $x = -3$, $x' = 6$

8. $x = 6$, $x' = -3$

9. $x = -2$, $x' = -7$

10. $x = -4\frac{1}{2}$, $x' = -\frac{1}{2}$

11. $x = 7.1$, $x' = 0$

12. $x = \sqrt{3} - 2$, $x' = 2\sqrt{3} - 1$

On a coordinate line graph the solutions of the following inequalities.

13. $x > \frac{2}{3}$

14. $x < -2$

15. $x > 1$ or $x < 0$

16. $x < 1$ or $x > 0$

17. $x < 1$ and $x > 0$

18. $x(x - 1) < 0$

19. $x(x - 1) > 0$

20. $x(x - 2)(x + 2) < 0$

On a coordinate line graph the solutions of the following sentences.

21. $x \leq -1$ or $x \geq 1$

22. $x < 5$ and $x > -2$

23. $|x - 2| = 6$

24. $|x - 2| < 6$

25. $|x - 2| > 6$

26. $-4 \leq x \leq -1$

27. $|x| < 1$

28. $|x| < 1/x$

Set B

29. Suppose the coordinates of A, B, and C are a, b, and c, respectively, and B is between A and C. If D is a point such that $|AC| = |BD|$, show that the coordinate of D is $b - (c - a)$ or $b + (c - a)$.

30. A, B, and C are points on a coordinate line with coordinates a, b, and c.
(a) Prove that $AB + BC + CA = 0$.
(b) Can $|AB| + |BC| + |CA| = 0$?

31. A and B are points on a line with coordinates 6 and 14, respectively. Show that 10 is the coordinate of a point C equidistant from A and B.

32. A and B are points on a line with coordinates -7 and 9, respectively. Determine the coordinate of a point C such that $|AC| = |BC|$.

33. Let A, B, and C be points on a line with coordinates -6, -2, and 3, respectively. Determine the possible coordinates of a point D if $|AC| = |BD|$.

Set C

34. Prove that if x and x' are the coordinates of the endpoints of $\overline{P_x P_{x'}}$, then the coordinate of the midpoint of the segment is $\dfrac{x + x'}{2}$.

[*Hint:* Show that the directed distance from P_x to the midpoint is equal to the directed distance from the midpoint to $P_{x'}$.

35. Show that $|x - a| < 3$ is equivalent to $a - 3 < x < a + 3$. Then graph the solution.

36. Using a coordinate system, argue geometrically that

$$|x - y| \le |x - z| + |z - y|.$$

[*Hint:* Consider the possible orders of P_x, P_y, P_z.]

37. Use the result of Problem 36 to show that $|x + y| \le |x| + |y|$.

Calculator Problem

Let S be the set of real numbers x such that

$$x = \left(1 + \frac{1}{n}\right)^n \qquad \text{where } n = 1, 2, 3, 4, \ldots.$$

(a) Find values of x for the following values of n: 1, 2, 3, 4, 5, 6, 7, 8, 9, 10, 10^2, 10^3, 10^4.

(b) Does the set S seem to have an upper bound? Give a decimal approximation of lub S.

The set S is bounded above and by the Completeness Axiom must have a least upper bound. The least upper bound of S is an important number in mathematics and is denoted by the letter e. The number e is the base of natural logarithms. $e \doteq 2.71828$.

1-4   Coordinatization of a Plane

We shall now use coordinate systems on lines to define coordinate systems in the plane. Given a plane, a number of choices must be made.

Let us choose a point 0 in the plane, called the *origin of coordinates.* Next we select two *perpendicular* lines through 0. Then we choose positive sides of 0 on these two lines and decide on a unit length. We choose one line, call it the *first axis,* and call the other the *second axis.* Our next step is to coordinatize* each of the axes, with the point 0 as origin, P_0, for each coordinate system.

We now consider an arbitrary point P and the (unique) lines through P parallel to the axes. (These parallels might coincide with an axis if P is on an axis.) The line through P parallel to the second axis will intersect the first axis at a point corresponding to some real number a. This number is called the *first coordinate* (or *abscissa*) of P. The line through P parallel to the first axis will intersect the second axis at a point corresponding to some real number b.

---

*Ordinarily we use the same unit segment for both axes, but this is not necessary in order to set up a coordinate system on a plane.

This number is called the *second coordinate* of P (or *ordinate*). The real numbers a and b are the coordinates of P, and we indicate the point and coordinates by P(a, b), or by (a, b). In Fig. 7 the point P(−2, 3) is plotted.

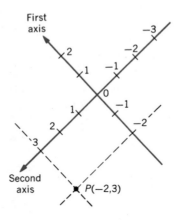

FIGURE 7

Definition 1-4

A *coordinate system on the plane* is a one-to-one correspondence between the set of ordered pairs of real numbers and the set of points in the plane, as constructed above.

Remarks

1. Frequently we shall refer to the ordered pair of real numbers (a, b) as a point.

2. To *plot a point,* with given coordinates, in the coordinate plane is to mark on your paper as nearly as possible the point with the given coordinates.

3. Usually one gives names to the two axes related to the variables that are used to denote the coordinates. Thus, if we use x to denote any first coordinate, it is convenient to call the first axis the x-axis. And so if y denotes any second coordinate, we call the second axis the y-axis. In this way it becomes natural to speak of the x- and y-coordinates of a point. Because the axes were chosen to be perpendicular, the coordinates, x and y, of a point (x, y) are called *rectangular coordinates,* and the coordinate system is called a *rectangular coordinate system.* Since we have called the axes the x-axis and y-axis, we call the plane the *xy-plane.*

Of course there is nothing special about the letters x and y. Any other letters would do as well. Furthermore, as indicated in Fig. 7, there is no single way to orient the axes in a plane. But one commonly finds the figure drawn so that, as one views the page, the positive x-axis is to the right and the positive y-axis upward.

4. The coordinate axes separate the plane into four sets of points, called *quadrants,* that are numbered I, II, III, and IV, as in Fig. 8. The first quadrant consists of the set of all points for which both coordinates are positive. The second quadrant consists of points whose first coordinate is negative and whose second coordinate is positive. Similar definitions are made for the other quadrants.

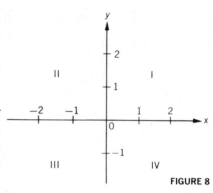

FIGURE 8

Problems

Set A

Plot the following points using the same coordinate axes.

1. $(3, 5)$ **2.** $(-4, 5)$ **3.** $(-3, -3)$

4. $(5, -1)$ **5.** $(0, 0)$ **6.** $(2.\overset{.}{5}, -3.5)$

7. $(0, -3)$ **8.** $(-6, 0)$ **9.** $\left(-\frac{3}{2}, \frac{7}{3}\right)$

10. $\left(\pi, \frac{\pi}{2}\right)$

11. $\left(-\frac{1}{\sqrt{2}}, \frac{1}{\sqrt{2}}\right)$

12. $\left(\frac{\sqrt{3}}{2}, -\frac{1}{2}\right)$

Give the quadrant number in which the point lines.

13. $(-\frac{1}{2}, 5)$ **14.** $(1.7, 3.4)$

15. $(-2, -5)$ **16.** $(1\frac{1}{4}, -3\frac{1}{2})$

17. (a, b) where $a < 0$ and $b > 0$

18. (c, d) where $c < 0$ and $d < 0$

19. Three of the vertices of a square are $(-1, 4)$, $(3, 3)$, and $(2, -1)$. Plot the points and determine the coordinates of the fourth vertex of the square.

20. Three vertices of a parallelogram are $(-2, 2)$, $(2, 3)$, and $(1, -1)$. Determine all possible locations for the remaining vertex.

Set B

21. A point is on the y-axis. What can you say about its x-coordinate? What can you say about its y-coordinate if the point is on the same side of the x-axis as $(5, -3)$?

22. A point is in the same half-plane determined by the x-axis as the point $(0, 1)$. What can you say about the y-coordinate of $P(x, y)$ in this half-plane?

23. A point is on a line that is parallel to the y-axis and passes through the point $(-2, 7)$. What is the x-coordinate of the point? Conversely, what is the set of all points (x, y) for which $x = -2$? What is the set of all points (x, y) for which $x = 0$? for which $x = \pi$?

24. A point $P(x, y)$ lies on a line parallel to, and 3 units from, the x-axis. What is an equation satisfied by the coordinates of P?

25. Give an algebraic definition for each of the four quadrants.

26. What is the distance between $(-1, 3)$ and $(-1, -4)$? between $(-1, a)$ and $(-1, a - 7)$? between $(-1, a)$ and $(-1, b)$?

27. Two points lie on a line parallel to the y-axis. Explain how to find the distance between them. What is a formula for this distance if the points are (x_1, y_1) and (x_1, y_2)?

Set C

28. What is the set of all points (x, y) for which $x + 2 < 0$? for which $x + 2 \leq 0$?

29. What is the set of all points (x, y) for which $x^2 > 0$?

30. Sketch the set of points (x, y) whose coordinates satisfy the following statement. $x = \pm 3$ and $-3 \leq y \leq 3$, or $-3 \leq x \leq 3$ and $y = \pm 3$, or $-2 < x < -1$ and $y = 2$, or $1 < x < 2$ and $y = 2$, or $x = \pm\frac{3}{2}$ and $1 < y < 2$, or $-1 < x < 1$ and $y = -1$, or $-2 < x < 2$ and $y = -2$.

31. Draw a graph of the set of points (x, y) whose coordinates satisfy the statement $|x| > 1$ or $|y| > 1$. Do the same for the statement $|x| < 1$ and $|y| < 1$.

32. It is not necessary, in coordinatizing the plane, to choose axes at right angles. Describe how one can assign coordinates for the plane using any two intersecting lines as axes.

Calculator Problem

Which number is the best approximation of π?

(a) $\frac{22}{7}$ (b) $\frac{355}{113}$ (c) $\sqrt{9.869}$ (d) $(1.4645)^3$

1-5   The Distance Formula

We shall see how to find the distance between two points $P(x_1, y_1)$ and $P(x_2, y_2)$ with given coordinates. We assume that $x_1 \neq x_2$, $y_1 \neq y_2$, and the same unit segment is chosen for both axes.

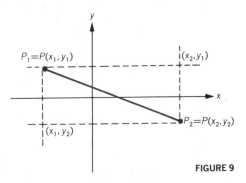

FIGURE 9

Consider the four lines through the two points and parallel to the two axes, as shown in Fig. 9. Two pairs of these will be parallel and the two pairs will intersect in the points (x_1, y_2) and (x_2, y_1). Then the two given points form a right triangle with either one of the points (x_1, y_2) or (x_2, y_1). The lengths of the sides of this triangle are $|x_1 - x_2|$ and $|y_1 - y_2|$. Finally, from the Pythagorean Theorem, we obtain

[distance from (x_1, y_1) to $(x_2, y_2)]^2 = |x_1 - x_2|^2 + |y_1 - y_2|^2$, or the desired *distance formula:*

$$|P_1P_2| = \sqrt{(x_1 - x_2)^2 + (y_1 - y_2)^2}.$$

(Remember that $\sqrt{a^2} = |a|$ for all real numbers a.)

Example   The distance between $(-3, -2)$ and $(-1, 5)$ is

$$\sqrt{(-3 + 1)^2 + (-2 - 5)^2} = \sqrt{53} \doteq 7.28.$$

Problems

Set A

Find the distance between the following.

1. $(2, 4)$ and $(-2, 1)$
2. $(5, 3)$ and $(-7, -2)$
3. $(0, 10)$ and $(-8, 4)$
4. $(4, -2)$ and $(4, -7)$
5. $(0, 0)$ and $(1, 1)$
6. $(0, 0)$ and $(-1, -1)$
7. $(0, 0)$ and $\left(\dfrac{1}{\sqrt{2}}, \dfrac{1}{\sqrt{2}}\right)$
8. $(1 - \sqrt{2}, 1 - \sqrt{3})$ and $(1 + \sqrt{2}, 1 + \sqrt{3})$
9. $(0, 0)$ and (a, b)
10. (a, b) and $(a + c, b + d)$

Set B

11. Show that the points $(-3, 1)$, $(2, 4)$, and $(0, -4)$ are vertices of a right triangle. What theorem from geometry must you use?

12. Is the point $(0, 4)$ inside or outside the circle of radius 4 with center at $(-3, 1)$? Draw a figure.

13. Determine y so that $(0, y)$ will be on the circle of radius 4 with center at $(-3, 1)$.

14. Show that a triangle whose vertices are $(0, 0)$, $(3, 3)$, $(7, 0)$ is congruent to a triangle whose vertices are $(0, 0)$, $(-3, -4)$, and $(-3, 3)$.

15. Show that the point $(3, \sqrt{7})$ is on a circle of radius 4 with center at the origin.

16. Using the circle of Problem 15, determine the coordinates of the point of intersection of the x-axis and the tangent to the circle through $(3, \sqrt{7})$.

17. Quadrilateral $ABCD$ has vertices at $A (-4, -3)$, $B (4, -1)$ $C (1, 3)$, and $D (-3, -3)$. What is the length of the longer diagonal of $ABCD$?

18. Show that $(0, 0)$, $(a, 0)$ and $\left(\dfrac{a}{2}, \dfrac{a\sqrt{3}}{2}\right)$ are the vertices of an equilateral triangle.

Set C

19. Show that the distance formula gives the correct number $|y_2 - y_1|$ as the distance between (x_1, y_1) and (x_1, y_2).

20. Show that if the line through (x_1, y_1) and (x_2, y_2) is perpendicular to the line through (x_1, y_1) and (x_3, y_3), then

$$(y_2 - y_1)(y_1 - y_3) + (x_2 - x_1)(x_1 - x_3) = 0.$$

21. Consider the circle of radius r with center at the origin. Show that if (x, y) is on this circle, then the line through $(-r, 0)$ and (x, y) is perpendicular to the line through (x, y) and $(r, 0)$. What theorem does this prove?

Calculator Problem

Triangle ABC has vertices at $(2, -2)$, $(3, 4)$, and $(-3, 2)$. Compute the perimeter of the triangle to the nearest hundredth of a unit.

Summary

1. The set of real numbers with the operations of addition and multiplication is a field. This means that both operations are associative and commutative, that there exist identity elements with respect to both operations, that each real number has an additive inverse, and that each non-zero real number has a multiplicative inverse. Finally, multiplication is distributive over addition.

2. The real numbers can be ordered; the real numbers form an ordered field.

3. The real number field is complete. This means that any non-empty subset of real numbers that has an upper bound must have a least upper bound.

4. There is a one-to-one correspondence between the real numbers and the points on a line. The distance between any two points is the absolute value of the difference of their corresponding coordinates.

5. There is a one-to-one correspondence between the set of ordered pairs of real numbers and the points in a plane. This correspondence enables us to coordinatize the plane with a rectangular coordinate system.

6. The distance between two points with coordinates (x_1, y_1) and (x_2, y_2) is

$$\sqrt{(x_1 - x_2)^2 + (y_1 - y_2)^2}.$$

Chapter 1   Test

1-2   **1.** Let S be the set of real numbers x such that $x^2 < 5$.

(a) Is 2 an upper bound of S?
(b) Is 3 an upper bound of S?
(c) What is lub S?

Write the following without absolute value signs.

2. $|-9|$

3. $|\frac{3}{2}|$

4. $|a|$ where $a < 0$

1-3   Give the distance between points on the real line with the given coordinates.

5. -3 and -5

6. 7 and -15

7. -10 and 10

Find the directed distance from P_x to $P_{x'}$.

8. $x = 3$, $x' = -6$

9. $x = 0.5$, $x' = -8.5$

10. $x = a$, $x' = b$

Show the graph of the solutions to the inequalities on a coordinate line.

11. $|x| < 4$

12. $|x| > 2$

13. $|x - 2| \leq 3$

1-4   **14.** A point lies on the x-axis. What is its y-coordinate?

15. In which quadrant does the point $(5, -3)$ lie?

16. Line s is parallel to the x-axis and contains the point $(5, 2)$. Line t is parallel to the y-axis and contains the point $(-4, -3)$. What are the coordinates of the point of intersection of s and t?

1-5   Find the distance between the two points in the coordinate plane.

17. $(-3, -1)$ and $(1, -4)$

18. $(1, 1)$ and $(-2, 4)$

19. (x_1, y_1) and (x_2, y_2)

20. Use the distance formula and the converse of the Pythagorean Theorem to show that $(3, 1)$, $(1, 2)$, and $(-1, -2)$ are vertices of a right triangle.

14   Real Numbers and Coordinates

Historical Note

René Descartes
(1596–1650)

Descartes was an important philosopher and mathematician. He is universally acclaimed as the founder of analytic geometry. His works in philosophy, principally *Discourse on Method*, have had lasting effect. Apparently, his philosophy was greatly influenced by the mathematics and science of his day, since he attempted to start with a minimum number of assumptions and build upon these logically.

The phrase, *Cogito ergo sum* (I think, therefore I am) expresses his goal of starting with experience.

His life overlapped those of several other intellectual giants. His contemporaries include Fermat, Pascal, Galileo, Newton, and Leibniz.

Descartes' one book on mathematics, *Geometry,* was published in 1637 as an appendix to the *Discourse on Method*. Its main purpose was to show how a systematic use of real-number coordinates could vastly simplify geometric arguments. By applying the techniques of algebra to geometry, he introduced a simple method of solution to a great variety of problems.

The idea of combining algebra and coordinates in geometry was not conceived by Descartes in a single stroke. It had been used previously in Greek geometry and by Pierre Fermat. However, Descartes was the first to assign unique coordinates to every point in the plane. His ideas contributed significantly to the advancement of physics and opened the door to the early invention of calculus by Isaac Newton in 1666 (and independently by Gottfried Leibniz a bit later).

Moreover, he greatly simplified algebraic notation, improving upon the already modern notation of Francois Viete.

Descartes was a prominent and worldly man of his times. His techniques of analytic geometry will certainly be significant in mathematics for many centuries.

Chapter 2
Functions and Their Graphs

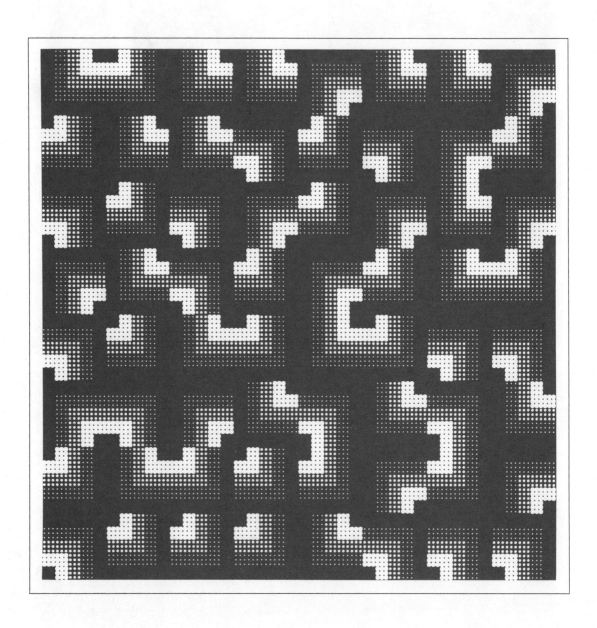

2-1   Introduction

One of the most important concepts in mathematics is the idea of a *function.* You will see that a function is a special relationship between the elements of two sets of objects. For example, the amount of gasoline used in a car is a function of the number of kilometers driven; your height is a function of your age in years; the circumference of a circle is a function of the radius of the circle.

You are already partly familiar with some of the special functions that are called *elementary functions,* and in succeeding chapters you will study these functions in detail. In this chapter you will study the definition of a function, special notation for functions, graphs and general properties of functions. You will also learn how functions can be combined to produce other functions.

2-2   Definition of Function

Functions can be defined in several equivalent ways, each of which has its own advantages. For each such definition there must be

(a) a set called the *domain,*
(b) a set called the *image set.*
(c) a *correspondence* or *association* between the elements of the two sets so that each element of the domain is paired with a *unique* element of the image set.

Definition 2-1   Let X and Y be any two sets. A *function F on X into Y* is a set of ordered pairs (x, y), where x is an element of X and y is an element of Y, such that for *each* x in X there is *exactly one* ordered pair (x, y) in F.

The set X in the definition above is called the *domain* of the function F. The set Y is the *image set.* The *range* of F is the set of all elements y for pairs (x, y) in F. If F is a function on X into Y, then the range is a subset of Y but need not be all of Y. If (x, y) is in F, then y is called the *value of F at x*, and is denoted by $F(x)$. We say that y is the *image* of x under the function F.

Example 1   Let $X = \{1, 2, 3, 4\}$ and $Y = \{a, b, c\}$. Let G be the set of ordered pairs $\{(1, a),\ (2, b),\ (3, a),\ (4, b)\}$. Then, by Definition 2–1, G is a function on X into Y. Note that the range of G is the set $\{a, b\}$, which is a proper subset of Y. (Fig. 1.)

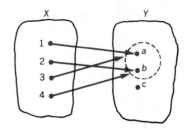

FIGURE 1

Definition 2–1 is closely related to the idea of a graph. Indeed, if X and Y are subsets of the set of real numbers, **R**, then the function can be identified with its graph (Fig. 2).

Example 2   Let $X = Y = \textbf{R}$, and let f be the set of all (x, y) such that $y = 2x - 1$. Then f is a function. The graph of f is shown in Fig. 2.

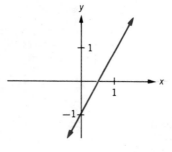

FIGURE 2

3   Let X be the set of topics listed in the index for a newspaper as shown above. Let Y be the corresponding page numbers in which these topics occur. Let I be the set of ordered pairs given by the index. Then I is *not* a function because there is not a *unique* element of Y for each element of X. For example, (Sports, 10) and (Sports, 11) are two different ordered pairs of I.

Figure 3 shows that a function may be regarded as a kind of machine that takes the elements of the domain X, processes them, and produces elements of the range.

When graphs of relations between ordered pairs of real numbers are given, there is an easy test to determine whether or not the graph represents a function. Any vertical line can

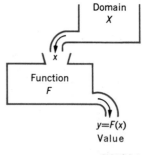

FIGURE 3

intersect the graph of a function in at most one point (Figs. 4 and 5).

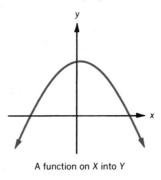

A function on X into Y

FIGURE 4

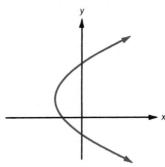

Not a function on X into Y

FIGURE 5

Problems

Set A

In Problems 1–8, $X = \{1, 2, 3, 4, 5\}$ and $Y = \{-2, -1, 0, 1, 2\}$. Which sets of ordered pairs are functions on X into Y?

1. $f = \{(1, 0), (2, -1), (3, 1), (4, -2), (5, 2)\}$

2. $g = \{(1, 1), (2, 1), (3, 1), (4, 1), (5, 1)\}$

3. $h = \{(1, 1), (2, 2), (3, 0), (4, 0), (5, 0)\}$

4. $F = \{(0, 1), (1, 2), (-1, 3), (2, 4), (-2, 5)\}$

5. $G = \{(1, -2), (2, -1), (3, 0), (1, 1), (2, 2)\}$

6. $H = \{(1, 2), (3, 0), (5, 2)\}$

7. $k = \{(1, -2), (2, 2), (4, 0), (5, 1), (6, -1)\}$

8. $p = \{(5, -2), (4, -1), (1, 0), (3, 1), (2, -1)\}$

9. The figure below illustrates a function on X into Y. What is the domain of the function? What is the range of the function? What is the image of -2? What is the image of 2?

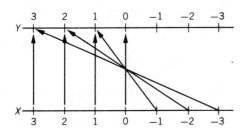

The figures below are subsets of a coordinate plane. Which are graphs of functions? Which appear to be graphs of functions with domain X equal to R? Which have range Y equal to R?

10.

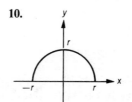

11.

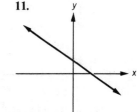

12.

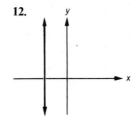

13.

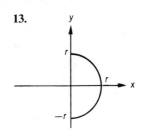

14.

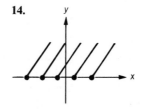

15.

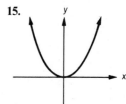

Set B

16. Explain how the students in your mathematics class and the grades they receive on a mathematics test can define a function.

17. Does the time of day and the length of your shadow suggest a function? Explain.

18. Let X be a set of parents and Y be the set of all children of the parents in X. Does the set of all (x, y) where x is a parent of y define a function?

19. Let $X = Y = \boldsymbol{R}$, and let f be the set of all (x, y) such that $y = 3x - 4$. Thus f is a function. What is y when $x = 1$? $x = 5$? $x = -4$? $x = 0$?

20. Let E be a function whose domain is the set of nonnegative integers, whose value is 1 at the odd integers, and whose value is 0 at the even integers. What is the value of the function at (1000)? at (999)? at $(2k + 1)$, where k is a nonnegative integer? What is the range of E?

Set C

Let $X = Y = \boldsymbol{R}$. Which of the following equations define a function on X into Y?

21. $x + 4y = 5$ **22.** $y = x^2$

23. $x = y^2$ **24.** $x^2 + y^2 = 25$

25. Describe a function for first class postage. What is the domain and range?

26. Describe a function that relates the length of the side of a square to its area.

27. Describe a function that relates the length of the edge of a cube to its volume.

28. Give examples of at least three functions that can be found in most daily newspapers.

Calculator Problem

Compute $\sqrt{2} - \sqrt[4]{3}$ on your calculator. Now define a function f as follows. If the digit in the kth decimal place of $\sqrt{2} - \sqrt[4]{3}$ is even, set $f(k) = 0$. If the digit is odd, set $f(k) = 1$. Find $f(1)$ through $f(7)$. What is the range of f?

2-3   Functions: Notation, Language, and Graphs

There is a wide variety of notation and language for functions with which you should become familiar.

A function f is often called a *mapping* or *transformation* because f "maps" or "transforms" x into y or $f(x)$, as indicated in Fig. 6. The mapping is symbolized in various ways:

$$f: X \rightarrow Y, \qquad f: x \rightarrow y, \qquad X \xrightarrow{f} Y,$$

$$x \xrightarrow{f} y, \qquad x \rightarrow f(x).$$

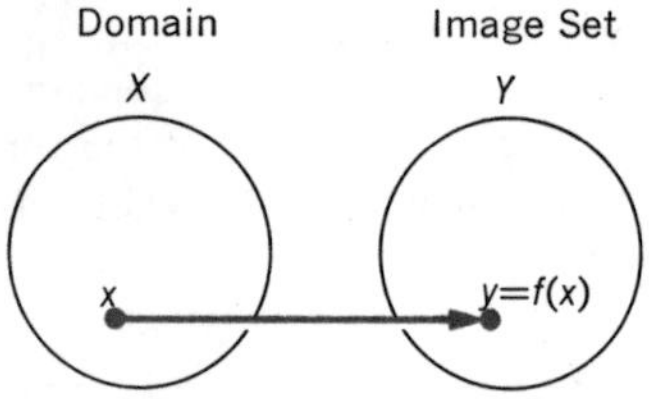

FIGURE 6

If f is a function mapping X into Y, and x is a variable representing elements of the domain, then x is called the *independent variable*. A variable y representing elements in the range of f is called the *dependent variable*. Sometimes a function is described as a process that assigns to each value of the independent variable a unique value of the dependent variable.

Although the descriptions of some functions are extremely complicated, the functions we shall study are given by simple *formulas*. If a function is to be determined by a formula, the domain of the function must be explicitly stated. In this text, unless otherwise stated, the domain will be some subset of the real numbers R.

Example 1

The function f is given by the formula $f(x) = 2x + 1$ for all x in R. The value of this function at $x = 2$ is 5 because $2 \cdot 2 + 1 = 5$. We write $f(2) = 5$. Also $f(0) = 1$, $f(-3) = -5$, $f(3) = 7$ and $f(-100) = -199$.

If a function has domain and range that are subsets of R, then the function has a graph that is a subset of the coordinate plane. The graph of the function f is shown by Fig. 7.

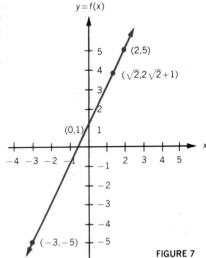

FIGURE 7

2

Suppose that F has domain R and is defined by the formula

$$F(x) = x^3 - 1, \qquad \text{for all } x \text{ in } R.$$

Then $F(0) = -1$, $F(1) = 0$, $F(10) = 999$, and $F(-10) = -1001$. A portion of the graph of F is shown in Fig. 8.

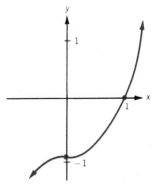

FIGURE 8

Remark

Note that in Examples 1 and 2 *portions* of the graphs are shown. If the domain of a function is "large," say the set of all real numbers, then obviously we cannot picture all the points on the graph. We must be content to show only a portion of the graph. The portion sketched depends upon our interests and the application of the function in question.

When we say, in the future, "the graph is shown," we shall mean that a *portion of the graph is shown—the interesting portion.*

When we say, "sketch the graph," we shall mean *sketch enough of the graph to see how the rest goes.*

Definition 2-2   If F is a function that maps X into Y, and every element y of Y is the image of at least one x in X, then F maps X *onto* Y. If F is an *onto mapping,* that is, F maps X onto Y, and if it is true that when x_1 and x_2 are distinct elements of X, $F(x_1) \neq F(x_2)$, then F is a *one-to-one mapping of X onto Y.*

In a one-to-one mapping, every element y of Y is equal to $f(x)$ for exactly one x in X.

Figure 9 shows a function h that maps X onto Y, but h is not a one-to-one mapping. Figure 10 shows a function g that maps X onto Y, and g is also a one-to-one mapping.

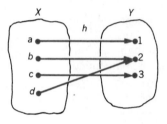

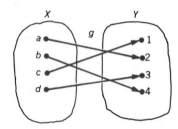

FIGURE 9   FIGURE 10

Definition 2-3   Two functions, f and g, are *equal* or *identical* if f and g have the same domain X and the same image set Y, and for each x in X, $f(x) = g(x)$.

Suppose f and g are defined as follows (see Fig. 11).

$$f(x) = |x|, \quad \text{for all } x,$$
$$g(x) = x, \quad \text{for all } x.$$

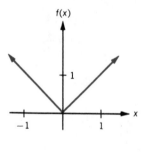

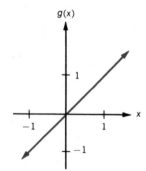

FIGURE 11

Then f and g are distinct functions, even though their graphs are identical over *part* of their domains. But even though $f(x) = g(x)$ for $x \geq 0$, f and g are not equal functions.

The function g shown in Fig. 11 is called the *identity function.* The identity function is sometimes denoted Id; that is, $\text{Id}(x) = x$ for all x in X.

A function F is a *constant function* if the range of F consists of a single element. That is, there is one element k in Y such that $F(x) = k$ for all x in X.

If F has domain R then the graph of F is a line parallel to the x-axis as shown in Fig. 12.

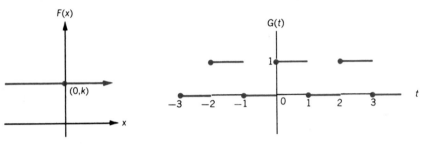

FIGURE 12   FIGURE 13

The function G maps R into R according to the formula

$$G(t) = 1, \quad \text{if } 2k \leq t < 2k + 1, \text{ where } k \text{ is an integer,}$$
$$G(t) = 0, \quad \text{otherwise.}$$

A portion of the graph of G is shown in Fig. 13. G is an example of a *step function*.

Problems

Set A

Given $f(x) = 4x - 3$ where $X = Y = R$, determine the following values.

1. $f(1)$ **2.** $f(3)$

3. $f(-2)$ **4.** $f(0)$

5. $f(-10)$ **6.** $f(7)$

7. $f(5) - f(4)$ **8.** $f(a)$

Given $g(x) = x^2 - x + 1$ where $X = Y = R$, determine the following values.

9. $g(1)$ **10.** $g(-1)$

11. $g(0)$ **12.** $g(5)$

13. $g(-5)$ **14.** $g(\frac{1}{2})$

15. $g(1.5)$ **16.** $g(-1.5)$

Draw the graphs of the following functions.

17. $F(x) = x^2$ for all real x

18. $G(x) = \frac{1}{2}x$ for $0 \leq x \leq 2$

19. $P(x) = \sqrt{x}$ for $0 \leq x \leq 9$

20. $H(x) = 1 - x^2$ for all x in R

21. $J(x) = x^2 - 1$ for all x in R

22. $B(x) = |x| - 2$ for $-3 \leq x \leq 3$

Set B

23. Let A be a function whose domain is the set of students in your mathematics class and whose value for each student is that student's age in years. Is A a constant function? Can you determine the range of A?

24. The function G is a one-to-one function and the domain of G contains exactly 10 elements. What can you conclude about the range of G?

25. Functions f and g are defined as follows

$$f(x) = \frac{x^2 - 1}{x - 1} \quad \begin{array}{l}\text{for all real } x \\ \text{except } x = 1.\end{array}$$

$$g(x) = x + 1 \qquad \text{for all } x \text{ in } \mathbf{R}.$$

Draw the graphs of f and g. Is $f = g$?

26. K is a constant function for all x in $\mathbf{R}$. $K(2) = -1$. What is $K(0)$?

27. If Id is the identity function for all x in $\mathbf{R}$, what is $\text{Id}(1 + \sqrt{2})$?

Set C

28. Draw the graph of the function f given by

$$f(x) = \sqrt{x^2 - 1} \qquad \text{for } |x| \geq 1.$$

29. Draw the graph of the function g given by

$$g(x) = \sqrt{4 - x^2} \qquad \text{for } |x| \leq 2.$$

30. What is the range of function g in Problem 29?

31. Sketch the graph of a function W defined as follows: the domain of W is the set of real numbers x such that $x \leq |a|$.

$$\begin{aligned} W(0) &= 0 \\ W(x) &= 1 \qquad \text{for } 0 < x < a/2 \\ W(a/2) &= \tfrac{1}{2} \\ W(x) &= 0 \qquad \text{for } a/2 < x \leq a \\ W(-x) &= -W(x) \end{aligned}$$

32. The *greatest integer function, G,* is defined as follows:

$$G(x) = \text{greatest integer} \leq x.$$

Then $G(3) = 3$, $G(-2) = -2$, $G(\pi) = 3$, $G(\tfrac{1}{2}) = 0$. A commonly used notation for this function is $G(x) = [x]$. Sketch the graph of G.

33. Sketch the graph of the function ψ given by

$$\psi(x) = (x - 10^{10})^2 + 1.$$

[*Hint:* Sketch only the *interesting* portion of the graph.]

Calculator Problem

A function f with domain $\mathbf{R}$ is given by the formula

$$f(x) = x^3 - 2.$$

The sketch of f at the right shows that the graph crosses the x-axis between $x = 1$ and $x = 2$.

For each value of x below tell whether $f(x)$ is positive or negative.

(a) 1.1   (b) 1.2   (c) 1.3

(d) 1.4   (e) 1.25   (f) 1.259

(g) 1.2599   (h) 1.25999

(i) For what value of x is $f(x) = 0$?

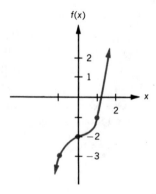

The Algebra of Functions

For certain functions it is possible to define operations called addition, multiplication, subtraction, and division. Such definitions are possible if the domains are identical and the range of the functions is in some field. In this chapter we shall be concerned with functions whose domains and ranges are subsets of the real number field. Such functions are called *real* functions.

We first consider an example of addition of two functions.

Example 1 Suppose f and g are functions with domain R and

$$f(x) = \tfrac{1}{2}x + 1$$

and

$$g(x) = 4 - x.$$

The graphs of f and g are shown in Figure 14 by the dotted lines. Now if for each x in the domains of f and g we compute $f(x) + g(x)$, we obtain the graph shown by the solid line in Figure 14.

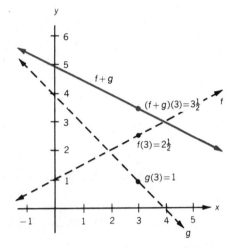

FIGURE 14

The mapping

$$x \rightarrow (f(x) + g(x))$$

is also a function which we call the *sum* of f and g and denote by $f + g$. Hence $(f + g)(x) = f(x) + g(x)$.

When the graphs of f and g are given, we can sketch the graph of $f + g$ using *graphical addition*. For example, from the graphs we see that $g(3) = 1$ and $f(3) = 2\tfrac{1}{2}$. Therefore $(f + g)(3) = 1 + 2\tfrac{1}{2} = 3\tfrac{1}{2}$. Other points on the graph of $f + g$ can be found in a similar manner.

A second method of graphing $f + g$ is to compute the formula for the sum of the functions. Since $f(x) = \tfrac{1}{2}x + 1$ and $g(x) = 4 - x$ we have

$$(f + g)(x) = f(x) + g(x)$$
$$= (\tfrac{1}{2}x + 1) + (4 - x)$$
$$= -\tfrac{1}{2}x + 5.$$

Note that for $f(x) + g(x)$ to make sense two requirements must be met. The element x must be in the domains of both functions f and g, and the image elements $f(x)$ and $g(x)$ must be things that can be *added*. If f and g are functions with different but overlapping domains, then $f + g$ can be defined only on the intersection of their domains as illustrated in Example 2.

Example 2   If f and g are given by

$$f(x) = \sqrt{x^2 - 1}, \qquad \text{for } |x| \geq 1,$$
$$g(x) = \sqrt{4 - x^2}, \qquad \text{for } |x| \leq 2,$$

then the domain of $f + g$ is the union of the two intervals

$$-2 \leq x \leq -1 \qquad \text{and} \qquad 1 \leq x \leq 2.$$

The graphs of f, g, and $f + g$ are shown in Fig. 15.

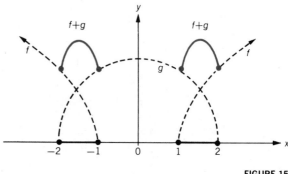

FIGURE 15

The formal definition of addition of functions is given below.

Definition 2-4   If f and g are real functions with domains X_1 and X_2 such that

$$X_1 \cap X_2 = X,$$

where X is not the empty set, then $f + g$ is a function with domain X given by

$$(f + g)(x) = f(x) + g(x).$$

Subtraction of functions can be similarly defined, and the graph of the difference of two functions can be constructed graphically from the separate graphs of the functions. Likewise, one can define the product $f \cdot g$ of two functions but in this case there is no simple construction of the graph of the product function.

Division of functions is defined in a similar way, *except that we must be careful not to divide by zero.* The method is illustrated in the next example.

Example 3   Suppose that f and g have domain R and that $f(x) = x + 1$ and $g(x) = x - 1$. Then $(f/g)(x)$ is given by

$$\frac{f}{g}(x) = \frac{f(x)}{g(x)} = \frac{x + 1}{x - 1},$$

provided that $g(x) \neq 0$, and we construct the following table of values.

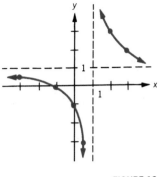

x	$f(x)$	$g(x)$	$(f/g)(x)$
0	1	-1	-1
2	3	1	3
3	4	2	2
-1	0	-2	0
-3	-2	-4	$\frac{1}{2}$
$\frac{1}{2}$	$\frac{3}{2}$	$-\frac{1}{2}$	-3

FIGURE 16

Since $g(x) = 0$ only for $x = 1$, we see that the domain of f/g is all of R except for the number 1. The graph of f/g is shown in Fig. 16 where the vertical and horizontal dashed lines correspond to numbers not in the domain and range, respectively.

Problems

Set A

In Problems 1–3, place a thin piece of paper over the graphs and sketch the graphs of $f + g$.

1.

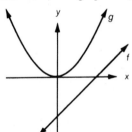

3.

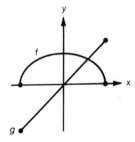

2.

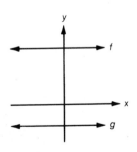

Graph the following pairs of real functions, then construct the graph of the sum of the functions. Find a formula for the sum of the two functions. What is the domain of the sum?

4. $f(x) = 2x$ and $g(x) = 1 - x$, for all x in R

5. $A(x) = x$ and $B(x) = 1 - x^2$, for all x in R

6. $f(x) = x^2$, for $-2 \leq x \leq 2$; and $g(x) = 1$, for $x \geq 0$

7. $F(t) = 2 - t$ and $G(t) = t - 1$, for $t \geq 0$

Graph the following pairs of functions, then draw the graph of $f - g$. Obtain a formula for $f - g$. What is the domain of $f - g$?

8. $f(x) = 1$ and $g(x) = x$, for $x \geq 0$

9. $f(x) = x^2$ and $g(x) = x$, for all x in R

10. $f(x) = x^2$ and $g(x) = -x$, for all x in R

11. $f(x) = x^3$ and $g(x) = -x$, for all x in R

Graph the following pairs of functions. Then draw the graph of $f \cdot g$.

12. $f(x) = x$ and $g(x) = 2$, for all x in R

13. $f(x) = x$ and $g(x) = x$, for all x in R

14. $f(x) = x$ and $g(x) = |x|$, for all x in R

15. $f(x) = x$ and $g(x) = 2 - x$, for $x \geq 0$

Graph the function f/g for each of the pairs of functions. Give the domain of f/g.

16. $f(x) = x + 2$ and $g(x) = x - 2$, for all x in R

17. $f(x) = |x|$ and $g(x) = x$, for all x in R

Set B

18. Define $f - g$, the difference of two functions f and g.

19. Define $f \cdot g$, the product of two functions f and g.

20. Let f be a function that matches each person in your class to the color of eyes that person has. Let g be a function which matches each person in your class to that person's age in years. Can $f + g$ be defined for these functions? Why?

21. Let f be the function that matches each person in the senior class with that person's height in centimeters. Let g be the function that matches each person in the sophomore class with that person's height in centimeters. Can $f + g$ be defined for these functions? Why?

Set C

22. If $R(x) = 1/x$ for all $x \neq 0$ and $\text{Id}(x) = x$ for all x, obtain a formula for $R \cdot \text{Id}$ and construct its graph. What is the domain of the product function, $R \cdot \text{Id}$?

23. f, g, and h are functions, with domain R, given by the formulas

$$f(x) = 2x, \quad g(x) = x, \quad \text{and} \quad h(x) = -3.$$

Obtain a formula for $((f \cdot g) + h)$ and sketch its graph.

24. f has as its domain the set of rational numbers and $f(x) = 1$ for all x in its domain. g has as its domain the set of irrational numbers and $g(x) = -1$ for all x in its domain. Are both $f(x)$ and $g(x)$ defined? Is $f + g$ defined?

Calculator Problem

Compute the following sums. Make a generalization.

$$1^3 + 2^3$$
$$1^3 + 2^3 + 3^3$$
$$1^3 + 2^3 + 3^3 + 4^3$$
$$1^3 + 2^3 + 3^3 + 4^3 + 5^3$$
$$\vdots$$

2-5 Composition of Functions

Besides combining functions by the operations of addition, multiplication, subtraction, and division, one can also often form the *composition* of two functions.

Definition 2-5 If g is a function with domain X and range Y and if f is a function with domain containing Y and range Z, then the *composition of f and g,* denoted by $f \circ g$,* is defined on the domain X, and

$$[f \circ g](x) = f(g(x)).$$

Diagrammatically, we have

$$X \xrightarrow{g} Y \xrightarrow{f} Z, \ X \xrightarrow{f \circ g} Z.$$

The pattern can also be shown as in Fig. 17.

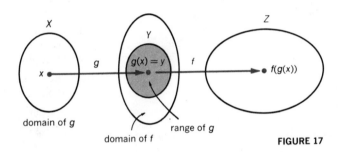

FIGURE 17

Example 1 Let $g(x) = x + 2$ for all x, and $f(x) = x^2 + 1$ for all x. Then $f \circ g$ is a function whose rule is

$$f(g(x)) = f(x + 2) = (x + 2)^2 + 1$$
$$= x^2 + 4x + 5.$$

2 Let g and f be the functions of Example 1. Then $g \circ f$ is a function whose rule is

$$g(f(x)) = g(x^2 + 1) = (x^2 + 1) + 2$$
$$= x^2 + 3.$$

3 If $g(x) = x^2 - 2$ for all x and $f(x) = 4x + 1$ for all x, then the value of $f \circ g$ at $x = 3$ is

$$f(g(3)) = f(3^2 - 2) = f(7)$$
$$= 4(7) + 1 = 29$$

---

*The composition of f and g may also be denoted by $f(g)$. Thus $f(g)(x) = f(g(x))$.

Example 4   If $F(x) = \sqrt{x^2 + 1}$, then F can be considered to be the composition of two functions, $f \circ g$, where $f(x) = \sqrt{x}$ for $x \geq 0$ and $g(x) = x^2 + 1$. Thus,

$$F(x) = [f \circ g](x) = f(g(x)) = f(x^2 + 1) = \sqrt{x^2 + 1}.$$

5   One can combine composition of functions with addition, subtraction, multiplication, or division of functions. Thus, if $F(x) = (1 - \sqrt{x})^3 - 3x$ for $x \geq 0$, then $F = (h \circ k) - g$, where $g(x) = 3x$, $k(x) = 1 - \sqrt{x}$, $x \geq 0$, $h(x) = x^3$, and

$$F(x) = h(k(x)) - g(x) = h(1 - \sqrt{x}) - 3x = (1 - \sqrt{x})^3 - 3x.$$

Problems

Set A

Let f and g be functions given by

$$f(x) = x - 3 \quad \text{for all } x \text{ in } R \text{ and}$$
$$g(x) = 2x^2 \quad \text{for all } x \text{ in } R.$$

Find $f(g(x))$ for each of the following values of x.

1. 1   **2.** -1

3. 0   **4.** 3

5. -3 **6.** 5

7. 10   **8.** -10

For each f and g give the domains, assuming that the domains are as large as necessary for $f(x)$ and $g(x)$ to be real numbers. Then find $f \circ g$ and its domain.

9. $f(x) = 2x + 1$ and $g(x) = \dfrac{x - 1}{2}$

10. $f(x) = \dfrac{1}{x}$ and $g(x) = \dfrac{1}{x}$

11. $f(x) = \dfrac{1}{x^2 + 1}$ and $g(x) = x$

12. $f(x) = \dfrac{1}{x}$ and $g(x) = \dfrac{1}{x - 1}$

13. $f(x) = \dfrac{1}{x + 1}$ and $g(x) = \dfrac{1 - x}{x}$

14. $f(x) = x^2$ and $g(x) = \sqrt{x}$

15. $f(x) = 2x^2 - 1$ and $g(x) = 3$

16. $f(x) = g(x) = 1 - x$

17. $f(x) = x^2 + 2$ and $g(x) = \sqrt{x - 2}$

18. $f(x) = x^3$ and $g(x) = x^2$

Set B

19. Given $p(x) = x^2 + 1$ and $q(x) = x - 1$, for all x in R, what is a formula for $p(q(x))$? What is the formula for $q(p(x))$?

20. Is the composition of two functions commutative? That is, is $f \circ g = g \circ f$ for every pair of functions f and g?

Explain how each of the following functions is the composition of two functions.

21. $f(x) = 2(1 + x)^2 - 3$

22. $F(x) = 2\sqrt{1 + x} - 3$

23. $H(x) = \sqrt{\sqrt{x^2 + 2} + 3}$

24. $F(x) = (4 + x^2)^{1/3} - (4 + x^2)^{4/3}$

Set C

25. If Id is the identity function given by $\text{Id}(x) = x$ for all x, show that $[\text{Id} \circ f](x) = f(x)$ for every function f; that $[f \circ \text{Id}](x) = f(x)$.

26. S and R are functions given by the formulas $S(x) = (x + 1)/x$ for all $x \neq 0$, and $R(x) = x/(x^2 + 1)$ for all x. Find a formula for $R \circ S$. What is the domain of $R \circ S$?

27. If $g(x) = 2x + 1$ for all x, find f so that $g \circ f = \text{Id}$, the identity function. Is it also true that $f \circ g = \text{Id}$?

28. Suppose that functions f, g, and h are defined so that $f: X \to Y$, $g: Y \to Z$, $h: Z \to U$. Show that $h \circ (g \circ f) = (h \circ g) \circ f$.

Calculator Problem

Let $f(x) = x$ for all x and $g(x) = \dfrac{1}{x} + 1$ for all $x \neq 0$. Draw the graphs of f and g and note their points of intersection. Calculate the value of x at the points of intersection to the nearest thousandth. The real-number value of x at the point of intersection is called the *Golden Ratio*. Look up this topic in a mathematics reference book.

2-6   Inverse Functions

Recall in algebra, that if the product of two numbers is 1, the identity element for multiplication, the two factors are said to be *multiplicative inverses* of each other. Thus $\frac{1}{3}$ and 3 are multiplicative inverses because $\frac{1}{3} \cdot 3 = 1$. Each number 3 and $\frac{1}{3}$ "undoes" the work of the other.

A similar situation can prevail for functions. Some pairs of functions have compositions which produce the identity function, Id. Such pairs of functions are called *inverse functions*.

Example 1   Consider the functions $g(x) = x + 1$ and $f(x) = x - 1$, for all x. Then

$$[g \circ f](x) = g(f(x)) = (x - 1) + 1 = x, \qquad \text{for all } x.$$

Thus $g \circ f = $ Id for all x. For each real x, f simply "undoes" $g(x)$. In this case, the domains of both f and g are all of $\mathbf{R}$, and g is called the inverse of f.

More generally, a similar situation prevails whenever f is a one-to-one mapping onto its range.

Definition 2-6   If X and Y are any sets, and if f is a function that is a *one-to-one* mapping of X *onto* Y, then for each y in Y there is a unique x in X such that $f(x) = y$ (Fig. 18). We define a function g with domain Y and range X by agreeing that $g(y) = x$ if and only if $f(x) = y$. This function g is called the *inverse of f*, and is often denoted by f^{-1}. Then

$$f^{-1} \circ f = \text{Id on } X$$

and

$$f \circ f^{-1} = \text{Id on } Y.$$

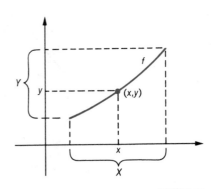

FIGURE 18

Not every function will have an inverse function, as the following example shows.

Example 2   Consider the function f where $f(x) = x^2$ for all real x. (See Fig. 19.) The range of this function consists of all nonnegative real numbers, and for each positive number in the range there are *two* numbers in the domain of f which map into this number. Therefore, f does not have an inverse because f is not a one-to-one mapping.

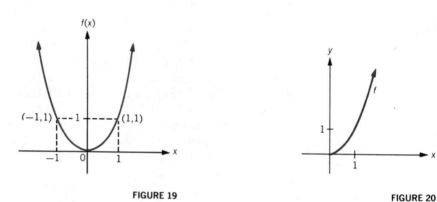

FIGURE 19   FIGURE 20

Now consider the function $f(x) = x^2$, for $x \geq 0$ as shown in Fig. 20. The function f is a one-to-one mapping and therefore has an inverse function.

If the graph of f is available, there is a quick test to see whether f is a one-to-one mapping. Simply check to see whether there are any horizontal lines that intersect the graph of f in more than one point; if there are, then f is not a one-to-one mapping. The graphs in Figs. 21 and 22 illustrate this point.

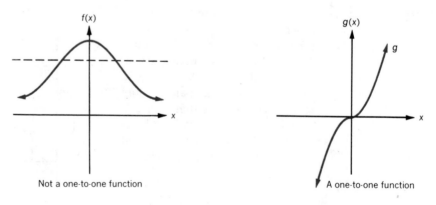

FIGURE 21   FIGURE 22

There is a simple but important relation between the graph of a function f and its inverse function f^{-1}. Suppose f maps the real number d in its domain into the real number r in its range, that is, $f(d) = r$. Then if f has an inverse f^{-1}, it follows that f^{-1} maps r into d, that is, $f^{-1}(r) = d$. Therefore, if the ordered pair (d, r) belongs to f, then the ordered pair (r, d) belongs to f^{-1}.

This relation between the pairs of f and f^{-1} is shown in Fig. 23. Observe that the points of the graph of f and f^{-1} are symmetric with respect to the line $y = x$, so that if the graph of f is given, we could construct the graph of f^{-1} by "reflecting" the graph of f in the line $y = x$.

For some functions whose values are found by simple algebraic formulas, we may easily determine the rule for the inverse of the functions.

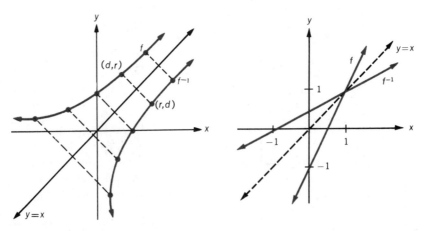

FIGURE 23   FIGURE 24

Example 3   Find the rule for the inverse of

$$f(x) = 2x - 1.$$

Solution. Set $y = 2x - 1$. Solving this equation for x, we get $x = (y + 1)/2$. Therefore, f^{-1} is a function such that

$$f^{-1}(y) = \frac{y + 1}{2}.$$

In graphing functions, we are accustomed to picturing the domain of functions along the horizontal or x-axis. Therefore, we replace the variable y in the rule for f^{-1} by x, getting

$$f^{-1}(x) = \frac{x + 1}{2}.$$

The graphs of f and f^{-1} are shown in Fig. 24. Observe that the graphs are symmetric with respect to the line $y = x$.

Problems

Set A

For each function whose graph is shown below, tell which functions have inverses. Make a sketch of the inverse function if it exists.

1.
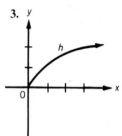

2.
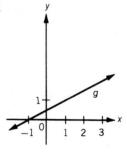

3.
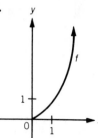

4.
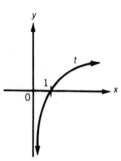

5.
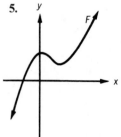

6.
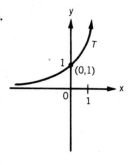

7. Which pairs of functions in Exercises 1–6 appear to be inverses of each other?

8. If f is a function that has an inverse and $f(-2) = 7$, what is $f^{-1}(7)$?

9. If $g(1) = -4$ and g has inverse g^{-1}, what is $(g^{-1} \circ g)(1)$?

10. Consider the function that assigns to each person in your class his age in years. Is there an inverse of this function?

11. A function f is the set of ordered pairs $\{(1, 2), (2, 3), (3, 5), (4, 7)\}$. Show that f has an inverse. What is the domain of f^{-1}? the range?

12. A function g is the set of ordered pairs $\{(0, 1), (1, 1), (2, 3), (3, 5)\}$. Does g have an inverse?

Set B

Give the inverse f^{-1} of f for each of the following.

13. $f(x) = x + 2$ **14.** $f(x) = x - 4$

15. $f(x) = 3x$ **16.** $f(x) = x/7$

17. $f(x) = 2x + 1$ **18.** $f(x) = -x$

19. $f(x) = 3 - x$ **20.** $f(x) = 1/x$

21. $f(x) = \dfrac{1}{x + 1}$

22. $f(x) = x^2 + 1$ for $x > 0$

23. $f(x) = \sqrt{x + 2}$ for $x > -2$

24. $f(x) = \dfrac{x}{x + 1}$ for $x > -1$

Set C

25. Explain why the function f, where $f(x) = \sqrt{16 - x^2}$, $-4 \le x \le 4$, does not have an inverse. How could one restrict the domain of f so the function with the restricted domain would have an inverse? [*Hint:* Sketch the graph of f.]

Show that each of the following real functions has an inverse. Sketch the graph of each and find a formula for the inverse function. What is its domain?

26. $f(x) = x^3$

27. $f(x) = \sqrt{3(x + 1)} + 1$

28. $f(x) = \begin{cases} x \text{ if } x \ge 0, \\ \frac{1}{2}x \text{ if } x < 0 \end{cases}$

29. $f(x) = x^4 + x^2$, $x \ge 0$

30. Show that a constant function whose domain consists of at least two numbers does not have an inverse.

31. If f has an inverse, show that $f^{-1}(f(x)) = x$ for all x in the domain of f, and that $f(f^{-1}(r)) = r$ for all r in the range of f. Give an example different from any previously met.

32. Does the absolute value function, $f(x) = |x|$, have an inverse? Why or why not?

33. Sketch the graph of $f(x) = x^2 + x - 2$ for all x in $\mathbf{R}$. Does f have an inverse? On what restricted domain would f have an inverse?

34. Show that if $f(x) = \dfrac{x}{x-1}$ then $f = f^{-1}$. Sketch the graph of f.

Calculator Problem

The function f has the set of positive integers as its domain and $f(x) = x^2 - x + 41$. Then $f(1) = 41$, $f(2) = 43$, $f(3) = 47$ and 41, 43, and 47 are all prime numbers. Compute other values of f at x. Are the values prime numbers? What is the smallest positive integer in the domain of f so that $f(x)$ is not a prime number?

2-7   General Properties of Functions

Functions may have a bewildering variety of properties, many of which you will encounter as you continue your study of mathematics. In this section and the next we call attention to three of these. These properties are concerned with *boundedness*, whether a function is *increasing* or *decreasing*, and *continuity*. Each property has a simple geometric interpretation.

For a discussion of these properties, one needs to have some terminology and symbolism. The definitions given below provide us with this information.

Definition 2-7   The set of all real numbers x such that $a < x < b$ is called the *open interval* determined by the real numbers a and b, or the *open interval* bounded by *end points* a and b. It is denoted by $\langle a, b \rangle$. (See Fig. 25.)

If just one of the end points is included in the set, then the interval is called *half-open* and is denoted by $[a, b \rangle$ or $\langle a, b]$.

If both end points are included in the set, the interval is called a *closed interval* and is denoted by $[a, b]$.

We say that a function is *defined on an interval* if each number in the interval is in the domain of the function.

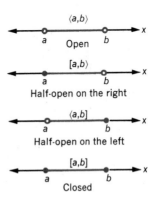

FIGURE 25

Definition 2-8   A function f defined on an interval is said to be *increasing on that interval* if whenever x_1 and x_2 are in that interval and $x_1 < x_2$, then $f(x_1) < f(x_2)$. A function g, defined on an interval, is said to be *decreasing on that interval* if whenever x_1 and x_2 are in that interval and $x_1 < x_2$, then $g(x_1) > g(x_2)$.

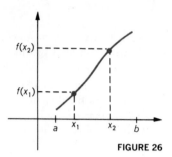

FIGURE 26

See Fig. 26 for the graph of an increasing function. Observe that as x increases so does $f(x)$. Thus the graph of f goes "uphill." Similarly, the graph of a decreasing function would go "downhill."

Example 1   Show that $f(x) = x - 4$ is an increasing function.

Solution. Suppose x_1 and x_2 are any two numbers in the domain of f and $x_1 < x_2$. We must show that $f(x_1) < f(x_2)$.

$$f(x_1) = x_1 - 4 \text{ and } f(x_2) = x_2 - 4.$$
$$f(x_2) - f(x_1) = (x_2 - 4) - (x_1 - 4) = x_2 - x_1.$$

Since $x_1 < x_2$ it follows that $(x_2 - x_1) > 0$ and thus $f(x_2) - f(x_1) > 0$ so that $f(x_1) < f(x_2)$.

Definition 2-9   A real function f defined on an interval with end points a and b is said to be *bounded above in that interval* if there is a number M such that $f(x) \le M$ for all x in the interval.

The function f is *bounded below in that interval* if there is a number m such that $m \le f(x)$ for all x in that interval.

If f is both bounded above and bounded below, then f is *bounded in that interval* (see Fig. 27).

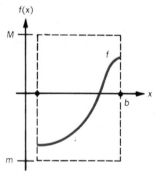

FIGURE 27

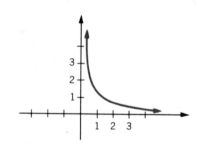

FIGURE 28

Example 2   Suppose that f is defined by $f(x) = 1/x$ for $x > 0$. The graph is shown in Fig. 28.

We see that f is not bounded above on the interval $\langle 0, 1]$. However, f is bounded below because $0 < f(x)$ for all x in the interval.

On the interval $[1, 2]$ the function is bounded. In fact, f is bounded on any closed interval $[a, b]$ if $a > 0$.

Problems

Set A

For each graph, tell whether the function is increasing or decreasing.

1.

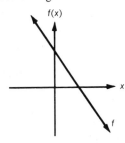

2.

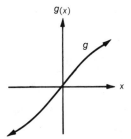

3.

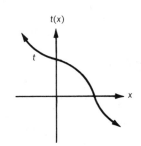

Graph the set of points on the real number line that are in the following intervals.

4. $\langle -3, 2 \rangle$ **5.** $[0, 1\rangle$ **6.** $\langle -1, 0]$

7. $[-4, 2]$ **8.** $\langle -6, -4 \rangle$ **9.** $\langle 0, 0.5]$

10. $[2, \pi]$ **11.** $\langle \pi, 4]$ **12.** $\langle a - e, a + e \rangle$

Which of the following functions are bounded above? bounded below? bounded?

13. $f(x) = 5$ for all x

14. $t(x) = x$ for all x

15. $g(x) = x^2$ for all x

16. $P(x) = -2x^2$ for all x

Set B

17. Is the identity function $\mathrm{Id}(x) = x$ an increasing or decreasing function?

18. On what part of its domain is the absolute value function $A(x) = |x|$ decreasing? On what part of the domain is it increasing?

Sketch a graph of each of the following functions. Tell whether the functions are bounded above or below or both.

19. $g(x) = \begin{cases} 1 \text{ if } x \geq 0 \\ 0 \text{ if } x < 0 \end{cases}$

20. $h(x) = \begin{cases} 1/x \text{ if } x \neq 0 \\ 2 \text{ if } x = 0 \end{cases}$

21. $H(x) = 1/x$ for $1 \leq x \leq 5000$

22. $Q(t) = \sqrt{t^2 - 1}$ for $t \geq 1$

23. $F(x) = \begin{cases} 1 \text{ if } x \text{ is rational} \\ 0 \text{ if } x \text{ is irrational} \end{cases}$

24. $f(x) = 4 - x^2$ for all x

Set C

25. Prove that the function f with domain $\boldsymbol{R}$ given by $f(x) = 2x - 5$ is an increasing function.

26. Prove that a function, $F(x) = mx + b$, where m and b are constants, is increasing if and only if $m > 0$.

27. Graph the function given by $x \to 1/x$ where $x > 0$. Prove that this function is decreasing for all $x > 0$.

28. Prove that if $0 < x_1 < x_2$, then $(x_1)^2 < (x_2)^2$. Hence prove that the function s, given by $s(x) = x^2$, is increasing for $x > 0$.

29. Prove that if g is an increasing function and $g(1) = 3$, then $g(2) \neq 0$.

30. Give an example of a decreasing function that has an inverse. Show that the inverse function is also decreasing.

31. Discuss the bounds, if any, of the function

$$P(x) = x^{16} + x^{12} + x^{10} + x^8 + x^2 + 1 \text{ for all } x.$$

32. Prove that if f is an increasing function then f has an inverse and this inverse is also an increasing function. Give an example of this theorem.

Calculator Problem

Calculate $f(x)$ for x in $[1, 2]$ for the function

$$f(x) = 1 - \frac{1}{x} + \frac{1}{x^2} - \frac{1}{x^3}.$$

Use x in increments of 0.1, that is $1, 1.1, 1.2, 1.3$ etc. Sketch a graph of f in the interval.

2-8   Continuity

The last of the three properties that we shall consider is continuity. This is a concept that you will meet again and again if you continue to study mathematics. Although continuity has a strong appeal to the intuition, its precise definition is surprisingly troublesome, and proofs of continuity are hard to manage unless the meaning of the definition is discussed in depth. For these reasons we shall confine ourselves here to a description of the idea, since an intuitive understanding of the concept is of first importance.*

There are two aspects to the notion of continuity—a local one and a global one. There is *continuity at a point* and *continuity in an interval*.

Definition 2-10 Let f be a function defined on $\langle a, b \rangle$ and let c be a point of the interval, that is, $a < c < b$. Then f is *continuous at* c if "for x very close to c, $f(x)$ is very close to $f(c)$" (Fig. 29).

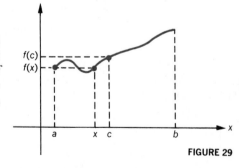

FIGURE 29

___
*For more discussion of continuity with an indication of how proofs of continuity are made, see Section 10-8.

Another way of stating this is to say that f is continuous at c if "the difference $|f(x) - f(c)|$ can be made as small as one likes by choosing x sufficiently close to c." That is, the closer we choose x to c, the smaller the difference $|f(x) - f(c)|$.

Definition 2-11 If f is defined on an interval, then f is *continuous on that interval* provided that f is continuous at each point of the interval.

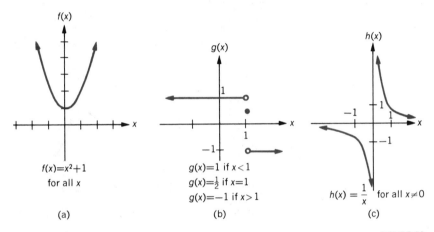

$f(x) = x^2 + 1$
for all x

(a)

$g(x) = 1$ if $x < 1$
$g(x) = \frac{1}{2}$ if $x = 1$
$g(x) = -1$ if $x > 1$

(b)

$h(x) = \dfrac{1}{x}$ for all $x \neq 0$

(c)

FIGURE 30

Figure 30(a) shows the graph of a function f that is continuous at every point in its domain. The graph of the function g in Fig. 30(b) shows that g is *discontinuous* at 1. The function is not continuous on any closed interval that contains 1. As "x gets close to 1, $g(x)$ does not get close to $g(1)$."

The graph of the function h in Fig. 30(c) must be considered carefully. We note that this function is not defined at 0, and so it does not make sense to discuss continuity at this point. However, on any interval that does not contain 0, the function is continuous.

Remarks

1. It is natural to ask how one goes about proving that a particular function is continuous at a point. Ultimately all such proofs rest upon the definition of continuity at a point, but we need a definition more precise than the one given here. We shall see in a moment that continuity in an interval implies that the graph has a certain property. In our problems *we shall rely upon the graph to decide upon the continuity of the function.*

2. It can be proved that the graph of a function *continuous on an interval* has no "breaks." The graph comes in "one piece."

Furthermore, one can prove that each polynomial function (see Chapter 3) is continuous. Therefore, we will be essentially correct in drawing the graph of a polynomial, when we connect the points we find by a continuous curve.

Continuous functions possess an important property which we shall use later. This is the *intermediate-value* property.

Theorem

INTERMEDIATE-VALUE THEOREM. *Suppose that f is continuous on the closed interval [a, b] and f(a) ≠ f(b), and suppose that d is a number between f(a) and f(b); then there is at least one number c such that a < c < b and d = f(c).*

The theorem is illustrated in Fig. 31, where for this particular number d, there are three possible values for the number c. The proof requires a more intensive study of continuity, and we shall assume its truth here.

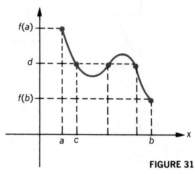

FIGURE 31

Example

The function f given by $f(x) = \frac{1}{8}(x^3 - 3x^2 - 9x + 2)$ takes on the values given in the table below.

x	0	1	2	3	4	5	−1	−2	−3
$f(x)$	0.25	−1.1	−2.5	−3.1	−2.2	0.9	0.9	0	−3.1

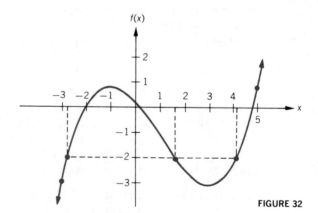

FIGURE 32

At 0 the function is positive, while at 1 it is negative. By the Intermediate Value Theorem the function must have the value 0 somewhere in the interval $\langle 0, 1 \rangle$. According to the graph in Fig. 32, this value appears to be approximately $x = 0.2$.

Because $f(-3) = -3.1$ and $f(5) = 0.9$, there must be at least one x in $\langle -3, 5 \rangle$ for which $f(x) = -2$. We see from the graph in Fig. 32 that there are, in fact, three such numbers, namely $x = -2.7, 1.7, 4.2$, approximately.

We note that the graph of the function in this example is continuous. Observe also that the function is bounded on each closed interval. Of course there is no one number that is an upper bound for the range of the entire function and so we say that it is *unbounded* on the whole set of real numbers.

From the graph we see that for $x > 3$ the function is increasing. Between -1 and 3 it is decreasing, and for $x < -1$ the function is again increasing.

Problems

Set A

1. The graph of a function F is shown in the figure below.
  (a) Is F bounded?
  (b) In what interval is F increasing?
  (c) In what interval is F decreasing?
  (d) Is F a continuous function? If not, where is F discontinuous?

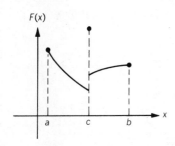

Sketch the graph of each function. Then tell whether or not the function is continuous for all real numbers.

2. $f(x) = 2x - 1$ for all x

3. $g(x) = x$ for $x \geq 0$
  $g(x) = x^2$ for $x < 0$

4. $h(x) = x + 1$ for $x \geq -1$
  $h(x) = 1 - x$ for $x < -1$

5. $t(x) = \dfrac{1}{x}$ for $x \geq 1$
  $t(x) = x$ for $x < 1$

6. Sketch the graph of $f(x) = 2x^2 - 5$ for all x. Find $f(1)$ and $f(2)$. Does $f(x) = 0$ for some x in $\langle 1, 2 \rangle$?

7. Find $f(-1)$ and $f(-2)$ for $f(x) = 2x^2 - 5$. Does $f(x) = 0$ for some x in $\langle -2, -1 \rangle$?

8. Sketch the graph of $f(x) = x^3 + x^2 + 1$. Show that $f(x) = 0$ for some x in $\langle -2, -1 \rangle$.

Set B

9. Sketch the graph of a continuous function whose domain is $\boldsymbol{R}$, which is increasing, and is unbounded.

10. Sketch the graph of a function that is defined on [0, 1], is bounded, and is continuous everywhere, except at $\frac{1}{2}$. Sketch another function with domain [0, 1] that is unbounded and continuous except at $\frac{1}{2}$.

11. If a function is continuous on some closed interval [a, b], will it be bounded on that interval?

12. If a function is bounded on some closed interval, will it necessarily be continuous on that interval?

13. Sketch the graph of the function f defined by

$$f(x) = x^3 - \tfrac{1}{2}x^2 - \tfrac{9}{4}x + \tfrac{9}{8},$$

with domain R. Show that there is some number x in each of the intervals $\langle -2, -1 \rangle$, $\langle 0, 1 \rangle$, and $\langle 1, 2 \rangle$ such that $f(x) = 0$. Can you determine any of the numbers x exactly?

Set C

14. Sketch the graph of $p(x) = x(x - 1)(x + 2)$ for x in $[-2, 1]$. Is p continuous in this interval? Is p bounded on this interval? Find an upper bound of the function. Find a lower bound of the function.

15. Sketch the graph of $f(x) = x^2$ for $x \geq 0$. Assuming continuity on any closed interval in the domain of this function, show that there is a positive real number whose square is 2; that is, show that $\sqrt{2}$ exists.

16. Sketch a graph of a function that will illustrate that *without* the requirement of continuity on an interval, the conclusion of the Intermediate-Value Theorem will not be valid.

17. Show, algebraically, that $\sqrt{x}$, $x \geq 0$, is an unbounded increasing function.

Calculator Problem

Let f be the function $f(x) = x^4 - 3x^2 + 1$ for all x. Use the Intermediate Value Theorem to show that $f(x) = 0$ for some x in $\langle 0, 1 \rangle$. Find x to the nearest tenth in this interval such that $f(x) = 0$.

Summary

The important ideas of the chapter can be summarized briefly as follows.

1. The definition of a function:

   domain, image set, range,

   notations: $f: X \to Y$, $f: x \to y$, $X \xrightarrow{f} Y$, $x \to f(x)$.
   the identity function, Id.

2. The algebra of functions: $f + g, f - g, f \cdot g, f/g$.

3. The composition of functions:

$$X \xrightarrow{g} Y \xrightarrow{f} Z$$
$$f \circ g$$

4. Inverses: $f^{-1} \circ f = $ Id on the domain of f, $f \circ f^{-1} = $ Id on the range of f.

5. General properties of functions:
   (a) defined on an interval
   (b) increasing or decreasing
   (c) continuity on an interval
   (d) the Intermediate Value Theorem

Chapter 2   Test

2-2   **1.** Which graph below shows the graph of a function on X into Y?

(a) 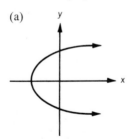   (b) 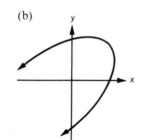   (c)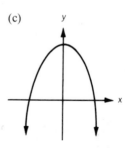

2-3   Given $f(x) = x^2 - 3x + 1$ for all x in R. Find the following.

    2. $f(2)$ **3.** $f(-3)$ **4.** $f(5)$ **5.** $f(a)$

    6. The function k is a constant function and $k(-2) = 3$. What is $k(0)$?

    7. Sketch the graph of the identity function Id, with domain R.

    8. Sketch the graph of the function f where $f(x) = 4 - x^2$ for $-2 \le x \le 2$.

2-4   **9.** $f(x) = 2x + 1$ and $g(x) = 3 - x$ both with domain R. Find a rule for $f + g$.

    10. $p(x) = 3x$ and $q(x) = 2x - 5$ both with domain R. Find a rule for $p - q$.

    11. $H(x) = \frac{1}{2}x$ and $J(x) = 2x - 6$ both with domain R. Find a rule for the product function $H \cdot J$.

    12. $K(x) = 2$ and $\mathrm{Id}(x) = x$ for all x in R. Find a rule for the quotient function $K \div \mathrm{Id}$. What is the domain for $K \div \mathrm{Id}$?

2-5   If $f(x) = 3x + 2$ and $g(x) = 2x$, find the following.

    13. $[f \circ g](1)$ **14.** $[f \circ g](-1)$

    15. $[g \circ f](2)$ **16.** $[g \circ f](\frac{1}{2})$

    17. If $F(x) = x^2 + 1$ and $H(x) = x - 4$, find a rule for $[F \circ H](x)$. What is its domain?

2-6   **18.** How are the graphs of f and f^{-1} related to the graph of the identity function, Id?

    19. If $f(4) = -3$ and f has an inverse, what is $f^{-1}(-3)$?

    20. If $f(x) = 3x - 2$, find a rule for $f^{-1}(x)$.

2-7   **21.** Sketch the graph of $f(x) = 10 - x^2$ for x in $[1, 3]$. Is f increasing or decreasing in this interval?

    22. Sketch the graph of $g(x) = \dfrac{1}{x}$ for $x > 0$. Is g increasing or decreasing? Is g bounded below? Is g bounded above?

2-8   **23.** Complete: A function f is continuous at a point c, if for x very close to c, $f(x)$ is . . . .

    24. Graph the function $f(x) = x - 2$ for all x except 3. $f(3) = 2$. Is f continuous for all x in the domain?

Chapter 3
Polynomials

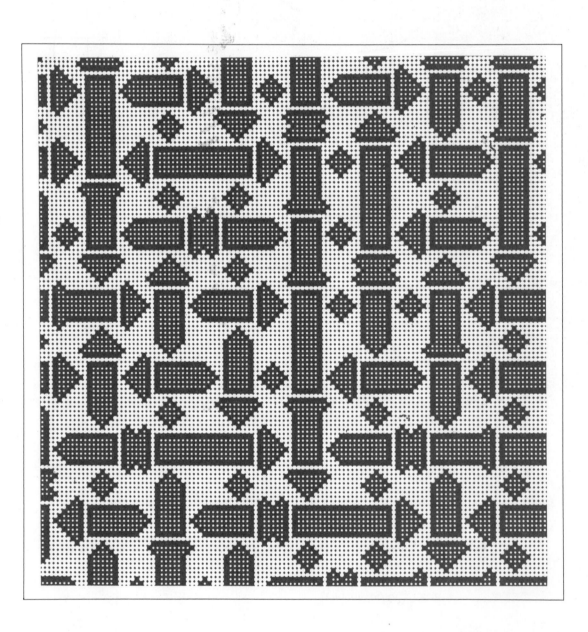

3-1   Introduction

We now consider a special class of functions which can be generated by restricting our attention to constant functions, $f(x) = a$ for all x in R, the identity function, $g(x) = x$ for all x in R, and the operations of addition and multiplication of functions. For example, if we have the functions $f(x) = 2$, $g(x) = x$, and $h(x) = -1$, each with domain R, then we may generate a new function, $f \cdot g + h$, given by

$$(f \cdot g + h)(x) = 2x - 1 \qquad \text{for all } x \text{ in } R.$$

Similarly, if

$$g(x) = x, \qquad f(x) = \tfrac{3}{4}, \qquad h(x) = \sqrt{3}, \qquad \text{and} \qquad s(x) = 17$$

for all x in R, then $f \cdot (g \cdot g) + h \cdot g + s$ is a function given by

$$(f \cdot (g \cdot g) + h \cdot g + s)(x) = \tfrac{3}{4}x^2 + \sqrt{3}x + 17 \qquad \text{for all } x \text{ in } R.$$

The functions that can be constructed in this manner are called *polynomial functions*. With the kinds of functions and operations we have chosen, we *cannot* generate functions such as

$$F(x) = \frac{1}{x}, \qquad G(x) = \sqrt{x - 1},$$

$$R(x) = 5^x, \qquad \text{or} \qquad Q(x) = \frac{x + 2}{x - 1}.$$

3-2   Polynomial Functions

Definition 3-1   A *polynomial function P* over the real numbers is a function given by

$$P(x) = a_0 x^n + a_1 x^{n-1} + \cdots + a_{n-1}x + a_n,$$

where $a_0, a_1, \ldots, a_n$, the *coefficients* of P, are real numbers, $a_0 \neq 0$, and n is a positive integer or 0.

When we speak of a polynomial function *over* the real numbers, the coefficients of the function are real numbers. However, we may consider polynomials in which the coefficients are restricted to be rational numbers or are permitted to be any complex numbers. Such polynomial functions are respectively called *polynomials over the rational numbers* and *polynomials over the complex numbers.*

The *degree* of a polynomial is n if $a_0 \neq 0$ and $n \geq 0$. Note that for $n = 0$, the polynomial of *degree zero* is $P(x) = a_0$, $a_0 \neq 0$, and it is called a *constant polynomial.* The special constant polynomial, $P(x) = 0$, called the *zero polynomial,* is not assigned a degree. The coefficient a_0 is called the *leading coefficient.*

Example 1 Several polynomial functions are shown below with their degrees and leading coefficients.

Polynomial function	Degree	Leading coefficient
$f(x) = \frac{1}{2}x^4 - 3x^2 + 2x - \frac{1}{2}$	4	$\frac{1}{2}$
$p(x) = -7x^3 + x^2 + \frac{1}{2}x - \sqrt{2}$	3	-7
$g(x) = 4x^7$	7	4
$h(x) = 5$	0	5
$t(x) = 0$	None	None

Usually one writes the expression for a polynomial with the term of highest degree first, and the remaining terms in order of decreasing degree.

In some of the polynomials, some of the powers did not occur. It is sometimes convenient when we are computing with polynomials to fill in the "empty places" by 0 times the corresponding power of the variable. For example,

$$f(t) = 3t^8 - 3t^4 - \tfrac{1}{2}t^2 + 7t - 5$$
$$= 3t^8 + 0t^7 + 0t^6 + 0t^5 - 3t^4 + 0t^3 - \tfrac{1}{2}t^2 + 7t - 5.$$

We say that the coefficients of the polynomial above are, in order, 3, 0, 0, 0, -3, 0, $-\frac{1}{2}$, 7, -5.

Definition 3-2 The *zeros* of a function f are those numbers x in the domain of f for which $f(x) = 0$.

Example 2 The polynomial $p(x) = 2x^2 + 5x - 3$ has zeros at -3 and $\frac{1}{2}$. That is, $p(-3) = 0$ and $p(\frac{1}{2}) = 0$. These zeros were found by setting $2x^2 + 5x - 3 = 0$ and solving for x.

We may be able to find the zeros of polynomials of degrees 1 and 2 but for polynomials of higher degrees the zeros may not be easy to find.

It is obvious, but difficult to prove, that a polynomial function completely determines its coefficients. In other words, each polynomial has exactly one set of coefficients. This is an important fact, needed so often in the following pages that we state it as a theorem without proof.

Theorem 3-1   *Two polynomial functions are identical if and only if their corresponding coefficients are identical.*

The *if* part of the theorem is trivial. It is the *only if* part that is too difficult to prove here. The *only if* part of the theorem assures us, for example, that if $P(x) = ax^3 + bx^2 + cx + d$ and $P(x) = 4x^3 + 7x - 4$ for all real x, then $a = 4$, $b = 0$, $c = 7$, $d = -4$.

Problems

Set A

If $g(x) = x$, $f(x) = 3$, and $h(x) = -2$ for all real x, give the polynomial functions generated by the following operations on f, g, and h.

1. $f \cdot g + h$

2. $h \cdot g \cdot g$

3. $f \cdot g \cdot g + h \cdot g + f \cdot h$

4. $g \cdot g \cdot g + f \cdot g \cdot g + h$

Give the coefficients of each of the following polynomials. Then give the degree and leading coefficient of each polynomial.

5. $f(x) = 7x^5 + 2x^3 - x^2 - 7$

6. $h(x) = x^6 + x^4 + x^2 + 1$

7. $s(x) = 5$

8. $g(x) = -5 - 2x^3 + \frac{7}{2}x^4 + x$

9. $q(x) = ax^2 + bx + c$

10. $p(x) = 1 - x^4$

11. $F(x) = c + bx + ax^3$

12. $P(t) = t^{50}$

Write polynomials whose coefficients are in the order indicated in each of the following.

13. $5, 2, -1$

14. $1, 2, 3, -4$

15. $1, 0, 5$

16. $\frac{1}{3}, 0, 0, 0, 1$

17. $2, -1, -1, 3, 5$

18. -6

Set B

19. Show that 2 and -3 are zeros of the polynomial $p(x) = x^2 + x - 6$.

20. Find the zero of $p(x) = 4x - 2$.

21. Find one real-number zero of $p(x) = x^3 + x^2 + x + 1$.

22. Polynomials f and g are identical:

$$f(x) = ax^2 + bx + c,$$
$$g(x) = 3x^2 - 4x + 7.$$

Determine a, b and c.

23. Polynomials f and g are identical:

$$f(x) = 3x^2 - 7x + 5,$$
$$g(x) = (a + 1)x^2 + 2bx + c^2.$$

Determine a, b, and c.

Set C

24. Give a polynomial in x of degree 7 and with leading coefficient 1. Choose the polynomial so that it has the value 3 when $x = 0$.

25. If $F(x) = x^2 + bx + 4$ and $F(2) = 10$, determine b.

26. If $p(x) = ax^2 + 7x + 1$ and $p(-2) = -21$, determine a.

Decide whether each polynomial below can be considered to be: (a) a polynomial over the rational field, (b) a polynomial over the real field, (c) a polynomial over the complex field.

27. $p(x) = x^3 + \frac{2}{3}x^2 + x + 1$

28. $r(x) = x^3 + \sqrt{3}x + 5$

29. $t(x) = x^3 + 3ix^2 + 4$

30. $q(x) = x^3 + i^2x^2 + \sqrt{\frac{4}{9}}x + 3$

31. The polynomial

$$P(x) = (r - 2)x^2 + (s + 3)x + t - 4$$

is the zero polynomial. Determine r, s, and t.

Calculator Problem

Graph the polynomial function $p(x) = \sqrt{2}x^2 - \sqrt{3}x - \sqrt{5}$ by finding values for $p(x)$ at $x = -2, -1, 0, 1, 2,$ and 3. Estimate the zeros of the polynomial to the nearest tenth. Then check your estimates of the zeros.

3–3   Graphs of Polynomial Functions

In graphing a polynomial it is useful to know that polynomials over the real numbers are continuous functions. This is a theorem that is an immediate consequence of four facts: (1) The identity function is continuous; (2) the constant functions are continuous; (3) a sum of continuous functions is continuous; and (4) a product of continuous functions is continuous.

Although the graphs of some polynomial functions may be difficult to construct, graphs of some simple polynomials are easy to draw. Because polynomial functions are continuous functions, we calculate a number of points on the graph and connect them by a smooth curve.

Example 1   Graph the polynomial p described by the formula $p(x) = x^2 - 1$.

Solution.

x	0	± 1	± 2	$\pm\frac{1}{2}$	$\pm\frac{3}{2}$
$p(x)$	-1	0	3	$-\frac{3}{4}$	$\frac{5}{4}$

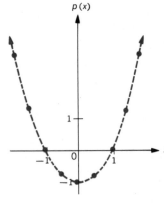

$p(x)$

FIGURE 1

The graphs of the nine number pairs given in the table are shown in Fig. 1, and the graph of the polynomial is sketched as the dashed curve. The arrows on the graph indicate how the function behaves for larger and smaller values of x.

In Section 3–1 it was stated that the zeros of a function f are those numbers x in the domain of f for which $f(x) = 0$. In terms of the graph of f the zeros are the points where the graph intersects the x-axis. If a polynomial is completely factored into real *linear* factors, it is easy to see the zeros or the points where the graph crosses the x-axis. Knowing this fact makes it easier to sketch the graph of a function.

Example 2   Sketch the graph of $P(x) = \frac{1}{2}(x + 1)(x)(x - 1)(x - 3)$.

Solution. The zeros of P are $-1, 0, 1$, and 3. For other values of x it is easy to determine whether the factors in x are positive or negative and hence whether $P(x) > 0$ or $P(x) < 0$, as follows.

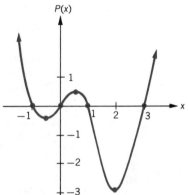

$$P(x) > 0 \quad \text{if } x < -1,$$
$$P(x) < 0 \quad \text{if } -1 < x < 0,$$
$$P(x) > 0 \quad \text{if } 0 < x < 1,$$
$$P(x) < 0 \quad \text{if } 1 < x < 3,$$
$$P(x) > 0 \quad \text{if } x > 3.$$

x	-1.5	-0.5	0.5	2	3.5
$P(x)$	4.2	-0.66	0.47	-3	9.8

FIGURE 2

Therefore, all that remains to be done is to obtain additional points on the graph in order to sketch it. Some of these are given in the table above, and all this information is shown in Fig. 2, along with a more complete sketch of the graph of P.

If a polynomial f, with real coefficients, is factored as completely as possible into *real* factors that are not all linear, then the graph is less easy to sketch.

Example 3   Sketch the graph of

$$f(x) = \frac{1}{4}(x^2 + 2x + 2)(x - 2).$$

Solution. Because there is no real number x such that $x^2 + 2x + 2 = 0$,* the only zero of f is 2. Therefore

$$f(x) > 0 \quad \text{if} \quad x > 2$$
and
$$f(x) < 0 \quad \text{if} \quad x < 2.$$

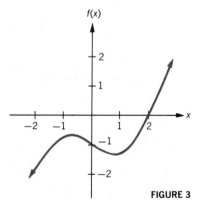

FIGURE 3

---

*The sentence $x^2 + 2x + 2 = 0$ is equivalent to the sentence $(x + 1)^2 + 1 = 0$, which is a false statement for all real numbers x.

In this problem, to draw the curve reasonably well, we must compute the coordinates of enough points on the graph of f.

x	0	1	-1	3	-2	-0.5	0.5	1.5
$f(x)$	-1	-1.25	-0.75	4.25	-2	-0.8	-1.3	-0.9

The graph of f is shown in Fig. 3.

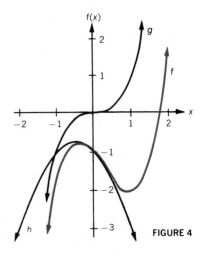

If we cannot factor a polynomial, then the principal means at our disposal for sketching the graph is that of plotting many points. However, in some cases, the method of adding ordinates graphically will permit one to sketch a graph quickly. For example, if $f(x) = x^3 - x^2 - x - 1$, let $g(x) = x^3$ and $h(x) = -x^2 - x - 1$. Then $f = g + h$, and both g and h have graphs that are easily sketched. The graphs of g, h and f are shown in Fig. 4.

FIGURE 4

Problems

Set A

Sketch the graphs of the following polynomials.

1. $p(x) = x^2 + \frac{1}{2}$
2. $g(x) = \frac{1}{2}x^2$
3. $H(x) = x^3$
4. $h(x) = (-x)^3$
5. $f(x) = \frac{1}{4}x^3 + 1$
6. $q(t) = 2t - 1$
7. $R(x) = -x^2$
8. $P(x) = x^2 - \frac{1}{2}$
9. $h(x) = -\frac{1}{2}x + 1$
10. $F(x) = x^4$
11. $k(t) = \frac{1}{4}t^3 - 1$
12. $Q(t) = \frac{1}{2}t^3 - t$
13. $R(x) = -x^2 - x - 1$
14. $t(x) = \frac{1}{10}x^5$

Sketch the graphs of the polynomial functions given below. Give the real zeros of each function.

15. $f(x) = (x + 1)x(x - 1)$
16. $P(x) = x(x - 1)(x - 2)$
17. $g(x) = (x - 1)(x - 2)(x - 3)$
18. $G(t) = t(t - 1)(t - 2)(t - 3)$
19. $T(x) = \frac{1}{10}(x + 2)(x + 1)(x - 1)x(x - 2)$
20. $R(s) = \frac{1}{3}(s^2 + s + 1)(s + 1)$

Set B

21. Graph on the same coordinate axes the polynomials $\frac{1}{4}x^2$ and $\frac{1}{4}x^4$, for $-2 \le x \le 2$.

22. Graph on the same coordinate axes the polynomials $\frac{1}{3}x$, $\frac{1}{3}x^3$, and $\frac{1}{3}x^5$, for $-1.5 \le x \le 1.5$.

23. How does the graph of $-ax^n$ compare with the graph of ax^n? If $a > 0$, how does ax^n behave as x increases, if n is odd? if n is even?

24. Sketch the graph of the polynomial $x^3 - x + 1$ and from the graph find, approximately, the real zeros of the polynomial.

25. Sketch the graph of $P(x) = (x + 1)^2(x - 1)(x - 3) + 1$ and obtain the real zeros of P from the graph.

26. Sketch the graph of $F(x) = \frac{1}{2}x^4 - x^3 - 2$ by sketching the graphs of $g(x) = \frac{1}{2}x^4$ and $h(x) = -x^3 - 2$ and then sketching the graph of $g + h$ using graphical addition.

Set C

Sketch the graphs of the polynomial functions given in Exercises 27 through 32.

27. $H(t) = t^2(t - 1)(t - 2)$

28. $Q(s) = (s - 1)^2(s + 1)^2$

29. $f(s) = s^2(s - 1)^3$

30. $P(s) = \frac{1}{4}(s^2 + 1)(s^2 - 1)$

31. $S(x) = \frac{1}{4}(x^2 + 4)(x^2 + 1)$

32. $f(x) = -\frac{1}{4}x^2(x^2 - 1)$

33. Sketch the graph of the polynomial function f, where $f(x) = (x - 2)^2 + 4$. Determine the "lowest" point of the graph of f; that is, find the minimum value of $f(x)$.

34. Sketch the graph of the polynomial function g, where $g(x) = 4 - (x - 2)^2$. Determine the "highest" point on the graph of g; that is, find the maximum value of $g(x)$.

Calculator Problem

Determine, to the nearest tenth, the lowest point of the graph of the function f, where $f(x) = 10x^2 + 14x - 12$. Sketch the graph of f.

3-4   Division of Polynomials

It is possible to prove that the sum, difference, and product of any two polynomials is a polynomial. However the quotient of two polynomials does not always result in a polynomial. The situation is similar to that of the integers. Just as $\frac{2}{3}$ and $-\frac{7}{8}$ are not integers, so also functions given by the formulas

$$\frac{x - 3}{x + 2}, \qquad \frac{x + 1}{2x^2 + x + 1}, \qquad \frac{x^2 + x + 1}{x}$$

are not polynomials. However, sometimes division is possible. For example, if $P(x) = 3x^2 + 5x - 2$ and $D(x) = x + 2$ then the quotient $Q = P/D$ is a polynomial. That is, $Q(x) = 3x - 1$. To verify this, we note that

$$Q(x) \cdot D(x) = (3x - 1)(x + 2) = 3x^2 + 5x - 2 = P(x).$$

Definition 3-3   If P, D, Q are polynomials and $D \neq 0$, and if $P = QD$, then we say that D *divides* P, or that P *is exactly divisible by D,* and write this as $P \div D = Q$ or $P/D = Q$. The polynomial P is called the *dividend,* D is called the *divisor,* and Q the *quotient.*

A polynomial may not always be exactly divisible by another polynomial. Just as in arithmetic where $17 \div 7$ gives quotient 2 with remainder 3, so also

$$(x^2 - 3x + 4) \div (x - 2) \qquad \text{gives quotient } x - 1 \text{ with remainder } 2.$$

That is, division of polynomials leads to a polynomial quotient with a polynomial remainder. This property of polynomials is a theorem that we state without proof.

Theorem 3-2

THE DIVISION ALGORITHM. Given two polynomials P and D with $D \neq 0$, there are unique polynomials Q and R such that either $R = 0$ or the degree of R is less than the degree of D and

$$P = QD + R.$$

D is called the divisor, Q the quotient, and R the remainder.

We first illustrate Theorem 3–2 for *monomial* divisors, that is, polynomials of the form ax^n.

Example 1

Suppose $P(x) = 2x^4 - 3x^3 + 3x^2 + 2x - 1$ and $D(x) = 3x^2$. We seek $Q(x)$ such that

$$2x^4 - 3x^3 + 3x^2 + 2x - 1 = Q(x) \cdot 3x^2 + R(x),$$

where R either is 0 or has degree less than 2. Clearly, Q must be of degree 2 in order that $Q(x) \cdot 3x^2$ be a fourth-degree polynomial.

$$
\begin{array}{r}
\frac{2}{3}x^2 - x + 1 \\
3x^2 \overline{\smash{\big)}\ 2x^4 - 3x^3 + 3x^2 + 2x - 1} \\
\underline{2x^4 \phantom{{}- 3x^3 + 3x^2 + 2x - 1}} \\
-3x^3 + 3x^2 + 2x - 1 \\
\underline{-3x^3 \phantom{{}+ 3x^2 + 2x - 1}} \\
3x^2 + 2x - 1 \\
\underline{3x^2 \phantom{{}+ 2x - 1}} \\
2x - 1
\end{array}
$$

Therefore, $Q(x) = \frac{2}{3}x^2 - x + 1$ and $R(x) = 2x - 1$. So

$$\frac{2x^4 - 3x^3 + 3x^2 + 2x - 1}{3x^2} = (\tfrac{2}{3}x^2 - x + 1) + \frac{2x - 1}{3x^2}.$$

Now consider divisors which are polynomials that are not monomials.

Example 2

Find $Q(x)$ and $R(x)$ such that

$$3x^3 + 2x^2 + 1 = Q(x) \cdot (2x^2 + x + 1) + R(x),$$

where R either is 0 or has degree less than 2.

Solution. It is helpful to include monomials in the polynomial dividend which have zero coefficients when carrying out the division.

$$\begin{array}{r} \frac{3}{2}x \ + \frac{1}{4} \\ 2x^2 + x + 1\overline{\smash{\big)}\ 3x^3 + 2x^2 + 0x + 1} \\ \underline{3x^3 + \frac{3}{2}x^2 + \frac{3}{2}x} \\ \frac{1}{2}x^2 - \frac{3}{2}x + 1 \\ \underline{\frac{1}{2}x^2 + \frac{1}{4}x + \frac{1}{4}} \\ -\frac{7}{4}x + \frac{3}{4} \end{array}$$

Therefore, $Q(x) = \frac{3}{2}x + \frac{1}{4}$ and $R(x) = -\frac{7}{4}x + \frac{3}{4}$.

Problems

Set A

Find the quotient and remainder (of degree less than that of the divisor) for each of the following.

1. $(6x^2 - 10x) \div 2x$

2. $(5x^3 + 10x^2 - 20x) \div 5x$

3. $(9x^2 + 3x) \div 3x$

4. $(2x^4 + 3x^3 + x + 1) \div 3x$

5. $(2x^4 + 3x^3 + x + 1) \div 3x^2$

6. $(9x^2 + 3x) \div 2x$

7. $(x^3 + 2x^2 - x + 1) \div (x - 1)$

8. $(4x^2 - 5x + 1) \div (4x - 1)$

9. $(x^3 - 8) \div (x - 2)$

10. $(x^4 - 1) \div (x^2 - 1)$

11. $(2x^4 + 3x^3 + x + 1) \div (3x^2 + x)$

12. $(2x^4 + 3x^3 + x + 1) \div (3x^2 + x + 1)$

Set B

Find the quotient and remainder.

13. $(y^4 - 16) \div (y + 1)$

14. $(x^4 - 16) \div (x + 2)$

15. $(y^4 - 16) \div (y^2 + y + 1)$

16. $(6t^5 - 5t^4 - 6t^2 + 2t + 3) \div (2t^2 - t - 1)$

17. $(x^4 - 7x^3 + x^2 + x - 5) \div (x^2 - x - 1)$

18. $(x^6 - a^6) \div (x^5 + ax^4 + a^2x^3 + a^3x^2 + a^4x + a^5)$

19. $(z^4 + z^2 + 1) \div (z^2 - z + 1)$

20. $(a^2x^2 - b^2) \div (ax - b)$

21. $(ax^2 + 2bx + b^2/a) \div (x + b/a)$

Set C

22. Does $2x - 1$ divide $4x^2 + 8x - 5$? If so find the quotient.

23. Does $2x + 3$ divide $2x^3 + 5x^2 + x - 3$?

24. Does $x^2 - x - 1$ divide $2x^3 - 3x^2 - 5x - 5$?

25. Find a real number k such that $6x^2 + kx + 6$ is divisible by $2x - 3$. [*Hint:* $R = 0$.]

26. Show that there is no polynomial p such that $x^2 + 1 = (x + 1)p(x)$. What does this say about the divisibility of $x^2 + 1$ by $x + 1$?

27. Show by an example that R in Theorem 3–2 is not unique unless we specify that the degree of R is less than the degree of D.

Calculator Problem

Let $p(x) = 1.8x^4 - 2.7x^3 + 1.3x^2 - 4.5x + 7.4$. Calculate $\dfrac{p(-1.3) - p(2.1)}{p(0.8)}$.

Synthetic Division

If the divisor of a polynomial is of the form $D(x) = x - a$, the division process may be simplified by a method called *synthetic division*. This method is illustrated in the examples that follow.

Example 1   Divide $3x^4 - 2x^3 - 7x^2 + 3x - 9$ by $x - 2$.

Solution.

$$
\begin{array}{r}
3x^3 + 4x^2 + 1x + 5 \\
x - 2 \overline{\smash{\big)}\, 3x^4 - 2x^3 - 7x^2 + 3x - 9} \\
\underline{3x^4 - 6x^3} \\
4x^3 - 7x^2 \\
\underline{4x^3 - 8x^2} \\
1x^2 + 3x \\
\underline{1x^2 - 2x} \\
5x - 9 \\
\underline{5x - 10} \\
1
\end{array}
$$

Therefore, $Q(x) = 3x^3 + 4x^2 + x + 5$ and $R(x) = 1$.

The coefficients of the quotient and where these coefficients first appear in the division are shown in color. If you examine the division carefully, you may discover that each coefficient of the quotient results from multiplying the coefficient that precedes it by (-2) and subtracting that product from the corresponding coefficient of the dividend. Thus the coefficient 4 results from $-2 - 3(-2)$. Similarly, the coefficient 1 (printed in this problem for clarity) results from $-7 - 4(-2)$. Since the leading coefficient of the quotient will always be the same as the leading coefficient of the dividend, we may start with this information and determine all the coefficients and the remainder successively. The work may be arranged in a convenient schematic manner. In order to further simplify the process, instead of multiplying by (-2) and subtracting, we shall multiply by 2 and add.

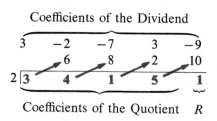

Coefficients of the Dividend

Coefficients of the Quotient   R

Example 2   Find the quotient and remainder if $5x^4 - 2x^2 + 1$ is divided by $x + 3$; use synthetic division.

Solution. We must include the zero coefficients of the dividend and since $x + 3 = x - (-3)$, the factor we use at each step in the synthetic process is -3.

$$5x^4 - 2x^2 + 1 = 5x^4 + 0x^3 - 2x^2 + 0x + 1$$

$$
\begin{array}{r|rrrrr}
 & 5 & 0 & -2 & 0 & 1 \\
 & & -15 & 45 & -129 & 387 \\
\hline
-3 & 5 & -15 & 43 & -129 & \big|\ 388
\end{array}
$$

Therefore, the quotient is $5x^3 - 15x^2 + 43x - 129$ and the remainder is 388.

Problems

Set A

Use synthetic division to find the quotient and remainder.

1. $(x^3 - x^2 + x - 1) \div (x - 1)$

2. $(2x^3 - 6x^2 + x - 5) \div (x - 6)$

3. $(x^3 + 6x^2 + 6x + 2) \div (x + 2)$

4. $(2x^4 - x^2 + 3x - 5) \div (x + 3)$

5. $(x^5 - 2x^4 - 4x^2 + 2) \div (x - 1)$

6. $(x^5 + 1) \div (x + 1)$

7. $(4x^4 + 2x^2 - 1) \div (x - \frac{1}{2})$

8. $(3x^3 + ax^2 + a^2x + 2a^3) \div (x - a)$

9. $(3x^4 + 22x^3 - 19x^2 - 22x + 16) \div (x + 8)$

10. $(x^6 - 64) \div (x - 2)$

Set B

Find the quotient and remainder for each problem given the following coefficients of the dividend and divisors.

11. $1, 3, -2, 2$; Divisor: $x - 3$

12. $1, 0, 0, -1$; Divisor: $x - 1$

13. $2, -4, -3$; Divisor: $x + 1$

14. $4, -5, 0, -6, -1$; Divisor: $x + 4$

15. $1, -1, 1, -1, 1, -1$; Divisor: $x - 1$

16. $3, 2, 0, -5$; Divisor: $x - 2$

17. $-1, 7, 0, 2, 0, -5$; Divisor: $x + 6$

18. $8, 53, -21$; Divisor: $x - 7$

19. $7, 56, -56, 63$; Divisor: $x + 9$

Set C

20. Find k so that when $4x^3 - 2x^2 - 3x + k$ is divided by $x - 2$, the remainder is 0.

21. Find the coefficient t if $3x^2 - tx + 4$ is exactly divisible by $x + 1$.

22. Explain how the method of synthetic division may be applied if the divisor is of the form $ax + b$ instead of $x - a$. Illustrate the method by dividing $3x^4 - 6x^3 - 9x + 1$ by $3x - 6$.

23. Use synthetic division to find the quotient and remainder when $x^3 + \frac{1}{6}x^2 - \frac{5}{12}x + \frac{1}{12}$ is divided by $x - \frac{1}{3}$.

Calculator Problem

Use synthetic division to find the quotient and remainder.

$$(1.8x^3 - 3.9x^2 - 4.5x + 4.4436) \div (x - 0.7)$$

Factors and Zeros of Polynomials

The roots of a polynomial equation $P(x) = 0$ are called the *zeros* of the polynomial P. An important theorem, known as the Remainder Theorem, will be helpful in our search for factors and zeros of polynomials.

Theorem 3-3

THE REMAINDER THEOREM. Let P be any polynomial and a any number. Let P(x) be divided by x − a:

$$P(x) = Q(x) \cdot (x - a) + R,$$

where R is a constant. Then R = P(a).

Proof

By the Division Algorithm, Theorem 3-2, we know that

$$P(x) = Q(x) \cdot (x - a) + R,$$

where R is of degree less than 1, and hence is a constant polynomial. Since this equality holds for every number x, it holds in particular for $x = a$. Hence, $P(a) = Q(a) \cdot (a - a) + R = 0 + R = R$.

Example 1

If $P(x) = x^3 - 2x^2 + 1$ is divided by $(x - 2)$, then the remainder $R = P(2) = 1$.

Theorem 3-4

THE FACTOR THEOREM. The polynomial P is divisible by the polynomial x − a if and only if P(a) = 0.

The proof of the Factor Theorem is left to the student.

Example 2

The polynomial P, where $P(x) = x^3 + 1$, has $(x + 1)$ as a factor, since $P(-1) = 0$.

The Remainder Theorem can be used with the method of synthetic division to find the value of a polynomial at various real numbers.

Example 3

Given $P(x) = x^4 - 38x^2 + 5x + 42$, find $P(6)$.

Solution. We use synthetic division to find the remainder R, which is the same as $P(6)$ when the polynomial is divided by $x - 6$.

$$
\begin{array}{r|rrrrr}
 & 1 & 0 & -38 & 5 & 42 \\
 &   & 6 & 36 & -12 & -42 \\
\hline
6 & 1 & 6 & -2 & -7 & 0 \\
\end{array}
$$

Hence $P(6) = 0$, and we see that 6 is a zero of the given polynomial.

For certain polynomials it is simpler to substitute directly in the formula for the polynomial than to use synthetic division. For example, we may find $Q(1)$ in the polynomial

$$Q(x) = 2x^8 - x + 1$$

by direct substitution since

$$Q(1) = (2 \cdot 1) - 1 + 1 = 2.$$

Usually one can tell from the complexity of the polynomial which method is more advantageous.

The problem of finding zeros of polynomials may often be difficult. However, for some polynomials, we can determine whether or not the zeros are rational numbers.

Theorem 3-5   **THE RATIONAL ROOT THEOREM.** *If $P(x) = a_0 x^n + a_1 x^{n-1} + \cdots + a_{n-1} x + a_n$ has integral coefficients and r/s is a rational zero of P, and r/s is in lowest terms, then r is a factor of a_n and s is a factor a_0.*

Proof   If r/s is a zero of P, then

$$a_0 \left(\frac{r}{s}\right)^n + a_1 \left(\frac{r}{s}\right)^{n-1} + \cdots + a_{n-1}\left(\frac{r}{s}\right) + a_n = 0. \qquad (1)$$

Multiplying both sides of (1) by s^n we get

$$a_0 r^n + a_1 s r^{n-1} + \cdots + a_{n-1} s^{n-1} r + a_n s^n = 0, \qquad (2)$$

or

$$r(a_0 r^{n-1} + a_1 s r^{n-2} + \cdots + a_{n-1} s^{n-1}) = -a_n s^n. \qquad (3)$$

Equation (3) shows that r is a factor of $-a_n s^n$. Since r is not a factor of s^n, r must be a factor of a_n. Equation (2) may also be written in the form

$$a_1 s r^{n-1} + \cdots a_{n-1} s^{n-1} r + a_n s^n = -a_0 r^n. \qquad (4)$$

Removing the factor s from the left-hand side gives

$$s(a_1 r^{n-1} + \cdots + a_{n-1} s^{n-2} r + a_n s^{n-1}) = -a_0 r^n.$$

Using an argument similar to that for r above, we can show that s must be a factor of a_0.

Example 4   Find any rational zeros of $p(x) = 3x^3 + 4x^2 + 8x - 8$.

Solution. If p has a rational zero r/s, then r must be a factor of -8 and s must be a factor of 3. Therefore, the only choices for r are 1, -1, 2, -2, 4, -4, 8, and -8, and the only choices for s are 1, -1, 3, and -3. Since there are eight choices for r and four choices for s, it would seem that we need to check 32 rational numbers as possible rational zeros of p. Actually we need only check 16 numbers. (Why?) Of course, it is tedious to check 16 numbers, but this is certainly better than checking *every* rational number. The student can show that $\frac{2}{3}$ is the only rational zero of the polynomial.

Corollary　　　*If $P(x) = a_0x^n + a_1x^{n-1} + \cdots + a_{n-1}x + a_n$ is a polynomial with integral coefficients, and t is an integral zero of P, then t is a factor of a_n.*

Example 5　　If $P(x) = x^3 - 2x^2 + x + 4$, then the only possible integral zeros of P are 1, $-1, 2, -2, 4$, and -4. It is not hard to show that -1 is the only integral zero of P.

Problems

Set A

Use the Remainder Theorem to find the remainder when

1. $x^3 + 4x^2 - 7x + 3$ is divided by $x - 2$.

2. $x^4 + 4x^3 + 3x^2 - 7x - 28$ is divided by $x + 2$.

3. $x^3 + 3x^2 - 4$ is divided by $x + 2$.

4. $2x^5 - 5x^3 + 6x - 7$ is divided by $x - 1$.

5. $2x^4 - 8x^3 + 2x^2 - 8x + 33$ is divided by $x + 4$.

6. $17x^{10} - 3$ is divided by $x - 1$.

7. $43x$ is divided by $x - 2$.

8. $x^2 - x + 41$ is divided by $x - 41$.

Use the Factor Theorem to decide if the first polynomial is a factor of the second polynomial.

9. $x + 4$, $2x^2 + 7x - 4$

10. $x - 3$, $3x^3 - 11x + 6$

11. $x - 2$, $x^3 - 4x^2 - x + 10$

12. $x + 1$, $x^5 + x^4 - x^3 + x^2 - x - 1$

Set B

13. Show that $(z - 2)$ is a factor of $z^5 - 32$. Find the other factor by synthetic division.

14. Factors of $x^3 + x^2 - 4x - 4$ are $(x - 2)$, $(x + 2)$, and $(x + 1)$. What are the zeros of the polynomial? Check.

15. Given $p(x) = 2x^4 - 3x^3 - 12x^2 + 7x + 6$, find the following.
　(a) $p(1)$　　　(b) $p(2)$　　　(c) $p(3)$
　(d) $p(-1)$　　(e) $p(-2)$　　(f) $p(-3)$
　(g) What are some of the factors of the polynomial?

16. Given that the zeros of $x^3 - 6x^2 + 11x - 6$ are 1, 2, and 3, what are the factors of the polynomial? Check by multiplication.

17. The only zeros of polynomial function P are 1, 2, and -3.
　(a) Give three linear factors of the polynomial.
　(b) Give a quadratic factor of the polynomial.
　(c) Give the polynomial if $P(3) = 60$.

18. Verify that

$$2x^3 - 3x^2 - 3x + 2 = (2x - 1)(x - 2)(x + 1).$$

Graph the polynomial function.

19. Graph the polynomial $P(x) = x^3 - 3x^2 - 6x + 9$. Obtain from the graph approximations to the zeros of $P(x)$. Hence obtain approximations to the factors of $P(x)$.

20. Show that $\frac{2}{3}$ is a zero of $p(x) = 3x^3 + 4x^2 + 8x - 8$.

Set C

21. (a) Solve the equation $x^2 + x - 1 = 0$ by using the quadratic formula.
(b) What are the zeros of $p(x) = x^2 + x - 1$?
(c) Factor the polynomial $p(x) = x^2 + x - 1$.

22. Factor the polynomial $f(x) = x^2 - 3x + 2$. What are the solutions of the equation $x^2 - 3x + 2 = 0$?

23. Use the Factor Theorem to show that $x^4 + x^2 + 1$ is not divisible by $x - a$ for any real number a.

24. Prove the Factor Theorem.

25. (a) List all the possible rational zeros of $f(x) = 6x^2 + x - 1$.
(b) Determine which numbers are actually zeros of f.

26. The polynomial $g(x) = x^3 - 4x^2 + 6x - 4$ has one integral zero. What is it?

27. Determine all the rational roots of
$$p(x) = x^4 + x^3 - 5x^2 + x - 6 = 0.$$

28. Prove the corollary given in this section.

Calculator Problem

Show that 0.5, -0.7, and -0.3 are zeros of

$$P(x) = x^3 + 0.5x^2 - 0.29x - 0.105.$$

Sketch the graph of the polynomial function.

3–7   The Fundamental Theorem of Algebra

We have seen that if $(x - a)$ is a factor of a polynomial, then a is a zero of the polynomial. Conversely, if a is a zero of a polynomial, then $x - a$ is a factor of the polynomial. However, if we are given a polynomial, the Factor Theorem will not help us locate zeros of the polynomial. In fact, we do not know at this time whether there exist polynomials (other than constants) without zeros or whether every polynomial must have a zero. The following fundamental theorem will give us some insight into this problem.

Theorem 3–6   *THE FUNDAMENTAL THEOREM OF ALGEBRA. If P is any polynomial function of degree $n > 0$ with complex coefficients, then P has a zero that is a complex number.*

The German mathematician Karl Friedrich Gauss (1777–1855) was the first to prove the theorem above. We shall not prove it here. We will, however, use this theorem to show that no polynomial function of degree $n > 0$ can have more than n zeros.

For example, suppose P is a fourth-degree polynomial function with complex coefficients. Then by Theorem 3–6, there is a complex number c_1 such that $P(c_1) = 0$. Hence by the Factor Theorem, $P = (x - c_1)P_1$, where P_1 is a polynomial of degree 3. By Theorem 3–6, P_1 has a complex zero, say

c_2, so that $P = (x - c_1)(x - c_2)P_2$ and P_2 is a polynomial of degree 2. It should be clear that by continuing the argument, we have

$$P(x) = a_0(x - c_1)(x - c_2)(x - c_3)(x - c_4), \qquad \text{where } a_0 \neq 0.$$

Now, if x is any number different from all the numbers c_1, c_2, c_3, and c_4, then $P(x) \neq 0$, and so P does not have more than four zeros. Of course, not all the numbers c_1, c_2, c_3, and c_4 need be distinct. But it is convenient to say, even in this case, that P has four zeros. With this agreement on the use of language, we can say that each polynomial function of degree $n > 0$ has exactly n zeros.

Example 1

P is a polynomial of degree 4 having leading coefficient 5. The zeros of P are $-2, 1, 3, 6$. Therefore, the complete factorization of $P(x)$ is

$$P(x) = 5(x + 2)(x - 1)(x - 3)(x - 6).$$

If the coefficients of P are real, then the complex (nonreal) zeros of P must occur in pairs, as the next theorem states.

Theorem 3-7

If the polynomial P has real coefficients and $P(a + bi) = 0$, with $b \neq 0$, then $P(a - bi) = 0$.

Recall that the numbers $a + bi$ and $a - bi$ are *complex conjugates* of each other. We shall prove this theorem only for the case of second degree polynomials.

Suppose $P(x) = Ax^2 + Bx + C$, where A, B and C are real numbers and $A \neq 0$.

$$\begin{aligned} P(a + bi) &= A(a + bi)^2 + B(a + bi) + C \\ &= (Aa^2 - Ab^2 + Ba + C) + (2Aab + Bb)i \end{aligned} \tag{1}$$

$$\begin{aligned} P(a - bi) &= A(a - bi)^2 + B(a - bi) + C \\ &= (Aa^2 - Ab^2 + Ba + C) - (2Aab + Bb)i \end{aligned} \tag{2}$$

Now if $P(a + bi) = 0$, then both the real and imaginary parts of the complex number given in the right hand side of equation (1) are zero. That is $(Aa^2 - Ab^2 + Ba + C) = 0$ and $(2Aab + Bb) = 0$. But the complex number for $P(a - bi)$ in equation (2) has the same real and imaginary parts. Hence $P(a - bi) = 0$.

Example 2

The polynomial $P(x) = x^2 - 2x + 5$ has $1 + 2i$ as a zero because

$$\begin{aligned} P(1 + 2i) &= (1 + 2i)^2 - 2(1 + 2i) + 5 \\ &= (1 - 4 + 4i) - 2 - 4i + 5 \\ &= 0. \end{aligned}$$

Since $P(1 + 2i) = 0$, we know that $P(1 - 2i) = 0$.

Example 3

The polynomial $P(x) = x^3 - 2x + 4$ has one zero equal to $1 + i$, that is, $P(1 + i) = 0$, as may be easily verified. Since the coefficients of P are real, $1 - i$ must also be a zero: $P(1 - i) = 0$.

4 One zero of the polynomial $f(x) = x^2 + 1$ is i. Since the coefficients of f are real, the other zero has to be $-i$. Hence

$$f(x) = x^2 + 1 = (x + i)(x - i).$$

Problems

Set A

1. Show that the zeros of $x^3 - x^2 + x - 1$ are 1, i and $-i$.

2. Is $2 + 3i$ a zero of $x^2 - 4x + 13$? What is another zero of the polynomial?

3. Show that 1 and -1 are zeros of $x^3 - x^2 - x + 1$. Could the other zero of the polynomial be a complex number?

4. Show that the zeros of $x^3 - 4x^2 + 6x - 4$ are $1 + i$, $1 - i$, and 2.

5. Show that i is a zero of $x^3 + 3x^2 + ix + 4 + i$. Factor this polynomial as a product of first- and second-degree polynomials.

Set B

6. A second-degree polynomial with real coefficients has a leading coefficient of 1 and $2 + i$ as one of its zeros. What is the other zero? Find the polynomial.

7. One zero of a second-degree polynomial with real coefficients is $3 + 4i$. What are the coefficients of the polynomial if $P(0) = 25$?

8. It is given that two of the roots of the equation

$$x^4 - 6x^3 + 18x^2 - 30x + 25 = 0$$

are $1 + 2i$ and $2 - i$. Determine the other roots of this equation and factor the polynomial over the real numbers.

9. Construct a third-degree polynomial with real coefficients that has the complex numbers 2 and $3 + 2i$ for zeros.

10. P is a polynomial of degree 5 having leading coefficient 3. Using the notation of Section 3-7, if P has for a zero the number 2, P_1 has the zero 1, P_2 has the zero -1, P_3 has the zero 2, and P_4 has the zero 5, write out a complete factorization of P.

11. P is a polynomial of degree 4. The leading coefficient of P is $\frac{2}{3}$. Zeros of P, P_1, P_2, P_3 are respectively 6, i, $\sqrt{2}$, $2 - i$. Write out a complete factorization of P.

12. Give in factored form a polynomial of degree 10 and leading coefficient 3 that has no zero except the complex number $\sqrt{3}$.

Set C

13. If $P(x) = x^3 + 2x^2 - 3x + 1$, show that $P(2 + i)$ is the conjugate of $P(2 - i)$.

14. Show that if $P(x) = x^2 + 2x + 2$, then $P(x) > 0$ for every real number x.

15. Give a polynomial of degree 5 whose only root is 2; one of degree 4 whose only roots are i and $\sqrt{2}$.

16. Prove that a polynomial equation of degree 3 cannot have four distinct roots.

17. Prove that if P is a polynomial of degree n, and if P has distinct zeros $b_1, b_2, \ldots, b_n$, then $P(x) \neq 0$ if $x \neq b_i$, $i = 1, 2, \ldots, n$.

18. Prove that every polynomial of degree 3 and with real coefficients must have at least one zero that is a real number.

19. Find a third-degree polynomial with leading coefficient 4 and whose zeros are

$$\tfrac{1}{2}(3 + \sqrt{2}i), \qquad \tfrac{1}{2}(3 - \sqrt{2}i), \qquad \text{and} \qquad i.$$

Calculator Problem

What does a prevaricator do awake or asleep?

To find out multiply 19.99 by the largest prime number less than 20 and multiply the result by the cube root of 2744. Read the answer upside down on the calculator.

3-8   Rational Functions

So far in this chapter, we have systematically studied only polynomials. As we know from algebra, the sum and product of polynomials is again a polynomial, and hence addition and multiplication do not lead to new functions. For division the situation is different. In the first place, we have to be careful not to divide by 0. But, because a polynomial, not the zero polynomial, can have only a finite set of zeros, we need to watch the behavior of a quotient function only at a finite set of numbers.

Definition 3-4   If f and g are polynomials with no common nonconstant factors, then the *quotient of f divided by g,* denoted by f/g, is the function defined by

$$\frac{f}{g}(x) = \frac{f(x)}{g(x)}, \qquad \text{for all } x \text{ for which } g(x) \neq 0.$$

The function f/g, a quotient of polynomials, is called a *rational function.*

Observe the similarity between the terminology used for functions and that used for numbers. Rational numbers are quotients of integers. Rational functions are quotients of polynomials. For this reason, polynomials are often called *rational integral functions.*

One other remark about rational functions should be made. The domain of a rational function does not contain the zeros of the polynomial in the denominator. Further, if $g(a) = 0$, and $f(a) \neq 0$, then, because of continuity, $g(x)$ must be very small for x near a, and hence $|f(x)/g(x)|$ must be large near a. In other words, near a zero of the denominator, the rational function f/g must be unbounded.

Example 1   Graph the rational function F defined by $F(x) = x/(x + 1)$. The domain of F consists of all real numbers except -1.

Solution. Several points on the graph of F are computed in the table below.

x	-3	-2	-1.5	-0.5	0	1	2
$F(x)$	1.5	2	3	-1	0	0.5	0.7

To sketch the graph of F, we must recognize that F is continuous every-where in its domain, but is not defined at -1. Moreover, we must recognize that $|F(x)|$ is large for x near -1. Indeed F is unbounded in any open interval having -1 for an end point. If $x < -1$, then $F(x) > 1$. If $-1 < x < 0$, then $F(x) < 0$. We also note that

$$\frac{x}{x+1} = \frac{x+1-1}{x+1} = 1 - \frac{1}{x+1}.$$

From this we see that if x is a very large positive number, then $F(x)$ is near 1 but less than 1. However, if x is negative and $|x|$ is large, then $F(x)$ is also near 1, but is greater than 1. The graph is shown in Fig. 5.

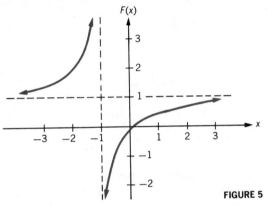

FIGURE 5

Example 2 Graph the rational function G given by $G(x) = x^2/(1 - x^2)$. The domain consists of all real numbers except 1 and -1.

Solution.

$$\begin{array}{lll} \text{If} & |x| < 1, & \text{then} & G(x) \geq 0. \\ \text{If} & |x| > 1, & \text{then} & G(x) < -1. \end{array}$$

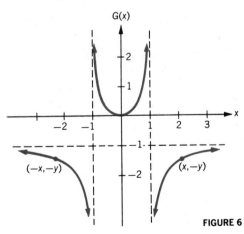

FIGURE 6

This last example illustrates several properties of graphs. From Fig. 6 we see that the graph has *symmetry*. The left half is a mirror image of the right half. We say that the graph is symmetric with respect to the y-axis. Symmetry with respect to the y-axis can easily be determined from the formula for a function. A graph has this symmetry if and only if for each point (x, y) on the graph, the point $(-x, y)$ is also on the graph. In other words, we must have $F(x) = F(-x)$ for every x in the domain of F. A function with this property is called an *even* function.

We can also have symmetry with respect to a point, as in the next example.

Example 3   The graph of the function g given by

$$g(x) = \frac{-1}{x}$$

is shown in Fig. 7. Here we have symmetry with respect to the origin 0. If (x, y) is a point on the graph, then so is $(-x, -y)$. The function g has the property

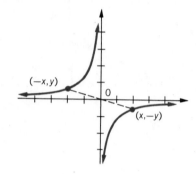

$$g(-x) = -g(x).$$

FIGURE 7

A function with this property is called an *odd* function. All functions are not necessarily odd or even; that is, many functions are neither odd nor even.

Figures 5, 6, and 7 are pictures of graphs having *asymptotes*. In Fig. 5 we observe from the graph that when $|x|$ is large, $F(x)$ is very near to 1. We say that the line $y = 1$ is a *horizontal asymptote* of F. Also, in the same figure, when x is near -1, $F(x)$ is unbounded. The line $x = -1$ is a *vertical asymptote* of F.

In Fig. 6, we observe that

$$G(x) = \frac{x^2}{1 - x^2} = \frac{1}{(1/x^2) - 1},$$

so that when $|x|$ is large, $G(x)$ is near -1. Thus the line $y = -1$ is a horizontal asymptote. Also, when $|x|$ is near 1, $G(x)$ is unbounded. Hence the lines $x = \pm 1$ are vertical asymptotes.

In Fig. 7, we observe that the x- and y-axes are asymptotes.

In these examples the asymptotes were either horizontal or vertical lines. One might ask whether a rational function could have an asymptote not parallel to either axis. The following example shows that this can occur.

Example 4   Figure 8 shows the graph of the function f given by

$$f(x) = \frac{x^2 + 1}{x} = x + \frac{1}{x}$$

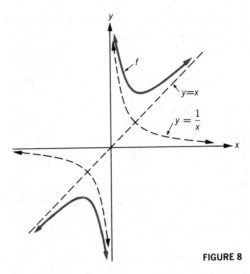

FIGURE 8

When $|x|$ is large, $f(x)$ is very near x. Therefore the line $y = x$ is an asymptote. The curve was drawn by graphical addition of the graphs of $y = x$ and $y = 1/x$.

It will be convenient, for graphing and for later uses, to introduce the symbols $+\infty$ and $-\infty$, called "infinity" and "minus-infinity." *These symbols do not represent numbers.* They are symbols which represent a more complicated idea. We explain uses of these symbols in the following definition.

Definition 3-5
(a) "x approaches $+\infty$" or "x becomes positively infinite" means that we are considering arbitrarily large numbers x. In other words, for any number B, we shall consider numbers larger than B.

(b) "x approaches $-\infty$" means that for any number B, we shall consider numbers less than B.

(c) $[a, +\infty\rangle$ is the interval that includes all real numbers x such that $x \geq a$. Similarly, $\langle -\infty, +\infty\rangle = \mathbf{R}$.

(d) "If x approaches a, then $F(x)$ approaches $+\infty$," which is expressed symbolically by "If $x \to a$, then $F(x) \to +\infty$," means that given any number B, if x is close enough to a, then $F(x) > B$.

We can now better describe horizontal and vertical asymptotes of the graph of a function f.

Definition 3-6
A vertical line, $x = a$, is a *vertical asymptote* if as x approaches a from one side or the other, then $f(x) \to +\infty$ or $f(x) \to -\infty$.

A horizontal line, $y = b$, is a *horizontal asymptote* if $f(x) \to b$ as either $x \to +\infty$, or $x \to -\infty$.

Problems

Set A

Sketch the graphs of the following rational functions. Find all horizontal and vertical asymptotes. What is the domain of each function?

1. $f(x) = \dfrac{x}{x^2 + 1}$ **2.** $W(x) = \dfrac{x^2}{x^2 + 1}$

3. $h(x) = \dfrac{x^2 - 1}{x^2 + 1}$ **4.** $F(x) = \dfrac{x^2 + 1}{x^2 - 1}$

5. $G(x) = \dfrac{1}{(x^2 - 1)^2}$ **6.** $T(x) = \dfrac{3x^2}{x^2 - 4}$

7. $g(x) = \dfrac{x - 1}{x^2(x - 2)}$ **8.** $S(x) = \dfrac{x}{2x - 1}$

9. $U(x) = \dfrac{x^2 - 1}{(x - 2)^2}$ **10.** $V(x) = \dfrac{x^2 - 1}{x - 1}$

Set B

11. Which functions in Problems 1–10 are odd functions? Which are even functions? Which are neither odd nor even?

12. Sketch the graph of

$$t(x) = \frac{x^2 - 1}{x} = x - \frac{1}{x}$$

by sketching the graphs of $f(x) = x$ and $g(x) = -(1/x)$ and then adding f and g graphically.

13. Describe the asymptotes, if any, of the function t of Problem 12.

14. Sketch the graph of

$$r(x) = \frac{x^3 - x + 1}{x} = x^2 - 1 + \frac{1}{x} \text{ by}$$

sketching the graphs of $f(x) = x^2 - 1$ and $g(x) = \dfrac{1}{x}$ and then adding f and g graphically.

Calculator Problem

Set C

15. Does the quotient of the polynomials

$$\frac{x^2 - 1}{x + 1}$$

define a rational function? Explain.

16. Show that the graph of the equation

$$x^3y + 2x^2y + 4xy + y + x^2 + x + 1 = 0$$

is the graph of a rational function.

17. Show that the rational function

$$f(x) = \frac{x^{10}}{x^{12} + 17}$$

has a horizontal asymptote.

18. If $f(x) = -1/(x - 1)$ and if y is in the interval $\langle -\infty, 0 \rangle$, show that there is a unique x in the interval $\langle 1, \infty \rangle$ such that $f(x) = y$.

19. Show that every rational function satisfies an equation of the form

$$P_0(x)F(x) + P_1(x) = 0,$$

where P_0 and P_1 are polynomials with no common nonconstant polynomial factors.

Sketch the graph of $f(x)$ and find the maximum and minimum values if

$$f(x) = \frac{1}{x + \dfrac{1}{x}} \quad \text{for all real } x \neq 0.$$

Algebraic Functions

We have now exhausted the possible functions that can be defined directly in terms of the operations of addition, subtraction, multiplication and division of polynomial functions. To get more functions we introduce a new operation, namely that of solving algebraic equations whose coefficients are polynomials. This will introduce a larger class of functions called *algebraic functions*.

Example 1 Consider the equation

$$xy^2 + 2xy + x - 1 = 0. \tag{1}$$

This equation can be thought of as a quadratic equation in y whose coefficients are polynomials in x. Thus (1) can be thought of as

$$P_1(x)y^2 + P_2(x)y + P_3(x) = 0 \tag{2}$$

where $P_1(x) = x$, $P_2(x) = 2x$ and $P_3(x) = x - 1$. If quadratic equation (1) is solved for y we get

$$y = -1 + \frac{1}{\sqrt{x}}$$

or

$$y = -1 - \frac{1}{\sqrt{x}}.$$

Each solution of the equation defines a function. Thus

$$F(x) = -1 + \frac{1}{\sqrt{x}}$$

and

$$G(x) = -1 - \frac{1}{\sqrt{x}}$$

where the domain of both F and G is $\langle 0, +\infty \rangle$.

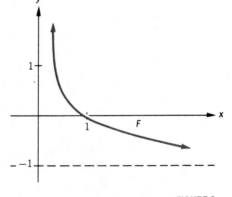

FIGURE 9

The functions F and G are examples of algebraic functions. The graph of F is shown in Figure 9. What is the graph of G?

Definition 3-7 If f is a continuous function and if $y = f(x)$ and x and y satisfy an algebraic equation,

$$P_0(x)y^n + P_1(x)y^{n-1} + \cdots + P_n(x) = 0, \tag{3}$$

where $P_0, P_1, \ldots, P_n$ are polynomials in x, then f is called an *algebraic function*.

Example 2   Show that $f(x) = 1/x + \sqrt{x}$ is an algebraic function.

Solution. We must show that $y = f(x)$ satisfies an equation of the form of (3) in Definition 3–7. If

$$f(x) = y = \frac{1}{x} + \sqrt{x}$$

then

$$\left(y - \frac{1}{x}\right)^2 = (\sqrt{x})^2.$$

Squaring and clearing of fractions we have

$$x^2 y^2 - 2xy + 1 - x = 0.$$

Thus $y = f(x)$ satisfies an algebraic equation of the form given in Definition 3–7. In this example $n = 2$ and $P_0(x) = x^2$, $P_1(x) = -2x$ and $P_2(x) = 1 - x$.

3   Consider the equation

$$(x^4 - 3x^2 + 5)y^{12} + (x^{10} + 1)y^7 + (x - 2)y^3 - y - 7 = 0$$

and suppose that it has been solved. By this we mean that for each real number x, the roots of the equation are known. In general, there will be 12 values of y for each x, so that the equation will define not one function but many. Each of these functions is an algebraic function.

Remark   In general, because of our limited algebraic skills, we will be unable to handle equation (3) if $n > 2$. However, some special equations of higher degree can be considered. For example, if $(x^2 + 1)y^3 - (x - 1) = 0$, then the algebraic function

$$f(x) = y = \sqrt[3]{\frac{x - 1}{x^2 + 1}}$$

satisfies the equation. The other two functions that satisfy this equation involve complex numbers.

Problems

Set A

Graph the following algebraic functions. In each case prove that the function is algebraic by showing that $y = f(x)$ satisfies an equation of the form in Definition 3–6.

1. $f(x) = \dfrac{1}{\sqrt{x}}, \; x \geq 0$

2. $f(x) = \sqrt{4 - x^2}, \; -2 \leq x \leq 2$

3. $f(x) = \sqrt{x} - 1, \; x \geq 0$

4. $f(x) = \sqrt[3]{x} + 1$ for all x

5. $f(x) = 2 - \sqrt{1 - (x - 1)^2}, 0 \leq x \leq 2$

6. $f(x) = 1 - 2\sqrt{x + 2}, \; x \geq -2$

7. $f(x) = \frac{2}{3}\sqrt{x^2 - 9}, \; x \geq 3$ or $x \leq -3$

8. $f(x) = \frac{2}{3}\sqrt{9 - x^2}, \; -3 \leq x \leq 3$

9. $f(x) = \sqrt[3]{x^2}$ for all x

10. $f(x) = \dfrac{1 - x + \sqrt{x^2 + 4}}{2x}, \; x \neq 0.$

Set B

11. Solve $4y^2 - 4y + (1 - x) = 0$ for y. What two algebraic functions does this equation define?

12. Solve $2y - 3x + 1 = 0$ for y. What algebraic function does this equation define? Is this function also a polynomial function?

13. Find one real function defined by the equation $x^2 y^3 - 1 = 0$. Sketch a graph of the function.

14. Given that $f(x) = \sqrt{x} + (1/\sqrt{x}) + 1$, show that f is an algebraic function.

Set C

15. Show that every polynomial function is an algebraic function.

16. Prove that rational functions are algebraic functions.

17. If n is the smallest positive integer for which x and y satisfy an equation of the form (3), then f is said to be an algebraic function of degree n. Give an example of an algebraic function of degree 4.

18. Show that if F is a rational function and $f(x) = \sqrt{F(x)}$, then f is an algebraic function.

Calculator Problem

Graph the function $f(x) = \sqrt[3]{x} - x$ for x in $[-1, 1]$. Evaluate $f(x)$ at successive tenths in this interval. Estimate the "maximum" and "minimum" values of $f(x)$ in the interval. What algebraic equation has a solution which defines the function f?

Summary

1. Polynomials are functions that are generated from the identity function, $\mathrm{Id}(x) = x$ for x in $\mathbf{R}$, the constant functions, $f(x) = a$ for x in $\mathbf{R}$, and the operations of addition and multiplication of functions.

2. A polynomial function P has the form

$$P(x) = a_0 x^n + a_1 x^{n-1} + \cdots + a_{n-1} x + a_n.$$

The numbers $a_0, a_1, \ldots, a_n$ are the *coefficients* of P and the degree of P is n if $a_0 \neq 0$.

3. Polynomials are continuous functions, so the graph of a polynomial is in "one piece."

4. The sum, difference, and product of two polynomials is a polynomial. The quotient of two polynomials is not necessarily a polynomial.

5. The Division Algorithm:

$$P(x) = Q(x) \cdot D(x) + R(x).$$

6. When the divisor $D(x)$ is of the form $x - a$, synthetic division is convenient.

7. The Remainder Theorem:

$$\text{If } P(x) = Q(x)(x - a) + R, \qquad \text{then } R = P(a).$$

8. The Factor Theorem:

$$\text{If } P(a) = 0, \qquad \text{then } P(x) = Q(x)(x - a).$$

9. The rational zeros of a polynomial with *integral* coefficients can be found by trial from the Rational Root Theorem.

10. The Fundamental Theorem of Algebra asserts that every polynomial of positive degree has at least one zero. It follows then that polynomials of degree $n > 0$ have exactly n zeros.

11. Rational functions are quotients of polynomial functions. They include the polynomial functions.

12. Algebraic functions satisfy algebraic equations with polynomial coefficients. They include the rational functions. (See Fig. 10.)

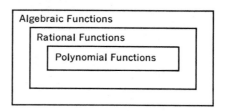

FIGURE 10

Chapter 3   Test

3-2 1. Give the degree and list all coefficients, including zero coefficients, of the polynomial function $p(x) = 3x^4 - 2x^2 + 1$.

2. A polynomial has a coefficient set of $(3, 1, 0, 4, -1)$. What is the value of the polynomial at $x = -2$?

3-3 3. Sketch a graph of the polynomial $p(x) = x^2 - 5x + 6$.

4. Sketch a graph of the polynomial $q(x) = \frac{1}{4}(x - 4)(x + 2)(x + 4)(x - 1)$. What are the zeros of q?

3-4 5. Find the quotient: $(2x^3 - 3x^2 + 8x - 12) \div (2x - 3)$.

6. Find the quotient and remainder: $(6x^3 - 7x^2 - x + 1) \div (3x - 2)$.

3-5 Use synthetic division to find the quotients and remainder.

7. $(2x^4 - 3x^3 + x^2 - 2x + 1) \div (x - 1)$

8. $(x^3 - 27) \div (x - 3)$

3-6 9. Find only the remainder when $3x^4 - 5x^2 - 1$ is divided by $x - 2$.

10. Is $2x^2 - 7x + 5$ divisible by $x - 1$? Use the Remainder Theorem.

11. A polynomial p is such that $p(3) = 0$ and $p(-1) = 0$. What are two linear factors of $p(x)$?

12. (a) What are the possible rational zeros of $p(x) = 4x^3 - 2x^2 - x - 1$?
    (b) Which of the numbers are rational zeros of p?

3-7 13. The polynomial $R(x) = x^2 - 2x + 2$ has $1 + i$ as a zero. What is another zero of R?

14. Given the polynomial $s(x) = x^3 + x^2 + x + 1$,

(a) show that -1 is a rational zero.
(b) show that i is a complex zero.
(c) find a third zero of s.

3-8 15. Sketch the graph of the rational function

$$F(x) = \frac{x}{x - 3}.$$

Determine the asymptotes of F.

16. If $g(x) = (x + 1)/(x^2 - 9)$, what real numbers are excluded from the domain of g?

17. Sketch a graph of the function g of Problem 16.

3-9 18. Sketch the graph of the algebraic function $f(x) = \sqrt{16 - x^2}$. What is the domain of f?

19. Sketch the graph of $g(x) = x^2 - \sqrt{x}$ for $x \geq 0$.

20. Find two algebraic functions that are solutions to $xy^2 - 2xy - x - 1 = 0$.

Chapter 4
Exponential and Logarithmic Functions

4-1 Introduction

There are many functions defined on the real numbers other than algebraic functions. Functions that are not algebraic are called *transcendental functions*. Some nonalgebraic functions occur so frequently that they are referred to as the *elementary* transcendental functions. The first transcendental functions we will study are the *exponential* functions. Later, we shall consider other transcendental functions, such as the *logarithmic* functions and the *trigonometric* functions.

Logarithms were invented by Napier in the early part of the seventeenth century. The use of logarithms in calculation of planetary orbits and other celestial problems was a great aid to astronomers. It has been said that the invention of logarithms "by shortening labors, doubled the life of the astronomer."

Today, hand-held calculators or computers can readily solve problems involving difficult calculations. However the theory of logarithms is still as important as ever.

4-2 Exponents

Before studying the exponential functions it will be convenient to recall some definitions and theorems concerning integral exponents.

Definition 4-1 If x is any real number and n is any positive integer, then

(a) if $n = 1$, $x^n = x$. (b) if $n > 1$, $x^n = x \cdot x^{n-1}$.
(c) if $x \neq 0$, $x^{-n} = 1/x^n$. (d) if $x \neq 0$, $x^0 = 1$.

We call x^n the nth *power of* x. The integer n is called *the exponent of x^n to the base x.*

Having defined integral exponents, we can prove that the five laws of exponents listed in Theorem 4-1 hold.

Theorem 4–1   *For any integers m and n, and x $\neq$ 0, y $\neq$ 0,*

$$(a)\ x^n \cdot x^m = x^{n+m}, \qquad (b)\ x^n/x^m = x^{n-m} = 1/x^{m-n},$$
$$(c)\ (x^n)^m = x^{nm}, \qquad\qquad (d)\ (xy)^n = x^n y^n,$$
$$(e)\ (x/y)^n = x^n/y^n.$$

At this stage we have only exponents that are *integers*. However, we would like to give useful meanings to such symbols as $3^{1/2}$, $3^{-1/2}$, $x^{1/3}$, $a^{-2/3}$. We shall see that it is possible to give definitions such that the five laws of exponents are valid for rational exponents. It would be very inconvenient if the laws for rational exponents were different from the laws for integral exponents. The desire to preserve these laws leads us to our definitions. Consider the following examples.

Example 1   Suppose we have defined $3^{1/2}$ to be a number and the definition has been made so that the laws of exponents are valid for rational exponents. Then by Theorem 4–1(c), we have

$$(3^{1/2})^2 = 3^{(1/2) \cdot 2} = 3^1 = 3.$$

Hence $3^{1/2}$ must be a number whose square is 3. The only possible definition for $3^{1/2}$ that preserves our laws of exponents is that $3^{1/2}$ is one of the two square roots of 3.

2   Consider $5^{1/3}$. Using the same argument as in Example 1, we have

$$(5^{1/3})^3 = 5^{(1/3) \cdot 3} = 5^1 = 5.$$

Hence $5^{1/3}$ must be defined to be a number whose cube is 5, that is, a cube root of 5.

3   Consider $(-4)^{1/2}$. If we assign a meaning to this symbol, clearly we shall wish it to represent a number whose square is -4. This means that we must choose between $2i$ and $-2i$, for $(2i)^2 = 4i^2 = -4$ and $(-2i)^2 = 4i^2 = -4$. However, in this chapter we are primarily interested in real numbers, and for the time being we shall not define symbols like $(-4)^{1/2}$.

In order to define rational exponents, we first define $x^{1/n}$. If $x \geq 0$ and n is a positive integer, then $x^{1/n}$ is the unique *nonnegative* real number such that

$$(x^{1/n})^n = x.$$

If x is *any* real number and n is *odd*, then $x^{1/n}$ is the unique real number such that

$$(x^{1/n})^n = x.$$

If $x < 0$ and n is even, then $x^{1/n}$ is not defined as a real number. (Why?) Having defined the meaning of symbols like $x^{1/n}$, we must still attach meaning to symbols like $4^{2/3}$, $5^{-3/8}$, and, in general, $x^{p/q}$. It is easy to see how these definitions must be made if we are to retain our laws of exponents.

Definition 4-2 If $r = p/q$, where p and q are integers, $q > 0$, and p/q is in lowest terms, then, provided $x^{1/q}$ is defined as a real number, we agree that

$$x^r = x^{p/q} = (x^p)^{1/q} = (x^{1/q})^p.$$

Example 4 We apply this definition in the four following cases.

$$4^{3/2} = (4^3)^{1/2} = (2^6)^{1/2} = 2^3$$
$$(\tfrac{1}{25})^{-3/2} = [(\tfrac{1}{25})^{-3}]^{1/2} = (25^3)^{1/2} = (5^6)^{1/2} = 5^3$$
$$3^{2/3} = (3^2)^{1/3} = 9^{1/3}$$
$$16^{-3/4} = (16^{-1/4})^3 = (2^{-1})^3 = \tfrac{1}{8}$$

Note that if x is negative and q is an even integer, then $x^{p/q}$ is *not* defined. Give an example to illustrate this.

Now that definitions have been made to govern the use of rational exponents, we could prove that the five laws are valid for rational exponents. However, we shall omit their proofs. The problems and examples will show that we have stated the definition for rational exponents so that the five laws of exponents are valid.

Theorem 4-2 *For all rational numbers r and s and for all real numbers x and y for which the expressions below are defined,*

(a) $x^r \cdot x^s = x^{r+s}$, (*Multiplication Law*)
(b) $x^r/x^s = x^{r-s}$, (*Division Law*)
(c) $(x^r)^s = x^{rs}$, (*Power of a Power Law*)
(d) $(xy)^r = x^r \cdot y^r$, (*Power of a Product Law*)
(e) $(x/y)^r = x^r/y^r$. (*Power of a Quotient Law*)

Example 5 Four illustrations of the above theorem follow.

If $a > 0$, $a^{1/2} \cdot a^{-1/2} = a^0 = 1$.

$$\frac{1}{x^r} = \frac{x^0}{x^r} = x^{-r}$$

$$10^a \cdot 10^{-b} = 10^{a-b}$$

$$\left(\frac{2y^{-1}}{5x}\right)^{-3} = \frac{(2y^{-1})^{-3}}{(5x)^{-3}} = \frac{2^{-3}y^3}{5^{-3}x^{-3}} = \frac{5^3 y^3 x^3}{2^3}$$

Problems

Set A

Write each of the following as simply as possible.

1. x^3/x^6
2. $2^7/2^{11}$
3. $y^{-5}y^2$
4. $(ax)^{-3}$
5. $(-5)^0$
6. $a^n \cdot a^{-n}$
7. $3x^{-5}/y^{-3}$
8. $3^{-5}/3$
9. $(2^{-2})^{-3}$
10. $(a^{-2}/b^{-4})^{-2}$
11. $(2x)^{-3}(4y)^2$
12. $5(a+b)^m/2(a+b)^r$
13. $(2x^2)^{-5}$
14. r^{-n+2}/r^{-m-n}
15. x^3/y^3
16. $(3a)^0$
17. $(1+2\sqrt{xy})^0$
18. u^a/u^{3a}
19. $(x^{-2}y^{-3}z^2)^{-2}$
20. $(x^{-1}y^2/z^{-2})^{-3}$
21. $(3^{-1/2})^2$

What rational numbers are represented by the following?

22. $32^{-1/5}$
23. $16^{3/2}$
24. $(\frac{9}{4})^{-3/2}$
25. $(-32)^{2/5}$
26. $(-32)^{-3/5}$
27. $27^{2/3}$
28. $(0.027)^{-1/3}$
29. $4^{-7/2}$
30. $(\frac{1}{64})^{-2/3}$
31. $8^{-5/3}$
32. $25^{-3/2}$
33. $-25^{-3/2}$

Write the following without negative exponents.

34. $2n^{-3/2} \cdot an^{-5/2}$
35. $5x^{-5} \cdot 3x^2$
36. $x^{-1/3}/x^{2/3}$
37. $(16y^{1/3})^{-1/2}$
38. $8^{-2/3} + 3a^0 - (\frac{1}{81})^{-1/4}$
39. $(y^{1/3})^{-3/2}$
40. $(x^{1/2}y^{-1/6}z^{-1/2})^{-4}$
41. $(9x^4/4y^{-2})^{-1/2}$ $(y > 0)$
42. $(x^2)^{1/2}$
43. $(a^4b^2)^{-1/2}$
44. $\dfrac{32x^{-5/2}y^{1/2}}{2^{4/3}x^{-2}y^{-3/2}}$
45. $(2x^{-2}/9y)^{-2}$

Set B

Determine x.

46. $3^{-2} = x$
47. $(\frac{1}{2})^{-3} = x$
48. $(10^{-1})^{-2} = x$
49. $(-2)^{-4} = x$

Compute the exponent x if

50. $2^x = \frac{1}{16}$.
51. $10^x = 0.001$.
52. $(\frac{1}{3})^x = 27$.
53. $(0.02)^x = 2500$.
54. $4^x = \frac{1}{2}$.
55. $(\frac{9}{16})^x = \frac{4}{3}$.
56. $4^x = 8$.
57. $27^x = 9$.
58. $9^x = 3^{10}$.

Compute the *positive* base x if

59. $x^3 = 8^2$.
60. $x^4 = 25^2$.
61. $x^{-2} = \frac{1}{4}$.
62. $x^{-4} = 81$.
63. $x^{-3} = 0.001$.
64. $x^{-1} = \frac{11}{13}$.
65. $x^{3/2} = 64$.
66. $x^{5/3} = -32$.
67. $x^{-3/2} = \frac{8}{27}$.

Determine x.

68. $(5^{2/3})^x = 25$
69. $16^{3/x} = 8$
70. $27^{x/3} = 81$
71. $x^{3/4} = \frac{1}{8}$

Set C

72. Is $(-1)^{1/2}$ a real number? $(-1)^{2/4}$? $[(-1)^2]^{1/4}$?

73. Find all pairs of positive integers x and y such that $x \neq y$ and $x^y = y^x$.

74. Prove that there is no real number r such that $r^{-3/4} = -3$.

75. Locate the positive number x between two integers if $x^6 = 35,714$.

76. Locate the positive number x between two consecutive integers if $x^{5/3} = 20$.

Calculator Problem

Find an integer x such that $(\frac{1}{8})^{-3/4} < x < (\frac{1}{9})^{-3/4}$.

4-3 Exponential Functions

In the last section we defined a^r for every rational number r and every real number $a > 0$. Now we want to extend the domain of exponents to the set $\boldsymbol{R}$ of real numbers in such a way that the laws of exponents still remain valid.

To see how this extension is possible, let us consider the function

$$f(x) = 2^x \qquad \text{for all rational numbers } x.$$

The graph of this function is shown in Fig. 1, where the graph is dashed to emphasize that the domain is the set of rational numbers and not the set of all real numbers. Several items are clear from the graph, namely, that the function is increasing, is not bounded above, is always positive or bounded below by the x-axis, and assumes arbitrarily small positive values as $x \to -\infty$.

Now we want to extend the domain of this function so as to include all real numbers. That is, we wish to know what numbers to assign to

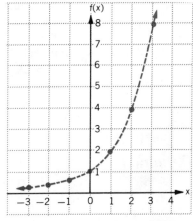

FIGURE 1

symbols such as $2^{\sqrt{2}}, 2^\pi, 2^{\sqrt[3]{4}}$. Since the exponents are irrational numbers, the definition of the previous section for rational exponents does not apply. However, from the graph of f it is clear what would be desirable.

Let us consider the specific case of $2^{\sqrt{2}}$. If we desire to keep the property that f is continuous and increasing, then for rational numbers r and s such that $r < \sqrt{2} < s$, we should have

$$2^r < 2^{\sqrt{2}} < 2^s.$$

The real number $\sqrt{2}$ may be approximated as closely as we desire by rational numbers. For example, because we know that

$$
\left.
\begin{array}{l}
1.4 \quad < \sqrt{2} < 1.5 \\
1.41 \quad < \sqrt{2} < 1.42 \\
1.414 \: < \sqrt{2} < 1.415 \\
1.4142 < \sqrt{2} < 1.4143 \\
\vdots
\end{array}
\right\}
\text{we should have}
\left\{
\begin{array}{l}
2^{1.4} \quad < 2^{\sqrt{2}} < 2^{1.5}, \\
2^{1.41} \quad < 2^{\sqrt{2}} < 2^{1.42}, \\
2^{1.414} \: < 2^{\sqrt{2}} < 2^{1.415}, \\
2^{1.4142} < 2^{\sqrt{2}} < 2^{1.4143} \\
\vdots
\end{array}
\right.
$$

A calculator with an exponential key, y^x, can be used to find the approximate value of the rational powers of 2. For example

$$2^{1.4142} \approx 2.6651190 \qquad \text{and} \qquad 2^{1.4143} \approx 2.6653038.$$

Thus we should have $2.6651190 < 2^{\sqrt{2}} < 2.6653038$. By considering better and better approximations for $\sqrt{2}$, we may further narrow down the choice of the number to be assigned to $2^{\sqrt{2}}$. Thus, if we consider the set of numbers S_1,

$$S_1 = \{2^{1.4}, 2^{1.41}, 2^{1.414}, 2^{1.4142}, \ldots\},$$

where all the exponents are rational numbers less than $\sqrt{2}$, we see that S_1 is a set of numbers that is *bounded above*. For example, we see that $2^{1.5}$ is an upper bound of S_1. Other upper bounds of S_1 are $2^{1.6}$, 2^2, 5, and 10. Since S_1 is indeed bounded above (the Completeness Axiom), there is a unique real number that is the least upper bound of S_1. We *define* $2^{\sqrt{2}}$ to be the least upper bound of S_1.

This means that for the coordinate $\sqrt{2}$ on the x-axis there exists a real number $2^{\sqrt{2}}$, and hence there exists the point $(\sqrt{2}, 2^{\sqrt{2}})$ on the graph of $f(x) = 2^x$. Since we could discuss all the other irrational powers of 2 in a similar manner, we know that $f(x) = 2^x$ is defined for all real x.

Analogous to the example of $f(x) = 2^x$, we can assign meaning to a^x for all real numbers x and for any real positive base a.

Definition 4-3   Let $a \geq 1$, and let x be any real number. Let S be the set of all numbers a^t, for all rational numbers $t < x$. Then a^x is the *least upper bound* of S.

Definition 4-4   For each real number $a \geq 1$, $f(x) = a^x$ defines a function whose domain is the set of all real numbers. We call each of these functions an *exponential function*. Its value at x is the number a^x. If $0 < a < 1$, we define

$$a^x = \left(\frac{1}{a}\right)^{-x}.$$

The following important theorem can now be proved, although the proof of each assertion is not at all easy. We shall assume that this theorem is valid.

Theorem 4-3   *The exponential function $f(x) = a^x$, where x is a real number,*

(a) *is increasing if $a > 1$, decreasing if $0 < a < 1$, constant if $a = 1$,*
(b) *is continuous,*
(c) *is a one-to-one mapping of the real numbers onto the positive real numbers, if $a \neq 1$,*
(d) *obeys the laws of exponents:*

For all real numbers x and y,
(1) $a^x \cdot a^y = a^{x+y}$,   (2) $a^x / a^y = a^{x-y}$,
(3) $(a^x)^y = a^{xy}$,   (4) $(a \cdot b)^x = a^x \cdot b^x$,
(5) $(a/b)^x = a^x / b^x$.

Example 1   Sketch the graph of $f(x) = a^x$ for $a = 2$.

Solution. We use the following table and connect these points by a smooth continuous curve. (See Fig. 2.)

x	$f(x) = 2^x$
-3	$\frac{1}{8}$
-2	$\frac{1}{4}$
-1	$\frac{1}{2}$
0	1
1	2
2	4
3	8

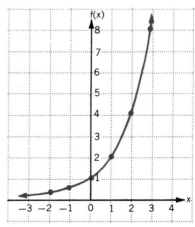

FIGURE 2

2 $10^2 \cdot 10^{-3} = 10^{-1}$, $7^{1.53} \cdot 7^{2.44} = 7^{3.97}$,
    $10^{\sqrt{2}} \cdot 10^2 = 10^{(2+\sqrt{2})}$, $(\frac{2}{3})^{1.472} = 2^{1.472}/3^{1.472}$,
    $3^{\sqrt{2}}/3^1 = 3^{(\sqrt{2}-1)}$

3   Find x if $2^x = 32$. Since $2^5 = 32$, we have $2^x = 2^5$ and $x = 5$. There can be only one root of this equation because 2^x is increasing. That is, if $x > 5$, $2^x > 2^5$, and if $x < 5$, $2^x < 2^5$.

Problems

Set A

Write each of the following as a power of one number.

1. $3^{1/2} \cdot 3^2$

2. $6^{-2} \cdot 6^3$

3. $5^{2.3} \cdot 5^{1.4}$

4. $\dfrac{x^{1/2}}{x^{1/4}}$

5. $2^3 \cdot 2^2$

6. $\dfrac{4^{-3}}{32^{1/4}}$

7. $a^5 \cdot a^{-3}$

8. $10^7 \cdot 10^{-5}$

9. $3^{-1.53} \cdot 3^{-2.71}$

10. $\dfrac{2^y}{8^y}$

11. $a^x \cdot a^y \cdot a^s$

12. $\dfrac{a^u \cdot a^v}{a^w}$

13. $2^{-3.4} \cdot 8$

14. $100 \cdot 10^{-1.47}$

15. $\frac{1}{100} \cdot 10^{4.32}$

Find x in each equation.

16. $2^x = 2$

17. $2^x = 1$

18. $(\frac{2}{3})^x = \frac{3}{2}$

19. $\dfrac{1}{3^x} = 27$

20. $\dfrac{1}{2^x} = \dfrac{1}{8}$

21. $2^{x-1} = 4$

22. $4^{x-1} = 64$

23. $10^{x-1} = 0.1$

24. $10^{2x-1} = 10^a$

Graph each of the following functions. Obtain the value of each at $x = 1.5$ and $x = -1.5$ from the graph.

25. 3^x

26. $(\frac{1}{2})^x$

27. 2^{-x}

28. 4^x

29. 4^{-x}

30. $(\frac{1}{3})^x$

31. $3 \cdot 2^x$

32. $2^x - 2$

Set B

33. Sketch as accurately as you can a graph of 10^x for x between -1 and 1. Then read from your graph the following numbers.

    (a) $10^{0.3}$ (b) $10^{0.9}$

    (c) $10^{-0.9}$ (d) $10^{-0.3}$

    (e) $10^{0.25}$ (f) $10^{-0.25}$

    (g) $10^{0.75}$ (h) $10^{-0.75}$

    (i) $10^{0.1}$ (j) $10^{-0.1}$

    (k) x if $10^x = 2$ (l) x if $10^x = \frac{1}{2}$

    (m) x if $10^x = 3$ (n) x if $10^x = \frac{1}{3}$

    (o) t if $10^t = 5$ (p) t if $10^t = 0.2$

    (q) s if $10^s = 9$ (r) s if $10^s = \frac{1}{9}$

    (s) x if $10^x = 3.2$ (t) x if $10^x = 0.63$

34. Why are exponential functions not defined for $a < 0$? for $a = 0$? Describe the graph of a^x if $a = 1$.

Set C

Some of the following exponential functions are very useful in applied mathematics. Graph each function.

35. $f(x) = 2^{-x^2}$

36. $f(x) = 2^{x^2}$

37. $f(x) = 2^{1/x},\ x \neq 0$

38. $f(x) = 2^{-1/x^2},\ x \neq 0$

39. $f(x) = 2^x + 2^{-x}$

40. $f(x) = 2^x - 2^{-x}$

41. Sketch a graph of $f(x) = -(2^{-(1/2)x})$. Discuss the range, bounds, and asymptotes of f.

42. Prove that if f is an exponential function and x_1 and x_2 are numbers in the domain of f, then $f(x_1 + x_2) = f(x_1) \cdot f(x_2)$.

43. Prove that if f is an exponential function and x_1 and x_2 are in the domain of f, then $f(x_1 - x_2) = f(x_1)/f(x_2)$.

44. Sketch an approximate graph of $f(x) = (\sqrt{2})^x$. From the graph give a rational approximation of $(\sqrt{2})^{\sqrt{2}}$.

45. If $f(x) = 2^{-x}$ for all x, and $g(x) = (\frac{1}{2})^x$ for all x, is $f = g$? Prove your answer.

Calculator Problem

Use the y^x key on a calculator to find x to the nearest thousandth in the equations,

$$3^x = 2.626$$
$$x^x = 2$$

4-4   Applications of the Exponential Functions

Exponential functions occur in many applications, most importantly as a means of expressing the law of growth or decay in mathematical terms.

Example 1   The number, N, of bacteria in a pure nutrient solution tend to increase according to the law

$$N = N_0 2^{kt},$$

where t is time measured in some units, k is a positive constant depending on the unit of time, the kind of bacteria, and the nutrient, and N_0 is the number of bacteria present at time $t = 0$.

Suppose that initially 10^4 bacteria are present in the solution, and $k = 1$ when time is measured in hours. Then at time t the number of bacteria present would be $N = 10^4 \cdot 2^t$. Hence at the end of $\frac{5}{2}$ hours,

$$N = 10^4 \cdot 2^{2.5} = 10^4(5.7) = 57{,}000, \text{ approximately.}$$

2   Radioactive substances tend to decay according to the law $S = S_0 2^{-kt}$, where t is time measured in some units, k is a positive constant depending upon the substance, S_0 is the quantity of the substance present at time $t = 0$, and S is the quantity at time t.

The element actinium decays according to the law $A = A_0 2^{-0.05t}$, where t is measured in years. Then at the end of 10 years, the quantity left would be

$$A = A_0 2^{-0.5} = A_0(0.707).$$

In discussing radioactive decay, one customarily works with the *half-life*, which is the time required to reduce A_0 to $A_0/2$, instead of using the constant k. In this example, if T is the half-life, then

$$\frac{A_0}{2} = A_0 2^{-0.05T}, \qquad 2^{-1} = 2^{-0.05T},$$

and hence $2 = 2^{0.05T}$, and $0.05T = 1$ or $T = 20$ years.

3   Uranium 238 has a half-life of about 4.5×10^9 years. Thus it would take 4.5×10^9 years for 4 milligrams of U_{238} to decay to 2 milligrams and another 4.5×10^9 years for the remaining mass to decay to 1 milligram. If A_0 is the original amount, then for U_{238} we have

$$\frac{A_0}{2} = A_0 2^{-k \cdot 4.5 \times 10^9}.$$

Solving for k we have

$$2^{-1} = 2^{-k \cdot 4.5 \times 10^9},$$
$$k \doteq 0.22 \times 10^{-9}.$$

Problems

Set A

Solve each equation for T, where T is the half-life in years.

1. $\dfrac{A_0}{2} = A_0 2^{-0.04T}$

2. $\dfrac{A_0}{2} = A_0 2^{-0.005T}$

3. $\dfrac{A_0}{2} = A_0 2^{-0.001T}$

4. $\dfrac{A_0}{2} = A_0 2^{-0.025T}$

Set B

5. The number of a certain kind of bacterium tends to increase according to the formula $N = N_0 2^{(1/2)t}$, where time t is measured in hours and N_0 is the number present when $t = 0$. If there were approximately 10^3 bacteria present at the start of an experiment, how many would be present after one day? How many would be present after four days? after ten days?

6. An isotope of strontium, Sr^{90}, has a half-life of 25 years. How long would it take 4 milligrams of Sr^{90} to decay to a mass of 1 milligram?

7. Scientists can determine the age of some objects by a method called *radiocarbon dating*. This method utilizes the fact that an isotope of carbon, C^{14}, has a half-life of 5700 years. How many years would it take for a given amount of C^{14} to reduce to one-eighth the given amount?

8. In three days a certain amount of manganese-52, Mn^{52}, decays to $1/\sqrt{2}$ of its original amount. What is the half-life of Mn^{52}?

9. After a period of 90 days a certain amount of Silver-110, Ag^{110}, has decayed to about 80 percent of its original amount. Find the approximate half-life of Ag^{110}.

10. Suppose the amount of technical and scientific information available in the world tends to double every ten years. Let A_0 represent the amount of scientific information available in some kind of units at the present time. Write a formula for the amount of information available at any time t in years.

11. Bacteria in a nutrient solution double at the end of 2 hours. How many are present after $3\frac{1}{2}$ hours?

Set C

12. An isotope of thorium, Th^{232}, has a half-life of 1.39×10^{10} years. Find a formula for the present amount A of Th^{232} in terms of the original amount A_0 and the time t in years.

13. The isotope Ra^{226} has a half-life of 1590 years. Find a formula for the present amount A in terms of the original amount A_0 and the time t in years.

Calculator Problem

Suppose that the cost of an article in the year 1980 was $1.00. Assume that the annual increase in the cost of the article due to inflation is 12%.

(a) In what year will the cost of the article be about $2.00?

(b) What would be the cost of the article in the year 2000?

4-5 Logarithmic Functions

We now can define the logarithmic functions. The exponential function given by $f(x) = a^x$, where a is some fixed positive number different from 1, has for domain the set of real numbers and for range the set of positive real numbers. Furthermore, f maps the domain R one-to-one onto the set of positive real numbers. Therefore, f has an inverse. Note, however, that we cannot give a simple rule for the inverse of the exponential function. For if $f(x) = y = a^x$, we do not have, at the present moment, a way of solving this equation for x. But because we know that the inverse to the exponential function exists, we shall define it to be the *logarithmic* function.

Definition 4-5 The inverse of the function f defined by $f(x) = a^x$ is called the *logarithmic function with base a*, and is denoted by $\log_a$.
The value of this function at y is that unique number x such that

$$y = a^x, \text{ that is, } \log_a y = x.$$

We read this as "the logarithm of y to the base a is x."

Observe that one can express the definition above in words as follows. "The logarithm of a number to the base a is the exponent of that power of a which is equal to the given number." Hence, we sometimes say, abusing the language, *logarithms are exponents*.
The graph of the exponential function with base $a > 1$ is shown in Fig. 3.

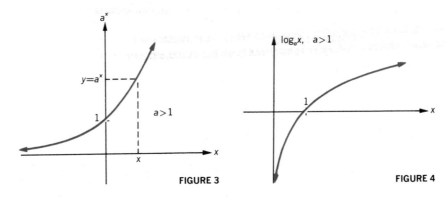

FIGURE 3   FIGURE 4

The graph of the logarithmic function with base $a > 1$ is shown in Fig. 4. Observe that the logarithmic function is increasing, unbounded, and continuous, and is defined for x in $\langle 0, +\infty \rangle$. Also note that as x approaches 0, $\log_a x$ approaches $-\infty$ if $a > 1$.
If $a = 10$, the logarithmic function is called the *common* logarithmic function, and we usually omit the base, writing "log 5" and "log 6.34" instead of "$\log_{10} 5$" and "$\log_{10} 6.34$."

Example 1　Write an equivalent exponential statement for $\log_4 \frac{1}{64} = -3$.

Solution. If $\log_4 \frac{1}{64} = -3$, then, by definition of logarithm,

$$4^{-3} = \tfrac{1}{64}.$$

2　$\log 100 = 2$ because $10^2 = 100$, $\log 0.1 = -1$ because $10^{-1} = 0.1$

3　Since $8^{2/3} = 4$, $\log_8 4 = \frac{2}{3}$

Problems

Set A

Write equivalent statements for the following, using logarithmic functions.

1. $2^5 = 32$
2. $3^4 = 81$
3. $8^{1/3} = 2$
4. $10^3 = 1000$
5. $10^{-2} = 0.01$
6. $2^{1/2} = 1.414$
7. $5^0 = 1$
8. $9^{1.5} = 27$
9. $10^{1/2} = 3.162$
10. $3^5 = 243$
11. $8^{-1} = 0.125$
12. $5^{-2} = 0.04$
13. $10^x = y$
14. $a^r = s$
15. $t^u = v$

Write statements equivalent to the following, using exponential functions.

16. $\log 1 = 0$
17. $\log_a 1 = 0$
18. $\log 10 = 1$
19. $\log 100 = 2$
20. $\log_a z = w$
21. $\log 2 = 0.3010$
22. $\log 5 = 0.699$
23. $\log \frac{1}{2} = -0.301$
24. $\log_2 32 = 5$
25. $\log_4 64 = 3$

Set B

Evaluate.

26. $\log_2 8$
27. $\log_2 \sqrt{8}$
28. $\log_3 \frac{1}{9}$
29. $\log_x 1$
30. $\log \frac{1}{10}$
31. $\log_5 \frac{1}{125}$

Copy and complete the following logarithm tables.

32.

N	$\log_{10} N$
0.001	
0.01	
0.1	
1	
10	
100	
1000	

33.

N	$\log_2 N$
$\frac{1}{8}$	
$\frac{1}{4}$	
$\frac{1}{2}$	
1	
2	
4	
8	

34. Between what two consecutive integers are the common logarithms of numbers between 10 and 100? between 1 and 10? between 0.001 and 0.01?

Set C

35. Show that if $1 \le x < 10$, then $0 \le \log_{10} x < 1$.

36. What is $\log_a a$? $\log_a a^t$? $a^{\log_a x}$? Give your explanations in terms of the definition.

Give the values of the following.

37. $10^{\log 100}$
38. $10^{\log 1000}$
39. $10^{\log 0.1}$
40. $10^{\log 2}$

Calculator Problem

Find x if $\pi^x = 2^\pi$.

Graphs and Properties of the Logarithmic Functions

The graph of $y = \log x$ is easily obtained from that of the exponential function with base 10. The graph is shown in Fig. 5, where the vertical scale is exaggerated in order to have a more informative graph. From the graph we can read approximate values for the common logarithms of numbers between 1 and 10. Except for larger and smaller numbers, the graph is sufficiently accurate. For example, $\log 2$ is approximately 0.3. Note that this logarithmic function is increasing.

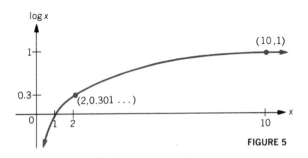

FIGURE 5

The logarithmic functions have a number of important properties corresponding to the various laws of exponents. These properties give the logarithmic functions their wide range of application.

Theorem 4-4

(a) *The logarithm of a product of positive numbers is equal to the sum of the logarithms of the factors:*

$$\log_a xy = \log_a x + \log_a y.$$

(b) *The logarithm of a quotient of positive numbers is equal to the difference of the logarithms of dividend and divisor:*

$$\log_a \frac{x}{y} = \log_a x - \log_a y.$$

(c) *The logarithm of a power of a positive number is equal to the exponent of that power times the logarithm of the number:*

$$\log_a x^y = y \log_a x.$$

Because logarithms are exponents, the laws of exponents are reflected in these properties. A proof of the theorem must therefore depend upon the corresponding theorem concerning exponents.

Proof   **Part (a).** Suppose that $\log_a x = u$ and $\log_a y = v$. Then $x = a^u$ and $y = a^v$. (Why?) Hence

$$xy = a^u \cdot a^v = a^{u+v}, \qquad \text{(Why?)}$$

and

$$\log_a xy = u + v,$$

so

$$\log_a xy = \log_a x + \log_a y.$$

Proofs of parts (b) and (c) are left as problems (Set C, 28 and 29).

Example 1   Three illustrations of Theorem 4–4 follow.

$$\log_2 16 \cdot 8 = \log_2 16 + \log_2 8 = 4 + 3 = 7$$
$$\log_2 \tfrac{64}{16} = \log_2 64 - \log_2 16 = 6 - 4 = 2$$
$$\log_{10} 100^5 = 5 \cdot \log_{10} 100 = 5 \cdot 2 = 10$$

2   If $\log 2 = 0.3010$, then

$$\log 200 = \log 100 \cdot 2 = \log 100 + \log 2 = 2 + 0.3010,$$
$$\log 0.02 = \log \tfrac{1}{100} \cdot 2 = \log \tfrac{1}{100} + \log 2 = -2 + 0.3010,$$
$$\log 200{,}000 = 5 + 0.3010,$$
$$\log 0.000002 = -6 + 0.3010.$$

The logarithmic functions are inverses of the exponential functions and the exponential functions obey the laws of exponents for real numbers (Theorem 4–3). Therefore, the laws of logarithms (Theorem 4–4) have a formulation in terms of exponents as shown below.

THE LAWS OF EXPONENTS AND LAWS OF LOGARITHMS

For real numbers $a > 1$, $u > 0$, $v > 0$,

$$a^x \cdot a^y = a^{x+y} \qquad \textit{and} \qquad \log_a uv = \log_a u + \log_a v,$$

$$\frac{a^x}{a^y} = a^{x-y} \qquad \textit{and} \qquad \log_a \frac{u}{v} = \log_a u - \log_a v,$$

$$(a^x)^y = a^{xy} \qquad \textit{and} \qquad \log_a u^z = z \log_a u.$$

Sometimes it is necessary to change from one base to another in dealing with logarithmic functions. The next theorem gives the way that this can be accomplished.

Theorem 4-5   *For real numbers $a > 1$, $b > 1$, and $N > 0$,*

$$\log_a N = \log_b N \cdot \log_a b.$$

Proof   Let $\log_b N = x$ and $\log_a b = y$. Then $b^x = N$ and $a^y = b$ by the definition of logarithms. Therefore, $(a^y)^x = a^{xy} = N$, so that

$$\log_a N = xy = \log_b N \cdot \log_a b.$$

Example 3   Find $\log_2 6$ if $\log 6 = 0.7782$ and $\log 2 = 0.3010$.

    Solution. By Theorem 4-5 we must have $\log 6 = \log_2 6 \cdot \log 2$. Thus

$$0.7782 = \log_2 6 \cdot 0.3010 \quad \text{and} \quad \log_2 6 = \frac{0.7782}{0.3010} = 2.5854.$$

    Historically, logarithms were invented to shorten the enormous labor of astronomical calculations. The English mathematician, Henry Briggs (1556–1631) first suggested the advantage of using base 10 for logarithms. Tables of logarithms have been carefully computed and can be used in calculations. A table of common logarithms can be found in the Appendix as well as instruction in computing with logarithms. Since the hand-held calculator is readily accessible for ordinary calculations and the large computer available for very complex calculations, the use of logarithms as an aid in calculating is less important today than in the past.

Problems

Set A

Assume that the variables in the following problems are suitably restricted so that all expressions have meaning.

1. Draw a graph of $f(x) = 10^x$ for $-1 \le x \le 1$. Make the graph as large as possible on a single sheet of graph paper. Use the graph to construct the graph of the inverse of the function. That is, construct a graph of the function

$$f(x) = \log x \quad \text{for } \tfrac{1}{10} \le x \le 10.$$

2. From the graph constructed in Problem 1 estimate the following.
   - (a) $\log 2$
   - (b) $\log 3$
   - (c) $\log 4$
   - (d) $\log 5$
   - (e) $\log 6$
   - (f) $\log 7$
   - (g) $\log 8$
   - (h) $\log 9$

3. Use the graph of Problem 1 to find x approximately if
   - (a) $\log x = 0.25$.
   - (b) $\log x = 0.5$.
   - (c) $\log x = 0.75$.
   - (d) $\log x = 1$.
   - (e) $\log x = 0.9$.
   - (f) $\log x = 0.4$.

4. If $\log 3 = 0.477$ and $\log 4 = 0.602$, what is $\log 12$?

5. If $\log 5 = 0.699$, what is $\log 5^7$?

6. If $\log 21 = 1.322$ and $\log 3 = 0.477$, what is $\log \tfrac{21}{3} = \log 7$?

If $\log a = 0.369$ and $\log b = 0.202$, find the following:

7. $\log ab$.

8. $\log a/b$.

9. $\log a^2$.

10. $\log \sqrt{b}$.

11. $\log a^2 b$.

12. $\log \sqrt[3]{ab}$.

Set B

Use Theorem 4–4 to explain why the following are true.

13. $\log_a 100 = \log_a 10 + \log_a 10 = 2 \log_a 10$

14. $\log_a \frac{2}{3} = \log_a 2 - \log_a 3$

15. $\log 23.6 = 1 + \log 2.36$

16. $\log 23{,}600 = 4 + \log 2.36$

17. $\log 0.0236 = -2 + \log 2.36$

18. $\log 10^k x = k + \log x$

19. $\log_a 1 \cdot x = \log_a 1 + \log_a x = \log_a x$

Sketch the graphs of the following functions.

20. $f(x) = \log_2 x$

21. $f(x) = \log_3 x$

22. $f(x) = \log_{1/2} x$

23. $f(x) = \log_2 1/x$

24. $f(x) = \log_2 2x$

25. $f(x) = \log_2 \sqrt{x}$

26. $f(x) = \log_2 (-x)$

27. $f(x) = (\log_2 x)^2$

Set C

28. Prove that $\log_a x/y = \log_a x - \log_a y$.

29. Prove that $\log_a x^k = k \log_a x$.

30. Using Theorem 4–4, prove that

$$\log_a \sqrt[n]{x} = \frac{1}{n} \log_a x.$$

31. Using Theorem 4–4, prove that

$$\log_a xyz = \log_a x + \log_a y + \log_a z.$$

32. Graph and discuss $\log_2 (\log_2 x)$.

33. Find $\log_5 9$ if $\log 9 = 0.9542$ and $\log 5 = 0.6990$.

34. If $\log 7 = 0.8451$, determine $\log_7 100$.

35. Show that $\log_a 1/N = -\log_a N$.

36. Graph $f(x) = x \log_2 x$.

37. Compute $\log_b a \cdot \log_c b \cdot \log_a c$.

38. Compute x if $\log x - 4 \log 5 = -2$.

39. Determine x if $\log_{3x} 729 = x$.

40. Determine x if $\log_a x \cdot \log_4 a = 2$.

Explain how each of the following real functions can be expressed as the composition of two functions.

41. $f(x) = 3^{x^2+1}$

42. $F(x) = \log_2 \sqrt{x}$

43. $H(x) = 2^{2x} + (3 \cdot 2^x) - 3$

44. $L(x) = \log_2 (\log_2 x)$; what is the domain?

45. $E(x) = 10^{10^x}$

46. $T(x) = \log_a (3x^3 + x^2 + 7)$

Calculator Problem

(a) Try to find $\log(\log(\log 10))$ using a calculator that has a log key. Explain the outcome.

(b) Which is the larger number

$$\log 2^{\log 2^{\log 2}} \quad \text{or} \quad ((\log 2)^{\log 2})^{\log 2}?$$

Exponential and Logarithmic Equations

Occasionally one encounters equations whose solutions require knowledge of logarithmic or exponential functions. Some of these are quite simple and occur frequently; therefore, they merit our attention.

In some of the examples and problems that follow, base 10 logarithms of certain numbers will be required. These values can be obtained from calculators that have a log capability or from Table I, Four-Place Logarithms of Numbers. Appendix A-1 explains the use of this table.

Some new terminology will be useful at this time.

Definition 4-6   If $\log N = z$, then N is called the *antilogarithm* of z, and is written "$N = \text{antilog } z$." In other words, antilog $z = 10^z$.

Example 1   Since $\log_3 81 = 4$, then antilog$_3$ $4 = 3^4 = 81$.

2   Since $\log 5 = 0.6990$, then antilog $0.6990 = 10^{0.6990} = 5$.

3   Solve the equation $4^x = 10$.
   Solution. If $4^x = 10$, then $\log 4^x = \log 10$, and

$$x \log 4 = 1,$$

$$x = \frac{1}{\log 4} = \frac{1}{0.6021} = 1.661.$$

4   Solve the equation $\log_3 (3x + 1) = 2.5$.
   Solution. We have $3x + 1 = 3^{2.5}$. Using a calculator we can compute $3^{2.5} = 15.59$. Hence $3x + 1 = 15.59$, $3x = 14.59$ and $x = 4.86$. We may also use logarithms to solve the same problem. We have

$$\log 3 = 0.4771,$$
$$\log 3^{2.5} = 2.5 \log 3 = 1.1928.$$

So $3^{2.5} = $ antilog $1.1928 = 15.59$; therefore, $3x + 1 = 15.59$, and

$$x = 4.86.$$

5   Solve the equation $x^5 = 200$.
   Solution.

$$\log x^5 = \log 200,$$
$$5 \log x = 2.3010,$$
$$\log x = 0.4602,$$
$$x = \text{antilog } 0.4602 = 2.885.$$

Problems

Set A

Solve the following equations.

1. $2^x = 10$
2. $7^{2x-3} = 12$
3. $2^{x^2-x} = 64$
4. $6^{x-1} = 25$
5. $8^{x^2} = 50$
6. $5^{y+2} = 5^2$
7. $64 = 2^{-x}$
8. $10^x = 28.52$

Set B

Solve the following equations.

9. $\log x - \log 4 = 2$
10. $3 \log 2 + \log x = 1$
11. $\log 2^x = 5$
12. $\dfrac{\log 8}{\log x} = \log 2$
13. $3^{2x-1} = 7$
14. $(0.3)^{x+1} = 0.5$
15. $x^3 = 343$
16. $x^7 = 128$

Set C

Solve the following equations.

17. $\begin{cases} 5^{x+2y} = 10, \\ x - y = 3 \end{cases}$
18. $\begin{cases} 4^{x+y} = 60, \\ 3^{x-y} = 5 \end{cases}$

19. If a body at temperature T_1 is surrounded by air at temperature T_0, it will gradually cool so that the temperature T, t minutes later, is given approximately by

$$T = T_0 + (T_1 - T_0)10^{-kt}.$$

This is Newton's law of cooling. The constant k depends on the particular body. If a given body is initially at temperature $100°$ and in air of temperature $40°$, find the temperature after 19 minutes if $k = 0.055$. What is the approximate temperature of the body for very large values of t? for very small values of t?

20. Using Newton's law of cooling from Problem 19, find k for a certain body if, when the initial temperature is $60°$ and the air is at $30°$, the temperature after 12 minutes is $40°$. What will be the temperature after 24 minutes?

Calculator Problem

The formula for compound interest on an annual basis is

$$A = P(1 + r)^t$$

where

A = total amount,
P = principal or original amount,
r = yearly interest rate,
t = time in years.

If 1¢ had been invested at 6% interest compounded annually beginning in the year 1 A.D., what would be the total amount of this investment in the present year?

4-8   The Number e and Natural Logarithms

There are two special exponential functions that are used more than any others. The first of these is the function 10^x. This exponential function is important because our system of writing numbers is based upon 10.

The second of these functions has an irrational number for its base. This number is denoted by e and is approximately 2.71828. The symbol e was chosen in honor of the Swiss mathematician Leonhard Euler (1707–1783).

The number e arises in calculus in the following way. Consider the graph of the function

$$f(x) = \frac{1}{x},\ x > 0.$$

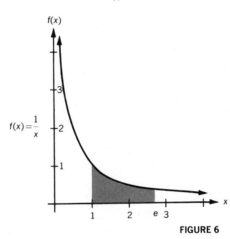

FIGURE 6

(See Fig. 6.) Using methods of calculus, the area under this curve from $x = 1$ to $x = n$ can be calculated. When $x = e$ the area under this curve is 1 square unit.

The number e also occurs naturally as a limit:

$$e = \lim_{n \to \infty} \left(1 + \frac{1}{n}\right)^n.$$

The limit concept will be discussed in Chapter 10.

For convenience, a few approximate values of e^x for selected values of x are given in the following table.

x	0	0.5	1	1.5	2	2.5
e^x	1	1.6487	2.7183	4.4817	7.3891	12.182

A more extensive table for e^x is found in the Appendix.

The graph of $y = e^x$ is shown in Fig. 7. Since $y = e^x$ is continuous and increasing, we see that the exponential function e^x must have an inverse. This inverse function is the *natural logarithm function*. That is, if

$$y = e^x, \qquad \text{then} \quad \log_e y = x.$$

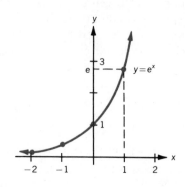

FIGURE 7

Instead of the notation $\log_e$ for the natural logarithm function it is customary to use *ln* to distinguish it from other logarithm functions.

Example 1 $\ln e = 1$ because $e^1 = e$.

2 $\ln e^2 = 2 \ln e = 2 \cdot 1 = 2$.

3   If $e^{1.5} = 4.4817$, then $\ln 4.4817 = 1.5$.

Problems

Set A

Write equivalent statements using natural logarithms.

1. $e^0 = 1$ 2. $e^{0.1} = 1.105$
3. $e^{-1} = 0.3679$ 4. $e^1 = e$
5. $e^{1.2} = 3.320$ 6. $e^3 = 20.086$

Write equivalent statements using exponential functions with base e.

7. $\ln 2 = 0.6931$ 8. $\ln 10 = 2.303$
9. $\ln 0.5 = -0.6931$ 10. $\ln 54.6 = 4$
11. $\ln 0.1353 = -2$ 12. $\ln 1/e = -1$

Set B

13. Draw a graph of e^x. Then answer the following questions.
    (a) If $e^x = e$, what is x?
    (b) If $e^x = e^2$, what is x?
    (c) If $e^x = 1/e$, what is x?
    (d) If $e^x = 1$, what is x?
    (e) If $e^x = 4$, between what two integers is x?
    (f) If $e^x = \frac{1}{4}$, between what two integers is x?

Simplify each expression.

14. $e^{\ln e}$ 15. $e^{-2} \cdot e^3$ 16. $e^{\ln 1/e}$
17. $\ln e^3$ 18. $\ln e^{-1}$ 19. $\ln \sqrt{e}$

Set C

20. Prove that $\ln 1/x = -\ln x$.

21. Graph $\frac{1}{2}e^x$ and $\frac{1}{2}e^{-x}$ on the same coordinate axis. Then graph the sum, $\frac{1}{2}(e^x + e^{-x})$, using graphical addition. The graph of the sum of the two functions is a *catenary*. It has the shape of a chain suspended from its end points.

22. Graph the function defined by e^{-x^2}. This function is of great importance in statistics.

23. Graph the function f, where

$$f(x) = \left(1 + \frac{1}{x}\right)^x \qquad \text{for real } x > 0.$$

It can be shown that this function is bounded above. Estimate the least upper bound.

Calculator Problem

Using a calculator with an exponential key, y^x, and the function f given in Problem 23, find $f(x)$ for the following values of x.

(a) $x = 100$ (b) $x = 1000$ (c) $x = 1,000,000$

Compare the values of $f(x)$ with $e = 2.7182818\ldots$ What do you think is the least upper bound of f?

Summary

In this chapter we have studied the first two elementary transcendental functions: the exponential functions and the logarithmic functions.

1. The exponential function f where $f(x) = a^x$, $a > 0$ and x is any real number, is a continuous function with the following properties.

(a) $a^x \cdot a^y = a^{x+y}$

(b) $(a^x)^y = a^{xy}$

(c) $\dfrac{a^x}{a^y} = a^{x-y}$

(d) $\left(\dfrac{a}{b}\right)^x = \dfrac{a^x}{b^x}$

(e) $(a \cdot b)^x = a^x \cdot b^x$

2. Logarithmic functions are inverses of the exponential functions.

(a) $\log_a xy = \log_a x + \log_a y$

(b) $\log_a \dfrac{x}{y} = \log_a x - \log_a y$

(c) $\log_a x^y = y \log_a x$

3. Common logarithms have a base of 10.

4. Natural logarithms have a base of e, where $e = 2.71828\ldots$.

Chapter 4   Test

4-2   Give a simple expression for each of the following.

1. $8^{2/3}$ 2. $16^{5/4}$ 3. $9^{-(1/2)}$

4. $125^{2/3}$ 5. $3x^0$ 6. $(-4a)^0$

7. $\dfrac{x^7}{x^{-3}}$ 8. $y^7 \cdot y^{-8}$ 9. $(a^{-2}y^{-1}b^2)^3$

10. $\dfrac{r^5}{r^6}$ 11. $(x^{-(1/2)})^2$ 12. $\dfrac{s^3 \cdot t^{-2}}{s^{-2} \cdot t^{-2}}$

13. (a) Is $(-16)^{1/4}$ a real number?
    (b) Is $(16)^{-(1/4)}$ a real number?

4-3   Compute the exponent x.

14. $3^x = \frac{1}{9}$ 15. $(\frac{1}{2})^x = 4$

16. $23^x = 1$ 17. $(\frac{1}{4})^x = \frac{1}{2}$

18. $8^x = 16$ 19. $10^x = 0.01$

20. Sketch a graph of the function f where $f(x) = \frac{1}{3}(5^x)$ for all x.

4-4   21. A certain radioactive substance has a half-life of 50 years. How long will it take for the substance to lose seven-eighths of its radioactive material?

4-5   Write each exponential statement as a logarithmic statement.

22. $2^x = 8$ 23. $10^3 = y$ 24. $a^{-b} = c$

Write each logarithmic equation in terms of exponents.

25. $\log 100 = x$ 26. $\log_2 \frac{1}{16} = -4$ 27. $\log N = x$

4-6   28. If $\log 5 = 0.6990$ and $\log 6 = 0.7781$, compute $\log 30$.

29. If $\log 24 = 1.3802$ and $\log 8 = 0.9031$, compute $\log 3$.

30. If $\log 2 = 0.3010$, what is $\log 2^5$?

4-7   Solve the following equations.

31. $3^x = 16$ 32. $2^{x-1} = 50$

33. $\log x - \log 3 = 1$ 34. $\log 2x + \log 2 = 2$

4-8   Express in terms of natural logarithms.

35. $e^{1.3} = 3.669$ 36. $e^{-2} = 0.1353$ 37. $e^e = 15.154$

Express in terms of the exponential function with base e.

38. $\ln 6 = 1.7917$ 39. $\ln 1 = 0$ 40. $\ln \pi = 1.1447$

Historical Note

Pascal's Arithmetical Machine (1642)

The use of logarithms in computations has become outdated with the increased availability of electronic hand-held calculators.

The development of calculators began in 1642 when Blaise Pascal (1623–1662) invented one of the first machines that could add and subtract. In 1671 Gottfried Liebniz (1646–1716) proposed a 4-operation machine, "The Stepped Reckoner." Liebniz had the idea that his machine could be used to develop various tables. It was built in 1694.

The Difference Engine, the first machine to calculate a table of logarithms, was envisioned by Charles Babbage in 1812. Babbage also wanted his machine to produce the output so that no human error could occur. Babbage also had ideas for a machine, the Analytical Engine, which would have accomplished similar tasks to the modern day computer. This machine would follow a sequence of steps fed into it by a series of punched cards.

Babbage was supported by the British government for ten years, but aid was withdrawn because the machines were too complicated for the mechanics of the time. The Difference Engine was constructed by George Scheutz in 1855. The Analytical Engine was never constructed. Mechanical calculators first became available commercially around 1820.

Babbage's ideas were incorporated into the design of the first electro-mechanic computer, the Mark I, in 1944. In this machine the calculations were done by electro-magnetic relay circuits.

The first completely electronic computer was developed in 1945 at the University of Pennsylvania, the ENIAC. This machine used vacuum tubes instead of relay circuits and was over 1000 times as fast as the Mark I. The development of computers has since progressed at an incredible rate.

The first electronic hand-held calculator was not produced until 1965. It was as expensive as the electromechanical calculator. However, with the development of integrated circuits and transistors, the price has decreased considerably while the capabilities of the calculators have increased. Today's programmable calculators can now accomplish as much as the giant ENIAC computer, built in 1945.

Chapter 5
The Circular Functions

5-1   Introduction

Up to this point the only elementary functions that we have studied are the algebraic functions (which include rational and polynomial functions), exponential functions, logarithmic functions, and those functions that can be obtained from these by addition, subtraction, multiplication, division, and composition. Now, in this chapter we shall study six additional elementary functions called the *circular functions* or *trigonometric functions*. We shall define these functions and study some of their properties. In later chapters we shall consider other properties and some applications of these functions.

Before introducing these new functions, we briefly review some ideas of angle measurement.

5-2   Angle Measurement

In geometry an angle is defined as the set of points on two noncollinear rays originating from a single point (Fig. 1).

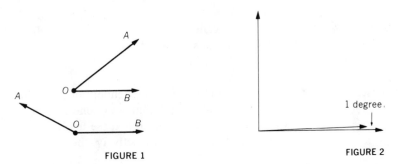

FIGURE 1

FIGURE 2

Associated with each angle is a real number called the *measure of the angle*. This number depends upon the choice of a *unit angle*. The unit angle most often used in elementary mathematics is the *degree*. To visualize an angle of 1 degree, imagine a right angle divided into 90 congruent angles. Each of the small angles has a measure of 1 degree (Fig. 2).

In your study of mathematics in this course and in later courses, the unit angle will often be the *radian*. Radian measure of angles is based upon the concept of *length of circular arc*. We shall not attempt to make this concept precise, but will assume that the idea of the length of a circular arc is intuitively clear.

If $\angle AOB$ is a central angle of a circle with radius r, then there is a unique positive real number L, the length of the arc subtended by $\angle AOB$ (Fig. 3). Note that L is less than half of the circumference, so that $0 < L < \pi r$. Conversely, in a circle with center O and radius r let A be a point on the circle (Fig. 3). Then, if L is a real number such that $0 < L < \pi r$, there are exactly two points, B and B', on the circle and on opposite sides of the line through A and O, such that the lengths of the arcs subtended by $\angle AOB$ and $\angle AOB'$ are both equal to L.

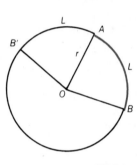

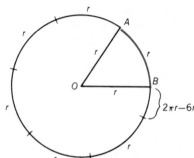

FIGURE 3   FIGURE 4

Definition 5–1   If $\angle AOB$ is a central angle of a circle with radius r and if $\angle AOB$ subtends an arc of length r, then the measure of $\angle AOB$ is one *radian* (Fig. 4). The phrase "the measure of $\angle AOB$" will be denoted by $m(\angle AOB)$.

Definition 5–2   If $\angle AOB$ is a central angle of a circle with radius r (Fig. 3), and if L is the length of the arc subtended by $\angle AOB$, then $m(\angle AOB) = L/r$ (radians).

Remarks   1. Angle measurement is independent of the radius, r, because on different circles, congruent central angles subtend arcs of length proportional to the radii. Thus, if $\angle A \cong \angle A'$ and these angles subtend arcs of L and L' on circles of radii r and r', respectively, then

$$\frac{L}{r} = \frac{L'}{r'}.$$

Hence, the number L/r depends only upon the angle and not upon the circle chosen.

2. A right angle subtends an arc of length $\pi r/2$ and therefore has measure equal to $\pi/2$. The sum of the measures of two right angles is equal to π. It is customary to say that "there are 2π radians in a circle."

3. We found it convenient to introduce the idea of directed length to combine the concepts *length of segment* and *direction along a line*. In Section 5–4 we shall see that by introducing "directed angles" we may consider angles whose measures are negative, zero, or greater than or equal to π.

Because the radian measure of a right angle is $\pi/2$, whereas its degree measure is 90, it follows that an angle of 1 degree is an angle of $\pi/180$ radian, or approximately 0.017 radian. An angle of 1 radian is an angle of $180/\pi$ degrees, or approximately 57.3 degrees.

Example   An angle of measure $\pi/3$ has degree measure of

$$\frac{\pi}{3} \cdot \frac{180}{\pi} = 60.$$

An angle whose degree measure is 36 has radian measure of

$$36 \cdot \frac{\pi}{180} = \frac{\pi}{5}.$$

Remark   We shall follow the customary practice of using real numbers, such as $\pi/3$, 0.7438, 2, etc., as measures of angles without specifically referring to the fact that we are using the radian as the unit angle. However, when we use degree measure, we shall denote this by the usual symbol; thus we shall write 23°, 45°, etc.

Problems

Set A

What are the radian measures of angles whose degree measures are the following?

1. 150	**2.** 75	**3.** 30	**4.** 45
5. 60	**6.** 120	**7.** 80	**8.** 72
9. 135	**10.** 67.5	**11.** 22.5	**12.** 15

Find the degree measures of the angles whose radian measures are given below.

13. $\dfrac{5\pi}{9}$ **14.** $\dfrac{1}{2}$ **15.** $\dfrac{7\pi}{12}$ **16.** $\dfrac{11\pi}{14}$

17. 1.2   **18.** $\dfrac{\pi}{36}$ **19.** $\dfrac{5\pi}{6}$ **20.** $\dfrac{2\pi}{3}$

21. $\dfrac{7\pi}{18}$ **22.** $\dfrac{\pi}{15}$ **23.** $\dfrac{3\pi}{10}$ **24.** 3

Set B

25. A 60° central angle of a circle subtends an arc of length $4\pi/3$ units. What is the radius of the circle?

26. A central angle of a circle with radius 10 has measure of $3\pi/4$. What is the length of the arc subtended by this angle?

27. A central angle of $7\pi/8$ subtends an arc that is 14π units in length. What is the radius of the circle?

28. The radian measure of two angles of a triangle are $\pi/2$ and $\pi/3$. What is the measure of the third angle of the triangle?

Set C

29. $\angle AOB$ is a central angle of a circle. $\overline{AC}$ is a diameter of the circle. If $m(\angle ACB) = \pi/8$, what is $m(\angle AOB)$?

30. A three-speed record player can be set so that the turntable will rotate at $33\frac{1}{3}$, 45, or 78 rpm. Through how many radians will a point on the turntable move in one second at each of these speeds?

31. A wheel rotates at 700 revolutions per minute (rpm). Through how many radians does a spoke of the wheel rotate in one second?

32. A bicycle has wheels with a radius of 33 cm. If the bicycle is moving so that a point on a wheel turns through 8π radians in one second, about how far would the bicycle travel in one hour?

33. Design a radian protractor.

Calculator Problem

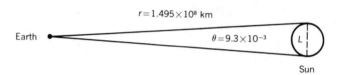

The distance from the earth to the sun is about 1.495×10^8 km. Viewed from the earth, the sun subtends an angle of about 9.3×10^{-3} radians. Since the diameter of the sun is small in comparison to its distance from the earth, the length L of the subtended arc gives an approximation of the diameter of the sun. Compute the approximate diameter of the sun.

5-3   The Wrapping Function, W—Intuitive Description

In this section we shall describe, in an intuitive way, a new function which we shall call the "wrapping function" and denote by the symbol W. This function will help us formulate precise definitions of the circular or trigonometric functions which we shall meet later in the chapter.

Suppose that a point P on a circle of radius 1 touches a coordinate line at the origin, as shown in Fig. 5(a). If the circle rolled along the line, each point of the circle would touch a point of the line. After it has rolled so that point Q touches the line at point x (Fig. 5(b)), the length of arc PQ is the distance from 0 to x, namely x. After one complete revolution of the circle (wheel), the point P again touches the line at the point 2π. Hence to each real number between 0 and 2π, there corresponds a unique point on the circle. Numbers greater than 2π also correspond to points on the circle, as do negative real numbers. In the latter case, correspondence is obtained by rolling the circle in the other direction.*

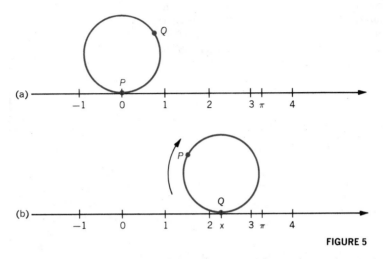

FIGURE 5

The above describes the wrapping function W. The domain of W is the set of real numbers, and the range of W is the set of points on the circle whose radius is 1.

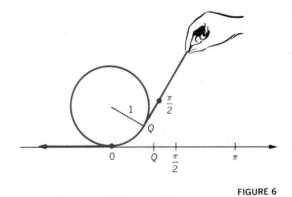

FIGURE 6

Another way of thinking of the wrapping function W is illustrated in Fig. 6. Imagine the real line as a flexible, but nonstretchable, string which is wrapped around the circle. Each real number is mapped (wrapped) into a unique point of the circle. Note that this is not a one-to-one mapping, because many real numbers correspond to the same point on the circle.

---

*We are *not* interested here in the path of the point P as the circle rolls. The point P describes a curve called a cycloid.

Problems

Set A

Imagine that a circle of radius 1 is tangent to the real number line so that a point P of the circle touches the line at 0. Give the coordinate of the point on the real line that will be tangent to the circle for each roll of the circle.

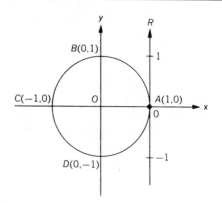

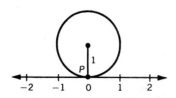

1. 2 revolutions in the positive direction of the line

2. 7 revolutions in the negative direction of the line

3. $\frac{1}{2}$ revolution in the negative direction

4. $\frac{1}{4}$ revolution in the positive direction

5. $1/2\pi$ revolution in the positive direction

6. $1/\pi$ revolution in the negative direction

Consider the unit circle with center at the origin, and the real number line tangent to the circle so that 0 on the line corresponds to the point $A = (1, 0)$, as shown in the figure. Imagine the real line R wrapped around the circle.

7. What is the smallest positive number that will correspond to point B?

8. What is the largest negative number that will correspond to point B?

9. Develop a formula for all real numbers that map into point B by the wrapping function.

10. Repeat Problems 7, 8, and 9 for points $C(-1, 0)$, $D(0, -1)$, and $A(1, 0)$.

Calculator Problem

What is the shortest path from A to B along the semicircles? What is the longest path?

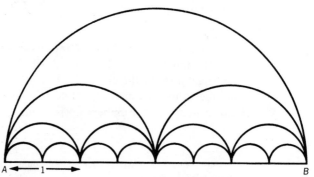

The Definition of W

In Section 5-3 we gave an intuitive description of the function W which mapped the real numbers onto a circle of radius 1. We now give a precise definition of this function.

Definition 5-3   Let C_1 be the circle of radius 1 with center at the origin. The function W is the function with domain R, that maps the real numbers onto C_1 as follows. (See Fig 7.)

    (a) $W(0) = A = (1, 0)$,
            $W(\pi) = C = (-1, 0)$,
            $W(2\pi) = A = (1, 0)$.

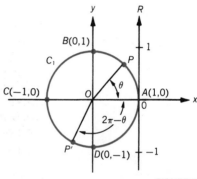

FIGURE 7

    (b)   If θ is a real number such that $\quad 0 < \theta < \pi$, $\quad$ then $W(\theta) = P$, where P is a point of C_1 on the same side of the x-axis as the point $B = (0, 1)$ and such that $m(\angle AOP) = \theta$.

    (c)   If $\quad \pi < \theta < 2\pi$, $\quad$ then $W(\theta) = P'$, where P' is a point of C_1 on the side of the x-axis opposite to B and such that $m(\angle AOP') = 2\pi - \theta$.

    (d)   Now let θ be any real number. There is an integer k (positive, negative, or zero) such that

$$2\pi k \leq \theta < 2\pi(k + 1).$$

Then $0 \leq \theta - 2\pi k < 2\pi$ and $W(\theta) = W(\theta - 2\pi k)$.

Remarks

1. The definition first defines the wrapping function, W, for $0 \leq \theta \leq 2\pi$ and then the definition is extended so that the values of W are repeated. Thus, if two real numbers differ by an integral multiple of 2π then W maps each number into the same point of C_1. The positive real numbers map onto C_1 by "wrapping counterclockwise," whereas the negative real numbers map onto C_1 by "wrapping clockwise."

2. For simplicity, we often speak of "the angle θ" instead of using the more lengthy expression, "the angle AOP, where $P = W(\theta)$."

3. We can now clarify the remark made earlier concerning "negative angles."

As an example, let us show that $W(3\pi/4) = W(-5\pi/4)$. Since $0 < 3\pi/4 < \pi$, then by part (b) of Definition 5-3, $W(3\pi/4) = P$, where P is a point of C_1 in the upper half-plane such that the measure $\angle AOP = 3\pi/4$. (See Fig. 8.) We now consider the real number $-5\pi/4$ and observe that by part (d) of Definition 5-3, letting $k = -1$,

$$-2\pi < \frac{-5\pi}{4} < 0,$$

so that

$$0 < \frac{-5\pi}{4} - (-2\pi) < 2\pi.$$

Hence

$$W\left(\frac{-5\pi}{4}\right) = W\left(\frac{-5\pi}{4} - (-2\pi)\right)$$

$$= W\left(\frac{3\pi}{4}\right) = P.$$

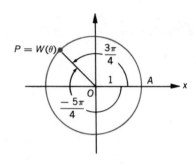

FIGURE 8

While we may use language such as "the negative angle, $-5\pi/4$," we wish to emphasize that this is mathematical slang and that we really mean $\angle AOP$, where $W(-5\pi/4) = P$. The measure of $\angle AOP$ is $3\pi/4$, a number between 0 and π. Similar remarks hold for "angles greater than π."

Example   The points $W(\theta)$ for various θ from 0 to 2π are shown in Fig. 9. It will be helpful to keep the location of these points in mind when locating the points for other values of θ.

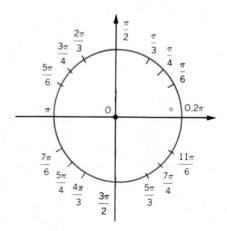

FIGURE 9

Problems

Set A

Find a real number θ, so that $0 \leq \theta < 2\pi$ for each equation.

1. $W(5\pi) = W(\theta)$

2. $W\left(\dfrac{17\pi}{4}\right) = W(\theta)$

3. $W(-3\pi) = W(\theta)$

4. $W\left(\dfrac{-\pi}{2}\right) = W(\theta)$

5. $W\left(\dfrac{25\pi}{6}\right) = W(\theta)$

6. $W(-100\pi) = W(\theta)$

7. $W\left(\dfrac{8\pi}{3}\right) = W(\theta)$

8. $W\left(\dfrac{-13\pi}{2}\right) = W(\theta)$

9. $W\left(\dfrac{-\pi}{3}\right) = W(\theta)$

10. $W\left(\dfrac{-11\pi}{6}\right) = W(\theta)$

11. $W\left(\dfrac{13\pi}{3}\right) = W(\theta)$

12. $W(-20\pi) = W(\theta)$

Set B

13. Graph $W(\theta)$ for $\theta = 2\pi$, $-\pi/6$, $7\pi/6$, $-5\pi/6$, $5\pi/12$, 1, -1, 2, -2, 3, 0.5, -2.5, $-\pi/4$, $-5\pi/4$, $21\pi/4$, $15\pi/2$, 17π.

14. What integer is k in part (d) of Definition 5-3 if $\theta = 20$? $11\pi/3$? $-15\pi/6$?

15. Show that $W(11\pi/4) = W(-5\pi/4)$.

16. Given that $W(\pi/4) = P$, determine the coordinates of P.

17. Determine the coordinates of Q, where $W(\pi/3) = Q$.

18. What are the coordinates of $W(-\pi/3)$?

19. If $W(\theta) = P$, where is $W(-\theta)$ on C_1?

Set C

20. Show that if $W(\theta) = P(x, y)$, then $x^2 + y^2 = 1$. [*Hint:* Use the Pythagorean Theorem.]

21. Show that for any real number θ, there is a unique real number θ_1 such that $0 \leq \theta_1 < 2\pi$ and $W(\theta) = W(\theta_1)$.

22. Show that $W(\theta + 2\pi) = W(\theta)$. More generally, show that if k is an integer, then $W(\theta + 2\pi k) = W(\theta)$.

Calculator Problem

In which quadrant is the point P if $W(\theta) = P$ and $\theta = \pi^\pi$?

5-5   The Sine and Cosine Functions

We now have the preliminaries out of the way and are able to define the principal *circular functions*. These functions are called the *sine* and *cosine* and are abbreviated as *sin* and *cos*.

Definition 5-4   If θ is a real number and

$$W(\theta) = P = (x, y),$$

then

$$\sin(\theta) = \sin\theta = y,$$
$$\cos(\theta) = \cos\theta = x.$$

(See Fig. 10.)

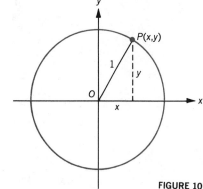

FIGURE 10

Remarks

1. If $\pi/2 < \theta < \pi$, then $W(\theta) = P(x, y)$ is in the second quadrant; hence $x < 0$ and $y > 0$.

2. Similarly, if $\pi < \theta < 3\pi/2$, then $W(\theta) = P(x, y)$ is in the third quadrant, and both $x < 0$ and $y < 0$. If $3\pi/2 < \theta < 2\pi$, then $x > 0$ and $y < 0$.

3. The signs of the circular functions can be determined for any θ by locating the quadrant of which $W(\theta) = P(x, y)$ is a member.

The following theorem is basic and will be applied in many instances in your study of trigonometry. Usually $(\sin \theta)^2$ is written $\sin^2 \theta$, and $(\cos \theta)^2$ is written $\cos^2 \theta$.

Theorem 5-1   *For all real θ, $\sin^2 \theta + \cos^2 \theta = 1$.*

Proof   Suppose $W(\theta) = P(x, y)$. (See Fig. 11.) Then $x = \cos \theta$ and $y = \sin \theta$. By the Pythagorean Theorem $x^2 + y^2 = 1$. Hence,

$$(\cos \theta)^2 + (\sin \theta)^2 = 1,$$

or

$$\sin^2 \theta + \cos^2 \theta = 1.$$

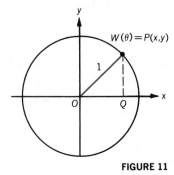

FIGURE 11

Example 1   Find $\sin \theta$ and $\cos \theta$ when $\theta = \pi/4$.

Solution. The real number $\pi/4$ maps into the point $P(x, y)$ in the first quadrant on the unit circle such that $x = y$. (See Fig. 12.) By the Pythagorean Theorem, or by Theorem 5–1 we have

$$x^2 + y^2 = 1.$$

Since $x = y$, then

$$2x^2 = 1 \quad \text{and} \quad x = y = \frac{1}{\sqrt{2}} = \frac{\sqrt{2}}{2}.$$

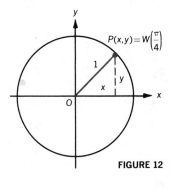

FIGURE 12

Hence

$$x = \cos \frac{\pi}{4} = \frac{\sqrt{2}}{2} \doteq 0.7071,$$

$$y = \sin \frac{\pi}{4} = \frac{\sqrt{2}}{2} \doteq 0.7071.$$

Note that the positive square roots were chosen because both x and y are positive since $P(x, y)$ is in quadrant I.

Example 2   If $\theta = 3\pi/4$, then

$$\cos \theta = x = -\frac{\sqrt{2}}{2} \doteq 0.7071$$

$$\sin \theta = y = \frac{\sqrt{2}}{2} \doteq 0.7071$$

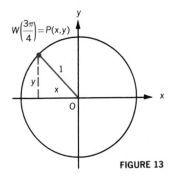

FIGURE 13

In this example, note that x is negative and y is positive because $P(x, y) = W(3\pi/4)$ is a point in the second quadrant. (See Fig. 13.)

3   If $\theta = 7\pi/6$, then $W(\theta) = P(x, y)$ is in the third quadrant and both x and y are negative. (See Fig. 14.) In right triangle OPQ, the length of $\overline{PQ}$ is one-half the length of $\overline{OP}$. Therefore

$$\sin \theta = y = -\tfrac{1}{2} = -0.500,$$

$$\cos \theta = x = -\frac{\sqrt{3}}{2} \doteq -0.866.$$

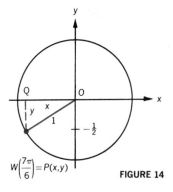

FIGURE 14

Problems

Set A

Compute the following.

1. $\sin 0$
2. $\cos 0$
3. $\sin \frac{\pi}{2}$
4. $\cos \frac{\pi}{2}$
5. $\sin \frac{\pi}{4}$
6. $\cos \frac{\pi}{4}$
7. $\sin \pi$
8. $\cos \pi$
9. $\sin 2\pi$
10. $\cos -4\pi$
11. $\sin 15\pi$
12. $\sin \frac{15\pi}{2}$
13. $\sin \frac{3\pi}{4}$
14. $\cos \frac{3\pi}{4}$
15. $\sin \frac{\pi}{6}$
16. $\cos \frac{\pi}{6}$
17. $\sin \frac{\pi}{3}$
18. $\cos \frac{\pi}{3}$
19. $\sin \frac{5\pi}{6}$
20. $\cos \frac{-5\pi}{6}$
21. $\cos \frac{-\pi}{6}$
22. $\sin \frac{-\pi}{6}$
23. $\sin \frac{3\pi}{2}$
24. $\cos \frac{11\pi}{6}$

Set B

25. Verify Theorem 5-1 for each of the following.

   (a) $\frac{\pi}{4}$ (b) $\frac{\pi}{2}$ (c) $\frac{\pi}{6}$

26. In which quadrant is point P, where $W(\theta) = P(x, y)$, if

   (a) both $\sin \theta$ and $\cos \theta$ are positive?
   (b) both $\sin \theta$ and $\cos \theta$ are negative?
   (c) $\sin \theta$ is negative and $\cos \theta$ is positive?
   (d) $\sin \theta$ is positive and $\cos \theta$ is negative?

27. As θ increases from 0 to $\pi/2$ does $\sin \theta$ increase or decrease? Does $\cos \theta$ increase or decrease in this interval?

28. Are there real numbers θ such that $\sin \theta = 2$?

Set C

29. $W(\theta)$ maps into a point in the first quadrant such that $\sin \theta = 0.6$. What is $\cos \theta$? [*Hint:* Use Theorem 5-2.]

30. $W(\theta)$ maps into a point in the fourth quadrant such that $\cos \theta = 2\sqrt{2}/3$. What is $\sin \theta$?

31. Show that if $0 < \theta < \pi/2$, then $\sin (\pi/2 - \theta) = \cos \theta$.

32. Construct a graph of $f(\theta) = \sin \theta$ for θ in $[0, 2\pi]$. Assume f is continuous in the interval.

33. Construct the graph of $g(\theta) = \cos \theta$ for θ in $[0, 2\pi]$.

34. Use the graphs of f and g in Problems 32 and 33 to graph $f + g$ in the interval $[0, 2\pi]$.

35. Sketch the graph of $h(\theta) = \sin^2 \theta + \cos^2 \theta$ for all real numbers θ.

Calculator Problem

If $\sin^2 \theta = 0.0625$, give all possible values of $\sin \theta$ and $\cos \theta$.

5-6   Other Circular Functions

There are six trigonometric functions. So far, we have defined only the sine and cosine functions. We now give definitions of all six functions.

Definition 5-5   If W is the wrapping function and if $W(\theta) = P(x, y)$ (Fig. 15), then

$$\begin{aligned}
\text{sine of } \theta = \sin \theta &= y, \\
\text{cosine of } \theta = \cos \theta &= x, \\
\text{tangent of } \theta = \tan \theta &= y/x && \text{if } x \neq 0, \\
\text{cotangent of } \theta = \cot \theta &= x/y && \text{if } y \neq 0, \\
\text{secant of } \theta = \sec \theta &= 1/x && \text{if } x \neq 0, \\
\text{cosecant of } \theta = \csc \theta &= 1/y && \text{if } y \neq 0.
\end{aligned}$$

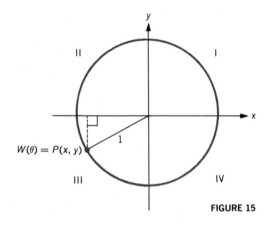

FIGURE 15

Remarks

1. The domains of the sine and cosine functions are both **R**, that is, the set of real numbers.

2. The tangent and the secant are not defined if $x = 0$. We have $x = 0$ when $W(\theta) = P$ is a point on the y-axis and this occurs when θ is an odd multiple of $\pi/2$.

3. The cotangent and cosecant are not defined if $y = 0$. We have $y = 0$ when $W(\theta) = P$ is a point on the x-axis and this occurs when θ is any multiple of π.

4. When $W(\theta) = P$ is a point in the first quadrant, then all the circular functions have positive values at the real number θ. For θ corresponding to points in the other quadrants, some of the circular functions will have positive values, and others will have negative values. For example, in Quadrant III only the tangent and the cotangent functions have positive values because both x and y are negative in this quadrant.

Example 1   Find the other four trigonometric functions of θ if $y = \sin\theta = -1/\sqrt{5}$ and $x = \cos\theta = 2/\sqrt{5}$.

Solution.

$$\tan\theta = \frac{y}{x} = \frac{\dfrac{-1}{\sqrt{5}}}{\dfrac{2}{\sqrt{5}}} = -\frac{1}{2} \qquad \cot\theta = \frac{x}{y} = -2$$

$$\sec\theta = \frac{1}{x} = \frac{\sqrt{5}}{2} \qquad \csc\theta = \frac{1}{y} = -\sqrt{5}$$

2   One can estimate the values of the functions for any given real number θ by drawing a reasonably accurate figure. For example, if

$$\theta = \tfrac{9}{4} = 2.25,$$

then $m(\angle AOP)$ in degrees is approximately $129°$. Then angle can be drawn with a protractor to obtain Fig. 16. Using the figure we can estimate the values of each function at 2.25. Thus

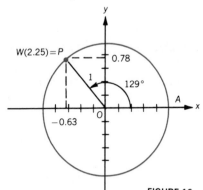

FIGURE 16

$$\sin 2.25 = 0.78, \qquad\qquad \csc 2.25 = \frac{1}{0.78} = 1.28,$$

$$\cos 2.25 = -0.63, \qquad\qquad \sec 2.25 = \frac{1}{-0.63} = -1.59,$$

$$\tan 2.25 = \frac{0.78}{-0.63} = -1.24, \qquad \cot 2.25 = \frac{-0.63}{0.78} = -0.81.$$

Problems

Set A

Find the other four trigonometric functions of θ.

1. $\sin \theta = \frac{4}{5}$, $\cos \theta = \frac{3}{5}$

2. $\sin \theta = \frac{1}{2}$, $\cos \theta = \frac{-\sqrt{3}}{2}$

3. $\sin \theta = \frac{-2}{\sqrt{13}}$, $\cos \theta = \frac{-3}{\sqrt{13}}$

4. $\sec \theta = \sqrt{2}$, $\csc \theta = -\sqrt{2}$

5. Which trigonometric functions have positive values in
   (a) Quadrant I?   (b) Quadrant II?
   (c) Quadrant III?   (d) Quadrant IV?

Set B

Construct a circle of radius 1 on graph paper and obtain approximate values of the trigonometric functions of θ for each of the following.

6. $\theta = 1$ 7. $\theta = 0.5$ 8. $\theta = -7$
9. $\theta = -0.1$ 10. $\theta = \pi + 0.3$ 11. $\theta = 2$
12. $\theta = -2$ 13. $\theta = 20$ 14. $\theta = -20$

15. Draw an angle with measure θ so that $W(\theta)$ is in Quadrant I and $\sin \theta = 0.25$.

16. Draw an angle in the second quadrant so that $\sin \theta = 0.25$. Is there an angle in the third quadrant whose sine is 0.25?

17. Draw an angle in the second quadrant whose cosine is $-\frac{2}{3}$. What is the value of the secant of this angle?

18. If $\sin \theta = -\frac{2}{3}$, and $W(\theta) = P$ is in the third quadrant, what are $\tan \theta$ and $\sec \theta$?

19. If $\cos \theta = -\frac{1}{4}$, and $P = W(\theta)$ is in the second quadrant, what are the values of the other functions of θ?

Set C

20. What is $\sin \theta / \cos \theta$ if θ is not an odd multiple of $\pi/2$?

21. What is $\cos \theta / \sin \theta$ if θ is not a multiple of π?

22. What is $1/\sin \theta$ if θ is not a multiple of π?

23. What is $1/\cos \theta$ if θ is not an odd multiple of $\pi/2$?

Calculator Problem

Most scientific calculators have sin, cos, and tan keys but do not have keys for cot, sec, and csc. Since the latter three functions are simply reciprocals of the first three, the values of these functions can be found by finding the reciprocals of the sin, cos, or tan functions.

For example

$$\sin 2 = 0.90929743$$
$$\cos 2 = -0.41614684$$
$$\tan 2 = -2.1850399$$

(a) Find the value of the other three functions at 2 radians.

(b) Choose some real numbers. Find the value of all six functions for these real numbers.

(c) What happens with your calculator when you try to find $\tan \pi/2$? (Use the π key on the calculator, not an approximation for π.)

(d) $\pi/2 = 1.5707963$ approximately. What is $\tan 1.5707963$? Compare with part (c).

Special Angles

For certain angles, the exact coordinates of $P(x, y) = W(\theta)$ can be found from our knowledge of elementary geometry. These angles are the multiples of $\pi/6$ or $30°$ and $\pi/4$ or $45°$. In order to obtain the exact coordinates of $W(\theta)$ in these cases, we need a clear mental picture of the right triangles shown in Fig. 17.

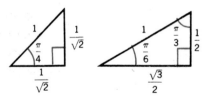

FIGURE 17

Example 1 Find the six trigonometric functions of $2\pi/3$.

Solution. The angle with radian measure of $2\pi/3$ has degree measure of $120°$. Thus we have $W(2\pi/3)$ in the second quadrant and

$$W\left(\frac{2\pi}{3}\right) = \left(-\frac{1}{2}, \frac{\sqrt{3}}{2}\right),$$

as shown in Fig. 18.

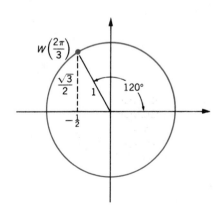

FIGURE 18

Therefore,

$$\sin\frac{2\pi}{3} = \frac{\sqrt{3}}{2} \doteq 0.866, \qquad \csc\frac{2\pi}{3} = \frac{2}{\sqrt{3}} \doteq \frac{2\sqrt{3}}{3} \doteq 1.155,$$

$$\cos\frac{2\pi}{3} = -\frac{1}{2} = -0.5, \qquad \sec\frac{2\pi}{3} = -2,$$

$$\tan\frac{2\pi}{3} = -\sqrt{3} \doteq -1.732, \qquad \cos\frac{2\pi}{3} = -\frac{1}{\sqrt{3}} = \frac{-\sqrt{3}}{3} \doteq -0.577.$$

Example 2   Find the six trigonometric functions of $5\pi/4$.

Solution. The point P, where $W(5\pi/4) = P$, is in Quadrant III, and $m(\angle AOP) = 2\pi - 5\pi/4 = 3\pi/4$ or $135°$. Therefore $m(\angle POQ) = \pi/4$ or $45°$. Thus we have

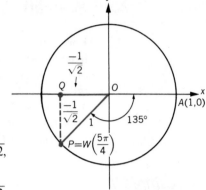

FIGURE 19

$$\sin \frac{5\pi}{4} = \frac{-1}{\sqrt{2}}, \qquad \csc \frac{5\pi}{4} = -\sqrt{2},$$

$$\cos \frac{5\pi}{4} = -\frac{1}{\sqrt{2}}, \qquad \sec \frac{5\pi}{4} = -\sqrt{2},$$

$$\tan \frac{5\pi}{4} = 1, \qquad \cot \frac{5\pi}{4} = 1.$$

3   Find the trigonometric functions of $-5\pi/2$.

Solution. From Fig. 20 we see that

$$W\left(\frac{-5\pi}{2}\right) = (0, -1).$$

Then

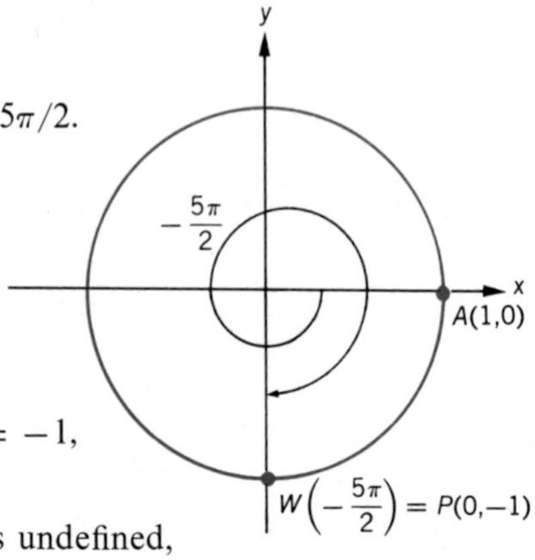

FIGURE 20

$$\sin \frac{-5\pi}{2} = \frac{-1}{1} = -1, \qquad \csc \frac{-5\pi}{2} = -1,$$

$$\cos \frac{-5\pi}{2} = \frac{0}{1} = 0, \qquad \sec \frac{-5\pi}{2} \text{ is undefined,}$$

$$\tan \frac{-5\pi}{2} \text{ is undefined,} \qquad \cot \frac{-5\pi}{2} = \frac{0}{-1} = 0.$$

Problems

Set A

Find the following values of trigonometric functions.

1. $\sin \dfrac{-\pi}{6}$ 2. $\cos \dfrac{-\pi}{3}$ 3. $\tan -9\pi$

4. $\tan \dfrac{5\pi}{2}$ 5. $\sec \dfrac{5\pi}{2}$ 6. $\sin 13\pi$

7. $\sin \dfrac{-5\pi}{4}$ 8. $\cos \dfrac{-7\pi}{4}$ 9. $\sin \dfrac{5\pi}{6}$

10. $\sin \dfrac{7\pi}{6}$ 11. $\tan \dfrac{-3\pi}{4}$ 12. $\sec \dfrac{-3\pi}{4}$

13. $\sin \dfrac{11\pi}{6}$ 14. $\sin \dfrac{2\pi}{3}$ 15. $\sin \dfrac{4\pi}{3}$

16. $\sin \dfrac{7\pi}{3}$ 17. $\cos \dfrac{2\pi}{3}$ 18. $\cos \dfrac{4\pi}{3}$

19. $\cos \pi$ 20. $\cos \dfrac{5\pi}{3}$ 21. $\cos \dfrac{3\pi}{2}$

22. $\cot \dfrac{-\pi}{2}$ **23.** $\tan \dfrac{-\pi}{3}$ **24.** $\tan \dfrac{-2\pi}{3}$

25. $\tan -\pi$ **26.** $\tan \dfrac{-4\pi}{3}$ **27.** $\tan \dfrac{-5\pi}{3}$

28. $\csc \dfrac{5\pi}{6}$

Set B

For each of the following find all θ, such that $0 \le \theta < 2\pi$.

29. $\sin \theta = \frac{1}{2}$ **30.** $\sin \theta = 0$

31. $\sin \theta = 1$ **32.** $\sin \theta = \dfrac{\sqrt{3}}{2}$

33. $\sin \theta = -1$ **34.** $\cos \theta = -\dfrac{1}{\sqrt{2}}$

35. $\cos \theta = -\dfrac{\sqrt{3}}{2}$ **36.** $\cos \theta = -1$

37. $\tan \theta = 0$ **38.** $\tan \theta = \dfrac{1}{\sqrt{3}}$

39. $\tan \theta = 1$ **40.** $\tan \theta = \sqrt{3}$

41. $\sin \theta = -\frac{1}{2}$ **42.** $\sin \theta = \dfrac{-\sqrt{3}}{2}$

43. $\sin \theta = \dfrac{1}{\sqrt{2}}$ **44.** $\sin \theta = \dfrac{-1}{\sqrt{2}}$

45. $\cos \theta = 0$ **46.** $\tan \theta$ is undefined

47. $\cot \theta = 0$ **48.** $\cot \theta = \dfrac{1}{\sqrt{3}}$

49. $\cot \theta = 1$ **50.** $\cot \theta = \sqrt{3}$

51. $\cot \theta$ is undefined **52.** $\tan \theta = \dfrac{-1}{\sqrt{3}}$

53. $\cos \theta = \frac{1}{2}$ **54.** $\cos \theta = \dfrac{1}{\sqrt{2}}$

55. $\cos \theta = \dfrac{\sqrt{3}}{2}$ **56.** $\cos \theta = 1$

57. $\cos \theta = -\frac{1}{2}$ **58.** $\tan \theta = -1$

59. $\tan \theta = -\sqrt{3}$ **60.** $\cot \theta = -\dfrac{1}{\sqrt{3}}$

61. $\cot \theta = -1$ **62.** $\cot \theta = -\sqrt{3}$

63. $\sec \theta = 0$ **64.** $\sec \theta = \dfrac{2}{\sqrt{3}}$

65. $\sec \theta = \sqrt{2}$ **66.** $\sec \theta = 2$

67. $\sec \theta = \dfrac{-2}{\sqrt{3}}$ **68.** $\sec \theta = -\sqrt{2}$

69. $\sec \theta = -2$ **70.** $\csc \theta = \dfrac{-2}{\sqrt{3}}$

71. $\csc \theta = \sqrt{2}$ **72.** $\csc \theta = -2$

73. $\csc \theta$ is undefined

Set C

74. Prove that $\sin (\theta + 2\pi) = \sin \theta$ for all θ in $\boldsymbol{R}$.

75. Prove that $\cos (\theta + 2n\pi) = \cos \theta$ for all integers n and all θ in $\boldsymbol{R}$.

76. Prove that $\cos [(2n + 1)\pi] = -1$ for all integers n.

77. Prove that $\tan (k\pi - \pi/4) = -1$ if k is an odd integer.

Calculator Problem

If you can buy widgets at a price of 9 for 1¢ and sell them 8 for 1¢ and you sell one million widgets a day, how long will it take you to make a million dollars in the widget business?

Graphs

Since a clear mental picture of the graphs of each of the six circular functions and the ability to sketch these graphs quickly are of vital importance in our work, we shall discuss both aspects in some detail. Our method in sketching the graphs will be to plot a few points, make some observations about those intervals in the domain where the functions are increasing or decreasing, and then draw the graph, remembering that for each circular function f,

$$f(\theta + 2n\pi) = f(\theta)$$

if n is an integer.

The sine function is 0 at $n\pi$, is 1 at $\pi/2 + 2n\pi$, and is -1 at $-\pi/2 + 2n\pi$, where n is any integer. The function is increasing in the interval $[0, \pi/2]$ and decreasing in the interval $[\pi/2, \pi]$. The graph is shown in Fig. 21.

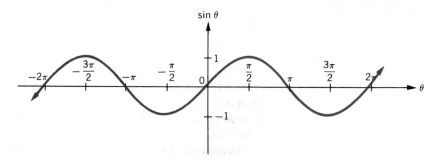

FIGURE 21

The cosine function takes on the same values as the sine function but at different values of θ. The cosine function is decreasing in the interval $[0, \pi]$. Its graph is shown in Fig. 22.

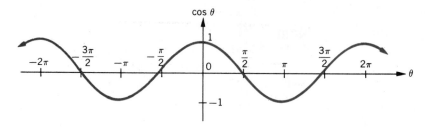

FIGURE 22

The tangent function is not defined at odd multiples of $\pi/2$, and its graph has vertical asymptotes at these points. It is increasing in the interval $\langle -\pi/2, \pi/2 \rangle$. The graph is shown in Fig. 23.

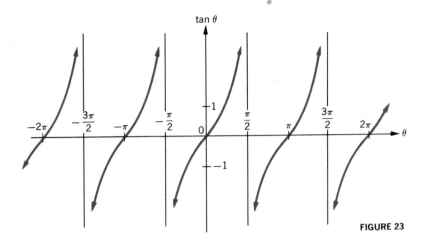

FIGURE 23

As is evident from the graphs, the sine and cosine functions are continuous. Because the tangent is not defined at $\pm\pi/2, \pm 3\pi/2, \ldots$, it does not make sense to speak of continuity at these values of θ, but the tangent is continuous on any interval on which it is defined.

The graphs of the other three circular functions are left as exercises.

In Section 4–1 we defined *transcendental functions* to be nonalgebraic functions. The trigonometric functions are six of those functions, known as the *elementary* transcendental functions. A proof that these functions are not algebraic, and are therefore transcendental, requires more mathematics than we have presented at this point.

Problems

Set A

1. In the interval from 0 to 2π, when is the sine function increasing? When is it decreasing?

2. In the interval from 0 to 2π, when is the cosine function decreasing? When is it increasing?

3. In the interval from $-\pi/2$ to $\pi/2$ is the tangent increasing or decreasing?

4. What is the range of the sine and cosine functions?

5. What is the range of the tangent and cotangent functions?

6. What is the range of the secant and cosecant functions?

Set B

7. Graph on coordinate paper the sine function in the interval $[0, \pi/2]$. Plot those points for which the sine is known exactly and using the definition, plot a few other points.

8. Repeat Problem 7 for the cosine function.

9. Draw the graph of the cotangent function. What is its domain? its range?

10. Draw the graph of the secant function. What is its domain? Can it assume all real values?

11. Draw the graph of the cosecant function. What is its domain? Can it assume all real values?

Set C

12. If f is any one of the trigonometric functions, show that $f(\theta \pm 2\pi) = f(\theta)$. What does this indicate about its graph?

13. From the graph of the tangent function, prove that for any real number y, there is exactly one real number x, $-\pi/2 < x < \pi/2$, such that $y = \tan x$.

14. From the graph of the sine function, prove that if $-1 \leq y \leq 1$, then there is exactly one real number x, $-\pi/2 \leq x \leq \pi/2$, such that $y = \sin x$.

15. From the graph of the cosine function, prove that if $-1 \leq y \leq 1$, then there is exactly one real number x, $0 \leq x \leq \pi$, such that $y = \cos x$.

Calculator Problem

Find $\sin \theta$ and $\cos \theta$, θ in Quadrant I, so that $\sin \theta = 2 \cos \theta$.

5-9   Other Graphs

There are certain other functions that are closely related to the trigonometric functions. These are compositions of linear and trigonometric functions.

Example 1   Sketch the graph of the equation

$$y = 3 \sin 2x. \tag{1}$$

Solution. Equation (1) defines a mapping, $x \xrightarrow{F} 3 \sin 2x$. This mapping is the composition of three functions, $F = f \circ (g \circ h)$, where $h(x) = 2x$, $g(x) = \sin x$ and $f(x) = 3x$. Thus

$$[f \circ (g \circ h)](x) = f(g(h))(x) = f(g(2x)) = f(\sin 2x) = 3 \sin 2x.$$

x	0	$\pi/8$	$\pi/4$	$\pi/12$	$\pi/6$	$3\pi/8$	$\pi/2$
$2x$	0	$\pi/4$	$\pi/2$	$\pi/6$	$\pi/3$	$3\pi/4$	π
$3 \sin 2x$	0	$3/\sqrt{2}$	3	$3/2$	$\frac{3}{2}\sqrt{3}$	$3/\sqrt{2}$	0

One method for obtaining the graph of this composite function is that of plotting points. When the points in the table are plotted, a pattern emerges, and the graph is easy to draw. It is shown in Fig. 24.

Note that if x increases from 0 to π, then in the interval $[0, \pi)$, $W(2x) = P$ takes all possible positions on the unit circle. Hence in this interval, $\sin 2x$ must complete a full cycle of values. There must be "one wave" between $x = 0$ and $x = \pi$. But the wave must be of "height" or "amplitude" 3 because of the factor 3 in $y = 3 \sin 2x$. Thus we see that it would be possible to sketch the graph of $y = 3 \sin 2x$ without making a table of values. All that is necessary is to observe the "length" and amplitude of the wave.

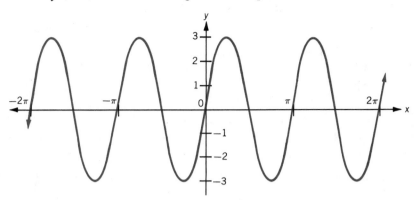

FIGURE 24

Remark   If $y = A \sin kx$ or $y = A \cos kx$ where A and k are real numbers, then

$$|A| = \text{Amplitude or wave height,}$$
$$\frac{2\pi}{k} = \text{length of one wave.}$$

Example 2   Sketch the graph of $y = 2 \cos (x/2)$.

Solution. Although we could make a table of values, we shall, instead, use the short-cut method described above. Recall the general shape of the graph of the cosine function in Fig. 22. We note that the amplitude will be 2 and that $k = \frac{1}{2}$. Therefore, the length of one wave of the curve will have a length of $2\pi/\frac{1}{2}$ or 4π. We therefore only need to sketch a cosine wave of the appropriate length and height, as shown in Fig. 25.

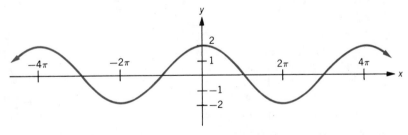

FIGURE 25

Similar considerations apply to graph of $y = A \tan \alpha x$, as well as to graphs involving compositions of the other functions. Note that the tangent function is repetitive but repeats in intervals of length π rather than 2π, as is the case for the sine and cosine functions.

In many cases, it will be convenient to use different scales on the two axes to fit the graph better to the coordinate paper.

Problems

Set A

Sketch the graphs of the following equations. Before drawing the graph determine the amplitude and the length of one wave of the curve.

1. $y = \sin 3x$ **2.** $y = \sin(x/3)$

3. $y = 2(\sin 3x)$ **4.** $y = 2 \sin \pi x$

5. $y = \frac{1}{2} \cos(x/2)$ **6.** $y = 5 \cos(\pi x/2)$

7. $y = \sqrt{2} \sin 2\pi x$ **8.** $y = -\sqrt{3} \cos(\pi x/3)$

9. $y = \sin(\pi x/2)$ **10.** $y = \cos 2x$

Set B

Sketch the graphs of the following.

11. $y = \tan(\pi x/2)$ **12.** $g(v) = \cos(v/2)$

13. $y = 2 \sec(x/3)$ **14.** $f(t) = \tan 2t$

15. $F = 2 \cot \pi x$ **16.** $g(x) = \sin \pi x$

17. $T(x) = \tan(x/3)$ **18.** $C(x) = \cot(x/3)$

19. $S(x) = \sec(\pi x/3)$ **20.** $y = 2 \tan 2x$

21. $m(x) = \csc(\pi x/2)$ **22.** $y = 3 \csc(x/2)$

Set C

23. Write an equation in terms of the sine function whose graph is a curve with amplitude 3 and the length of one wave of the curve is π. The value of the function at 0 is 0.

24. Sketch the graph of the curve of problem 23.

25. Write an equation in terms of the cosine function whose graph is a curve with amplitude 5 and a wave length of 6π. The value of the function at 0 is 5.

26. Sketch a graph of the curve of problem 25.

Write an equation for each curve below.

27.

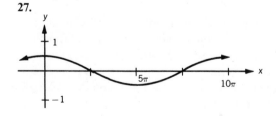

28.

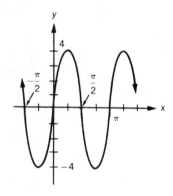

29.

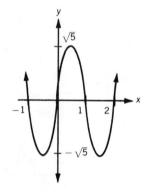

30.

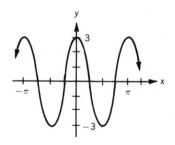

Calculator Problem

Sketch the graph of $f(x) = (\sin x)/x$ for all real x except 0 in $[-\pi, \pi]$. In particular, compute $f(x)$ for values of x very close to 0 such as $x = 0.1, 0.01, 0.001, -0.001, -0.01,$ and -0.1. How could f be defined so that it would be continuous in $[-\pi, \pi]$?

5-10   Periodic Functions

From the graphs we see that the circular functions repeat themselves again and again. Functions with this repetitive property are called *periodic functions*.

Definition 5-6   If f is a function with domain R and there is a number $p > 0$ such that

$$f(x + p) = f(x)$$

for all x in R, then f is said to be *periodic*. If p is the smallest positive number with this property, then we call p *the period of f.*

Examples of periodic functions are shown in Fig. 26. The function f in part (a) is also continuous, but the function F of part (b) is not. There is an infinite variety of periodic functions, and such functions occur again and again in applications of mathematics.

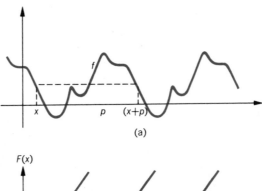

(a)

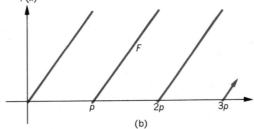

(b)

FIGURE 26

You are already familiar with some periodic functions, namely the circular functions. The period of the sine function, for example, is 2π. To prove this, we observe that for every real number θ, $\sin(\theta + 2\pi) = \sin\theta$, since $P(x, y) = W(\theta) = W(\theta + 2\pi)$ and $y = \sin\theta$ by definition. (See Problem 22, p. 105.) The sine, therefore, is periodic and 2π is a period of the sine function. To show that 2π is the smallest positive period of the sine function, suppose that there is a real number p, $0 < p < 2\pi$, and $\sin(\theta + p) = \sin\theta$ for all real numbers θ. Then for $\theta = 0$, we have $\sin p = \sin 0 = 0$. There is exactly one real number p, $0 < p < 2\pi$, such that $\sin p = 0$, namely π. But π is not a period of the sine function, for if it were, then $\sin(\theta + \pi) = \sin\theta$ for every real number θ. But for $\theta = \pi/2$, we have

$$\sin\theta = \sin\frac{\pi}{2} = 1,$$

whereas

$$\sin(\theta + \pi) = \sin\left(\frac{\pi}{2} + \pi\right) = \sin\frac{3\pi}{2} = -1.$$

Hence the period of the sine function is 2π. The proofs of periodicity of the other circular functions are left as exercises.

Problems

Set A

The graphs of some functions are shown below. Which are graphs of periodic functions? Determine, by inspection, the periods of those functions that are periodic.

1.

3.

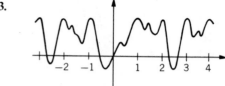

2.

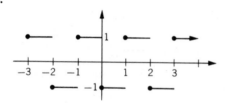

4.

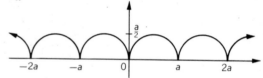

5.

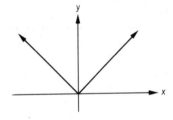

6.

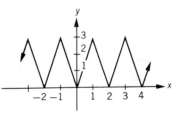

Set B

Each function below is periodic. Find the period of each function.

7. $f(x) = \sin 2x$

8. $g(x) = \cos \dfrac{x}{3}$

9. $T(x) = 4 \cos 10x$

10. $h(x) = \sqrt{2} \sin 4x$

11. $K(x) = 2 \sin (2\pi x)$

12. $R(x) = 1.5 \cos \left(\dfrac{\pi x}{4} \right)$

Set C

13. Prove that if a function is periodic with period $p > 0$, then $2p$ is also a period of the function.

14. Prove that the cosine, secant, and cosecant all have period 2π.

15. Prove that the tangent and cotangent have period π.

16. Is the wrapping function, W, a periodic function? If so, what is the period?

17. Show that if f is periodic with period p, then $1/f$ is periodic with period p.

18. Consider the constant function $f: x \to c$ for all real numbers x. Is f periodic? Does it have a unique period? Is it correct to speak of *the* period of f?

19. (a) Graph the function f with domain $\mathbf{R}$ defined by

$$f(x) = 1, \quad \text{if } x \text{ is rational,}$$
$$f(x) = -1, \quad \text{if } x \text{ is irrational.}$$

(b) Prove that every positive rational number is a period of f.

(c) Prove that no irrational number is a period of f.

(d) Why does it not make sense to speak of *the* period of f?

Calculator Problem

Graph the functions below for x in $[0, \pi/2]$.

$$f(x) = \cos x$$
$$g(x) = x$$

Estimate, from the graph, the real number x such that

$$x = \cos x.$$

Use a calculator to find x correct to at least 4 decimal places.

Sums of Periodic Functions

We have seen that from the circular functions one can obtain periodic functions with periods different from 2π. We shall now see how to get other periodic functions from the circular functions.

Example 1   We can show that the sum of two periodic functions with the same period is a periodic function with that period. Consider the function f defined by $f(x) = \sin x + 2 \cos x$.

To obtain the graph of f we could, of course, prepare a table of values of f and plot points. It is easier, and quicker, to sketch the graph of f by graphical addition. The graphs of $y = \sin x$ and $y = 2 \cos x$ are drawn dashed in Fig. 27. The graph of f, which is shown in color, clearly shows that f has period 2π. It appears to be a "sine wave" somewhat shifted sideways, and with height slightly more than 2. Such is indeed the case, and in Chapter 6 we shall prove it.

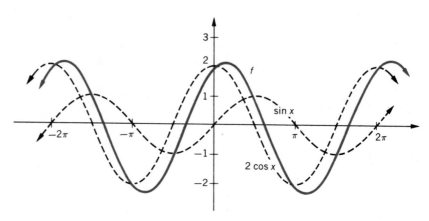

FIGURE 27

2   We now add two functions, the period of one being twice the period of the other. Consider f given by $f(x) = \sin x + 2 \cos 2x$. As in the previous example, we graph

$$y = \sin x \qquad \text{(period } 2\pi\text{),}$$
$$y = 2 \cos 2x \qquad \text{(period } \pi\text{),}$$

and obtain Fig. 28. The figure shows that f has period 2π but is not a pure sine wave.

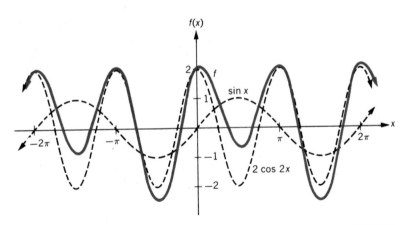

FIGURE 28

Example 3   In this example we graph a function that is a pure sine wave with altered period and height, and that has been "shifted along the horizontal." Consider

$$f(x) = 2 \sin \left(2x + \frac{\pi}{3}\right).$$

To graph this function one could prepare a table and plot points, but this is too laborious. First observe that the "angle" $(2x + \pi/3)$ is 0 when $x = -\pi/6$. So, the graph of f must "start" at $-\pi/6$. Next we find the "end point" of f. Since the period of the sine function is 2π, we must have, for some x, $(2x + \pi/3) = 2\pi$. Hence $x = 5\pi/6$. Thus, in the interval from $-\pi/6$ to $5\pi/6$, $f(x)$ has a full cycle of its values, and the period of f must be

$$\frac{5}{6}\pi - \left(-\frac{\pi}{6}\right) = \pi.$$

Clearly, the height, or amplitude, of the wave is 2. A sketch of one period of this function is shown in Fig. 29.

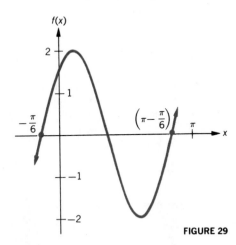

FIGURE 29

This last example illustrates the behavior of functions given by

$$f(x) = A \sin (kx + \alpha),$$

and

$$g(x) = A \cos (kx + \alpha).$$

The periods of both f and g are $2\pi/|k|$ and both have height, or *amplitude,* equal to $|A|$. The graphs are sine or cosine waves starting where $kx + \alpha = 0$ or at $x = -\alpha/k$. Therefore the graphs of f and g can usually be sketched very quickly.

Problems

Set A

Sketch the graphs of the following functions by graphical addition or subtraction. What is the period of each?

1. $y(x) = \sin x + \cos x$

2. $y(x) = \sin x - \cos x$

3. $f(x) = 2 \sin x - 3 \cos x$

4. $F(x) = \frac{1}{2} \sin x - \cos 3x$

Determine the period, amplitude, and starting point, and then sketch the graphs by drawing a suitable wave.

5. $y(x) = 2 \sin \left(\pi x - \frac{\pi}{4}\right)$

6. $f(x) = 3 \sin (2x - \frac{1}{2})$

7. $F(x) = 4 \sin \left(\frac{x}{2} - 2\right)$

8. $G(x) = 8 \cos \left(\frac{x}{3} + 1\right)$

Set B

Find the period and amplitude of the following functions and then sketch the graphs. Check your graph by evaluating the functions at one or two values of the independent variable.

9. $F(x) = \sqrt{2} \sin 2\pi x$

10. $F(x) = 2 \cos \frac{\pi x}{3}$

11. $y(t) = 3 \sin \frac{t}{2}$

12. $E(t) = -\frac{1}{2} \sin 3t$

13. $I(t) = 10 \cos \dfrac{\pi t}{1000}$ (use different t-, I-scales)

14. $V(t) = 110 \sin 120 \pi t$ (use different t-, V-scales)

15. $g(x) = 1.5 \cos 6x$

16. $A(t) = A_0 \sin kt, \ k > 0$

17. $E(t) = 110 \sin \left(120\pi t + \dfrac{2\pi}{3}\right)$ (use different t-, E-scales)

18. $H(t) = 3 \sin (t - 1)$

19. $R(t) = 2 \cos \dfrac{t - 1}{3}$

Set C

Sketch a graph of each function.

20. $g(x) = \sin x - \frac{1}{8} \sin 4x$

21. $E(t) = \sin t + \sin 2t + \sin 3t$

22. $K(t) = 1.5 \cos \frac{1}{2}t - 2 \sin 2t$

23. Let f and g be periodic functions with the same period p. Prove that $f + g$ is periodic and that

$$[f + g](x) = [f + g](x + p).$$

24. Give an argument similar to the one of Example 3 above to show that

$$f(x) = A \sin (kx + \alpha)$$

has period $2\pi/|k|$ and amplitude $|A|$.

Calculator Problem

There are certain functions that are combinations of the exponential functions e^x and e^{-x}. Two of these functions are the *hyperbolic cosine* function, denoted by *cosh* and the *hyperbolic sine* function denoted by *sinh*. These two functions are defined as follows:

$$\cosh x = \tfrac{1}{2}(e^x + e^{-x})$$
$$\sinh x = \tfrac{1}{2}(e^x - e^{-x}).$$

Both functions have the set of real numbers as their domains.

Use a calculator to compute values of each function. Then sketch a graph of each function.

Summary

1. The wrapping function W maps each real number θ into a point $P(x, y)$ on the unit circle with center at the origin.

2. If W is the wrapping function and $W(\theta) = P(x, y)$ then the six circular functions are defined as follows:

$$y = \sin\theta \qquad \tan\theta = y/x,\ x \neq 0 \qquad \sec\theta = 1/x,\ x \neq 0$$
$$x = \cos\theta \qquad \cot\theta = x/y,\ y \neq 0 \qquad \csc\theta = 1/y,\ y \neq 0$$

3. Radian measure is often used with the circular functions. A right angle has a measure of $\pi/2$ radians. We say "there are 2π radians in a circle." 1 radian $\approx 57.3°$.

4. If θ is any real number, $\sin^2\theta + \cos^2\theta = 1$.

5. The circular functions are examples of periodic functions.

6. If $y = A\sin(kx + \alpha)$ or $y = A\cos(kx + \alpha)$, then the

$$\text{amplitude} = |A|,$$
$$\text{period} = \frac{2\pi}{k},$$

and graphs are sine or cosine waves "beginning" at $x = -\alpha/k$.

7. Functions which are sums or differences of sine and cosine functions can be sketched by graphical addition or subtraction.

Chapter 5   Test

5-2 1. How many degrees is $\pi/5$ radians?

2. How many radians is $20°$?

5-4 3. What are the coordinates of point $P(x, y)$ on the unit circle if $W(11\pi/2) = P(x, y)$?

4. Find a real number θ where $0 \le \theta < 2\pi$ such that $W(-9\pi/4) = W(\theta)$.

5-5 5. $W(\theta) = P(-1/\sqrt{5}, 2/\sqrt{5})$. What is $\sin \theta$? What is $\cos \theta$?

6. Complete: For every real number θ, $\sin^2 \theta + \cos^2 \theta = $ ___?___

5-6 7. If $\sin \theta = \frac{3}{5}$ and $\cos \theta = -\frac{4}{5}$, find $\tan \theta$, $\cot \theta$, $\sec \theta$ and $\csc \theta$.

8. Which of the six trigonometric functions are positive for points in Quadrant IV?

5-7 Give exact values of the trigonometric functions.

9. $\sin \dfrac{\pi}{4}$ 10. $\cos \dfrac{\pi}{6}$ 11. $\tan \dfrac{3\pi}{4}$

12. $\cos \dfrac{-2\pi}{3}$ 13. $\sec \dfrac{7\pi}{4}$ 14. $\sin \dfrac{5\pi}{6}$

5-8 15. In the interval from $\pi/2$ to $3\pi/2$ is the sine function increasing or decreasing?

16. Is there a real number θ such that $\sec \theta = \frac{1}{2}$?

5-9 17. Sketch the graph of $y = \frac{1}{2} \cos 2x$.

18. Sketch the graph of $y = 5 \sin (x/4)$.

5-10 Without graphing, determine the period and amplitude of each of the following functions.

19. $f(x) = 3 \sin 4\pi x$

20. $g(t) = -10 \cos (2t + \pi/2)$

21. $F(x) = 5 \cos (\pi x + \pi/4)$

22. $f(\theta) = 3 \sin (5\theta + 2\pi/3)$

5-11 23. Write an equation for the function shown below.

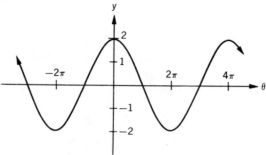

24. Sketch, by graphical addition

$$y = 2 \cos \theta + \sin (\theta/2), \qquad 0 \le \theta \le 4\pi.$$

Historical Note

François Viète
1540–1603

In the ancient world, astronomy was the principal science and the only one that made much use of mathematics. The world's first great astronomer was Hipparchus of Nicaea (second century B.C.), whose goal was to give a mathematical description of the motions of the planets. He apparently invented trigonometry to help him in this endeavor.

As seen from the earth, the planets seem to move in an irregular way on the surface of a large sphere, the celestial sphere (the word planet means wanderer). Hence, to describe their positions with respect to one another and with respect to the stars, *spherical* trigonometry, the study of triangles on the surface of a sphere, was developed. Consequently, one must be familiar with the trigonometric, or circular, functions. Hipparchus was able to compile a crude table of sines.

The historical note of Chapter 6 contains some remarks on the manner in which early writers conceived the trigonometric functions. Here we are concerned mainly with the grad-

ual evolution of the subject. During antiquity, and long after, trigonometry was inseparable from astronomy. All books on astronomy contained a discussion of spherical trigonometry, and there were no books on trigonometry alone. It was not until the thirteenth century that an Arab astronomer Nasir-Eddin (1201-1274) wrote the first treatise on trigonometry, independent of astronomy.

During the Middle Ages, the culture of the Greeks and the Hindus was preserved and enriched by the Arabs. Among the names that may be mentioned, we give only that of Mohammed Ibn Musa Al-Khowarizmi, who (in 825 A.D.) wrote a book entitled, *al-jebr w' almuquabala,* which means "restoration and reduction." From the title we derive our word "algebra" and from the author's name, the term "algorithm."

Eventually, via the Moslems in Spain, the Greek-Hindu-Arabic culture reached Europe and sparked the revival of the arts and sciences which historians call the renaissance period. Mathematics played an important part in this general intellectual upsurge. By the end of the sixteenth century, elementary, or computational, trigonometry was almost in its modern form, and the word "trigonometry" appeared for the first time.

This reformulation of trigonometry was in large measure the work of François Viète (1540-1603) who, by his systematic use of algebra, substantially simplified the exposition. He also extended the circular function tables (to 7 places for every second) begun by the German, Rhaeticus. These extensive and quite accurate tables were computed by hand, without the use of logarithms and without the use of the convenient formulas derived in the calculus. Rhaeticus was also the first to define the six circular functions as the ratios of the sides of a right triangle.

Chapter 6
Applications of the Circular Functions

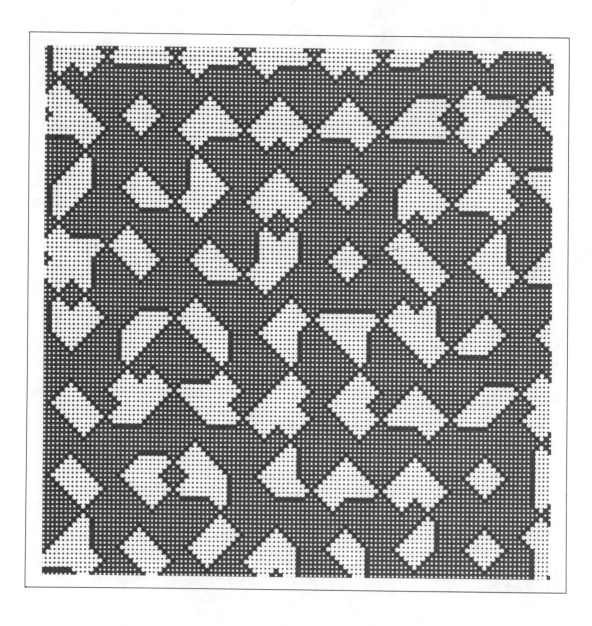

6-1   Introduction

Circular functions have two essentially different types of applications. One kind of application is to geometry, where the circular functions are the proper tool for solving problems related to triangles. This application to triangles is sometimes called *numerical trigonometry*. Historically, it is this application which aroused interest in the subject. The word *trigonometry* means "three angle measurement".

A second kind of application arises because of the periodic nature of the circular functions. Applications of this kind abound in the physics of sound, light, electricity and mechanics.

6-2   Functions and Cofunctions

For numerical applications one must be able to find, or compute, the values of the trigonometric functions for any value of the independent variable. Conversely, given the value of one of the trigonometric functions, one must be able to find a real number that gives that value of the function. If one has a calculator with the trigonometric functions, both of these problems can be handled directly. If one does not have a calculator, then tables of the trigonometric functions must be used.

Since each of the functions has as its domain the set of real numbers, it would seem that such a table of values would have to be endless. However, since each of the six functions are periodic with a period of 2π, it is necessary to tabulate the functions at most between 0 and 2π.

We next observe that the value of a trigonometric function, for θ in any quadrant, differs at most in sign from the value of the same function for a number r, where $0 \leq r \leq \pi/2$. The angle whose measure is r is called the *reference angle*.

For example, $\sin \pi/6$ and $\sin 5\pi/6$ have the same value, 0.5000. Likewise, $\sin 7\pi/6$ and $\sin 11\pi/6$ are both negatives of this value, namely, -0.5000. For all four of these angles, the first quadrant angle, $\pi/6$, is the reference angle.

Fig. 1 shows the various positions of $P = (x, y) = W(\theta)$, in each quadrant, having the same reference angle AOP_1.

In Fig. 1, we have

$$P_1(x_0, y_0) = W(\theta_1),$$
$$P_2(-x_0, y_0) = W(\theta_2),$$
$$P_3(-x_0, -y_0) = W(\theta_3),$$
and
$$P_4(x_0, -y_0) = W(\theta_4),$$

all having the same reference angle AOP_1. By definition,

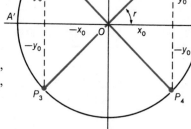

$\sin\theta_1 = y_0,$	$\cos\theta_1 = x_0,$
$\sin\theta_2 = y_0,$	$\cos\theta_2 = -x_0,$
$\sin\theta_3 = -y_0,$	$\cos\theta_3 = -x_0,$
$\sin\theta_4 = -y_0,$	$\cos\theta_4 = x_0.$

Therefore

FIGURE 1

$$|\sin\theta_1| = |\sin\theta_2| = |\sin\theta_3| = |\sin\theta_4|$$

and

$$|\cos\theta_1| = |\cos\theta_2| = |\cos\theta_3| = |\cos\theta_4|.$$

That is, except for their signs, the sines and the cosines of θ_1, θ_2, θ_3, and θ_4 are the same. Note that

$$m(\angle AOP_1) = m(\angle A'OP_2) = m(\angle A'OP_3) = m(\angle AOP_4).$$

This fact helps in determining the reference angles of any $P(x, y) = W(\theta)$.

Since a similar argument can be made for tangent and cotangent, it follows that only the functions on the part of the domain between 0 and $\pi/2$ must be tabulated.

Example 1   In Fig. 1, if $r = \pi/6$, what are the values of θ_2, θ_3, and θ_4?
Solution.

$$\theta_2 = \pi - m(\angle A'OP_2) = \pi - r = \frac{5\pi}{6},$$

$$\theta_3 = \pi + m(\angle A'PO_3) = \pi + r = \frac{7\pi}{6},$$

$$\theta_4 = 2\pi - m(\angle AOP_4) = 2\pi - r = \frac{11\pi}{6}.$$

2   Determine the values of the sine and cosine functions for θ_1, θ_2, θ_3, and θ_4 of Example 1.
Solution.

$$\sin\theta_1 = \sin\frac{\pi}{6} = \frac{1}{2}, \qquad \cos\theta_1 = \cos\frac{\pi}{6} = \frac{\sqrt{3}}{2},$$

$$\sin \theta_2 = \sin \frac{\pi}{6} = \frac{1}{2}, \qquad \cos \theta_2 = -\cos \frac{\pi}{6} = -\frac{\sqrt{3}}{2},$$

$$\sin \theta_3 = -\sin \frac{\pi}{6} = -\frac{1}{2}, \qquad \cos \theta_3 = -\cos \frac{\pi}{6} = -\frac{\sqrt{3}}{2},$$

$$\sin \theta_4 = -\sin \frac{\pi}{6} = -\frac{1}{2}, \qquad \cos \theta_4 = \cos \frac{\pi}{6} = \frac{\sqrt{3}}{2}.$$

Example 3 $\sin 3 = \sin (\pi - 3)$, because the measure of the reference angle is $\pi - 3$ (Fig. 2).

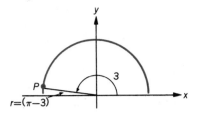

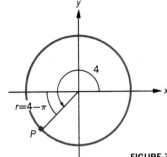

FIGURE 2   FIGURE 3

4    $\cos 4 = -\cos (4 - \pi)$, because the measure of the reference angle is $4 - \pi$ and the cosine is negative in the third quadrant (Fig. 3).

5    $$\tan \frac{2\pi}{3} = -\tan \left(\pi - \frac{2\pi}{3} \right) = -\tan \frac{\pi}{3},$$

because the measure of the reference angle is $\pi - 2\pi/3 = \pi/3$ and the tangent is negative in the second quadrant (Fig. 4).

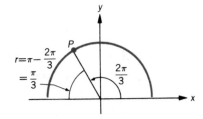

What has been shown so far is that we need only tables between 0 and $\pi/2$. There is yet another relation that will permit the tables to be just half this large.

FIGURE 4

Let us look at the names of the functions. There are functions and *co*-functions:

sine and *co*sine,
tangent and *co*tangent.

We shall agree that the *co*-cosine is the sine, and the *co*-cotangent is the tangent. We shall now prove that for $0 < \theta < \pi/2$,

$$\text{function of } \theta = \text{cofunction of } \left(\frac{\pi}{2} - \theta\right).^*$$ (1)

Consider Fig. 5. Triangle $\triangle PQO$ is a right triangle with right angle PQO;

$$m(\angle PQO) = \pi/2,$$
$$m(\angle POQ) = \theta,$$
$$m(\angle OPQ) = \pi/2 - \theta,$$
$$OQ = x_0, \quad \text{and} \quad PQ = y_0.$$

We now choose P' with coordinates (y_0, x_0), that is, $x = y_0$ and $y = x_0$.

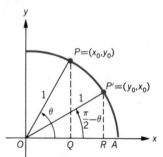

FIGURE 5

We immediately see that $\triangle PQO \cong \triangle ORP'$, and since this is true for any $P(x_0, y_0)$ and $P'(y_0, x_0)$, we can make the following general statement. If $P = (x, y) = W(\theta)$, then

$$P' = (y, x) = W\left(\frac{\pi}{2} - \theta\right).$$

So directly from the definition of the functions, we have

$$\sin \theta = y = \cos\left(\frac{\pi}{2} - \theta\right), \quad \tan \theta = \frac{y}{x} = \cot\left(\frac{\pi}{2} - \theta\right),$$

$$\cos \theta = x = \sin\left(\frac{\pi}{2} - \theta\right), \quad \cot \theta = \frac{x}{y} = \tan\left(\frac{\pi}{2} - \theta\right).$$

Therefore tables need give the circular functions of θ only for $0 \le \theta \le \pi/4$.

Example 6   Express $\sin 2\pi/3$ in terms of its cofunction and reference angle.
Solution.

$$\sin \frac{2\pi}{3} = \sin \frac{\pi}{3} = \cos\left(\frac{\pi}{2} - \frac{\pi}{3}\right) = \cos \frac{\pi}{6}$$

7   Express $\tan 2$ in terms of its cofunction and reference angle.
Solution.

$$\tan 2 = -\tan(\pi - 2) = -\cot\left[\frac{\pi}{2} - (\pi - 2)\right] = -\cot\left(2 - \frac{\pi}{2}\right)$$

---

*The relation (1) is actually correct for all θ, as will be shown in Chapter 7. At the moment, we need the relation only for the restricted values of θ: $0 < \theta < \pi/2$.

Problems

Set A

Express each function in terms of the reference angle θ where $0 \le \theta \le \pi/2$.

1. $\sin \dfrac{7\pi}{4}$ **2.** $\cos \left(\dfrac{-\pi}{4} \right)$ **3.** $\tan \dfrac{3\pi}{4}$

4. $\sec \dfrac{9\pi}{4}$ **5.** $\sin \dfrac{5\pi}{3}$ **6.** $\cot \dfrac{5\pi}{4}$

7. $\tan \left(\dfrac{-2\pi}{3} \right)$ **8.** $\cos \dfrac{5\pi}{6}$ **9.** $\csc \dfrac{2\pi}{3}$

Express each function in terms of its cofunction.

10. $\cos \dfrac{\pi}{4}$ **11.** $\tan \dfrac{\pi}{6}$ **12.** $\sin \dfrac{\pi}{2}$

13. $\sec \dfrac{\pi}{6}$ **14.** $\cot \dfrac{\pi}{3}$ **15.** $\csc \dfrac{\pi}{6}$

16. $\sin \dfrac{\pi}{3}$ **17.** $\tan \dfrac{\pi}{4}$ **18.** $\cos \dfrac{\pi}{6}$

19. $\cot \dfrac{\pi}{4}$ **20.** $\csc \dfrac{\pi}{3}$ **21.** $\sin 0$

Set B

22. $\sin (\pi/6) = \frac{1}{2}$. Determine the values for $\sin (5\pi/6)$, $\sin (7\pi/6)$, and $\sin (11\pi/6)$.

23. $\cos (7\pi/6) = -\sqrt{3}/2$. Determine the values for $\cos (11\pi/6)$, $\cos (\pi/6)$, and $\cos (5\pi/6)$.

24. $W(\theta_1)$, $W(\theta_2)$, $W(\theta_3)$, and $W(\theta_4)$ all have the same reference angle but are in different quadrants, as shown in the figure. If $\theta_1 = \pi/3$, then what are the smallest positive values of θ_2, θ_3, and θ_4?

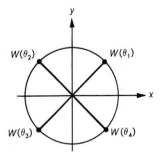

Set C

Which of the following numbers are positive?

25. $\sin 0.5$ **26.** $\sin 2$ **27.** $\cos 1.4$ **28.** $\sin 4$

29. $\tan 3.5$ **30.** $\cot 5$ **31.** $\csc 4$ **32.** $\sec 6$

Find the values for $\sin \theta$, $\cos \theta$, and $\tan \theta$, if the coordinates of $P(x, y) = W(\theta)$ are as follows.

33. $\left(\dfrac{1}{3}, \dfrac{2\sqrt{2}}{3} \right)$ **34.** $\left(-\dfrac{5}{13}, \dfrac{12}{13} \right)$

35. $\left(-\dfrac{1}{\sqrt{5}}, -\dfrac{2}{\sqrt{5}} \right)$ **36.** $\left(\dfrac{40}{41}, -\dfrac{9}{41} \right)$

Calculator Problem

Find a real number θ in $[0, \pi/2]$ such that

$$\tan \theta = \cos \theta.$$

Tables of Values of Trigonometric Functions

Originally circular functions were primarily used to solve triangle problems and, in particular, problems that arose in physical applications, notably astronomy, where degree measure was customary. Therefore in applications it is traditional and convenient to continue the practice of using the measure of the reference angle in degrees. Thus instead of writing $\sin \pi/6$, we can write $\sin 30°$. There need be no confusion about this change of notation because it will always be clear from the context what is meant.

Deg.	Sin	Tan	Cot	Cos	Deg.
36.0	0.5878	0.7265	1.3764	0.8090	**54.0**
.1	.5892	.7292	1.3713	.8080	53.9
.2	.5906	.7319	1.3663	.8070	.8
.3	.5920	.7346	1.3613	.8059	.7
.4	.5934	.7373	1.3564	.8049	.6
.5	.5948	.7400	1.3514	.8039	.5
.6	.5962	.7427	1.3465	.8028	.4
.7	.5976	.7454	1.3416	.8018	.3
.8	.5990	.7481	1.3367	.8007	.2
.9	.6004	.7508	1.3319	.7997	53.1
$\sim\sim\sim$					
.8	.6401	.8332	1.2002	.7683	.2
.9	.6414	.8361	1.1960	.7672	50.1
Deg.	Cos	Cot	Tan	Sin	Deg.

FIGURE 6

Figure 6 shows a portion of Table II after the Appendix. Angles less than, or equal to, 45° are listed in the left-hand column, and the name of the function appears at the top of the table. Angles greater than 45° are in the right-hand column, and the name of the function appears at the bottom of the table.

Example 1 Find $\sin 36.8°$.

Solution. Since $36.8 < 45°$, this measure is found in the left hand column. Under the column labeled sin *at the top* of the chart we find $\sin 36.8° = 0.5990$.

2 Find $\tan 53.2°$.

Solution. This measure is found in the right hand column since $53.2° > 45°$. Locate the tan column *at the bottom* of the chart. Opposite 53.2° in this column we read $\tan 53.2° = 1.3367$.

3 Find $\cos 143.6°$.

Solution. The reference angle is $(180.0° - 143.6°) = 36.4°$. Therefore $\cos 143.6° = -\cos 36.4° = -0.8049$.

Example 4   Find A such that $0 < A < 90$ if cot $A° = 0.7563$.

Solution. The value 0.7563 is located in the column with cot at the bottom of the table. The measure for A is therefore found in the right hand side of the table. Therefore $A = 52.9$.

Most of the numbers in the body of the table are approximations correct to four significant digits. Calculators will give values of the functions accurate to seven or more significant digits. For example, by calculator, sin 36.8° = 0.5990235. (Compare with Example 1 above.)

Problems

Set A

From Table II in the Appendix find the following.

1. sin 23.3°   **2.** cos 19.5°   **3.** tan 40.1°

4. sin 53.2°   **5.** sin 84.0°   **6.** cos 63.8°

7. cot 33.2°   **8.** tan 68.7°   **9.** cos 75.7°

10. sin 46.6°   **11.** sin 57.9°   **12.** tan 3.8°

Find A such that $0 < A < 90$.

13. sin $A° = 0.2113$ **14.** cos $A° = 0.3987$

15. tan $A° = 0.9004$ **16.** sin $A° = 0.8462$

17. cos $A° = 0.4003$ **18.** cot $A° = 2.971$

19. tan $A° = 5.850$ **20.** sin $A° = 0.9823$

21. cos $A° = 0.6547$ **22.** cot $A° = 0.4899$

23. sin $A° = 0.7570$ **24.** cos $A° = 0.9982$

Set B

Find each of the following.

25. sin 124°   **26.** cos 138°   **27.** sin 163°

28. tan 132.4°   **29.** cos 113.7°   **30.** sin 103.8°

31. tan 164.5°   **32.** sin 154.9°   **33.** cos 133.3°

Find A to the nearest tenth of a degree, where $0 < A < 90$.

34. sin $A° = 0.2625$ **35.** cos $A° = 0.4941$

36. cos $A° = 0.8229$ **37.** sin $A° = 0.7183$

38. tan $A° = 2.777$ **39.** tan $A° = 0.4343$

Set C

Write the following functions as $\pm$ the same function of a real number between 0 and $\pi/2$. That is, express each of them in terms of the reference angle.

40. tan 2   **41.** sin 2   **42.** cos $\dfrac{2\pi}{3}$

43. cot 2.5   **44.** sin 2.5   **45.** cos 2.9

46. tan 1.7   **47.** cot 1.83   **48.** cos $(\pi - 0.1)$

Calculator Problem

Measures of angles are sometimes given in degrees, minutes and seconds. For calculator use, such a measure must be expressed in degrees as a decimal. Thus

$$27°32'45'' = 27° + \tfrac{32}{60}° + \tfrac{45}{3600}° = 27.5458333°$$

Find the value of each of the following.

(a) sin 33°12′29″   (b) cos 54°35′55″   (c) tan 20°43′17″
(d) cos 63°38′24″   (e) tan 84°52′30″   (f) sin 19°7′12″

Right Triangles

Geometric application of the circular functions to right triangles depends upon properties of similar triangles. Suppose that one has a right triangle, $\triangle ABC$, with the right angle at C and sides of lengths a, b, c opposite the corresponding angles. Let us choose the coordinate axes as in Fig. 7 with vertex A at the origin and C on the x-axis. Consider the right triangle, $\triangle APQ$, with the right angle at Q and $|AP| = 1$. Then $\triangle APQ$ is similar to $\triangle ABC$, and

$$\sin A = \frac{a}{c} = \frac{\text{length of opposite side}}{\text{length of hypotenuse}},$$

$$\cos A = \frac{b}{c} = \frac{\text{length of adjacent side}}{\text{length of hypotenuse}},$$

$$\tan A = \frac{a}{b} = \frac{\text{length of opposite side}}{\text{length of adjacent side}},$$

$$\cot A = \frac{b}{a} = \frac{\text{length of adjacent side}}{\text{length of opposite side}}.$$

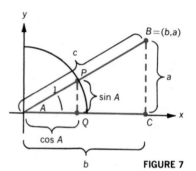

FIGURE 7

The equations above are immediate consequences of the definitions of the functions. The opposite-adjacent-hypotenuse language is often used in formulating definitions of the circular functions of acute angles.

Example　In a right triangle the measure of one angle is 34.4° and the length of the hypotenuse is 77.8 m. Find the measure of the other angle and the lengths of the remaining sides.

Solution. Labeling the triangle as in Fig. 8, we have, on using the table of functions,

$$\sin A° = 0.5650 = \frac{a}{77.8}.$$

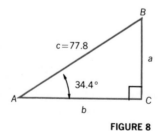

FIGURE 8

Therefore
$$a = (0.5650)(77.8) = 44.0 \text{ to three significant figures.}$$

And since
$$\cos A° = 0.8251 = \frac{b}{77.8},$$

$b = (77.8)(0.8251) = 64.2$ m to three significant figures. Also $m(\angle B) = 90° - 34.4° = 55.6°.$

Problems

Set A

In the triangles below, A, B, C are the angles, with C a right angle and a, b, c the lengths of the sides opposite these angles, respectively. Find the part designated. Draw a figure in each case.

1. $a = 12.5$ cm, $m(\angle A) = 31.7°$. Find c.
2. $b = 4.86$ m, $m(\angle A) = 62.6°$. Find c.
3. $c = 86.2$ cm, $m(\angle A) = 18.8°$. Find b.
4. $c = 3.88$ km, $m(\angle A) = 44.5°$. Find a.
5. $a = 36.8$ m, $c = 51.2$ m. Find $m(\angle A)$.
6. $a = 3.44$ m, $b = 6.89$ m. Find $m(\angle B)$.

Set B

7. A freeway exit is 300 meters long. The exit drops 12 m in this distance. What is the measure of the angle that the exit makes with the horizontal? That is, find the measure of $\angle A$ in the drawing.

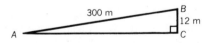

8. A street up a hill in San Francisco rises 94.5 m through a distance of 315 m along the street. What is the measure of the angle of inclination of the street ($\angle X$)?

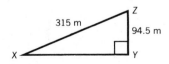

9. From a photograph of the moon a scientist estimated the length of a shadow of a crater wall to be 424 m. The sun was at an angle of 24.4° when the photograph was taken. What was the height h of the crater wall?

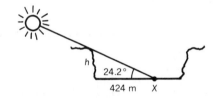

10. A gable roof has a rise of 1.8 m and a run of 7.2 m. (See diagram.) What is the measure of the angle of inclination, $\angle A$, of the roof?

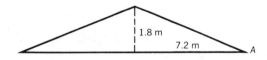

Set C

11. The diagram shows the cross section of a V-thread. Find the depth d of the thread.

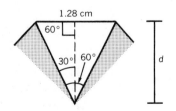

12. A plane is flying at an altitude of 5 kilo-
    meters. The pilot wants to descend into an
    airport so that the path of the plane makes
    an angle of 4° with ground. How far from
    the airport (horizontal distance) should the
    descent begin?

13. A ladder 7.5 m long leans against the side of
    a building with the foot of the ladder 1.8 m
    from the building. What angle does the
    ladder make with the ground, to the nearest
    degree?

14. The base angles of an isosceles trapezoid
    have measures of 39.2°. The top and bottom
    edges have lengths of 8.62 and 18.53
    centimeters. What is the altitude of the
    trapezoid?

15. What is the height of the tree in the diagram
    to the nearest whole meter?

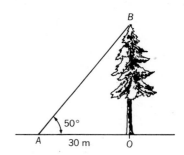

16. The side of a regular pentagon is approxi-
    mately 11.83 units. Find the radii of the
    inscribed and circumscribed circles.

Calculator Problem

According to the ancient Greeks, a rectangle is a
Golden Rectangle if the length l and width w are
such that

$$\frac{l}{w} = \frac{w}{l-w}.$$

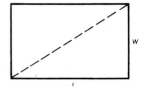

Solve this proportion for l in terms of w, then find the ratio l/w. This ratio is called
the Golden Ratio.

In a Golden Rectangle what is the measure of the angle that one of the diagonals
of the rectangle makes with the shorter side of the rectangle?

6–5   Oblique Triangles: Laws of Sines and Cosines

In applying the circular functions to triangles other than right triangles, one
can proceed in several ways. One can subdivide the given triangles into right
triangles or one can use new formulas relating the sides and angles of any
triangle. It turns out that these new formulas have applications in other
situations and so are important in their own right. We shall now consider
these formulas.

Let us recall from geometry that a triangle is uniquely determined if
either

(1) angle-side-angle are given (ASA),
(2) side-angle-side are given (SAS),
(3) side-side-side are given (SSS).

Our problem is that of devising formulas to find the other three parts of the given triangle for these cases. The desired formulas are called the *Law of Sines* and the *Law of Cosines* and are derived below.

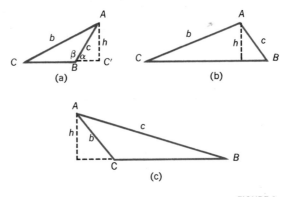

FIGURE 9

Consider $\triangle ABC$ as in Fig. 9 where we have two cases depending on whether C is acute or obtuse. In all three cases, we have

$$h = c \sin B = b \sin C,$$

$$\frac{c}{\sin C} = \frac{b}{\sin B}.$$

Note that in the case shown in Fig. 9(a), $\sin \beta = \sin \alpha$. And because $m \angle CBA < 180°$ or π, the reference angle for $\angle CBA$ has a measure equal to $m \angle C'BA$. If the perpendicular of length h had been dropped to side b, we would have obtained

$$\frac{c}{\sin C} = \frac{a}{\sin A}.$$

Combining these equations, we have a theorem called the Law of Sines.

LAW OF SINES

In every triangle with angles A, B, C and opposite sides of lengths a, b, c, respectively,

$$\frac{a}{\sin A} = \frac{b}{\sin B} = \frac{c}{\sin C}.$$

Clearly, knowing two angles and a side will enable us to compute the other sides. Hence the Law of Sines solves case (1) for us.

Example 1   In $\triangle ABC$, $c = 32.7$ cm, $m(\angle A) =$ 31.5°, and $m(\angle B) = 44.8°$. Find the length of side a. (Fig. 10.)

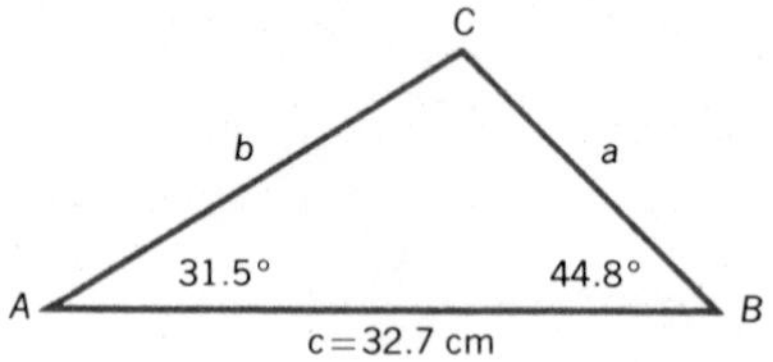

$$m(\angle C) = 180° - (31.5° + 44.8°)$$
$$= 103.7°$$

From the Law of Sines, we have

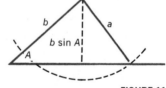

$$\frac{a}{\sin A} = \frac{c}{\sin C}$$

or

$$a = \sin A \left(\frac{c}{\sin C}\right).$$

FIGURE 10

Computing we find

$$a = 0.5225 \left(\frac{32.7}{0.9715}\right) = 17.6 \text{ cm.}$$

The Law of Sines can also be used when two sides and the angle opposite one of them are given. For example, suppose that a, b, and angle A are given, as in Fig. 11. This is the so-called ambiguous case (see Problems 11–15 below) which has

no solution   if $a < b \sin A$,
one solution   if $a = b \sin A$,
two solutions   if $b \sin A < a < b$,
one solution   if $a \geq b$.

FIGURE 11

We now turn to the Law of Cosines and for its derivation apply the distance formula in a coordinate plane. Given $\triangle ABC$, suppose that the axes are chosen so that C is at the origin, A on the positive x-axis, and B is above the x-axis, as in Fig. 12.

The coordinates of B are $(a \cos C, a \sin C)$, and the coordinates of A are $(b, 0)$. Note that by $\angle C$ we mean $\angle BCA$, and further that

$$\cos C = \cos \alpha = -\cos \beta$$

in the case shown in Fig. 12. In general, if C is greater than 90°, then the cosine for that angle will be a negative number.

The distance formula gives us

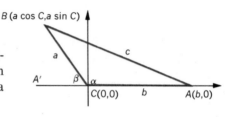

FIGURE 12

$$c^2 = (a \cos C - b)^2 + (a \sin C - 0)^2$$
$$= a^2(\cos^2 C + \sin^2 C) + b^2 - 2ab \cos C.$$

Because $\sin^2 \theta + \cos^2 \theta = 1$ for all angles θ, we get

$$c^2 = a^2 + b^2 - 2ab \cos C.$$

Clearly, similar formulas must hold for a^2 and b^2. We have thus obtained the Generalized Pythagorean Theorem, or a theorem called the Law of Cosines.

LAW OF COSINES

In every triangle, with angles A, B, C and opposite sides of lengths a, b, c, respectively,

$$a^2 = b^2 + c^2 - 2bc \cos A,$$
$$b^2 = c^2 + a^2 - 2ca \cos B,$$
$$c^2 = a^2 + b^2 - 2ab \cos C.$$

Example 2   In $\triangle ABC$, $a = 1.23$ m, $c = 2.62$ m, $m(\angle B) = 100°$ (Fig. 13). Find side b.

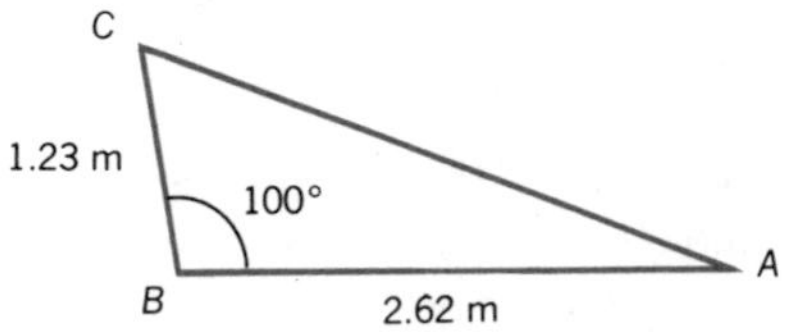

Solution.

$$\cos 100° = -\cos(180 - 100)°$$
$$= -\cos 80°.$$

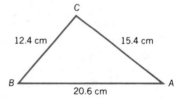

FIGURE 13

$$b^2 = c^2 + a^2 - 2ca \cos B$$
$$b^2 = (2.62)^2 + (1.23)^2 - 2(2.62)(1.23)(-0.1736)$$
$$b^2 = 9.4961867$$
$$b = \sqrt{9.4961867} = 3.08 \text{ m to three significant digits}$$

3   In $\triangle ABC$, $a = 12.4$ cm, $b = 15.4$ cm and $c = 20.6$ cm. Find $m(\angle C)$. (Fig. 14.)

Solution. Solving one of the forms of the Law of Cosines for $\cos C$, we have

$$\cos C = \frac{a^2 + b^2 - c^2}{2ab}.$$

FIGURE 14

Thus

$$\cos C = \frac{(12.4)^2 + (15.4)^2 - (20.6)^2}{2(12.4)(15.4)},$$

$$\cos C = \frac{-33.44}{381.92} = -0.0876,$$

$$m(\angle C) = 95.0°.$$

Problems

Set A

In each of the following problems, find the remaining sides and angles of $\triangle ABC$.

1. $m(\angle A) = 17.5°$, $a = 62.0$, $b = 42.0$
2. $m(\angle A) = 24.9°$, $c = 7.5$, $b = 12.6$
3. $m(\angle A) = 72.0°$, $m(\angle B) = 56.1°$, $c = 32.8$
4. $m(\angle B) = 71.2°$, $m(\angle C) = 12.1°$, $a = 14.2$
5. $m(\angle C) = 125.6°$, $a = 12.8$, $c = 20.7$
6. $m(\angle B) = 53.1°$, $m(\angle C) = 21.5°$, $c = 14.3$
7. $a = 18.0$, $c = 25.0$, $m(\angle B) = 60.0°$
8. $a = 10.0$, $b = 12.5$, $c = 16.0$
9. $a = 1.25$, $b = 1.25$, $c = 2.00$
10. $a = 150$, $b = 109$, $c = 210$

Set B

In Problems 11–15, determine whether there is no solution, one solution, or two solutions.

11. $m(\angle A) = 35.0°$, $a = 24$, $b = 17$
12. $m(\angle A) = 62.5°$, $a = 9.6$, $b = 12.0$
13. $m(\angle A) = 30°$, $a = 7.2$, $b = 14.4$
14. $m(\angle A) = 29.4°$, $a = 27$, $b = 27$
15. $m(\angle A) = 46.4°$, $a = 28.3$, $b = 32.4$
16. Find the remaining parts of $\triangle ABC$ if $m(\angle A) = 37.3°$, $a = 15.2$, $b = 22.0$. There are two solutions.
17. A boat at point A sights a lighthouse at point C making an angle of 28° with the direction of the boat. When the boat reaches point B, 3.5 km from A, the lighthouse makes an angle of 53° with the boat's path. How far from the lighthouse is the boat at point B?

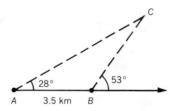

18. A machinist must drill three holes at A, B and C in a steel plate. If $a = 20.9$ cm, $b = 23.4$ cm and $c = 27.4$ cm, what is the measure of $\angle ABC$?

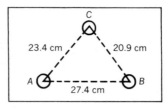

19. The lengths of two sides of a parallelogram are 2.8 cm and 5.5 cm. The angle between the two sides has a measure of 64°. Find the length of the longer diagonal of the parallelogram.

20. The measures of two angles of a triangle are 40° and 28°. The length of the side between these angles is 5 cm. What is the perimeter of the triangle?

Set C

21. Show that the Pythagorean Theorem is a special case of the Law of Cosines.

22. Show that if angle C of a triangle is obtuse, then $c^2 > a^2 + b^2$.

23. Show that the area of any triangle is given by area $= \frac{1}{2}ab \sin C$.

24. In $\triangle ABC$, $a = 3.56$ m, $b = 7.15$ m, $m(\angle C) = 118°$. What is the area of $\triangle ABC$?

25. Show that if $\angle AOB$ is a central angle of a circle with center at O and radius r, and if $m(\angle AOB) = \theta$, then

$$|AB| = r\sqrt{2(1 - \cos\theta)}.$$

If $\angle AOB$ is a straight angle, what does the formula give?

26. Parallelogram $OPRQ$ has vertex O at the origin. The coordinates of P and Q are $(2, 6)$ and $(5, 2)$, respectively. What is the measure of the angle between the positive x-axis and ray OR?

27. R is the radius of the circumscribed circle of $\triangle ABC$, and s is one-half its perimeter. Prove each of the following.

(a) $R(\sin A + \sin B + \sin C) = s$

(b) $2R = \dfrac{a}{\sin A} = \dfrac{b}{\sin B} = \dfrac{c}{\sin C}$

Calculator Problem

The hypotenuse and one leg of a right triangle have lengths 372.5 m and 237.4 m, respectively. Find the length of the other side

(a) by the Pythagorean Theorem,
(b) by trigonometry.

6-6   **Simple Harmonic Motion**

Many motions in physics are periodic. Examples include the oscillations of a pendulum, the vibrations of a tuning fork, or the variations of the voltage of alternating electrical current. Periodic motions or displacements which have mathematical models that are pure sine or cosine waves are given the special name *simple harmonic motions*.

Example 1   A piston of an engine is attached by a rod to a crankshaft. (Fig. 15). When the crankshaft turns at a constant speed, the piston moves up and down in its cylinder in simple harmonic motion. For example, in an engine in which the radius of the crankshaft is 5 cm and the shaft is rotating 20 times a second, the distance between the piston and its central position is given by

$$d = 5 \sin 40\pi t$$

where d is distance in centimeters and t is time in seconds.

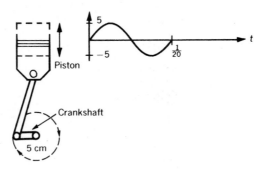

FIGURE 15

Definition 6-1   If d is any displacement in distance, pressure, or voltage such that

$$d = A \sin \omega t \qquad \text{or} \qquad d = A \cos \omega t, \tag{1}$$

where A and ω are real constants and t is the time, then the displacement is said to be a *simple harmonic motion* of *amplitude* $|A|$.

Remark   Displacements given by $d = A \sin [\omega(t - \alpha)]$ or $d = A \cos [\omega(t - \beta)]$, where α and β are constants, are also simple harmonic motions. The cycle simply "begins" at $t = \alpha$ or $t = \beta$.

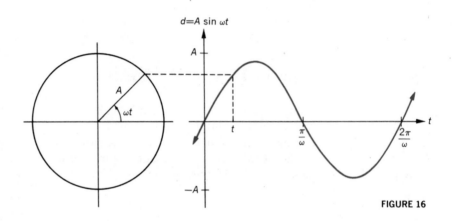

FIGURE 16

A simple construction of the graph of $d = A \sin \omega t$ is shown in Fig. 16.

Example 2   Figure 16 is closely related to the simple harmonic voltage variations in an alternating current generator. Figure 17 represents an idealized generator. The armature is a rectangular loop of wire which rotates about its axis at a speed of ω radians per second. It is suspended between the poles of a magnet. As the armature rotates, the wires pass through the magnetic field and generate an electromotive force, or voltage, E. If the armature is vertical (as

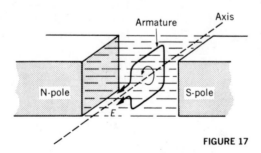

FIGURE 17

shown) at time $t = 0$, then the voltage is proportional to $\sin \omega t$: $E = E_0 \sin \omega t$, where E_0 is a constant related to the strength of the magnet. If the armature were inclined to the vertical at angle α when $t = 0$, then the voltage variation would be given by $E = E_0 \sin (\omega t + \alpha)$.

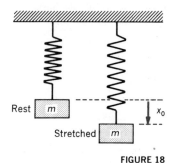

FIGURE 18

Example 3   Consider a mass m suspended from a weightless spring (Fig. 18). Let x measure the displacement of the mass from its position at rest, where x is positive if the displacement is downward.

Suppose that the mass is pulled down a short distance x_0 and then released. The mass will oscillate on either side of the rest position. Neglecting air resistance and friction in the spring, one shows in physics that the mass will execute the simple harmonic motion given by

$$ x = x_0 \cos \sqrt{\frac{k}{m}}\, t, $$

where k is a constant associated with the spring. The period of the motion is seen to be $2\pi / \sqrt{k/m}$. Thus heavier masses on the same spring will oscillate more slowly than lighter ones, because the period is larger for the heavier mass.

In Chapter 5 we defined the period, p, of a periodic function. If the independent variable measures time, the period is the time for one full cycle, or oscillation. Definitions follow for two other terms often encountered.

Definition 6–2   If F is a periodic function with period p (so that $F(t + p) = F(t)$ for all t, and p is the least positive number with this property), then

  (a) the *frequency* of $F = 1/p = \nu$,
  (b) the *circular frequency* of $F = 2\pi\nu = \omega$.

The number ν is *the number of cycles per unit time*. The number ω is the *number of radians per unit time* and is the same ω that appeared in equation (1).

Example 4   Let F be the function given by $F(t) = 5 \sin 2t$. F is periodic with period $p = \pi$. The frequency of $F = \nu = 1/\pi$ (cycles per unit time). The circular frequency of $F = \omega = 2\pi(1/\pi) = 2$ (radians per unit time).

Problems

Set A

Find the period, frequency, circular frequency, and amplitude of simple harmonic motions given by the following.

1. $d = 20 \sin 4\pi t$

2. $d = 8 \sin 10\pi t$

3. $e = 110 \sin 120\pi t$

4. $x = 4 \sin 2t$

5. $k = 3 \sin \pi t$

6. Sketch a graph of one period of the simple harmonic motion given by
$d = 5 \sin (t - \pi/4)$.

Set B

7. A simple harmonic motion has frequency equal to 3 cycles per second and amplitude 4. Write a formula for such a displacement and sketch its graph.

8. A simple harmonic motion has amplitude 10 and a circular frequency of 12π radians per second. Write a formula for the displacement d at any time t.

9. What is the period of the simple harmonic motion in problem 8?

10. Show that the circular frequency of a simple harmonic motion of period p is $2\pi/p$.

11. The frequency of a periodic function is 2 cycles per second. What is the period of the function?

Set C

12. A spring weighted by a mass m oscillates in simple harmonic motion given by the equation
$$d = d_0 \cos \frac{8\pi t}{\sqrt{m}}.$$

(a) What is the period of the motion for a mass of 16 g?

(b) What is the period of the motion for a mass of 4 g?

13. The position of a pendulum determined by the angle θ describes, very nearly, a simple harmonic motion. (See the figure below.) Given that at $t = 0$, the pendulum hangs vertically downward, the period of the pendulum is 2 seconds, and the maximum angular displacement is $\frac{1}{10}$ radian, write a formula giving θ as a function of time t, in seconds.

14. A particle moves in simple harmonic motion between two points on a line that are 10 centimeters apart. (See the figure below). How far will the particle move during the first $\frac{1}{8}$ period after passing the midpoint? during the first $\frac{1}{6}$ period? during the first $\frac{1}{4}$ period?

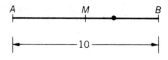

Calculator Problem

The shortest distance between two points on Earth is along the great circle connecting the two points. In the figure a, b, and c are arcs of the polar triangle in which Dallas, Texas and New York City are two of the vertices of the triangle. Point A is the North Pole. The great circle distance along arc a can be computed if the latitude and longitude of the two cities is given. The basic formula is

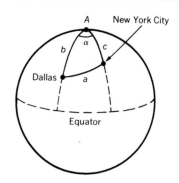

$$\cos a = \cos \alpha \sin b \sin c + \cos b \cos c$$

where

α = positive difference in the longitude of the two cities,
$b = 90°$ − latitude of Dallas,
$c = 90°$ − latitude of New York City,
a = measure of the great circle arc in degrees.

Assuming that the earth is spherical, an arc of $1°$ of a great circle has a length of about 111.12 km. Compute the great circle distance between Dallas and New York City given the latitude and longitude below.

	Latitude	Longitude
Dallas	32.8°	96.8°
New York City	40.8°	74.0°

6-7   Harmonic Analysis

In Section 5–11 we saw that the sum of two periodic functions *with the same period* is another periodic function.

If, however, the two functions have different periods, then their sum may not be periodic at all. For example, the function f given by

$$f(x) = \sin x + \sin \pi x$$

is not periodic, for the two addends never quite repeat together. In general, if f_1 and f_2 are periodic with periods p_1 and p_2, respectively, then $f_1 + f_2$ is not periodic if the ratio p_1/p_2 is irrational.

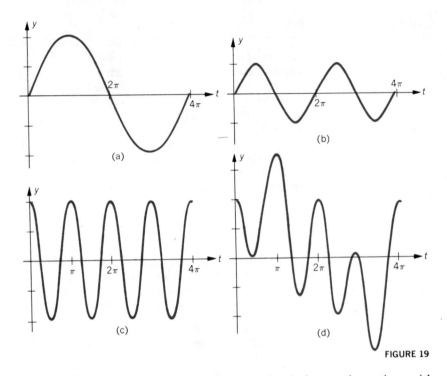

FIGURE 19

In Fig. 19 parts (a), (b), and (c) illustrate simple harmonic motions with periods 4π, 2π, and π, respectively. Motion (b) has twice the frequency of (a), and (c) has twice the frequency of (b). Thus each motion repeats itself every 4π units of time. The sum of these three functions is shown in Fig. 19(d) and is seen to have period 4π. It is not a simple harmonic motion even though it is the sum of such motions, yet it is a periodic motion.

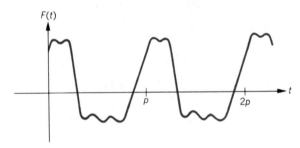

FIGURE 20

A natural question now arises: Given some "nonsimple" periodic function, such as F in Fig. 20, is it a sum of simple harmonic functions? In other words, can we resolve any periodic function into simple harmonic components? Surprisingly, the answer to this question is *yes*. This fact is the celebrated theorem of the French mathematician and physicist J. B. J. Fourier (1768–

1830). This theorem, stated below, has innumerable ramifications in both mathematics and the physical sciences. A complete statement and proof of the theorem requires calculus, but the intuitive content should be clear and the applications to physics meaningful.

Theorem

FOURIER'S THEOREM. If F is any smooth* continuous periodic function of frequency ν, then $F(t)$ can be approximated as closely as one desires by a sum of simple harmonic functions of frequencies that are whole-number multiples of ν:

$$a_0 + a_1 \cos 2\pi\nu t + b_1 \sin 2\pi\nu t$$
$$+ a_2 \cos 4\pi\nu t + b_2 \sin 4\pi\nu t + \cdots$$
$$+ a_n \cos 2\pi n\nu t + b_n \sin 2\pi n\nu t.$$

The calculation of the numbers $a_0, a_1, b_1, a_2, b_2, \ldots$, which are called *Fourier coefficients,* is called *harmonic analysis.*

Example

Sound is pressure pulsation in the air. A *pure tone* is a simple harmonic variation from the normal pressure P_0. If $P(t)$ is the pressure at time t of a pure tone of frequency ν, then $P(t)$ can be expressed by

$$P(t) = P_0 + A \sin 2\pi\nu t.$$

A tuning fork, Fig. 21, emits a tone which is very nearly pure. For example, the tone of middle C has a frequency $\nu = 256$ vibrations per second. Hence the pressure variation for a pure tone of middle C would be given by

FIGURE 21

$$P(t) = P_0 + A \sin 512\pi t.$$

Loud tones correspond to large values of A.

Other musical tones are combinations, that is, sums, of pure tones. For a given note, most musical instruments produce, besides the ground tone, or *fundamental,* some of the *higher harmonics.* For example, middle C on a violin might consist not only of the fundamental at 256 vibrations per second, but may also comprise tones at double (512) and triple (768) the frequency:

$$P(t) = P_0 + A_1 \sin 512\pi t + A_2 \sin 1024\pi t + A_3 \sin 1536\pi t.$$

The higher harmonics, in different intensities, give a musical note its particular character, or timbre, and enable one to distinguish between the same note played on different instruments.

---

*The adjective "smooth" means that the tangent line to the graph of F turns continuously.

The human ear-brain combination is a harmonic analyzer, because it can recognize subtle differences in the character of the sound, that is, the presence, or absence, of higher harmonics.

Noise is a sum of random pure sounds of different intensities and frequencies.

6-8

Radio

Two different methods are used today to transmit sound (and pictures) by means of electromagnetic waves. In this section, we *sketch* the *mathematical aspects* of these two systems, called *amplitude modulation* (AM) and *frequency modulation* (FM).

In either system the voltage variation E of the *carrier wave* is a pure sine wave (Fig. 22).

$$E(t) = E_0 \sin 2\pi\nu t,$$

where ν is the frequency of the transmitter. The carrier wave produces no sound in a receiver.

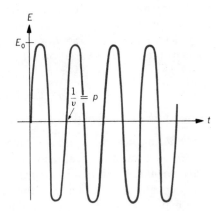

FIGURE 22

In *amplitude modulation* (AM) radio, the amplitude E_0 of the carrier wave is a function of time. For a pure tone, E_0 would be a simple sine variation from a constant,

$$E_0(t) = A_0 + A_1 \sin 2\pi n t, \tag{1}$$

where n is the frequency of the tone. In practice, the frequency of the carrier wave is at least 1000 times as large as that of the tone, $v > 1000n$. The modulated carrier wave appears as in Fig. 23. Note that the amplitude, A, of the carrier wave is modulated; that is, the amplitude of the sound wave is added to, or subtracted from, the amplitude of the carrier wave. The antenna voltage $E(t)$ is then given by

$$E(t) = (A_0 + A_1 \sin 2\pi nt) \sin 2\pi vt.$$

Thus we can say that the carrier wave has been *modulated* by equation (1).

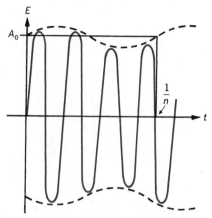

FIGURE 23

A radio receiver receives from the station a *signal* like that shown in Fig. 23 but much diminished in strength. The receiver then amplifies the signal and changes it into a pulsating voltage $V(t)$ of frequency n (Fig. 24). The loudspeaker responds to the final output signal, $V(t)$. The information (sound) of the modulation (1) has then been recovered.

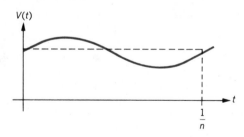

FIGURE 24

In *frequency modulation* radio (FM), the alteration (modulation) of the carrier wave is obtained by a change in the *frequency* of the carrier wave, $E(t) = E_0 \sin 2\pi vt$. In this case, E_0 is constant, and v is no longer constant but varies. For a pure tone, v would vary sinusoidally (in the form of a sine wave),

$$v(t) = v_0 + v_1 \sin 2\pi nt, \qquad (2)$$

where n is the frequency of the tone. Then

$$E(t) = E_0 \sin 2\pi (v_0 + v_1 \sin 2\pi nt)t.$$

A graph of $E(t)$ for this case is shown in Fig. 25. The graph gives the appearance of being squeezed together in places and stretched out in others, in an accordion-like fashion.

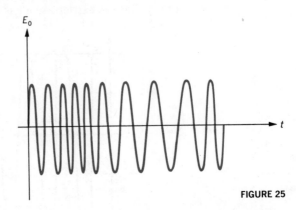

FIGURE 25

The FM receiver is able to take a signal such as the one shown in Fig. 25, recover a copy of the pure tone, $v_1 \sin 2\pi nt$, and impart to the loudspeaker a signal like that graphed in Fig. 24.

Problems

Set A

1. Which graph shows an AM carrier wave? Which shows an FM carrier wave?

   (a)   (b)

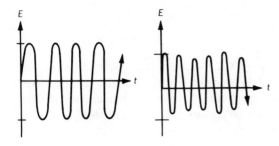

2. Consider the functions f and g where

$$f(x) = \sin 3x$$

and

$$g(x) = \sin \frac{8x}{3}.$$

What are the periods of these functions? Now consider the sum of f and g. Is $f + g$ periodic? If $f + g$ is periodic, what is its period?

3. Is the function F given by
$$F(x) = \cos 3x + \cos \pi x \text{ periodic?}$$

Set B

4. The musical tone high C has a frequency of 1024 vibrations per second. Write a formula for the pressure variation of this tone in terms of time t in seconds, where A is the amplitude and P_0 is the normal pressure.

5. A carrier wave has a frequency of 8 cycles per second. The amplitude of the carrier wave is modulated by a pure tone of frequency of 1 cycle per second. Write a formula for the modulated wave. Sketch a graph.

Set C

6. Sketch the graphs of $y = 3 + 2 \sin \pi t$ and $y = 2 \cos (\pi t + \pi/2)$ on the same axes and find their sum by graphical addition.

7. Concert pitch A has a frequency of 440 vibrations per second. If A, as produced by a flute, has first and second harmonics that are $\frac{1}{4}$ and $\frac{1}{8}$ the amplitude of the fundamental, what is a formula for the pressure variation in terms of t in seconds?

Calculator Problem

Sketch the graph of an amplitude modulated wave given by the formula

$$E(t) = (\sin \pi t)\sin 10\pi t, \quad \text{for } t \text{ in } [0, 1].$$

For convenience, use values of t in twentieths. That is use $t = 0, \frac{1}{20}, \frac{2}{20}, \frac{3}{20}, \ldots, \frac{19}{20}, 1$.

Summary

The significant topics of the chapter are the following.
1. Functions and cofunctions
2. Tables of the circular functions
3. Solution of right triangles. In right triangle ABC with sides a, b, and c and $\angle C$ a right angle,

$$\sin A = \frac{a}{c}, \quad \cos A = \frac{b}{c}, \quad \text{and} \quad \tan A = \frac{a}{b}.$$

4. The Law of Sines. In any triangle ABC,

$$\frac{a}{\sin A} = \frac{b}{\sin B} = \frac{c}{\sin C}.$$

5. The Law of Cosines. In any triangle ABC,

$$a^2 = b^2 + c^2 - 2bc \cos A,$$
$$b^2 = c^2 + a^2 - 2ca \cos B,$$
$$c^2 = a^2 + b^2 - 2ab \cos C.$$

6. Solution of oblique triangles using the Law of Sines or Law of Cosines
7. Simple harmonic motion, amplitude, period, frequency, circular frequency
8. Periodic functions as sums of simple harmonic functions

Chapter 6   Test

6-2   Express each function in terms of its cofunction.

1. $\sin \frac{\pi}{3}$ **2.** $\tan \frac{\pi}{6}$ **3.** $\cos \frac{\pi}{4}$

Express each of the following as a function of a real number between 0 and $\pi/4$, and find the value of each.

4. $\cos \frac{14\pi}{3}$ **5.** $\sin \frac{-\pi}{6}$ **6.** $\tan \frac{5\pi}{6}$

7. $\sin \frac{11\pi}{6}$ **8.** $\cos \frac{-5\pi}{3}$ **9.** $\tan \frac{-2\pi}{3}$

6-3   Use a table of trigonometric functions to find values for the following.

10. $\tan 27.5°$ **11.** $\cos 53.7°$ **12.** $\sin 18.1°$

13. $\cos 133.6°$ **14.** $\sin 158.2°$ **15.** $\tan 99.2°$

6-4   **16.** Triangle ABC is a right triangle, and $\angle C$ is the right angle. Compute the length of the hypotenuse c, given that $m(\angle A) = 37.2°$, and $a = 45.00$.

17. Compute the height h of $\triangle ABC$ shown at the left below.

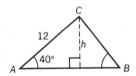
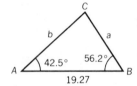

6-5   **18.** Find the lengths a and b, and $m(\angle C)$ in $\triangle ABC$ shown at the right above.

19. Find the measure of the largest angle of a triangle whose sides have lengths 5, 7, and 8.

20. The lengths of two sides of a triangle are 5 and 6 units, and the measure of the included angle is $2\pi/3$. Find the length of the third side.

6-6   **21.** Write a formula for the displacement d of a particle undergoing a simple harmonic motion which has amplitude 2 and a frequency of 4 cycles per second.

22. A simple harmonic motion has amplitude 6 and circular frequency of 100π radians per second. Write a formula for the displacement d at any time t. What is the period of the simple harmonic motion?

6-7, 6-8   **23.** Two functions have the same domain and are periodic with periods p_1 and p_2. What relation between p_1 and p_2 will make the sum of the functions a nonperiodic function?

24. Which kind of modulation is represented by the equation

$$E(t) = E_0 \sin 2\pi (v_0 + v_1 \sin 2\pi nt)t,$$

frequency modulation or amplitude modulation?

Historical Note

Ptolemy
(Second Century A.D.)

Let us look back at the tables of the circular functions as they existed in ancient times.

Both Greeks and Hindus divided the circle into four quadrants of 90 degrees each, and each degree into 60 minutes—a procedure that they inherited from the Babylonians. For the sine, the Greeks used the whole chord, $|AC|$, subtended by twice the angle (or arc). The Hindus, on the other hand, used the half-chord, $|AB|$, subtended by double the arc. (See Fig. 26.) Observe that the Hindu definition would correspond to the modern one if the radius, R, of the circle were 1. Various radii were used. Ptolemy (second century A.D.) used

$R=60$. Most Hindu astronomers used $R=120$ (observe that with $R=120$ the Hindu entries in their tables were the same as the Greek entries). One Hindu astronomer, Aryabhata (born 476 A.D.), used $R=3468$.

Remember that in those days numerical work was not the easy task it is today. For most of the time (perhaps up to 600 A.D. in India and 1200 A.D. in Europe) our convenient decimal notation, based on the Hindu-Arabic numerals, was not known. Therefore, the representation of the length of the chord (or half-chord), even though it might be a whole number, was a complex problem that required special skill.

Many of the ancient tables, for example the one computed by Ptolemy, gave the entries only for every $3°45'$, and often with little accuracy. The standard method of computing tables at this time was a Hindu invention. They started with the known values for $30°$, $45°$, and $60°$ and, using the half-angle formula (see Chapter 7), $\sin^2 \frac{1}{2}\theta = \frac{1}{2}(1 - \cos\theta)$, were able to compute the sines of $15°$, $22°30'$, and then $7°30'$, $11°15'$, and $3°45'$. The next step would be to find sines of half of these angles. Eventually, with some interpolation, they obtained tables with entries for every $3°45'$.

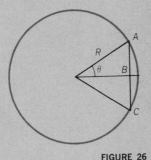

FIGURE 26

Chapter 7
Analytic Trigonometry

7-1   Introduction

The trigonometric functions arise in all sorts of ways in all branches of mathematics, both pure and applied. Although the functions have their origin in a rather simple geometric situation, their uses are much broader, as might be expected from the discussion of Chapter 6 concerning harmonic analysis of periodic functions. The study of the special properties that circular functions possess as "functions" is called *analytic trigonometry*. The word "analytic" comes from *analysis,* which refers to a general study of functions.

The fundamental topics of this chapter are

(a) the elementary identities,
(b) the addition formulas,
(c) the double- and half-angle formulas.

You should learn to derive all of these formulas; there are about 20 of them. You will also find it helpful to memorize most of them.

7-2   The Elementary Identities

Identities have been encountered before this. For example:

(a) $x^2 - 1 = (x - 1)(x + 1)$ for all real numbers x,

(b) $2x^2 - x - 1 = (2x + 1)(x - 1)$ for all real numbers x,

(c) $\dfrac{x^3 - 1}{x - 1} = x^2 + x + 1$ for all real numbers x, $x \neq 1$,

(d) $\dfrac{x^3 + x}{x^2 + 1} = x$ for all real numbers x,

(e) $(x + 1)^4 = (x^2 + 2x + 1)^2$ for all real numbers x.

In other words, an identity states that two functions or expressions represent the same number for all values of the variable in some domain which is usually clear from the context.

Definition 7-1 Suppose that *f* and *g* are functions with domains that overlap on a set *D*, and suppose that

$$f(x) = g(x) \qquad \text{for all } x \text{ in } D. \tag{1}$$

Then we say that (1) is an *identity* in *D*.

(See Fig. 1.) In other words, an identity is a statement that two functions are identical on a certain set. It is vital to be certain what this set, or domain, is. We could also denote such an identity by $f = g$ on *D*. In practice one does not often specifically mention what the domain *D* of the identity happens to be, but leaves it to the reader to see from the context what it must be. We shall proceed in both ways. At first we shall be quite specific about the domain and then later relax our vigilance.

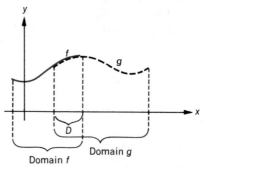

FIGURE 1   FIGURE 2

All the elementary trigonometric identities arise directly from the definitions of the circular functions. We have (see Fig. 2)

$$W(\theta) = P = (x, y), \qquad x = \cos \theta, \qquad y = \sin \theta,$$

from which it immediately follows that

$$\tan \theta = \frac{y}{x} = \frac{\sin \theta}{\cos \theta}, \qquad \text{for all } \theta \neq \frac{\pi}{2}(2k + 1), \ k \text{ an integer;}$$

$$\cot \theta = \frac{x}{y} = \frac{\cos \theta}{\sin \theta}, \qquad \text{for all } \theta \neq k\pi, \ k \text{ an integer;}$$

$$\sec \theta = \frac{1}{x} = \frac{1}{\cos \theta}, \qquad \text{for all } \theta \neq \frac{\pi}{2}(2k + 1), \ k \text{ an integer;} \tag{2}$$

$$\csc \theta = \frac{1}{y} = \frac{1}{\sin \theta}, \qquad \text{for all } \theta \neq k\pi, \ k \text{ an integer.}$$

The above are the simplest of the elementary identities. There are three more elementary ones, called the *Pythagorean identities*.

Recall that

$$x^2 + y^2 = 1,$$

$$1 + \frac{y^2}{x^2} = \frac{1}{x^2} \qquad \text{if} \quad x \neq 0,$$

$$\frac{x^2}{y^2} + 1 = \frac{1}{y^2} \qquad \text{if} \quad y \neq 0.$$

From these we obtain the Pythagorean identities

$$\sin^2 \theta + \cos^2 \theta = 1, \qquad \text{for all } \theta;$$
$$1 + \tan^2 \theta = \sec^2 \theta, \qquad \text{if } \theta \neq (\pi/2)(2k + 1), \ k \text{ an integer;} \qquad (3)$$
$$\cot^2 \theta + 1 = \csc^2 \theta, \qquad \text{if } \theta \neq k\pi, \ k \text{ an integer.}$$

The identities of (2) and (3) are the *elementary identities,* and should be memorized, since they will be used to establish other identities.

Example 1   Establish the identity

$$\frac{1}{\cos \theta} - \cos \theta = \tan \theta \cdot \sin \theta \qquad (4)$$

and determine the domain for which it is valid.

Solution. We have

$$\frac{1}{\cos \theta} - \cos \theta = \frac{1 - \cos^2 \theta}{\cos \theta}, \qquad \text{where } \theta \neq \frac{\pi}{2}(2k + 1),$$

$$= \frac{\sin^2 \theta}{\cos \theta}$$

$$= \frac{\sin \theta}{\cos \theta} \cdot \sin \theta$$

$$= \tan \theta \cdot \sin \theta.$$

In this problem we have worked with *one* side of the supposed identity and, by a succession of steps, reduced it to the other. This method is, perhaps, the most elegant way of proceeding, but one can work with both sides. Thus

$$\frac{1}{\cos \theta} - \cos \theta = \frac{1 - \cos^2 \theta}{\cos \theta}$$

$$= \frac{\sin^2 \theta}{\cos \theta},$$

whereas

$$\tan \theta \cdot \sin \theta = \frac{\sin \theta}{\cos \theta} \cdot \sin \theta = \frac{\sin^2 \theta}{\cos \theta}.$$

Therefore both sides of the presumed identity (4) are equal [for all $\theta \neq (\pi/2)(2k + 1)$] to $\sin^2 \theta / \cos \theta$, and so

$$\frac{1}{\cos \theta} - \cos \theta = \tan \theta \cdot \sin \theta \qquad \text{if } \theta \neq \frac{\pi}{2}(2k + 1).$$

In this example we have been careful about the domain of the variable θ. But this domain can really be seen from the context. The tangent function is not defined for $\theta = (\pi/2)(2k + 1)$ and $\cos \theta = 0$ for $\theta = (\pi/2)(2k + 1)$. Therefore the functions given by the left- and right-hand sides of (4) are defined if and only if $\theta \neq (\pi/2)(2k + 1)$. From this point of view, the identity (4) is a statement that two functions are the same function, and we may delete the variable θ and write

$$\frac{1}{\cos} - \cos = \tan \cdot \sin.$$

The proof in this form is precisely the same:

$$\frac{1}{\cos} - \cos = \frac{1 - \cos^2}{\cos}$$

$$= \frac{\sin^2}{\cos} = \frac{\sin}{\cos} \cdot \sin$$

$$= \tan \cdot \sin.$$

Example 2   Establish that

$$\frac{\sin \theta}{1 + \cos \theta} = \frac{1 - \cos \theta}{\sin \theta},$$

and determine the domain of validity.

Solution. First we observe that $1 + \cos \theta = 0$ if θ is an *odd* multiple of π, whereas $\sin \theta = 0$ if θ is *any* multiple of π. Therefore the identity can be valid only if $\theta \neq k\pi$, where k is an integer. With this restriction on the domain of θ, we can drop the variable θ and write

$$\frac{\sin}{1 + \cos} = \frac{\sin}{1 + \cos} \cdot \frac{1 - \cos}{1 - \cos}$$

$$= \frac{\sin (1 - \cos)}{1 - \cos^2}$$

$$= \frac{\sin (1 - \cos)}{\sin^2} = \frac{1 - \cos}{\sin}.$$

We have been representing the variable in the circular functions by θ, where θ is a real number. However, one may use any convenient letter for the argument of the functions, even x or y. Of course, if this is done, then x and y do not refer to the coordinates of the point P which is the image of the wrapping function W.

Problems

Set A

Establish the following identities. In each case state the domain on which the identity is valid.

1. $\sin \theta = \dfrac{1}{\csc \theta}$

2. $\cos x = \dfrac{1}{\sec x}$

3. $\tan t = \dfrac{\sec t}{\csc t}$

4. $\cot \theta = \dfrac{1}{\tan \theta}$

5. $\sin x \csc x = 1$

6. $\cos u \sec u = 1$

7. $\cot z \tan z = 1$

8. $\cos^2 a = 1 - \sin^2 a$

9. $\cot^2 \theta = \dfrac{1 - \sin^2 \theta}{\sin^2 \theta}$

10. $(1 + \tan \theta)^2 = \sec^2 \theta + 2 \tan \theta$

Express each of the functions below in terms of sine and/or cosine. In each case, give the domain on which the function is defined.

11. $\sec x - \tan x$

12. $\dfrac{1}{\sec^2 y} - \dfrac{1}{\tan^2 y}$

13. $(\sec u - \tan u)^2$

14. $(\csc t - \cot t)^2$

15. $\dfrac{1 - \tan^2}{1 + \tan^2}$

16. $\dfrac{\tan + \cot}{\sec \csc}$

17. $\dfrac{\cot \theta + 1}{\cot \theta - 1}$

18. $\dfrac{\tan}{1 - \cot} + \dfrac{\cot}{1 - \tan}$

19. $\dfrac{1 - \cos^2 \theta}{\sin \theta}$

20. $\dfrac{1 + \tan^2 a}{\sec a}$

Set B

Establish the following identities,* and give the domain of validity for each.

21. $\cot \theta + \tan \theta = \sec \theta \csc \theta$

22. $(1 - \sin x)(1 + \sin x) = \dfrac{1}{1 + \tan^2 x}$

23. $\dfrac{1}{\sec^2 x} + \dfrac{1}{\csc^2 x} = 1$

24. $\sec^2 \theta - \csc^2 \theta = \tan^2 \theta - \cot^2 \theta$

25. $\sin^2 y \cot^2 y + \cos^2 y \tan^2 y = 1$

26. $\dfrac{\sec t}{\tan t + \cot t} = \sin t$

27. $(\csc A - \cot A)^2 = \dfrac{1 - \cos A}{1 + \cos A}$

28. $\dfrac{\tan x - \sec x + 1}{\tan x + \sec x - 1} = \dfrac{\cos x}{1 + \sin x}$

29. $\dfrac{\csc^2 \theta - 1}{\csc^2 \theta} = \cos^2 \theta$

30. $\tan u(1 - \cot^2 u) + \cot u(1 - \tan^2 u) = 0$

31. $\sin^3 \theta \cos \theta + \cos^3 \theta \sin \theta = \sin \theta \cos \theta$

32. $\dfrac{\sec^2 x}{1 + \sin x} = \dfrac{\sec^2 x - \sec x \tan x}{\cos^2 x}$

33. $\dfrac{2 \sin \alpha \cos \alpha}{\cos^2 \alpha - \sin^2 \alpha} = \dfrac{2 \tan \alpha}{1 - \tan^2 \alpha}$

34. $\dfrac{\frac{1}{2}}{1 - \sin v} + \dfrac{\frac{1}{2}}{1 + \sin v} = 1 + \tan^2 v$

35. $(1 + \cot 2\theta - \csc 2\theta)(1 + \tan 2\theta + \sec 2\theta) = 2$

36. $\dfrac{\sin x}{\csc x} - 1 = -\dfrac{\cos x}{\sec x}$

37. $\sin^4 3\theta - \cos^4 3\theta = 1 - 2 \cos^2 3\theta$

38. $2 \sin^2 \alpha - 1 = \dfrac{\tan \alpha - \cot \alpha}{\tan \alpha + \cot \alpha}$

---

* When one is faced with a presumed identity, a thorough familiarity with the basic identities will usually suggest a convenient method of attack. When no obvious procedure is apparent, it will often help to express all the functions in terms of sines and cosines.

39. $\tan A + \cot A = \sec A \csc A$

40. $\sec^2 x + \csc^2 x = \sec^2 x \csc^2 x$

41. $(1 + \tan^2 z)(1 - \sin^2 z) = 1$

42. $\sec^4 x - \tan^4 x = 1 + 2 \tan^2 x$

Set C

Express each of the other circular functions in terms of the one cited. The angle θ may be in any one of the quadrants. In each case, state what signs to use on the radicals when θ is in the different quadrants.

43. sine   **44.** cosine   **45.** tangent

46. cotangent   **47.** secant   **48.** cosecant

Express the following in terms of sine and cosine.

49. $\dfrac{\sin x + \tan x}{1 + \sec x}$ **50.** $\dfrac{\csc \theta}{\csc \theta - 1} + \dfrac{\csc \theta}{\csc \theta + 1}$

51. $\dfrac{1 - \tan^2}{1 + \tan^2}$ **52.** $(\csc + \cot)^2$

53. $(\sec + \csc)^2 \tan$ **54.** $\cot + \tan$

Establish each identity.

55. $\dfrac{\tan^2 - 1}{\tan^2 + 1} = 2 \sin^2 - 1$

56. $\dfrac{\sin + \tan}{\cot + \csc} = \sin \tan$

57. $\dfrac{1 + \csc x}{\csc x - 1} = \dfrac{1 + \sin x}{1 - \sin x}$

58. $\dfrac{1 + \tan^2}{\tan^2} = \csc^2$

59. $\dfrac{2 \sin^2 - 1}{\sin \cos} = \tan - \cot$

60. $\sin^6 + \cos^6 = 1 - 3 \sin^2 \cos^2$

61. $\sec^2 (A + \sqrt{2} B)$
$\quad - \sin^2 (A + \sqrt{2} B) \sec^2 (A + \sqrt{2} B) = 1$

62. $\sin \tan = \sec - \cos$

63. $\dfrac{\tan + \sec}{\cos - \tan - \sec} = -\csc$

64. $\sin + \cos + \dfrac{\sin}{\cot} = \sec + \csc - \dfrac{\cos}{\tan}$

65. $\sin \cos \tan \cot \sec \csc = 1$

66. $\dfrac{\sin}{\csc - \cot} = 1 + \cos$

67. $\dfrac{\sin \alpha \cos \beta + \cos \alpha \sin \beta}{\cos \alpha \cos \beta - \sin \alpha \sin \beta} = \dfrac{\tan \alpha + \tan \beta}{1 - \tan \alpha \tan \beta}$

68. $\cos \theta \sqrt{\sec^2 \theta - 1} = \sin \theta$ if θ is in Quadrants I, III

69. $\cos \theta \sqrt{\sec^2 \theta - 1} = -\sin \theta$ if θ is in Quadrants II, IV

70. $\dfrac{1}{\sqrt{1 - \sin^2 \theta}} = -\sec \theta$ if θ is in Quadrants II, III

71. Prove that $\csc \theta \neq \cot \theta$ for any real number for which the functions are defined.

Calculator Problem

Which is larger, $\sin (\cos 1)$ or $\cos (\sin 1)$? Try to decide mentally. Then use your calculator to check your choice.

The Addition Formulas

Among the important identities for the circular functions are those which express functions of the sum, or difference, of two real numbers in terms of functions of each number. We will now obtain these formulas. It is important that the development of these formulas be understood. The formulas themselves should be memorized.

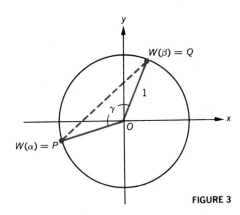

FIGURE 3

If α, β are real numbers and $P = W(\alpha)$, $Q = W(\beta)$, where W is the wrapping function, then the points O, P, Q will, in general,* form a triangle, $\triangle OPQ$. (See Fig. 3.) The angle, $\angle POQ$, has a radian measure $\gamma = \pm(\alpha - \beta) + k \cdot 2\pi$, where k is some integer. We will now obtain the number $|PQ|^2$ in two ways. From the distance formula, using the coordinates of $P(\cos \alpha, \sin \alpha)$ and $Q(\cos \beta, \sin \beta)$, we have the following.

$$
\begin{aligned}
|PQ|^2 &= (\cos \alpha - \cos \beta)^2 + (\sin \alpha - \sin \beta)^2 \\
&= \cos^2 \alpha - 2 \cos \alpha \cos \beta + \cos^2 \beta + \sin^2 \alpha - 2 \sin \alpha \sin \beta + \sin^2 \beta \\
&= 2 - 2 \cos \alpha \cos \beta - 2 \sin \alpha \sin \beta.
\end{aligned}
\tag{1}
$$

By the law of cosines, we obtain

$$
\begin{aligned}
|PQ|^2 &= 1 + 1 - 2 \cos \gamma = 2 - 2 \cos \gamma \\
&= 2 - 2 \cos [\pm(\alpha - \beta) + k \cdot 2\pi] = 2 - 2 \cos [\pm(\alpha - \beta)] \\
&= 2 - 2 \cos (\alpha - \beta).
\end{aligned}
\tag{2}
$$

---

*If $P = Q$, or if P, O, and Q are collinear, the formula for $\cos (\pi - \beta)$ is easily checked and found to be correct.

$(\cos(\pm\theta) = \cos\theta$ because cosine is an *even* function.*) From (1) and (2) we have

$$2 - 2\cos(\alpha - \beta) = 2 - 2\cos\alpha\cos\beta - 2\sin\alpha\sin\beta,$$

or

$$\cos(\alpha - \beta) = \cos\alpha\cos\beta + \sin\alpha\sin\beta. \tag{3}$$

Identity (3) is the first of the new identities. We shall obtain others from this one.

Because the cosine is an *even* function and the sine is an *odd*† function, we have for all real numbers θ,

$$\cos(-\theta) = \cos\theta \qquad \text{and} \qquad \sin(-\theta) = -\sin\theta.$$

Therefore

$$\cos(\alpha + \beta) = \cos[\alpha - (-\beta)]$$

$$= \cos\alpha\cos(-\beta) + \sin\alpha\sin(-\beta),$$

or

$$\cos(\alpha + \beta) = \cos\alpha\cos\beta - \sin\alpha\sin\beta. \tag{4}$$

This is the second of the new identities.

To obtain corresponding formulas for the sine function, we digress first to examine functions of the "complementary angle." You are familiar with complementary acute angles. What is new, perhaps, is our agreement to call $\pi/2 - \theta$ the *complement of θ* for any real number θ. Then from (3), we find that

$$\cos\left(\frac{\pi}{2} - \beta\right) = \cos\frac{\pi}{2}\cos\beta + \sin\frac{\pi}{2}\sin\beta$$

$$= 0 \cdot \cos\beta + 1 \cdot \sin\beta.$$

Therefore

$$\cos\left(\frac{\pi}{2} - \beta\right) = \sin\beta, \qquad \text{for all } \beta. \tag{5}$$

Because β is arbitrary in (5), if we set $\beta = (\pi/2 - \theta)$, we obtain

$$\cos\left[\frac{\pi}{2} - \left(\frac{\pi}{2} - \theta\right)\right] = \sin\left(\frac{\pi}{2} - \theta\right)$$

---

*A function f is *even* if $f(-x) = f(x)$ for all x. The graph of an even function possesses line symmetry. The cosine is an even function because if $W(\theta) = (x, y)$, then $W(-\theta) = (x, -y)$. Therefore $\cos(-\theta) = x = \cos\theta$. See Chapter 3, p. 64.

†A function f is *odd* if $f(-x) = -f(x)$ for all x. The graph of an odd function possesses point symmetry. The sine is an odd function because if $W(\theta) = (x, y)$, then $W(-\theta) = (x, -y)$. Therefore $\sin(-\theta) = -y = -\sin\theta$. See Chapter 3, p. 64.

or

$$\sin\left(\frac{\pi}{2} - \theta\right) = \cos\theta, \qquad \text{for all } \theta. \tag{6}$$

Formulas analogous to (5) and (6) are valid for the tangent (see Problem 23 of this section) and cotangent, and for the secant and cosecant. Thus in every case the circular functions satisfy the formula

$$\text{function of } \theta = \text{cofunction of } \left(\frac{\pi}{2} - \theta\right).$$

We can now apply (5) and (6) to obtain addition formulas for the sine. We have

$$\sin(\alpha + \beta) = \cos\left[\frac{\pi}{2} - (\alpha + \beta)\right]$$

$$= \cos\left[\left(\frac{\pi}{2} - \alpha\right) - \beta\right]$$

$$= \cos\left(\frac{\pi}{2} - \alpha\right)\cos\beta + \sin\left(\frac{\pi}{2} - \alpha\right)\sin\beta$$

$$= \sin\alpha\cos\beta + \cos\alpha\sin\beta,$$

or

$$\sin(\alpha + \beta) = \sin\alpha\cos\beta + \cos\alpha\sin\beta. \tag{7}$$

To obtain $\sin(\alpha - \beta)$, we can either proceed in the same way or consider $\sin(\alpha - \beta) = \sin[\alpha + (-\beta)]$. The derivation is left as an exercise. The result is

$$\sin(\alpha - \beta) = \sin\alpha\cos\beta - \cos\alpha\sin\beta. \tag{8}$$

To obtain a formula for $\tan(\alpha + \beta)$, we use the elementary identities and our formulas for $\sin(\alpha + \beta)$ and $\cos(\alpha + \beta)$. That is,

$$\tan(\alpha + \beta) = \frac{\sin(\alpha + \beta)}{\cos(\alpha + \beta)} = \frac{\sin\alpha\cos\beta + \cos\alpha\sin\beta}{\cos\alpha\cos\beta - \sin\alpha\sin\beta}.$$

Dividing numerator and denominator of this last fraction by $\cos\alpha\cos\beta$ gives

$$\tan(\alpha + \beta) = \frac{\tan\alpha + \tan\beta}{1 - \tan\alpha\tan\beta}. \tag{9}$$

Similarly, one obtains

$$\tan(\alpha - \beta) = \frac{\tan\alpha - \tan\beta}{1 + \tan\alpha\tan\beta}. \tag{10}$$

Formulas for $\cot(\alpha + \beta)$ and $\cot(\alpha - \beta)$ can also be obtained, but they are not commonly used. One seldom sees formulas for $\sec(\alpha + \beta)$ or

$\csc(\alpha + \beta)$, since they are neither elegant nor necessary. For convenient reference, we list the addition formulas below.

$$\cos(\alpha \pm \beta) = \cos\alpha\cos\beta \mp \sin\alpha\sin\beta,$$

$$\sin(\alpha \pm \beta) = \sin\alpha\cos\beta \pm \cos\alpha\sin\beta,$$

$$\tan(\alpha \pm \beta) = \frac{\tan\alpha \pm \tan\beta}{1 \mp \tan\alpha\tan\beta}.$$

Example The addition formulas permit us to extend the set of numbers for which exact values of the functions are known. Thus

$$\sin\frac{\pi}{12} = \sin\left(\frac{\pi}{3} - \frac{\pi}{4}\right)$$

$$= \sin\frac{\pi}{3}\cos\frac{\pi}{4} - \cos\frac{\pi}{3}\sin\frac{\pi}{4}$$

$$= \frac{\sqrt{3}}{2}\cdot\frac{\sqrt{2}}{2} - \frac{1}{2}\cdot\frac{\sqrt{2}}{2}$$

$$= \frac{\sqrt{6} - \sqrt{2}}{4}.$$

Problems

Set A

Find exact values of the following.

1. $\cos\dfrac{\pi}{12}$ 2. $\tan\dfrac{7\pi}{12}$ 3. $\sin\dfrac{11\pi}{12}$

4. $\cos\dfrac{5\pi}{12}$ 5. $\sin\dfrac{13\pi}{12}$ 6. $\tan\dfrac{5\pi}{12}$

7. Develop the formula for $\sin(\alpha - \beta)$ by using the formula for $\sin(\alpha + \beta)$.

8. Complete the development of the formula for $\tan(\alpha + \beta)$. For what numbers α and β is it valid?

9. Derive the formula for $\tan(\alpha - \beta)$.

10. Obtain a formula for $\cot(\alpha + \beta)$ in terms of $\cot\alpha$ and $\cot\beta$.

11. Obtain a formula for $\cot(\alpha - \beta)$ in terms of $\cot\alpha$ and $\cot\beta$.

Set B

Establish the following identities.

12. $\sin(x + y) + \sin(x - y) = 2\sin x\cos y$

13. $\tan(x + \pi/4) - \tan(x - 3\pi/4) = 0$

14. $\sin(x + y)\sec x\sec y = \tan x + \tan y$

15. $\tan(\theta + \pi/4) = \dfrac{\cos\theta + \sin\theta}{\cos\theta - \sin\theta}$

16. $\cos(\pi/3 + x) - \sin(\pi/6 - x) = 0$

17. $\sin(\pi/4 + x) + \cos(\pi/4 - x) = 2\sin(x + \pi/4)$

18. $\sin(x - y)\cos y + \cos(x - y)\sin y = \sin x$

19. $\cos(x + y)\cos y + \sin(x + y)\sin y = \cos x$

20. $\cos\theta = \cos\left(\dfrac{\theta}{2} + \dfrac{\theta}{2}\right) = 2\cos^2\dfrac{\theta}{2} - 1$

21. Show that $\cos(x + y) + \cos(x - y) = 2\cos x\cos y$. Let $x + y = A$ and $x - y = B$ to obtain

$$\cos A + \cos B = 2\cos\frac{A + B}{2}\cos\frac{A - B}{2}.$$

22. Obtain formulas similar to that in Problem 21 for $\cos A - \cos B$, $\sin A + \sin B$, and $\sin A - \sin B$.

23. Show that $\tan(\pi/2 - x) = \cot x$ for all x that is not an integral multiple of π.

24. Show that if $\alpha + \beta + \gamma = \pi$, then $\sin \alpha = \sin \beta \cos \gamma + \cos \beta \sin \gamma$.

Set C

25. Show that $\sin(x + y + z) =$
$$\sin x \cos y \cos z - \sin x \sin y \sin z$$
$$+ \cos x \sin y \cos z + \cos x \cos y \sin z.$$

26. Find a formula for $\cos(x - y + z)$ similar to that of Problem 25.

Establish the following identities.

27. $\dfrac{\tan(x + y) - \tan x}{1 + \tan(x + y)\tan x} = \dfrac{\sin y}{\cos y}$

28. $\sin(A + B)\sin(A - B) = \sin^2 A - \sin^2 B$

29. $\cos(A + B)\sin(A - B) = \sin A \cos A - \sin B \cos B$

30. Suppose that A, B, and C are the measures of the angles of a triangle. Prove

(a) $\tan A + \tan B + \tan C = \tan A \tan B \tan C$.
(b) $\cos^2 A + \cos^2 B + \cos^2 C +$
$$2 \cos A \cos B \cos C = 1.$$

31. The Greeks were familiar with the addition formulas in the form of Ptolemy's Theorem: If $ABCD$ is any quadrilateral inscribed in a circle (see figure), then

$$|AB| \cdot |CD| + |AD| \cdot |BC| = |AC| \cdot |BD|.$$

Show that Ptolemy's Theorem implies the formula for $\sin(\alpha + \beta)$. [*Hint:* Select a quadrilateral so that $\overline{BD}$ is a diameter in a circle of diameter 1. Then show that $|AB| = \sin \alpha$, $|AD| = \cos \alpha$, $|BC| = \sin \beta$, $|CD| = \cos \beta$, and $|AC| = \sin(\alpha + \beta)$.]

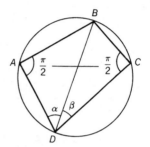

Calculator Problem

In the figure for Problem 31, suppose that $|AB| = 0.8$, $|BC| = 0.4$, and $|AD| = 0.6$. Find $|CD|$, $|AC|$, and $(\alpha + \beta) = m\angle ADC$.

7–4   Applications of the Addition Formulas

The addition formulas may be applied in a wide variety of problems. We shall consider a few examples in this section.

Example 1   *Reduction formulas* are simple consequences of the addition formulas. For example,

$$\cos(\pi - \theta) = \cos \pi \cos \theta + \sin \pi \sin \theta$$
$$= -1 \cdot \cos \theta + 0 \cdot \sin \theta$$
$$= -\cos \theta,$$

and

$$\sin\left(\frac{3\pi}{2} + \theta\right) = \sin\frac{3\pi}{2}\cos\theta + \cos\frac{3\pi}{2}\sin\theta$$

$$= -1 \cdot \cos\theta + 0 \cdot \sin\theta$$
$$= -\cos\theta.$$

Example 2 The problem is to find $\sin(\alpha - \beta)$ and $\cos(\alpha - \beta)$ given that $\sin\alpha = -\frac{5}{13}$ and $\cos\beta = \frac{3}{5}$, with α in the third quadrant and β in the fourth.

Solution. We shall first find $\cos\alpha$ and $\sin\beta$. From Fig. 4 we see that

$$W(\alpha) = (-\tfrac{12}{13}, -\tfrac{5}{13}), \qquad W(\beta) = (\tfrac{3}{5}, -\tfrac{4}{5});$$

therefore

$$\cos\alpha = -\tfrac{12}{13} \quad \text{and} \quad \sin\beta = -\tfrac{4}{5}.$$

Then

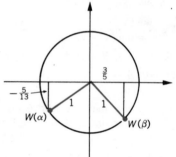

FIGURE 4

$$\sin(\alpha - \beta) = \sin\alpha\cos\beta - \cos\alpha\sin\beta$$
$$= (-\tfrac{5}{13})(\tfrac{3}{5}) - (-\tfrac{12}{13})(-\tfrac{4}{5})$$
$$= -\tfrac{63}{65},$$

$$\cos(\alpha - \beta) = \cos\alpha\cos\beta + \sin\alpha\sin\beta$$
$$= (-\tfrac{12}{13})(\tfrac{3}{5}) + (-\tfrac{5}{13})(-\tfrac{4}{5})$$
$$= -\tfrac{16}{65}.$$

We observe that $\sin(\alpha - \beta) < 0$ and $\cos(\alpha - \beta) < 0$, so that $\alpha - \beta$ must be in the third quadrant.

3 An important application of the addition formulas occurs in electrical circuit work. The sum of a sine and a cosine function (of the same period) is again a sine, or cosine, function with a new amplitude and the graph shifted sideways. We first consider a special numerical case. We start with the function F, given by

$$F(\theta) = 2\sin\theta + 3\cos\theta.$$

Let us multiply and divide by $\sqrt{2^2 + 3^2} = \sqrt{13}$. Then

$$F(\theta) = \sqrt{13}\left(\frac{2}{\sqrt{13}}\sin\theta + \frac{3}{\sqrt{13}}\cos\theta\right).$$

We see that the point $(2/\sqrt{13}, 3/\sqrt{13})$ is on the unit circle (Fig. 5), and there is a real number α, $0 < \alpha < \pi/2$, such that

$$W(\alpha) = \left(\frac{2}{\sqrt{13}}, \frac{3}{\sqrt{13}}\right);$$

so

$$\cos\alpha = \frac{2}{\sqrt{13}} \quad \text{and} \quad \sin\alpha = \frac{3}{\sqrt{13}}.$$

Hence

$$F(\theta) = \sqrt{13}\,(\cos\alpha\,\sin\theta + \sin\alpha\,\cos\theta) = \sqrt{13}\,\sin\,(\theta + \alpha).$$

This is the desired result. The formula makes it easy for us to graph the function F.

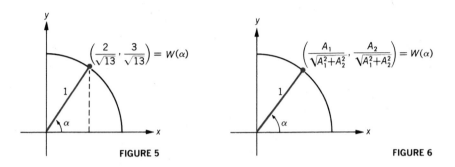

FIGURE 5   FIGURE 6

We now turn to the general situation and consider

$$I(t) = A_1 \sin 2\pi ft + A_2 \cos 2\pi ft,$$

where we are thinking of t as time measured in, say, seconds. Then f is the frequency of the motion, and A_1 and A_2 are some given constants. If this is an electrical application, $I(t)$ might be the current in an electrical circuit at a given time. The numbers A_1 and A_2 will be determined by the components of the circuit. We shall suppose here that $A_1 > 0$ and $A_2 > 0$. Then

$$I(t) = \sqrt{A_1^2 + A_2^2}\left(\frac{A_1}{\sqrt{A_1^2 + A_2^2}}\sin 2\pi ft + \frac{A_2}{\sqrt{A_1^2 + A_2^2}}\cos 2\pi ft\right),$$

and there is a real number α, such that $0 < \alpha < \pi/2$ and

$$\cos\alpha = \frac{A_1}{\sqrt{A_1^2 + A_2^2}}, \qquad \sin\alpha = \frac{A_2}{\sqrt{A_1^2 + A_2^2}}.$$

(See Fig. 6.) Then

$$I(t) = \sqrt{A_1^2 + A_2^2}\,(\cos\alpha\,\sin 2\pi ft + \sin\alpha\,\cos 2\pi ft)$$
$$= \sqrt{A_1^2 + A_2^2}\,\sin\,(2\pi ft + \alpha),$$

where $0 < \alpha < \pi/2$.

We see that, in general, *the sum of two simple harmonic motions of the same period is again a simple harmonic motion of the same period but with an amplitude that depends on the amplitudes of the summands. There is also a sideways shift, or phase shift.*

Problems

Set A

Establish the identities below.

1. $\cos(\pi + \theta) = -\cos\theta$
2. $\sin(\pi + \theta) = -\sin\theta$
3. $\sin(3\pi/2 - \theta) = -\cos\theta$
4. $\cos(\theta - 3\pi/2) = -\sin\theta$
5. $\sin(\pi/2 + \theta) = \cos\theta$
6. $\cos(\pi/2 + \theta) = -\sin\theta$

Given that $\sin\alpha = \frac{1}{3}$ and $\cos\beta = \frac{2}{3}$ and α and β are in Quadrant I, find the following.

7. $\sin(\alpha + \beta)$
8. $\cos(\alpha - \beta)$
9. $\tan(\alpha + \beta)$
10. $\tan(\alpha - \beta)$
11. $\sec(\alpha + \beta)$
12. $\csc(\alpha - \beta)$
13. Find $\cos(\alpha + \beta)$ if $\tan\alpha = -\frac{12}{5}$ and $\sec\beta = -\frac{5}{3}$. Give all possibilities.
14. Show that
$$\tan\left(\frac{\pi}{2} - \theta\right) = \cot\theta.$$
15. Obtain a reduction formula for
$$\sin\left[(2k + 1)\frac{\pi}{2} + \theta\right],$$ where k is an integer.
16. Obtain a reduction formula for
$$\sin(k\pi + \theta),$$
where k is an integer.
17. Obtain a reduction formula for
$$\tan\left[(2k + 1)\frac{\pi}{2} - \theta\right],$$ where k is an integer.

Set B

Express the following in terms of $\sin\theta$ and $\cos\theta$.

18. $\sin(\pi/3 + \theta)$
19. $\cos(\pi/4 - \theta)$
20. $\sec(\theta - \pi/6)$
21. $\sin(\theta - \pi/4)$
22. $\tan(\theta - \pi/4)$
23. $\cos(\pi/6 - \theta)$

Express the following functions in the form $A\sin(\theta + \alpha)$. Be sure to specify α.

24. $3\sin\theta + 4\cos\theta$
25. $3\sin\theta - 4\cos\theta$

26. $B\sin\theta + B\cos\theta,\ B > 0$
27. $\sqrt{3}\sin\theta + \sqrt{7}\cos\theta$
28. $\sqrt{3}\sin\theta - \sqrt{7}\cos\theta$
29. $A\sin\theta + B\cos\theta;\ A, B > 0$
30. $A\sin\theta + B\cos\theta,\ A > 0, B < 0$
31. $\sin\theta + \cos\theta$

Set C

Given that $\sin\alpha = u$ and $\cos\beta = v$, find the following in terms of u and v.

32. $\sin(\alpha + \beta)$; α is in Quadrant I, β in Quadrant I
33. $\tan(\alpha - \beta)$; α is in Quadrant I, β in Quadrant II
34. $\tan(\alpha + \beta)$; α is in Quadrant I, β in Quadrant III
35. Derive a formula for $\sin 2\alpha$ from $\sin(\alpha + \beta)$.
36. Derive a formula for $\cos 2\alpha$.
37. Simplify: $\sin 3 \cos 2 - \sin 2 \cos 3$.
38. The right triangle ABC is inscribed in a semicircle of radius a. Show that the sides shown in the figure have the lengths indicated, and then derive the formula for $\sin 2\alpha$.

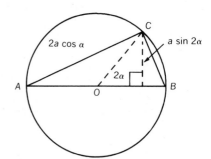

Establish the following identities.

39. $\dfrac{1}{1 + \sin^2 2\theta} = \dfrac{\csc^2 2\theta}{2 + \cot^2 2\theta}$

40. $\dfrac{\sin 2x}{\sin x} - \dfrac{\cos 2x}{\cos x} = \sec x$

41. $\dfrac{1 - \cos 2\theta}{\sin 2\theta} = \tan \theta$

42. $\sin^3 y \cos y - \sin^5 y \cos y = \sin^3 y \cos^3 y$

43. $\dfrac{\sin 3\theta}{\sec 2\theta} - \dfrac{\cos 3\theta}{\csc 2\theta} = \sin \theta$

44. $(\sin x + \sec x)^2 + (\cos x + \csc x)^2 = (1 + \sec x \csc x)^2$

45. $\sin 4\theta = 2 \sin 2\theta - 8 \sin^3 \theta \cos \theta$

46. $\cos^2 \theta + \cos^2 (\tfrac{2}{3}\pi + \theta) + \cos^2 (\tfrac{2}{3}\pi - \theta) = \tfrac{3}{2}$

47. $\tan (\theta + \pi/3) \tan (\theta - \pi/3) +$
$\tan \theta \tan (\theta + \pi/3) + \tan (\theta - \pi/3) \tan \theta = -3$

48. $(\cos \theta + \sin \theta)^4 + (\cos \theta - \sin \theta)^4 = 3 - \cos 4\theta$

Calculator Problem

Let $F(\theta) = \sqrt{5} \sin \theta + \sqrt{3} \cos \theta$. Compute $F(1.2)$ in two ways:

(a) By direct substitution in the equation.
(b) By expressing $F(\theta)$ as $F(\theta) = A \big(\sin (\theta + \alpha)\big)$, finding α, and then substituting in the derived formula.

7-5   Double- and Half-Angle Formulas

From the basic addition formulas we easily obtain (where $\theta = \alpha = \beta$)

$$\sin 2\theta = 2 \sin \theta \cos \theta,$$

$$\cos 2\theta = \cos^2 \theta - \sin^2 \theta = 1 - 2 \sin^2 \theta = 2 \cos^2 \theta - 1, \qquad (1)$$

$$\tan 2\theta = \frac{2 \tan \theta}{1 - \tan^2 \theta}.$$

From these, in turn, we can derive formulas for the functions of half an angle. Thus, setting $2\theta = x$ so that $\theta = x/2$, we have

$$\cos x = 2 \cos^2 \frac{x}{2} - 1 = 1 - 2 \sin^2 \frac{x}{2}.$$

Therefore

$$\cos^2 \frac{x}{2} = \frac{1 + \cos x}{2},$$

$$\sin^2 \frac{x}{2} = \frac{1 - \cos x}{2}. \qquad (2)$$

Taking square roots of both sides, we have

$$\cos \frac{x}{2} = \pm \sqrt{\frac{1 + \cos x}{2}},$$

$$\sin \frac{x}{2} = \pm \sqrt{\frac{1 - \cos x}{2}}, \qquad (3)$$

where the sign used depends on the quadrant to which $x/2$ belongs. From (3) we obtain a formula for $\tan x/2$:

$$\tan \frac{x}{2} = \pm \sqrt{\frac{1 - \cos x}{1 + \cos x}}. \tag{4}$$

However, (4) is not the best possible formula, as there is another form free from radicals and ambiguity in sign, and that is

$$\tan \frac{x}{2} = \frac{\sin \dfrac{x}{2}}{\cos \dfrac{x}{2}} = \frac{\sin \dfrac{x}{2} \sin \dfrac{x}{2}}{\cos \dfrac{x}{2} \sin \dfrac{x}{2}}$$

$$= \frac{\sin^2 \dfrac{x}{2}}{\dfrac{1}{2} \cdot 2 \sin \dfrac{x}{2} \cos \dfrac{x}{2}} = \frac{\dfrac{1}{2}(1 - \cos x)}{\dfrac{1}{2} \sin 2 \cdot \dfrac{x}{2}},$$

or

$$\tan \frac{x}{2} = \frac{1 - \cos x}{\sin x}. \tag{5}$$

By a similar argument, one can also obtain the following equation:

$$\tan \frac{x}{2} = \frac{\sin x}{1 + \cos x}. \tag{6}$$

Example 1 Find $\cos (\pi/12)$.

Solution. We do this in the following manner:

$$\cos \frac{\pi}{12} = \cos \frac{1}{2} \cdot \frac{\pi}{6} = \sqrt{\frac{1 + \sqrt{3}/2}{2}} = \frac{\sqrt{2 + \sqrt{3}}}{2}.$$

The above result is perfectly satisfactory, but it may be given a different form as follows:

$$\frac{\sqrt{2 + \sqrt{3}}}{2} = \frac{\sqrt{2}\sqrt{2 + \sqrt{3}}}{\sqrt{2} \cdot 2} = \frac{\sqrt{4 + 2\sqrt{3}}}{2\sqrt{2}} = \frac{\sqrt{(1 + \sqrt{3})^2}}{2\sqrt{2}}$$

$$= \frac{1 + \sqrt{3}}{2\sqrt{2}} = \frac{\sqrt{2} + \sqrt{6}}{4}.$$

This is the answer that we would have obtained if we had used the fact that $\pi/12 = \pi/3 - \pi/4$, so that

$$\cos \frac{\pi}{12} = \cos \left(\frac{\pi}{3} - \frac{\pi}{4} \right) = \cos \frac{\pi}{3} \cos \frac{\pi}{4} + \sin \frac{\pi}{3} \sin \frac{\pi}{4}$$

$$= \frac{1}{2} \cdot \frac{\sqrt{2}}{2} + \frac{\sqrt{3}}{2} \cdot \frac{\sqrt{2}}{2} = \frac{\sqrt{2} + \sqrt{6}}{4}.$$

Most *binomial surds* (that is, of the form $a \sqrt{b} + c \sqrt{d}$, where a, b, c, d are positive integers) do not have square roots that are also binomial surds. The example is an exceptional case.

Observe that by the continued halving of an angle we could find the values of the circular functions for arbitrarily small angles and we could determine these values as accurately as we wished. From these values, using the addition formulas and some interpolation, we could, in time, construct a very accurate table of the circular functions. This is *not* the method used to construct the tables, but it does show that we are able to compute accurate tables if we so desire.

Example 2 If $\sin \alpha = -\frac{3}{5}$ and α is in Quadrant III, what is $\sin 2\alpha$? Also find $\sin \alpha/2$ if $\pi < \alpha < 3\pi/2$.

Solution. We have $\cos \alpha = -4/5$ and

$$\sin 2\alpha = 2 \cdot \frac{-3}{5} \cdot \frac{-4}{5} = \frac{24}{25}.$$

Then

$$\sin \frac{\alpha}{2} = +\sqrt{\frac{1 - (-4/5)}{2}} = \frac{3}{\sqrt{10}},$$

where the positive root is taken because $\pi/2 < \alpha/2 < 3\pi/4 < \pi$.

Problems

Set A

Find $\sin 2x$, $\cos 2x$, and $\tan 2x$ given the following.

1. $\cos x = -\frac{5}{13}$

2. $\sin x = -\frac{9}{41}$ and x is in Quadrant IV

3. $\csc x = \frac{3}{2}$ and x is in Quadrant II

4. $\cot x = 2$

5. $\tan x = 1/\sqrt{2}$

6. $\cos x = -\frac{3}{5}$

7. $\sin x = a$ and x is in Quadrant III

8. Determine $\sin (\pi/8)$, using a half-angle formula.

9. Find the exact value of $\sin 15°$ using a half-angle formula.

10. Find $\cos (3\pi/8)$ using a half-angle formula.

Set B

11. Find $\tan \pi/12$ using two different formulas.

Derive formulas for the following.

12. $\sin 2\theta$ **13.** $\cos 2\theta$ **14.** $\tan 2\theta$

15. Find all the functions of $x/2$ given that $\sin x = \frac{3}{4}$ and x is in Quadrant II.

16. Derive the formula $\cos 2\theta = \cos^2 \theta - \sin^2 \theta$
   (a) using the formula for $\cos^2 x/2$.
   (b) using the formula for $\sin^2 x/2$.

17. Derive the formula
   $\tan (x/2) = \sin x/(1 + \cos x)$.

18. Show that $\cos 3x = 4 \cos^3 x - 3 \cos x$.

19. Obtain a formula for $\sin 3x$ in terms of $\sin x$.

20. Derive a formula for $\tan 3x$ in terms of $\tan x$.

Set C

Show that the following are identities.

21. $2 - 2 \tan x \cot 2x = \sec^2 x$

22. $\dfrac{1 - \cos 2\alpha}{1 + \cos 2\alpha} = \tan^2 \alpha$

23. $\tan \left(\dfrac{\pi}{4} + \theta \right) = \dfrac{1 + \sin 2\theta}{\cos 2\theta}$

24. $\dfrac{\sin^3 x + \cos^3 x}{\sin x + \cos x} = 1 - \frac{1}{2} \sin 2x$

25. $\tan 3x - \tan x = 2 \sin x \sec 3x$

26. $\cos 2x = \cos^4 x - \sin^4 x$

27. $\dfrac{1 + \sin 2\theta}{1 + \cos 2\theta} = \frac{1}{2}(1 + \tan \theta)^2$

28. $\dfrac{2 \tan x}{1 + \tan^2 x} = \sin 2x$

29. $\dfrac{2 \cot x}{1 + \cot^2 x} = \sin 2x$

30. $\dfrac{\cot \frac{1}{2} x - \tan \frac{1}{2} x}{\cot \frac{1}{2} x + \tan \frac{1}{2} x} = \cos x$

31. $\dfrac{\sin 2\alpha}{\sin \alpha} - \dfrac{\cos 2\alpha}{\cos \alpha} = \sec \alpha$

32. $\dfrac{\sin 2\alpha}{\sin \alpha} + \dfrac{\cos 2\alpha}{\cos \alpha} = \dfrac{2 \sin 3\alpha}{\sin 2\alpha}$

33. $\csc 2\theta - \cot 2\theta = \tan \theta$

34. $\csc 2\theta + \cot 2\theta = \cot \theta$

35. $\cot \frac{1}{2}\theta = \dfrac{1}{\csc \theta - \cot \theta}$

36. $\tan \frac{1}{2}\theta = \dfrac{1}{\csc \theta + \cot \theta}$

Given that $A + B + C = \pi$, show that the following are true.

37. $\sin A + \sin B + \sin C =$
   $\qquad 4 \cos (A/2) \cos (B/2) \cos (C/2)$

38. $\sin A + \sin B - \sin C =$
   $\qquad 4 \sin (A/2) \sin (B/2) \cos (C/2)$

Calculator Problem

Verify the formula given in Problem 37 if

$$A = \frac{3\pi}{10}, \qquad B = \frac{\pi}{6} \qquad \text{and} \qquad C = \frac{8\pi}{15}.$$

Complex Numbers

In this section we use the addition formulas to obtain a graphical interpretation of the product of two complex numbers. Recall that addition of complex numbers had a simple geometric representation in terms of the parallelogram law.

Our first step in obtaining an interpretation of the product will be to define the *polar form of a complex number*.

Suppose that z is any non-zero complex number. Then

$$z = x + iy,$$

where x and y are real and not both 0, and i is the imaginary unit. We will let P be the point representing z in the complex plane (Fig. 7), and P_1 be the intersection of the ray OP with the unit circle. Then there is a real number θ (in fact, infinitely many of them) such that $W(\theta) = P_1$. Let $r = \sqrt{x^2 + y^2}$. Observe that $r = |OP|$.

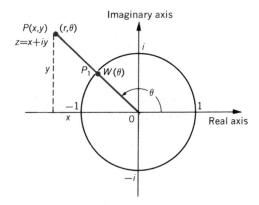

FIGURE 7

Definition 7-2   With the notation as above, the numbers r and θ are *polar coordinates** of $P(x, y)$, and are written as the ordered pair (r, θ). If $|OP| = 0$, then its polar coordinates are $(0, \theta)$, where θ is arbitrary.

Remark   Because θ (for $r \neq 0$) is determined only to a multiple of 2π, each point has infinitely many polar coordinates, $\theta + 2\pi k$, where k is an integer.

For the complex number $x + iy$, we have

$$x = r \cos \theta, \qquad y = r \sin \theta \qquad \text{and} \qquad x + iy = r(\cos \theta + i \sin \theta). \quad (1)$$

---

*See Chapter 19 for a full discussion of polar coordinates.

Definition 7-3 With the notation as above, the *polar form* of the complex number $z = x + iy$ is given by*

$$z = x + iy = r(\cos \theta + i \sin \theta).$$

The absolute value of a complex number, $z = x + iy$, is the number

$$|x + iy| = \sqrt{x^2 + y^2}.$$

Since for any $P(x, y)$, the number $r = \sqrt{x^2 + y^2}$, we can conclude that $|x + iy| = r$. The number r is called the *absolute value*, or *modulus*, of z. The number θ (not unique) is called an *amplitude*, or *argument*, of z.

Example 1 To put $-2 + 2\sqrt{3}\,i$ in polar form, we first compute the modulus

$$r = |(-2 + 2\sqrt{3}\,i)| = \sqrt{4 + 12} = 4.$$

Then

$$-2 + 2\sqrt{3}\,i = 4\left(-\frac{1}{2} + \frac{\sqrt{3}}{2}i\right),$$

and from Fig. 8 we observe that

$$W\left(\frac{2\pi}{3}\right) = \left(-\frac{1}{2}, \frac{\sqrt{3}}{2}\right).$$

Therefore

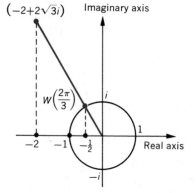

FIGURE 8

$$-2 + 2\sqrt{3}\,i = 4\left(\cos \frac{2\pi}{3} + i \sin \frac{2\pi}{3}\right).$$

Let us now use the polar form to consider the product of two complex numbers,

$$z_1 = r_1(\cos \theta_1 + i \sin \theta_1) \quad \text{and} \quad z_2 = r_2(\cos \theta_2 + i \sin \theta_2).$$

---

*In reading other books you may encounter the shorthand form "cis θ" which stands for

$$\cos \theta + i \sin \theta.$$

In more advanced mathematics it is shown that the exponential function, e^z, where $e = 2.7182\ldots$, which we have defined only for real z, can have its domain extended to all complex numbers. When this extension is made, we find that

$$e^{i\theta} = \cos \theta + i \sin \theta.$$

This astonishing result (known as Euler's formula) implies, for example, that

$$e^{i\pi} = \cos \pi + i \sin \pi = -1.$$

Then

$$z_1 z_2 = r_1 r_2 (\cos \theta_1 + i \sin \theta_1)(\cos \theta_2 + i \sin \theta_2)$$
$$= r_1 r_2 [(\cos \theta_1 \cos \theta_2 - \sin \theta_1 \sin \theta_2) + i(\sin \theta_1 \cos \theta_2 + \cos \theta_1 \sin \theta_2)]$$
$$= r_1 r_2 [\cos (\theta_1 + \theta_2) + i \sin (\theta_1 + \theta_2)].$$

We state this important result as Theorem 7–1.

Theorem 7–1

The absolute value of the product of two complex numbers is the product of their absolute values. An amplitude of their product is the sum of their amplitudes.

$$[r_1(\cos \theta_1 + i \sin \theta_1)][r_2(\cos \theta_2 + i \sin \theta_2)] =$$
$$r_1 r_2 [\cos (\theta_1 + \theta_2) + i \sin (\theta_1 + \theta_2)].$$

Corollary

The absolute value of the quotient of two complex numbers is the quotient of their absolute values. An amplitude of their quotient is the difference of their amplitudes:

$$\frac{r_1(\cos \theta_1 + i \sin \theta_1)}{r_2(\cos \theta_2 + i \sin \theta_2)} = \frac{r_1}{r_2} [\cos (\theta_1 - \theta_2) + i \sin (\theta_1 - \theta_2)].$$

If we let the quotient be $r(\cos \theta + i \sin \theta)$, then

$$r_1(\cos \theta_1 + i \sin \theta_1) = [r(\cos \theta + i \sin \theta)][r_2(\cos \theta_2 + i \sin \theta_2)],$$

and Theorem 7–1 applies. The details are left to the reader.

Observe the following special case:

$$\frac{1}{r(\cos \theta + i \sin \theta)} = \frac{1}{r}(\cos \theta - i \sin \theta).$$

Example 2

Compute the product $(-1 + \sqrt{3}\,i)(2\sqrt{3} + 2i)$ using both rectangular and polar forms; then compare the results.

Solution. In rectangular form we have

$$(-1 + \sqrt{3}\,i)(2\sqrt{3} + 2i) = -2\sqrt{3} - 2i + 6i - 2\sqrt{3} = -4\sqrt{3} + 4i.$$

Since

$$-1 + \sqrt{3}\,i = 2\left(-\frac{1}{2} + \frac{\sqrt{3}}{2}i\right) = 2\left(\cos \frac{2\pi}{3} + i \sin \frac{2\pi}{3}\right),$$

and

$$2\sqrt{3} + 2i = 4\left(\frac{\sqrt{3}}{2} + \frac{1}{2}i\right) = 4\left(\cos \frac{\pi}{6} + i \sin \frac{\pi}{6}\right),$$

we have, in polar form,

$$(-1 + \sqrt{3}\,i)(2\sqrt{3} + 2i) = 2\left(\cos\frac{2\pi}{3} + i\sin\frac{2\pi}{3}\right) \cdot 4\left(\cos\frac{\pi}{6} + i\sin\frac{\pi}{6}\right)$$

$$= 8\left[\cos\left(\frac{4\pi}{6} + \frac{\pi}{6}\right) + i\sin\left(\frac{4\pi}{6} + \frac{\pi}{6}\right)\right]$$

$$= 8\left(\cos\frac{5\pi}{6} + i\sin\frac{5\pi}{6}\right) = 8\left(-\frac{\sqrt{3}}{2} + \frac{1}{2}i\right)$$

$$= -4\sqrt{3} + 4i.$$

Theorem 7–1 is of particular interest when the factors are equal. We have

$$[r(\cos\theta + i\sin\theta)]^2 = r^2(\cos 2\theta + i\sin 2\theta),$$

and, by an inductive argument,* we get, for any positive integer n,

$$[r(\cos\theta + i\sin\theta)]^n = r^n(\cos n\theta + i\sin n\theta). \tag{2}$$

Formula (2) is known as de Moivre's Theorem.† The main application of this theorem is its use "in reverse" to find roots of complex numbers. Suppose that $z = r(\cos\theta + i\sin\theta)$ is any given complex number, and n is a positive integer. We seek a complex number $R(\cos\phi + i\sin\phi)$ such that

$$[R(\cos\phi + i\sin\phi)]^n = r(\cos\theta + i\sin\theta).$$

Clearly there will be such a number if and only if $R^n = r$ and $n\phi = \theta + 2\pi k$, where k is any integer.

In other words, we must have

$$R = \sqrt[n]{r} \quad \text{and} \quad \phi = \frac{\theta + 2\pi k}{n}. \tag{3}$$

Observe that we get distinct complex numbers $R(\cos\phi + i\sin\phi)$ if $k = 0, 1, 2, \ldots, n - 1$. For larger integral values of k, the numbers recur. Observe also that by the fundamental theorem of algebra, a complex number A can have, at most, n roots; these roots are the solutions of the equation $z^n - A = 0$ which is of nth degree. Since formula (3) gives n different roots, it must give all of them. We state these results as Theorem 7–2.

Theorem 7–2   **The complex number $r(\cos\theta + i\sin\theta)$, $r > 0$, has n nth roots given by**

$$\sqrt[n]{r}\left(\cos\frac{\theta + 2\pi k}{n} + i\sin\frac{\theta + 2\pi k}{n}\right), \qquad k = 0, 1, \ldots, n - 1.$$

---

*For a discussion of induction see Section 9–4.

†Abraham de Moivre (1667–1754) was an English mathematician of French extraction.

Example 3　Find the cube roots of -1. (See Fig. 9.)

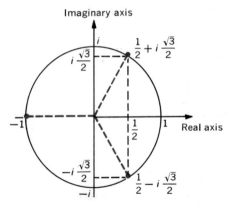

Imaginary axis

FIGURE 9

Solution. We have

$$-1 = 1(\cos \pi + i \sin \pi);$$

hence the cube roots are

$$\sqrt[3]{1}\left(\cos \frac{\pi}{3} + i \sin \frac{\pi}{3}\right)$$

$$= 1\left(\frac{1}{2} + \frac{i\sqrt{3}}{2}\right) = \frac{1 + i\sqrt{3}}{2},$$

$$\sqrt[3]{1}\left(\cos \frac{\pi + 2\pi}{3} + i \sin \frac{\pi + 2\pi}{3}\right) = 1(-1 + 0) = -1,$$

$$\sqrt[3]{1}\left(\cos \frac{\pi + 4\pi}{3} + i \sin \frac{\pi + 4\pi}{3}\right) = 1\left(\frac{1}{2} + i\frac{-\sqrt{3}}{2}\right) = \frac{1 - i\sqrt{3}}{2}.$$

4　Find the square roots of i.

Solution. We have

$$i = 1\left(\cos \frac{\pi}{2} + i \sin \frac{\pi}{2}\right),$$

and the square roots of i are

$$\sqrt{1}\left(\cos \frac{\pi}{4} + i \sin \frac{\pi}{4}\right) = \frac{1}{\sqrt{2}} + i\frac{1}{\sqrt{2}} = \frac{1 + i}{\sqrt{2}},$$

$$\sqrt{1}\left(\cos \frac{5\pi}{4} + i \sin \frac{5\pi}{4}\right) = \frac{-1}{\sqrt{2}} + i\frac{-1}{\sqrt{2}} = \frac{-1 - i}{\sqrt{2}}.$$

Problems

Set A

Find the polar forms of the following complex numbers. Graph each to check your answer.

1. 3
2. $-2i$
3. $-\sqrt{3} - i$
4. $\sqrt{2} - \sqrt{2}\,i$
5. $-1 - i$
6. $-1/2 + \sqrt{3}/2\,i$

Express the following in the form $x + yi$ by evaluating the circular functions.

7. $2\left(\cos \frac{3\pi}{4} + i \sin \frac{3\pi}{4}\right)$

8. $2\left(\cos \frac{11\pi}{4} + i \sin \frac{11\pi}{4}\right)$

9. $4\left(\cos\dfrac{4\pi}{3} + i\sin\dfrac{4\pi}{3}\right)$

10. $2\left(\cos\dfrac{3\pi}{2} + i\sin\dfrac{3\pi}{2}\right)$

11. $1\left(\cos\dfrac{5\pi}{6} + i\sin\dfrac{5\pi}{6}\right)$

12. $8(\cos\pi + i\sin\pi)$

13. Compute the product $(1 + i)(1 - i)$ using both rectangular and polar forms. Compare the results.

14. Compute the quotient $(1 + i)/(1 - i)$ using both rectangular and polar forms.

Set B

Plot the following pairs of complex numbers and find each product. Put them in polar form and obtain the product using Theorem 7–1. Plot the product and check graphically.

15. $(1 + i)i$

16. $(-\sqrt{3} + i)(2 - 2\sqrt{3}\,i)$

17. $(-\sqrt{3} + i)(-\sqrt{3} - i)$

18. $(2 + 2i)(-2 + 2i)$

19. $(-1 + \sqrt{3}\,i)^2$

20. $(1 + i)^2$

Obtain the following powers.

21. $\left[2\left(\cos\dfrac{\pi}{8} + i\sin\dfrac{\pi}{8}\right)\right]^4$

22. $\left[2\left(\cos\dfrac{\pi}{12} + i\sin\dfrac{\pi}{12}\right)\right]^6$

23. $\left[1\left(\cos\dfrac{2\pi}{3} + i\sin\dfrac{2\pi}{3}\right)\right]^3$

24. $\left[\sqrt{2}\left(\cos\dfrac{\pi}{4} + i\sin\dfrac{\pi}{4}\right)\right]^4$

Find the two square roots of the following.

25. $-4i$ 26. $1 + \sqrt{3}\,i$

Find the three cube roots of the following.

27. 1 28. -8 29. i

Set C

30. What is the formula for
$$\frac{r_1(\cos\theta_1 + i\sin\theta_1)}{r_2(\cos\theta_2 + i\sin\theta_2)}?$$
Prove your assertion.

31. Give, in polar form, a complex number which when multiplied by
$$2\left(\cos\frac{\pi}{3} + i\sin\frac{\pi}{3}\right)$$
gives a product equal to 1.

32. If $|z| = 1$ and the complex number z and its three cube roots are plotted, what is the geometric relation between z and its three roots? between z and its n nth roots?

Solve these equations.

33. $z^3 + i = 0$ 34. $z^6 + 8 = 0$

35. $z^2 + 1 + i = 0$

Calculator Problem

Find the three cube roots of $3 + 4i$. Plot the cube roots in the complex plane. Express the roots as complex numbers in rectangular form.

Summary

The principal identities and formulas are listed, for reference, below. You should be able to derive all of them.

1. Elementary identities:

$$\tan \theta = \frac{\sin \theta}{\cos \theta} = \frac{1}{\cot \theta}, \qquad \cot \theta = \frac{\cos \theta}{\sin \theta} = \frac{1}{\tan \theta},$$

$$\sec \theta = \frac{1}{\cos \theta}, \qquad \csc \theta = \frac{1}{\sin \theta},$$

$$\sin^2 \theta + \cos^2 \theta = 1, \qquad 1 + \tan^2 \theta = \sec^2 \theta, \qquad 1 + \cot^2 \theta = \csc^2 \theta.$$

2. The addition formulas:

$$\sin (\alpha \pm \beta) = \sin \alpha \cos \beta \pm \cos \alpha \sin \beta,$$

$$\cos (\alpha \pm \beta) = \cos \alpha \cos \beta \mp \sin \alpha \sin \beta,$$

$$\tan (\alpha \pm \beta) = \frac{\tan \alpha \pm \tan \beta}{1 \mp \tan \alpha \tan \beta}.$$

3. Double- and half-angle formulas:

$$\sin 2\theta = 2 \sin \theta \cos \theta,$$

$$\cos 2\theta = \cos^2 \theta - \sin^2 \theta = 2 \cos^2 \theta - 1 = 1 - 2 \sin^2 \theta,$$

$$\tan 2\theta = \frac{2 \tan \theta}{1 - \tan^2 \theta},$$

$$\sin \frac{\theta}{2} = \pm \sqrt{\frac{1 - \cos \theta}{2}}, \qquad \cos \frac{\theta}{2} = \pm \sqrt{\frac{1 + \cos \theta}{2}},$$

$$\tan \frac{\theta}{2} = \pm \sqrt{\frac{1 - \cos \theta}{1 + \cos \theta}} = \frac{1 - \cos \theta}{\sin \theta} = \frac{\sin \theta}{1 + \cos \theta}.$$

4. These identities and formulas were used in the chapter in the following ways:

(a) To establish new identities from the elementary ones.

(b) To find exact values of the circular functions at points other than 0, $\pi/6$, $\pi/4$, $\pi/3$, $\pi/2$, for example at $\pi/12$.

(c) To obtain reduction formulas, for example, $\sin (\pi + \theta) = -\sin \theta$.

(d) To obtain functions of 2θ and $\theta/2$ when a function of θ is known.

(e) To add two simple harmonic motions of the same period and obtain a simple harmonic motion.

(f) To find powers and roots of complex numbers using de Moivre's theorem.

7-2   Give another, possibly simpler, form for each of the following.

     1. $\dfrac{\sin \theta}{\cos \theta}$ **2.** $1 - \sin^2 \theta$

     3. $1 + \cot^2 \theta$ **4.** $\dfrac{1}{\sec \theta}$

     Establish the following identities and determine the domain of validity.

     5. $\dfrac{\csc^2 \theta}{\csc^2 \theta - 1} = \sec^2 \theta$ **6.** $\dfrac{1 + \tan x}{1 + \cot x} = \tan x$

7-3   **7.** Use the fact that $5\pi/12 = 2\pi/3 - \pi/4$ to find an exact value of $\sin 5\pi/12$.

     8. What relation does one get from the addition formula for $\cos (\alpha - \beta)$ if $\alpha = \beta$?

7-4   **9.** Given that $\sin \alpha = \frac{1}{3}$, with α in Quadrant I, and $\cos \beta = -\frac{2}{3}$, with β in Quadrant II, find $\cos (\alpha + \beta)$ and $\sin (\alpha + \beta)$.

    10. Given that $\sin \alpha = \frac{2}{3}$, with α in Quadrant II, and $\cos \beta = \frac{1}{2}$, with β in Quadrant IV, find $\cos (\alpha - \beta)$ and $\tan (\alpha + \beta)$.

     Express each of the following in the form $A \sin (\theta + \alpha)$.

    11. $2 \sin \theta + 2 \cos \theta$
    12. $\sqrt{3} \sin \theta + \cos \theta$

7-5   **13.** If $\sin \theta = \sqrt{5}/3$, and θ is in Quadrant I, find all the functions of 2θ.

    14. Determine $\tan (\pi/8)$ using a half-angle formula.

7-6   Write each complex number below in polar form.

    15. $2 - 2i$ **16.** $\sqrt{3} + i$

    17. 4 **18.** $-5i$

     Write the following in the form $a + bi$.

    19. $10 \left(\cos \dfrac{\pi}{4} + i \sin \dfrac{\pi}{4} \right)$

    20. $7 \left(\cos \dfrac{3\pi}{2} + i \sin \dfrac{3\pi}{2} \right)$

    21. Find the product of the complex numbers z_1 and z_2, given that

$$z_1 = 3 \left(\cos \frac{\pi}{2} + i \sin \frac{\pi}{2} \right)$$

     and

$$z_2 = 5 \left(\cos \frac{\pi}{6} + i \sin \frac{\pi}{6} \right).$$

    22. Find the 4 fourth roots of $16i$.

Historical Note

Leonhard Euler
(1707–1783)

Trigonometry was originally used in astronomy and for the solution of triangles (see Historical Notes of Chapter 5 and 6). Today spherical trigonometry is seldom studied in schools. The study of the properties of circular functions, however, has become very important because of their applications to wave theory in light, sound, electricity, etc. With the rise of science as a major discipline, beginning in the seventeenth century, and the application of calculus to the solution of physical and mathematical problems, the importance of circular functions gradually became apparent. It is truly remarkable that these few functions have found so many uses in so many different branches of mathematics.

The key to this universality is the fact that they are, in some sense, the simplest of the periodic functions, and that every other periodic function can be represented in terms of them by means of Fourier's Theorem.

The analytical theory of the circular functions began during the period of the development of the calculus. Leonhard Euler (1707–1783) advanced the theory by showing that the elementary functions, including the circular functions, can be extended to have domains which include complex numbers. Thus it can be shown that it makes sense to speak of the exponential functions, e^z, with *complex exponents z*. A particularly interesting example is Euler's formula, $e^{i\theta} = \cos\theta + i\sin\theta$, where $i^2 = -1$ and θ is a real number.

Chapter 8
Inverse Circular Functions and
Trigonometric Equations

8-1   Introduction

In this chapter we define inverses of some of the circular functions. But because the circular functions are not one-to-one mappings, it is necessary to restrict their domains in order to get inverses. The situation is analogous to that encountered in Chapter 2 with the square-root function. Then if f is the squaring function with domain R, we have

$$f(x) = x^2.$$

The range of f is the interval $[0, \infty)$. Since for each real number $b > 0$ there are two real numbers a such that $a^2 = b$, it is necessary to restrict attention to *one* of them in order to get a unique inverse function. We then select the *principal value,* that is, the *positive* number whose square is b. See Fig. 1(a).

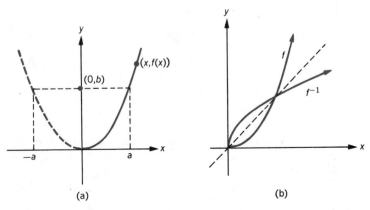

(a)   (b)

FIGURE 1

When we restrict the domain of f to the interval $[0, \infty)$, then the inverse function is the square-root function

$$f^{-1}(x) = \sqrt{x}.$$

The graphs of f and f^{-1} are shown in Fig. 1(b). Observe that the graph of the inverse function is obtained by "reflecting" the graph of f in the line $y = x$.

8-2   The Inverse Circular Functions

Recall that the graphs of sine, cosine, and tangent appear as in Fig. 2. It should be clear from the graphs of the functions that none of the functions are one-to-one mappings. In order to discuss the inverses of the circular

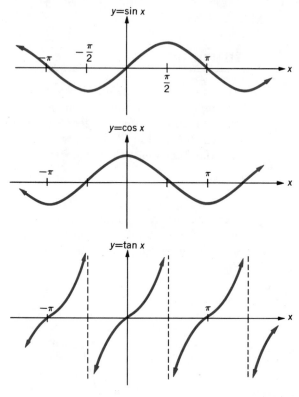

FIGURE 2

functions, we must restrict the domain of the functions so that in the restricted domain the functions will be one-to-one mappings. In the case of the sine function, we note that the mapping is one-to-one and has its full range of values on many intervals. Although one could choose any of these intervals, it is generally agreed to use $[-\pi/2, \pi/2]$ as the domain of the inverse function for the sine.

This convention is adopted in the following definitions.

Definition 8-1   The *Sine* function (capital S is used to distinguish it from the ordinary sine function) is the function Sin defined by

$$\text{Sin } \theta = \sin \theta \quad \text{for} \quad -\frac{\pi}{2} \leq \theta \leq \frac{\pi}{2}.$$

Definition 8-2   The inverse of the Sine function is called the *Arcsine* function and is abbreviated to Arcsin (or Sin^{-1}).* If $y = \text{Sin}\,\theta$, then $\theta = \text{Arcsin}\,y$ (or $\theta = \text{Sin}^{-1}\,y$).

The graphs of $y = \text{Sin}\,\theta$ and $\theta = \text{Sin}^{-1}\,y$ are shown in Fig. 3(a) and (b).

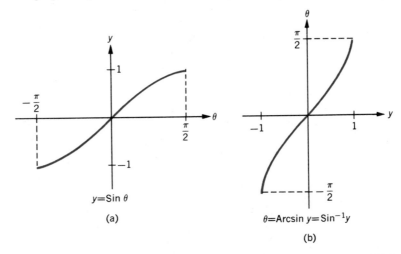

(a)

$y = \text{Sin}\,\theta$

(b)

$\theta = \text{Arcsin}\,y = \text{Sin}^{-1}y$

FIGURE 3

Arcsin y is often interpreted as "the number (or arc) whose sine is y." On the other hand, if *any* number whose sine is y is intended, one often sees "arcsin y" rather than "Arcsin y."

In a similar manner, we get a unique inverse to $y = \cos\theta$ if we restrict θ to the interval $0 \le \theta \le \pi$.

Definition 8-3   The *Cosine* function is the function Cos defined by

$$\text{Cos}\,\theta = \cos\theta \qquad \text{for} \quad 0 \le \theta \le \pi.$$

The inverse of Cos is the *Arccos* function (also denoted by Cos^{-1}). If $y = \text{Cos}\,\theta$, then

$$\theta = \text{Arccos}\,y = \text{Cos}^{-1}\,y.$$

The graphs of $y = \text{Cos}\,\theta$ and $\theta = \text{Cos}^{-1}\,y$ are shown in Fig. 4.

The mapping is one-to-one from $[0, \pi]$ to $[-1, 1]$. We have

$$0 \le \text{Arccos}\,y \le \pi \qquad \text{or} \qquad 0 \le \text{Cos}^{-1}y \le \pi.$$

Similarly, by restricting the domain of the tangent function, we get a unique inverse to the tangent function.

---

*Both notations, *Arcsin* and *Sin*$^{-1}$, are used by mathematicians and so we shall use both in this text.

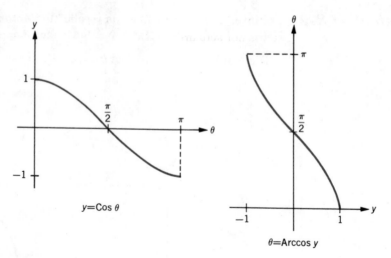

$y=\cos\theta$

$\theta=\text{Arccos } y$

FIGURE 4

Definition 8-4 The *Tangent* function is the function Tan defined by

$$\text{Tan } \theta = \tan \theta \qquad \text{for} \quad -\frac{\pi}{2} < \theta < \frac{\pi}{2}.$$

The inverse of Tan is the function *Arctan* (also denoted by Tan^{-1}). Then if $y = \text{Tan } \theta$, $\theta = \text{Arctan } y = \text{Tan}^{-1} y$.

The graphs of $y = \text{Tan } \theta$ and $\theta = \text{Arctan } y$ are shown in Fig. 5.

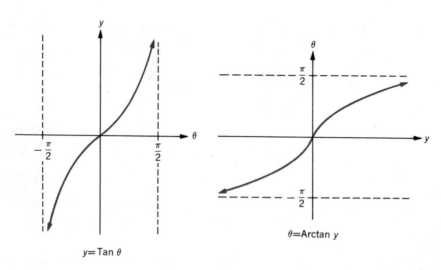

$y=\text{Tan } \theta$

$\theta=\text{Arctan } y$

FIGURE 5

In the same manner, one *can* define inverses of the other circular functions, but it is not actually necessary to do so. For example, one might define the inverse cosecant as follows. Set

$$\text{Csc } \theta = \csc \theta = t \qquad \text{for} \quad -\frac{\pi}{2} \le \theta \le \frac{\pi}{2}, \quad \theta \ne 0.$$

Then

$$\text{Sin } \theta = \frac{1}{t} \qquad \text{and} \qquad \theta = \text{Arccsc } t = \text{Arcsin } \frac{1}{t}.$$

Thus it is not necessary to define the other inverse functions. The inverses of the sine, cosine, and tangent will suffice. Furthermore, not all mathematicians agree on the domain of definition for Csc^{-1} and Sec^{-1}. For Cot^{-1} there is a natural choice. See Problem 34 below.

Remark

In many situations, one wishes to discuss all possible values for inverse relations of the circular functions, not necessarily just the ones above which are the principal values. When this is the case, the capital letter is not used and one simply writes arcsin, arccos, and arctan. Then, for example, one would have

$$\arcsin \frac{1}{2} = \frac{\pi}{6}, \frac{5\pi}{6}, \frac{\pi}{6} \pm 2\pi, \frac{5\pi}{6} \pm 2\pi, \text{ etc.,}$$

$$\arccos \left(-\frac{1}{2} \right) = \frac{2\pi}{3}, \frac{4\pi}{3}, \frac{2\pi}{3} \pm 2\pi, \frac{4\pi}{3} \pm 2\pi, \text{ etc.,}$$

$$\arctan \left(-1 \right) = \frac{3\pi}{4}, \frac{3\pi}{4} \pm \pi, \frac{3\pi}{4} \pm 2\pi, \text{ etc.}$$

The numbers Arcsin θ, Arccos θ, and Arctan θ are just the selected *principal values* of the relations arcsin θ, arccos θ, and arctan θ.

Example 1 $\quad \text{Arcsin } \frac{1}{2} = \text{Sin}^{-1} \frac{1}{2} = \frac{\pi}{6}$

2 $\quad \text{Arcsin } \frac{-1}{2} = \text{Sin}^{-1} \frac{-1}{2} = -\frac{\pi}{6}$

3 $\quad \text{Arctan } 1 = \text{Tan}^{-1} 1 = \frac{\pi}{4}$

4 $\quad \text{Arccos } \left(-\frac{1}{2} \right) = \text{Cos}^{-1} \frac{-1}{2} = \frac{2\pi}{3}$

Problems

Set A

Compute the following.

1. $\text{Sin}^{-1}\,1$ **2.** $\text{Cos}^{-1}\,1$

3. $\text{Arcsin}\,(\sqrt{3}/2)$ **4.** $\text{Arccos}\,(-\sqrt{3}/2)$

5. $\text{Tan}^{-1}\,(-1)$ **6.** $\text{Tan}^{-1}\,(-\sqrt{3})$

7. $\text{Cos}^{-1}\,(-1/\sqrt{2})$ **8.** $\text{Sin}^{-1}\,(-1/\sqrt{2})$

9. $\text{Sin}^{-1}\,(1/\sqrt{2})$ **10.** $\text{Arccos}\,0$

11. $\text{Arctan}\,\sqrt{3}$ **12.** $\text{Tan}^{-1}\,1$

13. $\text{Tan}^{-1}\,0$ **14.** $\text{Arccos}\,(-1)$

15. $\text{Arcsin}\,(-\sqrt{3}/2)$ **16.** $\text{Tan}^{-1}\,(-1/\sqrt{3})$

Use the trigonometric tables or a calculator to compute the following.

17. $\text{Sin}^{-1}\,0.3987$ **18.** $\text{Cos}^{-1}\,0.5577$

19. $\text{Arctan}\,0.3038$ **20.** $\text{Tan}^{-1}\,0.6009$

21. $\text{Arccos}\,0.2974$ **22.** $\text{Arcsin}\,0.7501$

Set B

Give all possible values of the following.

23. $\arcsin\,(-1)$ **24.** $\arctan\,\sqrt{3}$

25. $\arccos\,(-\sqrt{3}/2)$ **26.** $\arccos\,1/\sqrt{2}$

27. $\arcsin\,(-0.1236)$ **28.** $\arctan\,(-2)$

Evaluate the following.

29. $\text{Arcsin}\left(\sin\dfrac{5\pi}{4}\right)$ **30.** $\text{Arccos}\left(\cos\dfrac{\pi}{3}\right)$

31. $\text{Arctan}\left(\tan\dfrac{2\pi}{3}\right)$ **32.** $\text{Arccos}\left(\sin\dfrac{-5\pi}{6}\right)$

33. Why would we not want to define $\text{Cos}^{-1}\,z$ such that

$$-\frac{\pi}{2} \le \text{Cos}^{-1}\,z \le \frac{\pi}{2}?$$

34. Define $\text{Cot}^{-1}\,y$.

Set C

Which statements below are true and which are false?

35. $\text{Sin}^{-1}\,1 + \text{Sin}^{-1}\,(-1) = 0$

36. $\text{Cos}^{-1}\,1 + \text{Cos}^{-1}\,(-1) = 0$

37. $\text{Sin}^{-1}\,x = -\text{Sin}^{-1}\,(-x)$ for all x in the domain of Sin^{-1}

38. $\text{Arccos}\,x = \text{Arccos}\,(-x)$ for all x in the domain of Arccos

39. If $\theta = \text{Arccos}\,t$, express t as a function of θ. What is the domain of the function you have written?

40. If $r = \frac{1}{2}\,\text{Sin}^{-1}\,u$, express u as a function of r. What is the range of u as a function of r?

41. Solve

$$3y = 4 - 2\,\text{Cos}^{-1}\,x$$

for x in terms of y. What is the domain of the function of y?

42. Solve

$$a^2 = b^2 + c^2 - 2bc\,\text{Cos}\,A$$

for A.

43. For what real number x is $\text{Arcsin}\,(2x^2 - 2x) = -\pi/6$?

44. For what real number x is $\text{Cos}^{-1}\,(3x - 1) = \pi/3$?

Calculator Problem

For what real number x is

$$\text{Sin}^{-1}\,(0.9x - 1.3) = \pi/5?$$

Applications of the Inverse Functions

We consider some examples.

Example 1   The law of cosines states that in a triangle, with the usual notation,

$$a^2 = b^2 + c^2 - 2bc \cos A.$$

Because in any triangle $m(\angle A)$ is a number in $\langle 0, \pi \rangle$, we have

$$\cos A = \frac{b^2 + c^2 - a^2}{2bc},$$

and, by definition,

$$A = \text{Arccos} \frac{b^2 + c^2 - a^2}{2bc}.$$

2   Find $\sin (\text{Arcsin } u)$.

Solution. Evidently the answer is u, for u is the sine of any number (or angle) whose sine is u: $\sin (\text{Arcsin } u) = u$.

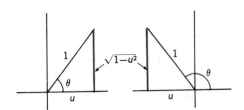

FIGURE 6

However, if we try to find $\sin (\text{Arccos } u)$, the problem is more difficult. Suppose $y = \sin (\text{Arccos } u)$. Let $\theta = \text{Arccos } u$. Then $u = \text{Cos } \theta$ and $y = \sin \theta$. By the definition of Cos, θ must be in $[0, \pi]$, so the two graphs in Fig. 6 apply to the problem. If $u \geq 0$, then $0 \leq \theta \leq \pi/2$ and $\sin \theta = \sqrt{1 - u^2}$. If $u < 0$, then $\pi/2 < \theta \leq \pi$ and $\sin \theta = \sqrt{1 - u^2}$. Thus in all cases, $\sin (\text{Arccos } u) = \sqrt{1 - u^2}$.

3   Show that $\text{Arctan } \frac{3}{4} + \text{Arctan } \frac{1}{4} = \text{Arctan } \frac{16}{13}$.

Solution. Let $x = \text{Arctan } \frac{3}{4}$, $y = \text{Arctan } \frac{1}{4}$ and $z = \text{Arctan } \frac{16}{13}$. We are to show that $x + y = z$.

$$\tan (x + y) = \frac{\frac{3}{4} + \frac{1}{4}}{1 - \frac{3}{4} \cdot \frac{1}{4}} = \frac{1}{1 - \frac{3}{16}} = \frac{16}{13} = \tan z.$$

Since $\tan (x + y) = \tan z$, it follows that $x + y = z$.

Problems

Set A

Find the following.

1. $\sin(\text{Sin}^{-1}\frac{1}{2})$

2. $\cos\left(\text{Cos}^{-1}\frac{\sqrt{3}}{2}\right)$

3. $\cos(\text{Sin}^{-1}\frac{3}{5})$

4. $\sin\left(\text{Cos}^{-1}\frac{-1}{\sqrt{2}}\right)$

5. $\tan\left(\text{Sin}^{-1}\frac{1}{\sqrt{2}}\right)$

6. $\tan(\text{Cos}^{-1}\frac{8}{17})$

7. Find $\cos(\text{Sin}^{-1} t)$ in terms of t.

8. Show that

$$\sin(\text{Cos}^{-1} x + \text{Sin}^{-1} y)$$
$$= \sqrt{1-x^2}\sqrt{1-y^2} + xy.$$

9. Show that

$$\sin(\text{Arcsin } x + \text{Arcsin } y)$$
$$= x\sqrt{1-y^2} + y\sqrt{1-x^2}.$$

10. Find $\tan(\text{Arctan } x + \text{Arctan } y)$ in terms of x and y.

Set B

11. Show that

$$\text{Arctan}\frac{1}{2} + \text{Arctan}\frac{1}{3} = \frac{\pi}{4}.$$

12. Show that

$$2\,\text{Arctan}\frac{1}{3} + \text{Arctan}\frac{1}{7} = \frac{\pi}{4}.$$

13. Show that

$$4\,\text{Tan}^{-1}\frac{1}{5} - \text{Tan}^{-1}\frac{1}{239} = \frac{\pi}{4}.$$

(Problems 11, 12, and 13 can be used with a calculus formula for Tan^{-1}, to compute $\pi/4$, and hence π.)

14. Show that $\text{Arcsin } x + \text{Arccos } x = \pi/2$.

15. Show that $2\,\text{Arctan}\frac{2}{3} = \text{Arctan}\frac{12}{5}$.

Set C

Compute the following.

16. $\cos(\frac{1}{2}\,\text{Sin}^{-1}\frac{4}{5})$

17. $\tan[2\,\text{Cos}^{-1}(-\frac{3}{5})]$

18. $\tan[\text{Tan}^{-1}(2+\sqrt{3}) - \text{Tan}^{-1}(2-\sqrt{3})]$

19. $\cos[\text{Sin}^{-1}(-\frac{1}{2}) + \text{Cos}^{-1}(-\frac{1}{2})]$

20. $\cos(2\,\text{Tan}^{-1}\frac{3}{4})$

21. $\sin(\text{Sin}^{-1}\frac{63}{65} + 2\,\text{Tan}^{-1}\frac{1}{5})$

22. Find $\tan[\text{Arcsin}(-\frac{8}{17}) + \text{Arccos}\frac{4}{5}]$.

Sketch the graphs of the following functions.

23. $f(x) = \text{Arctan}(\cot x)$

24. $h(x) = \text{Arccos}(\cos x)$

25. $g(x) = \text{Arcsin}(\cos x)$

26. A soccer player attempts a goal from point S in a soccer field. S is d units from the goal line and x units to the right of one side of the goal which is g units in width. Show that effective angle α for the kick to the goal is given by

$$\alpha = \text{Tan}^{-1}\frac{g+x}{d} - \text{Tan}^{-1}\frac{x}{d}.$$

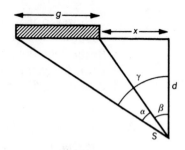

Calculator Problem

Find the measure of the angle α in Problem 26 where $d = 20$ m, $x = 5.5$ m and $g = 7.3$ m.

Trigonometric Equations

Equations involving the trigonometric functions, or their inverses, occur in applications with considerable frequency. Solutions of such equations can be either quite trivial or quite difficult. There are no general rules, so we shall examine a few equations.

Example 1 Solve $\sin \theta = 1/\sqrt{2}$ for θ.

Solution. Clearly,

$$\theta = \frac{\pi}{4} + 2\pi n \quad \text{or} \quad \theta = \frac{3\pi}{4} + 2\pi n, \text{ where } n \text{ is an integer.}$$

2 Solve $\tan x + \cot x = -2$.

Solution. We have

$$\tan x + \frac{1}{\tan x} = -2,$$

which is equivalent to the *quadratic* equation

$$\tan^2 x + 2 \tan x + 1 = 0,$$
$$(\tan x + 1)^2 = 0.$$

Then

$$\tan x = -1,$$

$$x = -\frac{\pi}{4} + n\pi,$$

where n is an integer. Substituting x into the original equation, we have

$$\tan \left(-\frac{\pi}{4} + n\pi \right) + \cot \left(-\frac{\pi}{4} + n\pi \right) = -2;$$

using the addition formulas (and the fact that $\tan (n\pi)$ is 0 where n is an integer), we get $-1 + (-1) = -2$, and our solution is correct.

3 Solve $\tan x + x = \pi/4$.

Solution. This innocent-appearing problem is much more troublesome to handle than the previous problem. Let us write the equation in the equivalent form

$$\tan x = \frac{\pi}{4} - x,$$

and let us graph the two functions

$$y = \tan x, \quad y = \frac{\pi}{4} - x.$$

Their graphs are the colored and dashed curves, respectively, in Fig. 7.

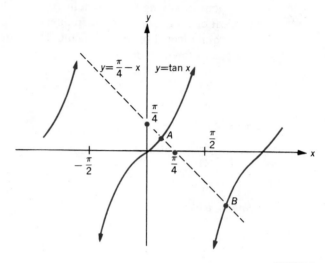

FIGURE 7

From the graphs we see that there are crossings at A, B, and infinitely many other points.

Let us try to locate A with some accuracy. From a table or a calculator we find that

$$\tan \frac{\pi}{8} = 0.4142,$$

whereas

$$\frac{\pi}{4} - \frac{\pi}{8} = \frac{\pi}{8} = 0.3927.$$

Therefore the solution is somewhat less than $\pi/8$. A process of successive trial and error with use of the tables or calculator would enable us to find the x-coordinate of A more accurately. Thus when $x = 0.38275$,

$$\tan 0.38275 = 0.4026049$$

and

$$\frac{\pi}{4} - 0.38275 = 0.4026481$$

But there is no direct method giving an exact decimal answer. The best one can hope for is a sequence of consecutively better approximations. In calculus, there are quick methods which will give excellent approximations to the roots of such equations.

Problems

Set A

Find all θ, $0 < \theta < 2\pi$, such that:

1 $\sin \theta = -\sqrt{3}/2$ **2.** $\cos \theta = 1/\sqrt{2}$

3. $\tan \theta = -1$ **4.** $\cos \theta = -1$

5. $\sin \theta = 1$ **6.** $\tan \theta = -1/\sqrt{3}$

Find all A, $0 < A < 360$, such that:

7. $\sin A° = 0.2334$ **8.** $\tan A° = -2.322$

9. $\cos A° = 0.8059$ **10.** $\sin A° = -0.5592$

11. $\cos A° = -0.6401$ **12.** $\tan A° = -1.753$

Set B

Solve for θ, $0 \le \theta < 2\pi$.

13. $4 \sin^2 \theta + 1 = 8 \cos \theta$

14. $4 \cot \theta - \tan \theta = 3$

15. $\sin^2 \theta + \sin \theta - 1 = 0$

16. $2 \sin^2 \theta + \cos \theta = 1$

17. $2 \cos^2 \theta - 3 \sin \theta = 0$

18. $2 \sin \theta + \csc \theta = 3$

19. $4 = 2 \sin^2 \theta + 5 \cos \theta$

20. $\sin 2\theta = \frac{1}{2}$

21. $3 \cot \theta = \tan \theta$

22. $\tan 3\theta = 1$

23. $\sin^2 \theta + 3 \cos^2 \theta = 2$

24. $\sin 2\theta = -\frac{1}{3}$

Set C

Solve for θ.

25. $\cos 2\theta + 3 \cos \theta - 1 = 0$

26. $\sin 2\theta = \sin \theta$

27. $\cos \theta + \cos 2\theta = 0$

28. $\cos 2\theta = \cos^2 \theta$

29. $\cos \theta + \cos 2\theta + 2 \sin^2 \theta = 0$

30. $\sin 4\theta - \sin 2\theta = \cos 3\theta$

31. $\cos 3\theta + \cos \theta = 0$

32. $\sin 2\theta = 2 \cos \theta$

33. $\cos 5\theta + \cos 3\theta = 0$

Find the θ such that $|\theta|$ is as small as possible, given that:

34. $2 \sin \theta - \theta = 0$ **35.** $\cos \theta = \theta$

36. $\cos \theta = \theta^2$ **37.** $\tan \theta = 1 + \theta$

Calculator Problem

Locate θ correct to the nearest ten-thousandth of a radian so that $\cos \theta = \frac{1}{2}\theta - 1$.

Summary

1. In order to define *functions* inverse to the circular functions, it was necessary to restrict the domains of the circular functions. Thus, the Sin, Cos, and Tan functions were defined by

$$\text{Sin } \theta = \sin \theta, \qquad -\frac{\pi}{2} \le \theta \le \frac{\pi}{2};$$

$$\text{Cos } \theta = \cos \theta, \qquad 0 \le \theta \le \pi;$$

$$\text{Tan } \theta = \tan \theta, \qquad -\frac{\pi}{2} < \theta < \frac{\pi}{2}.$$

The inverses to these functions are

$$\begin{aligned}
\text{Arcsin } x &= \text{Sin}^{-1} x, & -1 &\le x \le 1; \\
\text{Arccos } x &= \text{Cos}^{-1} x, & -1 &\le x \le 1; \\
\text{Arctan } x &= \text{Tan}^{-1} x & -\infty &< x < \infty.
\end{aligned}$$

You should also know the graphs, as well as the definitions, of these functions.

2. Trigonometric equations are easy to solve if they can be reduced to the form

(a circular function of θ) = (a number).

Then one can obtain θ from tables of the functions. However, not all equations can be reduced to this simple form.

Chapter 8   Test

8-2   Give the range and domain of the following.

  1. Arcsine   **2.** Arccosine   **3.** Arctangent

  4. Sketch a graph of $\theta = \text{Sin}^{-1} y$.

  5. Sketch a graph of $\theta = \text{Tan}^{-1} y$.

  Answer true or false.

  6. $\text{Tan}^{-1}(-x) = -(\text{Tan}^{-1} x)$

  7. $\text{Sin}^{-1}(-x) = -(\text{Sin}^{-1} x)$

  8. $\text{Cos}^{-1}(-x) = -(\text{Cos}^{-1} x)$

  9. Why is the following statement false?

$$\text{Cos}^{-1}\left(-\frac{1}{2}\right) = \text{Sin}^{-1}\frac{\sqrt{3}}{2}$$

8-3   Compute the following.

  10. $\text{Cos}^{-1}\left(-\dfrac{\sqrt{3}}{2}\right)$

  11. $\tan^{-1}(1)$ (Give all possible values.)

  12. $\cos\left(\text{Cos}^{-1}\frac{12}{13}\right)$

  13. $\text{Tan}^{-1}\left(\tan\dfrac{\pi}{7}\right)$

  Compute the following.

  14. $\sin\left[\text{Tan}^{-1}(-1)\right]$

  15. $\sin\left(2\,\text{Tan}^{-1}\dfrac{1}{\sqrt{3}}\right)$

  16. $\sin\left(2\,\text{Sin}^{-1}\frac{4}{5} + \text{Cos}^{-1}\frac{1}{3}\right)$

  17. $\cos\left(2\,\text{Sin}^{-1}\frac{4}{5} + \text{Cos}^{-1}\frac{1}{3}\right)$

  18. Prove that $\text{Sin}^{-1} x + \text{Cos}^{-1} x = \pi/2$.

8-4   **19.** Solve the equation for x.

$$6\sin^2 x - \sin x - 1 = 0$$

  20. Given $4\cos\theta - 4\sin^2\theta + 5 = 0$, find θ such that $0 \le \theta \le 2\pi$.

  21. Show that the only real numbers in $[0, \pi]$ satisfying $\sin\theta + \cos\theta = 1$ are 0 and $\pi/2$.

  22. Find all real numbers θ in $(0, 2\pi)$ such that $\sin^2\theta - \cos^2\theta - \cos\theta = 1$.

  23. Solve $2\cos\theta = \theta - \pi/3$ for θ by graphing. Estimate θ as accurately as you can.

Chapter 9
Functions on the Natural Numbers

9-1   Introduction

This chapter is concerned with a variety of topics that have a common theme. In each topic one encounters functions whose domains are the set of *natural numbers*, $N = \{1, 2, 3, \ldots, n, \ldots\}$.

Any function whose domain is N is called a sequence, and we first consider sequences whose image set is the real numbers. Then other sequences will occur.

In the course of all this we will meet combinatorial problems (that is, problems of counting) and also the important proof technique called mathematical induction.

9-2   Sequences

A *sequence* is simply a function whose domain is the set of natural numbers, $N = \{1, 2, 3, \ldots, n, \ldots\}$. Its most general form is given by the following definition.

Definition 9-1   Let Y be any set of objects and let f be a function whose domain is N and whose range is in Y. Then f is called a *Y-valued sequence*. If $Y = R$ the sequence is called a *real* sequence.

Thus, a sequence f is known when its nth term $f(n)$ is known. Instead of representing sequences by the usual functional symbols f, g, a, etc., and their values at n by $f(n)$, $g(n)$, $a(n)$, etc., it is customary to use a subscript notation. The values of the sequences at the natural number n are denoted by f_n, g_n, a_n, ... The sequences as a whole are denoted by $\{f_n\}$, $\{g_n\}$, $\{a_n\}$, ...

In this chapter we shall be concerned mostly with real sequences.

Remark   The sequences we have defined are usually called *infinite* sequences because their domains are the infinite set N. In practice, however, one also encounters *finite* sequences. These are functions defined only for natural numbers not exceeding some fixed number. Thus, we say that f is a *finite sequence* if f is defined only on the set $\{1, 2, \ldots, n\}$ for some given natural number n.

There is a bewildering variety of sequences, some of which are quite bizarre. The two important types we wish to consider are:

1. *Arithmetic sequences* (progressions*):

$$a, a + d, a + 2d, \ldots, a + (n - 1)d, \ldots,$$

where a and d are given numbers (the *first term* and the *common difference*) and n is a natural number. The nth term of the sequence is $a + (n - 1)d$.

2. *Geometric sequences* (progressions):

$$a, ar, ar^2, \ldots, ar^{n-1}, \ldots,$$

where a and r are given numbers (the *first term* and the *common ratio*) and n is a natural number. The nth term of the sequence is ar^{n-1}.

Example 1   Sequences can be given by simple formulas. For example, if the nth term of a sequence is given by

$$a_n = n^2 - 1 \quad \text{for} \quad n = 1, 2, 3, \ldots,$$

then the terms of the sequence are

$$a_1 = 0, \quad a_2 = 3, \quad a_3 = 8, \quad \ldots, \quad a_n = n^2 - 1, \quad \ldots.$$

2   Let p_n be the perimeter of a regular polygon of n sides inscribed in a circle of radius a. (Necessarily now $n \geq 3$.) We have the sequence

$$3\sqrt{3}\,a, \, 4\sqrt{2}\,a, \ldots, p_n, \ldots.$$

When n is large, what does p_n approach?

3   Consider the decimal expansion of π,

$$\pi = 3.141592653589 \ldots.$$

Let a_n be 0 if the digit in the nth decimal place is even. Let a_n be 1 if the nth digit is odd. We get the sequence

$$1, 0, 1, 1, 1, 0, 0, 1, 1, 1, 0, 1, \ldots, a_n, \ldots.$$

4   *Harmonic sequences* are sequences whose terms are reciprocals of the terms of arithmetic sequences. When we speak of *the* harmonic sequence we mean the special sequence

$$1, \frac{1}{2}, \frac{1}{3}, \ldots, \frac{1}{n}, \ldots.$$

In many applications one has to add the successive terms of a real sequence. This leads to the concept of the sum of the first n terms of a sequence.

---

*The term "progression" is sometimes used for sequence, especially in older books, and with reference to arithmetic or geometric sequences.

Definition 9-2 For a real sequence, $a_1, a_2, a_3, \ldots, a_n, \ldots$, the successive sums are

$$S_1 = a_1,$$
$$S_2 = a_1 + a_2,$$
$$\vdots$$
$$S_n = a_1 + a_2 + \cdots + a_n.$$

These sums form a new sequence, $\{S_n\}$.

In Definition 9-2 we have a lengthy indicated sum for S_n. Because such sums occur frequently, a shorthand notation is convenient. The notation uses the Greek letter Σ (sigma) to suggest sum. The following definition and example will explain its use.

Definition 9-3 Given the sequence $\{a_n\}$, $S_n = \displaystyle\sum_{k=1}^{n} a_k = a_1 + a_2 + \cdots + a_n.$

Remark The letter k is a so-called *dummy variable*. Any letter would do as well.

Example 5 If $a_k = 2k - 1$ for $k \in \{1, 2, 3, \ldots\}$, then

$$\sum_{k=1}^{5} a_k = \sum_{k=1}^{5} (2k - 1) = 1 + 3 + 5 + 7 + 9.$$

Our first objective is to find formulas for the first n terms of arithmetic and geometric sequences. These sums are

$$A_n = a + (a + d) + \cdots + [a + (n - 1)d] = \sum_{k=1}^{n} [a + (k - 1)d],$$

$$G_n = a + ar + \cdots + ar^{n-1} = \sum_{k=1}^{n} ar^{k-1}.$$

Formulas for both these sums can be found by a little manipulation. For A_n we can reverse the order of addition to obtain

$$A_n = \quad a \quad + \quad (a + d) \quad + \cdots + [a + (n - 1)d],$$
$$A_n = [a + (n - 1)d] + [a + (n - 2)d] + \cdots + \quad a$$

Then, by addition of the two forms for A_n, we get

$$2A_n = [2a + (n - 1)d] + [2a + (n - 1)d] + \cdots + [2a + (n - 1)d],$$

from which, since there are n terms on the right-hand side, we have

$$2A_n = n[2a + (n - 1)d] \quad \text{and} \quad A_n = \tfrac{1}{2}n[2a + (n - 1)d].$$

Since the last, or nth, term of the arithmetic sequence is $a_n = a + (n - 1)d$, we can also write

$$A_n = \tfrac{1}{2}n(a + a_n) = n\left(\frac{a + a_n}{2}\right).$$

The sum is n times the arithmetic mean of the first and last terms.

Example 6   The sum of the first seven terms of the arithmetic sequence with first term 13 and common difference $d = -2$ is

$$A_7 = 13 + 11 + 9 + 7 + 5 + 3 + 1 = \tfrac{1}{2}(7)(13 + 1) = 49.$$

Note that the last, or seventh term is $13 + (7 - 1)(-2) = 1$.

7   To find the common difference of an arithmetic sequence if the first term is 2 and the sum of the first eight terms is 58, we have

$$A_8 = \tfrac{1}{2}(8)[2(2) + (7)d] = 58.$$

Solving for d gives $d = \tfrac{3}{2}$.

For G_n the sum of the first n terms of a geometric sequence, we proceed differently. On the one hand,

$$G_{n+1} = a + ar + \cdots + ar^{n-1} + ar^n = G_n + ar^n.$$

But we also have

$$G_{n+1} = a + r(a + ar + \cdots + ar^{n-1}) = a + rG_n.$$

Equating these two formulas for G_{n+1} and solving for G_n, we get

$$G_n + ar^n = a + rG_n,$$
$$G_n(1 - r) = a - ar^n,$$

so that

$$G_n = \frac{a - ar^n}{1 - r}.$$

Example 8   The sum of the first eight terms of the geometric sequence with first term 2 and common ratio 2 is

$$G_8 = 2 + 4 + 8 + 16 + 32 + 64 + 128 + 256$$
$$= \frac{2 - (2)2^8}{1 - 2}$$
$$= 2^9 - 2 = 510.$$

Problems

Set A

Write the first six terms of the sequences whose general terms are given.

1. $a_n = \dfrac{n}{2}$ **2.** $a_n = 2n - 1$

3. $a_n = 2n$ **4.** $a_n = n^2$

5. $a_n = \frac{1}{2}(2^n)$ **6.** $a_n = |2 - n|$

7. $a_n = 2(\frac{1}{3})^{n-1}$ **8.** $a_n = \dfrac{n(n + 1)}{2}$

9. $a_n = (-1)^n \cdot \dfrac{1}{n}$

10. The first term of an arithmetic sequence is 3 and the common difference is $-\frac{1}{3}$. Find the seventh term and the sum of the first seven terms.

11. What are the first five terms of the arithmetic sequence with $a = 5$ and $d = -\frac{2}{3}$? Find the sum of 32 terms.

12. The first two terms of an arithmetic sequence are 11 and $9\frac{1}{2}$, respectively. Find the sum of the first ten terms.

13. The first and second terms of an arithmetic sequence are 7 and 4, respectively. Is -17 one of the terms? If so, which one? Is -52 one of the terms?

14. The first term of a geometric sequence is 5 and the common ratio is $-\frac{1}{2}$. Find the tenth term and the sum of ten terms.

15. The first two terms of a geometric sequence are 1 and $\frac{2}{3}$, respectively. Find the sum of the first six terms.

16. The first two terms of a geometric sequence are 2 and -1. Is $\frac{1}{8}$ one of the terms? If so, which one? Is $-\frac{1}{128}$ one of the terms?

Set B

Find the stated term in the arithmetic sequence.

17. The ninth term of $2, -1, -4, \ldots$

18. The twelfth term of $2, 5, 8, \ldots$

19. The eighth term of $\frac{2}{3}, 1, \frac{4}{3}, \ldots$

20. A ball rolls down an inclined plane, traveling 34.3 cm during the first second. In each succeeding second it travels 68.6 cm more than in the preceding one. How far does it roll in eight seconds?

21. An object falling in a vacuum falls 4.9 m the first second. In each succeeding second it falls 14.7 m more than it did in the previous second. How far would the object fall in ten seconds?

Write out the terms in each of the following. You need not find the sums.

22. $\displaystyle\sum_{i=1}^{6} (2i - 1)$ **23.** $\displaystyle\sum_{k=1}^{5} k^2$

24. $\displaystyle\sum_{n=1}^{7} \dfrac{1}{n}$ **25.** $\displaystyle\sum_{k=1}^{9} k$

26. $\displaystyle\sum_{k=1}^{4} |1 - n|$ **27.** $\displaystyle\sum_{i=1}^{6} (-1)^i i^2$

Which of the following are sums of terms of arithmetic sequences? of geometric sequences?

28. $\displaystyle\sum_{k=1}^{7} (3k + 1)$ **29.** $\displaystyle\sum_{n=1}^{5} (1 - 2n)$

30. $\displaystyle\sum_{n=1}^{5} 3(\frac{1}{2})^n$ **31.** $\displaystyle\sum_{k=1}^{8} (k + 1)^2$

32. $\displaystyle\sum_{m=1}^{1000} (-1)^m 2^{2m}$ **33.** $\displaystyle\sum_{n=1}^{10} (-1)^n (1 - n + n^2)$

Set C

34. The fifth term of an arithmetic sequence is 3; the fifteenth term is 8. What is the sequence?

35. Obtain a formula for the sum of the first n natural numbers.

36. Obtain a formula for the sum of the first n odd numbers.

37. Obtain a formula for the sum of the first n even numbers.

38. Find the sum of ten terms of the geometric sequence with $a = 1$ and $r = 2$. About how many digits has the sum of 50 terms?

39. A person contributes 1 cent to a charity and writes letters to two friends requesting each to contribute 1 cent and write similar letters to two friends. Let us assume that all comply. How many dollars would the charity receive after 100 sets of letters were written?

40. The *Fibonacci sequence** is a famous sequence with many interesting properties. It is defined as follows:

$$a_1 = 1, \quad a_2 = 1, \quad \text{and} \quad a_n = a_{n-1} + a_{n-2}$$
for $n > 2$.

(a) Write the first 15 terms of this sequence.
(b) Find the sum of the first three terms of the sequence.
(c) Find the sum of the first four terms of the sequence.
(d) Find the sum of the first five terms of the sequence.
(e) The sum of the first k terms of the Fibonacci sequence is 143. What number is k?
(f) Give a formula for the sum of the first n terms of the sequence.

Calculator Problem

Suppose you accepted a job in which your pay for each day's work for a month of 31 days is 1 cent for the first day, 1 cent for the second day, 2 cents for the third day, 3 cents for the fourth day, 5 cents for the fifth day and so on so that the number of cents earned each day form the Fibonacci sequence. (See Problem 40 above.)

(a) Find the total amount you would earn in 31 days.
(b) Show that the ratio of the 31st Fibonacci number to the 30th Fibonacci number is a good approximation of the "Golden Ratio," $(1 + \sqrt{5})/2$.

9–3   Series

In many applications one has to add the successive terms of a real sequence. There is a difficulty, however, because one cannot add infinitely many numbers. This leads to the notion of an infinite series.†

Definition 9–4   For the real sequence $a_1, a_2, a_3, \ldots, a_n, \ldots$, the indicated sum of the terms is called an *infinite series:*

$$a_1 + a_2 + a_3 + \cdots + a_n + \cdots = \sum_{n=1}^{\infty} a_n.$$

---

*Named after Leonardo of Pisa, an Italian mathematician of the thirteenth century whose nickname was Fibonacci, which means the "stutterer."

†The reader should not confuse the words "sequence" and "series." In common English usage the two words are synonymous, but in mathematics they are distinct. A sequence is a function on the natural numbers and a series is an "infinite sum."

The partial sums of this series are the following numbers:

$$S_1 = a_1,$$
$$S_2 = a_1 + a_2,$$
$$\vdots$$
$$S_n = a_1 + a_2 + \cdots + a_n = \sum_{k=1}^{n} a_k.$$

They form a new sequence, $\{S_n\}$, the sequence of partial sums.

The infinite series defined above can now be given meaning in terms of S_n.

Definition 9-5 The sum of the infinite series

$$\sum_{n=1}^{\infty} a_n = a_1 + a_2 + a_3 + \cdots + a_n + \cdots$$

is the *limit* of its sequence of partial sums (if that limit exists):

$$S = \lim_{n \to \infty} S_n. \tag{1}$$

By this we mean that as n becomes infinite, the partial sums S_n approach, arbitrarily closely, the number S.

Here the object of study is *defined* to be a limit. Just as in geometry, where the circumference of a circle is defined to be the limit of the perimeters of inscribed polygons, so the object of our study is a limit of a sequence of finite approximations.

In this section we shall be concerned only with infinite geometric series, and we shall see that if the absolute value of the common ratio is less than 1, then the limit (1) exists. For geometric series it is easy to see what the limit must be. The reader who would like a more systematic discussion of limits should consult Section 9-8.

For the geometric series

$$a + ar + ar^2 + \cdots = \sum_{n=1}^{\infty} ar^{n-1}$$

the nth partial sum is

$$G_n = \frac{a - ar^n}{1 - r} = \frac{a}{1 - r} - \frac{ar^n}{1 - r}. \tag{2}$$

When n is very large the second term in (2) is very small and approaches 0 as n becomes infinite if $|r| < 1$ Therefore, the limit of the sequence is

$$G = \lim_{n \to \infty} G_n = \lim_{n \to \infty} \frac{a - ar^n}{1 - r} = \frac{a}{1 - r} \qquad \text{if} \quad |r| < 1.$$

Example 1   The geometric series

$$\frac{1}{2} + \frac{1}{4} + \frac{1}{8} + \cdots + \frac{1}{2^n} + \cdots$$

has as its first term $a = \frac{1}{2}$ and as its ratio $r = \frac{1}{2}$. Since $|r| < 1$, the sum of the series, by the formula above, is

$$\frac{\frac{1}{2}}{1 - \frac{1}{2}} = 1.$$

FIGURE 1

The geometric significance of this series on the real line is shown in Fig. 1. The partial sums G_n "sneak up" on 1.

2   Repeating decimals are infinite geometric series. For example,

$$0.78\overline{18181} = 0.7 + 0.081 + 0.00081 + \cdots,$$

where the bar over the digits 81 means that they repeat indefinitely. The terms following the first form a geometric series with ratio $r = 0.01$. Therefore

$$0.78\overline{18181} = 0.7 + \frac{0.081}{1 - 0.01} = \frac{7}{10} + \frac{81}{990}$$

$$= \frac{7}{10} + \frac{9}{110} = \frac{86}{110} = \frac{43}{55}.$$

We can check this by dividing 43 by 55 to obtain the original decimal.

Problems

Set A

Find the sum of the following infinite series.

1. $\frac{1}{3} + (\frac{1}{3} \cdot \frac{2}{3}) + \cdots + \frac{1}{3}(\frac{2}{3})^n + \cdots$

2. $\frac{1}{10} + \frac{1}{10^2} + \cdots + \frac{1}{10^n} + \cdots$

3. $0.3 + 0.03 + 0.003 + \cdots$

4. $2 + 1 + \frac{1}{2} + \frac{1}{4} + \cdots$

5. $0.9 + 0.09 + 0.009 + \cdots$

6. $0.1 + 0.06 + 0.036 + 0.0216 + \cdots$

Use geometric series to express as quotients of integers the rational numbers given by the following repeating decimals.

7. $0.444\ldots$ **8.** $0.\overline{27}$ **9.** $31.\overline{09}$

10. $-2.2\overline{3}$ **11.** $0.\overline{245}$ **12.** $1.2\overline{34}$

Set B

Find the sum of the following infinite series.

13. $\displaystyle\sum_{k=1}^{\infty} (-\frac{1}{2})^k$ **14.** $\displaystyle\sum_{n=1}^{\infty} \frac{3}{(\sqrt{2})^n}$

15. $\displaystyle\sum_{n=1}^{\infty} (\frac{1}{3})^{2n}$ **16.** $\displaystyle\sum_{n=1}^{\infty} 2(0.1)^n$

17. $\displaystyle\sum_{n=1}^{\infty} \frac{5}{(\sqrt{5})^n}$ **18.** $\displaystyle\sum_{n=1}^{\infty} \left(\frac{1}{e}\right)^n$

19. A ball is dropped from a height h and bounces to 0.9 its previous height after each bounce. What is the total distance traveled?

Set C

20. Show that the sum of the infinite geometric series, with $|x| < 1$,

$$1 + x + x^2 + x^3 + \cdots + x^n + \cdots,$$

is $1/(1 - x)$. Use long division on this result to recover the original series.

21. Show that if the common ratio r in a geometric series is such that $|r| > 1$, then the sequence of partial sums cannot have a limit.

22. Suppose that $d > 0$ in an arithmetic sequence. Show that the sum, A_n, of the first n terms becomes arbitrarily large as n becomes infinite. What happens if $d < 0$?

Calculator Problem

Show that the infinite series

$$\frac{1}{4} + \frac{1}{16} + \frac{1}{64} + \frac{1}{256} + \cdots + \frac{1}{4^n} + \cdots$$

has a sum of $\frac{1}{3}$. Use a calculator to find how many terms of the series must be added together to give the sum correct to five decimal places, that is 0.33333.

9-4   Mathematical Induction

In this section we are concerned with a method of proof called mathematical induction. The situation that prevails is that we have a *sequence of statements,* $P(1), P(2), \ldots, P(n), \ldots$ for each natural number n, and we wish to prove that each is a true statement.

Observe that we do have a sequence in the sense of Definition 9–1: For each n the value of the function, $P(n)$, is not a number but a *statement.* Thus $\{P(n)\}$ is a statement-valued sequence instead of a real-valued sequence.

The method of mathematical induction depends on a fundamental property possessed by the natural numbers, $N = \{1, 2, 3, \ldots, n, \ldots\}$, called the Induction Principle.

THE INDUCTION PRINCIPLE

If S is a set of natural numbers such that

    (a) *1 is in S, and,*

    (b) *whenever k is in S, this implies that k + 1 is in S,*

then S is the set of all natural numbers: S = N.

This principle simply describes the set which we *define* as the natural numbers. It states carefully what each of us learned as a child. "The whole numbers are those you get by counting from 1—that is, starting with 1 and adding 1 again and again."

One amusing way of looking at the principle is to regard it as the "domino effect." Imagine an infinite set of dominoes (one for each natural number) lined up not too far apart (Fig. 2). Then, if the first one is toppled over, eventually each one must fall. But

(a) one must be sure to topple the first domino;
(b) one must be sure that the kth domino topples the $(k + 1)$th domino.

FIGURE 2

Part (a) of the Induction Principle is called the *anchor*. If part (a) is true, the induction is *anchored*. Part (b) begins "whenever k is in S..." The assumption "k is in S" is called the *inductive hypothesis*. Let us see how the Induction Principle can supply proofs.

Example 1   Prove that the sum of the first n natural numbers is $n(n + 1)/2$; that is, the statement P_n is true for all natural numbers n, where

$$P_n: \quad 1 + 2 + 3 + \cdots + n = \frac{n(n + 1)}{2}.$$

Solution.

Let S be the set of all natural numbers n for which P_n is true. To prove that P_n is true for all n we must show that $S = N$. We do this as follows.

(a) 1 is in S because P_1 asserts that

$$1 = \frac{1(1 + 1)}{2} = 1,$$

which is true. The induction is *anchored*.
(b) Suppose k is in S. Then P_k is true, that is,

$$1 + 2 + 3 + \cdots + k = \frac{k(k + 1)}{2}. \tag{1}$$

This is the *inductive hypothesis*. We must show that this statement implies P_{k+1}.

We have, by the inductive hypothesis,

$$1 + 2 + \cdots + k = \frac{k(k + 1)}{2}.$$

Adding $k + 1$ to both sides of equation (1) we get

$$1 + 2 + \cdots + k + (k + 1) = \frac{k(k + 1)}{2} + (k + 1) = \frac{(k + 1)(k + 2)}{2}.$$

But this is precisely P_{k+1}. By assuming that k is in S, we have shown that $k + 1$ must be in S. This proves part (b) and completes the induction; $S = N$ and P_n is true for all n.

Remark

What we have done in the example is establish that our *guess* for the formula is really correct. But no hint is given as to how one guesses what to try. Observe that in this particular example we did not need to guess because 1, 2, ..., n, ... is an arithmetic sequence and the formula for A_n in Section 9–2 could have been used. The importance of the Induction Principle lies in its use in proofs where some simple trick fails to work.

Example 2

Find the sum of the first n odd numbers.

Solution. With no clues as to how to proceed we do some computing:

$$1 = 1^2,$$ the first odd number,
$$1 + 3 = 4 = 2^2,$$ the sum of the first two odd numbers,
$$1 + 3 + 5 = 9 = 3^2,$$ the sum of the first three odd numbers.

Because the nth odd number is $2n - 1$, we conjecture that

$$P_n: \quad 1 + 3 + \cdots + (2n - 1) = n^2, \text{ for all natural numbers } n.$$

We prove our conjecture by induction.

(a) The induction is anchored by the computation that led to the conjecture, that is, $1 = 1^2$.

(b) Assume that P_k is true. Then $1 + 3 + 5 + \cdots + (2k - 1) = k^2$.

The $(k + 1)$th odd number is $2k + 1$; hence by the inductive hypothesis, and by adding $2k + 1$ to both sides of the equation for P_k, we have

$$1 + 3 + \cdots + (2k - 1) + (2k + 1) = k^2 + (2k + 1),$$
$$1 + 3 + \cdots + (2k - 1) + (2k + 1) = (k + 1)^2.$$

But this is precisely the statement of P_{k+1}. This completes the induction. P_n is true for all natural numbers n.

3

One can also establish inequalities by induction. Let P_n be the statement

$$P_n: \quad (1 + x)^n \geq 1 + nx \quad \text{if} \quad 1 + x > 0.$$

This is called *Bernoulli's inequality* and is often useful in proofs in advanced analysis.

(a) To anchor the induction we have $P_1: \quad (1 + x)^1 = 1 + x \geq 1 + 1 \cdot x$.

(b) The inductive hypothesis is $P_k: \quad (1 + x)^k \geq 1 + kx$.

To show that P_k implies P_{k+1} we multiply both sides of the statement P_k by $1 + x$ and obtain

$$(1 + x)^k(1 + x) = (1 + x)^{k+1} \geq (1 + kx)(1 + x).$$

Because $1 + x > 0$, the sense of the inequality is preserved. Then

$$(1 + x)^{k+1} \geq (1 + kx)(1 + x) = 1 + (k + 1)x + kx^2,$$
$$(1 + x)^{k+1} \geq 1 + (k + 1)x, \quad \text{as} \quad kx^2 \geq 0.$$

The last inequality is simply P_{k+1}, and the proof is complete.

Problems

Set A

Prove by induction that the following statements are true for all natural numbers n.

1. $2 + 4 + \cdots + 2n = n(n + 1)$

2. $1 + 4 + 7 + \cdots + (3n - 2) = \frac{1}{2}n(3n - 1)$

3. $2 + 7 + 12 + \cdots + (5n - 3) = \frac{1}{2}n(5n - 1)$

4. $1^2 + 2^2 + \cdots + n^2 = \frac{1}{6}n(n + 1)(2n + 1)$

5. $1^2 + 3^2 + \cdots + (2n - 1)^2$
   $= \frac{1}{3}n(2n - 1)(2n + 1)$

6. $1^3 + 2^3 + \cdots + n^3 = \frac{1}{4}n^2(n + 1)^2$

7. $\frac{1}{2} + \frac{1}{2^2} + \frac{1}{2^3} + \cdots + \frac{1}{2^n} = 1 - \frac{1}{2^n}$

8. $100 + 97 + 94 + \cdots + (103 - 3n) = \frac{1}{2}n(203 - 3n)$

Set B

Prove by mathematical induction.

9. $2^n > n$

10. $3^n \geq 2n + 1$

11. $r^n < s^n$ if $0 < r < s$

12. $n^3 + 2n$ is divisible by 3

13. $3^{2n} - 1$ is divisible by 8

14. $\frac{1}{1 \cdot 2} + \frac{1}{2 \cdot 3} + \cdots + \frac{1}{n(n + 1)} = \frac{n}{n + 1}$

   [*Hint:* There is a neat short proof if one observes that

   $$\frac{1}{k(k + 1)} = \frac{1}{k} - \frac{1}{k + 1}.]$$

Set C

15. Using induction, prove the formula for the sum A_n of an arithmetic series,

    $$A_n = \frac{1}{2}n[2a + (n - 1)d].$$

16. Using induction, prove the formula for the sum G_n of a geometric series,

    $$G_n = \frac{a - ar^n}{1 - r}.$$

Prove by mathematical induction.

17. $x^n - y^n$ is divisible by $x - y$

18. $x^{2n+1} + y^{2n+1}$ is divisible by $x + y$

19. $1 \cdot 2 + 2 \cdot 3 + \cdots + n(n + 1)$
    $= \frac{1}{3}n(n + 1)(n + 2)$

20. $\cos x + \cos 3x + \cdots + \cos(2n - 1)x$
    $= \frac{\sin 2nx}{2 \sin x}$

21. The laws of exponents for positive-integer exponents can be established by induction. Recall that $a^{n+1} = a \cdot a^n$ by definition. To prove that $a^n \cdot a^m = a^{n+m}$ for all positive integers n and m (natural numbers), we proceed as follows.

    Let S be the set of all positive integers n such that $a^n \cdot a^m = a^{n+m}$ is true for *all positive integers* m. Explain why each of the following is true.

(a) 1 is in S because $a^1 \cdot a^m = a^{m+1}$. (Why?)
(b) If k is in S, then $a^k \cdot a^m = a^{k+m}$. (Why?)

Then

$$
\begin{aligned}
a^{k+1} \cdot a^m &= (a \cdot a^k) \cdot a^m && \text{(Why?)} \\
&= a \cdot (a^k \cdot a^m) && \text{(Why?)} \\
&= a \cdot a^{k+m} && \text{(Why?)} \\
&= a^{k+m+1} && \text{(Why?)} \\
&= a^{(k+1)+m} && \text{(Why?)}
\end{aligned}
$$

This completes the induction. (Why?)

22. Using induction, prove that $(ab)^n = a^n b^n$ for all natural numbers n.

23. Using induction, prove that

$$(a^n)^m = a^{nm}$$

for all natural numbers n and m. [*Hint:* First fix n and prove the statement for all m. Then make an induction on n.]

24. What is wrong with the "proof" of the following "theorem"?

In any group of people, all members are of the same sex.

The proof is by induction on the number in a group.

(a) If there is only one person in the group, the theorem is obvious. This anchors the induction.

(b) Suppose that the theorem is true for groups of k persons and consider a group of $k + 1$ members. Take one person aside. This will leave k persons, and all of these necessarily are of the same sex. Now return the person you took aside to the group and remove another. Again the remaining group is all of one sex. Therefore the person first taken aside has the same sex as the others.

Calculator Problem

Compute each number below. Check to see if each number is divisible by 8.

(a) $3^2 - 1$ (b) $3^4 - 1$ (c) $3^6 - 1$ (d) $3^8 - 1$
(e) $3^{10} - 1$ (f) $3^{12} - 1$ (g) $3^{14} - 1$ (h) $3^{16} - 1$

Write a conjecture about all such statements of the form (a) through (h). Prove your conjecture using mathematical induction.

9–5   Permutations

In this section and the next we are concerned with certain combinatorial problems—*counting* problems in which we count the ways in which finite sets of objects can be arranged or selected. The formulas that we derive have important applications to probability and statistics, but we pursue them here for their own interest.

It is worth noting that the formulas that are obtained here for permutations are just special functions defined for certain pairs of integers.

Basic to problems of counting is the following principle.

COUNTING PRINCIPLE

If an event can occur in m ways, and if a second independent event can occur in n ways, then the two events can occur in mn ways.

Let us suppose that we have a set of n distinct objects and we select $r (\leq n)$ of them. We shall derive a formula for the number of ways in which r objects of the set of n objects can be arranged on a line.

Example 1 We have three objects a, b, and c. Using two of the three objects, let us enumerate all the arrangements (permutations) that can be made. They are

$$ab, \ ac, \ ba, \ bc, \ ca, \ cb.$$

If we list all the arrangements obtained by using all three objects, we have

$$abc, \ acb, \ bac, \ bca, \ cab, \ cba.$$

In each case there are six possible arrangements.

How many arrangements can one make of four objects, using all the objects each time? List all possibilities. (There are 24 arrangements.)

Definition 9-6 A *permutation* of a set of n different objects is an arrangement of the n objects in order, so that there is a first, a second, a third, . . . , an nth object.

Every permutation* of a set of r objects taken from a set of n different objects is called a *permutation of n objects taken r at a time.*

The number of different permutations of n objects taken r at a time is denoted† by $P(n, r)$.

From Example 1 we observe that $P(3, 2) = 6$ and $P(3, 3) = 6$. It was noted above that $P(4, 4) = 24$. It is an easy conjecture that

$$P(n, n) = n(n - 1)(n - 2) \cdots (1). \tag{1}$$

The right-hand member of equation (1) occurs with great frequency in all parts of mathematics and hence is denoted by the special symbol "$n!$":

$$n! = n(n - 1)(n - 2) \cdots (1),$$

where, of course, n must be a natural number. The number $n!$ is called "n-factorial." Then $1! = 1$, $2! = 2$, $3! = 6$, $4! = 24$, etc.

Let us verify the conjecture mentioned above:

$$P(n, n) = n!.$$

The result is really quite obvious because of the Counting Principle: The first object can be selected in n ways. This leaves $n - 1$ objects from which to choose a second object. Therefore the first two objects can be selected in $n(n - 1)$ ways. The next object can be selected in $n - 2$ ways, *and so on.* Continuing in this manner, we obtain the desired result.

---

*Thus a permutation on n distinct objects is a function, f, that maps the integers $1, \ldots, n$ one-to-one onto the set of n objects. Then $\{f(1), f(2), \ldots, f(n)\}$ is a finite sequence that includes all the n objects.

†The notation $_nP_r$ is also used.

We can also give an inductive proof that avoids the phrase "and so on."

(a) If $n = 1$, there is only one arrangement and $1 = 1!$. This anchors the induction.

(b) If $P(k, k) = k!$, then a permutation of $k + 1$ objects is made by first selecting one object ($k + 1$ possible ways to select the first in order). When this has been done, there remain k objects, and furthermore it is a different set of k objects for each choice of the first object. For each of the $k + 1$ sets of k objects there are, by the inductive hypothesis, $k!$ ways of arranging them. Therefore, by the Counting Principle

$$P(k + 1, k + 1) = (k + 1)P(k, k) = (k + 1)k! = (k + 1)!.$$

This completes the induction and the proof.

We now wish to find a formula for $P(n, r)$. We first prove that

$$P(n, r) = P(n, r - 1)(n - r + 1).$$

We can select a permutation of $r - 1$ objects in $P(n, r - 1)$ ways. Then the next object can be selected in $n - r + 1$ ways. Every permutation r of the objects is obtained in this manner. Therefore, by the Counting Principle,

$$P(n, r) = P(n, r - 1)(n - r + 1).$$

Theorem 9-1* $P(n, r) = n(n - 1) \cdots (n - r + 1) = \dfrac{n!}{(n - r)!}.$

Proof   This proof is by induction.

(a) $P(n, 1) = n = n!/(n - 1)!$. The induction is anchored.

(b) If $P(n, k) = n!/(n - k)!$ and $k < n$, then

$$P(n, k + 1) = P(n, k)(n - k)$$

$$= \frac{n!}{(n - k)!}(n - k)$$

$$= \frac{n!}{(n - k - 1)!},$$

which is the correct formula for $P(n, k + 1)$. The induction is complete.

The formula for $P(n, r)$ is almost obvious. The first of the r objects can be chosen in n ways, the second in $n - 1$ ways, *and so on,* until one reaches the rth object, which can be chosen in $n - r + 1$ ways.

Observe that $P(n, r)$ is defined for all natural numbers n and all whole numbers $r \leq n$. Thus the "permutation function" has for domain the set of all ordered pairs, (n, r), with $n \geq r$.

---

*If $r = n$, then the denominator $(n - r)! = 0!$. To make this formula valid in this case, we *define* $0! = 1$.

Example 2   A president, vice-president, and secretary are to be selected from a group of 15 people. How many different slates of candidates are possible?

Solution. A direct solution based on the Counting Principle is possible. The president can be one of 15, the vice-president one of 14, and the secretary one of 13. There are therefore $15 \cdot 14 \cdot 13 = 2730$ different slates.

Theorem 9–1 also provides a solution. There will be $P(15, 3)$ slates, because when three are selected one must be first, one second, and one third: $P(15, 3) = 15 \cdot 14 \cdot 13 = 2730$.

Problems

Set A

Evaluate the following.

1. $P(4, 3)$ **2.** $P(7, 2)$ **3.** $P(5, 5)$ **4.** $P(10, 4)$

5. If $8! = 40{,}320$, what is $9!$?

6. Six persons compete in a race. In how many different orders can the six persons finish the race if there are no ties?

7. How many different batting orders for a baseball team are possible?

8. How many three-letter "words" can be made from the alphabet if no letter is to be used more than once?

9. An automobile manufacturer makes three differently named cars, with five body types and three types of engines available for each. How many different kinds of autos does the manufacturer make?

10. What is $P(n, 1)$ if $n \geq 1$?

Set B

11. A coin is tossed eight times in succession. How many different outcomes are there for the eight tosses?

12. Prove that the number of different permutations of n objects of which p are the same and q are the same (but different from the p objects) is $n!/p! \, q!$.

13. How many different three-digit numbers (count 012 as a three-digit number) can be formed from 0, 1, 2, . . . , 9 if

(a) no repetition is permitted?
(b) repetition is permitted?

14. How many different arrangements are there of the letters of the words

(a) pester?   (b) Mississippi?

15. Show that

$$\frac{(n + 1)!}{(n - 1)!} = n^2 + n.$$

16. Show that $n[n! + (n - 1)!] = (n + 1)!$.

Set C

17. Prove that
$$P(n, r) = P(n, r - 1) + (n - r)P(n, r - 1).$$

18. A combination lock has numbers 1, 2, . . . , 10 on its dial. If an opening combination consists of dialing (after clearing the tumblers by a full rotation left to 1) three distinct numbers, right, then left, then right, how many combinations are there?

19. Four dice are tossed. What is the total number of ways they can come up? How many of these have exactly one 5 showing?

20. Four people are seated at a round table. How many seating arrangements are there? ("Rotations" of an arrangement do not change the arrangement.) Suppose five people are at the table. How many seating plans are possible? Generalize your result.

Calculator Problem

Arrange the numbers below in order of size from least to greatest.

(a) 2^{30} (b) $P(100, 4)$ (c) $\tan{(\pi/2 - 0.0000001)}$

(d) $P(13, 13)$ (e) 10^8

9-6   Combinations

We have been counting the number of permutations, or arrangements, of r objects from a set of n. We now turn to the number of such sets of r objects *without regard to order.*

Definition 9-7   A *subset* of r objects from a set of n objects is called a *combination of n objects taken r at a time.* The number of combinations of n objects taken r at a time is denoted* by $C(n, r)$.

Theorem 9-2

$$P(n, r) = r! \, C(n, r),$$

$$C(n, r) = \frac{n!}{r!(n - r)!}.$$

Note that when we apply this formula for $C(n, r)$ to the case $r = n$, we obtain

$$C(n, n) = \frac{n!}{n! \, 0!}.$$

We must use the convention of the footnote on page 213, that $0! = 1$. Then the number of combinations of n things taken n at a time comes out to be 1.

Proof   One gets all permutations by choosing a combination of r objects (this may be done in $C(n, r)$ ways) and then arranging these r objects in all ways (there are $r!$ ways). Therefore, by the Counting Principle, $P(n, r) = C(n, r)r!$.

The formula for $C(n, r)$ follows from the one for $P(n, r)$.

Observe that a "combination function" is a function defined for certain pairs of natural numbers. It has the same domain as the permutation function.

---

*There are several other notations for $C(n, r)$, the most common being $_nC_r$ and $\binom{n}{r}$. We shall use the notation $\binom{n}{r}$ in the next section.

Example 1   Three representatives (of equal rank) are to be selected from a group of 15 persons. How many different sets of representatives are possible?

Solution. Since there is no concern with order, there are $C(15, 3)$ sets:

$$C(15, 3) = \frac{15!}{(3!)(12!)} = \frac{15 \cdot 14 \cdot 13}{3 \cdot 2 \cdot 1} = 455.$$

2   How many different five-digit numbers can be formed from the digits 3, 4, 6, 6, 6?

Solution. Had the digits been all different the answer would be $P(5, 5) = 5! = 120$. However, there are three "6's" which in any five-digit number could be permuted amoung themselves without affecting the number. Since there are 3! such permutations of the "6's," the number of different numbers is $5!/3! = 20$.

Problems

Set A

Compute the following.

1. $C(7, 3)$ 2. $C(10, 2)$
3. $C(8, 7)$ 4. $C(6, 3)$

5. A student must write a report on any two books out of a choice of 8 books. How many combinations of reports are possible?

6. On a ten-question True-False quiz four of the statements are false. How many combinations of the false statements are possible?

7. How many different basketball teams (without regard to position) can be selected from 12 players?

8. If $C(n, 3) = 20$, what is n?

9. In how many different ways is it possible to arrange the letters in the word "cool"?

10. Using the digits 3, 3, 4, 4, 5, 6
    (a) how many different six-digit numbers can be formed?
    (b) how many different three-digit numbers can be formed?

Set B

11. A committee of four is to be chosen from five Republicans and six Democrats and at least one from each party must be selected. How many committees are possible? How does this number compare with the total number of committees of four that could be selected from the eleven possibilities?

12. Three cards are drawn from an ordinary pack of 52 cards. What is the total number of three-card sets possible? Of these, how many consist only of spades?

13. Thirteen cards are dealt from a pack of 52. How many different hands are possible? Leave your answer as a product, but estimate its magnitude.

14. An examination has ten questions from which the student is to select six to work on. How many different selections can be made?

15. Prove that $C(n, r) = C(n, n - r)$.

16. Prove that $C(n, r) = C(n - 1, r - 1) + C(n - 1, r)$, where $1 < r < n$.

Set C

Warning: One of the troublesome features of some of the problems that follow is an initial decision as to whether the problem is one in which order is important (so one has permutations) or one in which order is not important. One simply has to work some problems (perhaps with errors) to be able to proceed with confidence.

17. In how many ways can ten persons form two groups of four and six persons?

18. In a ten-team league, how many league games are there if each team plays all other teams twice? Why is this number $P(10, 2)$?

19. In how many ways can ten people be lined up so that a certain pair of them are

(a) always next to each other? [*Hint:* Arrange the other eight first.]
(b) never next to each other? [*Hint:* This part follows from part (a).]

20. Six boys and six girls are to be lined up in such a way that boys and girls alternate. In how many different ways can this be done if a certain boy and a certain girl

(a) must be together?
(b) must not be together?

21. Prove that $n!/(k! (n - k)!)$ is always an integer, where $0 \leq k \leq n$.

22. Prove that if p is a prime, then $(p - 1)(p - 2) \cdots (p - r + 1)$ is divisible by $r!$, where $0 < r < p$.

Calculator Problem

A ballot for the National League All Star baseball team lists 64 players, 8 players for each of eight positions except for the pitchers who are chosen by the manager of the team.

(a) How many different teams of 8 players would it be possible to vote for on the ballot?
(b) If each of the 64 players on the ballot could play any of the eight positions, how many teams of 8 players could be selected?

9-7   The Binomial Theorem

The polynomial $a + x$ is called a *binomial*. Our purpose in this section is to obtain a formula (the binomial theorem) for $(a + x)^n$, where n is a natural number. First we make a few computations to see what develops.

$$
\begin{aligned}
(a + x)^0 &= 1\\
(a + x)^1 &= a + x\\
(a + x)^2 &= a^2 + 2ax + x^2\\
(a + x)^3 &= a^3 + 3a^2x + 3ax^2 + x^3\\
(a + x)^4 &= a^4 + 4a^3x + 6a^2x^2 + 4ax^3 + x^4\\
(a + x)^5 &= a^5 + 5a^4x + 10a^3x^2 + 10a^2x^3 + 5ax^4 + x^5
\end{aligned}
\tag{1}
$$

A pattern is beginning to emerge. Before reading on, you may wish to guess what the coefficients are in the next row.

To get $(a + x)^6$ we multiply $(a + x)^5$ by $a + x$. Let us suppose that we wish to find the coefficient of a^4x^2 in $(a + x)^6$:

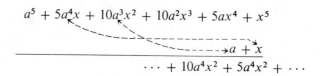

$$\cdots + 10a^4x^2 + 5a^4x^2 + \cdots$$

The dashed lines indicate the products that give "a^4x^2-terms," namely $10a^4x^2 + 5a^4x^2 = 15a^4x^2$. What will be the "$a^5x$-term"?

Examination of the products in (1) and the coefficients in the expansion of $(a + x)^6$ makes the following conjecture reasonable.

Having computed $(a + x)^n$, we find that:

   (a) the expansion of $(a + x)^{n+1}$ begins with a^{n+1} and ends with x^{n+1};

   (b) the coefficients are the same, in reverse order, at the end as they are at the beginning; and

   (c) we can obtain the coefficient of $a^k x^{n-k+1}$ in $(a + x)^{n+1}$ from the coefficients of $a^{k-1}x^{n-k+1}$, and of $a^k x^{n-k}$ in the expansion of $(a + x)^n$. The desired coefficient is the sum of the coefficients of these two terms.

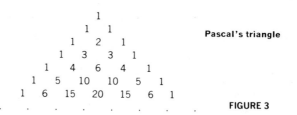

Pascal's triangle

FIGURE 3

The pattern of coefficients described by (a), (b), and (c) is called *Pascal's triangle* (after Blaise Pascal, 1623–1662) and is shown in Fig. 3. We therefore have an algorithm for computing any power of $(a + x)$.

Yet what we have is not all we might desire, for we do not have a formula for, say, the coefficient of $a^{12}x^{13}$ in $(a + x)^{25}$ without doing a great deal of extraneous computation. Nevertheless, the insight we get from Pascal's triangle can lead us quickly to the binomial theorem.

Let us consider, for example,

$$(a + x)^6 = (a + x)(a + x)(a + x)(a + x)(a + x)(a + x).$$

The separate terms in the expanded form are obtained by taking one factor (an a or an x) from within each pair of parentheses. If we always take the factor a, then we get the term a^6; there is only one way of doing this. To obtain terms a^5x we must choose the factor a five times and the factor x once. However, a factor a can be chosen from the six expressions in parentheses in $C(6, 5)$ ways. The coefficient of a^5x is therefore $C(6, 5)$. For the full expansion we would have

$$(a + x)^6 = C(6, 6)a^6 + C(6, 5)a^5x + C(6, 4)a^4x^2 + C(6, 3)a^3x^3$$
$$+ C(6, 2)a^2x^4 + C(6, 1)ax^5 + C(6, 0)x^6.$$

The same type of argument must be valid for any integral exponent. It is therefore inescapable that we must have the following theorem.

Theorem 9-3   **THE BINOMIAL THEOREM.** *For every natural number n,*
$$(a + x)^n = C(n, n)a^n + C(n, n - 1)a^{n-1}x + \cdots$$
$$+ C(n, r)a^rx^{n-r} + \cdots + C(n, 0)x^n.$$

Although the preceding argument should have convinced us of the truth of the binomial theorem, has it *proved* its validity? Rereading the preceding argument will show that what we have done is to show what the binomial theorem *ought* to be. A proof can now be made by induction.

Proof   (a) $(a + x)^1 = C(1, 1)a + C(1, 0)x = a + x$. The induction is anchored.
(b) Suppose that the theorem is true for $n = k$. Then
$$(a + x)^k = a^k + \cdots + C(k, r)a^rx^{k-r} + \cdots + x^r,$$

and

$$(a + x)^{k+1} = (a + x)(a + x)^k$$
$$= (a + x)[a^k + \cdots + C(k, r - 1)a^{r-1}x^{k-(r-1)}$$
$$+ C(k, r)a^rx^{k-r} + \cdots + x^k].$$

It suffices to examine the coefficient of a^rx^{k+1-r}. This coefficient is

$$C(k, r - 1) + C(k, r). \tag{2}$$

It would appear that we have failed because we did not get $C(k + 1, r)$. However, it is easy to show that (2) is actually $C(k + 1, r)$:

$$C(k, r - 1) + C(k, r) = \frac{k!}{(r - 1)!\,(k - (r - 1))!} + \frac{k!}{r!\,(k - r)!}$$

$$= \frac{k!}{(r - 1)!\,(k - r)!}\left(\frac{1}{k + 1 - r} + \frac{1}{r}\right)$$

$$= \frac{(k + 1)!}{r!\,(k + 1 - r)!}$$

$$= C(k + 1, r).$$

Therefore the coefficient of a^rx^{k+1-r} is $C(k + 1, r)$. This completes the induction and the proof.

Remarks

1. The numbers $C(n, r)$ of combinations of n things r at a time are also called *binomial coefficients.*

2. As we noted in the footnote on page 215, there is another notation for $C(n, r)$, namely

$$\binom{n}{r} = C(n, r) = C(n, n - r) = \binom{n}{n - r}.$$

If we use this notation in conjunction with the sigma notation for sums, the binomial theorem appears as follows:

$$(a + x)^n = \sum_{r=0}^{n} \binom{n}{r} a^{n-r} x^r.$$

3. If a particular term in the expansion of $(a + x)^n$ is needed, it can quickly be obtained from the Binomial Theorem. But is the theorem the quickest way of writing the entire expansion of a power of $(a + x)$, say $(a + x)^8$? The answer is "no." There is an algorithm one uses which is based on the following lemma.

Lemma $C(n, r - 1) = \dfrac{C(n, r)r}{n - r + 1}.$

Proof $C(n, r - 1) = \dfrac{n!}{(r - 1)!\,(n - (r - 1))!}$

$$= \frac{n!}{r!\,(n - r)!} \cdot \frac{r}{(n - r + 1)}$$

$$= \frac{C(n, r)r}{(n - r + 1)}.$$

We can now compute the binomial coefficients one after the other. Any coefficient can be obtained from the preceding term by multiplying its coefficient by the exponent k of a^k and dividing by one more than the exponent of x^{n-k}.

Example 1 $(a + x)^7 = 1 \cdot a^7 + \dfrac{1 \cdot 7}{1} a^6 x^1 + \dfrac{7 \cdot 6}{2} a^5 x^2 + \dfrac{21 \cdot 5}{3} a^4 x^3$

$$+ \frac{35 \cdot 4}{4} a^3 x^4 + \frac{35 \cdot 3}{5} a^2 x^5 + \frac{21 \cdot 2}{6} a x^6 + \frac{7 \cdot 1}{7} x^7$$

$$= a^7 + 7a^6 x + 21a^5 x^2 + 35a^4 x^3 + 35a^3 x^4 + 21a^2 x^5$$
$$+ 7ax^6 + x^7.$$

Example 2   Find $(1 - 2\sqrt{2})^5 = [1 + (-2\sqrt{2})]^5$.

Solution. Here $a = 1$, $x = -2\sqrt{2}$. Then

$$[1 + (-2\sqrt{2})]^5 = 1^5 + 5 \cdot 1^4 \cdot (-2\sqrt{2})^1 + 10 \cdot 1^3 \cdot (-2\sqrt{2})^2$$
$$+ 10 \cdot 1^2 \cdot (-2\sqrt{2})^3 + 5 \cdot 1^1 \cdot (-2\sqrt{2})^4 + (-2\sqrt{2})^5$$
$$= 1 - 10\sqrt{2} + 10(8) - 10(16\sqrt{2}) + 5(64) - 128\sqrt{2}$$
$$= 401 - 298\sqrt{2}.$$

3   What is the 4th term of $(a + x)^{10}$?

Solution. The coefficient of the rth term of $(a + x)^n$ is $C(n, n - r + 1)$. In this case we have $r = 4$ and $n = 10$. Therefore the fourth term is

$$C(10, 7)a^7x^3 = \frac{10 \cdot 9 \cdot 8}{1 \cdot 2 \cdot 3}a^7x^3 = 120a^7x^3.$$

Problems

Set A

1. Write out the first eleven rows of Pascal's triangle.

2. Use the ninth row of Pascal's triangle to write the expansion of $(a + x)^8$.

Expand the following binomial powers and simplify where it is natural to do so.

3. $(a - b)^5$

4. $(x - 1/x)^7$

5. $(a^{-1} + a^{-2})^3$

6. $(\sqrt{a/b} + \sqrt{b/a})^6$

7. $(2 + \sqrt{3})^7 + (2 - \sqrt{3})^7$

8. $(\frac{1}{2} + x)^8$

9. $(1 - ab)^7$

10. $(x - 2y)^9$

11. $(x^{1/3} - y^{1/3})^6$

12. $(a/2 - 2/a)^5$

Find the term indicated for the following binomial expansions.

13. $(a + b)^{11}$, the fifth term

14. $(\frac{1}{2} + \frac{1}{3})^{10}$, the fourth term

15. $(4x/5 - 5/2x)^{10}$, the eighth term

16. $(x^2 - y^2)^{10}$ the sixth term

17. $(1 - x^{1/3})^7$, the fourth term

18. $(x + 1)^{12}$, the seventh term

Set B

19. Compute $(0.99)^6$ to six decimal places. [*Hint:* $0.99 = 1 - 0.01$.]

20. Find (where $i^2 = -1$)

(a) $(1 + i)^4 + (1 - i)^4$.   (b) $(\sqrt{3} - i)^6$.

21. The fourth term of a binomial expansion is

$$\frac{9! \, (x/2)^6 y^3}{6! \, 3!}$$

What is the fifth term?

22. If $C(n, 5) = 21$, what is n?

23. Find the coefficient of x^{19} in $(2x^3 - 3x)^9$.

24. If a^k occurs in $(a + 1/a)^n$, what is the coefficient?

Expand and simplify.

25. $\displaystyle\sum_{r=0}^{5} \binom{5}{r} 2^r \cdot 1^{5-r}$

26. $\displaystyle\sum_{n=0}^{6} \binom{6}{n} a^r 2^n$

27. $\displaystyle\sum_{n=0}^{3} \binom{3}{n} (2a)^n (-3b)^{3-n}$

28. Show that $\displaystyle\sum_{r=0}^{n} \binom{n}{r} = 2^n$.

[*Hint:* Expand $(1 + 1)^n$.]

29. Show that $\displaystyle\sum_{r=0}^{n}(-1)^r\binom{n}{r}=0$.

[*Hint:* Expand $(1-1)^n$.]

30. Conclude from Problem 29 that the sum of the terms $\binom{n}{r}$ for r even is equal to the sum for r odd.

31. Find the middle term in the expansion of $(1+x)^{2n}$.

32. Use the binomial theorem to expand $(x^2-3x+1)^3=[x^2+(1-3x)]^3$.

Set C

33. Show that $C(n,1)+2C(n,2)+$
$$3C(n,3)+\cdots+nC(n,n)=n2^{n-1}.$$

34. Show that $C(n,0)+\dfrac{C(n,1)}{2}+$
$$\dfrac{C(n,2)}{3}+\cdots+\dfrac{C(n,n)}{n+1}=\dfrac{2^{n+1}-1}{n+1}.$$

35. Show that $\dfrac{C(n,1)}{C(n,0)}+\dfrac{2C(n,2)}{C(n,1)}+\dfrac{3C(n,3)}{C(n,2)}+$
$$\cdots+\dfrac{nC(n,n)}{C(n,n-1)}=\dfrac{n(n+1)}{2}.$$

In the calculus it is shown that the Binomial Theorem can be formulated for exponents that are not positive integers. The coefficients are computed by the algorithm that follows the lemma on page 220.

$$(1+x)^n = 1 + nx + \frac{n(n-1)}{2}x^2 +$$
$$\frac{n(n-1)(n-2)}{3!}x^3 + \cdots \quad (1)$$

If n is not a positive integer, the expansion (1) does not terminate. Nevertheless, a finite number of terms of (1) approximates $(1+x)^n$ for any x such that $|x|<1$.

Use this fact to compute the following to three decimal places by means of the Binomial Theorem.

36. $\sqrt{1.02}=(1+0.02)^{1/2}$ **37.** $\sqrt[3]{1.06}$

38. $(1.2)^{-1}$ **39.** $(\frac{5}{4})^{1/2}$

40. $\sqrt{48}=\sqrt{49-1}=7\sqrt{1-1/49}$

41. Expand $(1+x)^{-1}$ by the Binomial Theorem. Then obtain the same series by long division.

42. Assume that x is small enought that (for our purposes) one can neglect x^2, x^3, and higher powers in the binomial expansions. Find and simplify

$$\frac{(1+x/2)^{-4}+2(1+x)^{1/2}}{8(1+x/4)^{3/2}}.$$

Calculator Problem

If n is not an integer and if $a>1$ and $0<b<1$, then the first two terms of the expansion of $(a+b)^n$ give an approximation that is correct to about the nearest hundredth. That is

$$(a+b)^n \doteq a^n + na^{n-1}b.$$

Find approximations of the following numbers using the first two terms in the expansion above. Check by finding the roots on a calculator.

(a) $\sqrt{4.2}=(4+0.2)^{1/2}$ (b) $\sqrt{16.08}$ (c) $\sqrt[3]{8.27}$ (d) $\sqrt[5]{32.50}$

Much of elementary mathematics is concerned with combinations of, or relations among a finite number of objects. This aspect includes most of geometry too. However, there are certain mathematical concepts which, by their very definition, require the consideration of infinite sets. In many of these cases, the concept of "infinite" is essential because the notion of *limit* is involved.

You have already encountered examples of the need for limits. Thus the circumference C of a circle is *defined* to be the limit of perimeters p_n of polygons inscribed in that circle:

$$C = \lim_{n \to \infty} p_n.$$

In Section 9–3 the sum of the terms of an infinite geometric sequence was *defined* to be the limit of the sums G_n of the first n terms:

$$G = \lim_{n \to \infty} G_n.$$

In this section we formalize our earlier intuitive treatment of limits of sequences. It will be seen that the existence of limits is intimately associated with fundamental properties of the real number system. Therefore, a review of Section 1–2 is appropriate now with particular attention to the completeness axiom.

We wish to emphasize that at this time we are primarily concerned with *definitions*. The few problems and theorems are included solely to illuminate the concepts. Real facility in the use of limits will be attained in more advanced courses.

Example 1   If

$$a_n = \frac{n + 1}{3n}, \qquad n = 1, 2, \ldots,$$

then

$$a_1 = \tfrac{2}{3}, \quad a_2 = \tfrac{1}{2}, \quad a_3 = \tfrac{4}{9}, \quad \ldots, \quad a_n = \frac{1}{3} + \frac{1}{3n}, \ldots.$$

Clearly, when n is *large,* a_n is *close to* $\tfrac{1}{3}$. We then write $A = \lim_{n \to \infty} a_n = \tfrac{1}{3}$.

2   Let

$$S_n = \frac{1 - r^n}{1 - r},$$

which is the sum of the first n terms of the geometric sequence

$$1, r, r^2, r^3, \ldots, r^n, \ldots.$$

Then if $|r| < 1$, r^n is a very small number when n is a large number. Therefore, when n is *large*, S_n is *close to* $1/(1-r)$,

$$S = \lim_{n \to \infty} S_n = \frac{1}{1-r}.$$

These examples illustrate the general situation. The statement

$$\lim_{n \to \infty} f_n = L$$

means that "when n is *large*, then f_n is *close to* L." To make the idea precise and put in a form that can be used in proofs, it is necessary to clarify what "close to" means and how large "large" is. We need a definition.

Definition 9–8   Suppose that $\{a_n\}$ is a sequence of real numbers. Then $\{a_n\}$ has limit L as $n \to \infty$ if, given any *positive* number ϵ, there is a positive number N (which depends on ϵ) such that $|a_n - L| < \epsilon$ when $n \geq N$.

Remarks   1. The *given* positive number ϵ specifies the closeness to L that one wishes to get. The number N (which, in general, must get larger as ϵ gets smaller) specifies how large n should be for the specified degree of closeness, ϵ.

2. The definition does not predict or supply a way of computing L. What the definition does is supply a criterion with which one can *test a number L* to see whether it is actually the limit of the sequence $\{a_n\}$.

Example 3   Consider again the sequence of Example 1:

$$a_n = \frac{n+1}{3n} = \frac{1}{3} + \frac{1}{3n}.$$

We saw by inspection that the limit of the sequence is $\frac{1}{3}$. We must now verify this result by using Definition 9–8. We have

$$|a_n - L| = \left| a_n - \frac{1}{3} \right| = \frac{1}{3n}.$$

According to the definition, we must find, for any $\epsilon > 0$, a number N such that $1/3n < \epsilon$ if $n \geq N$.

Fortunately, this is easy; we simply choose $N > 1/3\epsilon$. Then if $n \geq N$,

$$n > \frac{1}{3\epsilon} \quad \text{and} \quad \epsilon > \frac{1}{3n}.$$

Now consider an infinite series

$$\sum_{n=1}^{\infty} a_n = a_1 + a_2 + \cdots + a_n + \cdots \tag{1}$$

In Section 9–3 we defined the sum of the series to be the limit (if there is a limit) of the sequence of partial sums. Then, when that is the case, the sum (1) is

$$S = \lim_{n \to \infty} S_n = \lim_{n \to \infty} (a_1 + a_2 + \cdots + a_n),$$

and we say that the series *converges*.

Therefore at this stage of development one must be able to find a "reasonable" formula for S_n in order to decide whether or not the limit exists. In most cases this is a formidable task, and other methods are developed in more advanced courses in order to decide whether the series converges. We cannot pursue these other methods here, and so we shall confine our attention to (1) geometric series for which a formula for S_n exists, and (2) a few special series for which a trick will get a formula for S_n. To illustrate the kind of trick we have in mind, consider this example.

Example 4   The series $\sum_{k=1}^{\infty} 1/(k(k + 1))$ has partial sums

$$S_n = \sum_{k=1}^{n} \frac{1}{k(k + 1)} = \frac{1}{1 \cdot 2} + \frac{1}{2 \cdot 3} + \cdots + \frac{1}{n(n + 1)}.$$

Now we observe that

$$\frac{1}{k(k + 1)} = \frac{1}{k} - \frac{1}{k + 1}.$$

Therefore, S_n becomes

$$S_n = \left(1 - \frac{1}{2}\right) + \left(\frac{1}{2} - \frac{1}{3}\right) + \cdots + \left(\frac{1}{n} - \frac{1}{n + 1}\right) = 1 - \frac{1}{n + 1}$$

because of cancellation (telescoping) of all except the first and last terms. Clearly now $\lim_{n \to \infty} S_n = 1$. A proof can be made as follows. Given $\epsilon > 0$, choose $N > 1/\epsilon$. Then

$$|S_n - 1| = \frac{1}{n + 1} < \frac{1}{N} < \epsilon \qquad \text{if} \quad n \geq N.$$

Problems

Set A

For each sequence, guess its limit L. Then show that given $\epsilon > 0$, there is a number N such that $|S_n - L| < \epsilon$ if $n \geq N$.

1. $S_n = 3 + 2/n$

2. $S_n = (2n - 1)/n$

3. $S_n = \dfrac{n}{n + 1}$

4. $S_n = \dfrac{n + 2}{2n + 3}$

5. $S_n = \dfrac{n + 2}{2n - 3}$

6. $S_n = \dfrac{n + 1}{n^2 + 3}$

Set B

Find the limit to each sequence. Prove that the limit is correct.

7. $S_n = \dfrac{2n^2}{n^2 + 1}$

8. $S_n = \dfrac{1 + n}{2n}$

9. $S_n = \dfrac{7n - 1}{3n + 2}$

10. $S_n = \dfrac{n^2}{n^3 + 2}$

Find the sum of each series. Prove your sum is correct.

11. $\displaystyle\sum_{n=1}^{\infty} \frac{1}{(n + 2)(n + 3)}$

12. $\displaystyle\sum_{n=1}^{\infty} \frac{2}{4n^2 - 1}$

13. $\displaystyle\sum_{k=1}^{\infty} x^k, \ |x| < 1$

14. $\displaystyle\sum_{k=1}^{\infty} (2x)^k, \ |x| < \tfrac{1}{2}$

Set C

Find the limit to each sequence. Prove that the limit is correct.

15. $S_n = a + (\sin n)/n$

16. $S_n = r^n, \ |r| < 1$

17. $S_n = \dfrac{n!}{(2n)!}$

18. $S_n = \sin\left(\dfrac{1}{n}\right)$

Find the sum of each series. Prove your sum is correct.

19. $\displaystyle\sum_{k=1}^{\infty} 2(2x - 1)^k, \ 0 < x < 1$

20. $\displaystyle\sum_{k=1}^{\infty} \frac{2}{k(k + 2)}$

Calculator Problem

Find the smallest positive integer k such that

$$\sum_{n=1}^{k} \frac{1}{n} \geq 5.$$

Summary

Each section in this chapter is at least in part concerned with sequences. For the most part these sequences are real sequences but some are sequences of inequalities and others are sequences of statements. The main topics are briefly as follows.

1. A sequence is a function whose domain is N.
2. A series is a sum of the terms of a sequence. This sum will exist if the partial sums of the series have a limit.
3. Special sequences are the arithmetic and geometric sequences:

$$a, a + d, a + 2d, \ldots, a + (n - 1)d, \ldots$$

and

$$a, ar, ar^2, \ldots, ar^{n-1}, \ldots.$$

The sums of n terms of these sequences are, respectively

$$A_n = \tfrac{1}{2}n(2a + (n - 1)d) = \tfrac{1}{2}n(a + a_n) \qquad \text{and} \qquad G_n = \frac{a - ar^n}{1 - r}.$$

4. The Greek letter sigma indicates sum:

$$\sum_{k=1}^{n} a_k = a_1 + a_2 + \cdots + a_n.$$

5. Of infinite series, the most important by far is the geometric series, which has a sum if $|r| < 1$:

$$\sum_{k=1}^{\infty} ar^{k-1} = a + ar + ar^2 + \cdots + ar^n + \cdots = \frac{a}{1 - r}.$$

6. Fractions representing repeating decimals can be found by regarding the decimal as a geometric series.
7. Mathematical induction is a potent tool for proofs. The Induction Principle is a basic property of the whole number system.
8. A permutation on n elements is an ordered arrangement of the n elements. It can be regarded as a function whose domain is the set $\{1, \ldots, n\}$. For the number of permutations of n things taken r at a time, we have
$$P(n, r) = \frac{n!}{(n - r)!}.$$

9. The number of combinations of n objects taken r at a time is
$$C(n, r) = \binom{n}{r} = \frac{P(n, r)}{r!} = \frac{n!}{r!\,(n - r)!}.$$

10. The Binomial Theorem states that the coefficient of $a^r x^{n-r}$ in the expansion of $(a + x)^n$ is equal to $C(n, r)$.
11. The sequence $\{a_n\}$, n a positive integer, has limit L if for every positive number ϵ there is a natural number N such that $|a_n - L| < \epsilon$ if $n \geq N$.

Chapter 9   Test

9-2   Write the first five terms of these sequences.

1. $a_n = 3n - 1$

2. $a_n = \dfrac{n!}{(n-1)!}$

3. $a_n = 2x^n$

4. $a_n = (n+1)! - n!$

Write the terms of these series. You need not find the sums.

5. $\displaystyle\sum_{k=1}^{5} \frac{1}{2k-1}$

6. $\displaystyle\sum_{k=1}^{6} \frac{(-1)^{k+1}}{(2k-1)^2}$

7. An arithmetic sequence has first term $\frac{1}{2}$ and common difference $\frac{3}{2}$. Find the sum of the first 11 terms.

8. Find the sum of the first ten terms of the geometric sequence whose first term is 1 and whose common ratio is $\frac{1}{10}$.

9-3   Find the sum of each infinite series.

9. $0.4 + 0.04 + 0.004 + 0.0004 + \ldots$

10. $\displaystyle\sum_{n=1}^{\infty} \frac{1}{4^n}$

9-4   11. Prove by induction that $1 - 2 - 5 - \cdots - (3n - 4) = [n(5 - 3n)]/2$.

12. Prove by induction that $2^{2n} - 1$ is divisible by 3 for every positive integer n.

9-5   13. If $n! \cdot 8 = 8!$, what is n?

14. Find $P(7, 3)$.

15. Eight runners enter a race with ribbons awarded to the first three runners to finish the race. How many possible arrangements of the ribbon winners are there?

9-6   16. Find $C(5, 2)$.

17. Ten cards are numbered from 1 to 10. Three of the cards are drawn. How many combinations of the three cards are possible?

9-7   18. Write out the expansion of $(2x - y)^7$.

19. What is the coefficient of $x^5 y^3$ in the expansion of $(x - 3y)^8$?

9-8   20. Using the definition of limit, prove that $\lim\limits_{n \to \infty} 2n/(3n + 1) = \frac{2}{3}$.

21. Find the sum of the infinite series

$$0.9 + 0.09 + 0.009 + 0.0009 + 0.00009 + \ldots.$$

Historical Note

Augustin-Louis Cauchy
(1789–1857)

1. The structure of the *real number* system needed clarification.
2. The concept of *function,* and continuity of functions, needed precise formulation.
3. The concept of *limit* needed a rigorous definition.

But in 1700 there was much confusion. There was no general definition of function. The reader had to know intuitively what was meant. Furthermore, mathematicians were overly concerned with functions as "nice formulas." They did not understand how vast even the class of continuous functions actually is. A few of the landmarks in the gradual evolution of the function concept are associated with the following mathematicians.

Leonhard Euler (1707–1783) was a great calculator, a great manipulator of formulas. He created the notation $f(x)$ for functions.

Augustin-Louis Cauchy (1789–1857) is the first to have approached a modern treatment of calculus, limits, and continuity. The publication of his lectures at the Ecole Polytechnique in 1821 set a definite pattern of exposition which is still used in the books of today.

Peter G. Lejeune Dirichlet (1805–1859) gave the first definition (in 1837) of a real function as a correspondence between two sets of real numbers.

Georg Cantor (1845–1918) during the 1870's developed abstract set theory—a step which has influenced the direction of mathematical development. Cantor's work led to the general concept of function as a mapping from sets to sets, a concept that is discussed in this book.

By 1700 calculus had been invented, by Newton and Leibniz (see the Historical Note of Chapter 10) and a host of followers were using the new method to attack problems that had been unsolvable previously. Yet, all the while, there were no satisfactory proofs that the processes of calculus were valid! Gradually, this lack of an adequate foundation became more and more worrisome, and although there were numerous attempts to put the processes of calculus on a firm basis, real progress was slow. Eventually it became clear that the difficulties were threefold:

Chapter 10
Introduction to Calculus

10-1　　Introduction

In this chapter we shall be concerned with two problems which had occupied mathematicians from ancient times (notably the Greek mathematician Archimedes), and which were the focus of attention for several of the great mathematicians of the middle seventeenth century. The problems are concerned with *tangents* to curves and *areas* under curves.

The names of some of the mathematicians who worked on these problems are Pierre de Fermat (1601–1665); Isaac Newton (1642–1727); Isaac Barrow (1630–1677), the teacher of Newton; and Gottfried Leibniz (1646–1716), who, independently of Newton, also discovered the calculus. For an excellent account of these men and their accomplishments, the student is urged to read *Men of Mathematics* by E. T. Bell.

The history of the two problems mentioned is long and interesting but we cannot pursue it here. After you have studied the calculus, you will find the history of the problems both entertaining and beneficial.

Although we shall be dealing with problems of the seventeenth century, we will be able to attack them with modern concepts and modern notation. Examples will be used to illustrate the problems. We have on purpose chosen simple functions so that the algebra will not obscure the ideas. We shall try to bring to your attention the need for simple rules of calculation. (Find the meaning of the word "calculus" in a dictionary.) We shall do a fair amount of arithmetical computation and we shall make a few definitions. For the most part, however, the formulation of the basic concepts will be left to you. If all goes well, you will be able to discover the solutions to the basic problems yourself.

In the first part of the chapter we shall consider the problem of tangents. Then we shall treat, in an introductory manner, the problem of areas. Finally we shall examine briefly the relation between these two problems.

10-2　　Slope of Lines

In the next section we shall discuss lines which are tangent to curves at some point. In order to discuss tangents we first need to introduce the meaning of *inclination* and *slope* of a line.

Definition 10-1 If a line is parallel to the *x*-axis, its *inclination* is 0. For other lines the inclination, θ, is the measure of the angle between the upward direction on *l* and the positive *x*-axis. (See Fig. 1.)

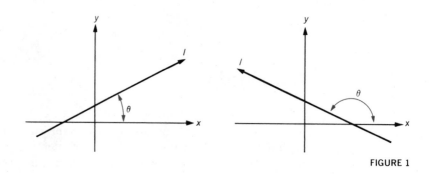

FIGURE 1

Note that the inclination of a line is always such that $0 \leq \theta \leq \pi$.

We can now define the slope of a line. It is usually denoted by the letter *m*.

Definition 10-2 The *slope m* of a line with inclination θ is

$$m = \tan \theta \qquad \text{if } \ \theta \neq \frac{\pi}{2}.$$

If $\theta = \pi/2$ (vertical lines), then the line has no slope.

Because two points determine a line, the slope of a non-vertical line must be determined by the coordinates of the two points. The theorem below gives the basic formula for slope of a line.

Theorem 10-1 *If (x_1, y_1) and (x_2, y_2) are distinct points on a nonvertical line, then the slope of the line is*

$$m = \frac{y_2 - y_1}{x_2 - x_1}.$$

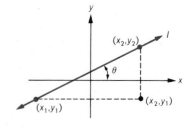

FIGURE 2

Proof The simplest proof, in the case where θ is acute, follows from an examination of Fig. 2. We need simply apply the definition of $\tan \theta$ to establish the theorem.

Example 1 A line has an inclination of $\pi/3$. The slope of the line is $m = \tan \pi/3 = \sqrt{3}$.

Example 2 The line containing the points $(-2, 1)$ and $(3, -2)$ has slope

$$m = \frac{1 - (-2)}{-2 - 3} = -\frac{3}{5}.$$

(See Fig. 3.) Note that the slope is negative. This is expected since the angle of inclination θ is $\pi/2 < \theta < \pi$ and $\tan \theta$ is negative in this interval.

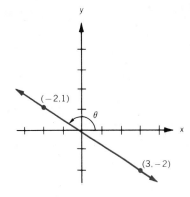

FIGURE 3

Problems

Set A

Give the slope of a line whose angle of inclination is the following.

1. $\dfrac{\pi}{6}$ **2.** $\dfrac{2\pi}{3}$ **3.** $\dfrac{\pi}{4}$

4. $72°$ **5.** $153.7°$ **6.** $84.2°$

Find the slope of a line containing two points whose coordinates are given below.

7. $(-2, 2), (4, 4)$ **8.** $(-1, 4), (3, 1)$

9. $(-5, -2), (4, 6)$ **10.** $(4, 0), (0, 3)$

11. $(-6, -4), (-1, -2)$

12. $(x, y), (x + 1, y + 2)$

Set B

13. Sketch a line that contains the point $(1, 2)$ and has an inclination of $\pi/6$.

14. Sketch a line that contains the point $(-3, 4)$ and has a slope of -1.

15. Sketch a line with 0 slope which contains the point $(1, -3)$.

16. A line contains the point $(-4, 2)$ and is parallel to the y-axis. What is the inclination of the line? What can be said of its slope?

Set C

17. Show that the formula for the slope of a line is independent of the order of the two points selected. That is, show that

$$m = \frac{y_1 - y_2}{x_1 - x_2} = \frac{y_2 - y_1}{x_2 - x_1}.$$

18. A line contains the point $(1, 2)$ and has an inclination of $\theta = \text{Arctan } \frac{1}{2}$. What are the coordinates of some other points on the line?

Calculator Problem

Find the angle of inclination of a line that contains the points $(-2.45, 0.96)$ and $(4.77, -3.18)$.

10-3   Tangents to Graphs of Functions

We will consider the graph of a function f that is continuous on its domain $[a, b]$, as in Fig. 4. The problem is to discover a device, rule, or algorithm that will enable one to compute easily the slope of the tangent line at an arbitrary point $(x_0, f(x_0))$ of the graph of f.

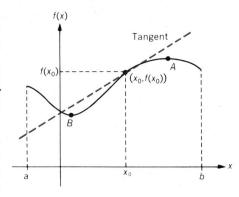

FIGURE 4

The usefulness of such a rule is easy to see. For example, it seems reasonable that if the slope of the tangent were positive for every point on the graph of f, then the function would be an increasing function. Another application might be the determination of "maximum points" or "minimum points" such as the points A and B in Fig. 4. At such points the slope of the tangent should be 0.

The first question that arises is: "What is a good definition of the tangent line?" Let us defer answering this question for the time being and instead consider a definition of *secant lines*.

Definition 10-3   A *secant line* of a continuous function f is a line joining points $(a, f(a))$ and $(b, f(b))$, $b \neq a$. (See Fig. 5.)

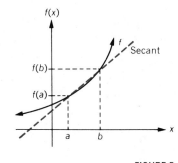

FIGURE 5

It follows from the definition of slope that the slope of the secant line containing the two points $(b, f(b))$ and $(a, f(a))$ is

$$m = \frac{f(b) - f(a)}{b - a}.$$

Example 1   Suppose that f is a linear function. Then every secant line of f coincides with the graph of f. (See Fig. 6.) The slope of the secant is constant, for if f is given by

$$f(x) = Ax + B,$$

then

$$f(a) = Aa + B \quad \text{and} \quad f(b) = Ab + B.$$

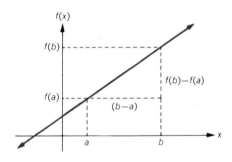

FIGURE 6

Then,

$$\text{slope of secant} = \frac{f(b) - (a)}{b - a} = \frac{(Ab + B) - (Aa + B)}{b - a}$$

$$= \frac{A(b - a)}{b - a} = A.$$

We have shown in this example that the slope of the secant line to $f(x) = Ax + B$ is simply what we have always called the slope of the line given by $f(x) = Ax + B$.

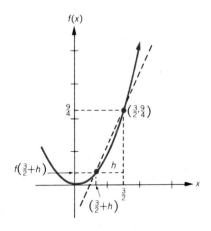

FIGURE 7

Example 2   Let f be the function given by $f(x) = x^2$ for all x, and consider the various secants that pass through $(\frac{3}{2}, \frac{9}{4})$ on the graph of f. (See Fig. 7.) We can select any real number $h \neq 0$ and consider the slopes of the secant lines through the points

$$(\tfrac{3}{2}, \tfrac{9}{4}) \quad \text{and} \quad ((\tfrac{3}{2} + h), (\tfrac{3}{2} + h)^2)$$

for different values of h. Computation yields the values listed in Table 1 below. From the table it appears that when h is small, the slope m of the secant line through $(\frac{3}{2}, \frac{9}{4})$ is near 3.

TABLE 1

h	$f(\frac{3}{2} + h)$	$m = \dfrac{f(\frac{3}{2} + h) - f(\frac{3}{2})}{h}$
-1	$\frac{1}{4}$	$2 = 3 - 1$
1	$\frac{25}{4}$	$4 = 3 + 1$
$-\frac{1}{2}$	1	$\frac{5}{2} = 3 - \frac{1}{2}$
$\frac{1}{2}$	4	$\frac{7}{2} = 3 + \frac{1}{2}$
$-\frac{1}{4}$	$\frac{25}{16}$	$\frac{11}{4} = 3 - \frac{1}{4}$
$\frac{1}{4}$	$\frac{49}{16}$	$\frac{13}{4} = 3 + \frac{1}{4}$
-0.1	1.96	$2.9 = 3 - 0.1$
0.1	2.56	$3.1 = 3 + 0.1$
h	$\frac{9}{4} + 3h + h^2$	$3 + h$

Particularly important is the last line of the table, which presents us with a formula for the slope of the secant for any choice of h. From this formula it is easy to see what happens to the slope m as h approaches 0.

Let us now develop a formula for the slope of the secants through *any* point (x_0, x_0^2) of the graph of f and for *any* choice of $h \neq 0$.

We have

$$f(x_0 + h) = x_0^2 + 2x_0 h + h^2,$$

so the slope of the secant is

$$m = \frac{f(x_0 + h) - f(x_0)}{(x_0 + h) - x_0}$$

$$= \frac{x_0^2 + 2x_0 h + h^2 - x_0^2}{h}$$

$$= 2x_0 + h. \tag{1}$$

From (1) we see that when h is small, the slope of the secant through (x_0, x_0^2) is near $2x_0$. Let us agree on the following rough definition of the tangent line at x_0.

Definition 10-4 The tangent line to the graph of a function f at x_0 is the line through $(x_0, f(x_0))$ that is the *limiting position* of the secant line through $(x_0, f(x_0))$ and $(x_0 + h, f(x_0 + h))$.

This definition is not precise because we have not been precise about the meaning of "the limiting position". What is meant is that the slope of the tangent line through $(x_0, f(x_0))$ is equal to the limit of the slope of the secant line through $(x_0, f(x_0))$ and $(x_0 + h, f(x_0 + h))$. We shall return to this idea in a later section. Thus the concept of tangent line and the slope of the tangent line requires the use of limits.

Problems

Set A

1. Complete the table below to find the slope m of the secant lines through $(1, 1)$ and $f(1 + h)$ for the function $f(x) = x^2$.

h	$f(1 + h)$	$m = \dfrac{f(1 + h) - f(1)}{h}$
1		
-1		
0.5		
-0.5		
0.25		
-0.25		
0.1		
-0.1		

2. Using a large scale, draw as accurately as possible the graph of $f(x) = x^2$ for $0 \le x \le 1.5$. Draw the secant lines through $(1, 1)$ for the values of h in the table in Problem 1.

3. Using Problems 1 and 2, what do you think is the slope of the tangent line to $f(x) = x^2$ at the point $(1, 1)$?

4. What is a formula for the slope of the tangent of $f(x) = x^2$ at the point where $x = x_0$? Use this formula to find the slope of the tangents and draw the tangent lines to the graph of f at the points where $x = -2$, -1, $-\frac{1}{2}$, 0, $\frac{1}{2}$, 1, and 2.

Set B

5. Sketch the graph of $f(x) = \frac{1}{2}x^2 + 4$ and the secant lines that pass through $(2, 6)$ for the choices of h in the table below. Complete the table.

h	$f(2 + h)$	$m = \dfrac{f(2 + h) - f(2)}{h}$
1		
-1		
$\frac{1}{2}$		
$-\frac{1}{2}$		
$\frac{1}{4}$		
$-\frac{1}{4}$		
0.1		
-0.1		
0.0001		

6. (a) Draw a graph of $f(x) = x^2$ using a large scale for $-1 \le x \le 0$.
   (b) Sketch what you think is the tangent line to the curve through $(-0.5, 0.25)$.
   (c) Measure the inclination of the tangent line with a protractor.
   (d) Find the slope of the tangent line from the inclination.
   (e) Compare the measured slope with the slope given by the formula in equation (1) of this section.

7. Compute the slope of the secant through the points $(x_0, f(x_0))$ and $(x_0 + h, f(x_0 + h))$ on the graph of $f(x) = \frac{1}{2}x^2 + 4$. What is the slope of the tangent line at $(x_0, f(x_0))$?

8. Compute the slopes of the secants through $(\frac{3}{2}, \frac{9}{4})$ of $f(x) = x^2$ for the following values of h.
   (a) 0.01   (b) 0.001
   (c) -0.01 (d) -0.001

9. (a) Consider the set of numbers one gets for the slope of the secants through $(\frac{3}{2}, \frac{9}{4})$ of $f(x) = x^2$ for $h > 0$. Is this set of numbers bounded below? What is the greatest lower bound of this set of numbers?
   (b) Consider the set of numbers that are slopes of the secants through $(\frac{3}{2}, \frac{9}{4})$ of the same function but for $h < 0$. Is this set bounded above? What is the least upper bound?
   (c) What do you think the slope of the tangent line is through $(\frac{3}{2}, \frac{9}{4})$?

10. Show that for the linear function f, where $f(x) = 3x + 4$, the slopes of the secants through any two points $(x_1, f(x_1))$ and $(x_2, f(x_2))$ are the same constant 3.

What are the slopes of the secants through any two points of

11. $f(x) = -\frac{1}{2}x - 7$?   12. $p(x) = 5x + 8$?
13. $g(x) = x + 1$?   14. $q(x) = 0.67x + 1.8$?
15. $h(x) = \frac{3}{4}x + \pi$?   16. $r(x) = 10 - x$?

Set C

17. (a) Sketch the graph of $f(x) = x^3$.
    (b) Draw several secant lines through $(\frac{1}{2}, \frac{1}{8})$, and $(\frac{1}{2} + h, f(\frac{1}{2} + h))$ for some $h > 0$ and some $h < 0$.
    (c) What is the slope of the tangent line through $(\frac{1}{2}, \frac{1}{8})$?
    (d) What is the slope of a secant line through $(x_0, f(x_0))$?
    (e) What is the slope of the tangent line through $(x_0, f(x_0))$?

18. (a) Sketch the graph of $y = f(x) = x - x^2$.
    (b) Draw several secant lines through $(\frac{1}{2}, \frac{1}{4})$, some for $h > 0$ and some for $h < 0$.
    (c) What is the slope of the tangent line through $(\frac{1}{2}, \frac{1}{4})$?
    (d) What is the slope of a secant line through $(x_0, f(x_0))$?
    (e) What is the slope of the tangent line through $(x_0, f(x_0))$?

19. (a) Sketch the graph of $y = f(x) = x^3 - x$.
    (b) Draw several secant lines through $(\frac{1}{2}, -\frac{3}{8})$.
    (c) What is the slope of the tangent line through $(\frac{1}{2}, -\frac{3}{8})$?
    (d) What is the slope of a secant line through $(x_0, f(x_0))$?
    (e) What is the slope of the tangent line at $(x_0, f(x_0))$?

Calculator Problem

Sketch a graph of $f(x) = x^5 - x$ for $0 < x < 1$ using a large scale. Use the graph to estimate a point through which the slope of the tangent is 0. Check your estimate by using the formula $m = 5x_0^4 - 1$.

The Derivative of a Function

If $m(x)$ is the slope of the tangent line to the graph of f at the point $(x, f(x))$, then one has a new function m, the slope function. (See Fig. 8.) There are many notations used for this function. We shall content ourselves with the one given in the following definition.

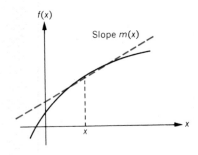

FIGURE 8

Definition 10–5 The slope function for the graph of f is called the *derived function* (or *derivative*) *of f*. It is denoted by f'. From f one gets another function $f': f \rightarrow f'$.

If the graph of f has been drawn, then the graph of the derived function, or derivative, can be roughly sketched as follows. We draw (approximately) several tangent lines and estimate their slopes, either "by eye" or by counting squares on the graph. These rough data will give several points on the graph of f'. With these points, it is usually not difficult to sketch the general shape of the graph of f'.

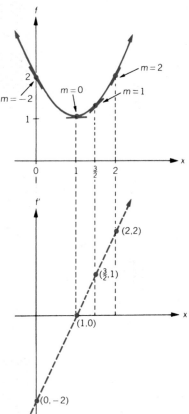

Example 1 The graph of $y = f(x) = 1 + (x - 1)^2$ is shown in Fig. 9 with the tangent lines sketched at $x = 0, 1, \frac{3}{2}$, and 2. Estimating slopes by eye, one has approximately

$$f'(0) = -2, \quad f'(1) = 0,$$
$$f'(\tfrac{3}{2}) = 1, \quad f'(2) = 2$$

These points are plotted in the graph directly below that of f. The points apparently lie on a straight line, the graph of f', shown dashed in the figure.

FIGURE 9

Example 2   Consider the function f whose graph is drawn in Fig. 10. The tangent lines are sketched at $x = -2, -1, 0, 2,$ and 4, where the slopes appear to be -2, $0, 1, \frac{1}{2},$ and $\frac{1}{8}$, respectively. The graph of f' must look something like that shown in the figure.

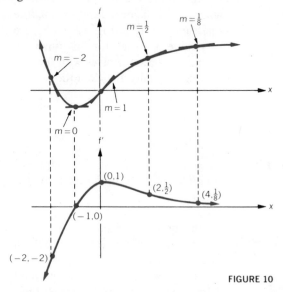

FIGURE 10

Even though a function is continuous, the graph need not have a tangent line at all points. There may be "corners" as in the next example.

Example 3   The graph of $f(x) = |x|$ is shown in Fig. 11. At $x = 0$ there is no line that satisfies Definition 10–4. At other values of $x, f'(x)$ is either $+1$ or -1. $f'(0)$ *does not exist;* it is *not defined.*

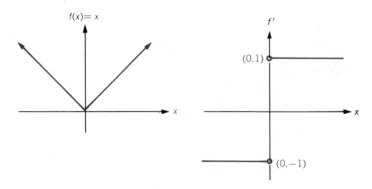

FIGURE 11

It can be shown that there are continuous functions f for which $f'(x)$ does not exist for any x in the domain of f, but they are exceedingly complicated.

For the elementary functions the derived function always exists, except perhaps at a finite set of points.

Much of the calculus notation in use today was invented by Leibniz in the seventeenth century. Among the notations that he introduced is the "Δ-notation" for increments. This notation is described in the next definition.

Definition 10-6 Suppose the real variable x changes from x_1 to x_2. Then the change in x is called the *increment* of x and is denoted by Δx (where the Greek letter Δ reminds us that it is a *difference*):

$$\Delta x = x_2 - x_1.$$

Thus, the increment of x as x changes from

$$
\begin{aligned}
2 \text{ to } 4 \quad &\text{is} \quad \Delta x = 4 - 2 = 2, \\
1 \text{ to } 1.3 \quad &\text{is} \quad \Delta x = 1.3 - 1 = 0.3, \\
x \text{ to } x + h \quad &\text{is} \quad \Delta x = (x + h) - x = h.
\end{aligned}
$$

If $y = f(x)$, then the change in y as x changes from x to $x + h$ (or $x + \Delta x$) is

$$\Delta y = f(x + h) - f(x) = f(x + \Delta x) - f(x).$$

Sometimes this increment is denoted by Δf. Then the slope of the secant line between $(x, f(x))$ and $(x + \Delta x, f(x + \Delta x))$ is

$$\frac{\Delta y}{\Delta x} = \frac{f(x + \Delta x) - f(x)}{\Delta x}. \tag{1}$$

To find the derived function f' for a function f, one must examine (1) to see what happens to $\Delta y / \Delta x$ as Δx approaches 0. In other words, what is $\Delta y / \Delta x$ close to for small Δx?

Example 4 Compute $\dfrac{\Delta y}{\Delta x}$ for $y = f(x) = \frac{1}{2}x^2 - 1$.

$$
\begin{aligned}
\frac{\Delta y}{\Delta x} &= \frac{\frac{1}{2}(x + \Delta x)^2 - 1 - (\frac{1}{2}x^2 - 1)}{\Delta x} \\[2mm]
&= \frac{\frac{1}{2}x^2 + x\,\Delta x + \frac{1}{2}(\Delta x)^2 - 1 - \frac{1}{2}x^2 + 1}{\Delta x} \\[2mm]
&= \frac{x\,\Delta x + \frac{1}{2}(\Delta x)^2}{\Delta x} \\[2mm]
&= x + \tfrac{1}{2}\Delta x
\end{aligned}
$$

Therefore as Δx approaches 0, $\Delta y / \Delta x$ approaches x.

Problems

Set A

Sketch the following graphs of functions on coordinate paper. Then sketch, as in Examples 1 and 2, the graphs of the derived functions *without doing any computations.*

1.

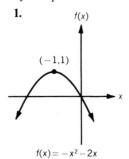

$$f(x) = -x^2 - 2x$$

2.

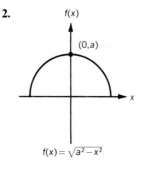

$$f(x) = \sqrt{a^2 - x^2}$$

3. **4.**

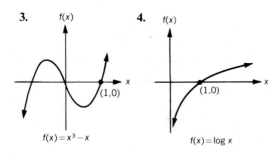

$$f(x) = x^3 - x \qquad f(x) = \log x$$

5. **6.**

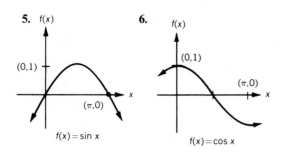

$$f(x) = \sin x \qquad f(x) = \cos x$$

Compute $\Delta y/\Delta x$ for each function $y = f(x)$.

7. $y = f(x) = \frac{1}{4}x^2$

8. $y = f(x) = (x - 2)^2$

9. $y = f(x) = 4x - 3$

10. $y = f(x) = 1/x, \; x > 0.$

11. For each of problems 7–10, give a rule for the derivative of f, by observing what happens to $\Delta y/\Delta x$ as Δx approaches 0.

Set B

12. Consider the function $y = f(x) = x^2$.
   (a) In what interval is f increasing?
   (b) Is $f'(x)$ positive or negative on that interval?
   (c) In what interval is f decreasing?
   (d) Is $f'(x)$ positive or negative in that interval?
   (e) What can be said of f when $f'(x) = 0$?

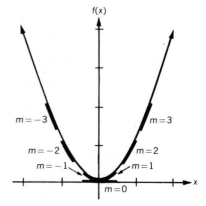

13. (a) Sketch the graph of the polynomial function g, where $g(x) = \frac{1}{4}x^2 + x$ for all x.
   (b) Sketch the graph of g' *without making any computations.*
   (c) Develop a formula for the slope of the secants of g through the points $(x_0, g(x_0))$ and $(x_0 + h, g(x_0 + h))$.
   (d) What is a formula for g'? Compare the graph of g' with your previous guess.
   (e) Show that if $x > -2$, then g is increasing. How does this check with your graph of g? with the graph of g'?

14. (a) Sketch the graph of the function f given by $f(x) = x^3$ for all x.

(b) Sketch the secants through $(1, 1)$ on the graph of f for the values of h given in the table below. Complete the table.

(c)

h	$f(1 + h)$	m
1		
-1		
$\frac{1}{2}$		
$-\frac{1}{2}$		
$\frac{1}{4}$		
$-\frac{1}{4}$		
0.1		
-0.1		

(d) Find a formula for the slope of the secants through (x_0, x_0^3) and $(x_0 + h, (x_0 + h)^3)$.

(e) What is the formula for the slope of the tangent of f at x_0? What is the slope of the tangent at $x = 1$? at $x = \frac{1}{2}$? at $x = 0$?

(f) Sketch the graph of f'. Is $f'(x)$ always positive?

Set C

15. What is the slope of the graph of a function h where $h(x) = f(x) + g(x)$ in terms of the slopes to the graphs of f and g?

16. Sketch the graph of $f(x) = x^3 + x^2 - 2x$. Make a guess as to the shape of the graph of f' by inspecting the graph of f. Compute $f'(x)$ and draw the graph of f'. Compare the graph of f' with your previous guess. Sketch several tangent lines to f.

17. Using a short cut, if you can, compute the slope of the tangent to the graph of

$$f(x) = x^4 - 2x^3 + 6x^2 - x - 2$$

at the point where $x = 1$; at the point where $x = 0.1$.

18. Draw the graph of $y = f(x) = e^x$. Use the graph to sketch the graph of f', the derived function. What relation does there appear to be between f and f'?

19. Suppose that f has domain $[0, 1]$, $f(0) = 1$, and also that $0 < f'(x) < 1$ for x in $[0, 1]$. How large do you think $f(1)$ can be? Why?

Calculator Problem

Draw the graph of $y = f(x) = \ln x$ for $0 < x \le 10$ using a large scale. It is shown, using calculus methods, that the derivative of this function is $f'(x) = 1/x$. Use this fact to draw accurately the tangent lines to f at several points along the curve.

In the last section we derived for certain functions f another function f', whose value at x was the slope of the tangent line at $(x, f(x))$. In this section we shall interpret this derived function f' in another way.

Example 1   Suppose that a tank is being emptied (see Fig. 12), and that the volume V of liquid in the tank, measured in liters, at any time t in minutes, is given by

$$V = f(t) = 4(t - 10)^2, \qquad 0 \le t \le 10.$$

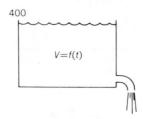

400

$V = f(t)$

FIGURE 12

At $t = 0$ there are 400 L in the tank, while at the end of ten minutes the tank is empty. Therefore, the *average rate of flow* is

$$\frac{\text{volume of liquid emptied}}{\text{elapsed time}} = \frac{400}{10} = 40 \text{ L/min}$$

At the end of five minutes there are 100 L left in the tank, therefore during the first five minutes the average rate of flow was

$$\frac{400 - 100}{5} = 60 \text{ L/min}.$$

During the first minute the average rate was

$$\frac{400 - 324}{1} = 76 \text{ L/min}.$$

These different rates are given by

$$\frac{f(0) - f(10)}{10}, \qquad \frac{f(0) - f(5)}{5}, \qquad \text{and} \qquad \frac{f(0) - f(1)}{1}.$$

The rates computed above are, *except for sign*, equal to the slopes of the secant lines through the points $(0, 400)$ and $(t, f(t))$ of the graph of $V = f(t)$ shown in Fig. 13. Our signs are reversed because we have computed the rate of *decrease* of V.

Let us compute the rate at which V changes over a time interval from t_0 to $t_0 + \Delta t$, where $t_0 + \Delta t \leq 10$. The change in V is

$$\Delta V = f(t_0 + \Delta t) - f(t_0).$$

The average rate of change of V is

$$\Delta V = \frac{f(t_0 + \Delta t) - f(t_0)}{\Delta t}$$

Therefore the average rate of change of V is

$$\Delta V = \frac{4[(t_0 + \Delta t) - 10]^2 - 4(t_0 - 10)^2}{\Delta t}$$

$$= \frac{8\,\Delta t(t_0 - 10) + 4\,\Delta t^2}{\Delta t}$$

$$= 8(t_0 - 10) + 4\,\Delta t.$$

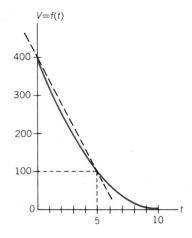

FIGURE 13

By examining our final result, we see that as Δt approaches 0, ΔV approaches $8(t_0 - 10)$. The limiting value of ΔV is the *instantaneous rate of change of V*. Thus the instantaneous rate of change of V at $t = 0$ is $8(0 - 10) = -80$ L/min. When $t = 4$, the instantaneous rate of change is $8(4 - 10) = -48$ L/min.

Example 2   A body falls from rest in a vacuum and after t seconds has fallen a distance S, in centimeters, given by (Fig. 14)

$$S = 490t^2.$$

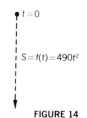

FIGURE 14

TABLE 2

t	0	0.1	0.5	1	2	2.1	2.5	3	4
S	0	4.90	122.5	490	1960	2160.9	3062.5	4410	7840

Let us compute the distance S at various times in order to obtain the average rates (velocities) in several time intervals. The values obtained are listed in Table 2. Since the average velocity v is given by

$$\frac{\text{distance}}{\text{elapsed time}},$$

then the average velocities for several time intervals starting at $t = 0$ are listed in Table 3.

TABLE 3

Time interval	Average velocity, v cm/sec
$t = 0$ to $t = 2$	$1960/2 = 980$
$t = 0$ to $t = 1$	$490/1 = 490$
$t = 0$ to $t = 0.5$	$122.5/0.5 = 245$
$t = 0$ to $t = 0.1$	$4.90/0.1 = 49$

From the table, it appears that as $t \to 0$, then $v \to 0$. Does this conform to the physical situation?

The average velocities starting at $t = 2$ over several time intervals are given in Table 4.

TABLE 4

Time interval	Average velocity, v cm/sec
$t = 2$ to $t = 3$	$(4410 - 1960)/1 = 2450$
$t = 2$ to $t = 2.5$	$(3062.5 - 1960)/0.5 = 2205$
$t = 2$ to $t = 2.1$	$(2160.9 - 1960)/0.1 = 2009$

Suppose we considered even smaller time intervals from $t = 2$. What happens to v? What do you think is meant by the *instantaneous velocity*? What is the instantaneous velocity at $t = 2$? at $t = t_0$?

In these two examples we have seen that the number obtained for the slope of a secant line could also be interpreted as a rate of change of the function in the case where the independent variable is *time*. But this physical (time) restriction is extraneous to the mathematics of the situation. Hence we make the following definition.

Definition 10-7 *The average rate of change of a function f over the interval x_0 to $x_0 + \Delta x$ is the number*

$$\frac{f(x_0 + \Delta x) - f(x_0)}{\Delta x}.$$

Example 3   The average rate of change of the function f given by $y = f(x) = 3x^2 - 2x + 1$ in the interval from $x = 1$ to $x = 3$ is

$$\frac{f(3) - f(1)}{2} = \frac{22 - 2}{2} = 10.$$

The average rate of change of f in the interval from $x = 1$ to $x = 2$ is

$$\frac{f(2) - f(1)}{1} = \frac{9 - 2}{1} = 7.$$

What do you think is the instantaneous rate of change of f at $x = 1$? To answer this question let us find the average rate of change of f over the interval x_0 to $(x_0 + \Delta x)$.

$$\Delta f = \frac{\Delta y}{\Delta x} = \frac{3(x_0 + \Delta x)^2 - 2(x_0 + \Delta x) + 1 - (3x_0{}^2 - 2x_0 + 1)}{\Delta x}$$

$$= \frac{6x_0 \, \Delta x - 2 \, \Delta x + 3\Delta x^2}{\Delta x}$$

$$= 6x_0 - 2 + 3 \, \Delta x.$$

This last result shows that as Δx approaches 0, Δf approaches $6x_0 - 2$. Hence the instantaneous rate of change of f at $x = 1$ is $6(1) - 2 = 4$.

Problems

Set A

Use the function

$$V = f(t) = 4(t - 10)^2$$

of Example 1 and compute the average rate of flow (rate of change of volume) in the time intervals below.

1. $t = 4$ to $t = 6$

2. $t = 4$ to $t = 5$

3. $t = 4$ to $t = 4.5$

4. $t = 4$ to $t = 4.2$

5. $t = 4$ to $t = 4.1$

6. $t = 4$ to $t = 4.01$

7. $t = t_0$ to $t = t_0 + \Delta t$

8. What is the instantaneous rate of flow at $t = 4$?

9. What is the instantaneous rate of flow at $t = t_0$?

A body falls from rest according to formula

$$S = 4.9t^2$$

where S is in meters at t in seconds. Compute the average velocity of the object in the following time intervals.

10. $t = 0$ to $t = 5$

11. $t = 1$ to $t = 5$

12. $t = 2$ to $t = 5$

13. $t = 4$ to $t = 5$

14. $t = 4.5$ to $t = 5$

15. $t = 4.9$ to $t = 5$

16. $t = t_0$ to $t = t_0 + \Delta t$

17. What is the instantaneous velocity at $t = 5$?

18. What is the instantaneous velocity at $t = t_0$?

Set B

A ball is thrown upward from ground level. The distance S in meters that the ball is from the ground at any time t in seconds is given by

$$S = 20t - 4.9t^2, \qquad 0 \le t \le 20/4.9.$$

Compute the average velocity of the ball in the following time intervals.

19. $t = 0$ to $t = 2$ **20.** $t = 0$ to $t = 1$

21. $t = 0$ to $t = 0.5$ **22.** $t = 0$ to $t = 0.1$

23. $t = t_0$ to $t = t_0 + \Delta t$

24. What is the instantaneous velocity at $t = 0$?

25. What is the instantaneous velocity at $t = t_0$?

26. Show that when $t = 20/9.8$, the instantaneous velocity of the ball is 0.

27. How far is the ball above the ground when its instantaneous velocity is 0?

28. If

$$f(x) = x^3 - x^2 + x - 1,$$

what is the average rate of change of f between x and $x + \Delta x$?

29. What is the instantaneous rate of change of f with respect to x for the function f of Problem 28?

Set C

A point "moves" on a coordinatized line so that its coordinate d at any time t is

$$d = f(t) = 3t^2 - 2t + 1.$$

30. Sketch the graph of f for $t \ge 0$.

Compute the average velocity of the point between the following times.

31. $t = 0$ and $t = 1$ **32.** $t = 0$ and $t = \frac{1}{2}$

33. $t = 0$ and $t = 0.1$ **34.** $t = 0$ and $t = h$

35. What is the instantaneous velocity at $t = 0$?

36. What is the average velocity in the interval from t_0 to $t_0 + h$?

37. What is the velocity at t_0?

38. Sketch a graph of the velocity function f'.

39. What is the velocity at $t = 2$? at $t = \frac{1}{2}$?

40. When is the point at rest? That is, at what time t is the velocity 0?

41. *Acceleration* is defined as the rate of change of velocity. What is the acceleration of the point? [*Hint:* Look at the graph of f'.]

42. What is the average rate of change of the area of a circle between radii of r and $r + \Delta r$? What is the instantaneous rate of change of the area with respect to the radius?

Calculator Problem

Let $f(\theta) = \sin \theta$. Calculate the average rate of change of f in the following intervals.

(a) $\frac{\pi}{3}$ to $\left(\frac{\pi}{3} + 0.5\right)$ (b) $\frac{\pi}{3}$ to $\left(\frac{\pi}{3} + 0.4\right)$ (c) $\frac{\pi}{3}$ to $\left(\frac{\pi}{3} + 0.3\right)$

(d) $\frac{\pi}{3}$ to $\left(\frac{\pi}{3} + 0.2\right)$ (e) $\frac{\pi}{3}$ to $\left(\frac{\pi}{3} + 0.1\right)$ (f) $\frac{\pi}{3}$ to $\left(\frac{\pi}{3} + 0.01\right)$

(g) $\frac{\pi}{3}$ to $\left(\frac{\pi}{3} + 0.001\right)$ (h) What is the instantaneous rate of change of f at $\theta = \pi/3$?

Area Under Graphs of Functions

Let us consider a function f that is continuous and always has positive values on $[a, b]$. We shall investigate the area of the set S of all points $P(x, y)$ such that

$$a \leq x \leq b \quad \text{and} \quad 0 \leq y \leq f(x).$$

Set S is the set of points between the graph of f and the x-axis in the interval from a to b (Fig. 15). Our approach will be to examine some cases for simple functions.

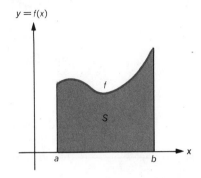

FIGURE 15

Example 1

Suppose f is the identity function, $f(x) = x$ for all x, and we wish to find the area under the graph of f between $x = 0$ and $x = a$ (Fig. 16(a)). Of course, from elementary geometry,

$$A(S) = \tfrac{1}{2}a^2,$$

but suppose we try to obtain this result in another way.

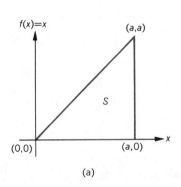

(a)

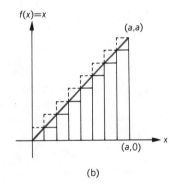

(b)

FIGURE 16

Let us partition the interval $[0, a]$ into n congruent subintervals of equal length, a/n. Then we obtain rectangular strips, as in Fig. 16(b), and we can calculate the sum of the areas of these strips.

Let $\underline{S}_n$ denote the *union* of the shorter rectangles plus their interiors. Then

$$A(\underline{S}_n) = \frac{a}{n} \cdot \frac{a}{n} + \frac{a}{n} \cdot \frac{2a}{n} + \frac{a}{n} \cdot \frac{3a}{n} + \cdots + \frac{a}{n} \cdot \frac{(n-1)a}{n}$$

$$= \frac{a^2}{n^2} (1 + 2 + 3 + \cdots + (n-1)).$$

Now it happens (fortunately) that the sum of the first $n - 1$ natural numbers (the sum in parentheses) is (see Chapter 9)

$$1 + 2 + 3 + \cdots + (n - 1) = \frac{n(n - 1)}{2}.$$

Therefore

$$A(\underline{S}_n) = \frac{a^2}{n^2} \cdot \frac{n(n - 1)}{2} = \frac{a^2}{2}\left(1 - \frac{1}{n}\right). \tag{1}$$

Evidently the number $A(\underline{S}_n)$ is a lower bound of the area of the set S.

In the same manner, if we denote the larger rectangles, those with the dotted tops in Fig. 16(b), plus their interiors by $\overline{S}_n$, then

$$A(\overline{S}_n) = \frac{a}{n} \cdot \frac{a}{n} + \frac{a}{n} \cdot \frac{2a}{n} + \frac{a}{n} \cdot \frac{3a}{n} + \cdots + \frac{a}{n} \cdot \frac{na}{n}$$

$$= \frac{a^2}{n^2}(1 + 2 + 3 + \cdots + n)$$

$$= \frac{a^2}{n^2} \cdot \frac{n(n + 1)}{2} = \frac{a^2}{2}\left(1 + \frac{1}{n}\right). \tag{2}$$

We see that the number $A(\overline{S}_n)$ given in (2) is an upper bound of the area of the set S. Therefore, if S is the set of points of the triangle plus its interior, then

$$\frac{a^2}{2}\left(1 - \frac{1}{n}\right) \leq A(S) \leq \frac{a^2}{2}\left(1 + \frac{1}{n}\right). \tag{3}$$

Now when the number n gets large, that is, the rectangular strips become very narrow, the fraction $1/n$ in (3) approaches 0 and $A(S)$ approaches $a^2/2$ as one would expect from the formula for the area of a triangle. Is it clear to you why this scheme is sometimes referred to as "the mathematical vise"?

Example 2   We now consider the area of the set of points under the graph of $f(x) = x^2$ and between $x = 0$ and $x = a$.

Elementary geometry does not supply an immediate answer in this case. We must try some scheme, and the one that was successful in the previous example suggests itself.

We partition the interval $[0, a]$ into n congruent subintervals of length a/n and construct the upper and lower rectangles, as shown in Fig. 17. Let $\underline{S}_n$ be the set of

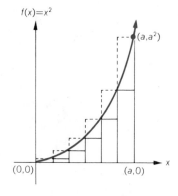

FIGURE 17

points of the lower rectangles plus their interiors. Then

$$A(\underline{S}_n) = \frac{a}{n} \cdot \left(\frac{a}{n}\right)^2 + \frac{a}{n} \cdot \left(\frac{2a}{n}\right)^2 + \frac{a}{n} \cdot \left(\frac{3a}{n}\right)^2 + \cdots + \frac{a}{n}\left[\frac{(n-1)a}{n}\right]^2$$

$$= \frac{a^3}{n^3}(1 + 4 + 9 + \cdots + (n-1)^2).$$

As in the previous example, there is a fine formula (see Chapter 9) for the sum of the squares of the first k integers:

$$1^2 + 2^2 + 3^2 + \cdots + k^2 = \frac{k(k+1)(2k+1)}{6}.$$

Therefore

$$A(\underline{S}_n) = \frac{a^3}{n^3} \cdot \frac{(n-1)(n)(2n-1)}{6} = \frac{a^3}{3}\left(1 - \frac{3}{2n} + \frac{1}{2n^2}\right). \qquad (4)$$

Similarly, we let $\overline{S}_n$ be the set of points in and on the upper rectangles. Then

$$A(\overline{S}_n) = \frac{a}{n} \cdot \left(\frac{a}{n}\right)^2 + \frac{a}{n} \cdot \left(\frac{2a}{n}\right)^2 + \cdots + \frac{a}{n} \cdot \left(\frac{na}{n}\right)^2$$

$$= \frac{a^3}{n^3}(1 + 2^2 + \cdots + n^2) = \frac{a^3}{n^3} \cdot \frac{n(n+1)(2n+1)}{6}$$

$$= \frac{a^3}{3}\left(1 + \frac{3}{2n} + \frac{1}{2n^2}\right). \qquad (5)$$

Therefore, if S is the set of points under the graph of $f(x) = x^2$ between $x = 0$ and $x = a$, then equations (4) and (5) imply that

$$\frac{a^3}{3}\left(1 - \frac{3}{2n} + \frac{1}{2n^2}\right) \leq A(S) \leq \frac{a^3}{3}\left(1 + \frac{3}{2n} + \frac{1}{2n^2}\right). \qquad (6)$$

Now suppose n becomes large. What happens to $A(S)$? What is the area under the graph of $f(x) = x^2$ from $x = 0$ to $x = a$?

Problems

Set A

1. If f is a constant function, $f(x) = c$ for all x, $c > 0$, show that the area under the graph of f for $0 \leq x \leq a$ is $a \cdot c$, using the technique of Examples 1 and 2 of this section.

2. What is the area under the graph of f where $f(x) = x + 2$, $0 \leq x \leq a$?

3. Compute, approximately, the area under the graph of $y = x^2$ between 0 and 1 by counting squares. Draw the curve on graph paper with each small square 0.1 unit on a side. Check by using the formula of Example 2.

4. What is the area under the graph of $f(x) = x^2$ between $x = 1$ and $x = 2$?

5. What is the area under the graph of $f(x) = 2x^2$ between $x = 0$ and $x = a$? Justify your answer.

6. How do the areas under the graphs of $y = Ax$ and $y = Bx$ between $x = 0$ and $x = a$ compare, if $A > B > 0$? (See the accompanying figure.)

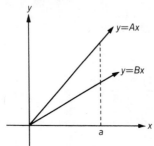

Set B

7. What is the area under the graph of $f(x) = x^2 + 1$ between $x = 0$ and $x = a$? Can you think of different ways of finding the area?

8. Obtain a formula for the area under $f(x) = x^2$ between $x = a$ and $x = b$, where $b > a$.

9. The figure below is a graph of a continuous, positive function f defined for $x > 0$. Draw an approximate graph of the area function, A, where $A(x)$ is the area under the graph of f between $x = 0$ and x.

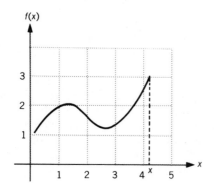

Set C

10. What is the area under $F(x) = \sqrt{x}$ between $x = 0$ and $x = a$?

11. Find the area under $f(x) = x^3$ between $x = 0$ and $x = a$. [*Hint:* Use the fact that

$$1^3 + 2^3 + 3^3 + \cdots + n^3 = \frac{n^2(n + 1)^2}{4}.]$$

12. Use your answer to Problem 11 to compute the area under $y = \sqrt[3]{x}$ between $x = 0$ and $x = a$.

13. What is the area of the shaded region shown in the figure below:

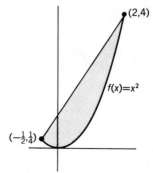

14. Suppose f is a function that is not always positive. What do you think is meant by the "area under the graph of f"? [*Hint:* We should, perhaps, like the process of the illustrative examples to be the same in all cases.]

15. In physics, when a constant force F acts in a straight line through a distance d, the work done is $F \cdot d$. Suppose that the force is not constant. How does one then compute the work? Suppose that the force is proportional to the distance x (as is the case of a spring stretched an amount x). What is the work in this case?

Calculator Problem

Let $y = f(x) = \dfrac{1}{x}$. Find the area of the upper and lower rectangles under the graph of f from $x = 1$ to $x = e = 2.718.\ldots$ Use rectangles of width 0.2 except for the last rectangle whose width is $e - 2.6$. Use the result of the calculations to guess the exact area under the curve in the interval $[1, e]$.

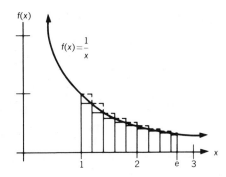

10-7 Differential and Integral Calculus

By the middle of the seventeenth century, mathematicians were familiar with all the results we have obtained to date in this chapter and many more. They could compute tangents to graphs of a considerable variety of functions. Furthermore, they could compute areas under a variety of curves—using the same painful methods that we have used. But there was no real system to all this work. Problems that today can be handled with dispatch often called for exceedingly clever algebraic manipulation. What was needed was a set of calculation rules, easy to apply, that would work on "most" of the functions and would solve each kind of problem. On reading the history of those times, the beginning student will probably wonder why the light did not dawn sooner.

One of the troubles was that each object to be calculated, namely slope of the tangent and area under the curve, was a *limit*.

For slope, the desired number is

$$m = \lim_{\Delta x \to 0} \frac{f(x_0 + \Delta x) - f(x_0)}{\Delta x} = f'(x_0). \tag{1}$$

The *differential calculus* consists of a set of *rules* that enable one to compute the limit in (1) for a large class of functions, *without doing* all the tedious details.

From our examples of slopes of tangents we know that

$$
\begin{aligned}
\text{if } \ f(x) &= x, &&\text{then } \ m = f'(x_0) = 1; \\
\text{if } \ f(x) &= x^2, &&\text{then } \ m = f'(x_0) = 2x_0; \\
\text{if } \ f(x) &= x^3, &&\text{then } \ m = f'(x_0) = 3x_0^2.
\end{aligned}
$$

You may have found other rules for other functions and, if so, you have begun to tackle the problem of differential calculus.

For area, one has areas of smaller and larger sets $\underline{S}_n$ and $\overline{S}_n$, and the true area $A(S)$ is

$$
\begin{aligned}
A(S) &= \lim_{n \to \infty} A(\underline{S}_n) \\
&= \lim_{n \to \infty} A(\overline{S}_n).
\end{aligned}
\tag{2}
$$

This common limit is called the *integral* of the function f over the given interval.

The *integral calculus* consists of a set of *rules* that enable one to compute the limit in (2) for a large class of functions, *without doing* all the tedious details.

From the examples in the previous section we know that the area $A(x)$ under the graph of f and over the interval from 0 to x_0 is

$$A(x_0) = x_0 \qquad \text{if} \quad f(x) = 1;$$

$$A(x_0) = \frac{x_0^2}{2} \qquad \text{if} \quad f(x) = x;$$

$$A(x_0) = \frac{x_0^3}{3} \qquad \text{if} \quad f(x) = x^2.$$

Hence, for these simple functions, both problems of differential and integral calculus are solved. For these functions we can calculate quite complicated limits by the simple rules given above.

It so happens that the problem of the differential calculus, namely, the discovery of algorithms for computing slopes of tangent lines, can be solved completely *for the elementary functions*. In other words, rules can be given such that for each elementary function f, the slope function f' can be written quite easily. To go into additional detail would be to write half of a calculus book. Let it suffice to say that there are no inherent difficulties here as soon as the notion of limit is made precise.

With regard to area, the problem is more complicated, and it apparently took the insight of men of genius (Newton and Leibniz) to see the "trick" involved. The trick, if we may call it that, lies in the observation that the two problems are related. The exercises below are chosen to suggest to you this relation. Once the relation between the problems is understood, the solution to the problem of the differential calculus furnishes a solution to the problem of the integral calculus.

Problems

Set A

1. What is the area $A(x_0)$ between 0 and x_0 under the graph of f if $f(x) = 1$ for all x? Graph the area function A. Compute the slope of the tangent at x on the graph of A.

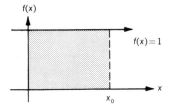

2. What is the area $A(x_0)$ between 0 and x_0 under the graph of f if $f(x) = x$ for all x? Graph the area function A. Compute the slope of the tangent at x on the graph of A.

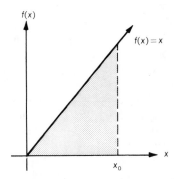

3. What is the area $A(x_0)$ between 0 and x_0 under the graph of f if $f(x) = x^2$ for all x? Graph the area function A. Compute the slope of the tangent at x on the graph of A.

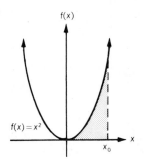

Set B

4. What is the area $A(x_0)$ between 0 and x_0 under the graph of f if $f(x) = \frac{1}{2}x + 2$ for all x? Graph the area function A. Compute the slope of the tangent at x on the graph of A.

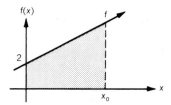

5. Show that the area under the graph of $f(x) = x^2 + 1$ from $x = 0$ to $x = 1$ is $1\frac{1}{3}$.

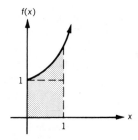

Set C

6. Suppose that f is an increasing function and is continuous. (The requirement that f be increasing is not necessary, but is convenient here for clarity.) Let $A(x)$ be the area under the graph of f between 0 and x. Obtain upper and lower bounds of $A(x + h) - A(x)$, $h > 0$. Show that the slope of $A(x)$ at x is between $f(x)$ and $f(x + h)$. From this result decide what $A'(x)$ is equal to.

Calculator Problem

Sketch a graph of $f(x) = \sin x$ for x in $[0, \pi]$. Divide the interval from 0 to π into ten subintervals of length $\pi/10$. Compute the sums $\underline{S}_n$ and $\overline{S}_n$ of the lower and upper rectangles. What do you think is the exact area under the curve in this interval?

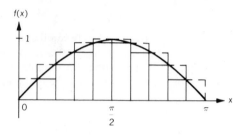

10-8   Limits and Continuity

At various places throughout this book we have spoken intuitively about limits of functions and continuity. Now, in this chapter, we have seen that in finding the slope of a tangent line to the graph of a function or the area under its graph *limits necessarily occur*. The object of study is *defined to be* a limit. (The same situation arose in Chapter 9 where we defined the sum of an infinite series.) There was no real difficulty in finding the limits of the simple functions that occurred, but in more complicated cases one might need to know precisely what must be done to prove that some limit exists or that some function is continuous.

It is the purpose of this section to give precise, arithmetic definitions for these concepts. There is no attempt to be complete. What we do wish to present is the *kind* of arguments one makes.

Definition 10-8 Suppose that c is a real number and f is a function whose domain contains an open interval with c as an end point. Then the "limit of $f(x)$ as x approaches c" is L

$$\lim_{x \to c} f(x) = L,$$

if to each positive number ϵ, there corresponds a *positive* number δ such that

$$|f(x) - L| < \epsilon \quad \text{if} \quad 0 < |x - c| < \delta.$$

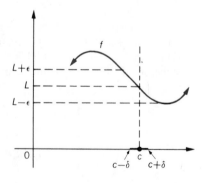

FIGURE 18

We see from Fig. 18 that if x is different from c and is located between $c - \delta$ and $c + \delta$, then $f(x)$ is between $L - \epsilon$ and $L + \epsilon$.

Remarks

1. The number ϵ specifies the closeness to L that one wants to achieve. The number δ specifies a closeness to c that will ensure that $f(x)$ is within a distance ϵ from L.

2. The definition does *not* provide a technique for calculating L. What the definition does is supply a criterion that one uses to *test* a number L to see whether it is actually the limit of $f(x)$ as x approaches c.

3. The value of f at c does not matter so far as the limit is concerned. Indeed, f need not even be defined at c.

Example 1 To determine $\lim_{x \to 2} (3x - 7)$, we first guess that

the limit $L = -1$. Hence we must show that

$$|f(x) - L| = |3x - 7 - (-1)| = |3x - 6|$$

is small when x is near 2. Let us suppose $\epsilon > 0$ is given; then

$$|f(x) - L| = |3x - 6| = 3|x - 2| < \epsilon$$

if

$$|x - 2| < \frac{\epsilon}{3}.$$

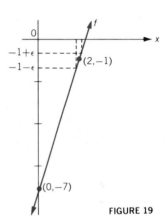

FIGURE 19

Therefore, if we choose $\delta = \epsilon/3$, we will have fulfilled the conditions of the definition. One can see from the graph in Fig. 19 that $\delta = \epsilon/3$ will work.

2 To prove that $\lim_{x \to 1} x^2 = 1$, we must show that $|x^2 - 1|$ is small if $|x - 1|$ is small enough. Hence, let us suppose that $\epsilon > 0$ is given and let us consider

$$|x^2 - 1| = |x - 1|\,|x + 1|.$$

If x is near 1, then $|x + 1|$ is not too large. If we restrict x to the interval $0 \le x \le 2$, then $|x + 1| \le 3$ and so

$$|x^2 - 1| \le 3|x - 1| \qquad \text{if} \qquad 0 \le x \le 2 \quad \text{or} \quad |x - 1| \le 1.$$

We are now in a satisfactory position to choose δ. We want to choose $\delta > 0$ such that $\delta \le 1$ and

$$3|x - 1| < \epsilon \qquad \text{if} \qquad |x - 1| < \delta.$$

Remember that we should have $\delta \le 1$ in order that $|x + 1| \le 3$. Therefore, if we choose

$$\delta = \text{minimum of } \frac{\epsilon}{3} \text{ and } 1,$$

then

$$|x^2 - 1| = |x - 1|\,|x + 1| < \frac{\epsilon}{3} \cdot 3 = \epsilon$$

if

$$|x - 1| < \delta.$$

The conditions of the definition are satisfied (Fig. 20).

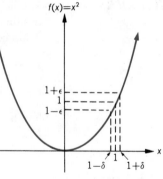

FIGURE 20

We return now to a consideration of continuity. First we give some examples of discontinuous functions to aid the intuition. Figure 21 represents three graphs of functions, f, g, and h, defined on a closed interval (shown as a heavy line) containing the point c. Each is discontinuous at c. In (a) the limits of $f(x)$, from either side of c, appear to exist but do not equal the value of f at c. In (b) $\lim_{x \to c} g(x)$ does not exist. The graph oscillates near c. In part (c) the function appears to become infinite near c, but at c it is finite.

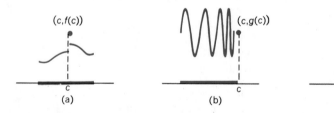

FIGURE 21

Definition 10-9 If f is defined on an interval containing c, then f is *continuous at c* if

$$\lim_{x \to c} f(x) = f(c).$$

In other words, when x is close to c, then $f(x)$ is close to $f(c)$. In terms of "epsilons and deltas" this means that given $\epsilon > 0$, there is a $\delta > 0$ such that

$$|f(x) - f(c)| < \epsilon \quad \text{if} \quad |x - c| < \delta.$$

Definition 10-9 defines continuity at a point. The functions in which one is usually interested are continuous at all points where they are defined.

Definition 10-10 A function defined on an interval, open or closed, is *continuous on that interval* if it is continuous at each point of the interval.

In Chapter 2 the Intermediate-Value Theorem was discussed and used. We restate this theorem here and give a proof. Observe that in the proof we have occasion to use the completeness property of the real number system.

Theorem 10-2   *Suppose that f is a real-valued function that is continuous on the interval [a, b], and that $f(a) < f(b)$. Suppose now that d is a number between $f(a)$ and $f(b)$, so that $f(a) < d < f(b)$. Then there is at least one number c between a and b such that $d = f(c)$.*

Proof   Let A be the subset of $[a, b]$ consisting of numbers x such that $f(x) < d$. (See Fig. 22.) Then A is not empty because a is in A. Furthermore, since every member of A is less than b, the set A is bounded above. Let $c = \text{lub } A$.

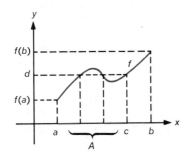

FIGURE 22

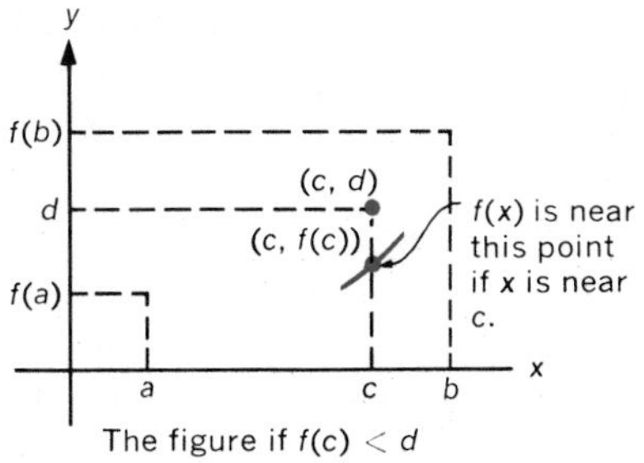

FIGURE 23

We shall prove that $f(c) = d$ by proving that $f(c) < d$ and $f(c) > d$ are impossible. Let us suppose that $f(c) < d$. (See Fig. 23.) We will apply the definition of continuity at c to obtain a contradiction. We denote by ϵ the difference $\epsilon = d - f(c)$, which is positive. There is a positive number δ such that

$$|f(x) - f(c)| < \epsilon \qquad \text{if} \qquad |x - c| < \delta.$$

So we have

$$f(c) - \epsilon < f(x) < f(c) + \epsilon \qquad \text{if} \qquad -\delta < x - c < \delta.$$

In particular, we have

$$f(x) < d \qquad \text{if} \qquad c < x < c + \delta.$$

But this last inequality implies that $f(x) < d$ for numbers x larger than c. This contradicts the choice of c as an upper bound of A. Therefore $f(c)$ cannot be less than d, so $f(c) \geq d$. A similar argument can be made to show that $f(c)$ cannot be greater than d. Hence $f(c) = d$, and the proof is complete.

There are many theorems concerning continuous functions. One studies these theorems in analysis. They are beyond the scope of this book. Two of these numerous theorems are stated without proof below.

Theorem 10-3   *If f is continuous on the closed interval [a, b], then f is bounded on that interval. Furthermore, if M is the least upper bound of f on the interval, then there is a point c of the interval such that f(c) = M.*

Theorem 10-4   *If both f and g are continuous functions on an interval, then f + g, f − g, f · g, and f/g (except where g is 0) are continuous functions on that interval.*

It is this last theorem that allows us to conclude rather easily that large classes of functions are continuous. Thus it is easy to see that constant functions are continuous. Likewise, it is easy to prove that the identity function, $f(x) = x$, also is continuous. Now we can use Theorem 10–4 to conclude that the functions given by the following formulas are continuous:

$$5x, \qquad x^2 = x \cdot x, \qquad 2x^2 - 3x + 7, \qquad x^3 = x^2 \cdot x, \qquad 7x^3 - 34x, \quad \text{etc.}$$

Continuing in this way, one sees that all polynomials are continuous functions. Moreover, again from Theorem 10–4, we can conclude that all rational functions are continuous at points where the function in the denominator does not vanish.

Problems

Set A

Guess what the following limits are. Then apply Definition 10–8 to prove that your guess is correct.

1. $\lim\limits_{x \to 6} (\frac{1}{3}x + 1)$ 2. $\lim\limits_{x \to -1} (2x + 5)$

3. $\lim\limits_{x \to 2} x^2$ 4. $\lim\limits_{x \to -2} (x - 4)$

5. Show that the function $f(x) = x^2$ for all real x is continuous at $x = 2$.

6. The function g defined by

$$g(x) = \tfrac{1}{2}x + \tfrac{3}{2} \quad \text{if} \quad -3 \leq x \leq 1,$$

$$g(x) = -x + 5 \quad \text{if} \quad 1 < x \leq 4,$$

is a discontinuous function. Sketch the graph of g and determine a point of discontinuity of g from the graph.

Set B

7. The function $f(x) = 3x^3 - x + 1$ is continuous for all x.
   (a) Use the Intermediate Value Theorem to prove that f has a zero between -1 and 0.
   (b) Approximate this zero of f to the nearest tenth.

8. The continuous function g is given by $g(x) = -x^2 + 4x - 1$ for all x.
   (a) Find the least upper bound of g in $[0, 3]$.
   (b) Find a number c in $[0, 3]$ such that $g(c) = M$ where M is the least upper bound of g in $[0, 3]$.

Set C

9. Graph the function

$$f(x) = \frac{x^2 - 4}{x - 2} \quad \text{for all } x \neq 2,$$

$$f(2) = 1.$$

Is f continuous at $x = 2$?

Guess the limit for each function. Then prove that your guess is correct.

10. $\lim\limits_{x \to -1} (x^2 + 3x)$

11. $\lim\limits_{x \to 1} \dfrac{x + 1}{x + 2}$

12. $\lim\limits_{x \to 1/2} \dfrac{1}{x}$

Calculator Problem

Compute

$$\frac{\sin\left(\dfrac{\pi}{6} + h\right) - \sin\dfrac{\pi}{6}}{h}$$

for $h = 0.1, 0.01, 0.001, 0.0001$, and compare with $\cos \pi/6$.

Summary

The basic problem in differential calculus and the basic problem in integral calculus have been examined in a very cursory way in this chapter. In this brief examination of the problems we have not gone into detail, nor have we attempted to pursue the innumerable applications of the calculus. All that we have done is present the two fundamental concepts, each of which is a *limit*. The two concepts are *derivative* and *integral*. The derivative we interpreted as a slope and a rate of change; the integral we interpreted as an area.

1. The derivative f' of a function f has, at a point x, the value

$$f'(x) = \lim_{\Delta x \to 0} \frac{f(x + \Delta x) - f(x)}{\Delta x}.$$

There are short-cut rules for calculating f' for the elementary functions. These rules comprise a part of the *differential calculus*. We have found a few of these rules.

2. The area under the graph of f over a given interval is also a limit, called the *integral* of f over the interval:

$$A(S) = \lim_{n \to \infty} A(\underline{S}_n) = \lim_{n \to \infty} A(\overline{S}_n).$$

There also exist short-cut rules for finding this limit. These short cuts exist because the problem of area is related to the problem of tangents.

10-2   **1.** What is the inclination of a line whose slope is 1?

2. A line has an inclination of $5\pi/6$. What is its slope?

3. What is the slope of a line containing the points $(4, 2)$ and $(-1, -2)$?

10-3   **4.** What is the slope of the tangent at any point of a constant function $f(x) = c$ for all x?

5. At what point is the slope of the tangent to the graph of $f(x) = x^2$ equal to 0?

6. Show that the slope of the secant of the function f given by

$$f(x) = \frac{1}{x}, \qquad x > 0,$$

through the points $(a, f(a))$ and $(b, f(b))$, $0 < a < b$, is $-1/ab$. What is $f'(a)$?

7. Find a formula for the slope of the secants through $(x_0, f(x_0))$ and $((x_0 + h), f(x_0 + h))$ of the function f of Problem 6. What is the slope of the tangent of f at x_0?

10-4   **8.** Compute $\Delta y/\Delta x$ for the function $f(x) = x^2 + 3x$.

9. Using the function f of Problem 8, compute the derivative $f'(x)$.

10-5   A car is moving according to the formula $d = 48t - 3t^2$, where d is distance in meters and t is time in seconds.

10. What is the average velocity in the interval from $t = 0$ to $t = 1$?

11. What is the average velocity in the interval from $t = 0$ to $t = 2$? Is the car accelerating or slowing down?

12. What is the instantaneous velocity at any time t_0?

13. At what time will the car be motionless?

10-6   **14.** The area under the graph of a function f from $x = 0$ to x is given by $A(x) = 2x^2$. What is a formula for $f(x)$?

15. Find the area of the region under the graph of the function f between $x = 2$ and $x = 5$ if $f(x) = x^2$.

10-7   **16.** Does differential calculus deal with the problem of finding tangents to functions or the area under the graph of a function?

10-8   **17.** Complete the following definition.

If f is defined on an interval containing c, then f is continuous at c if . . .

18. Prove that $\lim_{x \to 1} (2x + 1) = 3$.

Historical Note

Sir Issac Newton
(1642–1727)

Gottfried Wilhelm Leibniz
(1646–1716)

Sir Isaac Newton (1642–1727) was one of the great minds of all time. He is acclaimed by physicists for his mechanics, his theory of gravitation, and his optics. He is acclaimed by mathematicians for his discovery of the calculus.

Newton entered Trinity College, Cambridge, England in 1661 and soon became absorbed in mathematics and physics. He took his undergraduate degree in January 1664. The following year there was a recurrence of the bubonic plague, and the university was closed for about two years. In this time he invented the calculus (which he called the *method of fluxions*), discovered universal gravitation, and showed that white light is a blend of all colors.

Rather than have his work published, Newton was content to communicate his discoveries to friends in letters. Finally, at the continued and urgent insistence of his friends, he published his great masterpiece, *Philosophiae Naturalis Principia Mathematica* (*Mathematical Principles of Natural Philosophy*), in 1687, almost twenty years after his discovery of much of it.

Gottfried Wilhelm Leibniz (1646–1716) was largely self-taught when he began the study of law, obtaining a doctor's degree at the age of 20 in 1666.

In 1672 Leibniz persuaded the physicist Christian Huygens to tutor him in mathematics. It was at once clear that Leibniz was a natural mathematician, for he was soon making his own discoveries. He even invented a calculating machine.

By 1676 he had worked out the essential features of the calculus, both differential and integral, which he published in 1677. This was eleven years after Newton's discovery and ten years before Newton's *Principia*. Leibniz had developed a particularly appropriate notation, which is still in use today. Hence his ideas were seized upon by the mathematicians of continental Europe, who during the ensuing 20 years developed them into a powerful tool. In Newton's England, the calculus remained a curiosity.

Thus came about the bitter controversy over priority in the discovery of the calculus. The consensus of modern scholarship is that the two men made their discoveries independently of each other, a noteworthy example of new ideas occurring simultaneously to two people who have little or no connection with one another.

Part II
Analytic Geometry

Chapter 11
The Plane

11-1   Introduction

The invention of *analytic geometry,* usually accredited to Rene Descartes (1596–1650), was one of the significant developments in mathematics history. Plane analytic geometry relates algebra and plane geometry. This relation is made possible by the coordinatization of lines and planes. By establishing a one-to-one correspondence between the set of points of the plane and the set of ordered pairs of real numbers we can study the properties of geometric figures by algebraic methods.

In later chapters we shall see that space can be coordinatized much as the plane. Then we can study *space geometry* by analytic methods. In this chapter we will confine our attention to the plane and in particular to lines in the plane. In later chapters we shall consider planes and other surfaces and see that vectors can be used to help us in our study of geometry.

11-2   Lines

Everyone is familiar with locating towns on a map by giving distance, in kilometers, along a road. Figure 1 shows a road running approximately northeast. If we wish to find the location of Town B with respect to the crossroads through 0, we must obviously have a way of describing the direction of the road.

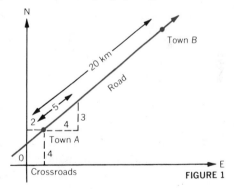

FIGURE 1

Suppose that for every 5 km traveled along the road one moves 3 km north. Then Town B must be 12 km north of Town A. It would also follow that traveling 5 km along the road would take one 4 km east. Then Town B would be 16 km east of Town A. The north and east coordinates of B from the crossroads are $N = 4 + \frac{3}{5} \cdot 20 = 16$, $E = 2 + \frac{4}{5} \cdot 20 = 18$. We can apply the idea of this example to any line.

Let l be any line in the plane and (x_0, y_0) a point on it. (See Fig. 2.) With (x_0, y_0) as the origin, we select one side of (x_0, y_0) on line l as the positive side of the line and coordinatize line l using the same choice of unit as for the x- and y-axes. Then each point (x, y) on l is uniquely determined by giving the directed distance from (x_0, y_0). Thus if line l is coordinatized as shown in the figure, then the directed distance along l from (x_0, y_0) to point R is 3 units, and the directed distance from (x_0, y_0) to point S is -2 units.

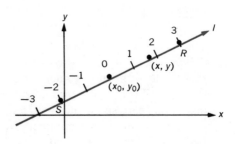

FIGURE 2

If (x_0, y_0) is the origin of coordinates, then there are two coordinatizations of l depending on which direction along l is the positive direction. These two coordinatizations are shown in Fig. 3.

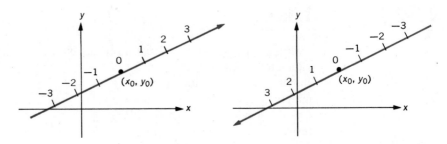

FIGURE 3

Remarks

1. Observe that there are *two coordinate systems* involved: the rectangular coordinates, x and y, in the plane, and the coordinate system on l which gives the directed distance from (x_0, y_0) on l.

2. The distance formula can be used to find the undirected distance between two points on a line where rectangular coordinates are known. Recall that if P_0 and P_1 are two points with coordinates (x_0, y_0) and (x_1, y_1), respectively, then $|P_0 P_1| = \sqrt{(x_1 - x_0)^2 + (y_1 - y_0)^2}$.

Example　A line containing the points $A(3, 1)$ and $B(-3, 3)$ is coordinatized with $(3, 1)$ as the origin and $(-3, 3)$ on the negative side of $(3, 1)$. (See Fig. 4.) Find the undirected and the directed distances from A to B.

Solution. The undirected distance from A to B is

$$|AB| = \sqrt{(-3-3)^2 + (3-1)^2}$$
$$= \sqrt{(-6)^2 + 2^2} = 2\sqrt{10}.$$

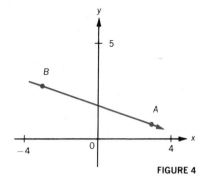

FIGURE 4

Since B is on the negative side of A, the directed distance from A to B is $AB = -2\sqrt{10}$.

Problems

Set A

1. A line l contains the points $(-4, 5)$ and $(2, 3)$. Suppose l is coordinatized with $(-4, 5)$ as the origin and $(2, 3)$ on the positive side of $(-4, 5)$. What is the directed distance d from $(-4, 5)$ to $(2, 3)$?

2. In Problem 1, if $(2, 3)$ had been the origin of coordinates and $(-4, 5)$ had been on the negative side of $(2, 3)$, what would have been the directed distance from $(2, 3)$ to $(-4, 5)$?

3. A line bisects the first and third quadrants. Find the rectangular coordinates of the two points on the line at a distance 5 from the origin. Find the coordinates of the two points on the line at a distance 5 from $(1, 1)$.

Set B

A line passes through $(0, 0)$ and $(3, 4)$ and is positively directed from $(0, 0)$ to $(3, 4)$.

4. Find the directed distance from $(0, 0)$ to $(3, 4)$.

5. Find the rectangular coordinates of a point whose directed distance from $(0, 0)$ is 10.

6. What are the coordinates of a point whose directed distance from $(0, 0)$ is -5?

7. What are the coordinates of a point whose directed distance from $(3, 4)$ is -5?

8. What are the coordinates of a point whose directed distance from $(3, 4)$ is -10?

9. A line passes through $(0, 0)$ and $(-3, 4)$, and is positively directed from $(0, 0)$ to $(6, -8)$. Determine the rectangular coordinates of the point whose directed distance from $(0, 0)$ is 10; whose directed distance from $(0, 0)$ is -10; whose directed distance from $(-3, 4)$ is -10.

10. A certain town, P_0, is 3 miles east and 2 miles north of a north–south and an east–west crossroads. A straight road runs northwesterly in such a way that if you travel 13 miles along the road, you will move 5 miles north.

    (a) How many miles west will you travel for each 13 miles along the road?

    (b) How many miles from P_0 must you travel along the road before reaching the north–south road?

Calculator Problem

The longest straight run of railroad track in the world is in Australia. It runs eastward from Loongana to Ooldea, a distance of 478 km. For every 100 km traveled along the railroad track eastward from Loongana, the distance traveled due north is 5.5 km and the distance traveled due east is 99.8 km. Assume that the earth is flat.

(a) How far north of Loongana is Ooldea?

(b) How far east of Loongana is Ooldea?

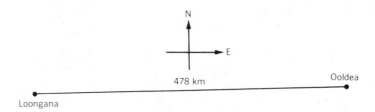

11-3   Parametric Equations of Lines

We continue our examination of a line l in the plane. We wish to express the coordinates of a point (x, y) on the line in terms of (x_0, y_0) and the directed-distance coordinate on l. Remember that there are *two* coordinate systems involved: the rectangular coordinates in the plane and the directed distance from (x_0, y_0) on l. For this purpose it will be convenient for us to consider the angles that a directed line makes with the coordinate axes.

Definition 11-1 Let l be any directed line. The angles formed by the positive ray of the directed line l and the positive x- and y-axes are called the *direction angles* of l and have measures denoted by α and β, respectively. (See Fig. 5.)

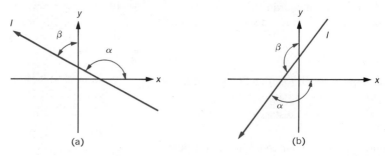

FIGURE 5

Remarks

1. Observe that for all α and β, $0 \le \alpha \le \pi$, and $0 \le \beta \le \pi$.

2. Clearly, the direction of l is known when α and β are known.

Now what arises naturally, as we shall see, are the cosines of the angles with measures α and β.

Definition 11-2 If α and β are the measures of the direction angles of a directed line l, then the *direction cosines* of l are $\cos \alpha$ and $\cos \beta$.

Remarks

3. The values of $\cos \alpha$ and $\cos \beta$ determine the direction angles uniquely. If $\cos \alpha \ge 0$, then $0 \le \alpha \le \pi/2$, and if $\cos \alpha < 0$, then $\pi/2 < \alpha \le \pi$. This is also true for β.

4. The measures of the direction angles of the oppositely directed line will be $\pi - \alpha$ and $\pi - \beta$, and therefore the direction cosines will be

$$\cos (\pi - \alpha) = -\cos \alpha \quad \text{and} \quad \cos (\pi - \beta) = -\cos \beta.$$

The relation between the rectangular coordinates of points on l, direction cosines, and directed distance along l is given by the following theorem.

Theorem 11-1 *Given the directed line l with direction angles whose measures are α and β, let (x, y) and (x_0, y_0) be distinct points on l with directed distance from (x_0, y_0) to (x, y) equal to d. (See Fig. 6.) Then*

$$\cos \alpha = \frac{x - x_0}{d} \quad \text{and} \quad \cos \beta = \frac{y - y_0}{d}. \tag{1}$$

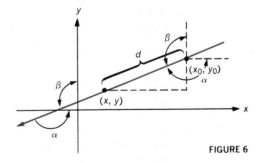

FIGURE 6

Proof For the directed line shown in Fig. 6, with (x, y) and (x_0, y_0) situated as shown, both α and β are obtuse and d is positive. From the right triangle in the figure it is clear that

$$|\cos \alpha| = \frac{|x - x_0|}{d} \quad \text{and} \quad |\cos \beta| = \frac{|y - y_0|}{d}. \tag{2}$$

Since α and β are greater than $\pi/2$, $\cos \alpha$ and $\cos \beta$ are negative. Also, from the figure, $x - x_0$ and $y - y_0$ are negative. Therefore from equations (2) we conclude that

$$\cos \alpha = \frac{x - x_0}{d} \qquad \text{and} \qquad \cos \beta = \frac{y - y_0}{d}.$$

If the point (x, y) were on the other side of (x_0, y_0), the same equations would hold. Both numerator and denominator in (1) would change sign.

Regardless of the direction of the line, a similar proof can be made. The result is always the same.

Remarks

5. Equations (1) provide a means for computing the direction cosines of a directed line if two points on the line are given.

6. Frequently we will use c_1 and c_2 for direction cosines. Then $c_1 = \cos \alpha$ and $c_2 = \cos \beta$. Sometimes c_1 is called the x-direction cosine and c_2 the y-direction cosine.

Theorem 11-2

Given a directed line l with direction cosines c_1 and c_2, a point $P(x, y)$ at a directed distance d from (x_0, y_0) on l has coordinates

$$\begin{cases} x = x_0 + c_1 d, \\ y = y_0 + c_2 d. \end{cases} \tag{3}$$

Conversely, if x and y are given by (3), then the point (x, y) is on l.

Proof If $d \neq 0$, then equations (1) are equivalent to (3). If $d = 0$, then $(x, y) = (x_0, y_0)$.

Conversely, if equations (3) are satisfied, and $d \neq 0$, then the point (x, y) is on l because equations (3) are then equivalent to equations (1):

$$\frac{x - x_0}{d} = c_1 = \cos \alpha \qquad \text{and} \qquad \frac{y - y_0}{d} = c_2 = \cos \beta,$$

so that (x, y) is on the directed line through (x_0, y_0) with direction angles of measures α and β. If $d = 0$, then $(x, y) = (x_0, y_0)$.

Equations (3) are *parametric equations** of the line, with *parameter d*. A *parameter* is merely a variable. The domain of the parameter is just the domain of the variable. It can be any non-empty set. In the parametric equations (3) the domain of the parameter d is the set of all real numbers.

_____

*Parametric equations of a line represent the line as a mapping of the real numbers into the plane. Other curves may also be represented by parametric equations. In general, as the parameter varies, the point in the plane "moves" along the curve.

Example

Find parametric equations of the line through $(-1, 3)$ and $(1, 1)$.

Solution. First we observe that there are several different sets of parametric equations. Either $(-1, 3)$ or $(1, 1)$ could be used as the origin of coordinates on l. Let us select $(1, 1)$. Now we must choose a direction on l as positive. Let us select the ray downward and to the right as the positive direction. (See Fig. 7.)

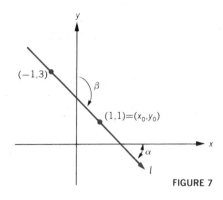

FIGURE 7

Next we must determine the numbers c_1 and c_2. Because we have two points on the line and can compute the distance between $(-1, 3)$ and $(1, 1)$, we can find c_1 and c_2 from equations (3). The distance from $(-1, 3)$ to $(1, 1)$ is

$$\sqrt{(-1 - 1)^2 + (3 - 1)^2} = \sqrt{8} = 2\sqrt{2}.$$

Then the parameter d for the point $(-1, 3)$ is $-2\sqrt{2}$ because $(-1, 3)$ is on the negative side of $(1, 1)$ on l. Hence

$$\cos \alpha = \frac{-1 - 1}{-2\sqrt{2}} = c_1 = \frac{1}{\sqrt{2}}, \qquad \cos \beta = \frac{3 - 1}{-2\sqrt{2}} = c_2 = -\frac{1}{\sqrt{2}}.$$

Observe that it is really evident from the figure that $\alpha = \pi/4$ and $\beta = 3\pi/4$. Parametric equations of the line therefore are

$$\begin{cases} x = 1 + \dfrac{1}{\sqrt{2}}d, \\[2ex] y = 1 - \dfrac{1}{\sqrt{2}}d. \end{cases}$$

By using these equations we can find coordinates of as many points on the line as we like. Thus using $d = 1$, we get the point

$$(1 + 1/\sqrt{2},\ 1 - 1/\sqrt{2}).$$

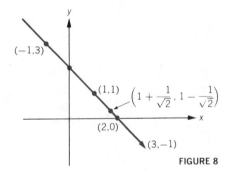

FIGURE 8

For $d = 2\sqrt{2}$, we get the point $(3, -1)$. For $d = -2\sqrt{2}$, we get the given point $(-1, 3)$. For $d = \sqrt{2}$, we get the point $(2, 0)$. (See Fig. 8.)

You should verify that if the other ray from $(1, 1)$ had been selected as the positive direction on l, then the parametric equations would have been

$$x = 1 - \frac{1}{\sqrt{2}}d, \quad \text{and} \quad y = 1 + \frac{1}{\sqrt{2}}d.$$

Likewise, if the point $(-1, 3)$ had been selected as the origin on l, we would have obtained the two sets of parametric equations:

$$\begin{cases} x = -1 + \dfrac{1}{\sqrt{2}}d, \\[2mm] y = 3 - \dfrac{1}{\sqrt{2}}d, \end{cases} \qquad \begin{cases} x = -1 - \dfrac{1}{\sqrt{2}}d, \\[2mm] y = 3 + \dfrac{1}{\sqrt{2}}d. \end{cases}$$

There is an important relation between the direction cosines of a line given in the following theorem.

Theorem 11-3   *If c_1 and c_2 are direction cosines of a directed line, then*

$$c_1^2 + c_2^2 = \cos^2 \alpha + \cos^2 \beta = 1.$$

Proof   From the distance formula

$$(x - x_0)^2 + (y - y_0)^2 = d^2,$$

where (x, y), (x_0, y_0), and d are as in Theorem 11–2. Therefore

$$c_1^2 + c_2^2 = \frac{(x - x_0)^2}{d^2} + \frac{(y - y_0)^2}{d^2} = \frac{(x - x_0)^2 + (y - y_0)^2}{d^2} = 1.$$

Let us suppose that we have a pair of real numbers, r and s, such that $r^2 + s^2 = 1$. Is there a line such that r and s are the direction cosines of the line? The answer to this question is "yes." Indeed, there are infinitely many lines such that r and s are the direction cosines of the lines.

Theorem 11-4   *If r and s are real numbers and $r^2 + s^2 = 1$, then there is a directed line whose direction cosines are the real numbers r and s.*

Proof   It is necessary to find only one such line. Consider the line (Fig. 9) through $(0, 0)$ and (r, s), and directed from 0 toward (r, s). The point (r, s) is at distance 1 from 0; therefore

$$c_1 = \frac{r}{1} = r$$

and

$$c_2 = \frac{s}{1} = s.$$

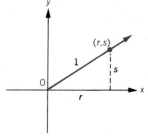

FIGURE 9

Problems

Set A

Find the direction cosines of a line through the following pairs of points. Assume that the positive direction of the line is from the first point to the second point.

1. $(-2, -4)$, $(6, 2)$ **2.** $(2, 2)$, $(-1, 5)$

3. $(0, 0)$, $(2\sqrt{3}, 2)$ **4.** $(-5, -4)$, $(7, 1)$

5. $(-4, 3)$, $(2, 3)$

6. (x_0, y_0), $(x_0 + r, y_0 + s)$

7. Find the direction cosines of line t in the figure below. Find the measures, α and β, of the direction angles.

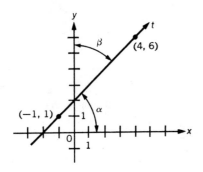

8. Sketch a line that contains the origin and has $c_1 = \frac{3}{5}$ and $c_2 = \frac{4}{5}$.

9. Sketch a line that contains the point $(-2, 3)$ with direction cosines $c_1 = 0$ and $c_2 = 1$.

10. How is the line of Problem 9 related to the coordinate axes?

Find parametric equations for the lines through the following pairs of points. Assume that the first point is (x_0, y_0).

11. $(0, 0)$ and $(3, 4)$ **12.** $(0, 0)$ and $(-3, 4)$

13. $(1, -2)$ and $(-4, -7)$

14. $(-3, -5)$ and $(-5, 2)$

15. $(-1, 1)$ and $(10, 3)$

16. (a, b) and $(a + e, b + f)$

Set B

17. Parametric equations of a line are

$$x = 6 + \frac{4d}{5}, \quad \text{and} \quad y = -8 + \frac{3d}{5}.$$

What are the rectangular coordinates of a point that is

(a) 5 units from $(6, -8)$?
(b) -5 units from $(6, -8)$?
(c) 5 units from $(2, -11)$?
(d) -5 units from $(2, -11)$?

18. If a line is parallel to the x-axis, show that $c_2 = 0$ and $c_1 = 1$ or -1. What are c_1 and c_2 for a line parallel to the y-axis?

19. Find parametric equations of the line through $(2, -3)$ and parallel to the x-axis; parallel to the y-axis.

20. Parametric equations of a line are

$$x = 5 + \frac{1}{\sqrt{5}}d, \quad \text{and} \quad y = -2 + \frac{2}{\sqrt{5}}d.$$

Find the coordinates of the point where the line intersects the x-axis. [*Hint:* The y-coordinate must be 0. Find d.]

21. Equations

$$x = -2 + \frac{1}{3}d \quad \text{and} \quad y = 3 - \frac{2\sqrt{2}}{3}d$$

are parametric equations of a line.

(a) Verify that $c_1^2 + c_2^2 = 1$.
(b) Find several points on the line.
(c) Find the coordinates of the point where the line intersects the y-axis.
(d) Give two other pairs of parametric equations of the line.
(e) Draw the line.

22. A line has parametric equations $x = a$ and $y = b + d$, where d is the parameter. Draw the line.

23. What is the set of points (x, y) such that $x = -2 + \frac{3}{5}d$, $y = 3 - \frac{4}{5}d$, if d is restricted to the interval $-1 \le d \le 4$?

Set C

24. Could the pair of numbers $-\frac{24}{25}$ and $\frac{7}{25}$ be direction cosines of a line? Could the pair $\frac{5}{6}$ and $\frac{1}{3}$ be direction cosines of a line?

25. Let a and b be any two real numbers where a and b are not both 0. Show that

$$\frac{a}{\sqrt{a^2 + b^2}} \quad \text{and} \quad \frac{b}{\sqrt{a^2 + b^2}}$$

are direction cosines of a directed line. Show this in two ways: (1) Use Theorem 11–4. (2) Consider the line through $(0, 0)$ and (a, b).

26. A line contains the point $(3, 0)$ and has direction angles $\alpha = \pi/6$ and $\beta = 2\pi/3$. What are parametric equations of the directed line?

27. Prove that the only point on the line in Problem 26 in which both the x- and y-coordinates are rational numbers is the point $(3, 0)$.

28. Consider the pair of equations,

$$\begin{cases} x = 2 - 2t, \\ y = -1 + 3t, \end{cases}$$

where t is a variable representing any real number.

(a) Find three ordered pairs of real numbers, (x, y), determined by this pair of equations by choosing three values for t.

(b) Show that the three points having the coordinates determined are collinear points.

(c) What are direction cosines of the line?

Calculator Problem

A line contains the point $(3, 3.6)$ and has direction angles $\alpha = \pi/10$ and $\beta = 2\pi/5$. Determine the coordinates of the points of intersection of the line with the x-axis and the y-axis.

11–4   Rectangular Equations of Lines

We have seen that direction cosines of a line tell us which "way" the line goes and that a pair of parametric equations of the line completely determine the line. However there is another way of describing lines in terms of the *slope* of the line.

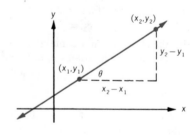

FIGURE 10

Recall that the slope m of a line containing the points (x_1, y_1) and (x_2, y_2) is

$$m = \frac{y_2 - y_1}{x_2 - x_1} = \tan \theta, \qquad \text{where } x_1 \neq x_2.$$

If the line is not parallel to the y-axis it will have a slope, and an equation is easy to find, as we shall see.

But let us first consider lines parallel to the y-axis. Such a line will meet the x-axis in a point $(a, 0)$. (See Fig. 11.) Every point on the line has its x-coordinate equal to a. Conversely, if a point has its x-coordinate equal to a, then the point is on the line through $(a, 0)$ parallel to the y-axis. Therefore the line has the equation $x = a$. Other equations equivalent to $x = a$ are $kx = ka$, where $k \neq 0$.

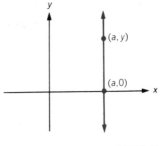

FIGURE 11

Now let us consider lines with slope. The following theorem is basic.

Theorem 11-5 *The point (x, y) is on the line with slope m through (x_1, y_1) if and only if*

$$y - y_1 = m(x - x_1). \tag{1}$$

Proof We prove first that if (x, y) is on the line, then x and y satisfy equation (1). If $(x, y) = (x_1, y_1)$, then (1) becomes $0 = m \cdot 0$, which is certainly true. If $x \neq x_1$, then the slope of the line is

$$m = \frac{y - y_1}{x - x_1},$$

and so $y - y_1 = m(x - x_1)$. This proves that (1) is satisfied if (x, y) is on the line.

Now suppose that x and y are such that $y - y_1 = m(x - x_1)$. If $x = x_1$, then $y = y_1$ and $(x, y) = (x_1, y_1)$, and so the point (x, y) is on the line. If $x \neq x_1$, then

$$\frac{y - y_1}{x - x_1} = m,$$

and we see that (x, y) is a point on the line with slope m through (x_1, y_1). This proves that if x and y satisfy (1), then (x, y) is on the line. This completes the proof.

Equation (1) is called the *point-slope* form for an equation of a line.

Formula (1) takes a particularly simple form if (x_1, y_1) is the point where the line intersects the y-axis. This point is called the y-intercept. It is customary to denote this point by $(0, b)$. Frequently, for brevity, the number b is called the y-intercept.

Corollary *The line with slope m and y-intercept b has an equation*

$$y = mx + b. \tag{2}$$

Equation (2) is often referred to as the *slope-intercept* form for the line.

Example 1   A line has slope $-\frac{1}{2}$ and passes through $(-2, 3)$. Find an equation of the line.

Solution. From Theorem 11-5 its equation is $y - 3 = -\frac{1}{2}(x + 2)$, or the equivalent equation $x + 2y - 4 = 0$.

[*Note:* Two equations are equivalent if they have the same solution sets.]

2   Find an equation of the line with slope $-\frac{2}{3}$ passing through $(0, 3)$. (See Fig. 12.)

Solution. Using the Corollary we get

$$y = -\tfrac{2}{3}x + 3,$$

or the equivalent equation

$$2x + 3y = 9.$$

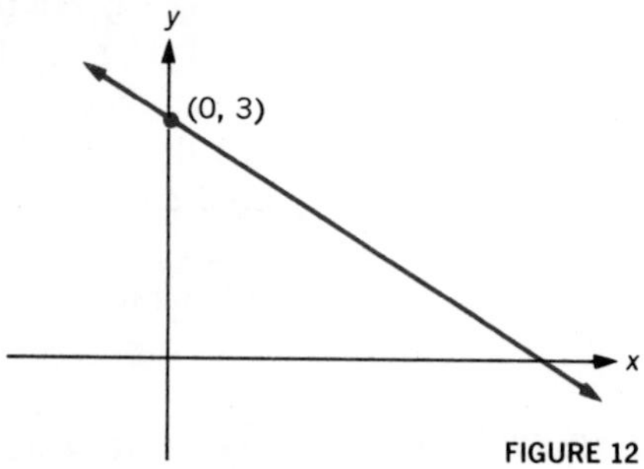

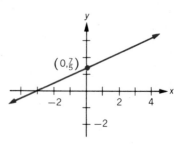

(0, 3)

FIGURE 12

3   We can use formula (1) to quickly obtain an equation for the line through two points. Suppose the points are $(-1, 2)$ and $(3, -4)$. Then

$$m = \frac{2 - (-4)}{-1 - 3} = -\frac{3}{2},$$

and the line is given by

$$y - 2 = -\tfrac{3}{2}(x + 1)$$

or

$$3x + 2y - 1 = 0.$$

Remark   To abbreviate, one often speaks of "the line $3x + 2y - 1 = 0$" instead of using the longer phrase "the line whose equation is $3x + 2y - 1 = 0$."

Example 4   Sketch the graph of $2x - 5y + 7 = 0$.

Solution. An equivalent equation is

$$y = \tfrac{2}{5}x + \tfrac{7}{5}.$$

We see from the Corollary that this is an equation for the line with slope $\frac{2}{5}$ and y-intercept $\frac{7}{5}$. (See Fig. 13.)

$(0, \tfrac{7}{5})$

FIGURE 13

Problems

Set A

Find equations of the lines through each pair of points.

1. $(4, 2)$ and $(-5, -1)$
2. $(-1, 2)$ and $(3, -1)$
3. $(-2, 1)$ and $(3, 4)$
4. $(-2, -\frac{2}{3})$ and $(3, -\frac{3}{2})$
5. $(-\frac{7}{3}, 0)$ and $(-\frac{5}{2}, 0)$
6. (x_0, y_0) and $(x_0 + a, y_0 + b)$, $a \neq 0$

Find an equation of a line through the given point with the given slope.

7. $(-1, -1)$ with slope $-\frac{1}{2}$
8. $(2, -4)$ with slope 2
9. $(0, 0)$ with slope $-\frac{2}{5}$
10. $(-\frac{3}{2}, \frac{5}{4})$ with slope $\frac{3}{4}$
11. $(-4, -\frac{7}{2})$ with slope 0
12. Through $(0, b)$ with slope m

Set B

Find the slope and the y-intercept, and draw the line.

13. $3x - y = 6$
14. $2x + 3y = 6$
15. $y = 2x + 2$
16. $x + y = 0$
17. $x + \pi y = 2$
18. $ax + by = b$, $b \neq 0$
19. $3x + 4y = k$, k is arbitrary
20. $\sqrt{2}x + (1 - \sqrt{2})y = 2$
21. Write an equation of a line parallel to the x-axis that passes through the point $(4, -2)$.
22. Write an equation of a line parallel to the y-axis that passes through the point $(4, -2)$.
23. Show that the points $(1, 0)$, $(4, -12)$ and $(2, -4)$ are collinear in two ways.
    (a) Show that the slope of the line between any two of the points is the same.
    (b) Write an equation for the line between two of the points. Then show that the coordinates of the third point satisfy the equation of the line.

Set C

24. A line has y-intercept b and x-intercept a where neither a nor b is 0. Show that an equation of the line has the form

$$\frac{x}{a} + \frac{y}{b} = 1.$$

Write rectangular equations of the line in each figure.

25.

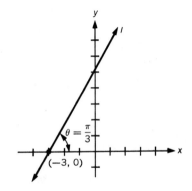

26.

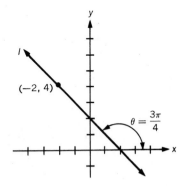

27. If c_1 and c_2 are direction cosines of a line, prove that the line has slope if and only if $c_1 \neq 0$. If it has slope, show that $m = c_2/c_1$.

Calculator Problem

Compute the x-intercept, the y-intercept and the slope of the line whose equation is

$$2.35x + 8.71y = 12.46.$$

Round the answers to the nearest hundredth.

11-5   The General Linear Equation

First we must have a definition.

Definition 11-3 A *linear* equation in x and y is an equation of the form

$$Ax + By = C, \tag{1}$$

where A and B are given real numbers and A and B are not both 0.

An equation of the form (1) is called "linear" because the graph of such an equation is always a straight line. Recall that the graph of any equation in x and y is the set of *all* points (x, y) and *only* those points whose coordinates satisfy the equation.

Theorem 11-6 *Every straight line is the graph of a linear equation. Conversely, every linear equation has a graph that is a straight line.*

Proof If a line is vertical, it has an equation $x = a$. This is a linear equation with $A = 1$, $B = 0$, and $C = a$. If a line is not vertical, it has a slope m and a y-intercept b, and is, by the corollary to Theorem 11-5, the graph of

$$y = mx + b.$$

This equation is equivalent to the equation

$$-mx + y = b,$$

which is a linear equation with $A = -m$, $B = 1$, and $C = b$. Therefore a line is the graph of a linear equation, and the first part of the theorem is proved.

Now, suppose we have a linear equation $Ax + By = C$. If $B = 0$, then $A \neq 0$ and the equation is $Ax = C$, which is equivalent to $x = C/A$. The graph of this equation is a line parallel to the y-axis.

If $B \neq 0$, then the linear equation is equivalent to

$$y = -\frac{A}{B}x + \frac{C}{B}.$$

By the corollary to Theorem 11–5 we recognize that the graph of this last equation is the straight line with

$$\text{slope } m = -\frac{A}{B} \quad \text{and} \quad y\text{-intercept } b = \frac{C}{B}.$$

Therefore, in all cases where A and B are not both 0, the graph of $Ax + By = C$ is a straight line.

Example 1   Draw the graph of $3x - 2y = 7$.

Solution. From Theorem 11–6 we know that the graph is a straight line. To draw the line it would suffice to find two points on the line. It is easily seen that $(0, -\frac{7}{2})$ and $(\frac{7}{3}, 0)$ are on the graph of the given equation. The graph appears as in Fig. 14.

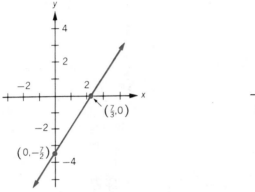

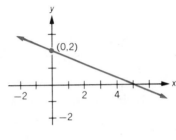

FIGURE 14   FIGURE 15

2   Find the slope of the line that has the equation $2x + 5y = 10$.

Solution. The equation is equivalent to $y = -\frac{2}{5}x + 2$. We recognize this equation as the slope-intercept form for the line with y-intercept 2 and slope $-\frac{2}{5}$. (See Fig. 15.)

Of course, we could also find the slope by getting two points on the line and then using the formula for slope. If we did this and selected the points $(0, 2)$ and $(5, 0)$, then the slope would be

$$m = \frac{2 - 0}{0 - 5} = -\frac{2}{5}.$$

3   Find the point of intersection of $3x + 4y = 10$ and $x - 2y = 5$.

Solution. The graphs of the equations are shown in Fig. 16. From the graph we might *estimate* the coordinates of the point of intersection. We can be more precise by attacking the problem algebraically.

We seek all those points and only those points (x, y) that satisfy

$$3x + 4y = 10 \qquad (2)$$

and

$$x - 2y = 5. \qquad (3)$$

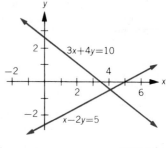

FIGURE 16

From (3) we have $x = 5 + 2y$, and substituting in (2), we have

$$3(5 + 2y) + 4y = 10.$$

Solving this equation for y, we find $y = -\frac{1}{2}$. Hence in (2) we must have $3x + 4(-\frac{1}{2}) = 10$ and therefore $x = 4$. Observe that the pair $(4, -\frac{1}{2})$ satisfies both equations (2) and (3), and so the point of intersection of the lines must be $(4, -\frac{1}{2})$.

Problems

Set A

Draw the lines whose equations are the following.

1. $2x - 3y = 6$ 　　　 2. $2x - \sqrt{3}\,y = \pi$
3. $x + y = \sqrt{7}$ 　　 4. $x + 7y = 1$
5. $y = 3x$ 　　　　　 6. $y = -3x$
7. $y = \frac{1}{3}x$ 　　　　 8. $y = -\frac{1}{3}x$
9. $2x = -5$ 　　　　 10. $y = -\frac{\pi}{2}$
11. $x = 2\pi$ 　　　　 12. $y = \frac{\sqrt{3}}{2}$

Find the slope and sketch the line whose equation is

13. $x + y = 9$. 　　　 14. $x - y = 9$.
15. $3x + y = -2$. 　　 16. $x + y = -2$.

Find the points of intersection of the following pairs of lines. Sketch the lines.

17. $3x - 2y = 5$ and $5x + 7y = -2$
18. $y = 2x - 7$ and $x + 2y = 5$
19. $7x - 3y = 11$ and $21x - 9y = 30$
20. $x = 5$ and $2x + 3y = 5$

Set B

Find a linear equation for the lines through the following pairs of points. Draw the lines.

21. $(-1, 1)$ and $(-2, 5)$ 　 22. $(2, -1)$ and $(5, 1)$
23. $(-1 - \sqrt{2}, 2 + \sqrt{2})$ and $(\sqrt{2}, \sqrt{2} - 1)$
24. $(\pi, 7)$ and $(\pi, -\sqrt{2})$ 　 25. $(0, 0)$ and $(1, m)$
26. $(a, 0)$ and $(0, b)$, where $a \neq 0 \neq b$
27. (x_1, y_1) and (x_2, y_2)
28. (x_0, y_0) and $(x_0 + 1, y_0 + 1)$
29. Find the vertices of the triangle whose sides are on the lines $y + 2x = 6$, $y - \frac{1}{2}x = 1$, and $y + \frac{3}{4}x = 1$. Then show in two ways that the triangle is a right triangle. What is the area of the triangle?
30. Show that the equations $x - 3y = 7$ and $2x - 6y - 14 = 0$ are equivalent. In other words, if x and y satisfy either of these equations, then they satisfy the other.
31. At what point do the lines with equations $x = 2$ and $y = 3$ meet? Sketch the lines.
32. Show algebraically that the lines with equations $2x + 3y = 5$ and $4x + 6y + 7 = 0$ do not intersect. Then sketch the lines.

33. Show that the medians of a triangle with vertices $(-1, 1)$, $(3, 3)$ and $(1, -3)$ meet at one point.

Set C

34. Graph the equation $mx - y = 2$. Choose several different values for m. Sketch the line for each value of m.

35. Graph the equation $y + 2x = b$. Choose several different values for b. Sketch the line for each value of b.

36. Find the point of intersection of the lines whose equations are $ax + by = c$ and $Ax + By = C$, where $aB - Ab \neq 0$.

37. Eliminate the parameter d from the pair of parametric equations

$$x = -1 + \frac{1}{\sqrt{2}}d, \quad \text{and} \quad y = 5 + \frac{-1}{\sqrt{2}}d,$$

to get a linear equation of the same line. [*Hint:* Add the equations.]

38. Find two points on the line whose parametric equations are

$$x = 4 + \frac{2}{\sqrt{5}}d, \quad \text{and} \quad y = -2 + \frac{1}{\sqrt{5}}d.$$

What is a linear equation of the line?

39. Show that if parametric equations of a line are

$$\begin{cases} x = x_0 + c_1 d, \\ y = y_0 + c_2 d, \end{cases}$$

then $c_2 x - c_1 y = c_2 x_0 - c_1 y_0$ is a linear equation of the line.

40. A linear equation of a line is $3x + 4y = 12$. What are direction cosines of the line? What are a pair of parametric equations for the line?

41. Show that the medians of a triangle with vertices (x_1, y_1), (x_2, y_2), (x_3, y_3) are concurrent.

Calculator Problem

Find the point of intersection of the lines $8.9x - 10y = -1$ and $8.9x - 10.1y = -1.1$. Then find the point of intersection of the lines $8.9x - 10y = -1$ and $8.9x - 10.01y = -1.1$. Draw the lines.

11-6   Parallel and Perpendicular Lines

The concept of slope is a convenient tool for studying parallel and perpendicular lines. The main objection to its use is that not all lines have slope, so that vertical lines must be discussed separately. However, because vertical lines have such simple equations there is no real problem.

Theorem 11-7   *If l_1 and l_2 are nonvertical lines and have respective equations*

$$a_1 x + b_1 y + c_1 = 0, \quad a_2 x + b_2 y + c_2 = 0,$$

then they are parallel or coincide if and only if they have the same slope. That is, if m_1 and m_2 are the slopes of l_1 and l_2, respectively, then

$$m_1 = -\frac{a_1}{b_1} = -\frac{a_2}{b_2} = m_2.$$

Proof The lines are parallel if and only if their inclinations are equal, $\theta_1 = \theta_2$. But this is the case if and only if $m_1 = \tan\theta_1 = \tan\theta_2 = m_2$.

A separate argument must be made for vertical lines. Suppose l_1 is vertical. How do you tell whether or not l_2 is parallel to l_1?

Now let us consider perpendicular lines. A horizontal and a vertical line are perpendicular, and this is the only pair of perpendicular lines where one of the lines does not have slope.

Theorem 11-8 *Suppose that lines l_1 and l_2 have slopes m_1 and m_2, respectively. Then l_1 is perpendicular to l_2 if and only if*

$$m_1 = -\frac{1}{m_2}$$

or, equivalently, $m_1 m_2 = -1$. (See Fig. 17.)

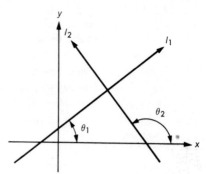

FIGURE 17

Proof The lines are perpendicular if and only if either

$$\theta_2 = \frac{\pi}{2} + \theta_1 \quad \text{or} \quad \theta_1 = \frac{\pi}{2} + \theta_2.$$

In the first case we have (by Section 7-3)

$$m_2 = \tan\theta_2 = \tan\left(\frac{\pi}{2} + \theta_1\right) = -\cot\theta_1 = -\frac{1}{\tan\theta_1} = \frac{-1}{m_1}.$$

The other case is treated similarly.

Slope and inclination are convenient for finding the measure of the angle between two lines. Suppose that l_1 and l_2 are nonvertical and nonhorizontal lines with inclinations θ_1 and θ_2. We define the angle with measure θ between the upward directions of l_1 and l_2, and from l_1 to l_2, to be

$$\theta = \theta_2 - \theta_1.$$

Then (see Fig. 18)

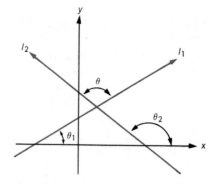

FIGURE 18

$$\tan\theta = \tan(\theta_2 - \theta_1) = \frac{\tan\theta_2 - \tan\theta_1}{1 + \tan\theta_1 \tan\theta_2},$$

and so

$$\tan \theta = \frac{m_2 - m_1}{1 + m_1 m_2}. \tag{1}$$

Therefore the measure of the angle θ between the lines l_1 and l_2 is

$$\theta = \tan^{-1} \frac{m_2 - m_1}{1 + m_1 m_2}. \tag{2}$$

Remarks

1. If $\theta = \pi/2$, then *tan* θ is undefined and the denominator in (1) must be 0. That is, $m_1 m_2 = -1$.

2. The sign of tan θ has significance. If tan $\theta < 0$, then the geometric angle *from l_1 to l_2 going clockwise is obtuse.*

Example 1

A line passes through $(-1, 3)$ and is parallel to the line $2x + 3y = 5$. (See Fig. 19.) Find an equation of the line.

Solution. The slope of the line is $-\frac{2}{3}$. Hence the desired line has an equation

$$y - 3 = -\tfrac{2}{3}(x + 1)$$

or, equivalently,

$$2x + 3y = 7.$$

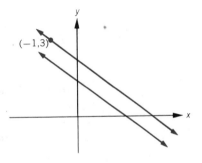

FIGURE 19

2 The lines $3x - 5y = 1$ and $6x - 10y + 7 = 0$ are parallel because both have slope $\frac{3}{5}$. The first line has an equation $y = \frac{3}{5}x - \frac{1}{5}$, and the second has $y = \frac{3}{5}x + \frac{7}{10}$.

3 Find an equation of the line that contains $(1, 5)$ and is perpendicular to the line $2x - 3y + 6 = 0$, as shown in Fig. 20.

Solution. The given line has slope $\frac{2}{3}$. By Theorem 11–8, a perpendicular to this line must have slope $-\frac{3}{2}$. Hence the line through $(1, 5)$ perpendicular to the given line is

$$y - 5 = -\tfrac{3}{2}(x - 1)$$

or

$$3x + 2y = 13.$$

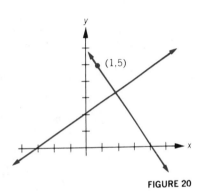

FIGURE 20

Example 4 Find the angle between the lines

$$l_1: y = -\tfrac{1}{4}x - 2$$

and

$$l_2: y = 2x + 3.$$

(See Fig. 21.)

Solution. The slopes of the lines are, respectively, $m_1 = -\tfrac{1}{4}$ and $m_2 = 2$. Using equation (1) above we have

$$\tan \theta = \frac{2 - (-\tfrac{1}{4})}{1 + (-\tfrac{1}{4})(2)} = 4.5,$$

$$\theta = \tan^{-1} 4.5 = 1.352 \text{ (or } 77.47°).$$

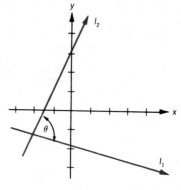

FIGURE 21

The two previous theorems imply the following theorem, which includes the cases of horizontal and vertical lines.

Theorem 11-9 *The lines l_1 and l_2,*

$$l_1: a_1 x + b_1 y + c_1 = 0, \qquad l_2: a_2 x + b_2 y + c_2 = 0,$$

are parallel (or identical) if and only if there is a number $k \neq 0$ such that

$$a_2 = ka_1 \quad and \quad b_2 = kb_1.$$

They are perpendicular if and only if

$$a_1 a_2 + b_1 b_2 = 0.$$

The proof is left to the student.

Example 5 The lines $7x + 5y = 3$ and $10x - 14y = 0$ are perpendicular because

$$(7)(10) + (5)(-14) = 0.$$

6 The line $ax + by = k$ is parallel (or identical) to $ax + by = c$, regardless of what number k is.

Similarly, $bx - ay = k$ is perpendicular to $ax + by = c$, regardless of what number k is.

7 Find the line which is perpendicular to the line $4x + 7y = 5$ and which passes through $(-1, 2)$.

Solution. The line $7x - 4y = k$ is perpendicular to the given line. If it passes through $(-1, 2)$, then $7(-1) - 4(2) = k = -15$. Hence the desired line has an equation $7x - 4y = -15$.

Problems

Set A

In Problems 1–12 sketch the graph of the lines on the same coordinate axes. Which pairs of lines are parallel? perpendicular? identical?

1. $3x + 2y = 0$ **2.** $x = 5$

3. $2x - 3y = 7$ **4.** $x = k$

5. $4x + 6y = 5$ **6.** $y = -3$

7. $6x = -4y$ **8.** $7y + 21 = 0$

9. $3x + 7y = 6$ **10.** $7x = 3y$

11. $15x + 35y = 31$ **12.** $4x - 6y = 0$

13. Find an equation of a line through $(2, -3)$ that is parallel to the line $x - 3y + 6 = 0$.

14. Find an equation of a line through $(2, -3)$ that is perpendicular to the line $x - 3y + 6 = 0$.

Set B

15. Using slope, show that the points $(1, -1)$, $(-\frac{39}{25}, 7)$, and $(\frac{29}{4}, 1)$ are vertices of a right triangle.

16. Show that the four lines

$$2x + 3y = 0, \qquad 2x + 3y = 5,$$
$$x - y = 1, \qquad 3x = 3y - 8$$

meet in four points which are vertices of a parallelogram.

17. The hypotenuse of a right triangle is a subset of the line $2x + 3y = 5$. The right angle has its vertex at $(1, -1)$. Given that one of the other vertices is at $(-2, 3)$, find the third vertex.

18. The line $5y + 3x = 47$ is tangent to a circle with center at $(1, 2)$. Find the point of tangency.

19. Show that the angle between these lines is $\pi/4$.

$$l_1: x + 3y = 3$$
$$l_2: x - 2y = 8$$

20. What is the perpendicular distance from $y = 7x + 7$ to $(6\frac{1}{2}, 4\frac{1}{2})$?

Set C

21. What is the angle between

$$l_1: x - \sqrt{3}\,y = -2\sqrt{3}$$

and

$$l_2: \sqrt{3}\,x - y = 4\sqrt{3}?$$

22. Sketch some of the lines with an equation $3x - 4y = k$, for different values of k.

23. Consider all the lines $ax + by = k$, where a and b are fixed, given numbers and k can have different values. How do these lines compare with all the lines $bx - ay = k$?

24. (a) Find the measure of the angle between the lines l_1 given by $2y - x = 7$ and l_2 given by $2y - 6x = 5$.

    (b) What is the measure of the angle between the line l_1 given by $2y - 6x = 5$ and any line l_2 parallel to the line $2y - x = 7$?

    (c) What is the measure of the angle between the line l_1 given by $2y - 6x = 5$ and any line l_2 perpendicular to the line $2y - x = 7$?

25. Prove Theorem 11–9.

26. Show that if $a > b > 0$, then $(0, 0)$, $(a, 0)$, $(a + \sqrt{a^2 - b^2}, b)$, and $(\sqrt{a^2 - b^2}, b)$ are vertices of a rhombus. Then show that the diagonals are perpendicular.

27. A triangle has vertices $(2, -1)$, $(-2, 3)$, and $(0, -3)$. Find its area by finding the length of a base and an altitude.

28. Show that the altitudes of the triangle whose vertices are $(-1, 2)$, $(4, 3)$, and $(1, -2)$ intersect in a point. Find the coordinates of the point of intersection.

29. Find the perpendicular distance from (x_1, y_1) to the line $ax + by + c = 0$.

30. Find equations of the three altitudes of the triangle whose vertices are (x_1, y_1), (x_2, y_2), and (x_3, y_3).

Calculator Problem

Sketch the three intersecting lines below.

$$l_1: x - 6y = 0, \qquad l_2: 2x + y = 8, \qquad l_3: x + 2y = 12.$$

Find the measure of each angle of the triangle formed by the three lines.

Summary

In this chapter we have given two kinds of equations that represent lines: parametric equations and rectangular equations. Both are important although you will encounter rectangular equations more often.

The highlights of the chapter are as follows.

1. Directed lines and directed distance along a line.

2. Direction angles and direction cosines:

$$\cos \alpha = \frac{x - x_0}{d}, \qquad \cos \beta = \frac{y - y_0}{d}.$$

3. Parametric equations of a line:

$$\begin{cases} x = x_0 + c_1 d, \\ y = y_0 + c_2 d. \end{cases}$$

4. $\cos^2 \alpha + \cos^2 \beta = 1$.

5. The slope m of a line containing the points (x_1, y_1), and (x_2, y_2) is

$$m = \frac{y_2 - y_1}{x_2 - x_1}.$$

6. The graph of $Ax + By = C$ is a line.

7. Two lines are parallel or identical if and only if they have the same slope.

8. Two lines both of which have slopes are perpendicular if and only if the product of their slopes is -1.

9. Equation of a line containing (x_0, y_0) with slope m: $y - y_0 = m(x - x_0)$.

10. Slope-intercept form of a line: $y = mx + b$, where $m = $ slope, $b = y$-intercept.

11. The angle between the lines l_1 and l_2 with given slopes m_1 and m_2 respectively is

$$\theta = \arctan \frac{m_2 - m_1}{1 + m_1 m_2}.$$

Chapter 11   Test

11-2   1. A line containing $(-3, -1)$ and $(1, 2)$ is coordinatized so that $(1, 2)$ is on the negative side of $(-3, -1)$. What is the directed distance from $(-3, -1)$ to $(1, 2)$?

11-3   2. A line is positively directed from $(-3, 3)$ to $(3, 5)$. What are the direction cosines of the line?

3. The x-direction cosine of a line is $-\frac{5}{13}$ and the y-direction cosine, c_2, is positive. What is c_2?

4. What are parametric equations of a line containing the points $(5, -4)$ and $(-2, 3)$?

5. Parametric equations of a line are

$$x = 2 + \frac{1}{\sqrt{5}}d \quad \text{and} \quad y = -3 - \frac{2}{\sqrt{5}}d.$$

At what point does the line intersect the y-axis?

11-4   6. A line contains the point $(1, -4)$ and has slope $m = \frac{1}{4}$. Find a rectangular equation of the line.

7. Give a rectangular equation of a line that contains the points $(7, -3)$ and $(1, 1)$.

8. Find the slope and y-intercept of the line given by $2x - 3y = 6$.

11-5   9. Find the point of intersection of the lines $3x + y = 5$ and $x - 3y = -5$.

10. What is the slope of the general linear equation $Ax + By + C = 0$ where neither A nor B is 0?

11-6   11. What is the relation between the slopes of two lines that are perpendicular? that are parallel?

12. Are the two lines $2x + 3y = 4$ and $9x - 6y = -2$ parallel or are they perpendicular?

13. Find an equation of a line through the point $(2, 3)$ that is perpendicular to the line $x - 2y = 7$.

14. Find an equation of a line through the point $(-4, 0)$ that is parallel to the line $3x + y = 5$.

15. Find the tangent of the angle between the lines l_1: $y = \frac{1}{2}x + \frac{3}{2}$ and l_2: $y = 3x - 1$. What is the measure of the angle between the lines?

16. Three lines have a common point of intersection at $(3,2)$.

$$l_1: x - 3y = -1$$
$$l_2: 3x + y = 11$$
$$l_3: 2x - y = 4$$

Show that l_3 bisects the angle between l_1 and l_2.

Chapter 12
Vectors in the Plane

12-1   Introduction

In this chapter we shall develop a new mathematical concept called a *vector*. The idea of a vector arises in geometry as a displacement in a given direction and given magnitude, and in physics as a force, or velocity, or acceleration.

Vectors are said to have both *direction* and *magnitude,* and so they cannot be described by single numbers. We shall see that, in the plane, two numbers are needed to describe a vector. In later chapters we shall study how vectors can be applied to problems in space.

12-2   Arrows

Imagine a picture of a line segment with end points P_1 and P_2 and with the point of an arrow at P_2, as in Fig. 1. There are several interpretations that we may give to the arrow. First, the arrow suggests *motion*. We might think of an object that *moves* or is *displaced* from the position P_1 to the position P_2. Second, we might think of the arrow as giving the position of P_2 with

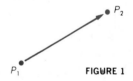

FIGURE 1

respect to P_1. Third, we might think of the arrow as a *force*, namely a force applied at P_1 in the direction of P_2 and whose magnitude is proportional to the length of the arrow. Finally, we may think of the arrow as a *velocity;* that is, if a point moves with constant speed along a line and at some instant is at P_1 and at a *unit time* later is at P_2, then the arrow denotes the velocity of the moving point. All these applications arise in mathematics and physics. Other applications occur in chemistry, biology, economics, and psychology.

Definition 12-1 If P_1 and P_2 are points, then the ordered pair of points (P_1, P_2) is called an *arrow*. The first point of the ordered pair is the *initial point* of the arrow and the second point is the *terminal point* or *end point* of the arrow. The magnitude of an arrow (P_1, P_2) is the length $|P_1P_2|$ of the segment $\overline{P_1P_2}$.

Example 1 The arrow (P_1, P_2) has initial point $P_1 = (-2, -3)$ and end point $P_2 = (2, 1)$. (See Fig. 2.) The magnitude of (P_1, P_2) is

$$|P_1 P_2| = \sqrt{[2 - (-2)]^2 + [1 - (-3)]^2} = \sqrt{4^2 + 4^2} = 4\sqrt{2}.$$

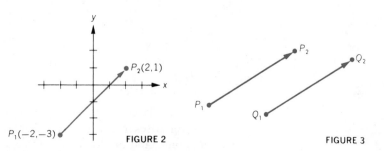

FIGURE 2   FIGURE 3

Next consider two arrows, (P_1, P_2) and (Q_1, Q_2), as in Fig. 3, and suppose that these two arrows have the same direction and the same magnitude. Are these arrows to be regarded as *equal* in some sense? Clearly they are not equal in the strict sense, since the arrows are two different ordered pairs of points. If the arrows are interpreted as forces, they have different physical effects because they are applied at different points. Since we want to reserve the term *equality* to mean identity, we shall say that these arrows are *equivalent*.

Definition 12-2 Two arrows are *equivalent* if they have the same direction and the same magnitude. The set of all arrows equivalent to a given arrow is an *equivalence class* of arrows.

Example 2 The arrows $(P_1, P_2) = ((-3, 5), (2, 2))$ and $(Q_1, Q_2) = ((-1, 2), (4, -1))$ are equivalent arrows. (See Fig. 4.) To prove this, we observe that

$$|P_1 P_2| = |Q_1 Q_2| = \sqrt{34}.$$

Furthermore, choosing P_1 as the origin and the distance from P_1 to P_2 positive, we find that the direction cosines of (P_1, P_2) are

$$c_1 = \frac{2 - (-3)}{\sqrt{34}} = \frac{5}{\sqrt{34}}$$

and

$$c_2 = \frac{2 - 5}{\sqrt{34}} = \frac{-3}{\sqrt{34}}.$$

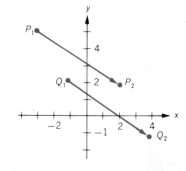

FIGURE 4

Similarly, for the arrow (Q_1, Q_2) with Q_1 as the origin and the distance from Q_1 to Q_2 positive, we find that

$$c_1 = \frac{4 - (-1)}{\sqrt{34}} = \frac{5}{\sqrt{34}} \qquad \text{and} \qquad c_2 = \frac{-1 - 2}{\sqrt{34}} = \frac{-3}{\sqrt{34}}.$$

Since the arrows have the same magnitude and the same direction (the same direction cosines), they are equivalent arrows and are in the same equivalence class.

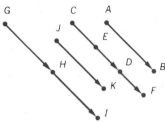

FIGURE 5

Figure 5 illustrates several arrows, (A, B), (C, D), (E, F), (G, H), (H, I), and (J, K), which are equivalent to one another.

It is helpful to conceive of an arrow whose initial point and end point are the same. Such an arrow has zero magnitude and its direction is undefined. Such an arrow might be called a *zero arrow* or a *null arrow*.

The following theorem is fundamental because it tells, in terms of the coordinates of points, when two arrows are equivalent.

Theorem 12-1 *If the points P_1, P_2, P_3, P_4 have the coordinates shown in Fig. 6, then the arrows (P_1, P_2) and (P_3, P_4) are equivalent if and only if*

$$\begin{aligned} x_2 - x_1 &= x_4 - x_3, \\ y_2 - y_1 &= y_4 - y_3. \end{aligned} \qquad (1)$$

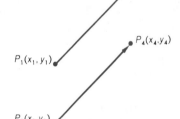

FIGURE 6

Proof   Suppose that equations (1) are true. Then the magnitudes of the arrows are the same, that is,

$$d = \sqrt{(x_2 - x_1)^2 + (y_2 - y_1)^2} = \sqrt{(x_4 - x_3)^2 + (y_4 - y_3)^2}. \qquad (2)$$

The direction cosines are also the same:

$$c_1 = \frac{x_2 - x_1}{d} = \frac{x_4 - x_3}{d}, \qquad c_2 = \frac{y_2 - y_1}{d} = \frac{y_4 - y_3}{d}. \qquad (3)$$

Therefore the two arrows are equivalent.

Conversely, suppose the two arrows are equivalent. Then they will have the same magnitude and direction. Therefore, equations (2) and (3) will be true, and these equations imply equations (1).

Problems

Set A

Sketch each arrow given by the following ordered pairs of points.

1. $((0, 0), (4, 1))$
2. $((-2, 4), (3, -3))$
3. $((-1, -1), (-2, -2))$
4. $((-4, 5), (6, 5))$
5. $((0, 6), (5, -6))$
6. $((-2, 2), (-2, -7))$

7. Find the magnitude of each arrow in Problems 1–6.

8. The arrow (P_1, P_2) is the ordered pair of points $((2, 3), (-1, 4))$. Represent this arrow in the plane and draw pictures of several other arrows that are in the equivalence class of arrows determined by the arrow (P_1, P_2).

9. Represent the arrow $(P_3, P_4) = ((3, 7), (8, -1))$ in the plane and draw pictures of several other arrows that are in this equivalence class of arrows.

10. The arrow (P, Q) is the ordered pair of points $((1, -2), (5, 4))$. (R, S) is an arrow equivalent to (P, Q), and R has coordinates $(-4, 1)$. What are the coordinates of S? Draw (R, S).

Set B

11. $(P, Q) = ((2, 3), (-2, 1))$. (X, Y) is equivalent to (P, Q), and Y has coordinates $(7, 0)$. Determine the coordinates of X.

12. What are the coordinates of the terminal point of an arrow equivalent to the arrows in Problem 11 if the initial point of the arrow is $(0, 0)$?

13. $(P_1, P_2) = ((-1, 2), (5, 6))$ and $(P_3, P_4) = ((2, -2), (8, 2))$. Is (P_1, P_2) equivalent to (P_3, P_4)? Draw a picture of the arrows.

14. Show that $(P_1, P_2) = ((1, 1), (4, 5))$ and $(P_3, P_4) = ((-2, 2), (-5, -2))$ have the same magnitude and lie on parallel lines but are not equivalent. Draw a picture.

15. Sketch the arrow $((-4, 2), (4, 8))$. Then sketch another arrow with initial point $(2, 3)$ which has the same direction as the first arrow but whose magnitude is only $\frac{1}{2}$ as much.

Set C

16. An arrow has initial point $(3, 4)$ and direction cosines $c_1 = \frac{3}{5}$ and $c_2 = \frac{4}{5}$. If the arrow has magnitude 5, what are the coordinates of the terminal point? Sketch the arrow.

17. How would you define *equal* arrows? Are equal arrows equivalent arrows? Are equivalent arrows necessarily equal arrows?

18. How many arrows are determined by 3 noncollinear points? How many arrows are determined by 4 points, no three of which are collinear?

19. Show that if (P_1, P_2) and (Q_1, Q_2) are equivalent, then so are (P_1, Q_1) are (P_2, Q_2).

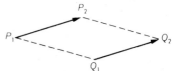

Calculator Problem

(P_1, P_2) is an arrow with magnitude of 1.75 units. The coordinates of P_1 are $(-1.36, 2.44)$. The direction cosines of the arrow are

$$c_1 = \frac{2}{\sqrt{13}} \quad \text{and} \quad c_2 = \frac{-3}{\sqrt{13}}.$$

Find the coordinates of P_2 rounded to the nearest hundredth. Sketch the arrow.

It is evident that given an arrow, there are infinitely many arrows equivalent to the given one. Note also that if two equivalence classes have an arrow in common, then they are identical. Furthermore, there are infinitely many different equivalence classes of arrows. Because all arrows in an equivalence class have the same direction and magnitude, we shall regard each equivalence class as a single object which we call a *vector*.

Definition 12-3   A *vector* is an equivalence class of arrows. Any arrow of an equivalence class of arrows may represent the vector. The *magnitude* of a vector is the magnitude of any arrow in the equivalence class that represents the vector.

Sometimes, for simplicity, we shall refer to an arrow as a *vector* instead of using the lengthy phrase, "*the vector represented by the arrow.*"

We shall denote vectors by letters in boldface type, for example, **a**, **b**, **r**, **s**, and **v**. The vector represented by the arrow (P_1, P_2) will be denoted by $\overrightarrow{P_1 P_2}$. The magnitude of **a** will be denoted by $|\mathbf{a}|$. Since you cannot write boldface letters with your pencil, you should use the arrow notation, $\vec{a}, \vec{b}, \vec{v}$, etc., to denote vectors.

A vector is a whole equivalence class of arrows. Each vector contains arrows of the same magnitude and direction. We can now say what we mean by the statement, *two vectors, **u** and **v**, are equal; **u** = **v**.* We mean that they contain the same arrows; that is, the two sets of arrows are the same. Another way of saying this is that the arrows of **u** and the arrows of **v** have the same direction and magnitude.

Definition 12-4   The *null vector* is the vector whose magnitude is zero. We denote the null vector by **0**.

The null vector is the set of all null arrows, that is, the set of all arrows of zero magnitude.

When we represent a vector **b** by an arrow emanating from the origin, we speak of it as the *position vector* of **v**. This convention on the use of language helps us to readily visualize any vector. For example if $\overrightarrow{P_1 P_2}$ is given by the ordered pair of points $((2, 4), (4, 6))$, the coordinates for the position vector for $\overrightarrow{P_1 P_2}$ can be found by applying Theorem

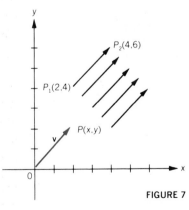

FIGURE 7

12–1. The initial point of $\overrightarrow{OP}$ is $(0, 0)$. If $P(x, y)$ is the terminal point, we have, by Theorem 12–1, $x - 0 = 4 - 2$ or $x = 2$, and $y - 0 = 6 - 4$ or $y = 2$. (See Fig. 7.) Thus the terminal point of the position vector is $(2, 2)$.

Problems

Set A

Vectors are represented by the following ordered pairs of points. Determine the magnitude of each vector. Sketch each arrow.

1. $((7, -1), (4, 3))$ 2. $((0, 0), (1, 0))$

3. $((0, 1), (1, 0))$ 4. $((3, -4), (3, 5))$

5. $((6, 5), (-1, 5))$ 6. $((11, -2), (51, 7))$

7. Represent each vector in Problems 1–6 by a position vector. Give the coordinates of the terminal point.

8. What is the magnitude of a position vector $\overrightarrow{OP}$ if $P = (12, 5)$? What are the coordinates of point P' if $\overrightarrow{OP}$ and $\overrightarrow{OP'}$ have the same magnitude but are opposite in direction?

Set B

9. How are $\overrightarrow{XY} = ((-5, -3), (-3, 2))$ and $\overrightarrow{OP} = ((0, 0), (2, 5))$ related?

10. How are $\overrightarrow{RS} = ((-1, 2), (-5, 4))$ and $\overrightarrow{OQ} = ((0, 0), (4, -2))$ related?

11. The vector $\mathbf{v}$ is represented by the arrow (P_1, P_2), and $\mathbf{r}$ is represented by the arrow (Q_1, Q_2). If $\mathbf{v} = \mathbf{r}$, what can you conclude?

12. If (X, Y) represents $\mathbf{a}$, (R, S) represents $\mathbf{b}$, and (X, Y) is equivalent to (R, S), what can you conclude?

Set C

13. What do the two vectors $\overrightarrow{AB} = ((-5, -5),$ $(3, 1))$ and $\overrightarrow{CD} = ((-3, 3), (1, 6))$ have in common? Sketch the vectors.

14. What do the two vectors $\overrightarrow{UV} = ((1, 4),$ $(-1, 0))$ and $\overrightarrow{YZ} = ((1, -3), (5, -1))$ have in common? Sketch the vectors.

15. Suppose that O, P_1, and P_2 are points, as shown in the figure. How does $|\overrightarrow{OP_2}|$ compare with $|\overrightarrow{OP_1}| + |\overrightarrow{P_1 P_2}|$?

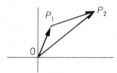

16. Is it possible for the points O, P_1, and P_2 in Problem 15 to be such that $|\overrightarrow{OP_2}| = 0$?

17. What must be the condition for the points of Problem 15 to be such that $|\overrightarrow{OP_1}| + |\overrightarrow{P_1 P_2}| = |\overrightarrow{OP_2}|$?

18. Show that if P_1 and P_2 are the points (x_1, y_1) and (x_2, y_2), then $\overrightarrow{P_1 P_2}$ is equivalent to the position vector, $\overrightarrow{OP}$, where $P = (x_2 - x_1, y_2 - y_1)$.

Calculator Problem

Sketch the vectors. Which two vectors are equal vectors?

$$\overrightarrow{P_1 P_2} = ((5.20, 2.50), (8.80, 5.20))$$
$$\overrightarrow{P_3 P_4} = ((1.50, 4.20), (5.34, 7.08))$$
$$\overrightarrow{P_5 P_6} = ((0.50, 6.20), (4.34, 9.08))$$

12-4 Operations with Vectors

In this section we shall see that vectors have many algebraic properties similar to the properties of the real numbers. One can add and subtract vectors and multiply them by real numbers.

If **v** is any vector and P is any point, then there is a unique point Q such that $\mathbf{v} = \overrightarrow{PQ}$. We shall use this fact in our definition of *addition* of vectors.

Definition 12-5 Suppose **a** and **b** are any two vectors. Choose point A so that $\mathbf{a} = \overrightarrow{OA}$. Choose point C so that $\mathbf{b} = \overrightarrow{AC}$. The *sum,* **a** + **b**, of **a** and **b** is the vector $\overrightarrow{OC}$ (Fig. 8).

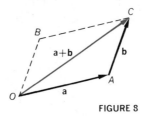

FIGURE 8

Remarks

1. If O, A, and C are not collinear, they are three of the vertices of a parallelogram $OACB$ such that $\mathbf{b} = \overrightarrow{OB}$, and the segment OC is a diagonal of the parallelogram. Because vectors can represent forces in physics, our definition of addition of vectors corresponds to the "parallelogram law" for the addition of forces. Sometimes the sum of two vectors is called the *resultant* of the vectors, a terminology borrowed from physics.

2. Although we denote the sum of **a** and **b** by **a** + **b**, using the familiar + sign, you should realize that this is not ordinary addition of real numbers.

3. It would be possible at this point to prove that vector addition is commutative, but we shall not do so, since commutativity will follow from the next theorem.

4. Definition 12-5 applies even if **a** or **b** is the null vector **0**, or if they have either the same direction or opposite directions.

Figure 9 shows **a** + **b** when the vectors **a** and **b** have either the same direction or opposite directions.

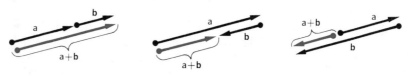

FIGURE 9

The following theorem is fundamental in problems dealing with vector addition.

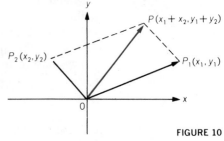

FIGURE 10

Theorem 12-2 *If $\overrightarrow{OP_1}$ and $\overrightarrow{OP_2}$ are position vectors with end points (x_1, y_1) and (x_2, y_2), respectively (as in Fig. 10), then $\overrightarrow{OP_1} + \overrightarrow{OP_2}$ is the position vector with end point P whose coordinates are $(x_1 + x_2, y_1 + y_2)$.*

Proof Let $\overrightarrow{OP}$ be the sum of $\overrightarrow{OP_1}$ and $\overrightarrow{OP_2}$ and suppose that P has coordinates (x, y). We must have $\overrightarrow{OP_1} = \overrightarrow{P_2P}$.

Therefore by Theorem 12–1,

$$x_1 - 0 = x - x_2, \qquad y_1 - 0 = y - y_2,$$

and hence

$$x = x_1 + x_2, \qquad y = y_1 + y_2.$$

Corollary *Addition of vectors is commutative: $a + b = b + a$.*

Proof If $\mathbf{a} = \overrightarrow{OP_1}$ and $\mathbf{b} = \overrightarrow{OP_2}$, in the notation of the theorem, then $\mathbf{a} + \mathbf{b} = \overrightarrow{OP}$ and $\mathbf{b} + \mathbf{a} = \overrightarrow{OP}$.

Sometimes we will want to discuss a vector that is three times as long, or k times as long, as another vector. To be able to do this we need the following definition.

Definition 12-6 If k is a real number and $\mathbf{v}$ is any vector, then $k\mathbf{v}$ is the vector such that

(a) $k\mathbf{v} = \mathbf{0}$ if $k = 0$,
(b) $k\mathbf{v}$ is a vector in the *same* direction as $\mathbf{v}$ and with magnitude $k|\mathbf{v}|$ if $k > 0$,
(c) $k\mathbf{v}$ is a vector in the *opposite* direction from $\mathbf{v}$ and with magnitude $|k| |\mathbf{v}|$ if $k < 0$.

Remarks

1. By (*b*) of Definition 12–6 we observe that $1\mathbf{v} = \mathbf{v}$.

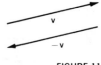

FIGURE 11

2. The vector $(-1)\mathbf{v}$ is denoted by $-\mathbf{v}$ and is called the *additive inverse* of $\mathbf{v}$, because $\mathbf{v} + -\mathbf{v}$ is the null vector. (See Fig. 11.)

3. The real number k of Definition 12–6 is often called a *scalar*.

Example In Fig. 12 arrows representing **v**, $\frac{1}{2}$**v**, $-$**v**, $-$2**v**, and 3**v** are shown.

Since each vector has an additive inverse, it is possible to define subtraction for vectors.

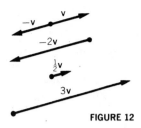

FIGURE 12

Definition 12-7 If **a** and **b** are vectors and **c** is a vector such that **c** + **b** = **a** then the difference **a** $-$ **b** of the vectors **a** and **b** is the vector **c**.

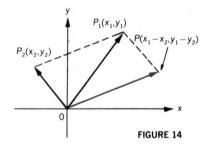

$c = a - b$

FIGURE 13

Remarks 4. Note that **a** is the diagonal of the parallelogram in which **b** and **c** are adjacent sides. (Fig. 13.)

5. Although the definition of subtraction is the same as for real numbers and the symbol "$-$" is used, the domain is vectors, not real numbers.

We can now prove a subtraction theorem corresponding to the addition theorem given by Theorem 12-2.

Theorem 12-3 **If $\overrightarrow{OP_1}$ and $\overrightarrow{OP_2}$ are position vectors with end points (x_1, y_1) and (x_2, y_2) respectively, (Fig. 14), then $\overrightarrow{OP_1} - \overrightarrow{OP_2}$ is a position vector whose end point is $(x_1 - x_2, y_1 - y_2)$.**

The proof is similar to that of Theorem 12-2.

FIGURE 14

Problems

Set A

Sketch each pair of vectors. Then sketch the sum, **a** + **b**, and the difference, **a** $-$ **b**, of the vectors.

1.
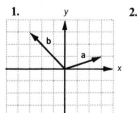

2.
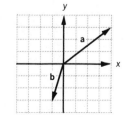

3.

4.
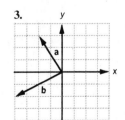

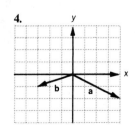

5. One vector has magnitude 2. A second vector has magnitude 5 and direction opposite to the first vector. What is the magnitude of their sum? What can you say about the direction of the sum of the vectors?

$\overrightarrow{OP}$ is a position vector to the point $P = (3, 0)$. What is the terminal point of the position vector for

6. $4\overrightarrow{OP}$?

7. $-3\overrightarrow{OP}$?

8. $4\overrightarrow{OP} + -3\overrightarrow{OP}$?

9. $\overrightarrow{OP} + (-1)\overrightarrow{OP}$?

Set B

10. The arrows representing two vectors are at right angles to each other. One vector has magnitude 4 and the other has magnitude 5. What is the magnitude of their sum?

11. Points P_1 and P_2 have coordinates $(2, -8)$ and $(-5, 10)$, respectively. Let P be a point such that $\overrightarrow{OP_1} + \overrightarrow{OP_2} = \overrightarrow{OP}$. What are the coordinates of P?

12. Q and R are points whose coordinates are $(11, 2)$ and $(8, 5)$, respectively. Determine the coordinates of a point X such that
$$\overrightarrow{OQ} - \overrightarrow{OR} = \overrightarrow{OX}.$$

13. $\overrightarrow{OQ}$ has a position vector with terminal point $Q = (2, 3)$. What are the coordinates of the terminal point for the position vectors for
(a) $2\overrightarrow{OQ}$?   (b) $-5\overrightarrow{OQ}$?
(c) $k\overrightarrow{OQ}$, where k is a real number?

14. If $P_1 = (-5, 1)$, $P_2 = (2, 6)$, and $P_3 = (6, 2)$, find the coordinates of a point P such that
$$(\overrightarrow{OP_1} + \overrightarrow{OP_2}) + \overrightarrow{OP_3} = \overrightarrow{OP}.$$

Set C

15. If $\mathbf{v}$ is any vector, is there always a vector $\mathbf{r}$ such that $\mathbf{v} + \mathbf{r} = \mathbf{0}$? What do you call the vector $\mathbf{r}$, if it exists?

16. Draw a picture of two position vectors for $\mathbf{a}$ and $\mathbf{b}$. Sketch the arrows representing $-\mathbf{b}$ and $[\mathbf{a} + (-\mathbf{b})]$. What is $[\mathbf{a} + (-\mathbf{b})] + \mathbf{b}$?

17. If $\mathbf{r}$ and $\mathbf{t}$ are any vectors, is there a vector $\mathbf{s}$ such that $\mathbf{r} + \mathbf{s} = \mathbf{t}$?

18. If A, B, and C are points as in the figure below, give an argument that shows that $(\overrightarrow{AB} + \overrightarrow{BC}) + \overrightarrow{CA} = \mathbf{0}$.

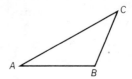

19. In the figure below which of the following statements are true?
(a) $\overrightarrow{XY} + \overrightarrow{YZ} = \overrightarrow{XZ}$
(b) $\overrightarrow{XY} - \overrightarrow{XZ} = \overrightarrow{YZ}$
(c) $\overrightarrow{XZ} - \overrightarrow{YZ} = \overrightarrow{XY}$

20. Prove Theorem 12-3.

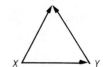

21. If $\mathbf{a}$ and $\mathbf{b}$ are vectors that have either the same direction or opposite directions, and $\mathbf{a} \neq \mathbf{0}$, prove that there is a unique real number k such that $k\mathbf{a} = \mathbf{b}$.

Calculator Problem

If $P_1 = (\sqrt{5}, \sqrt{2})$, $P_2 = (-\sqrt{3}, \sqrt{7})$ and $P_3 = (-\sqrt{2}, -\sqrt{6})$, find the coordinates of the point P, as a decimal, if $\overrightarrow{OP_1} + \overrightarrow{OP_2} + \overrightarrow{OP_3} = \overrightarrow{OP}$. Find the magnitude of $\overrightarrow{OP}$.

12-5   Unit Vectors

One of the most important theorems concerning vectors is that every vector in the plane can be represented as the sum of multiples of two fixed vectors that do not have either the same direction or opposite directions.

Theorem 12-4   *If* **a** *and* **b** *are two non-zero vectors that do not have either the same direction or opposite directions, and* **c** *is any other vector, then there exist unique real numbers p and q such that* **c** $= p$**a** $+ q$**b**.

Proof   Let **a** and **b** have two non-zero position vectors with end points A and B, respectively. (See Fig. 15.) By hypothesis, $\overrightarrow{OA}$ and $\overrightarrow{OB}$ do not have either the same direction or opposite directions. Let **c** have a position vector with end point C. Consider a line through C parallel to $\overrightarrow{OA}$. This line inter-

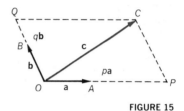

FIGURE 15

sects line OB at Q. Consider a line through C parallel to $\overrightarrow{OB}$. The line meets line OA at P. Then $\overrightarrow{OC} = \overrightarrow{OQ} + \overrightarrow{OP}$. Since **a** and $\overrightarrow{OP}$ have either the same direction or opposite directions, and **b** and $\overrightarrow{OQ}$ have either the same direction or opposite directions, then $\overrightarrow{OP} = p$**a** for some unique real number p and $\overrightarrow{OQ} = q$**b** for some unique real number q. (Recall Definition 12-6.) Hence $\overrightarrow{OC} = $ **c** $= p$**a** $+ q$**b**.

Theorem 12-4 shows that **c** is the sum of multiples of **a** and **b**, that is, **c** $= p$**a** $+ q$**b**, where p and q are real numbers. Vector **c** is said to be a *linear combination* of vectors **a** and **b**.

Example 1   The real numbers of Theorem 12-4 may be positive, negative, or zero. Figure 16 illustrates a situation in which q is evidently some negative real number. What must be the situation if one of the real numbers, p or q, is zero?

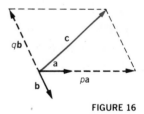

FIGURE 16

The fixed vectors, **a** and **b**, of Theorem 12-4 are said to be a *basis* for all vectors in the plane. While many pairs of vectors may be chosen as *basis vectors*, the usual and most convenient choice of basis vectors is a pair of *unit vectors* (vectors of unit length) directed, respectively, along the positive x- and y-axes. Let **i** denote the unit vector with the same direction as the positive x-axis and let **j** denote the unit vector with the same direction as the positive y-axis, as in Fig. 17. Then the position vector to any point $P(x, y)$ in the plane is (see Fig. 18) $\overrightarrow{OP} = \mathbf{r} = x\mathbf{i} + y\mathbf{j}$. Thus every vector $\mathbf{r}$ in the plane is a linear combination of the unit basis vectors $\mathbf{i}$ and $\mathbf{j}$.

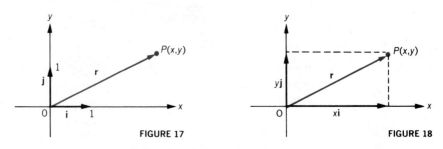

FIGURE 17   FIGURE 18

Definition 12-8 The *components* of $\mathbf{r}$ are the real numbers x and y such that $\mathbf{r} = x\mathbf{i} + y\mathbf{j}$. The component in the $\mathbf{i}$-direction is x, while the component in the $\mathbf{j}$-direction is y.

Example 2 The vector represented by the position vector to the point $(4, -3)$ is $4\mathbf{i} + (-3)\mathbf{j}$. The $\mathbf{i}$-direction component is 4 and the $\mathbf{j}$-direction component is -3.

Theorem 12-5 *Two vectors are equal if and only if they have the same components.*

The proof of this theorem is left to the student.

Example 3 If $3\mathbf{i} + y\mathbf{j} = x\mathbf{i} - \mathbf{j}$, then by Theorem 12-5 we must have $x = 3$ and $y = -1$.

Theorem 12-6 *If* $\mathbf{r}_1 = x_1\mathbf{i} + y_1\mathbf{j}$ *and* $\mathbf{r}_2 = x_2\mathbf{i} + y_2\mathbf{j}$, *then*

$$\mathbf{r}_1 + \mathbf{r}_2 = (x_1 + x_2)\mathbf{i} + (y_1 + y_2)\mathbf{j}.$$

The proof is left to the student.

Example 4 The sum, $\mathbf{r} + \mathbf{s}$, where

$$\mathbf{r} = 4\mathbf{i} + (-\mathbf{j})$$

and

$$\mathbf{s} = -\mathbf{i} + 3\mathbf{j},$$

is $(4 + -1)\mathbf{i} + (-1 + 3)\mathbf{j} = 3\mathbf{i} + 2\mathbf{j}$.
(See Fig. 19.)

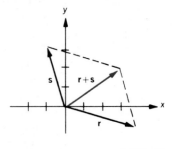

FIGURE 19

Problems

Set A

Sketch the following pairs of vectors, add them, and sketch their sum.

1. $2\mathbf{i} + 3\mathbf{j}$, $\mathbf{i} + \mathbf{j}$
2. $2\mathbf{i} + 3\mathbf{j}$, $-4\mathbf{i} + 2\mathbf{j}$
3. $-\mathbf{i} - \mathbf{j}$, $-\mathbf{i} + 3\mathbf{j}$
4. $4\mathbf{i} + 2\mathbf{j}$, $-3\mathbf{i} + 2\mathbf{j}$
5. $\frac{-1}{\sqrt{2}}\mathbf{j} + \mathbf{i}$, $\sqrt{2}\mathbf{i} + \mathbf{j}$
6. $-5\mathbf{i} + (-4)\mathbf{j}$, $4\mathbf{i} + 5\mathbf{j}$

Find the sums of the vectors.

7. $(3\mathbf{i} + 4\mathbf{j}) + (-2\mathbf{i} + 2\mathbf{j})$
8. $[-6\mathbf{i} + (-3\mathbf{j})] + (\mathbf{i} + \mathbf{j})$
9. $[9\mathbf{i} + (-5\mathbf{j})] + (-9\mathbf{i} + 5\mathbf{j})$
10. $(\frac{1}{3}\mathbf{i} + \frac{1}{4}\mathbf{j}) + [\frac{1}{2}\mathbf{i} + (-\frac{1}{2}\mathbf{j})]$
11. $\left(\frac{\sqrt{2}}{2}\mathbf{i} + 4\sqrt{3}\mathbf{j}\right) + \left(\sqrt{8}\mathbf{i} + \frac{-\sqrt{3}}{2}\mathbf{j}\right)$
12. $(\mathbf{i} + \mathbf{j}) + (-\mathbf{i} + \mathbf{j})$

Set B

13. If $\mathbf{v} = x\mathbf{i} + y\mathbf{j}$ what is the magnitude of $\mathbf{v}$ in terms of x and y?

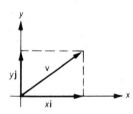

Find the magnitude of each vector.

14. $3\mathbf{i} + 4\mathbf{j}$
15. $2\mathbf{i} - 3\mathbf{j}$
16. $\mathbf{i} + \mathbf{j}$
17. $\frac{1}{\sqrt{5}}\mathbf{i} - \frac{2}{\sqrt{5}}\mathbf{j}$
18. $\mathbf{i}$
19. $\mathbf{i} + \sqrt{3}\mathbf{j}$
20. Vector $\mathbf{r}$ has x- and y-components of 7 and -2, respectively. Vector $\mathbf{s}$ has x- and y- components of -3 and 8, respectively. Express $(\mathbf{r} + \mathbf{s})$ as a linear combination of the unit basis vectors $\mathbf{i}$ and $\mathbf{j}$.

Determine the components x and y so that the sum is the null vector.

21. $(5\mathbf{i} + 2\mathbf{j}) + (x\mathbf{i} + y\mathbf{j}) = 0$
22. $[-2\mathbf{i} + (-\mathbf{j})] + (x\mathbf{i} + y\mathbf{j}) = 0$
23. The coordinates of two points are $(1, 5)$ and $(7, 7)$. What are the position vectors to these points? What is the sum of these two vectors?

Determine x and y in each equation below where $\mathbf{v} = x\mathbf{i} + y\mathbf{j}$.

24. $x\mathbf{i} + y\mathbf{j} = 3\mathbf{i} - 2\mathbf{j}$
25. $(x\mathbf{i} + y\mathbf{j}) + (2\mathbf{i} - 3\mathbf{j}) = -4\mathbf{i} - 5\mathbf{j}$
26. $(x\mathbf{i} + y\mathbf{j}) + (6\mathbf{i} + \mathbf{j}) = 0$
27. $(2x\mathbf{i} + 3y\mathbf{j}) - (\mathbf{i} - 2\mathbf{j}) = -4\mathbf{i} + \mathbf{j}$

Set C

28. Vector $\mathbf{c}$ has a position vector to the point $(2, 7)$, $\mathbf{a}$ has a position vector to the point $(4, -1)$, and $\mathbf{b}$ has a position vector to the point $(-2, 3)$. Determine real numbers p and q such that $p\mathbf{a} + q\mathbf{b} = \mathbf{c}$. Sketch the arrows.
29. Given that $\mathbf{r} = \mathbf{i} - 9\mathbf{j}$, $\mathbf{a} = \mathbf{i} + 2\mathbf{j}$, and $\mathbf{b} = 5\mathbf{i} - \mathbf{j}$, determine the real numbers s and t such that $\mathbf{r} = s\mathbf{a} + t\mathbf{b}$.
30. Prove Theorem 12–5.
31. Prove Theorem 12–6.
32. Prove that if $\mathbf{v}$ is a vector of length L, and c_1 and c_2 are the direction cosines of $\mathbf{v}$, then $\mathbf{v} = L(c_1\mathbf{i} + c_2\mathbf{j})$.
33. Prove that if $\mathbf{u} = a\mathbf{i} + b\mathbf{j}$ and $\mathbf{v} = x\mathbf{i} + y\mathbf{j}$ are perpendicular, then $ax + by = 0$.

Calculator Problem

Find the sum of the vectors

$$\mathbf{v}_1 = 3.41\mathbf{i} - 1.72\mathbf{j} \quad \text{and} \quad \mathbf{v}_2 = 0.48\mathbf{i} + 4.83\mathbf{j}.$$

Find the magnitude of the sum of the vectors. Then determine the angle that the position vector of the sum makes with the positive x-axis.

12-6   Theorems of Vector Algebra

We list below several important facts concerning vectors. Some are direct consequences of the definitions. Others are easily proved by means of Theorems 12–5 and 12–6. Note the similarity between these assertions for vectors and corresponding ones for real numbers.

1. The sum of two vectors is another vector and the product of a real number and a vector is another vector.

2. Vector addition is commutative; that is, if $\mathbf{a}$ and $\mathbf{b}$ are any vectors, then

$$\mathbf{a} + \mathbf{b} = \mathbf{b} + \mathbf{a}.$$

3. Vector addition is associative; that is, if $\mathbf{a}$, $\mathbf{b}$, and $\mathbf{c}$ are any vector, then

$$\mathbf{a} + (\mathbf{b} + \mathbf{c}) = (\mathbf{a} + \mathbf{b}) + \mathbf{c}.$$

4. If r and s are real numbers, and $\mathbf{v}$ is any vector, then

$$r(s\mathbf{v}) = (rs)\mathbf{v}.$$

5. If $\mathbf{v}$ is any vector, then

$$\mathbf{v} + \mathbf{0} = \mathbf{v} \quad \text{and} \quad 1\mathbf{v} = \mathbf{v}.$$

Thus the null vector, $\mathbf{0}$, is the *additive identity element* for vectors.

6. Multiplication of a sum of vectors by a real number is distributive; that is, if $\mathbf{a}$ and $\mathbf{b}$ are any vectors and k is a real number, then

$$k(\mathbf{a} + \mathbf{b}) = k\mathbf{a} + k\mathbf{b}.$$

7. Multiplication of a vector by a sum of real numbers is distributive; that is, if r and s are real numbers and $\mathbf{v}$ is any vector, then

$$(r + s)\mathbf{v} = r\mathbf{v} + s\mathbf{v}.$$

8. For each vector $\mathbf{v}$ there exists a vector $\mathbf{r}$ such that

$$\mathbf{v} + \mathbf{r} = \mathbf{0}.$$

Thus, $\mathbf{r}$ is the additive inverse of $\mathbf{v}$ and $\mathbf{r} = (-1)\mathbf{v} = -\mathbf{v}.$

Problems

Set A

1. Illustrate assertion 2 for the vectors

$$\mathbf{a} = 7\mathbf{i} + 2\mathbf{j} \quad \text{and} \quad \mathbf{b} = -3\mathbf{i} + (-4)\mathbf{j}.$$

2. Illustrate assertion 3 for the vectors

$$\mathbf{a} = \mathbf{i} + 3\mathbf{j},$$
$$\mathbf{b} = 4\mathbf{i} + (-2)\mathbf{j}$$

and

$$\mathbf{c} = 5\mathbf{i} + \mathbf{j}.$$

3. Is $-4(3\mathbf{v}) = -12\mathbf{v}$? Which assertion supports your answer?

4. Show that $0\mathbf{i} + 0\mathbf{j}$ is the zero vector. [*Hint*: Let $\mathbf{v} = x\mathbf{i} + y\mathbf{j}$ be any vector. Show that $0\mathbf{i} + 0\mathbf{j}$ is an *additive identity* vector for $\mathbf{v}$.]

Use assertion 6 to multiply the vectors by the real number.

5. $6(\mathbf{i} + \mathbf{j})$ **6.** $-4(\mathbf{i} + \mathbf{j})$

7. $3(2\mathbf{i} + 4\mathbf{j})$ **8.** $-1[-1\mathbf{i} + (-1\mathbf{j})]$

Write each sum as a multiple of vector $\mathbf{v}$.

9. $-4\mathbf{v} + 7\mathbf{v}$ **10.** $6\mathbf{v} + 8\mathbf{v}$

11. $3\sqrt{2}\,\mathbf{v} + (-2\sqrt{2}\,\mathbf{v})$ **12.** $\frac{2}{3}\mathbf{v} + (-\frac{3}{4}\mathbf{v})$

Give the additive inverse of each vector.

13. $3\mathbf{i}$ **14.** $-4\mathbf{j}$

15. $2\mathbf{i} + 3\mathbf{j}$ **16.** $6(\mathbf{a} + \mathbf{b})$

17. $(-3\mathbf{i} + 4\mathbf{j})$ **18.** $\mathbf{0}$

Set B

19. Use the figure to express vector $\mathbf{r}$ as a sum of vectors $\mathbf{a}$, $\mathbf{b}$, and $\mathbf{c}$ in two different ways. Which assertion of this section does this figure illustrate?

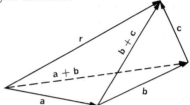

20. Draw a figure like that of Problem 19 for the vectors $\mathbf{a} = 6\mathbf{i} + \mathbf{j}$, $\mathbf{b} = -3\mathbf{i} + 4\mathbf{j}$ and $\mathbf{c} = -4\mathbf{i} + \mathbf{j}$.

Find the differences. Sketch the vectors.

21. $(3\mathbf{i} + 2\mathbf{j}) - (\mathbf{i} + \mathbf{j})$

22. $(-2\mathbf{i} + 7\mathbf{j}) - [-5\mathbf{i} + (-2\mathbf{j})]$

23. $(-\mathbf{i} + \mathbf{j}) - (0\mathbf{i} + 4\mathbf{j})$

24. $(2\sqrt{5}\,\mathbf{i} + \mathbf{j}) - [\sqrt{5}\,\mathbf{i} + (-\mathbf{j})]$

Set C

25. Sketch a picture of the arrows to illustrate assertion 6.

26. If $k\mathbf{a} + 4\mathbf{a} = (-3)\mathbf{a}$, where $\mathbf{a} \neq \mathbf{0}$, what real number is k?

27. Show that $\mathbf{v} + (-1)\mathbf{v} = \mathbf{0}$.

Calculator Problem

A vector $\mathbf{v}$ has a magnitude of 2.69 units and its position vector forms an angle of 2.34 radians with the positive x-axis. Express $\mathbf{v}$ as a linear combination of the unit vectors $\mathbf{i}$ and $\mathbf{j}$.

Vector Equations of Lines

In Chapter 11 we studied parametric and rectangular equations of lines. In this section we shall use vectors to represent lines. First we consider an example.

Example 1   A line is given by the rectangular equation $x + 2y = 6$ (Fig. 20). Several points on this line are

$$P_1 = (2, 2), \qquad P_2 = (4, 1), \qquad \text{and} \qquad P_3 = (-2, 4).$$

Let $\mathbf{r}_1$, $\mathbf{r}_2$, and $\mathbf{r}_3$ be the vectors $\overrightarrow{OP_1}$, $\overrightarrow{OP_2}$, and $\overrightarrow{OP_3}$, respectively. Then

$$\mathbf{r}_1 = 2\mathbf{i} + 2\mathbf{j}, \qquad \mathbf{r}_2 = 4\mathbf{i} + \mathbf{j}, \qquad \text{and} \qquad \mathbf{r}_3 = -2\mathbf{i} + 4\mathbf{j}.$$

Clearly, if $P(x, y)$ is any point on the line, then the position vector to the point P is $\overrightarrow{OP} = \mathbf{r} = x\mathbf{i} + y\mathbf{j}$.

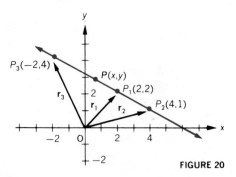

FIGURE 20

Let us consider the set of all position vectors having end points on the line $x + 2y = 6$, as shown in Fig. 21. We want to think of this set of vectors as representing the line. Our problem is that of finding a way of representing this set of vectors for any line.

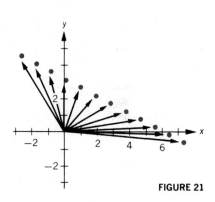

FIGURE 21

Suppose l is a line containing two points, $P_0 = (x_0, y_0)$ and $P_1 = (x_1, y_1)$, as in Fig. 22. Let $\mathbf{r}_0$ and $\mathbf{r}_1$ be the position vectors to these two points. By the definition of vector addition,

$$\mathbf{r}_1 = \mathbf{r}_0 + \overrightarrow{P_0P_1}. \qquad (1)$$

If $P = (x, y)$ is any point on l, then there is a unique real number t such that $\overrightarrow{P_0P} = t\overrightarrow{P_0P_1}$ because the vectors $\overrightarrow{P_0P}$ and $\overrightarrow{P_0P_1}$ have either the same direction or opposite direction. Then the position vector $\mathbf{r}$ to P is

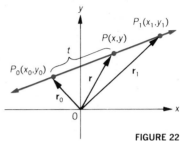

FIGURE 22

$$\mathbf{r} = \mathbf{r}_0 + t\overrightarrow{P_0P_1}. \qquad (2)$$

From (1) we have $\overrightarrow{P_0P_1} = \mathbf{r}_1 - \mathbf{r}_0$, and hence (2) can be written as

$$\mathbf{r} = \mathbf{r}_0 + t(\mathbf{r}_1 - \mathbf{r}_0). \qquad (3)$$

Equation (3) represents the position vector to any point P on the line l. By choosing different real values for t, we get position vectors to different points on the line. If we think of t as a parameter whose domain is the set of real numbers, then equation (3) represents the set of position vectors to all points of the line l. We shall refer to (3) or any equivalent statement as a *vector equation* of the line.

Example 2   Find a vector equation of the line through the points P_0 $(1, 4)$ and P_1 $(6, 7)$. (See Fig. 23.)

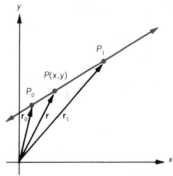

FIGURE 23

Solution. We have $\mathbf{r}_0 = \mathbf{i} + 4\mathbf{j}$ and $\mathbf{r}_1 = 6\mathbf{i} + 7\mathbf{j}$. From (3) we have

$$\mathbf{r} = (\mathbf{i} + 4\mathbf{j}) + t((6\mathbf{i} + 7\mathbf{j}) - (\mathbf{i} + 4\mathbf{j}))$$

$$= (\mathbf{i} + 4\mathbf{j}) + t(5\mathbf{i} + 3\mathbf{j}).$$

In the example above, note that when $t = 0$, $\mathbf{r} = \mathbf{i} + 4\mathbf{j} = \mathbf{r}_0$. When $t = 1$, $\mathbf{r} = (\mathbf{i} + 4\mathbf{j}) + 1(5\mathbf{i} + 3\mathbf{j}) = 6\mathbf{i} + 7\mathbf{j} = \mathbf{r}_1$. For other choices of t, $\mathbf{r}$ will be the position vector to other points on the line. Thus for $t = 2$, $\mathbf{r} = 7\mathbf{i} + 10\mathbf{j}$, hence $(7, 10)$ is a point on the line which is twice as far from P_0 as P_1 is from P_0. When $t = -1$, $\mathbf{r} = -4\mathbf{i} + \mathbf{j}$, hence $(-4, 1)$ is a point on the line which is the same distance from P_0 as P_1 is from P_0 but is in the opposite direction.

From (3) we may find the coordinates of the midpoint of segment $P_0 P_1$. Choosing $t = \frac{1}{2}$, we have

$$\mathbf{r} = \mathbf{r}_0 + \tfrac{1}{2}(\mathbf{r}_1 - \mathbf{r}_0)$$
$$= \tfrac{1}{2}(\mathbf{r}_0 + \mathbf{r}_1).$$

If $P_0 = (x_0, y_0)$ and $P_1 = (x_1, y_1)$, then expressing each vector in terms of components, we have

$$\mathbf{r} = x\mathbf{i} + y\mathbf{j},$$
$$\mathbf{r}_0 = x_0\mathbf{i} + y_0\mathbf{j},$$

and

$$\mathbf{r}_1 = x_1\mathbf{i} + y_1\mathbf{j},$$

so that

$$x\mathbf{i} + y\mathbf{j} = \tfrac{1}{2}(x_0\mathbf{i} + y_0\mathbf{j} + x_1\mathbf{i} + y_1\mathbf{j})$$
$$= \tfrac{1}{2}(x_0 + x_1)\mathbf{i} + \tfrac{1}{2}(y_0 + y_1)\mathbf{j}.$$

Since two vectors are equal if and only if their components are equal, it follows that

$$x = \tfrac{1}{2}(x_0 + x_1)$$

and

$$y = \tfrac{1}{2}(y_0 + y_1).$$

Thus we have proved the following theorem.

Theorem 12-7 **The midpoint (x, y) of a segment with end points (x_0, y_0) and (x_1, y_1) is**

$$(x, y) = \left(\frac{x_0 + x_1}{2}, \frac{y_0 + y_1}{2} \right).$$

Example 3 The coordinates of the midpoint of the segment whose end points are P_0 $(1, 4)$ and P_1 $(6, 7)$ are

$$x = \frac{1 + 6}{2} = \frac{7}{2} \quad \text{and} \quad y = \frac{4 + 7}{2} = \frac{11}{2}.$$

Problems

Set A

Determine a vector equation of the line through the following pairs of points.

1. $(3, 4)$ and $(0, -2)$
2. $(1, -3)$ and $(5, 0)$
3. $(-4, -1)$ and $(-1, -2)$
4. $(5, -3)$ and $(-5, 3)$
5. $(-4, 5)$ and $(7, 5)$
6. $(-6, 9)$ and $(-6, -1)$

Find the coordinates of two points on each line. Then give a vector equation of each line.

7. $x - 2y = 10$
8. $3x - y = 12$
9. $2x + y = 6$
10. $5x + 2y = 10$

Set B

Find the midpoints of the segments whose end points are given below.

11. $(-3, 8)$ and $(7, -2)$
12. $(0, 0)$ and $(-6, -8)$
13. $(-1, 7)$ and $(-3, 5)$
14. $(-1, 5)$ and $(8, 2)$
15. $(3.4, -2.5)$ and $(-1.8, 6.3)$
16. $(\pi, \pi/2)$ and $(\sqrt{2}, -\sqrt{2})$
17. $(-a, b)$ and $(a, -b)$, where $a < 0$ and $b < 0$
18. $(a, 0)$ and $(b, 0)$, where $a > 0$ and $b > 0$
19. $(a, 0)$ and $(b, 0)$, where $a < 0$ and $b > 0$
20. $(a, 0)$ and $(0, b)$, where $a > 0$ and $b > 0$
21. A point on the segment whose end points are $(-1, 3)$ and $(5, 2)$ is twice as far from the point $(-1, 3)$ as from $(5, 2)$. Find its coordinates.
22. What is a vector equation of the y-axis?
23. A line has parametric equations
$$\begin{cases} x = 3 + \tfrac{1}{3}d, \\ y = -2 + \dfrac{2\sqrt{2}\,d}{3}. \end{cases}$$

Write a vector equation of the line.

24. Obtain a formula for the coordinates of the points that trisect the segment between

$$(x_1, y_1) \quad \text{and} \quad (x_2, y_2).$$

Set C

25. Given P_1 and P_2 as below, determine the coordinates of the point P satisfying the condition indicated.
    (a) $P_1 = (-2, 3)$, $P_2 = (5, -1)$. Point P is between P_1 and P_2 and $|P_1P| = \tfrac{1}{3}|P_1P_2|$.
    (b) Same as part (a) except that P_1 is between P and P_2.
    (c) Same as part (a) except that P_2 is between P and P_1.

26. The points $(1, 3)$, $(4, -1)$, and $(-2, -2)$ are the midpoints of the sides of a triangle. Find the vertices of the triangle.

27. Show that the medians of the triangle with vertices (x_1, y_1), (x_2, y_2), and (x_3, y_3) meet at a point two-thirds the distance from a vertex to the midpoint of the opposite side. (See figure.)

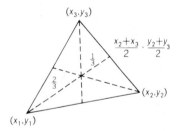

This point is called the *centroid* of the triangle. Its coordinates are

$$\left(\frac{x_1 + x_2 + x_3}{3}, \frac{y_1 + y_2 + y_3}{3} \right).$$

28. The points (a_1, b_1), (a_2, b_2), and (a_3, b_3) are the midpoints of the sides of a triangle. Find the vertices of the triangle.

Calculator Problem

Calculate the coordinates of the centroid of $\triangle ABC$ (see Problem 27) if $A = (-3.5, -2.4)$, $B = (\sqrt{10}, \sqrt{3})$ and $C = (-\sqrt{2}, \sqrt{19})$.

Summary

In this chapter we have studied vectors in the plane. Beginning with the simple idea of an *arrow* as an ordered pair of points, we have built a mathematical system containing elements called *vectors*. We have seen that vectors, while quite different from real numbers, have properties similar to some of the properties of real numbers. We have observed that vector addition is associative and commutative, that vectors may be multiplied by real numbers, and that multiplication by a real number is distributive with respect to vector addition.

The most important aid to computation with vectors is the theorem that every vector is a linear combination of two unit vectors directed along the positive x-axis and positive y-axis. Thus if $\mathbf{r}$ is any vector, then there exist unique real numbers x and y such that

$$\mathbf{r} = x\mathbf{i} + y\mathbf{j}.$$

In a later chapter we shall see that we can easily extend our concept of vectors in the plane to vectors in space. Still later we shall define some new operations for vectors. At the present, for example, we add vectors, but we have not defined any operations corresponding to multiplication for a pair of vectors.

Chapter 12 Test

12-2 **1.** What is the magnitude of the arrow given by the ordered pair of points $((1, 2), (6, 8))$?

2. Is the arrow $((-2, -2), (5, 1))$ equivalent to the arrow in Problem 1?

12-3 **3.** What are the coordinates of the terminal point of the position vector for $((5, 6), (-4, -3))$?

4. $\overrightarrow{OP}$ is a position vector and $P = (-2, 1)$. What is the magnitude of $\overrightarrow{OP}$?

12-4 **5.** Compare the directions and magnitudes of the vectors $-2\mathbf{v}$ and $4\mathbf{v}$.

6. Which statement is true about the vectors shown in the figure?

(a) $\mathbf{r} + \mathbf{s} = \mathbf{t}$
(b) $\mathbf{t} + \mathbf{r} = \mathbf{s}$
(c) $\mathbf{s} + \mathbf{t} = \mathbf{r}$

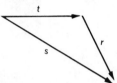

12-5 Find the sum of the vectors.

7. $[11\mathbf{i} + (-4\mathbf{j})] + (-6\mathbf{i} + 2\mathbf{j})$

8. $(\mathbf{i} + \sqrt{3}\,\mathbf{j}) + (7\mathbf{i} + \sqrt{3}\,\mathbf{j})$

9. Given that $\mathbf{r} = x\mathbf{i} + y\mathbf{j}$ is the sum of vectors $\overrightarrow{P_1P_2}$ and $\overrightarrow{P_3P_4}$, where $P_1 = (-1, 5)$, $P_2 = (-5, 2)$, $P_3 = (2, 3)$, and $P_4 = (5, 2)$, determine the components x and y of $\mathbf{r}$.

10. If $x\mathbf{i} + (-4)\mathbf{j} = 7\mathbf{i} + y\mathbf{j}$, determine x and y.

12-6 If $\mathbf{v} = 6\mathbf{i} + 4\mathbf{j}$ and $\mathbf{u} = -3\mathbf{i} + (-2\mathbf{j})$, what are the following?

11. $-\mathbf{u}$

12. $\mathbf{v} - \mathbf{u}$

13. $4\mathbf{u} + 5\mathbf{j}$

14. $-(\mathbf{u} + \mathbf{v})$

12-7 In Problems 15–18, suppose that l is a line containing the points A and B whose coordinates are $(2, 3)$ and $(5, 4)$, as shown in the figure.

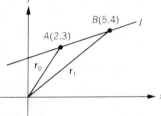

15. Write a vector equation of line l.

16. What are the components of vector $\overrightarrow{AB}$?

17. What are the coordinates of the midpoint of $\overline{AB}$?

18. What are the coordinates of a point C if A is between B and C and $\overline{CA} \cong \overline{AB}$?

19. Find two points on the line $3x - y = 7$. Then write a vector equation of the line.

20. A and B are points on a line and have coordinates $(-1, 5)$ and $(4, 6)$, respectively. Determine the coordinates of a point C on this line, given that $|\overrightarrow{AC}| = 4|\overrightarrow{BC}|$ and B is between A and C.

Chapter 13
Space

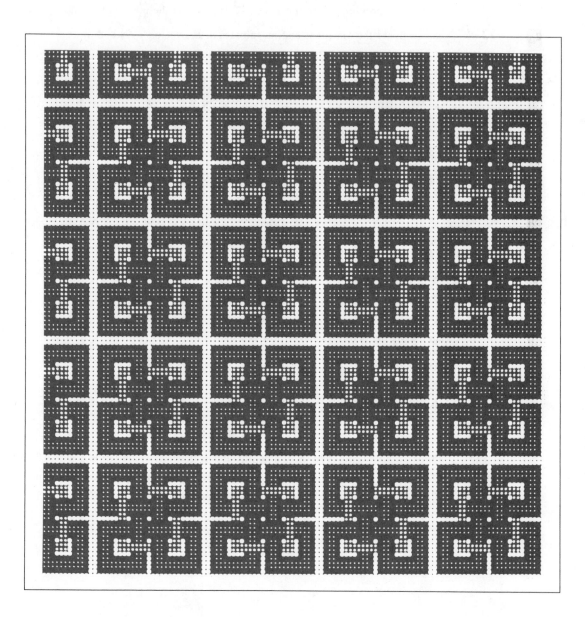

13-1 Introduction

In this chapter we shall see that we can coordinatize space in much the same way we did a plane. We shall also see further similarities: Parametric equations of a line in space are quite similar to those of a line in the plane. The distance formula is a simple extension of the formula in the plane. And finally, planes in space can be described simply by means of equations.

In this discussion we shall need certain facts about lines and planes in space. The required properties will be stated as postulates for space.

Postulates for Space

P1. There is a set of points called euclidean space. Certain subsets of space are called lines. Certain other subsets of space are called planes. Space contains at least four points not in any one plane.

P2. There is exactly one plane containing any three noncollinear points (Fig. 1).

FIGURE 1   FIGURE 2

P3. Each plane satisfies all the postulates for euclidean plane geometry. In particular, the line joining two points of a plane lies in that plane, and the postulates for congruence of segments and angles apply whether or not the segments and angles are in the same plane.

P4. Each plane separates space (Fig. 2). This means that the set of points not in the plane consists of two subsets on either side of the plane, called half-spaces, with the following properties:

(a) If two points are in the same subset, the segment joining them does not intersect the plane.

(b) If two points are in different subsets, the segment joining them does intersect the plane.

From these few postulates all the theorems of space, or *solid,* geometry can be derived. However, we will not prove any of these theorems in the text. All that is required is an understanding of the elementary aspects of space geometry and the ability to visualize and draw some space figures. In this regard, you should observe that the drawing problem is one of representing three-dimensional relations in a plane, in fact, in only a portion of a plane, namely a sheet of paper. Planes will be indicated by a drawing of a parallelogram, suggesting a portion of a plane. Lines that are behind planes as viewed by the observer (you) are dashed, as in Fig. 3.

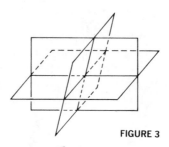

FIGURE 3

13-2   Space Coordinatization

Just as in the plane we defined a one-to-one mapping of ordered pairs of real numbers onto the points of the plane, so for space we analogously define a one-to-one mapping of ordered *triples* of real numbers onto space.

As was the case in the plane, the assigning of coordinates to space also depends on certain choices. These choices can be made in different ways.

Let us choose a unit of length and a point O, called the *origin of coordinates* (Fig. 4a). Next, let us choose three mutually perpendicular lines through O. We call any one of these lines the *first axis,* either of the other two the *second axis,* and the remaining line the *third axis.* The planes containing pairs of coordinate axes are called the *coordinate planes.*

Next we coordinatize each axis (Fig. 4b). This step involves choosing a positive direction on each axis. We can now define a mapping from the points of space to ordered triples of real numbers (Fig. 4c). For each point P, we consider the plane through P parallel to the coordinate plane of the second and third axes. This plane meets the first axis in a point with coordinate a_1, called the *first coordinate* of P. In the same manner, planes parallel to the other coordinate planes determine the second and third coordinates, a_2 and a_3, of P. We indicate the coordinates of point P by (a_1, a_2, a_3). Frequently we simply refer to the ordered triple (a_1, a_2, a_3) as a point.

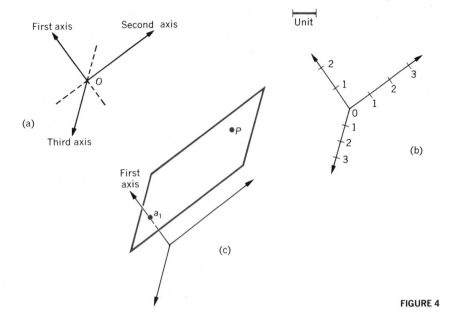

First axis

Second axis

Unit

(a)

Third axis

First
axis

●P

First
axis

●a_1

(b)

(c)

FIGURE 4

Because the planes through P parallel to the coordinate planes are unique, the definition of coordinates given above defines a function, or mapping, of points of space into ordered triples of real numbers. This mapping is one-to-one. Since we know that for each point there is a unique triple (a_1, a_2, a_3), it remains to show that each triple corresponds to exactly one point. This converse is left to the student.

A coordinate system provides a one-to-one mapping between the points of space and the set of all ordered triples of real numbers. The coordinates of a point are called *rectangular cartesian coordinates.* The word *rectangular* comes from our choice of axes which are mutually perpendicular. This choice is not necessary but is highly convenient. (See Problem 26 of the problem set.)

There are several conventions which are observed in coordinate space geometry. Usually we give names to the three axes, which are related to the variable used to denote the coordinate. Thus, if we use x to denote any first coordinate, and y and z to denote the second and third coordinates, respectively, then it is natural to speak of the x-, y-, and z-coordinates of a point, as well as the x-, y-, and z-axes. Of course, there is nothing compulsory about the use of the letters x, y, and z. Any letters would do as well. We could also have a-, b-, and c-axes, or u-, v-, and w-axes, etc.

Furthermore, there is no definite way to orient the axes, but it is customary in textbooks to picture the axes as shown in Fig. 5. The y- and z-axes are in the plane of the page, and the positive x-axis extends out from the page toward the reader. In the drawing, the x-axis is at an angle which is intended to convey a feeling of perspective, and the unit of length is shortened along the x-axis to enhance this effect. But these drawings are *not* perspective drawings, since parallel lines are not drawn to converge. Lines parallel in space are parallel in these drawings.

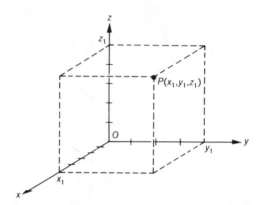

FIGURE 5

The plane containing the x- and y-axes is the *xy-coordinate plane,* or simply, the xy-plane. Likewise there are yz- and xz-coordinate planes. The coordinate planes separate space into eight *octants.* Usually only one of them is given a name; this is the *first octant,* which consists of the set of all points having positive coordinates only. The two sides of a plane are called *half-spaces.*

Remark

We have started with a geometric object, namely euclidean space, and have given it coordinates. But often, in the applications of mathematics to problems of physics, chemistry, engineering and other fields it is the converse situation that prevails. We are given ordered triples of real numbers and use space to illustrate graphically the relations between the ordered triples. In some cases there is no need to choose the same unit for all the coordinate axes. The following example illustrates this.

Example

A rectangular plate is heated, but not uniformly. Consider the temperature at each point of the plate. Discuss the problem of plotting temperature as a function of position. What is the relevant portion of space? (Fig. 6.)

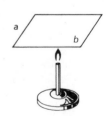

FIGURE 6

Solution. Let x and y denote the distances from one corner of the rectangular plate and t the temperature. Fig. 7 shows the temperature as a function of position. The graph would be a kind of surface, but not necessarily a plane, because the plate was not heated uniformly. Only the first octant would be needed to show the graph.

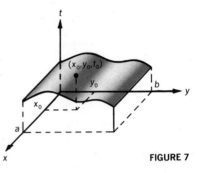

FIGURE 7

Problems

Set A

In the figure, the coordinates of point P are $(-2, 3, 1)$. Give the coordinates of each of these points.

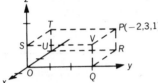

1. Q **2.** R **3.** S
4. T **5.** U **6.** V

7. Plot the following points on the same coordinate axis. $(0, 0, 0)$, $(0, 1, 2)$, $(0, -1, 2)$, $(1, -1, 2)$, $(-2, 2, -3)$, $(4, 0, 3)$, $(4, 0, -3)$, $(\pi, \pi/2, 0)$, $(-\sqrt{2}, \sqrt{2}, 0)$.

8. A point is on the y-axis. What can you say about its x- and z-coordinates? What equations in x, y, and z are satisfied if and only if the point (x, y, z) is on the y-axis?

Set B

9. Describe the eight octants in terms of the coordinates of points in them. Also describe the octants in terms of the half-spaces formed by the coordinate planes.

10. A plane is parallel to the xz-coordinate plane and passes through $(-1, 3, -4)$. What can you say about the coordinates of any point (x, y, z) in the plane?

11. What is the set of all points (x, y, z) for which $x = -2$? the set of all points (x, y, z) for which $x = 1$ and $y = -2$?

12. A point lies in the half-space formed by the yz-plane that contains the point $(-3, 4, 5)$. What can you say about the coordinates of any point (x, y, z) in this half-space?

13. What is the set of all points (x, y, z) for which $y < 0$?

14. What is the set of all points (x, y, z) for which $x + 2 \leq 0$?

15. What is the set of all points (x, y, z) for which $x^2 > 0$?

16. Draw a picture of the set of all points (x, y, z) for which $0 \leq x \leq 1$, $0 \leq y \leq 1$, and $0 \leq z \leq 1$.

17. A line is parallel to the z-axis and passes through $(-1, -2, -3)$. Find several other points on the line.

Set C

Plot the following pairs of points. Then draw the line segment connecting them. Draw a plane containing the segment that is parallel to the y-axis. Draw a second plane containing the segment parallel to the z-axis.

18. $(2, -2, 0)$, $(-1, 2, 3)$

19. $(3, 0, 2)$, $(0, 3, 3)$

20. $(3, 0, 3)$, $(0, 2, -1)$

21. $(2, 0, -2)$, $(0, 3, 1)$

22. A line passes through $(-1, -2, 3)$ and $(3, -2, 1)$. Find a pair of equations, one in x and z and the other in y, that are satisfied if and only if the point (x, y, z) is on the line.

23. What is the set of all points (x, y, z) such that $2x + 3y = 6$?

24. A particle moves along a straight line subject to a force that depends on its position and the time t. If the force is always in one direction and no greater than 100 lbs, discuss the portion of space relevant to plotting force as a function of distance and time.

25. The internal energy E of a given quantity of a gas depends on the pressure p and temperature T. What is the relevant portion of space?

26. In assigning coordinates for space, it is not necessary to choose mutually perpendicular axes. Describe how to set up a coordinate system for space using any three concurrent noncoplanar lines as axes.

27. Show that to each ordered triple of real numbers (a_1, a_2, a_3), there corresponds a unique point P in space.

Calculator Problem

A point P has space coordinates of $(\sqrt[3]{15}, -\sqrt{33}, \sqrt[4]{147})$. What are the coordinates of the point with *integer* coordinates that is closest to point P?

13-3   The Distance Formula

Let us consider any two points $P_1 = (x_1, y_1, z_1)$ and $P_2 = (x_2, y_2, z_2)$. We choose $P_3 = (x_2, y_2, z_1)$ (Fig. 8). Then the points P_1 and P_3 are in the plane parallel to the xy-coordinate plane where $z = z_1$. The distance $|P_1 P_3|$ is given by the distance formula in the plane,

$$|P_1 P_3| = \sqrt{(x_1 - x_2)^2 + (y_1 - y_2)^2}.$$

The points P_2 and P_3 are on a line parallel to the z-axis and

$$|P_2 P_3| = \sqrt{(z_1 - z_2)^2}$$
$$= |z_1 - z_2|.$$

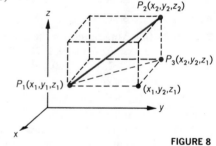

FIGURE 8

The triangle $P_1 P_2 P_3$ is a right triangle; hence by the Pythagorean Theorem,

$$|P_1 P_2|^2 = |P_1 P_3|^2 + |P_2 P_3|^2$$
$$= (x_1 - x_2)^2 + (y_1 - y_2)^2 + (z_1 - z_2)^2,$$

and we obtain the *distance formula*

$$|P_1 P_2| = \sqrt{(x_1 - x_2)^2 + (y_1 - y_2)^2 + (z_1 - z_2)^2}.$$

The distance formula in three dimensions is an extension of the distance formula in two dimensions. There is one extra term. If both P_1 and P_2 lie in the xy-plane, then $z_1 = z_2 = 0$ and we get the two-dimensional formula.

318   Space

Example   Find the distance between $P_1 = (-1, 1, 1)$ and $P_2 = (1, 2, 3)$.

Solution. Using the distance formula above, we have

$$|P_1P_2| = \sqrt{[1 - (-1)]^2 + (2 - 1)^2 + (3 - 1)^2}$$
$$= \sqrt{2^2 + 1^2 + 2^2} = \sqrt{9} = 3.$$

Problems

Set A

Plot the following pairs of points and find the distance between them.

1. $(2, 0, 1)$, $(10, 1, 5)$

2. $(2, -1, -1)$, $(-1, 3, 3)$

3. $(3, 2, 0)$, $(0, 0, 6)$

4. $(0, 0, 0)$, $(1, 1, 1)$

5. $(0, 0, 0)$, $(2, -9, 6)$

6. $(1 - \sqrt{2}, 1 + \sqrt{3}, 5)$, $(1 + \sqrt{2}, 1 - \sqrt{3}, 1)$

7. The eight vertices of a box have coordinates $(0, 0, 0)$, $(4, 0, 0)$, $(4, 5, 0)$, $(0, 5, 0)$, $(0, 5, 3)$, $(0, 0, 3)$, $(4, 0, 3)$, and $(4, 5, 3)$. Draw the box. Then find the length of the longest diagonal of the box.

8. The dimensions of a rectangular room are 4 m x 6 m x 3 m. What is the distance between a point on the floor in one corner and a point on the ceiling in the far opposite corner?

Set B

9. What is the distance between the pair of points whose coordinates are (a, b, c), $(a + d, b + e, c + f)$?

10. The vertices of $\triangle ABC$ are $A = (3, -2, 4)$, $B = (5, 5, 5)$ and $6 = (-4, 4, -2)$. Find the length of each side of the triangle.

11. The vertices of $\triangle XYZ$ are $X = (2, -1, 1)$, $Y = (4, 2, 1)$ and $Z = (2, -1, 4)$. Sketch the triangle. Show that the triangle is a right triangle by showing that the sum of the squares of two of the sides is equal to the square of the third side.

12. Are the points $(1, -1, 1)$, $(2, 2, 2)$, and $(4, -2, 1)$ vertices of a right triangle?

13. Show that $(2, 6, -3)$, $(-4, 3, -3)$, and $(-2, 7, 2)$ are vertices of an isosceles triangle.

Set C

14. Is the point $(1, 0, 4)$ inside or outside the sphere of radius π with center at $(2, 3, 3)$?

15. Determine x such that $(x, 0, 0)$ will be on the sphere of radius $3\sqrt{3}$ with center at $(2, 3, 3)$.

16. Give an equation in x, y, z that is satisfied if and only if the point (x, y, z) is on the sphere of radius r with center at the origin. Explain your reasoning.

17. Show that if a sphere of radius r has its center at (a, b, c) then any point $P(x, y, z)$ on the sphere has coordinates such that

$$r^2 = (x - a)^2 + (y - b)^2 + (z - c)^2.$$

18. Find an equation in x, y, and z satisfied by the coordinates of all points (x, y, z) that are equidistant from $(2, 3, -2)$ and $(6, 11, 8)$.

19. Find the points on the y-axis at a distance 6 from the point $(2, 1, 4)$.

20. Show that if the line through (x_1, y_1, z_1) and (x_2, y_2, z_2) is perpendicular to the line through (x_1, y_1, z_1) and (x_3, y_3, z_3), then

$$(x_2 - x_1)(x_1 - x_3) + (y_2 - y_1)(y_1 - y_3) + (z_2 - z_1)(z_1 - z_3) = 0.$$

21. Using the distance formula, show that $|P_1P_2| = |P_2P_1|$.

Calculator Problem

Heron of Alexandria (c. 50 A.D.) discovered a formula for the area of a triangle in terms of the lengths of the three sides of the triangle. Heron's formula for the area A of any triangle is

$$A = \sqrt{s(s - a)(s - b)(s - c)}$$

where a, b, and c are the lengths of the three sides and s is the semiperimeter of the triangle. That is, $s = \frac{1}{2}(a + b + c)$.

Use the distance formula to find the lengths of the three sides of a triangle whose vertices are $(6, 1, -4)$, $(4, 5, 3)$ and $(-2, -4, 7)$. Then use Heron's formula to find the area of the triangle.

13-4   Direction Cosines of Lines in Space

In the next section we will obtain parametric equations of lines in space in a manner analogous to that for lines in the plane. For this purpose we need to define direction angles and direction cosines of a line in space.

Let l be any line and (x_0, y_0, z_0) a point on it. Next we coordinatize the line with point (x_0, y_0, z_0) as the origin (Fig. 9). Then each point of l has associated with it a unique real number, d, the directed distance from (x_0, y_0, z_0). In

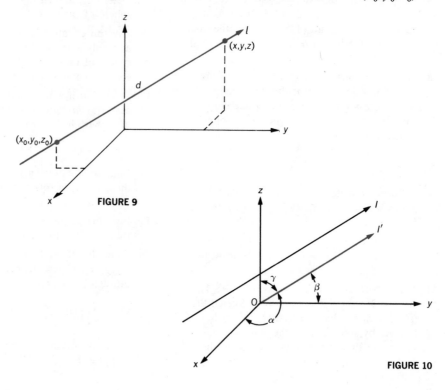

FIGURE 9

FIGURE 10

this way l becomes a directed line. To define direction angles we consider a directed line l' parallel to l and in the same direction (as in Fig. 10) and through the origin.

Definition 13-1 With the notation already described, the *direction angles* of the directed line l are the angles made by the positive ray from O on l' and the positive x-, y-, and z-axes. The angles have measure α, β, and γ, respectively.

Remark The oppositely directed line has direction angles with measures

$$\pi - \alpha, \qquad \pi - \beta, \qquad \pi - \gamma.$$

Definition 13-2 The *direction cosines* of the directed line l are the numbers c_1, c_2, c_3:

$$c_1 = \cos \alpha = \text{the } x\text{-direction cosine,}$$
$$c_2 = \cos \beta = \text{the } y\text{-direction cosine}$$
$$c_3 = \cos \gamma = \text{the } z\text{-direction cosine.}$$

Remark The oppositely directed line has these direction cosines:

$$\cos (\pi - \alpha) = -\cos \alpha,$$
$$\cos (\pi - \beta) = -\cos \beta,$$
$$\cos (\pi - \gamma) = -\cos \gamma.$$

What we now desire are equations that give the direction cosines of a line in terms of rectangular coordinates of points on the line. These are supplied by the following theorem, analogous to Theorem 11-1 for the plane.

Theorem 13-1 *Suppose l is a directed line in the plane. Let (x_0, y_0, z_0) and (x, y, z) be on l, and let d be the directed distance from (x_0, y_0, z_0) to (x, y, z). Then*

$$c_1 = \cos \alpha = \frac{x - x_0}{d},$$

$$c_2 = \cos \beta = \frac{y - y_0}{d}, \qquad (1)$$

$$c_3 = \cos \gamma = \frac{z - z_0}{d}.$$

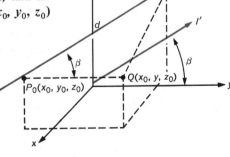

FIGURE 11

Proof We shall prove only the second equality. The others are proved similarly. Referring to Fig. 11, it is an easy exercise in geometry to see that $\angle PP_0Q$ is congruent to the y-direction angle if (x, y, z) is on the positive side of P_0. Because $\triangle PP_0Q$ is a right triangle with right angle at Q, we have

$$\cos \beta = \frac{y - y_0}{d}. \qquad (2)$$

If (x, y, z) is on the other side of (x_0, y_0, z_0), then both numerator and denominator change sign, so equation (2) remains valid.

Example What are the direction cosines of the line through $P(1, -1, 2)$ and $Q(1, 3, 6)$ if it is directed from P to Q? (See Fig. 12.)

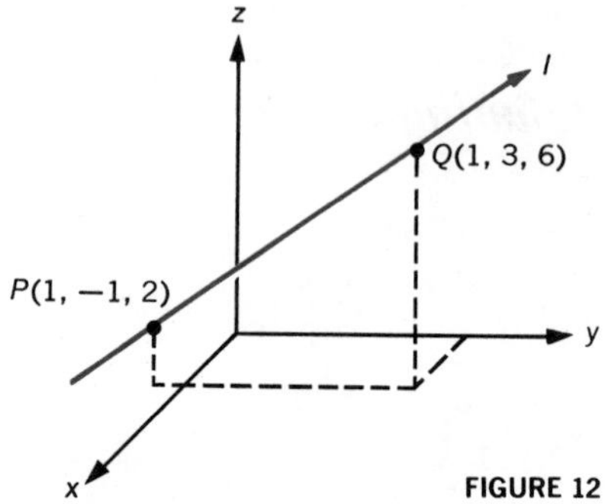

FIGURE 12

Solution. The directed distance from point P to Q is Q is

$$d = \sqrt{(1 - 1)^2 + (3 + 1)^2 + (6 - 2)^2}$$
$$= \sqrt{32} = 4\sqrt{2}.$$

From equations (1) we have

$$\cos \alpha = \frac{1 - 1}{4\sqrt{2}} = 0 \qquad \text{and so} \qquad \alpha = \frac{\pi}{2},$$

$$\cos \beta = \frac{3 + 1}{4\sqrt{2}} = \frac{1}{\sqrt{2}}, \qquad \text{and so} \qquad \beta = \frac{\pi}{4},$$

$$\cos \gamma = \frac{6 - 2}{4\sqrt{2}} = \frac{1}{\sqrt{2}}, \qquad \text{and so} \qquad \gamma = \frac{\pi}{4}.$$

Observe that even without equations (1) it is clear from Fig. 12 that $\alpha = \pi/2$ and $\beta = \gamma = \pi/4$.

There is an important relation connecting the direction cosines of any line in space, which we state as a theorem.

Theorem 13-2 *If c_1, c_2, c_3 are the direction cosines of a line, then*

$$c_1^2 + c_2^2 + c_3^2 = \cos^2 \alpha + \cos^2 \beta + \cos^2 \gamma = 1.$$

The proof is an easy application of the distance formula and equations (1), and is left to the student.

The result of Theorem 13-2 raises the question of whether there is a line with given direction cosines a, b, and c such that $a^2 + b^2 + c^2 = 1$. The answer to this question is given by Theorem 13-3, which is the converse of Theorem 13-2.

Theorem 13-3   *If a, b, and c are real numbers and $a^2 + b^2 + c^2 = 1$, then there is at least one line whose x-, y-, and z-direction cosines are a, b, and c, respectively.*

The proof of the theorem is left as an exercise and can easily be made by considering the line through $(0, 0, 0)$ and (a, b, c).

Problems

Set A

Find direction cosines of the lines through the following pairs of points, and directed from the first point to the second.

1. $(0, 0, 0)$, $(-3, 2, 6)$ 2. $(0, 0, 0)$, $(5, 0, 0)$

3. $(1, 2, 0)$, $(4, 0, 4)$ 4. $(3, 0, 2)$, $(0, 3, -1)$

5. $(0, 0, 0)$, (a, b, c)

6. (x, y, z), $(x + a, y + b, z + c)$

7. Verify that $c_1^2 + c_2^2 + c_3^2 = 1$ for Problems 1 through 6.

8. Give the direction cosines for Problems 1, and 3 if the lines are directed from the second point to the first.

Set B

9. The line through $(2, -3, 2)$ and $(-4, -3, 4)$ lies in a plane parallel to the xz-plane. Sketch the line. Find the direction cosines of the line.

10. A line is parallel to the xy-plane. Show that $c_3 = 0$.

11. A line is parallel to the z-axis. When directed, what direction cosines can it have? What direction angles?

12. Show that the three numbers $\frac{1}{2}$, $\frac{2}{3}$ and $\sqrt{11}/6$ are the direction cosines of some line.

13. Can a line have direction angles of $\pi/3$, $\pi/4$ and $\pi/3$?

14. Can one have direction angles

$$\alpha = \beta = \gamma = \pi/3?$$

Interpret geometrically. [*Hint:* Try holding a pencil so that it forms an angle of $\pi/3$ with each of the coordinate axes in space.]

Set C

15. What are the direction cosines of the directed line from $(0, 0, 0)$ to (a, b, c)? Suppose further that $a^2 + b^2 + c^2 = 1$. What theorem has been proved?

16. Prove Theorem 13-2.

17. Prove Theorem 13-3.

18. Suppose p, q, and r are real numbers such that not all three are zero. Show that if $k = \sqrt{p^2 + q^2 + r^2}$ then p/k, q/k, and r/k are direction cosines of some directed line.

19. If α, β, and γ are direction angles of a line, prove that $\sin^2 \alpha + \sin^2 \beta + \sin^2 \gamma = 2$.

Calculator Problem

A line has direction cosines $c_1 = c_2 = c_3$. Find these direction cosines and determine the direction angles of the line.

Parametric Equations of Lines

We shall obtain parametric equations of a line in space quite analogously to parametric equations of a line in the plane.

As in the development of parametric equations of a line in a plane, there are two coordinate systems associated with the parametric equations of a line in space. One is the rectangular coordinate system represented by the ordered triple (x, y, z) and the other is the coordinate system represented by the directed distance d.

Theorem 13-4   *Given a directed line l with direction cosines c_1, c_2, and c_3, let (x_0, y_0, z_0) be a point on l. Then a point (x, y, z) on l at a directed distance d from (x_0, y_0, z_0) has coordinates*

$$\begin{aligned} x &= x_0 + c_1 d, \\ y &= y_0 + c_2 d, \\ z &= z_0 + c_3 d. \end{aligned} \tag{1}$$

Conversely, if x, y, and z are given by equations (1), then the point (x, y, z) is on l. (See Fig. 13.)

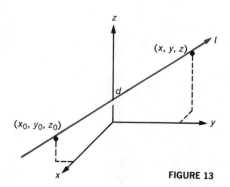

FIGURE 13

Proof   If (x, y, z) is on l and $(x, y, z) \neq (x_0, y_0, z_0)$, then $d \neq 0$ and one has, by Theorem 13–1,

$$c_1 = \frac{x - x_0}{d}, \qquad c_2 = \frac{y - y_0}{d}, \qquad c_3 = \frac{z - z_0}{d}. \tag{2}$$

These equations imply equations (1). If $(x, y, z) = (x_0, y_0, z_0)$, then $d = 0$ and equations (1) are valid.

Conversely, if equations (1) are satisfied and $d \neq 0$, then equations (2) are satisfied. But these imply that (x, y, z) is on a line through (x_0, y_0, z_0) with direction cosines c_1, c_2, c_3. If $d = 0$, then $(x, y, z) = (x_0, y_0, z_0)$.

Equations (1) are *parametric equations* of the line with *parameter d*.

Example   Find parametric equations of the line through $(1, 3, 1)$ and $(3, 0, 5)$.

Solution. We must first decide which point to use for (x_0, y_0, z_0). Let us suppose that $(1, 3, 1)$ is selected (Fig. 14). Then the positive direction on l must be chosen. Suppose that we select $(3, 0, 5)$ to be on the positive side. Then the distance between $(3, 0, 5)$ and $(1, 3, 1)$ is $\sqrt{29}$, and the direction cosines of the directed line are

$$c_1 = \frac{3-1}{\sqrt{29}} = \frac{2}{\sqrt{29}}, \qquad c_2 = \frac{0-3}{\sqrt{29}} = \frac{-3}{\sqrt{29}}, \qquad c_3 = \frac{5-1}{\sqrt{29}} = \frac{4}{\sqrt{29}}.$$

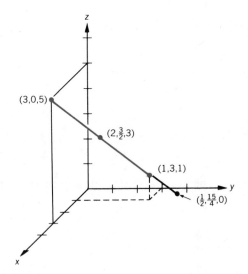

FIGURE 14

Had we selected the other ray from $(1, 3, 1)$ to be the positive side of l, the direction cosines would all have been opposite in sign.

Parametric equations of the line are therefore

$$\begin{cases} x = 1 + \dfrac{2}{\sqrt{29}}\, d, \\[2mm] y = 3 - \dfrac{3}{\sqrt{29}}\, d, \\[2mm] z = 1 + \dfrac{4}{\sqrt{29}}\, d. \end{cases}$$

Other points of the line are easily found by using different values for d. For example, the midpoint of the segment between $(1, 3, 1)$ and $(3, 0, 5)$ can be found by setting d equal to one-half the distance between the points or $\sqrt{29}/2$. The coordinates of the midpoint are

$$x = 1 + \frac{2}{\sqrt{29}} \cdot \frac{\sqrt{29}}{2} = 1 + 1 = 2$$

$$y = 3 - \frac{3}{\sqrt{29}} \cdot \frac{\sqrt{29}}{2} = 3 - \frac{3}{2} = \frac{3}{2}$$

$$z = 1 + \frac{4}{\sqrt{29}} \cdot \frac{\sqrt{29}}{2} = 1 + 2 = 3$$

The point at which the line pierces the xy-plane must have a z coordinate of 0. Setting

$$z = 1 + \frac{4}{\sqrt{29}} d = 0$$

we conclude that $d = -\sqrt{29}/4$, and the x- and y-coordinates are

$$x = 1 + \left(\frac{2}{\sqrt{29}} \cdot \frac{-\sqrt{29}}{4} \right) = \frac{1}{2},$$

$$y = 3 - \left(\frac{3}{\sqrt{29}} \cdot \frac{-\sqrt{29}}{4} \right) = \frac{15}{4}.$$

The point where the line pierces the plane is $(\frac{1}{2}, \frac{15}{4}, 0)$.

Problems

Set A

Find parametric equations of the lines through the following pairs of points. Use the first point as (x_0, y_0, z_0). Plot the pairs of points and find one other point on each line.

1. $(0, 0, 0)$, $(3, 2, 6)$
2. $(2, 2, -2)$, $(2, 5, 3)$
3. $(2, 4, 0)$, $(4, 0, 5)$
4. $(0, 0, 0)$, (e, f, g)
5. $(2, -1, 2)$, $(-1, 2, -1)$
6. (a, b, c), $(a + e, b + f, c + g)$

For Problems 7–11 use the line whose parametric equations are

$$x = 3 + \frac{2}{\sqrt{17}} d, \quad y = -1 - \frac{3}{\sqrt{17}} d,$$

$$\text{and } z = 3 + \frac{2}{\sqrt{17}} d.$$

7. Give the coordinates for (x, y, z) when $d = 0$.

8. Give the coordinates for (x, y, z) when $d = \sqrt{17}$.
9. Find the midpoint of the segment whose end points are those given in Problems 7 and 8.
10. Verify that $c_1^2 + c_2^2 + c_3^2 = 1$.
11. Find the point where the line pierces each of the coordinate planes.

Set B

12. A line contains the point $(4, 3, 1)$ and is perpendicular to the xy-plane. Draw the line. Find parametric equations of the line.
13. Draw the line that has parametric equations

$$x = 5, \quad y = 2 + \frac{1}{\sqrt{2}} d,$$

$$\text{and } z = -2 - \frac{1}{\sqrt{2}} d.$$

14. A line pierces the xy-plane at $A = (-2, 1, 0)$ and the xz-plane at $B = (-\frac{3}{2}, 0, 1)$. Find the point P on the line, directed from A to B, that is at a directed distance 3 from A.

15. Show that the segment with end points $A = (6, 4, -3)$ and $B = (2, 0, 5)$ and the segment with end points $C = (8, -5, -1)$ and $D = (0, 9, 3)$ have the same midpoint. What are the coordinates of the common midpoint?

Set C

16. A line has parametric equations $x = x_0$, $y = y_0$, and $z = z_0 + d$. Sketch the line. Show that the distance from (x, y, z) to (x_0, y_0, z_0) is $|d|$.

17. Given that (x_1, y_1, z_1) is on the line with parametric equations $x = x_0 + c_1d$, $y = y_0 + c_2d$, $z = z_0 + c_3d$, show that the line also has parametric equations

$$x = x_1 + c_1d',$$
$$y = y_1 + c_2d',$$
$$z = z_1 + c_3d',$$

where, of course, d' is not necessarily equal to d.

18. Show that if (x_1, y_1, z_1) and (x_2, y_2, z_2) are two points on a line, then the midpoint of the line segment with these endpoints will be

$$\left(\frac{x_1 + x_2}{2}, \frac{y_1 + y_2}{2}, \frac{z_1 + z_2}{2} \right).$$

Calculator Problem

A line has direction angles $\alpha = \pi/5$, $\beta = 2\pi/5$ and $\gamma = \pi/3$. Show that

$$c_1^2 + c_2^2 + c_3^2 = 1.$$

Suppose the line contains the point $(4, 3, 2)$. Find parametric equations of the line. Determine the coordinates of the points where the line pierces each of the three coordinate planes.

13-6   Planes

We shall return to the study of planes again in Chapter 15, where we shall prove that if A, B, C are real numbers, not all 0, then the set of points (x, y, z) such that

$$Ax + By + Cz + D = 0 \tag{1}$$

is a plane. Equation (1) is called an equation of the plane, and sometimes we simply say "the plane $Ax + By + Cz + D = 0$." Conversely, every plane has an equation of the form (1).

For now, we shall take this basic theorem for granted. We shall draw some planes and find equations of some.

Example 1   To sketch the plane $2x + 3y + 6z = 12$, it will suffice to find three points in the plane. Then we can "see" where it goes. If the plane is not parallel to any of the axes, it will cut each axis. These three *intercepts* are easy to obtain. For the given plane (Fig. 15) they are $(6, 0, 0)$, $(0, 4, 0)$, and $(0, 0, 2)$. The plane, or rather a triangular portion of the plane, is then easy to draw.

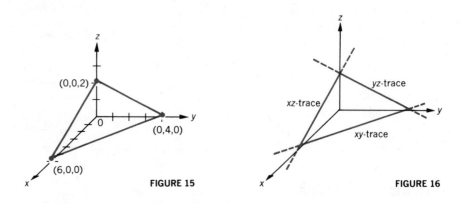

FIGURE 15   FIGURE 16

Another way of looking at the same problem is to examine the *traces* of the given plane in each of the coordinate planes (Fig. 16). The trace in any coordinate plane is the line of intersection of the given plane and that coordinate plane. Thus from Fig. 16 we see that the trace in the xy-plane is the intersection of the planes

$$z = 0, \qquad 2x + 3y = 12;$$

the trace in the yz-plane is the intersection of the planes

$$x = 0, \qquad 3y + 6z = 12;$$

the trace in the zx-plane is the intersection of the planes

$$y = 0, \qquad 2x + 6z = 12.$$

Example 2   Sketch the plane $3x + 2z = 6$.

Solution. What is striking here is that the variable y is missing from the equation. The x- and z-intercepts are at $(2, 0, 0)$ and $(0, 0, 3)$. There is no y-intercept because x and z cannot both be 0. Since the plane does not cut the y-axis, it is parallel to the y-axis, and the plane appears as in Fig. 17.

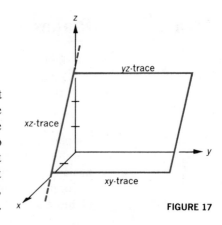

FIGURE 17

Example 3 Find an equation of the plane through the points $(0, -1, 1)$, $(6, 2, 1)$, and $(2, 1, 2)$.

Solution. Our first remark is that if the three points are collinear, there will be many planes through them. However, by finding direction cosines, it is easy to see that the three given points are *not* collinear, and so there is a unique plane. Therefore we wish to determine constants A, B, C, D such that the equation $Ax + By + Cz + D = 0$ is satisfied by the coordinates of all three points:

$$A(0) + B(-1) + C(1) + D = 0, \tag{2}$$
$$A(6) + B(2) + C(1) + D = 0, \tag{3}$$
$$A(2) + B(1) + C(2) + D = 0. \tag{4}$$

Although it may turn out that any one of A, B, C, or D is 0, we know that not all of A, B, C are 0 because the unique plane through the given points has an equation of the type we seek.

Let us see what we can discover about the relations of A, B, C, and D from equations (2), (3), and (4). From equations (2) and (3) we obtain by subtraction

$$6A + 3B = 0,$$

where $A = -\frac{1}{2}B$. If we use $-\frac{1}{2}B$ for A in equation (4), we obtain

$$-B + B + 2C + D = 0,$$

where $C = -\frac{1}{2}D$. Then equation (2) gives

$$B = C + D = -\tfrac{1}{2}D + D = \tfrac{1}{2}D.$$

Therefore

$$\begin{aligned} A &= -\tfrac{1}{2}B = -\tfrac{1}{4}D, \\ B &= \tfrac{1}{2}D, \\ C &= -\tfrac{1}{2}D, \end{aligned} \tag{5}$$

and the plane has an equation

$$-\tfrac{1}{4}Dx + \tfrac{1}{2}Dy + (-\tfrac{1}{2}Dz) + D = 0. \tag{6}$$

Certainly $D \neq 0$, for otherwise equation (6) is the triviality, $0 = 0$, and does not represent a plane. Hence equation (6) is equivalent to

$$x - 2y + 2z - 4 = 0,$$

and this is an equation of the plane we sought.

Remarks 1. What we have done in the above solution is to solve for three of the constants in terms of the fourth. We cannot tell in advance which one to select for the fourth; however, in practice this causes no trouble. We simply successively eliminate A, B, C, or D until we obtain a solution analogous to equations (5).

2. Equations (2), (3), and (4) are three equations in four unknowns. We are not actually interested in these numbers A, B, C, and D, but only in their ratios. In equation (6), D can be any non-zero number. In other words, the plane

$$Ax + By + Cz + D = 0 \qquad (1)$$

is also represented by

$$\frac{A}{D}x + \frac{B}{D}y + \frac{C}{D}z + 1 = 0$$

if $D \neq 0$. Then the three ratios, A/D, B/D, and C/D can be found from equations (2), (3), and (4), and the plane is determined.

But what happens if $D = 0$? Then we cannot divide equation (1) by D. Yet, there is a plane, $Ax + By + Cz = 0$, through the three given points, for which at least one of A, B, or C is not 0. Thus we may divide in equation (1) by any one of A, B, or C which is not 0. More generally, we can multiply equation (1) by any number $k \neq 0$ to obtain the equivalent equation

$$kAx + kBy + kCz + kD = 0. \qquad (7)$$

If $k = 1/D$, we have the situation of the example. If $k = 1/A$ ($A \neq 0$), then we would solve for the three ratios B/A, C/A, D/A.

If the intercepts of a plane are known, it is particularly easy to write an equation of the plane, as the following theorem shows.

Theorem 13-5 *If a plane has non-zero x-, y-, and z-intercepts of $(a, 0, 0)$, $(0, b, 0)$ and $(0, 0, c)$ respectively, then an equation of the plane is*

$$\frac{x}{a} + \frac{y}{b} + \frac{z}{c} = 1. \qquad (8)$$

Conversely, equation (8) is an equation of a plane with the given intercepts.

Proof Substituting the intercepts in (1) we have

$$Aa + D = 0, \qquad Bb + D = 0 \qquad \text{and} \qquad Cc + D = 0.$$

Therefore

$$A = \frac{-D}{a}, \qquad B = \frac{-D}{b} \qquad \text{and} \qquad C = \frac{-D}{c}.$$

Substituting these values in (1) gives

$$\frac{-D}{a}x + \frac{-D}{b}y + \frac{-D}{c}z = -D.$$

Dividing both sides of the equation by $-D$ gives the equation

$$\frac{x}{a} + \frac{y}{b} + \frac{z}{c} = 1.$$

Conversely, equation (8) is equivalent to equation (1) because $A = 1/a$, $B = 1/b$, $C = 1/c$ and $D = -1$. It is easy to show that equation (8) yields the desired intercepts.

Example   A plane has x-, y-, and z-intercepts of 3, -2, and 2 respectively. Find an equation of the plane.

Solution. From Theorem 13–5 an equation of the plane is

$$\frac{x}{3} + \frac{y}{-2} + \frac{z}{2} = 1$$

or equivalently

$$2x - 3y + 3z = 6.$$

A portion of the plane is shown in Fig. 18.

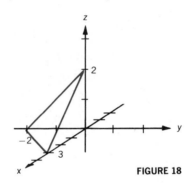

FIGURE 18

Problems

Set A

Sketch the following planes. In each case find the intercepts and the traces in the coordinate planes.

1. $x - y + 2z = 3$
2. $x + 2y = 5$
3. $x + y + z = a,\ a > 0$
4. $2y + 3z = 10$
5. $x - 2y - z + 4 = 0$
6. $2x - 2z + 5 = 0$

Find an equation of the plane passing through the following points.

7. $(1, 2, 2)$, $(3, 3, -1)$, $(-1, 5, 1)$
8. $(0, -1, 0)$, $(2, 1, -2)$, $(1, 0, -1)$
9. $(1, 1, 0)$, $(3, 0, 1)$, $(-1, 2, -1)$
10. $(2, 2, 1)$, $(4, 2, -1)$, $(6, -3, 2)$

Set B

Find an equation of the plane whose x-, y-, and z-intercepts are as follows. Sketch a portion of the plane.

11. $x = 4$, $y = -1$, $z = 3$

12. $x = -5$, $y = 6$, $z = 2$

13. $x = 3$, $y = 4$, $z = -4$

14. $x = -3$, $y = -3$, $z = 3$

15. Traces of a plane in each of the coordinate planes are given by

$$3x + 5z = 15,$$
$$2x - 5y = 10,$$

and

$$2z - 3y = 6.$$

Sketch a portion of the plane and find an equation of the plane with these traces.

Set C

Find the point or points of intersection, if any, of the following sets of three planes.

16. $x + y + z = 5$, $2x - y + z = 0$,
$3x - 4y + 5z + 4 = 0$

17. $x + 2y = 6$, $2x = y$, $z = 3$
(Draw the planes.)

18. $x = a$, $y = b$, $z = c$
(Draw the planes.)

19. $x + 2y - 3z = 5$, $2x + y + z = 6$,
$3x - y + 4z = -1$

20. $x + y + z = 5$, $x - y - z + 5 = 0$,
$3x - y - z + 5 = 0$. (Draw the planes.)

21. $x - y + 2z = 6$, $2x - 2y + 4z = -4$,
$5x - 5y + 10z = 15$ (Draw the planes.)

22. Show that if not all of A, B, and C are 0, then

$$A(x - x_0) + B(y - y_0) + C(z - z_0) = 0$$

is an equation of a plane through (x_0, y_0, z_0).

23. Given distinct planes

$$A_1 x + B_1 y + C_1 z + D_1 = 0$$

and

$$A_2 x + B_2 y + C_2 z + D_2 = 0$$

that are not parallel, and given a real number k, show that the set of all points (x, y, z) for which

$$A_1 x + B_1 y + C_1 z + D_1$$
$$+ k(A_2 x + B_2 y + C_2 z + D_2) = 0$$

is a plane through the line of intersection of the given planes.

24. Use Problem 23 to obtain an equation of the plane through the line of intersection of the planes $x - 3y + z = 5$ and $2x - y - z = 5$, and containing the point $(1, 1, 1)$.

25. The line through $(4, 4, 1)$ is perpendicular to a plane at $(3, 2, -1)$. Find an equation of the plane.

26. Show that if a line contains a point (a, b, c) and is perpendicular to a plane at (d, e, f), then

$$(a - d)x + (b - e)y + (c - f)z$$
$$+ (d^2 + e^2 + f^2 - ad - be - cf) = 0$$

is an equation of the plane.

Calculator Problem

Find the intercepts of the plane

$$3.66x - 8.34y + 6.83z = 2.18.$$

Round the coordinates of the intercepts to the nearest hundredth.

Summary

We have assumed in this chapter that you are familiar with the simpler aspects of space geometry. We observed that these space properties are consequences of only four postulates other than those of plane geometry. Then using the fact that a line can be assigned coordinates, we were able to coordinatize space, that is, to show the existence of a one-to-one correspondence between the points of space and the set of ordered triples (x, y, z) of real numbers. A distance formula between pairs of points in space was developed as a result of the establishment of a coordinate system.

Direction angles and direction cosines gave us parametric equations of a line in space in a manner analogous to that used for a line in the plane. In the plane, each line can be represented by two parametric equations. In space, a set of three parametric equations is needed to represent a line.

Finally, we considered rectangular equations of planes and observed that by considering the intercepts of a plane or the traces of the plane in the coordinate planes, it is quite easy to draw pictures of planes.

Some of the more important relations developed in this chapter are listed below.

1. The distance between two points (x_1, y_1, z_1) and (x_2, y_2, z_2):
$$d = \sqrt{(x_2 - x_1)^2 + (y_2 - y_1)^2 + (z_2 - z_1)^2}.$$

2. Direction cosines of a line: If d is the directed distance from (x_0, y_0, z_0) to (x_1, y_1, z_1), then the line containing these points has direction cosines

$$c_1 = \frac{x_1 - x_0}{d}, \qquad c_2 = \frac{y_1 - y_0}{d}, \qquad c_3 = \frac{z_1 - z_0}{d}.$$

3. Parametric equations of a line:

$$x = x_0 + c_1 d, \qquad y = y_0 + c_2 d, \qquad z = z_0 + c_3 d,$$

where d is the parameter and is the directed distance along the line.

4. Equation of a plane: Every plane has an equation of the form

$$Ax + By + Cz + D = 0,$$

where not all of the real numbers A, B, and C are 0. The set of all points (x, y, z) satisfying $Ax + By + Cz + D = 0$ is a plane.

5. Intercepts and traces of planes: The plane $Ax + By + Cz + D = 0$ has intercepts

$$\left(\frac{-D}{A}, 0, 0\right), \qquad \left(0, \frac{-D}{B}, 0\right), \qquad \text{and} \qquad \left(0, 0, \frac{-D}{C}\right)$$

If A, B, and C are not 0.
    Traces of the plane are given by

$$Ax + By + D = 0, \qquad By + Cz + D = 0, \qquad \text{and} \qquad Ax + Cz + D = 0.$$

13-2   **1.** In which coordinate plane is the point whose coordinates are $(6, 0, -3)$?

2. A plane is parallel to the xy-coordinate plane. What is true about all the coordinates (x, y, z) of points in this plane?

13-3   **3.** Find the distance from the origin to $(3, -4, 5)$.

4. Find the distance between $(2, 3, 1)$ and $(-2, 4, 5)$.

13-4   **5.** Can a line have direction angles of $\pi/3$, $\pi/4$ and $\pi/4$? Explain.

6. Find the direction cosines of the line from $(-2, -4, -1)$ directed toward $(0, -8, 3)$.

7. What are the direction angles of a line
(a) parallel to the y-axis?
(b) parallel to the xz-plane?

13-5   **8.** Find parametric equations of the line through $(-3, 5, 4)$ and $(-1, 2, 2)$. Use the first point as (x_0, y_0, z_0).

9. Parametric equations of a line are

$$x = 1 + \frac{3d}{5}, \qquad y = 4 - \frac{3d}{5}, \qquad z = -2 + \frac{\sqrt{7}d}{5}.$$

Find the coordinates of the point where the line pierces the yz-plane.

10. Find the coordinates of the midpoints of the segment joining $(7, -2, 5)$ and $(-3, 6, -3)$.

11. Parametric equations of a line are

$$x = 3 + \frac{1}{\sqrt{6}}d, \qquad y = -4 + \frac{2}{\sqrt{6}}d, \qquad z = 7 - \frac{1}{\sqrt{6}}d.$$

Find the coordinates of a point on the line when $d = 2\sqrt{6}$.

13-6   **12.** What are the intercepts of the plane $2x - 5y - 2z = 10$? Sketch a portion of the plane.

13. Give the equations of the traces of the plane $x - 3y + 2z = 6$ in each of the coordinate planes.

14. Find an equation of the plane that contains the three noncollinear points $(7, 0, 0)$, $(1, 1, 4)$, and $(7, 7, -2)$.

15. The traces of a plane are $2x + 5y = 10$, $3x + 5z = 15$, and $3y + 2z = 6$. What is a rectangular equation of the plane?

16. The three planes $2x + y + 2z = 7$, $x + y + z = 3$, and $x - y - z = 5$ have exactly one point in common. Find this point of intersection.

Historical Note

Title page of first translation of Euclid's Elements, printed in 1570.

Little is known of Euclid the man. The information we have is by inference from comments by other writers concerning his mathematics. What seems to be certain is that he lived around 300 B.C., that he learned his mathematics from pupils of Plato, and that he lived much of his life in Alexandria, where he taught and founded a school. His major work, *The Elements*, consists of thirteen "books," parts of which are familiar to high school students from either geometry or algebra. The word "elements" should not be construed in its common current sense to mean simple, or elementary. Rather, the word refers to the *foundations* or basic building blocks from which the entire edifice of mathematics (of his day) was to be constructed.

Of these books only XI and XIII are concerned with solid geometry. Most of the elementary theorems are to be found in Book XI among the first 19 propositions. The remaining propositions (20 to 39) of Book XI are concerned with solid polyhedra and their volumes. Euclid used no additional postulates for his geometry of space. More recently, however, mathematicians have determined the need for four additional postulates. Book XIII is devoted to propositions about the five regular polyhedra.

Chapter 14
Vectors in Space

14-1   Introduction

In Chapter 12 we discussed vectors in the plane. In this chapter we again consider vectors, but vectors in space. We shall see that lines in space can be represented by vector equations, and we shall also show that planes can be represented by vector equations.

14-2   Arrows and Vectors

The definitions for vectors in space are essentially the same as those for vectors in the plane. The same physical interpretations that were given for plane vectors may be made for vectors in space. We shall again denote vectors by boldface type; for example, $\mathbf{a}$, $\mathbf{v}$, $\mathbf{r}$, $\mathbf{s}$, and $\mathbf{u}$. The vector represented by the arrow (P_1, P_2) will be denoted by $\overrightarrow{P_1 P_2}$. The magnitude of $\mathbf{a}$ will be denoted by $|\mathbf{a}|$.

Recall that a vector is an equivalence class of arrows and that two arrows are equivalent if and only if they have the same direction and magnitude. The following theorem for arrows in space is analogous to the theorem for arrows in the plane.

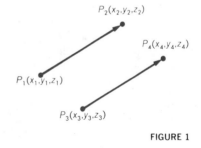

FIGURE 1

Theorem 14-1   *If the points P_1, P_2, P_3, and P_4 have the coordinates shown in Fig. 1, then the arrows (P_1, P_2) and (P_3, P_4) are equivalent if and only if*

$$
\begin{aligned}
x_2 - x_1 &= x_4 - x_3, \\
y_2 - y_1 &= y_4 - y_3, \quad \text{(1)} \\
z_2 - z_1 &= z_4 - z_3,
\end{aligned}
$$

Proof   We suppose that equations (1) are true. The magnitudes of the arrows are the same,

$$
\sqrt{(x_2 - x_1)^2 + (y_2 - y_1)^2 + (z_2 - z_1)^2}
$$
$$
= \sqrt{(x_4 - x_3)^2 + (y_4 - y_3)^2 + (z_4 - z_3)^2} = d, \quad \text{(2)}
$$

337

and the direction cosines are also the same,

$$c_1 = \frac{x_2 - x_1}{d} = \frac{x_4 - x_3}{d},$$

$$c_2 = \frac{y_2 - y_1}{d} = \frac{y_4 - y_3}{d}, \tag{3}$$

$$c_3 = \frac{z_2 - z_1}{d} = \frac{z_4 - z_3}{d}.$$

Therefore the two arrows are equivalent.

Conversely, let us suppose that the two arrows are equivalent. Then they have the same magnitude and direction. Therefore equations (2) and (3) will be true, and these equations imply equations (1).

Example The ordered pair of points $(P_0, P_1) = ((1, -2, 3), (-2, 2, 5))$ and $(Q_0, Q_1) = ((2, 1, 1), (-1, 5, 3))$ are equivalent arrows since each arrow has magnitude $\sqrt{29}$, and the ray from P_0 to P_1 has the same direction cosines as the ray from Q_0 to Q_1 (Fig. 2).

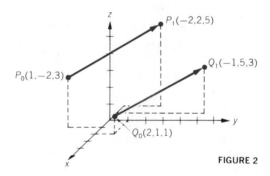

FIGURE 2

The definition of addition of vectors in space is the same as that given for plane vectors. Also we define multiplication of a vector by a real number in the same way. We repeat these definitions here.

Definition 14-1 If **a** and **b** are vectors and A and C are points such that $\mathbf{a} = \overrightarrow{OA}$ and $\mathbf{b} = \overrightarrow{AC}$, then $\mathbf{a} + \mathbf{b} = \overrightarrow{OC}$.

Observe that C is the fourth vertex of the parallelogram (possibly degenerate) whose other vertices are O, A, and B. (See Fig. 3.)

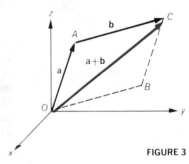

FIGURE 3

Cases for which **a** and **b** have the same direction or opposite directions are illustrated in Fig. 4.

FIGURE 4

Definition 14-2 If **v** is any vector and k is a real number, then $k\mathbf{v}$ is a vector with magnitude $|k| \cdot |\mathbf{v}|$. If $k > 0$, then $k\mathbf{v}$ has the same direction as **v**; if $k < 0$, then $k\mathbf{v}$ has direction opposite to that of **v**. In particular, $(-1)\mathbf{v} = -\mathbf{v}$.

The real number k in Definition 14–2 is often called a *scalar,* and we speak of "multiplication of a vector by a scalar."

The following theorem is fundamental in vector addition.

Theorem 14-2 *If* $\mathbf{v}_1 = \overrightarrow{OP_1}$ *and* $\mathbf{v}_2 = \overrightarrow{OP_2}$, *where* P_1 *and* P_2 *are points with coordinates as shown in Fig. 5, then* $\mathbf{v}_1 + \mathbf{v}_2 = \overrightarrow{OP}$, *where* P *is the point* $(x_1 + x_2, y_1 + y_2, z_1 + z_2)$.

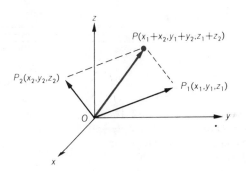

FIGURE 5

Proof Suppose that P has coordinates (x, y, z). Then (P_2, P) is equivalent to (O, P_1), and by Theorem 14–1,

$$x - x_2 = x_1 - 0, \quad y - y_2 = y_1 - 0, \quad z - z_2 = z_1 - 0.$$

Therefore, $(x, y, z) = (x_1 + x_2, y_1 + y_2, z_1 + z_2)$.

Problems

Set A

Give the magnitude and direction cosines of the vectors given by the ordered pairs of points.

1. $((0, 0, 0), (4, 4, 2))$

2. $((5, 4, 1), (1, -3, 3))$

3. $((-3, -3, 4), (0, 0, 0))$

4. $((0, a, 0), (b, 0, 0))$

5. What is the position vector for the ordered pair of points $((3, 3, 4), (5, -2, 1))$?

The terminal points of two position vectors are given. Find the coordinates of the terminal point of the vector that is the sum of the given vectors. Sketch the vectors.

6. $(0, 2, 3)$ and $(3, 1, 0)$

7. $(-1, 5, 1)$ and $(4, 1, 1)$

8. $(-2, -2, 4)$ and $(5, 6, -2)$

9. $(-2, 4, 4)$ and $(1, -2, -1)$

If $\mathbf{r}$ has a position vector with terminal point at $(3, -2, 1)$, what is the terminal point of the following vectors?

10. $3\mathbf{r}$　　　　　　**11.** $-\mathbf{r}$

12. $-5\mathbf{r}$　　　　　**13.** $4\mathbf{r} + (-4)\mathbf{r}$

14. $2\mathbf{r}$　　　　　　**15.** $6\mathbf{r} + (-5)\mathbf{r}$

Set B

16. An arrow has initial point $(-1, -2, 1)$ and direction cosines $c_1 = -\frac{1}{3}$, $c_2 = \frac{2}{3}$, $c_3 = \frac{2}{3}$. If the arrow has magnitude 6, what are the coordinates of the end point of the arrow?

17. If $P = (6, -6, -2)$ and $\overrightarrow{OP'}$ has the same magnitude as $\overrightarrow{OP}$ but is opposite in direction, what are the coordinates of P'? Sketch the arrows.

18. $|\overrightarrow{OP}| = 1$, and $\overrightarrow{OP}$ has direction cosines

$$\left(\frac{3}{\sqrt{14}}, \frac{-2}{\sqrt{14}}, \frac{1}{\sqrt{14}}\right).$$

What are the coordinates of P?

Set C

19. Vectors $\mathbf{v}_1$ and $\mathbf{v}_2$ have position vectors to points $(3, -4, 2)$ and $(-3, 4, -2)$, respectively. What are the coordinates of the point P such that

$$\overrightarrow{OP} = \mathbf{v}_1 + \mathbf{v}_2?$$

20. Does each vector in space have an additive inverse? That is, if $\mathbf{v}$ is any vector, is there a vector $\mathbf{r}$ such that $\mathbf{v} + \mathbf{r} = \mathbf{0}$?

21. If $\mathbf{r}$ and $\mathbf{t}$ are any vectors, is there a vector $\mathbf{s}$ such that $\mathbf{r} + \mathbf{s} = \mathbf{t}$?

22. Define subtraction for vectors.

23. Show that $\mathbf{v} + \mathbf{v} = 2\mathbf{v}$ for every vector $\mathbf{v}$.

24. If $\mathbf{a} = \overrightarrow{OA}$, $\mathbf{b} = \overrightarrow{OB}$, and $\mathbf{c} = \overrightarrow{OC}$, where $A = (3, 1, 2)$, $B = (-2, 2, -1)$, and $C = (4, 0, 3)$, find the coordinates of the point P such that $\overrightarrow{OP} = (\mathbf{a} + \mathbf{b}) + \mathbf{c}$. Find the coordinates of the point Q such that $\overrightarrow{OQ} = \mathbf{a} + (\mathbf{b} + \mathbf{c})$. Is addition of vectors associative?

In each figure, $\mathbf{c}$ is the difference of two vectors. Write the proper subtraction statement for each picture.

25.　　　　　　　　　　**26.**

　　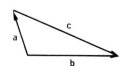

Calculator Problem

Find the coordinates of the terminal point of the position vector for $\overrightarrow{P_1 P_2}$ where $P_1 = (-2.6, 1.8, -3.7)$ and $P_2 = (4.5, -7.2, -5.1)$. Then find the magnitude, direction cosines and direction angles of the position vector.

14-3   Unit Basis Vectors

In Chapter 12 we saw that each vector in the plane can be represented as a linear combination of two unit vectors directed along the positive x- and positive y-axes. In a similar manner, we may show that every vector in space can be represented as a linear combination of three unit vectors. A most convenient choice of the unit vectors is the three unit vectors directed along the positive x-, y-, and z-axes, as shown in Fig. 6. We shall use **i**, **j**, and **k** to denote these unit vectors.

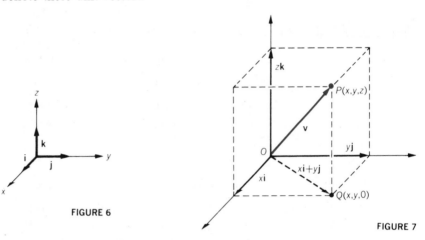

FIGURE 6

FIGURE 7

Let us consider a vector $\mathbf{v} = \overrightarrow{OP}$ as in Fig. 7. Then $x\mathbf{i}$, $y\mathbf{j}$, and $z\mathbf{k}$ are vectors directed along the axes, and

$$x\mathbf{i} + y\mathbf{j} = \overrightarrow{OQ}.$$

Because $\overrightarrow{QP} = z\mathbf{k}$,

$$\overrightarrow{OP} = \overrightarrow{OQ} + \overrightarrow{QP}$$

and

$$\mathbf{v} = \overrightarrow{OP} = (x\mathbf{i} + y\mathbf{j}) + z\mathbf{k}. \tag{1}$$

In the same way,

$$\mathbf{v} = x\mathbf{i} + (y\mathbf{j} + z\mathbf{k}). \tag{2}$$

Thus, if $P' \neq P$, then $\overrightarrow{OP'} \neq \overrightarrow{OP}$, and it follows that every vector is a sum of unique vectors directed along the axes. From equations (1) and (2), we see that the way in which the vectors are grouped, or associated, is immaterial. We therefore write

$$\mathbf{v} = x\mathbf{i} + y\mathbf{j} + z\mathbf{k}.$$

Definition 14-3 The *components* of $\mathbf{v} = x\mathbf{i} + y\mathbf{j} + z\mathbf{k}$ are the real numbers x, y, and z. The vectors $\mathbf{i}$, $\mathbf{j}$, and $\mathbf{k}$ are the *unit basis vectors* for this coordinate system.

Theorem 14-3 *Two vectors are equal if and only if the corresponding components of these vectors are equal relative to the same coordinate system.*

Proof The coordinates of P, which are the components of $\overrightarrow{OP}$, uniquely determine the vector $\overrightarrow{OP}$.

Theorem 14-4 *If $\mathbf{v}_1 = x_1\mathbf{i} + y_1\mathbf{j} + z_1\mathbf{k}$ and $\mathbf{v}_2 = x_2\mathbf{i} + y_2\mathbf{j} + z_2\mathbf{k}$, then*

$$\mathbf{v}_1 + \mathbf{v}_2 = (x_1 + x_2)\mathbf{i} + (y_1 + y_2)\mathbf{j} + (z_1 + z_2)\mathbf{k}.$$

Proof This is simply Theorem 14-2 expressed in terms of the unit basis vectors.

The following theorem exhibits several properties of vector addition. These properties are either immediate consequences of Definitions 14-1 and 14-2 or easy deductions from Theorem 14-4.

Theorem 14-5 *For all vectors $\mathbf{a}$, $\mathbf{b}$, $\mathbf{c}$ and real numbers r and s,*

(a) $\mathbf{a} + \mathbf{b} = \mathbf{b} + \mathbf{a}$, *(b)* $\mathbf{a} + (\mathbf{b} + \mathbf{c}) = (\mathbf{a} + \mathbf{b}) + \mathbf{c}$,
(c) $\mathbf{a} + \mathbf{0} = \mathbf{a}$, *(d)* $r(\mathbf{a} + \mathbf{b}) = r\mathbf{a} + r\mathbf{b}$,
(e) $(r + s)\mathbf{a} = r\mathbf{a} + s\mathbf{a}$, *(f)* $(rs)\mathbf{a} = r(s\mathbf{a})$,
(g) $0 \cdot \mathbf{a} = \mathbf{0}$, *(h)* $1 \cdot \mathbf{a} = \mathbf{a}$.

Proof (a) Let $\mathbf{a} = x_1\mathbf{i} + y_1\mathbf{j} + z_1\mathbf{k}$ and $\mathbf{b} = x_2\mathbf{i} + y_2\mathbf{j} + z_2\mathbf{k}$. By Theorem 14-4, commutativity of addition of real numbers, and Theorem 14-3 we have

$$\begin{aligned} \mathbf{a} + \mathbf{b} &= (x_1 + x_2)\mathbf{i} + (y_1 + y_2)\mathbf{j} + (z_1 + z_2)\mathbf{k} \\ &= (x_2 + x_1)\mathbf{i} + (y_2 + y_1)\mathbf{j} + (z_2 + z_1)\mathbf{k} \\ &= \mathbf{b} + \mathbf{a}. \end{aligned}$$

Proofs for some of the other parts of Theorem 14-5 are left for the student.

Problems

Set A

1. Sketch a picture as in Fig. 7 to show that a position vector $\overrightarrow{OP}$ may be represented as $\overrightarrow{OP} = (x\mathbf{i} + z\mathbf{k}) + y\mathbf{j}$.

2. If $P_1 = (7, 4, -1)$ and $P_2 = (3, -5, 4)$, what are the components of $\overrightarrow{P_1P_2}$? Express $\overrightarrow{P_1P_2}$ in terms of $\mathbf{i}$, $\mathbf{j}$, and $\mathbf{k}$.

Sketch the following vectors, add them, and sketch their sum.

3. $2\mathbf{i} + 3\mathbf{j}$, $\mathbf{j} + \mathbf{k}$
4. $2\mathbf{i} + \mathbf{j} + (-1)\mathbf{k}$, $-\mathbf{i} + \mathbf{j} + 2\mathbf{k}$
5. $3\mathbf{i}$, $-2\mathbf{k}$
6. $4\mathbf{i}$, $-2\mathbf{j} + 2\mathbf{k}$

Given that

$$r = \frac{\sqrt{3}}{2}i + 3j - \sqrt{2}k, \quad s = \sqrt{3}i - 6j + 2\sqrt{2}k,$$

$$t = 5j - 3k, \qquad u = i + 3j,$$

find the following.

7. $r + s$ 8. $s + t$ 9. $u + s + t$

10. $\frac{3}{4}r + \frac{3}{4}t$ 11. $r + 7u$ 12. $\frac{1}{2}(s + 3u)$

Set B

Find the magnitude of the following vectors.

13. $v = i + j + k$

14. $a = a_1i + a_2j + a_3k$

15. $r = 3i + (-4)j + k$

16. $u = \frac{3}{5}i + \frac{(-2)}{5}j + \frac{2\sqrt{3}}{5}k$

17. $t = xi + yj + zk$

Find real numbers x, y, and z such that

18. $xi + 2yj - zk + 3i - j = 4i + 3k.$

19. $7xi + (y - 3)j + 6k = 10i + 8j - 3zk.$

20. $(x + 4)i + (y - 5)j + (z - 1)k = 0.$

21. Verify that $a + (b + c) = (a + b) + c$ for the vectors

$$a = 2i - \tfrac{1}{2}j + 5k,$$
$$b = i - j - 2k,$$
$$c = -i + 3j - k.$$

22. Explain how the figure below illustrates the associative property of addition for vectors.

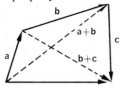

Set C

23. Prove part (b) of Theorem 14–5.

24. Prove part (d) of Theorem 14–5.

25. Let v be a position vector such that $|v| = L$. Given that the direction cosines of v are c_1, c_2, and c_3, show that $v = L(c_1i + c_2j + c_3k)$.

26. In the figure, $r_1 = x_1i + y_1j + z_1k$ and $r_2 = x_2i + y_2j + z_2k$. What are the components of $\frac{1}{2}(r_1 + r_2)$? What is this vector, geometrically?

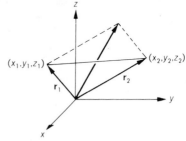

27. Three vectors with magnitudes 5, 12, and 13 have a sum equal to 0. Illustrate how this is possible.

28. If $u = a + b$ and $v = a - b$ are given, show how to find a and b geometrically. [*Hint:* What is $u + v$? What is $u - v$?]

29. If $P_1 = (3, -2, 2)$ and $P_2 = (4, 5, -1)$, show that $\overrightarrow{OP_1} \perp \overrightarrow{OP_2}$. [*Hint:* Use the distance formula and the converse of the Pythagorean Theorem.]

Calculator Problem

If $a + b = c$ and

$$a = 1.2i + 3.3j - 6.5k,$$
$$b = -0.9i - 1.7j + 2.1k,$$

find the components of c, the magnitude of c, and the direction cosines of c.

14-4   Vector Equations of Lines

In Chapter 12 we used vectors to represent lines in the plane. Here we repeat the same argument for lines in space. As in Chapter 12, a vector equation of a line is an equation for the position vectors of all points on the line.

Let l be the line through $P_0 = (x_0, y_0, z_0)$ and $P_1 = (x_1, y_1, z_1)$, and let $\mathbf{r}_0 = \overrightarrow{OP_0}$ and $\mathbf{r}_1 = \overrightarrow{OP_1}$ (Fig. 8). Choose a positive direction on l, say from P_0 to P_1, and let $\mathbf{u}$ be a unit vector in that direction.

If P is any point on l, let

$$\mathbf{r} = \overrightarrow{OP} = x\mathbf{i} + y\mathbf{j} + z\mathbf{k}.$$

If d is the directed distance along l from P_0, then

$$\mathbf{r} = \mathbf{r}_0 + d\mathbf{u}. \qquad (1)$$

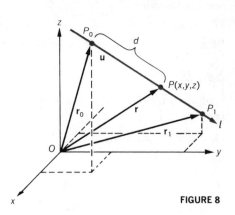

FIGURE 8

If c_1, c_2, and c_3 are the direction cosines of $\mathbf{u}$, then $\mathbf{u} = c_1\mathbf{i} + c_2\mathbf{j} + c_3\mathbf{k}$, so that equation (1) may be written

$$\begin{aligned} \mathbf{r} &= x\mathbf{i} + y\mathbf{j} + z\mathbf{k} \\ &= x_0\mathbf{i} + y_0\mathbf{j} + z_0\mathbf{k} + d(c_1\mathbf{i} + c_2\mathbf{j} + c_3\mathbf{k}) \\ &= (x_0 + c_1 d)\mathbf{i} + (y_0 + c_2 d)\mathbf{j} + (z_0 + c_3 d)\mathbf{k}. \end{aligned} \qquad (2)$$

It follows from Theorem 14–3 that

$$x = x_0 + c_1 d, \qquad y = y_0 + c_2 d, \qquad \text{and} \qquad z = z_0 + c_3 d.$$

These three equations are parametric equations of l. Thus the single vector equation (1) is equivalent to three parametric equations.

We may also write equation (1) in another way. Observe that for any point P on l, we have $d\mathbf{u} = \overrightarrow{P_0 P}$; and since $\overrightarrow{P_0 P}$ and $\overrightarrow{P_0 P_1}$ have the same direction or opposite direction, it follows that $\overrightarrow{P_0 P} = t\overrightarrow{P_0 P_1}$, where t is a real number. Thus equation (1) can be written

$$\mathbf{r} = \mathbf{r}_0 + t\overrightarrow{P_0 P_1}. \qquad (3)$$

Note that if $0 < t < 1$, then P lies between P_0 and P_1, that is, $P_0 P P_1$. If $t > 1$, then $P_0 P_1 P$. Figure 9 illustrates the case for $t > 1$. If $t = 0$, P coincides with P_0. If $t = 1$, P coincides with P_1.

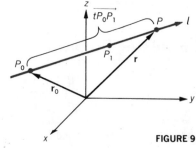

FIGURE 9

Example The coordinates of P_0 and P_1 are $(3, -2, 4)$ and $(-1, 3, 7)$, respectively. Find a vector equation of the line through P_0 and P_1. (Fig. 10.)

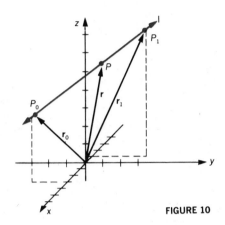

FIGURE 10

Solution. We have

$$\overrightarrow{OP_0} = \mathbf{r}_0 = 3\mathbf{i} + (-2)\mathbf{j} + 4\mathbf{k}$$

and

$$\overrightarrow{P_0P_1} = (-1 - 3)\mathbf{i} + (3 + 2)\mathbf{j} + (7 - 4)\mathbf{k}.$$
$$= -4\mathbf{i} + 5\mathbf{j} + 3\mathbf{k}$$

Therefore the vector $\mathbf{r}$ to any point P on the line P_0P_1 is

$$\mathbf{r} = \mathbf{r}_0 + t\overrightarrow{P_0P_1}$$
$$= 3\mathbf{i} + (-2)\mathbf{j} + 4\mathbf{k} + t(-4\mathbf{i} + 5\mathbf{j} + 3\mathbf{k})$$
$$= (3 - 4t)\mathbf{i} + (-2 + 5t)\mathbf{j} + (4 + 3t)\mathbf{k}.$$

Problems

Set A

Determine the vector equation of the line through each of the following pairs of points. (Let P_0 be the first point listed.)

1. $(0, 1, 2), (3, 0, 2)$

2. $(3, -1, 5), (2, 0, -5)$

3. $(4, 4, -2), (-3, 2, -1)$

4. $(-3, -1, -3), (3, 1, 3)$

5. $(a_1, b_1, c_1), (a_2, b_2, c_2)$

6. A line contains the point $(3, 2, 1)$ and is perpendicular to the xy-plane. Find a vector equation of the line.

A vector equation of a line is given by

$$\mathbf{r} = (4 + 2t)\mathbf{i} + (-1 + t)\mathbf{j} + (-3 + 4t)\mathbf{k}.$$

Find the coordinates of the terminal point of $\mathbf{r}$ for the following values of the parameter t.

7. 0   **8.** 1   **9.** -1

10. 2   **11.** $\frac{1}{2}$ **12.** $\frac{2}{3}$

Set B

13. Prove that the coordinates of the midpoint of a segment $\overline{P_1P_2}$, where $P_1 = (x_1, y_1, z_1)$ and $P_2 = (x_2, y_2, z_2)$, are

$$\left(\frac{x_1 + x_2}{2}, \frac{y_1 + y_2}{2}, \frac{z_1 + z_2}{2}\right).$$

Find the midpoints of the segments whose end points are

14. $(-1, 5, 2)$ and $(-3, 2, 7)$.

15. $(1, 2, 3)$ and $(4, 5, 6)$.

16. $(\pi, \pi/2, 2)$ and $(3, \sqrt{3}, \sqrt{2})$.

17. $(a, -b, c)$ and $(-a, b, -c)$.

18. $(a, 0, 0)$ and $(0, b, 0)$.

19. $(0, 0, 0)$ and (a, b, c).

20. A point P is between $P_0 = (-1, 3, 2)$ and $P_1 = (5, 2, 5)$ and is twice as far from P_0 as P_1. Find the coordinates of P.

21. A point P is on the line containing $P_0 = (-2, -4, 1)$ and $P_1 = (3, 2, 2)$. If P_1 is the midpoint of the segment $\overline{P_0P}$, what are the coordinates of P?

22. A line contains the points $P_0 = (5, 5, 3)$ and $P_1 = (1, -3, 8)$. Find all possible coordinates of a point P that is twice as far from P_1 as it is from P_0.

Set C

23. Obtain the coordinates of the points that trisect the segment whose end points are (x_1, y_1, z_1) and (x_2, y_2, z_2).

24. Parametric equations of a line are

$$x = -2 + \tfrac{2}{3}d, \ y = 5 + \tfrac{1}{3}d, \ z = 1 - \tfrac{2}{3}d.$$

Write a vector equation of the line.

25. A point "moves" on a line with constant speed. At time $t = 0$, it is at $(0, 0, 0)$. At the end of one second it is at $(2, 4, \sqrt{5})$. Give a formula for the position vector to the point at the end of t seconds. What is the speed in the x-direction? in the y-direction? in the z-direction?

26. The midpoints of the sides of a triangle are (a_1, b_1, c_1), (a_2, b_2, c_2), and (a_3, b_3, c_3). Using vectors, find the coordinates of the vertices of the triangle.

Calculator Problem

Find, as decimals, the midpoint of a segment whose end points are

$$(\sqrt{11}, \ln 29, \sin 4.7)$$

and

$$\left(\frac{\pi}{5}, e^{3.2}, \cos\frac{15\pi}{17}\right).$$

14-5   Vector Representation of Planes

We now turn to the vector representation of planes. Let us consider any plane π and a point $P_0 = (x_0, y_0, z_0)$ in π (Fig. 11). Let $\mathbf{u}$ and $\mathbf{v}$ be unit vectors (not necessarily perpendicular) such that arrows at P_0 representing $\mathbf{u}$ and $\mathbf{v}$ are in π and are not collinear. Let P be any point in the plane π and let $\mathbf{r}_0 = \overrightarrow{OP_0}$ and $\mathbf{r} = \overrightarrow{OP}$. Then

$$\mathbf{r} = \mathbf{r}_0 + \overrightarrow{P_0P}.$$

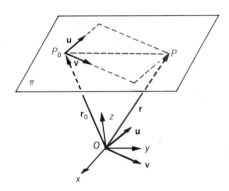

FIGURE 11

But $\overrightarrow{P_0P}$ is a sum of multiples of the unit vectors $\mathbf{u}$ and $\mathbf{v}$, that is, $\overrightarrow{P_0P} = s\mathbf{u} + t\mathbf{v}$, where s and t are real numbers uniquely associated with P. The real numbers s and t are the directed lengths of the sides of the parallelogram whose opposite vertices are P_0 and P. Thus

$$\mathbf{r} = \mathbf{r}_0 + s\mathbf{u} + t\mathbf{v}. \tag{1}$$

Now, if we think of s and t as parameters, that is, as variables that can be any real numbers, then the vector equation (1) represents the plane π. Note that the parameters have a simple geometric interpretation as lengths of the sides of parallelograms.

We have seen that three noncollinear points determine a unique plane. When we are given three such points, say P_0, P_1, and P_2, with coordinates (x_0, y_0, z_0), (x_1, y_1, z_1), and (x_2, y_2, z_2), respectively, it is convenient to use the vectors $\overrightarrow{P_0P_1}$ and $\overrightarrow{P_0P_2}$ instead of the unit vectors $\mathbf{u}$ and $\mathbf{v}$. Referring to Fig. 12, we then have

$$\mathbf{r} = \mathbf{r}_0 + s\overrightarrow{P_0P_1} + t\overrightarrow{P_0P_2}, \tag{2}$$

where s and t are parameters. Note that s and t do not represent the directed lengths of the sides of the parallelogram, as before. Considering the components of the vectors in equation (2), we find that

$$x = x_0 + s(x_1 - x_0) + t(x_2 - x_0),$$
$$y = y_0 + s(y_1 - y_0) + t(y_2 - y_0), \qquad (3)$$
$$z = z_0 + s(z_1 - z_0) + t(z_2 - z_0).$$

Equations (3) are parametric equations of the plane through P_0, P_1, and P_2.

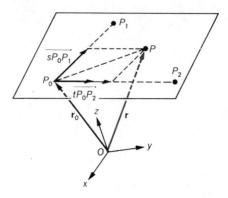

FIGURE 12

Remarks

1. In equations (1), (2), and (3), there are *two* parameters. Assigning values to these parameters determines a unique point in the plane and conversely. Thus we see that for a line, a single parameter covers all points of the line, whereas for a plane, two parameters are needed. This distinction is reflected in the common language that "a line is one-dimensional and a plane is two-dimensional."

2. A rectangular equation of the plane can be obtained by eliminating s and t from equations (3). One can solve the first pair of equations (3) for s and t and substitute the result in the third equation.

Example   Find parametric equations of the plane through the points $P_0(1, 2, 1)$, $P_1(3, -2, 0)$, and $P_2(-1, -3, 3)$. (See Fig. 13.) Then find a rectangular equation of the plane.

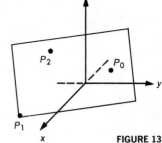

FIGURE 13

Solution. From equations (3) we obtain parametric equations of the plane:

$$x = 1 + s(3 - 1) + t(-1 - 1) = 1 + 2s - 2t, \qquad (a)$$
$$y = 2 + s(-2 - 2) + t(-3 - 2) = 2 - 4s - 5t, \qquad (b)$$
$$z = 1 + s(0 - 1) + t(3 - 1) = 1 - s + 2t. \qquad (c)$$

Eliminating t from equations (a) and (c) we have

$$x + z = 2 + s. \qquad (d)$$

Eliminating t from equations (a) and (b) we obtain

$$5x - 2y = 1 + 18s. \qquad (e)$$

Eliminating s from equations (d) and (e) we get the rectangular equation of the plane:

$$13x + 2y + 18z = 35. \qquad (f)$$

Note that if we choose $s = 2$ and $t = 1$ as values for the parameters, we find, from (a), (b) and (c), that

$$x = 1 + 2(2) - 2(1) = 3,$$
$$y = 2 - 4(2) - 5(1) = -11,$$

and

$$z = 1 - 2 + 2(1) = 1.$$

The point $(3, -11, 1)$ should be a point in the plane given by (f). This can be verified by substituting in (f). $13(3) + 2(-11) + 18(1) = 35$. Other values for the parameters s and t will give the coordinates of other points in the plane.

Problems

Set A

A vector equation of a plane is given by

$$\mathbf{r} = (2 + 3s + 4t)\mathbf{i} +$$
$$(-1 + 2s - 5t)\mathbf{j} + (4 - s + t)\mathbf{k}.$$

Find the coordinates of points in the plane determined by the following values of the parameters s and t.

1. $s = 0$ and $t = 0$ 2. $s = 0$ and $t = 1$

3. $s = 1$ and $t = 0$ 4. $s = 1$ and $t = 1$

5. $s = -1$ and $t = 0$ 6. $s = 0$ and $t = -1$

Write parametric equations of the planes through each of the following triples of points. Find several other points in the planes.

7. $(1, 0, 0)$, $(0, 1, 0)$, $(0, 0, 1)$

8. $(1, 1, 1)$, $(3, 0, 0)$, $(0, 2, 1)$

9. $(0, 0, 0)$, $(0, 2, 0)$, $(1, 0, 2)$

10. $(0, 1, 4)$, $(1, -2, 0)$, $(3, 0, 0)$

Set B

Sketch the planes having the following vector representations.

11. $\mathbf{r} = 3\mathbf{i} + s\mathbf{j} + t\mathbf{k}$

12. $\mathbf{r} = \mathbf{i} + \mathbf{j} + s\mathbf{j} + t\mathbf{k}$

13. $\mathbf{r} = \mathbf{i} + \mathbf{j} + (-\mathbf{i} + \mathbf{j})s + t\mathbf{k}$

14. $\mathbf{r} = (\mathbf{i} + 2\mathbf{j}) + s\mathbf{k} + t(-\mathbf{i} - \mathbf{j})$

15. $\mathbf{r} = 2\mathbf{k} - s\mathbf{k} + t(2\mathbf{i} + \mathbf{j})$

16. $\mathbf{r} = -2\mathbf{j} + s(2\mathbf{j} + \mathbf{k}) + t(3\mathbf{i} + 2\mathbf{j})$

17. Parametric equations of a plane are

$$x = 1 + s + t,$$
$$y = 2 - s + t,$$
$$z = 4 + 2s - 3t.$$

What is a rectangular equation of the plane?

18. Find three points in the plane $4x - y - z = 9$. Then write parametric equations of the plane.

Set C

19. Show how equations (3) of this section are derived from equation (2).

20. A line and a point not on the line determine a unique plane. Parametric equations of a line l are

$$x = 3 + \frac{2}{\sqrt{17}}d,$$

$$y = -5 + \frac{2}{\sqrt{17}}d,$$

$$z = 4 + \frac{3}{\sqrt{17}}d.$$

Let $P(2, 1, 1)$ be a point not on l. Find a vector equation of the plane containing P and l. Find a rectangular equation of the plane.

21. Two intersecting lines determine a unique plane. Find a vector equation and a rectangular equation of the plane containing the intersecting lines l_1 and l_2 whose parametric equations are given below.

$$l_1: \begin{cases} x = 2 + \dfrac{-1}{\sqrt{6}}d \\[2mm] y = 4 + \dfrac{1}{\sqrt{6}}d \\[2mm] z = -3 + \dfrac{2}{\sqrt{6}}d \end{cases} \quad l_2: \begin{cases} x = 2 + \dfrac{2}{3}d \\[2mm] y = 4 + \dfrac{2}{3}d \\[2mm] z = -3 + \dfrac{1}{3}d \end{cases}$$

22. Lines l_1 and l_2 are parallel lines whose parametric equations are given. Find a vector equation and a rectangular equation of the unique plane determined by the parallel lines.

$$l_1: \begin{cases} x = 1 + \dfrac{-1}{\sqrt{14}}d \\[2mm] y = -1 + \dfrac{2}{\sqrt{14}}d \\[2mm] z = 3 + \dfrac{3}{\sqrt{14}}d \end{cases} \quad l_2: \begin{cases} x = 5 + \dfrac{-1}{\sqrt{14}}d \\[2mm] y = 4 + \dfrac{2}{\sqrt{14}}d \\[2mm] z = -2 + \dfrac{3}{\sqrt{14}}d \end{cases}$$

23. $\mathbf{v}_1 = 2\mathbf{i} - 3\mathbf{j} + 4\mathbf{k}$, $\mathbf{v}_2 = \mathbf{i} + 2\mathbf{j} + \mathbf{k}$, $\mathbf{v}_3 = 3\mathbf{i} - \mathbf{j} - \mathbf{k}$, and $\mathbf{r} = 10\mathbf{i} - 15\mathbf{j} + 8\mathbf{k}$. Determine real numbers a, b, and c such that $a\mathbf{v}_1 + b\mathbf{v}_2 + c\mathbf{v}_3 = \mathbf{r}$.

24. A vector equation of a plane is

$$\mathbf{r} = (3\mathbf{i} + 2\mathbf{j}) + s(\mathbf{i} + 3\mathbf{j} + \mathbf{k}) + t(2\mathbf{i} - 2\mathbf{j}).$$

A vector equation of a line is

$$\mathbf{v} = (3\mathbf{i} + 6\mathbf{j} + \mathbf{k}) + d(5\mathbf{i} + 7\mathbf{j} + 3\mathbf{k}).$$

Show that the line lies in the plane.

Calculator Problem

A vector equation of a plane is given by

$$\mathbf{r} = (\sqrt{5} - \sqrt[3]{17}s - \sqrt{37}t)\mathbf{i} + (-\sqrt[3]{26} + \sqrt{19}s + \sqrt[4]{75}t)\mathbf{j}$$
$$+ (\sqrt[5]{127} + \sqrt[3]{91}s - \sqrt{57}t)\mathbf{k}.$$

Give the decimal approximation of the coordinates of three points in the plane for each of the following values of the parameters s and t.

(a) $s = 0, t = 0$ (b) $s = 1, t = -1$ (c) $s = 3, t = 5$

The properties of vectors that have been studied so far do not cover all the properties possessed by vectors. We have not yet discussed the angles that a vector makes with another vector or with a plane. Discussion of these properties will be found in the next chapter, where we shall show that vectors in space have additional algebraic properties.

In our discussion we have outlined the main algebraic properties of vectors in space, namely:

1. Vectors can be *added*. This addition is commutative and associative; the zero vector has special properties. Thus

$$\mathbf{a} + \mathbf{b} = \mathbf{b} + \mathbf{a},$$
$$\mathbf{a} + (\mathbf{b} + \mathbf{c}) = (\mathbf{a} + \mathbf{b}) + \mathbf{c},$$
$$\mathbf{a} + \mathbf{0} = \mathbf{a}.$$

For every vector **a** there is a vector −**a** (called the additive inverse, or opposite of **a**) such that

$$\mathbf{a} + (-\mathbf{a}) = \mathbf{0}.$$

2. Vectors can be *multiplied by real numbers to give vectors*. This multiplication by real numbers has the properties

$$\alpha(\mathbf{a} + \mathbf{b}) = \alpha\mathbf{a} + \alpha\mathbf{b},$$
$$(\alpha + \beta)\mathbf{a} = \alpha\mathbf{a} + \beta\mathbf{a},$$
$$\alpha(\beta\mathbf{a}) = (\alpha\beta)\mathbf{a},$$
$$0 \cdot \mathbf{a} = \mathbf{0},$$
$$1 \cdot \mathbf{a} = \mathbf{a},$$

where α and β are real numbers.

3. Each vector can be *uniquely represented as a linear combination of three basis vectors:*

$$\mathbf{v} = v_1\mathbf{i} + v_2\mathbf{j} + v_3\mathbf{k}.$$

Now it so happens that one encounters in mathematics and in its applications many sets of things with the three properties listed above—and yet these are not vectors as we have defined them, that is, equivalence classes of ordered pairs of points. However, any set of things that has these three properties listed above is called a *three-dimensional vector space* over the real numbers. The set of vectors in the plane is a two-dimensional vector space over the real numbers.

Properties 2 and 3 can be generalized. For instance, you will remember that the real numbers are only one of many mathematical systems that are called *fields*. The rational numbers comprise a field. The generalization of property 2 is that the scalars that are used as multipliers need not be the real numbers, but may be the objects in any field.

Property 3 is generalized in the natural way by having each vector uniquely represented as a sum of multiples of n basis vectors:

$$\mathbf{v} = v_1\mathbf{i}_1 + v_2\mathbf{i}_2 + \cdots + v_n\mathbf{i}_n,$$

where the basis vectors are $\mathbf{i}_1, \ldots, \mathbf{i}_n$.

Any set of things having these generalized properties is called an *n-dimensional vector space*. Here n can be any natural number. When $n = 2$, the situation is the same as in the plane, discussed in Chapter 12. When $n = 3$, we have vectors in space. When $n > 3$, we cannot visualize these objects any longer, and must learn to use them by relying only on their assumed algebraic properties. However, although we cannot visualize these objects for $n > 3$, we can carry over much of the geometric language that is natural to us for $n = 3$ to the case $n > 3$. Thus we speak of a vector as the position vector to a point. And we speak of $v_1, v_2, \ldots, v_n$ as the coordinates of this point, just as we speak of $v_1, v_2, \ldots, v_n$ as the components of the vector.

As an example of an n-dimensional vector space V, let V be the set of all polynomials in x of degree less than or equal to n. Then each member, $f(x)$, of V is a polynomial (which we consider a vector),

$$f(x) = a_0x^n + a_1x^{n-1} + \cdots + a_n,$$

where the coefficients $a_0, \ldots, a_n$ are arbitrary real numbers. It is now an easy matter to verify that (with the usual addition of polynomials and multiplication by real numbers) V is a vector space. That is, V has properties 1 and 2 given on page 351. The special polynomials $x^n, x^{n-1}, \ldots, x, 1$ form a basis for the vector space.

Summary

The development of vectors in space is quite analogous to that of plane vectors in Chapter 12. The main topics are as follows.

1. We began with the concept of *arrow*, that is an ordered pair (P_1, P_2) of points in space. An arrow has a magnitude equal to the distance between the two points, and a direction given by the direction cosines of the ray from P_1 through P_2.

2. Two arrows are *equivalent* if they have the same magnitude and direction. Hence it is true that the arrows (P_1, P_2) and (Q_1, Q_2) are equivalent if and only if the coordinate differences are the same for the two arrows (Theorem 14–1).

3. A *vector* is an equivalence class of arrows. It is the set of all arrows equivalent to a given arrow. Vectors are denoted by $\mathbf{u}$, $\mathbf{v}$, or $\overrightarrow{P_1 P_2}$, etc. A *position vector* has its initial point at the origin.

4. The *sum* of two vectors $\mathbf{a}$ and $\mathbf{b}$ is obtained by "tacking on" an arrow representing $\mathbf{b}$ to an arrow representing $\mathbf{a}$.

5. If $\mathbf{v}$ is a vector and k a real number, then $k\mathbf{v}$ is a vector with magnitude $|k|$ times the magnitude of $\mathbf{v}$ and is in the same or opposite direction according as k is positive or negative. Then if $\mathbf{v}$ and $\mathbf{w}$ are in the same direction or in opposite directions, there is a unique real number k such that $\mathbf{v} = k\mathbf{w}$.

6. Every vector can be represented as a linear combination of three noncoplanar vectors. Usually we choose these three noncoplanar vectors to be the unit vectors $\mathbf{i}, \mathbf{j}, \mathbf{k}$ with directions along the coordinate axes. Then, if $\mathbf{v} = x\mathbf{i} + y\mathbf{j} + z\mathbf{k}$, the numbers x, y, and z are the *components* of $\mathbf{v}$ with respect to the *basis vectors* $\mathbf{i}, \mathbf{j}, \mathbf{k}$.

7. If $\mathbf{a} = a_1\mathbf{i} + a_2\mathbf{j} + a_3\mathbf{k}$ and $\mathbf{b} = b_1\mathbf{i} + b_2\mathbf{j} + b_3\mathbf{k}$, then

$$\mathbf{a} + \mathbf{b} = (a_1 + b_1)\mathbf{i} + (a_2 + b_2)\mathbf{j} + (a_3 + b_3)\mathbf{k}.$$

8. Vectors have many (but not all) algebraic properties that the real numbers have. For all vectors $\mathbf{a}$, $\mathbf{b}$, and $\mathbf{c}$ and for all real numbers r and s, we have

$$\mathbf{a} + \mathbf{b} = \mathbf{b} + \mathbf{a},$$
$$\mathbf{a} + (\mathbf{b} + \mathbf{c}) = (\mathbf{a} + \mathbf{b}) + \mathbf{c},$$
$$\mathbf{a} + \mathbf{0} = \mathbf{a},$$
$$r(\mathbf{a} + \mathbf{b}) = r\mathbf{a} + r\mathbf{b},$$
$$(r + s)\mathbf{a} = r\mathbf{a} + s\mathbf{a},$$
$$(rs)\mathbf{a} = r(s\mathbf{a}),$$
$$0\mathbf{a} = \mathbf{0},$$
$$1\mathbf{a} = \mathbf{a}.$$

9. If P_0 and P_1 are points on a line l, and $\mathbf{r}_0 = \overrightarrow{OP_0}$, then a vector equation of the line l is $\mathbf{r} = \mathbf{r}_0 + t\overrightarrow{P_0 P_1}$.

10. If P_0, P_1, P_2 are three noncollinear points on a plane π, and $\mathbf{r}_0 = \overrightarrow{OP_0}$, then a vector equation of the plane π is $\mathbf{r} = \mathbf{r}_0 + s\overrightarrow{P_0 P_1} + t\overrightarrow{P_0 P_2}$.

Chapter 14   Test

14-2 **1.** If $P_1 = (3, 5, 7)$, $P_2 = (4, 4, 4)$, $P_3 = (5, -2, 4)$, and $\overrightarrow{P_1P_2} = \overrightarrow{P_3P_4}$, what are the coordinates of P_4?

2. $\overrightarrow{OP_1}$ is a position vector with end point $(2, 4, 3)$. $\overrightarrow{OP_2}$ is a position vector with end point at $(1, -2, 2)$. What are the coordinates of the end point of $\overrightarrow{OP_1} + \overrightarrow{OP_2}$?

3. **v** is a position vector with end point at $(3, 2, -\sqrt{3})$. What is the magnitude and end point of $-4\mathbf{v}$?

14-3 **4.** If $\mathbf{r} = 2\mathbf{i} - 2\mathbf{j} + \mathbf{k}$ what is $|\mathbf{r}|$? Sketch **r**.

5. If $(5\mathbf{i} - \mathbf{j} + 2\mathbf{k}) + \mathbf{b} = 4\mathbf{i} + 3\mathbf{j} - \mathbf{k}$, what are the components of **b**?

6. Find $\mathbf{r} + \mathbf{s}$ if $\mathbf{r} = -7\mathbf{i} + \mathbf{j} - 4\mathbf{k}$ and $\mathbf{s} = 5\mathbf{i} - 3\mathbf{j} + 10\mathbf{k}$.

14-4 **7.** A line contains the origin of the coordinate axes and the point $(2, 5, 3)$. Write a vector equation of the line.

8. Write a vector equation of a line containing the points $(-3, 5, 0)$ and $(2, -4, 6)$.

9. If $P_0 = (4, -4, 2)$ and $P_1 = (8, -6, 6)$, find the components of the vector to the midpoint of $\overline{P_0P_1}$.

10. A line contains the point $(2, 3, 0)$ and is perpendicular to the xy-plane. Write a vector equation of the line.

14-5 **11.** Write a vector equation of the plane containing the three points whose coordinates are $(2, 4, 2)$, $(3, 1, 1)$, and $(5, 3, 2)$.

12. Parametric equations of a plane are
$$x = 2 + 4s - t,$$
$$y = -1 + 2s + 3t,$$
$$z = 1 - s + 2t.$$

Find a rectangular equation of the plane.

13. The x-, y- and z-intercepts of a plane are 4, -3, and 5 respectively. Write a vector equation of the plane. Sketch a portion of the plane.

Historical Note

Sir William Rowan Hamilton
(1805–1865)

Historically, the concept of a vector (from the Latin *vehere,* "to carry") has its origin in the attempts to represent complex numbers geometrically. Complex numbers can be represented by points in a coordinate plane, as shown in Fig. 14. The complex number $a + bi$ is represented by the arrow (O,P). The vector $a\mathbf{i} + b\mathbf{j}$ is also represented by (O,P).

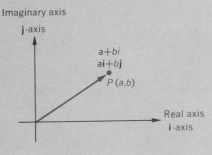

Imaginary axis
j-axis

$a+bi$
$a\mathbf{i}+b\mathbf{j}$
$P\,(a,b)$

Real axis
i-axis

FIGURE 14

Although the two concepts are related, they are not the same. Vectors and complex numbers do have the same additive properties. Complex numbers can also be multiplied. Multiplication of vectors will be discussed in the next chapter.

The complex numbers form a field. Mathematicians attempted to generalize complex numbers from objects in the plane to objects in space to provide a model for vectors in space. One approach is to add another component to $a + bi$ so that one would have $a + bi + cj$, where j is a new unit. This approach, however, is in error because it is not complete.

Sir William Rowan Hamilton (1805–1865), a professor of astronomy at the University of Dublin, developed the correct generalization of complex numbers in 1843. He called these new numbers quaternions. Quaternions have four components instead of three. They are of the form $r + ai + bj + ck$, where r, a, b, and c are real numbers, and i, j, and k are quaternion unit vectors. The numbers r, a, b, and c are called the components of the quaternion.

Two quaternions are equal if and only if their components are respectively equal. Quaternions are added by adding their components. Multiplication of quaternions is performed by means of the distributive property and the products of the units:

$$i^2 = j^2 = k^2 = -1,$$
$$i \cdot j = k, j \cdot k = i, k \cdot i = j,$$
$$j \cdot i = -k, k \cdot j = -i, i \cdot k = -j.$$

Observe that multiplication is not commutative. The quaternions form a noncommutative field.

To be sure that you understand how products are formed, you may verify that

$$(1 + 2i - 3j + k)(2 - i - j + 2k)$$
$$= -1 - 2i - 12j - k.$$

Chapter 15
Angles, Lines, and Planes

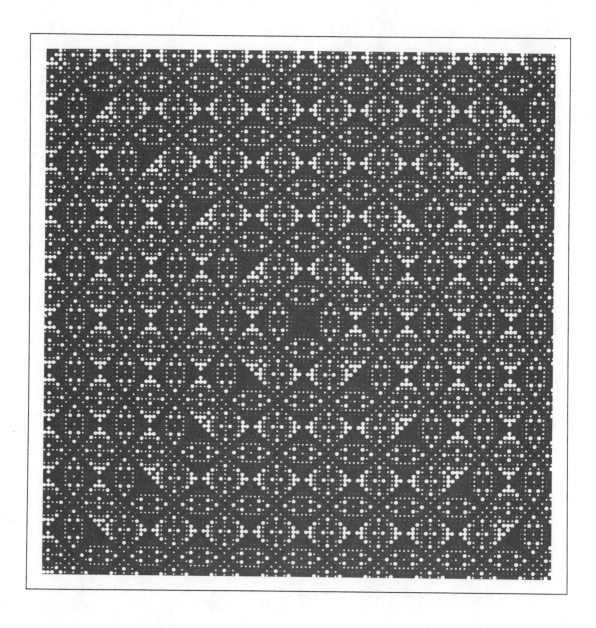

15-1   Introduction

In our study of coordinate geometry, we did not discuss the measure of angles between lines or planes nor did we find distances from points to lines or from points to planes. Now we discuss such problems.

The basic formula in this chapter concerns the angle between two vectors. Other formulas are simple consequences of this formula. We shall also define two new operations for vectors. Both operations are kinds of "multiplication," but one operation combines two vectors to produce a real number while the other operation combines two vectors to give another vector. These new operations have numerous applications and will help us deal efficiently with angles, lines, and planes.

15-2   The Angle Between Vectors

We define the angle between two vectors to be the angle between their position vectors; in Fig. 1, θ is the measure of the angle between vectors $\mathbf{v}$ and $\mathbf{v}'$.

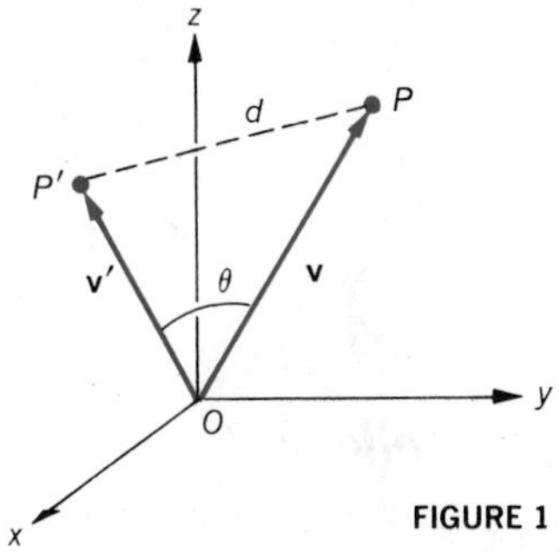

FIGURE 1

Theorem 15-1 *Suppose $\mathbf{v}$ has direction cosines c_1, c_2, c_3 and $\mathbf{v}'$ has direction cosines c_1', c_2', c_3'. Then if θ is the measure of the angle between the vectors,*

$$\cos \theta = c_1 c_1' + c_2 c_2' + c_3 c_3'. \quad (1)$$

Proof   Let $\mathbf{v} = \overrightarrow{OP}$, with $P = (x, y, z)$ and $\mathbf{v}' = \overrightarrow{OP'}$, with $P' = (x', y', z')$. The laws of cosines for the triangle OPP' and the distance formula provide two expressions for the distance d between P and P':

$$d^2 = |\mathbf{v}|^2 + |\mathbf{v}'|^2 - 2|\mathbf{v}|\,|\mathbf{v}'| \cos \theta \qquad \text{(by the law of cosines)},$$
$$d^2 = (x - x')^2 + (y - y')^2 + (z - z')^2 \quad \text{(by the distance formula)}.$$

357

Therefore

$$|v|^2 + |v'|^2 - 2|v|\,|v'|\cos\theta = (x - x')^2 + (y - y')^2 + (x - z')^2. \quad (2)$$

But

$$|v|^2 = x^2 + y^2 + z^2 \quad \text{and} \quad |v'|^2 = x'^2 + y'^2 + z'^2.$$

Then equation (2) becomes

$$-2|v|\,|v'|\cos\theta = -2xx' - 2yy' - 2zz'$$

or

$$\cos\theta = \frac{xx' + yy' + zz'}{|v|\,|v'|}. \quad (3)$$

But by the basic theorem for direction cosines,

$$c_1 = \frac{x}{|v|}, \qquad c_2 = \frac{y}{|v|}, \qquad c_3 = \frac{z}{|v|},$$

$$c_1' = \frac{x'}{|v'|}, \qquad c_2' = \frac{y'}{|v'|}, \qquad c_3' = \frac{z'}{|v'|},$$

and so equations (3) imply $\cos\theta = c_1 c_1' + c_2 c_2' + c_3 c_3'$.

Corollary 1   *If P_1, P_2 lie in the xy-plane, then $\cos\theta = c_1 c_1' + c_2 c_2'$.*

Corollary 2   *If the points P, P' are different from the origin O and have coordinates (x, y, z) and (x', y', z'), respectively (see Fig. 2), and θ is the measure of the angle between $\overrightarrow{OP}$ and $\overrightarrow{OP'}$, then*

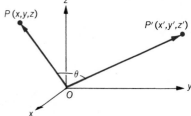

FIGURE 2

$$\cos\theta = \frac{xx' + yy' + zz'}{\sqrt{x^2 + y^2 + z^2}\sqrt{x'^2 + y'^2 + z'^2}}.$$

Corollary 3   *If neither of the vectors $v = v_1 i + v_2 j + v_3 k$ and $u = u_1 i + u_2 j + u_3 k$ are the zero vector, then θ, the measure of the angle between them is given by*

$$\cos\theta = \frac{u_1 v_1 + u_2 v_2 + u_3 v_3}{|u|\,|v|}.$$

Example 1   Find θ, the measure of the angle between the vectors $v = i + 2j + 3k$ and $v' = -i - j - 2k$.

Solution. The direction cosines of the vectors are

$$c_1 = \frac{1}{\sqrt{14}}, \qquad c_2 = \frac{2}{\sqrt{14}}, \qquad c_3 = \frac{3}{\sqrt{14}},$$

$$c_1' = \frac{-1}{\sqrt{6}}, \qquad c_2' = \frac{-1}{\sqrt{6}}, \qquad c_3' = \frac{-2}{\sqrt{6}}.$$

Therefore

$$\cos\theta = \left(\frac{1}{\sqrt{14}}\right)\left(\frac{-1}{\sqrt{6}}\right) + \left(\frac{2}{\sqrt{14}}\right)\left(\frac{-1}{\sqrt{6}}\right) + \left(\frac{3}{\sqrt{14}}\right)\left(\frac{-2}{\sqrt{6}}\right)$$

$$= \frac{-9}{2\sqrt{21}} = -0.9820,$$

$$\theta = \text{Arccos}\,(-0.9820) \doteq 2.9516\ (169.1°).$$

Example 2 Find the measure of $\angle BAC$, where $A = (-1, 2, 1)$, $B = (3, 4, 3)$, and $C = (1, 0, 0)$. (See Fig. 3.)

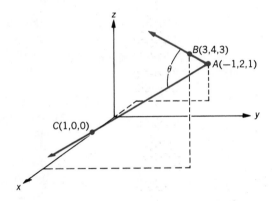

FIGURE 3

Solution. We have

$$\vec{AB} = 4\mathbf{i} + 2\mathbf{j} + 2\mathbf{k},$$
$$\vec{AC} = 2\mathbf{i} - 2\mathbf{j} - \mathbf{k}.$$

If $m(\angle BAC) = \theta$, then by Corollary 3,

$$\cos\theta = \frac{4(2) + 2(-2) + 2(-1)}{\sqrt{16 + 4 + 4}\,\sqrt{4 + 4 + 1}} = \frac{2}{(2\sqrt{6})3} = \frac{1}{3\sqrt{6}} = \frac{\sqrt{6}}{18},$$

$$\theta = \text{Arccos}\,\frac{\sqrt{6}}{18} \doteq \text{Arccos}\,0.1361 \doteq 1.4343\ (82.2°).$$

Problems

Set A

1. If $\mathbf{v}$ has direction cosines

$$c_1 = \frac{1}{2}, \qquad c_2 = -\frac{1}{2} \qquad \text{and} \qquad c_3 = \frac{1}{\sqrt{2}}$$

and $\mathbf{v}'$ has direction cosines

$$c_1' = \frac{1}{3}, \qquad c_2' = \frac{5}{6} \qquad \text{and} \qquad c_3' = -\frac{\sqrt{6}}{6},$$

find the cosine of the angle between $\mathbf{v}$ and $\mathbf{v}'$.

Find the cosine of the angle between the following pairs of vectors.

2. $(\mathbf{i} + \mathbf{k})$ and $(\mathbf{j} + \mathbf{k})$

3. $(\mathbf{i} + \mathbf{j} + \mathbf{k})$ and $(\mathbf{i} + \mathbf{j} + 2\mathbf{k})$

4. $(-\mathbf{i} + 3\mathbf{j} + 3\mathbf{k})$ and $(3\mathbf{i} + \mathbf{j} - 3\mathbf{k})$

5. $(\frac{2}{3}\mathbf{i} - \frac{2}{3}\mathbf{j} + \frac{1}{3}\mathbf{k})$ and $(2\mathbf{i} - 2\mathbf{j} + \mathbf{k})$

Find the cosine of the angle between two position vectors whose end points are given below.

6. $(3, 1, 1)$, $(-2, 4, -2)$

7. $(-4, 0, 3)$, $(0, 6, -3)$

8. $(2, 4, 3)$, $(2, -4, 3)$

9. (x, y, z), $(-x, -y, -z)$

Set B

10. Show that the angle between the unit basis vectors $\mathbf{i}$ and $\mathbf{j}$ is $\pi/2$.

11. Show that the angle between $\mathbf{i}$ and $-\mathbf{i}$ is π.

Find the cosine of the angle between the vectors $\overrightarrow{P_1P_2}$ and $\overrightarrow{P_3P_4}$ if P_1, P_2, P_3, and P_4 are, in order, the following points.

12. $(0, -1, 3)$, $(-2, 1, 2)$, $(-10, -2, -1)$, $(10, 3, 3)$

13. $(-2, -3, 1)$, $(0, 1, 2)$, $(-5, -2, 1)$, $(-2, 2, 3)$

14. $(7, -3, 1)$, $(4, 2, -2)$, $(6, 0, -3)$, $(-4, -4, 4)$

15. $(5, 3, 4)$, $(0, 0, 0)$, $(-3, -2, -1)$, $(1, 2, 3)$

16. Find the measure of the angles between $\mathbf{v} = 4\mathbf{i} - 2\mathbf{j} + 4\mathbf{k}$ and each of the positive coordinate axes.

17. Find the measure of angle XYZ if the coordinates of X, Y, and Z are $(5, 3, -1)$, $(4, -2, 6)$ and $(10, 10, 10)$ respectively.

18. Find the measure of the angle between $2\mathbf{i} + 3\mathbf{j} + 4\mathbf{k}$ and $-4\mathbf{i} + \mathbf{j} + 4\mathbf{k}$.

19. Find the measures of the angles between $\mathbf{v} = c\mathbf{i} + c\mathbf{j} + c\mathbf{k}$ and each of the positive coordinate axes.

20. Prove that $\mathbf{v}_1 = -\mathbf{i} + 3\mathbf{j} - 2\mathbf{k}$ and $\mathbf{v}_2 = 2\mathbf{i} + 2\mathbf{j} + 2\mathbf{k}$ are perpendicular.

Set C

21. Show that the line through $(1, 3, 5)$ and $(3, 0, 1)$ is perpendicular to the line through $(1, 11, -1)$ and $(-5, 3, 2)$.

22. A triangle has vertices $(-1, -1, 2)$, $(3, 2, -1)$, and $(0, 4, 3)$. Find the measure of the angle whose vertex is $(-1, -1, 2)$.

23. Prove that the vectors $\mathbf{a} = a_1\mathbf{i} + a_2\mathbf{j} + a_3\mathbf{k}$ and $\mathbf{b} = b_1\mathbf{i} + b_2\mathbf{j} + b_3\mathbf{k}$, neither of which is the null vector, are perpendicular if and only if $a_1b_1 + a_2b_2 + a_3b_3 = 0$.

24. A directed line has direction cosines $1/2$, $-\sqrt{3}/2$, 0. Find direction cosines of a directed line in the xy-plane perpendicular to the given line.

25. A directed line parallel to the xy-plane has direction cosines l, m, and 0. Show that a directed line perpendicular to the given line and also parallel to the xy-plane has direction cosines $\pm m$, $\mp l$, 0.

26. Show that the distinct points (x_1, y_1, z_1), (x_2, y_2, z_2), (x_3, y_3, z_3) are vertices of a right triangle with the right angle at (x_1, y_1, z_1) if and only if

$$(x_2 - x_1)(x_3 - x_1) + (y_2 - y_1)(y_3 - y_1) + (z_2 - z_1)(z_3 - z_1) = 0.$$

Calculator Problem

The vertices of $\triangle ABC$ are $A = (2, -2, 4)$, $B = (-3, 2, 5)$ and $C = (3, 2, -2)$. Find the following.

(a) The lengths of the sides of the triangle.
(b) The measures in degrees of each angle of the triangle.
(c) A rectangular equation of the plane of the triangle.

15-3   The Dot Product of Vectors

An important function defined on pairs of vectors is the *dot product*. Actually the term "product" is a misnomer because *this* "product" of two vectors is not a vector, but a real number, or scalar. Nevertheless, the name is not unreasonable because, as we shall see, this "product" does obey some of the same laws that ordinary multiplication does. This product of two vectors is called the *dot product* because of the "·" used to indicate this kind of multiplication. Sometimes it is also called the *inner product* or *scalar product*.

Definition 15-1   If **u** and **v** are vectors, neither the null vector, and θ is the measure of the angle between them, then the *dot product* of **u** and **v**, denoted by $\mathbf{u} \cdot \mathbf{v}$, is the real number $\mathbf{u} \cdot \mathbf{v} = |\mathbf{u}|\,|\mathbf{v}| \cos \theta$. If either **u** or **v** is the null vector, then $\mathbf{u} \cdot \mathbf{v} = 0$.

Because vectors are ordinarily given in terms of their components, it is desirable to be able to compute the dot product of two vectors in terms of their components. The next theorem gives the method for accomplishing this.

Theorem 15-2   *If* $\mathbf{u} = u_1\mathbf{i} + u_2\mathbf{j} + u_3\mathbf{k}$ *and* $\mathbf{v} = v_1\mathbf{i} + v_2\mathbf{j} + v_3\mathbf{k}$, *then*

$$\mathbf{u} \cdot \mathbf{v} = u_1 v_1 + u_2 v_2 + u_3 v_3.$$

Proof   See equation (3) of the proof of Theorem 15-1, page 358.

Examples 1 and 2 below show applications of dot products to geometry; Examples 3 and 4 show applications to physics.

Example 1   If $\mathbf{u} = u_1\mathbf{i} + u_2\mathbf{j} + u_3\mathbf{k}$, then from the definitions of dot product and direction cosines

$$\mathbf{u} \cdot \mathbf{i} = |\mathbf{u}| \cos \alpha = u_1, \quad \mathbf{u} \cdot \mathbf{j} = |\mathbf{u}| \cos \beta = u_2, \quad \mathbf{u} \cdot \mathbf{k} = |\mathbf{u}| \cos \gamma = u_3.$$

This result also follows directly from Theorem 15-2 because

$$\mathbf{i} = 1\mathbf{i} + 0\mathbf{j} + 0\mathbf{k} \quad \text{so that} \quad \mathbf{u} \cdot \mathbf{i} = u_1 \cdot 1 + u_2 \cdot 0 + u_3 \cdot 0 = u_1.$$

Example 2   If **n** is any unit vector, then $\mathbf{u} \cdot \mathbf{n} = |\mathbf{u}| \cos \theta$, where θ is the measure of the angle between **u** and **n**. This number is the length of the *projection* of **u** on **n**, as shown in Fig. 4. Note that $\mathbf{u} \cdot \mathbf{n}$ will be positive if $0 \leq \theta < \pi/2$, and negative if $\pi/2 < \theta \leq \pi$.

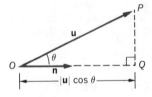 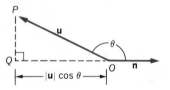

FIGURE 4

Later in this chapter we shall see how to use the dot product of vectors to study lines perpendicular to planes, or lines perpendicular to lines in a plane.

Example 3   *Work*. Let us suppose that F is a force, say measured in newtons. Then **F** is a vector, since it has both magnitude and direction. Let us assume that the force **F** acts through a distance given by a vector **d** whose magnitude is measured in meters. (See Fig. 5.) Let F_1 be the component of

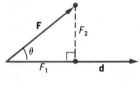

FIGURE 5

F along **d**, and F_2 the component of **F** that is perpendicular to **d**. By definition, the *work* performed by **F** acting through the distance $|\mathbf{d}|$ is $F_1|\mathbf{d}|$. But $F_1 = |\mathbf{F}| \cos \theta$, where θ is the measure of the angle between **F** and **d**. Hence the work J in joules (newton-meters) is

$$J = |\mathbf{F}| \, |\mathbf{d}| \cos \theta = \mathbf{F} \cdot \mathbf{d}.$$

Because there is no motion perpendicular to **d**, the component F_2 does no work.

For motion with velocity **v**, the *rate of doing work* equals $\mathbf{F} \cdot \mathbf{v}$.

Usually forces and displacements are resolved into components along three mutually perpendicular directions which one selects as directions of the x-, y-, and z-axes. If $\mathbf{F} = F_1\mathbf{i} + F_2\mathbf{j} + F_3\mathbf{k}$ and $\mathbf{d} = d_1\mathbf{i} + d_2\mathbf{j} + d_3\mathbf{k}$, then $\mathbf{F} \cdot \mathbf{d} = F_1 d_1 + F_2 d_2 + F_3 d_3$.

4   *Gravitational fields*. For many purposes the earth may be considered as flat with the acceleration due to gravity, **g**, constant in the downward direction. (See Fig. 6.) Then a mass m is pulled by a force $\mathbf{F} = m\mathbf{g}$.

If there is a vertical displacement **d**, then the work done will be

$$\mathbf{F} \cdot \mathbf{d} = m\mathbf{g} \cdot \mathbf{d}.$$

A horizontal displacement **d** gives $\mathbf{F} \cdot \mathbf{d} = m\mathbf{g} \cdot \mathbf{d} = 0$.

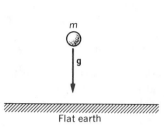

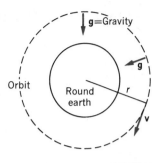

FIGURE 6

FIGURE 7

For a round earth, the gravitational force is exerted toward the center of the earth and is not constant. In fact (see Fig. 7),

$$|\mathbf{g}| = \frac{k}{r^2},$$

where k is the *gravitational constant* and r is the distance from the center of the earth. But in this case there is no work done if the motion is at a fixed distance r from the center of the earth. Thus a satellite in a circular orbit does no work, and so loses no energy because of the gravitational field, since $\mathbf{F} \cdot \mathbf{v} = 0$.

The following theorem is useful in applications.

Theorem 15–3   *If u and v are vectors, neither the null vector, then u and v are perpendicular if and only if u · v = 0.*

Proof   If $\mathbf{u} \cdot \mathbf{v} = |\mathbf{u}|\,|\mathbf{v}| \cos \theta = 0$, then since $|\mathbf{u}| \neq 0$ and $|\mathbf{v}| \neq 0$, we must have $\cos \theta = 0$. Therefore $\theta = \pi/2$ and $\mathbf{u} \perp \mathbf{v}$. Conversely, if $\mathbf{u} \perp \mathbf{v}$, $\cos \theta = \cos \pi/2 = 0$. Hence $\mathbf{u} \cdot \mathbf{v} = |\mathbf{u}|\,|\mathbf{v}| \cdot 0 = 0$.

Example 5   Show that $\mathbf{u} = 6\mathbf{i} - 4\mathbf{j} + 2\mathbf{j}$ and $\mathbf{v} = -\mathbf{i} + \mathbf{k} + 5\mathbf{j}$ are perpendicular.

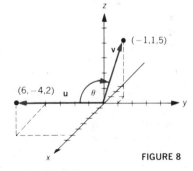

Solution.

$$\mathbf{u} \cdot \mathbf{v} = 6(-1) + (-4)1 + 2 \cdot 5 = 0$$

Since the dot product is zero, $\mathbf{u} \perp \mathbf{v}$. (See Fig. 8.)

FIGURE 8

We have called $\mathbf{u} \cdot \mathbf{v}$ a "product," and hence it is natural to expect that some properties of multiplication are valid. All that may be said is given by the following theorem.

Theorem 15-4   *For all vectors* **u**, **v**, *and* **w**,

$$\mathbf{u} \cdot \mathbf{v} = \mathbf{v} \cdot \mathbf{u} \qquad \textit{(commutative law)},$$

and

$$\mathbf{u} \cdot (\mathbf{v} + \mathbf{w}) = (\mathbf{u} \cdot \mathbf{v}) + (\mathbf{u} \cdot \mathbf{w}) \qquad \textit{(distributive law)}.$$

The theorem is an easy consequence of Theorem 15-2, and its proof is left to the student. Observe that there is no vector that acts as a multiplicative identity for dot products as the number 1 does for ordinary multiplication. Furthermore, there is no associative law for dot products.

Problems

Set A

Compute the dot product of the following pairs of vectors.

1. $2\mathbf{i} + 3\mathbf{j} + 4\mathbf{k}$, $\mathbf{i} - \mathbf{j} - \mathbf{k}$
2. $\mathbf{i} + 2\mathbf{j} - 5\mathbf{k}$, $2\mathbf{i} + 4\mathbf{j} + 2\mathbf{k}$
3. $3\mathbf{i} + \mathbf{j} - \mathbf{k}$, $-3\mathbf{i} - \mathbf{j} + \mathbf{k}$
4. $6\mathbf{i} - 9\mathbf{j} + 3\mathbf{k}$, $\frac{2}{3}\mathbf{i} + \frac{2}{3}\mathbf{j} + \frac{1}{3}\mathbf{k}$
5. $2\mathbf{i} + \mathbf{j} - 4\mathbf{k}$, $2\mathbf{i} + \mathbf{j} - 4\mathbf{k}$
6. $\mathbf{i} + \mathbf{j}$, $\mathbf{j} + \mathbf{k}$

Let **n** be a unit vector and $\mathbf{u} = -6\mathbf{i} + 3\mathbf{j} + 6\mathbf{k}$. What is the length of the projection of **u** on **n** if the measure of the angle between the two vectors is

7. 0.   8. $\pi/6$.   9. $\pi/4$.   10. $\pi/3$.
11. $\pi/2$.   12. $2\pi/3$.   13. π.   14. $5\pi/6$.

Set B

15. If $\mathbf{u} = \mathbf{i} + (-2)\mathbf{j} + 2\mathbf{k}$, what is $\mathbf{u} \cdot \mathbf{i}$? $\mathbf{u} \cdot \mathbf{j}$? $\mathbf{u} \cdot \mathbf{k}$?

16. Compute $\mathbf{a} \cdot (\mathbf{b} + \mathbf{c})$ where $\mathbf{a} = 3\mathbf{i} + 2\mathbf{j} - \mathbf{k}$, $\mathbf{b} = -\mathbf{i} + 3\mathbf{j} + 4\mathbf{k}$, $\mathbf{c} = 2\mathbf{i} - \mathbf{j} + \mathbf{k}$.

17. Compute $\mathbf{a} \cdot \mathbf{b} + \mathbf{a} \cdot \mathbf{c}$ using vectors **a**, **b** and **c** of Problem 16.

18. A force of 20 newtons moves an object along a line which forms an angle of 30° with the direction of the force. What is the component of the force along the line? What is the component of the force perpendicular to the line? How much work is done if the object is moved 8 m along the line?

19. A jet airplane flies southwest at 900 km/h in still air. The airplane encounters a jetstream of air moving due east at 150 km/h. What is the component of the jetstream along the line of flight of the plane? What will be the speed of the plane due to the wind?

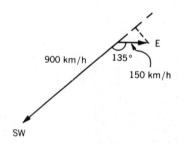

20. The unit vector $\mathbf{n} = \frac{3}{7}\mathbf{i} + (-\frac{6}{7}\mathbf{j}) + \frac{2}{7}\mathbf{k}$ is perpendicular to a plane, π. The point $P = (3, 1, 4)$ is in the plane. Find $\overrightarrow{OP} \cdot \mathbf{n}$. What does the dot product represent geometrically? What is the distance from the origin O to the plane at Q?

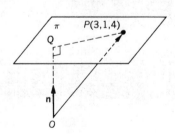

21. Show that there is no vector that behaves for the dot product as 1 does for ordinary multiplication.

22. Show that there is no associative law for dot products.

Set C

23. Find $(\mathbf{a} + \mathbf{b}) \cdot (\mathbf{a} - \mathbf{b})$, given that $\mathbf{a} = \mathbf{i} + 2\mathbf{j} + 3\mathbf{k}$ and $\mathbf{b} = 2\mathbf{i} - \mathbf{j} + \mathbf{k}$.

24. Prove that for every pair of vectors $\mathbf{a}$ and $\mathbf{b}$, $(\mathbf{a} + \mathbf{b}) \cdot (\mathbf{a} - \mathbf{b}) = |\mathbf{a}|^2 - |\mathbf{b}|^2$.

25. Prove that the distributive law holds for dot products; that is, prove that if $\mathbf{a}$, $\mathbf{b}$, and $\mathbf{c}$ are any vectors, then $\mathbf{a} \cdot (\mathbf{b} + \mathbf{c}) = \mathbf{a} \cdot \mathbf{b} + \mathbf{a} \cdot \mathbf{c}$.

26. In the statement of the distributive law for dot products, do the "+" symbols refer to the same operation on the same kind of objects in each case? Explain.

27. Prove that the commutative law holds for dot products.

28. Show that if $\mathbf{u} \cdot \mathbf{v} = \pm|\mathbf{u}|\,|\mathbf{v}|$, then the vectors are either in the same direction or opposite directions.

29. Dot products can be thought of as a function. What is the domain and range of this function?

30. Prove that $\mathbf{u} = \mathbf{v}$ if and only if $\mathbf{u} \cdot \mathbf{w} = \mathbf{v} \cdot \mathbf{w}$ for every vector $\mathbf{w}$.

Calculator Problem

Find all the relations of perpendicularity that exist among the four vectors below.

$$\mathbf{a} = 3.2\mathbf{i} - 6.1\mathbf{j} - 1.3\mathbf{k}$$
$$\mathbf{b} = 2.7\mathbf{i} - 5.4\mathbf{j} + 6.4\mathbf{k}$$
$$\mathbf{c} = 4.5\mathbf{i} + 1.7\mathbf{j} + 3.1\mathbf{k}$$
$$\mathbf{d} = -16.7\mathbf{i} - 15.77\mathbf{j} + 32.89\mathbf{k}$$

15-4   Normals to Lines in a Plane

A line is said to be *normal* to another line if the two lines are perpendicular to each other. The word "orthogonal"* is also used in reference to perpendicular lines. We shall also speak of vectors that are normal or orthogonal to lines or to other vectors.

If *l* is a line in the *xy*-plane, it should be evident that there are exactly two vectors of unit length in the plane that are normal to the line *l*. It is convenient to designate one of these vectors as the *positive unit normal* to the line. For the present, let us agree that the positive unit normal to a line is that unit vector whose position vector points from the origin to the line. Thus **n** in Fig. 9 represents the positive unit normal to the line *l*. If the line contains the origin, either unit normal may be chosen as the positive unit normal.

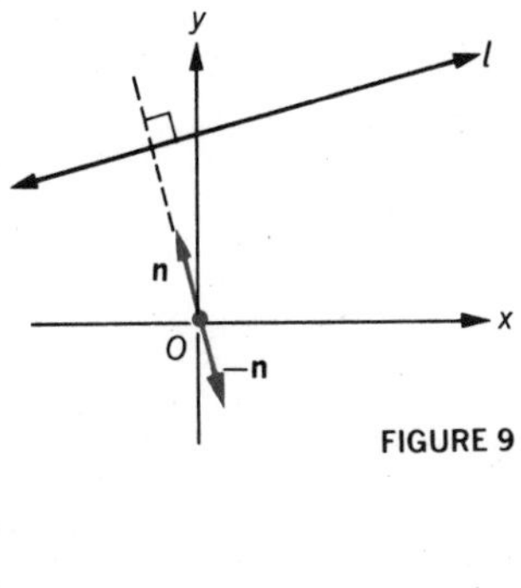

FIGURE 9

---

*From *ortho* meaning right and *gonia* meaning angular.

Theorem 15-5   *If a line l has an equation $ax + by + c = 0$, then the two unit normals to l are*

$$\frac{a}{\sqrt{a^2 + b^2}}\mathbf{i} + \frac{b}{\sqrt{a^2 + b^2}}\mathbf{j} \quad and \quad \frac{-a}{\sqrt{a^2 + b^2}}\mathbf{i} + \frac{-b}{\sqrt{a^2 + b^2}}\mathbf{j}.$$

Proof   If $P_0 = (x_0, y_0)$ and $P_1 = (x_1, y_1)$ are two points on the line $ax + by + c = 0$, as in Fig. 10, then

$$ax_0 + by_0 + c = 0 \qquad (1)$$

and

$$ax_1 + by_1 + c = 0. \qquad (2)$$

Subtracting equation (1) from equation (2), we obtain

$$a(x_1 - x_0) + b(y_1 - y_0) = 0. \quad (3)$$

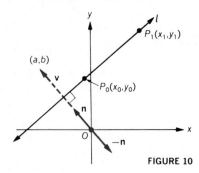

FIGURE 10

Now, $P_0P_1 = (x_1 - x_0)\mathbf{i} + (y_1 - y_0)\mathbf{j}$, and if we let $\mathbf{v} = a\mathbf{i} + b\mathbf{j}$, then

$$\mathbf{v} \cdot \overrightarrow{P_0P_1} = a(x_1 - x_0) + b(y_1 - y_0) = 0 \qquad (4)$$

from statement (3) above. Since the dot product $\mathbf{v} \cdot P_0P_1$ is 0, the two vectors are perpendicular by Theorem 15-3. Therefore $\mathbf{v}$ must be a vector normal to the line through P_0 and P_1. The direction cosines of $\mathbf{v}$ are

$$c_1 = \frac{a}{\sqrt{a^2 + b^2}} \quad and \quad c_2 = \frac{b}{\sqrt{a^2 + b^2}}.$$

The vector $-\mathbf{v}$ is also normal to the line l and has direction cosines

$$c_1 = \frac{-a}{\sqrt{a^2 + b^2}} \quad and \quad c_2 = \frac{-b}{\sqrt{a^2 + b^2}}.$$

Hence the two unit normals to l are

$$\frac{a}{\sqrt{a^2 + b^2}}\mathbf{i} + \frac{b}{\sqrt{a^2 + b^2}}\mathbf{j} \quad and \quad \frac{-a}{\sqrt{a^2 + b^2}}\mathbf{i} + \frac{-b}{\sqrt{a^2 + b^2}}\mathbf{j}.$$

Example 1   The two unit normals to the line $2x - 3y + 6 = 0$ are

$$\mathbf{n}_1 = \frac{2}{\sqrt{13}}\mathbf{i} + \frac{-3}{\sqrt{13}}\mathbf{j}$$

and

$$\mathbf{n}_2 = \frac{-2}{\sqrt{13}}\mathbf{i} + \frac{3}{\sqrt{13}}\mathbf{j}.$$

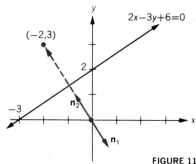

FIGURE 11

The line and the unit vectors are shown in Fig. 11. Observe that $\mathbf{n}_2$ appears to be the *positive* unit normal.

We can now develop a formula for computing the perpendicular distance from the origin to a line. First, if a line is parallel to one of the coordinate axes, no special formula is needed. (Why?) Second, if a line contains the origin, then its distance from the origin must be 0. A line with equation $ax + by + c = 0$ will contain the origin if and only if $c = 0$. (Why?)

Let l be a line with an equation $ax + by + c = 0$, and P_0 be the foot of the perpendicular from the origin O to l as in Fig. 12.

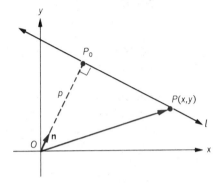

FIGURE 12

Then $|\overrightarrow{OP_0}| = p$ is the distance from the origin to the line. If $P = (x, y)$ is any other point on the line and $\mathbf{n}$ is the *positive* unit normal to the line, then

$$p = \overrightarrow{OP} \cdot \mathbf{n}. \quad \text{(Why?)}$$

We have seen that there are two unit normals to a line, namely,

$$\mathbf{n} = \frac{a\mathbf{i}}{\pm \sqrt{a^2 + b^2}} + \frac{b\mathbf{j}}{\pm \sqrt{a^2 + b^2}},$$

and our problem is to decide which of the two is to be the positive unit normal. Let us examine the dot products of $\overrightarrow{OP}$ and the unit normals:

$$p = \overrightarrow{OP} \cdot \mathbf{n} = (x\mathbf{i} + y\mathbf{j}) \cdot \left(\frac{a\mathbf{i}}{\pm \sqrt{a^2 + b^2}} + \frac{b\mathbf{j}}{\pm \sqrt{a^2 + b^2}} \right)$$

$$= \frac{ax + by}{\pm \sqrt{a^2 + b^2}}.$$

The sign of the radical must be chosen so that the dot product, p, is positive. But $ax + by = -c$, so that

$$p = \frac{-c}{\pm \sqrt{a^2 + b^2}},$$

and the sign of the radical must be chosen opposite to that of c. We have therefore proved the following theorem.

Theorem 15-6 *The positive unit normal to the line $ax + by + c = 0$ which does not contain the origin is*

$$\frac{a}{\sqrt{a^2 + b^2}}\mathbf{i} + \frac{b}{\sqrt{a^2 + b^2}}\mathbf{j} \quad if \quad c < 0,$$

or

$$\frac{a}{-\sqrt{a^2 + b^2}}\mathbf{i} + \frac{b}{-\sqrt{a^2 + b^2}}\mathbf{j} \quad if \quad c > 0.$$

The distance from the origin O to the line is

$$p = \frac{|c|}{\sqrt{a^2 + b^2}}.$$

Example 2 The positive unit normal to the line $3x - 4y + 7 = 0$ is

$$\mathbf{n} = -\tfrac{3}{5}\mathbf{i} + \tfrac{4}{5}\mathbf{j}.$$

The distance from the origin to the line is $p = \tfrac{7}{5}$.

Problems

Set A

Find the positive unit normal to each line. Sketch the line and the unit normal.

1. $3x + 4y - 1 = 0$ 2. $x + y - 4 = 0$
3. $2x - y + 5 = 0$ 4. $x + \sqrt{3}\,y + 2 = 0$

Find the distance from the origin to the lines whose equations are given below. Sketch each line.

5. $x - 3y + 10 = 0$ 6. $5x + 12y - 30 = 0$
7. $x + y + 8 = 0$ 8. $3x + 5y - 8 = 0$
9. $\sqrt{5}\,x - 7 = 0$ 10. $8y + 17 = 0$
11. $5x + 6y = 0$
12. $\sqrt{2}\,x + \sqrt{3}\,y + \sqrt{5} = 0$

17. A vector equation of a line is

$$\mathbf{r} = (3\mathbf{i} - 2\mathbf{j}) + t(\mathbf{i} + 4\mathbf{j})$$

where the parameter t is any real number. Find the distance from the origin to the line.

18. What is the distance from the origin to the line with parametric equations

$$\begin{cases} x = 4 + \dfrac{3}{\sqrt{10}}d, \\[2mm] y = 2 + \dfrac{-1}{\sqrt{10}}d\,? \end{cases}$$

Set B

Find the distance from the origin to the line through the following pairs of points. Sketch the lines.

13. $(1, 1)$ and $(-2, 4)$ 14. $(-3, 0)$ and $(0, 6)$
15. $(-4, 0)$ and $(12, 6)$
16. $(5, -2)$ and $(6, -1)$

Set C

19. A line has a positive unit normal

$$\mathbf{n} = \frac{2}{3}\mathbf{i} - \frac{\sqrt{5}}{3}\mathbf{j},$$

and the distance from the origin to the line is 3 units. Find a rectangular equation of the line.

20. The positive unit normal to a line is

$$\mathbf{n} = \frac{1}{\sqrt{5}}\mathbf{i} + \frac{2}{\sqrt{5}}\mathbf{j}.$$

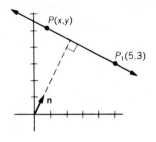

If the point $P_1 = (5, 3)$ is a point on the line, as in the figure, what is a rectangular equation of the line? [*Hint:* A point $P = (x, y)$ is on the line if and only if $\mathbf{n} \cdot \overrightarrow{P_1 P} = 0$.]

Calculator Problem

Find the distance from the origin to the line

$$7.48x + 3.81y - 18.44 = 0$$

to the nearest hundredth of a unit.

15-5 The Distance from a Point to a Line

We can now use Theorem 15-6 to derive a formula for the distance from a point $P_1 = (x_1, y_1)$ to the line $ax + by + c = 0$.

Referring to Fig. 13, we see that

$$d_1 = \mathbf{n} \cdot \overrightarrow{OP_1} = \frac{ax_1 + by_1}{\pm\sqrt{a^2 + b^2}}$$

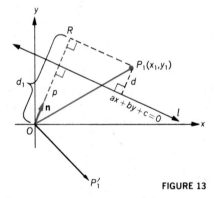

FIGURE 13

is the length of $\overline{OR}$, the projection of $\overrightarrow{OP_1}$ on the positive unit normal to the line l. The distance d_1 may be positive, as is the case for the point P_1 in the figure, or negative, as is the case for the point P_1', but in each case the distance d is

$$d = |\mathbf{n} \cdot \overrightarrow{OP_1} - p|$$

$$= \left| \frac{ax_1 + by_1}{\pm\sqrt{a^2 + b^2}} - \frac{-c}{\pm\sqrt{a^2 + b^2}} \right|$$

$$= \frac{|ax_1 + by_1 + c|}{\sqrt{a^2 + b^2}}.$$

This proves the following theorem.

Theorem 15-7 *The distance d from the point (x_1, y_1) to the line $ax + by + c = 0$ is*

$$d = \frac{|ax_1 + by_1 + c|}{\sqrt{a^2 + b^2}}.$$

Remark

We can get even more information from this theorem if we interpret the expression

$$\frac{ax_1 + by_1 + c}{\sqrt{a^2 + b^2}}. \tag{1}$$

The numerator of this expression will be positive, negative, or zero depending upon the relative positions of the point P_1, the line, and the origin. If $P_1 = (x_1, y_1)$ is any point, and expression (1) has the same sign as

$$\frac{c}{\sqrt{a^2 + b^2}},$$

then P_1 and the origin are on the same side of the line. If the signs are different, then P_1 is on the opposite side of the line from the origin. For $P_1 = (0, 0)$, we get the directed distance from the origin to the line, which may be positive, negative, or zero.

Example 1 The distance from the point $(-3, 2)$ to the line $2x - y + 4 = 0$ is

$$d = \frac{|2(-3) - 2 + 4|}{\sqrt{5}} = \frac{|-4|}{\sqrt{5}} = \frac{4}{\sqrt{5}}.$$

Because $2 \cdot 0 - 0 + 4 > 0$, whereas $2(-3) - 2 + 4 < 0$, the point $(-3, 2)$ and the origin $(0, 0)$ are on opposite sides of the line $2x - y + 4 = 0$, as may be seen from Fig. 14.

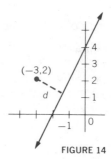

FIGURE 14

Finally, we can use the dot products of normals to lines to develop a formula for the cosines of the angles between two lines.

It is not difficult to show that the angles between two lines are congruent to the angles between the normals to the lines. Applying Theorem 15-1, we obtain the following theorem.

Theorem 15-8 *The cosines of the angles between the lines $l_1: a_1x + b_1y + c_1 = 0$ and $l_2: a_2x + b_2y + c_2 = 0$ are (see Fig. 15)*

$$\cos \theta = \frac{a_1a_2 + b_1b_2}{\pm \sqrt{a_1^2 + b_1^2}\sqrt{a_2^2 + b_2^2}}.$$

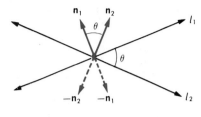

FIGURE 15

The proof of Theorem 15-8 is left to the student.

Example 2 Find the cosines of the angles between the lines $l_1: x + 2y - 7 = 0$ and $l_2: 3x - 2y + 10 = 0$ (Fig. 16).

Solution.

$$\cos \theta = \frac{1(3) + 2(-2)}{\pm \sqrt{5}\sqrt{13}}$$

$$= \frac{-1}{\pm \sqrt{5}\sqrt{13}} \doteq \pm 0.1240$$

If θ is acute, we choose the positive value of the cosine. The negative value is the cosine of $(\pi - \theta)$. In this example $\theta = \text{Arcos } 0.1240 = 1.446$ (82.9°).

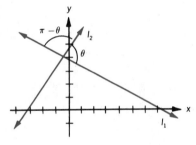

FIGURE 16

Problems

Set A

Find the distance to the line $3x - 2y + 12 = 0$ from each of the following points. Draw the line and plot each point.

1. $(1, 3)$

2. $(-1, 7)$

3. $(0, 0)$

4. $(-2, 3)$

5. $(2, -2)$

6. $(-3, -2)$

7. $(2, 9)$

8. $(-4, 4)$

Find the cosines of the angles between the following pairs of lines. Then find the measures of the angles. Draw figures in each case.

9. $x - 3y - 5 = 0$ and $x + y - 1 = 0$

10. $2x + 5y = 10$ and $y = 2$

11. $y = x$ and $x = 3$

12. $3x + 4y + 4 = 0$ and $4x - 3y - 10 = 0$

13. $x + y = 6$ and $x - 2y = 1$

14. $y = \frac{1}{2}x + 4$ and $y = -\frac{1}{3}x - 2$

Set B

15. Find the distance from the point $(-2, 3)$ to the line $3x - 2y + 1 = 0$. Is $(-2, 3)$ on the same side of the line as the origin, or is it on the opposite side?

16. A rectangular equation of a line is $4x - 3y + 12 = 0$. Find the coordinates of the point P_0 that is the foot of the perpendicular from the origin to the line. [*Hint:* $\overrightarrow{OP_0} = p \cdot \mathbf{n}$.]

17. Write equations of the two lines parallel to the line through $(1, 2)$ and $(4, 6)$ that are a distance of 3 units from the given line. Draw a figure.

18. Find the cosines of the angles between $x + 3y - 6 = 0$ and $4x - y + 8 = 0$.

19. Show from angle considerations that the lines $7x - 4y + 3 = 0$, $3x + 2y + 5 = 0$, and $x - 8y + 45 = 0$ intersect in the vertices of an isosceles triangle.

20. A triangle has its base vertices at the points $(-5, 6)$ and $(-1, 3)$. The area of the triangle is 10 square units. Find an equation satisfied by those points and only those points that could be the third vertex of the triangle.

Set C

21. Prove that the equation $bx - ay = k$, where k is arbitrary, represents a line normal to the line $ax + by + c = 0$.

22. Use the result of Problem 21 to write an equation of a line that is perpendicular to $6x + 2y + 5 = 0$ that contains the point $(4, -2)$. Draw a figure.

23. Find an equation of a line perpendicular to $3x - y - 5 = 0$ that contains the point $(-3, 2)$. Draw a figure.

24. Find an equation of a line perpendicular to $x - 4y - 1 = 0$ that contains the origin. Draw a figure.

25. Prove Theorem 15-8.

26. Find equations and draw figures of the two lines that bisect the angles formed by the lines

$$3x - 4y + 3 = 0 \quad \text{and} \quad 12x + 5y - 5 = 0.$$

[*Hint:* A point (x, y) is on a bisector if and only if it is equidistant from each line.]

27. Find an equation of the line bisecting the smaller angle between the lines $x + 3y - 10 = 0$ and $3x + y - 14 = 0$.

Calculator Problem

Find the cosines and the measures of the angles between the lines

$$1.8x - 3.6y + 6.4 = 0$$

and

$$4.3x + 0.8y - 9.5 = 0.$$

15-6   Normals to Planes

We now pursue the same ideas that were presented in Section 15-4, except that in this section, we shall apply them to space.

In our study of space in Chapter 13, we assumed that every plane has a linear equation of the form

$$Ax + By + Cz + D = 0, \qquad (1)$$

where not all the real numbers A, B, and C are 0. We shall prove this theorem now.

As was the case for lines in the xy-plane, every plane has two unit vectors that are normal to the plane. The unit vector that has a position vector pointing toward the plane is called the *positive unit normal* to the plane.

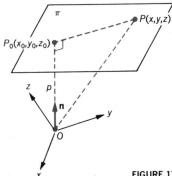

FIGURE 17

Let us suppose that we have a plane π with a positive unit normal $\mathbf{n} = c_1\mathbf{i} + c_2\mathbf{j} + c_3\mathbf{k}$, where c_1, c_2, and c_3 are the direction cosines of $\mathbf{n}$. (See Fig. 17.) Let $P_0 = (x_0, y_0, z_0)$ be the foot of the perpendicular from the origin O to the plane π. Then a point $P = (x, y, z)$ is a point in the plane if and only if

$$\mathbf{n} \cdot \overrightarrow{P_0P} = 0.$$

Since $\overrightarrow{P_0P} = (x - x_0)\mathbf{i} + (y - y_0)\mathbf{j} + (z - z_0)\mathbf{k}$,

$$\mathbf{n} \cdot \overrightarrow{P_0P} = c_1(x - x_0) + c_2(y - y_0) + c_3(z - z_0) = 0 \qquad (2)$$

or, equivalently,

$$c_1x + c_2y + c_3z - (c_1x_0 + c_2y_0 + c_3z_0) = 0. \qquad (3)$$

In equation (3), we see that

$$c_1x_0 + c_2y_0 + c_3z_0 = \mathbf{n} \cdot \overrightarrow{OP_0} = p,$$

where p is the perpendicular distance from the origin to the plane π.

Therefore an equation of the plane is

$$c_1x + c_2y + c_3z - p = 0. \qquad (4)$$

Clearly, if $k \neq 0$, an equivalent equation is

$$kc_1x + kc_2y + kc_3z - kp = 0. \qquad (5)$$

We have shown in equations (4) and (5) that the plane π has an equation of the form of equation (1): $Ax + By + Cz + D = 0$.

Conversely, let us suppose that equation (1) is given with not all A, B, and C equal to 0. There are exactly two units vectors with direction cosines proportional to the numbers A, B, and C. These vectors are

$$\mathbf{n} = \frac{A\mathbf{i}}{\pm\sqrt{A^2+B^2+C^2}} + \frac{B\mathbf{j}}{\pm\sqrt{A^2+B^2+C^2}} + \frac{C\mathbf{k}}{\pm\sqrt{A^2+B^2+C^2}}.$$

Dividing each term of equation (1) by $\pm\sqrt{A^2+B^2+C^2}$, we obtain

$$\frac{Ax}{\sigma} + \frac{By}{\sigma} + \frac{Cy}{\sigma} + \frac{D}{\sigma} = 0, \tag{6}$$

where

$$\sigma = \pm\sqrt{A^2+B^2+C^2}.$$

Comparing, we see that equation (6) has the same form as equation (4) except that we must choose the sign of the radical so that the coefficients of x, y, and z will be the components of the *positive unit normal* to the plane we seek. We also observe that we must have

$$p = \frac{-D}{\pm\sqrt{A^2+B^2+C^2}},$$

and since p must be ≥ 0, this will be the case if we choose the sign of the radical opposite to that of D. Hence we have proved that equation (1) is equivalent to equation (4) which is an equation of a plane π.

The following theorem gives a resume of what has been proved.

Theorem 15-9   (a) *The set of all points* (x, y, z) *satisfying an equation* $Ax + By + Cz + D = 0$, *where not all of* A, B, *and* C *are* 0, *is a plane; conversely, every plane has an equation of this form.*

(b) *The plane* $Ax + By + Cz + D = 0$ *has a positive unit normal*

$$\mathbf{n} = \frac{A\mathbf{i}}{\pm\sigma} + \frac{B\mathbf{j}}{\pm\sigma} + \frac{C\mathbf{k}}{\pm\sigma},$$

where $\sigma = \sqrt{A^2+B^2+C^2}$, *and the sign of* σ *is chosen opposite to that of* D.

(c) *The distance from the origin to the plane* $Ax + By + Cz + D = 0$ *is*

$$p = \frac{|D|}{\sqrt{A^2+B^2+C^2}}.$$

(d) *If a plane has a positive unit normal* $\mathbf{n} = c_1\mathbf{i} + c_2\mathbf{j} + c_3\mathbf{k}$ *and is at a distance* p *from the origin, then an equation of the plane is*

$$c_1x + c_2y + c_3z - p = 0.$$

Example 1 The positive unit normal to the plane $x - 2y + 2z - 6 = 0$ is
$$\mathbf{n} = \tfrac{1}{3}\mathbf{i} + (-\tfrac{2}{3})\mathbf{j} + \tfrac{2}{3}\mathbf{k}.$$
The distance from the origin to the plane is $p = |-6|/3 = 2$.

2 Find an equation of a plane that has a positive unit normal
$$\mathbf{n} = -\tfrac{6}{7}\mathbf{i} + \tfrac{2}{7}\mathbf{j} + (-\tfrac{3}{7})\mathbf{k}$$
and is 4 units from the origin.

Solution. From Theorem 15-9(d) we have for an equation of the plane
$$-\tfrac{6}{7}x + \tfrac{2}{7}y + (-\tfrac{3}{7})z - 4 = 0$$
or, equivalently, $6x - 2y + 3z + 28 = 0$.

Using the ideas developed in Theorem 15-2, we can now derive a formula for the distance from a point to a plane which will be quite analogous to the corresponding formula developed for the distance from a point to a line.

Theorem 15-10 *The distance from a point $P_1 = (x_1, y_1, z_1)$ to the plane $Ax + By + Cz + D = 0$ is*
$$d = \frac{|Ax_1 + By_1 + Cz_1 + D|}{\sqrt{A^2 + B^2 + C^2}}.$$

Proof Let $\mathbf{n}$ be the positive unit normal to the plane and
$$d_1 = \mathbf{n} \cdot \overrightarrow{OP_1}$$
be the length of the projection of $\overrightarrow{OP_1}$ on $\mathbf{n}$. Then d_1 can be positive, as for the point P_1 in Fig. 18, or zero, or negative, as for the point P_1' in the same figure. If d is the distance from P_1 to the plane, then in every case we have $d = |d_1 - p|$, where p is the distance from the origin to the plane. Now,
$$d_1 = \frac{Ax_1 + By_1 + Cz_1}{\pm\sqrt{A^2 + B^2 + C^2}}$$
and
$$p = \frac{-D}{\pm\sqrt{A^2 + B^2 + C^2}},$$
where the sign of the radical is chosen opposite to that of D. Hence
$$d = \frac{|Ax_1 + By_1 + Cz_1 + D|}{\sqrt{A^2 + B^2 + C^2}}.$$

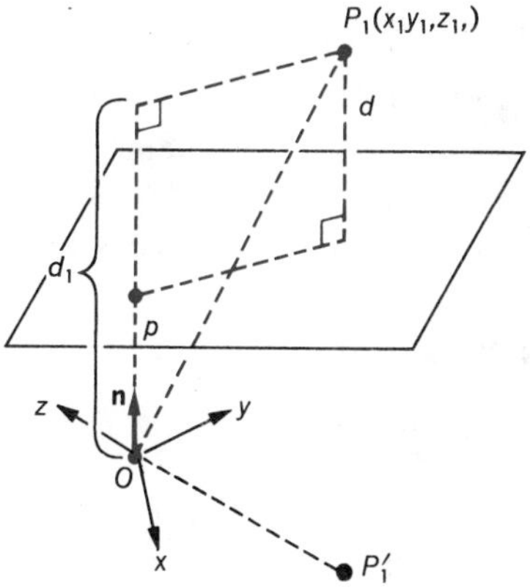

FIGURE 18

We observe that for $P_1 = (0, 0, 0)$, we have the formula for the distance from the origin to the plane,

$$d = p = \frac{|D|}{\sqrt{A^2 + B^2 + C^2}}.$$

If $P_2 = (x_2, y_2, z_2)$ is any other point and $Ax_2 + By_2 + Cz_2 + D$ has the same sign as D, then P_2 is on the same side of the plane as the origin, whereas if they are opposite in sign, P_2 is on the opposite side of the plane from the origin.

Example 3 The distance from the point whose coordinates are $(2, 3, 4)$ to the plane $3x + 3y + 4z - 12 = 0$ is

$$d = \frac{|3 \cdot 2 + 3 \cdot 3 + 4 \cdot 4 - 12|}{\sqrt{34}}$$

$$= \frac{|19|}{\sqrt{34}} = \frac{19}{\sqrt{34}}.$$

The distance from the origin to the plane is

$$p = \frac{|-12|}{\sqrt{34}} = \frac{12}{\sqrt{34}}.$$

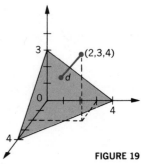

FIGURE 19

Since 19 and -12 are opposite in sign, we conclude that the point $(2, 3, 4)$ is on the opposite side of the plane from the origin. A sketch of a portion of the plane and the points in Fig. 19 substantiates, approximately, these results.

Problems

Set A

Find the distance from the origin to each of the following planes. Sketch a portion of the planes.

1. $x + y - z + 3 = 0$

2. $20x - 5y - 4z + 63 = 0$

3. $\sqrt{3}\, x + 9y - \sqrt{21} = 0$

4. $13x + 16 = 0$

5. $-6x - \dfrac{1}{\sqrt{2}}y - 2z + 18 = 0$

6. $\dfrac{1}{\sqrt{3}}x - \dfrac{1}{\sqrt{3}}y + \dfrac{1}{\sqrt{3}}z - 7 = 0$

7. $x + y + z = 6$

8. $5x - 2y - z = 20.$

Find the distance from each of the following points to the plane $x - 4y - 8z + 16 = 0$. Sketch.

9. $(2, 3, 4)$ 10. $(0, 0, 1)$ 11. $(-4, 1, 1)$

12. $(1, 5, 0)$ 13. $(-10, \frac{1}{2}, \frac{1}{2})$ 14. $(0, 0, 10^m)$

Set B

Find the distance from each of the given points to the planes and determine whether the point is on the same side of the plane as the origin or on the opposite side.

15. $(1, 1, 2)$ and $x + y + 2z - 4 = 0$

16. $(3, 0, -2)$ and $2x - 3y + z - 3 = 0$

17. $(-1, 2, 1)$ and $4x + 4y + 2z + 7 = 0$

18. $(-2, 3, 0)$ and $5x + 2y - 10 = 0$

19. $(2, 2, 2)$ and $3x + 4z - 12 = 0$

20. $(-5, -3, 6)$ and $x - 3y + 4z - 2 = 0$

21. What are the direction cosines of the positive unit normal to the plane $2x - y - z + a = 0$ if $a > 0$? if $a < 0$?

22. A plane has a positive unit normal

$$\mathbf{n} = \tfrac{1}{3}\mathbf{i} - \tfrac{2}{3}\mathbf{j} + \tfrac{2}{3}\mathbf{k}$$

and is 3 units from the origin. What is a rectangular equation of the plane?

23. A line has direction cosines

$$-\frac{1}{\sqrt{2}}, \quad -\frac{1}{\sqrt{3}}, \quad \frac{1}{\sqrt{6}}$$

and lies in a plane. If $P = (2, 3, 4)$, is $\overrightarrow{OP}$ perpendicular to that plane?

24. A rectangular equation of a plane is $3x - 2y - 4z - 12 = 0$. Find the coordinates of the point P_0 in the plane that is the foot of the perpendicular from the origin to the plane.

25. Find equations and sketch a picture of the two planes that are parallel to the plane $x - 2y + 2z - 6 = 0$ and are 4 units from the given plane.

26. A plane has a positive unit normal

$$\mathbf{n} = \frac{1}{\sqrt{14}}\mathbf{i} - \frac{2}{\sqrt{14}}\mathbf{j} + \frac{3}{\sqrt{14}}\mathbf{k},$$

and the point $P = (-2, 4, 5)$ lies in the plane. What is a rectangular equation of the plane?

27. Show that the planes $4x - 3y + z - 7 = 0$, and $4x - 3y + z + 6 = 0$ are parallel planes and find the distance between them.

28. Show that the planes $3x - 2y + z + 5 = 0$, and $-9x + 6y - 3z + 14 = 0$ are parallel planes and find the distance between them.

29. Show that a plane parallel to the plane

$$Ax + By + Cz + D = 0$$

and containing the point (x_0, y_0, z_0) has an equation

$$A(x - x_0) + B(y - y_0) + C(z - z_0) = 0.$$

Set C

30. Angles between two planes are defined as the angles between normals to the planes. What are the cosines of the angles between the planes whose equations are

$$2x + 3y - z + 5 = 0$$

and

$$-x + y + z + 1 = 0?$$

31. What are the measures of the angles formed by the plane $x + y - 2z = 0$ and the xy-coordinate plane?

32. The point $P = (x, y, z)$ is equidistant from the planes $2x - y - z + 6 = 0$ and $x + 2y - 7z + 12 = 0$. Write an equation satisfied by the coordinates (x, y, z). Prove that the set of all such points lies on two planes. What are these planes geometrically?

33. A plane is parallel to the plane $x - y + 3z = 1$ and is at a distance of 3 units from the point $P = (2, -1, 1)$. Find an equation of the plane. (There are two correct answers.)

34. Show that the planes $-2x + 5y - 3z + 8 = 0$ and $7x + 4y + 2z + 1 = 0$ are perpendicular planes.

Calculator Problem

Find the distance from the point $P = (-1.5, 3.8, -4.6)$ to the plane

$$\sqrt{3}x + 3.7y - \sqrt[3]{7}z + 0.8 = 0.$$

Vector Multiplication

In Section 15–3 the dot product of two vectors was defined to be a real number. In this section we define a new operation on vectors which will combine two 3-space vectors to produce another 3-space vector. We call this new operation *vector multiplication* and describe it in an intuitive manner.

Suppose $\mathbf{a} = \overrightarrow{OA}$ and $\mathbf{b} = \overrightarrow{OB}$ are vectors, and θ is the measure of the angle between them, $0 < \theta < \pi$. Consider the parallelogram $OAPB$ determined by these vectors. (See Fig. 20.) We define the *vector product* of $\mathbf{a}$ and $\mathbf{b}$, denoted by $\mathbf{a} \times \mathbf{b}$, to be a vector $\mathbf{c}$ that is perpendicular to the plane of $\mathbf{a}$ and $\mathbf{b}$. The magnitude of $\mathbf{c}$ is the real number that is the area of the parallelogram determined by $\mathbf{a}$ and

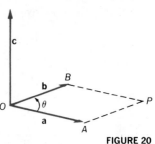

FIGURE 20

$\mathbf{b}$. Of course, there are two vectors perpendicular to the plane of $\mathbf{a}$ and $\mathbf{b}$, and so we must decide (if we wish $\mathbf{c}$ to be unique) which of these two vectors shall be the vector product of $\mathbf{a}$ and $\mathbf{b}$.

It is convenient to choose vector $\mathbf{c}$ as pointing in the same direction as is an advancing right-threaded screw when it is turned, or rotated, from $\mathbf{a}$ to $\mathbf{b}$ through the angle having measure θ. (See Fig. 21.)

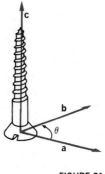

FIGURE 21

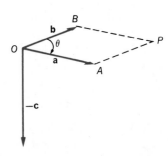

FIGURE 22

If we consider $\mathbf{b} \times \mathbf{a}$, then $\mathbf{b} \times \mathbf{a}$ would be a vector that is opposite in direction to $\mathbf{c}$. (See Fig. 22.) Thus

$$\mathbf{a} \times \mathbf{b} = \mathbf{c} \quad \text{and} \quad \mathbf{b} \times \mathbf{a} = -\mathbf{c}.$$

Example 1   Find $\mathbf{i} \times \mathbf{j}$.

Solution. Vectors $\mathbf{i}$ and $\mathbf{j}$ determine a parallelogram whose area is 1. (See Fig. 23.) Using the "right-hand" rule, we find that

$$\mathbf{i} \times \mathbf{j} = 1 \cdot \mathbf{k} = \mathbf{k}.$$

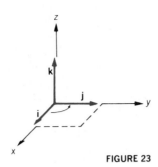

FIGURE 23

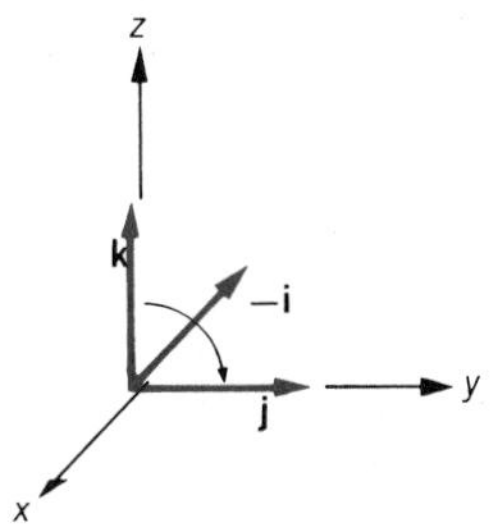

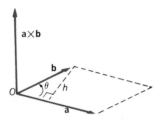

FIGURE 24

Example 2   From Fig. 24, we see that

$$\mathbf{k} \times \mathbf{j} = -\mathbf{i}.$$

3   If **a** and **b** are vectors and θ is the measure of the angle between them, then the area of the parallelogram determined by **a** and **b** is

$$|\mathbf{a}|(|\mathbf{b}| \sin \theta).$$

(See Fig. 25.) Hence

$$|\mathbf{a} \times \mathbf{b}| = |\mathbf{a}| \, |\mathbf{b}| \sin \theta.$$

FIGURE 25

Definition 15-2   If **a** and **b** are non-zero vectors, then the *vector product* of **a** and **b**, denoted by **a** × **b**, is the vector **c** that is perpendicular to the plane determined by **a** and **b** and whose direction is chosen as described above. The magnitude of **a** × **b** is $|\mathbf{a}| \, |\mathbf{b}| \sin \theta$, where θ is the measure of the angle between **a** and **b**.

The vector product of two vectors is also called the *cross product,* or *outer product,* of the vectors, to distinguish it from the inner, or dot, product. (See the historical note at the end of this chapter.)

Remarks   1. Note that $\mathbf{c} = (|\mathbf{a}| \, |\mathbf{b}| \sin \theta)\mathbf{n}$, where **n** is the unit vector in the direction of **c**.

2. If two vectors have the same direction or are opposite in direction, the parallelogram determined by the vectors will be a degenerate parallelogram and will have area zero. Therefore the vector product is the null vector.

Problems

Set A

1. Find the vector products for the table.

×	i	j	k
i			
j			
k			

Find the vector that is described as the vector product indicated. Sketch a picture of the vector in each case.

2. $2\mathbf{i} \times 3\mathbf{j}$ **3.** $-2\mathbf{i} \times -3\mathbf{j}$ **4.** $2\mathbf{i} \times -3\mathbf{j}$

5. $\mathbf{j} \times 4\mathbf{k}$ **6.** $(\mathbf{i} \times \mathbf{j}) \times \mathbf{k}$ **7.** $\mathbf{i} \times (\mathbf{j} \times \mathbf{k})$

Set B

8. Find $(3\mathbf{i} - 2\mathbf{j}) \times (2\mathbf{i} + 3\mathbf{j})$. Sketch the vectors.

9. Find $3\mathbf{i} \times (3\mathbf{i} + 3\mathbf{j})$. [*Hint:* What is the angle between the two vectors?]

10. Find $2\mathbf{j} \times (\sqrt{3}\,\mathbf{j} + \mathbf{k})$. What is the angle between the vectors?

11. Is $(\mathbf{i} \times 2\mathbf{j}) \times 3\mathbf{i} = \mathbf{i} \times (2\mathbf{j} \times 3\mathbf{i})$?

12. Is $(\mathbf{i} \times \mathbf{i}) \times \mathbf{j} = \mathbf{i} \times (\mathbf{i} \times \mathbf{j})$?

13. Is vector multiplication associative?

14. Is vector multiplication commutative?

15. If $|\mathbf{a}| = 4$ and $|\mathbf{b}| = 6$ and the angle between the vectors is $\pi/6$, what is the magnitude of $\mathbf{a} \times \mathbf{b}$?

16. Show that if $|\mathbf{r}| = \sqrt{2}$ and $|\mathbf{s}| = \sqrt{2}$ and the angle between the vectors is $5\pi/6$ then $\mathbf{r} \times \mathbf{s}$ is a vector of unit length.

Set C

17. Show that if $\mathbf{a}$ and $\mathbf{b}$ have position vectors $a_1\mathbf{i} + a_2\mathbf{j} + a_3\mathbf{k}$ and $b_1\mathbf{i} + b_2\mathbf{j} + b_3\mathbf{k}$, respectively, then an equation of the plane of $\mathbf{a}$ and $\mathbf{b}$ is

$$(a_2b_3 - a_3b_2)x + (a_3b_1 - a_1b_3)y + (a_1b_2 - a_2b_1)z = 0.$$

18. Show that the plane of Problem 17 has a unit normal

$$\mathbf{u} = \frac{(a_2b_3 - a_3b_2)}{d}\mathbf{i} + \frac{(a_3b_1 - a_1b_3)}{d}\mathbf{j} + \frac{(a_1b_2 - a_2b_1)}{d}\mathbf{k},$$

where
$$d = [(a_2b_3 - a_3b_2)^2 + (a_3b_1 - a_1b_3)^2 + (a_1b_2 - a_2b_1)^2.]^{1/2}$$

Calculator Problem

Find the angle between the vectors

$$\mathbf{a} = 3\mathbf{i} + 2\mathbf{j} + \mathbf{k}$$

and

$$\mathbf{b} = 4\mathbf{i} - 3\mathbf{j} + 5\mathbf{k}.$$

Then compute $|\mathbf{a} \times \mathbf{b}|$.

Use the results of Problems 17 and 18 to find the components of the vector product of $\mathbf{a}$ and $\mathbf{b}$.

The Computation of Vector Products

It is desirable to be able to compute the vector product of two vectors in terms of the components of the two vectors. The following theorem gives a formula for doing this.

Theorem 15-11 *If*

$$\mathbf{a} = a_1\mathbf{i} + a_2\mathbf{j} + a_3\mathbf{k} \qquad and \qquad \mathbf{b} = b_1\mathbf{i} + b_2\mathbf{j} + b_3\mathbf{k},$$

then

$$\begin{aligned} \mathbf{v} &= \mathbf{a} \times \mathbf{b} \\ &= (a_2b_3 - a_3b_2)\mathbf{i} + (a_3b_1 - a_1b_3)\mathbf{j} + (a_1b_2 - a_2b_1)\mathbf{k}. \end{aligned} \tag{1}$$

Proof Although it is possible to derive formula (1) without knowing it in advance, it is much easier to simply *verify* that (1) is, indeed, correct. This is what we shall do.

If either $\mathbf{a} = \mathbf{0}$ or $\mathbf{b} = \mathbf{0}$, then $\mathbf{a} \times \mathbf{b} = \mathbf{0}$ and formula (1) also gives $\mathbf{0}$. Suppose now that neither $\mathbf{a}$ nor $\mathbf{b}$ is $\mathbf{0}$ but that $\mathbf{b}$ has the same direction as, or the opposite direction from, $\mathbf{a}$. Then $\mathbf{b} = \lambda\mathbf{a}$ for some real number λ, and $\mathbf{a} \times \mathbf{b} = \mathbf{0}$. But if $\mathbf{b} = \lambda\mathbf{a}$, then $b_1 = \lambda a_1$, $b_2 = \lambda a_2$, $b_3 = \lambda a_3$, and the right-hand member of (1) is also $\mathbf{0}$. Hence in this case also, $\mathbf{a} \times \mathbf{b}$ is given by formula (1).

Suppose now that neither $\mathbf{a}$ nor $\mathbf{b}$ is $\mathbf{0}$ and $\mathbf{b} \neq \lambda\mathbf{a}$ for any real number λ. Then not all the numbers

$$a_2b_3 - a_3b_2, \qquad a_3b_1 - a_1b_3, \qquad a_1b_2 - a_2b_1 \tag{2}$$

are 0.* Therefore the vector $\mathbf{v}$ defined by

$$\mathbf{v} = (a_2b_3 - a_3b_2)\mathbf{i} + (a_3b_1 - a_1b_3)\mathbf{j} + (a_1b_2 - a_2b_1)\mathbf{k} \tag{3}$$

is not the zero vector.

We shall now verify by Theorem 15-3 that $\mathbf{v}$ is perpendicular to both $\mathbf{a}$ and $\mathbf{b}$ (Fig. 26), and therefore to the plane of $\mathbf{a}$ and $\mathbf{b}$. This will show that $\mathbf{v}$ has either the correct direction or the opposite direction.

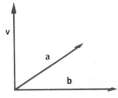

FIGURE 26

---

*This may be seen as follows. Since $\mathbf{a} \neq \mathbf{0}$, at least one of its components is not 0. Suppose that $a_1 \neq 0$ and that all the numbers in (2) are 0. Then

$$b_2 = \frac{a_2b_1}{a_1}, \qquad b_3 = \frac{a_3b_1}{a_1},$$

and

$$\mathbf{b} = b_1\mathbf{i} + \frac{a_2b_1}{a_1}\mathbf{j} + \frac{a_3b_1}{a_1}\mathbf{k} = \frac{b_1}{a_1}(a_1\mathbf{i} + a_2\mathbf{j} + a_3\mathbf{k}) = \frac{b_1}{a_1}\mathbf{a}.$$

But this equation asserts that $\mathbf{b} = \lambda\mathbf{a}$, with $\lambda = b_1/a_1$, which is contrary to assumption. If $a_1 = 0$, then either a_2 or a_3 does not equal 0, and a similar argument leads to a contradiction. Therefore if $\mathbf{b} \neq \lambda\mathbf{a}$, not all of the numbers (2) are 0.

We have

$$\mathbf{v} \cdot \mathbf{a} = (a_2 b_3 - a_3 b_2) a_1 + (a_3 b_1 - a_1 b_3) a_2 + (a_1 b_2 - a_2 b_1) a_3 = 0,$$
$$\mathbf{v} \cdot \mathbf{b} = (a_2 b_3 - a_3 b_2) b_1 + (a_3 b_1 - a_1 b_3) b_2 + (a_1 b_2 - a_2 b_1) b_3 = 0, \tag{4}$$

where it is easily checked that the right-hand members of (4) are 0.

We now verify that $\mathbf{v}$ has the correct magnitude. We have

$$|\mathbf{v}|^2 = (a_2 b_3 - a_3 b_2)^2 + (a_3 b_1 - a_1 b_3)^2 + (a_1 b_2 - a_2 b_1)^2$$

$$= a_2^2 b_3^2 + a_3^2 b_2^2 + a_3^2 b_1^2 + a_1^2 b_3^2 + a_1^2 b_2^2 + a_2^2 b_1^2$$
$$- 2a_2 a_3 b_2 b_3 - 2a_1 a_3 b_1 b_3 - 2a_1 a_2 b_1 b_2, \tag{5}$$

and, if θ is the measure of the angle between $\mathbf{a}$ and $\mathbf{b}$,

$$|\mathbf{a} \times \mathbf{b}|^2 = |\mathbf{a}|^2 |\mathbf{b}|^2 \sin^2 \theta = |\mathbf{a}|^2 |\mathbf{b}|^2 (1 - \cos^2 \theta)$$

$$= |\mathbf{a}|^2 |\mathbf{b}|^2 \left(1 - \frac{(\mathbf{a} \cdot \mathbf{b})^2}{|\mathbf{a}|^2 |\mathbf{b}|^2} \right)$$

$$= |\mathbf{a}|^2 |\mathbf{b}|^2 - (\mathbf{a} \cdot \mathbf{b})^2$$

$$= (a_1^2 + a_2^2 + a_3^2)(b_1^2 + b_2^2 + b_3^2) - (a_1 b_1 + a_2 b_2 + a_3 b_3)^2$$

$$= a_2^2 b_3^2 + a_3^2 b_2^2 + a_3^2 b_1^2 + a_1^2 b_3^2 + a_1^2 b_2^2 + a_2^2 b_1^2$$
$$- 2a_2 a_3 b_2 b_3 - 2a_1 a_3 b_1 b_3 - 2a_1 a_2 b_1 b_2. \tag{6}$$

Comparison of (5) and (6) shows that $|\mathbf{v}|^2 = |\mathbf{a} \times \mathbf{b}|^2$.

We have now proved that $\mathbf{v}$ is the correct magnitude and is perpendicular to $\mathbf{a}$ and $\mathbf{b}$. To verify that $\mathbf{v}$ has the correct one of the two possible directions requires an argument based on continuity which we omit here. For our purpose it suffices to observe that the formula for $\mathbf{v}$ gives $\mathbf{a} \times \mathbf{b}$ when $\mathbf{a}$ and $\mathbf{b}$ are pairs of the unit vectors $\mathbf{i}$, $\mathbf{j}$, $\mathbf{k}$. This last is left as an exercise for the student.

Remark

The components of $\mathbf{a} \times \mathbf{b}$ may seem difficult to remember, but after determinants are studied in Chapter 16 it will be easy to show that $\mathbf{a} \times \mathbf{b}$ can be expressed as a third-order determinant, namely,

$$\mathbf{a} \times \mathbf{b} = \begin{vmatrix} \mathbf{i} & \mathbf{j} & \mathbf{k} \\ a_1 & a_2 & a_3 \\ b_1 & b_2 & b_3 \end{vmatrix}$$

$$= (a_2 b_3 - a_3 b_2)\mathbf{i} + (a_3 b_1 - a_1 b_3)\mathbf{j} + (a_1 b_2 - a_2 b_1)\mathbf{k}$$

Furthermore, we may show that vector multiplication is distributive with respect to addition of vectors so that memorization of the components of $\mathbf{a} \times \mathbf{b}$ is not really necessary.

Theorem 15-12 *If* **a**, **b** *and* **c** *are any vectors,*

$$\mathbf{a} \times (\mathbf{b} + \mathbf{c}) = (\mathbf{a} \times \mathbf{b}) + (\mathbf{a} \times \mathbf{c}).$$

Proof Let $\mathbf{a} = a_1\mathbf{i} + a_2\mathbf{j} + a_3\mathbf{k}$, $\mathbf{b} = b_1\mathbf{i} + b_2\mathbf{j} + b_3\mathbf{k}$, and $\mathbf{c} = c_1\mathbf{i} + c_2\mathbf{j} + c_3\mathbf{k}$.

$\mathbf{a} \times (\mathbf{b} + \mathbf{c}) = \mathbf{a} \times [(b_1 + c_1)\mathbf{i} + (b_2 + c_2)\mathbf{j} + (b_3 + c_3)\mathbf{k}]$

$\quad = [a_2(b_3 + c_3) - a_3(b_2 + c_2)]\mathbf{i} + [a_3(b_1 + c_1) - a_1(b_3 + c_3)]\mathbf{j}$
$\quad\quad + [a_1(b_2 + c_2) - a_2(b_1 + c_1)]\mathbf{k}$ Theorem 15-11

$\quad = [(a_2b_3 - a_3b_2)\mathbf{i} + (a_3b_1 - a_1b_3)\mathbf{j} + (a_1b_2 - a_2b_1)\mathbf{k}]$
$\quad\quad + [(a_2c_3 - a_3c_2)\mathbf{i} + (a_3c_1 - a_1c_3)\mathbf{j} + (a_1c_2 - a_2c_1)\mathbf{k}]$

Associativity and commutativity for addition of vectors and distributivity

$\quad = (\mathbf{a} \times \mathbf{b}) + (\mathbf{a} \times \mathbf{c}).$ Theorem 15-11

Example Find $\mathbf{a} \times \mathbf{b}$ where $\mathbf{a} = 2\mathbf{i}$ and $\mathbf{b} = (4\mathbf{j} + 3\mathbf{k})$.

Solution.

$\mathbf{a} \times \mathbf{b} = 2\mathbf{i} \times (4\mathbf{j} + 3\mathbf{k})$
$\quad = (2\mathbf{i} \times 4\mathbf{j}) + (2\mathbf{i} \times 3\mathbf{k})$
$\quad = 8\mathbf{k} + (-6)\mathbf{j} = -6\mathbf{j} + 8\mathbf{k}$

The sketch in Fig. 27 substantiates the results.

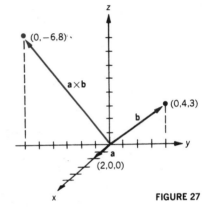

FIGURE 27

Problems

Set A

Use Theorem 15-11 to find the vector products below.

1. $(\mathbf{i} + \mathbf{j} - \mathbf{k}) \times (2\mathbf{i} - \mathbf{j} + \mathbf{k})$

2. $(2\mathbf{i} + \mathbf{j}) \times (3\mathbf{j} + 2\mathbf{k})$

3. $(4\mathbf{i} - \mathbf{k}) \times (2\mathbf{i} - \mathbf{j})$

4. $(2\mathbf{i} + 3\mathbf{j} + 4\mathbf{k}) \times (\mathbf{i} - 2\mathbf{j} + 2\mathbf{k})$

5. $(-\mathbf{i} + 5\mathbf{j} + 3\mathbf{k}) \times (3\mathbf{i} + \mathbf{j} - 4\mathbf{k})$

6. $(\mathbf{i} + \mathbf{j} + \mathbf{k})(2\mathbf{i} - 2\mathbf{j} - 2\mathbf{k})$

7. Give the area of the parallelogram determined by the position vectors in Problems 1 through 6.

Set B

Use the distributive law for vector multiplication to compute the following cross products.

8. $2\mathbf{i} \times (\mathbf{j} + 3\mathbf{k})$

9. $3\mathbf{i} \times (\mathbf{i} + \mathbf{j} + \mathbf{k})$

10. $(3\mathbf{i} + \mathbf{j}) \times (4\mathbf{j} + \mathbf{k})$

11. $(\mathbf{i} + \mathbf{j} + \mathbf{k}) \times (3\mathbf{i})$

12. $(3\mathbf{i} - \mathbf{j} + \mathbf{k}) \times (\mathbf{i} + 2\mathbf{j} - 3\mathbf{k})$

13. $(2\mathbf{i} + \mathbf{j} + 4\mathbf{k}) \times (-3\mathbf{i} + \mathbf{j} + 2\mathbf{k})$

Set C

14. Is $\mathbf{a} \times (\mathbf{b} + \mathbf{c}) = (\mathbf{b} \times \mathbf{a}) + (\mathbf{c} \times \mathbf{a})$?

15. Let $\mathbf{r} = \mathbf{i} + 2\mathbf{j} + \mathbf{k}$ and $\mathbf{s} = -3\mathbf{i} - \mathbf{j} - 4\mathbf{k}$. Find $\mathbf{r} \times \mathbf{s}$ and $\mathbf{s} \times \mathbf{r}$. What do you notice about the two cross products?

16. Prove that the cross product of two vectors $\mathbf{a}$ and $\mathbf{b}$ is *anticommutative*, that is, show that $\mathbf{a} \times \mathbf{b} = -(\mathbf{b} \times \mathbf{a})$.

17. Let $\mathbf{a} = 2\mathbf{i} + \mathbf{j} - \mathbf{k}$, $\mathbf{b} = \mathbf{i} + 3\mathbf{j} + 4\mathbf{k}$ and $\mathbf{c} = -5\mathbf{i} - 2\mathbf{j} + 3\mathbf{k}$. Verify for these vectors that $\mathbf{a} \times (\mathbf{b} \times \mathbf{c}) = (\mathbf{a} \cdot \mathbf{c})\mathbf{b} - (\mathbf{a} \cdot \mathbf{b})\mathbf{c}$.

18. Show that if $\mathbf{a}$, $\mathbf{b}$, and $\mathbf{c}$ are the vectors of Problem 16, then

$$(\mathbf{a} \times \mathbf{b}) \times \mathbf{c} = (\mathbf{a} \cdot \mathbf{c})\mathbf{b} - (\mathbf{b} \cdot \mathbf{c})\mathbf{a}.$$

19. Verify that the formula for $\mathbf{v}$ in Theorem 15–11 gives the correct vector when $\mathbf{a} = \mathbf{i}$ and $\mathbf{b} = \mathbf{j}$, where $\mathbf{i}$ and $\mathbf{j}$ are the unit vectors.

Calculator Problem

Find $\mathbf{a} \times (\mathbf{b} + \mathbf{c})$ where

$$\mathbf{a} = 4.2\mathbf{i} + 3.5\mathbf{j} + 2.3\mathbf{k},$$
$$\mathbf{b} = 0.5\mathbf{i} - 1.2\mathbf{j} - 0.8\mathbf{k},$$
$$\mathbf{c} = -2.6\mathbf{i} + 7.3\mathbf{j} - 3.2\mathbf{k}.$$

15-9 Applications of Vector Products

We wish to consider three special applications of vector products. The first of these concerns *areas of parallelograms and triangles in space*. Let us suppose that B, A, and C are successive vertices of a parallelogram, as in Fig. 28. Then by the definition of vector multiplication,

$$\text{area } \square BACD = |\overrightarrow{AB} \times \overrightarrow{AC}|$$

and

$$\text{area } \triangle BAC = \tfrac{1}{2}|\overrightarrow{AB} \times \overrightarrow{AC}|.$$

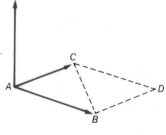

FIGURE 28

Example 1 Find the area of $\triangle ABC$, where $A = (2, 1, 3)$, $B = (-1, 0, 4)$ and $C = (4, 2, 2)$.

Solution. We proceed as follows:

$$\overrightarrow{AB} = -3\mathbf{i} - \mathbf{j} + \mathbf{k}, \qquad \overrightarrow{AC} = 2\mathbf{i} + \mathbf{j} - \mathbf{k}$$
$$\overrightarrow{AB} \times \overrightarrow{AC} = [(-1)(-1) - 1 \cdot 1]\mathbf{i} + [1 \cdot 2 - (-3)(-1)]\mathbf{j}$$
$$+ [(-3)1 - (-1)2]\mathbf{k} = -\mathbf{j} - \mathbf{k};$$
$$\text{area } \triangle ABC = \tfrac{1}{2}|\overrightarrow{AB} \times \overrightarrow{AC}| = \tfrac{1}{2}\sqrt{(-1)^2 + (-1)^2} = \sqrt{2}/2.$$

Our second application deals with finding equations for *planes perpendicular to two intersecting planes*. If a plane, π_3, is perpendicular to each of two intersecting planes, π_1 and π_2, then the normals of π_1 and π_2 must be perpendicular to the normals of π_3. (See Fig. 29.) Therefore the cross product of vectors normal to the intersecting planes π_1 and π_2 will produce a vector that will be normal to the set of planes perpendicular to π_1 and π_2.

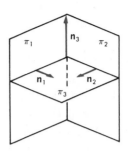

FIGURE 29

Example 2 Find an equation of the plane π that contains the point $P_1 = (3, 2, 4)$ and is perpendicular to each of the intersecting planes

$$\pi_1: x + y - z - 4 = 0 \qquad \text{and} \qquad \pi_2: x - 2y + 3z - 6 = 0.$$

Solution. The given planes have normals

$$\mathbf{n}_1 = \mathbf{i} + \mathbf{j} - \mathbf{k} \qquad \text{and} \qquad \mathbf{n}_2 = \mathbf{i} - 2\mathbf{j} + 3\mathbf{k},$$

respectively. The required plane will have a normal $\mathbf{n}$ given by

$$\mathbf{n} = \mathbf{n}_1 \times \mathbf{n}_2 = \mathbf{i} - 4\mathbf{j} - 3\mathbf{k}.$$

The plane π must contain $P_1 = (3, 2, 4)$; so if $P = (x, y, z)$ is any point in π, then $\mathbf{n} \cdot \overrightarrow{P_1 P} = 0$. Hence $(x - 3) \cdot 1 + (y - 2)(-4) + (z - 4)(-3) = 0$, so $x - 4y - 3z + 17 = 0$ is an equation of the plane π.

A final application of vector products is that dealing with *moment of force*. A force F acting on a lever of length d from a fixed point O tends to rotate the lever about O. (See Fig. 30.) The vector product, $\mathbf{d} \times \mathbf{F}$, is called the *moment of force* about O. Numerous applications of moments of force occur in physics.

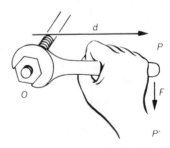

FIGURE 30

Example 3 The vector $\overrightarrow{PP'}$ acts on $\overrightarrow{OP}$ to produce a moment of force about O. What is this moment if $P = (2, 3, 1)$ and $P' = (-2, 6, 4)$?

Solution.

$$\overrightarrow{OP} = 2\mathbf{i} + 3\mathbf{j} + \mathbf{k},$$
$$\overrightarrow{PP'} = -4\mathbf{i} + 3\mathbf{j} + 3\mathbf{k},$$
$$\text{moment of force about } O = \overrightarrow{OP} \times \overrightarrow{PP'} = 6\mathbf{i} - 10\mathbf{j} + 18\mathbf{k}.$$

Problems

Set A

Using cross products, find the area of each triangle whose vertices have the following coordinates.

1. $(0, 0, 0)$, $(1, 1, 1)$, $(0, 0, 3)$
2. $(2, 0, 0)$, $(0, 2, 0)$, $(0, 0, 2)$
3. $(2, 0, 0)$, $(0, 3, 0)$, $(0, 0, 4)$
4. $(1, -1, 1)$, $(2, 2, 2)$, $(4, -2, 1)$
5. (x_1, y_1, z_1), (x_2, y_2, z_2), (x_3, y_3, z_3)
6. Three of the vertices of a parallelogram are $(1, 2, -1)$, $(4, 0, -4)$ and $(0, 6, 6)$. What is the area of the parallelogram?
7. The area of an equilateral triangle is $s^2\sqrt{3}/4$ where s is the length of one side of the triangle. Verify your result for the equilateral triangle in Problem 2.

Set B

8. Find an equation of a plane through $(0, 2, 0)$ that will be perpendicular to the pair of intersecting planes $x + 2z = 6$ and $x + y = 6$. Sketch a picture of all three planes.
9. Find an equation of a plane that contains the origin and is perpendicular to each of the planes $x + y + z = 4$ and $x - y + z = 4$. Sketch a picture.
10. Find the point of intersection of the three planes of Problem 9.
11. The volume of a tetrahedron is given by the formula $V = \frac{1}{3}Bh$, where B is the area of a base and h is the length of the altitude to this base. Find the volume of a tetrahedron whose triangular base has vertices at $(3, 1, 0)$, $(1, 4, 0)$, and $(5, 5, 0)$. The fourth vertex is at $(3, 1, 6)$.

Set C

In each problem, find an equation of the plane through the given noncollinear points. [*Hint:* In Problem 12, for example, the arrows $((1, 2, 2), (3, 3, -1))$ and $((1, 2, 2), (-1, 5, 1))$ lie in the plane. Therefore, the vector product of the vectors represented by these arrows, $(2\mathbf{i} + \mathbf{j} - 3\mathbf{k}) \times (-2\mathbf{i} + 3\mathbf{j} - \mathbf{k})$, will be a normal to the plane.]

12. $(1, 2, 2)$, $(3, 3, -1)$, $(-1, 5, 1)$
13. $(0, -1, 0)$, $(2, 1, -2)$, $(1, 0, 1)$
14. $(1, 1, 0)$, $(3, 0, 1)$, $(-1, 2, 1)$
15. $(1, 1, 1)$, $(2, 4, -2)$, $(5, 1, 0)$
16. $(2, 0, 0)$, $(0, 3, 0)$, $(0, 0, 4)$
17. $(2, 2, 1)$, $(4, 2, -1)$, $(6, -3, 2)$
18. A force $\mathbf{F} = 2\mathbf{i} - 4\mathbf{j} + \mathbf{k}$ acts at P, where $\overrightarrow{OP} = 5\mathbf{i} + 2\mathbf{j} + 4\mathbf{k}$. What is the moment of force about the point O? What is the magnitude of the moment of force?
19. In mechanics, a useful theorem due to Varignon states that the sum of the moments of force about a point O is equal to the moment of the sum of the forces about O. Use the diagram to verify that the sum of the moments of $\mathbf{F}_1$ and $\mathbf{F}_2$ about O is the same as the moment of force of $\mathbf{F}_1 + \mathbf{F}_2$ about O. What property of vectors does this illustrate?

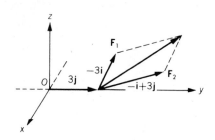

Calculator Problem

Use the cross product to calculate the area of $\triangle ABC$ if $A = (3.4, -1.1, 0.8)$, $B = (1.5, -3.1, 1.2)$ and $C = (0.4, 1.2, 2.8)$.

Summary

Some of the more important concepts and formulas developed in this chapter are listed below. You should make certain that you understand the concepts and can apply the formulas.

1. The angle between two vectors or two rays.

2. The cosine of the angle between the vectors $\mathbf{a} = a_1\mathbf{i} + a_2\mathbf{j} + a_3\mathbf{k}$ and $\mathbf{b} = b_1\mathbf{i} + b_2\mathbf{j} + b_3\mathbf{k}$:

$$\cos\theta = \frac{a_1b_1 + a_2b_2 + a_3b_3}{|\mathbf{a}|\,|\mathbf{b}|}.$$

3. The dot or scalar product of $\mathbf{a}$ and $\mathbf{b}$: $\mathbf{a}\cdot\mathbf{b} = |\mathbf{a}|\,|\mathbf{b}|\cos\theta$, where θ is the measure of the angle between $\mathbf{a}$ and $\mathbf{b}$.

4. If the components of $\mathbf{a}$ and $\mathbf{b}$ are (a_1, a_2, a_3) and (b_1, b_2, b_3), respectively, then $\mathbf{a}\cdot\mathbf{b} = a_1b_1 + a_2b_2 + a_3b_3$.

5. Two vectors $\mathbf{a}$ and $\mathbf{b}$ are perpendicular if and only if $\mathbf{a}\cdot\mathbf{b} = 0$.

6. The line $ax + by + c = 0$ has a positive unit normal

$$\mathbf{n} = \frac{a}{\pm\sqrt{a^2 + b^2}}\mathbf{i} + \frac{b}{\pm\sqrt{a^2 + b^2}}\mathbf{j},$$

where the sign of the radical is chosen opposite to that of c.
   The distance p from the origin to the line is

$$p = \frac{|c|}{\sqrt{a^2 + b^2}}.$$

The distance d of the point $P_1 = (x_1, y_1)$ from the line is

$$d = \frac{|ax_1 + by_1 + c|}{\sqrt{a^2 + b^2}}.$$

7. The plane $Ax + By + Cz + D = 0$ has a positive unit normal

$$\mathbf{n} = \frac{A\mathbf{i}}{\pm\sigma} + \frac{B\mathbf{j}}{\pm\sigma} + \frac{C\mathbf{k}}{\pm\sigma},$$

where $\sigma = \sqrt{A^2 + B^2 + C^2}$, and the sign of the radical is chosen opposite to that of D.
   The distance p from the origin to the plane is

$$p = \frac{|D|}{\sqrt{A^2 + B^2 + C^2}}.$$

The distance d from a point $P_1 = (x_1, y_1, z_1)$ to the plane is

$$d = \frac{|Ax_1 + By_1 + Cz_1 + D|}{\sqrt{A^2 + B^2 + C^2}}.$$

8. The cross product of vectors: If

$$\mathbf{a} = a_1\mathbf{i} + a_2\mathbf{j} + a_3\mathbf{k} \qquad \text{and} \qquad \mathbf{b} = b_1\mathbf{i} + b_2\mathbf{j} + b_3\mathbf{k},$$

then

$$\mathbf{a} \times \mathbf{b} = (a_2b_3 - a_3b_2)\mathbf{i} + (a_3b_1 - a_1b_3)\mathbf{j} + (a_1b_2 - a_2b_1)\mathbf{k}.$$

9. Vector multiplication is distributive with respect to vector addition: If $\mathbf{a}$, $\mathbf{b}$, and $\mathbf{c}$ are vectors, then

$$\mathbf{a} \times (\mathbf{b} + \mathbf{c}) = (\mathbf{a} \times \mathbf{b}) + (\mathbf{a} \times \mathbf{c}).$$

Chapter 15 Test

15-2 **1.** What is the cosine of the angle between $\overrightarrow{P_1P_2}$ and $\overrightarrow{P_3P_4}$ if $P_1 = (2, 1, 3)$, $P_2 = (-4, 4, 5)$, $P_3 = (0, 7, 0)$, and $P_4 = (-3, 4, -2)$?

2. Find the cosine of the angle between $\mathbf{a} = 4\mathbf{i} - \mathbf{j} + \mathbf{k}$ and $\mathbf{b} = \mathbf{i} + 3\mathbf{j} - 3\mathbf{k}$.

15-3 **3.** Find the dot product, $\mathbf{u} \cdot \mathbf{v}$, where $\mathbf{u} = -6\mathbf{i} + 2\mathbf{j} - 4\mathbf{k}$ and $\mathbf{v} = \mathbf{i} + 4\mathbf{j} - \mathbf{k}$.

4. If $\mathbf{a}$ and $\mathbf{b}$ are vectors, $\mathbf{a} \cdot \mathbf{b} = 0$, and neither $\mathbf{a}$ nor $\mathbf{b}$ is the null vector, what can you conclude?

5. What is $\mathbf{i} \cdot \mathbf{j}$, where $\mathbf{i}$ and $\mathbf{j}$ are the unit basis vectors along the x- and y-axes?

15-4 **6.** Find the positive unit normal to the line whose equation is $x - 2y - 2 = 0$.

7. What is the distance from the origin to a line with an equation $12x + 5y - 3 = 0$?

15-5 Find the distance from each point below to the line $3x - 4y + 7 = 0$.

8. $(6, 2)$ **9.** $(-2, -3)$ **10.** $(-4, 0)$

11. Find the cosines of the angles between the lines $x + 2y - 4 = 0$ and $x - y + 3 = 0$.

15-6 **12.** What is a positive unit normal to the plane $x - 2y + 2z - 3 = 0$?

13. Find the distance from the origin to the plane $4x + y - 5z - 9 = 0$.

14. Find the distance from the point $(2, -1, 3)$ to the plane $x + 4y + 5z = 1$.

15-7 Find the cross products.

15. $\mathbf{i} \times \mathbf{j}$ **16.** $\mathbf{j} \times \mathbf{i}$ **17.** $\mathbf{j} \times \mathbf{j}$

18. If the dot product of two vectors $\mathbf{a}$ and $\mathbf{b}$ is zero, where neither vector is the null vector, what is the magnitude of the vector $\mathbf{a} \times \mathbf{b}$?

15-8 Use the distributive property of vector multiplication with respect to addition to compute the cross products.

19. $3\mathbf{i} \times (2\mathbf{i} - 3\mathbf{j} + \mathbf{k})$ **20.** $(\mathbf{i} + 2\mathbf{j}) \times (3\mathbf{i} + 4\mathbf{j} + \mathbf{k})$

15-9 **21.** Use vector multiplication to find the area of a triangle whose vertices have coordinates $(2, 2, 0)$, $(0, 4, 3)$, and $(4, 0, 4)$.

22. Find an equation of the plane that contains the point $(1, 1, 1)$ and is perpendicular to each of the planes $2x - y + 4z - 3 = 0$ and $x + 5y - 2z + 10 = 0$.

Historical Note

Josiah Willard Gibbs
(1839–1903)

During the nineteenth century, physicists were looking for a notation and algebra of vectors that could be readily applied to the problems of mechanics.

In science for example, *work* is defined simply as the product of force and distance. More precisely, its value can be found by thinking of vectors and computing the dot product. If a constant force **F** acts through a displacement **d**, then the work done is **F · d**. *Torque*, or *moment*, is found by computing the vector product: If a force **F** acts at a point P with position vector $\overrightarrow{OP} = \mathbf{v}$, then the moment of the force is the vector **v × F**.

Physicists computed these scalars and vectors directly in terms of the rectangular components of the vectors. This direct approach of writing everything in terms of components was referred to as "cartesian methods." What was needed was an approach for dealing with the vector itself, without its components. Vector algebra enabled physicists to consider the physical concepts without doing all the computation.

Sir William Rowan Hamilton introduced quaternions in 1843 (See the Historical Note of Chapter 14). In quaternions one can find both dot and vector products.

Let $\qquad \mathbf{v} = ai + bj + ck$
and $\qquad \mathbf{F} = xi + yj + zk,$

where i, j, k are the quaternion units. Then the quaternion product of **F** and **v** is

$$\mathbf{vF} = (ai + bj + ck)(xi + yj + zk)$$
$$= -(ax + by + cz) + [(bz - cy)i$$
$$+ (cx - az)j + (ay - bx)k].$$

The real part of this quaternion is $-(ax + by + cz)$ and is simply the *negative* of the *dot product* $(\mathbf{v} \cdot \mathbf{F})$ of the vectors **F** and **v**. The vector part of this quaternion is $(bz - cy)i + (cx - az)j + (ay - bx)k$, and this is simply the *vector product* $(\mathbf{v} \times \mathbf{F})$ of the vectors **F** and **v**.

Although quaternions provided a vector algebra, they were never widely used. Later works continued to use cartesian methods.

The pure vector approach, which was introduced by Hermann Grassman (1809–1877) in *Die Lineale Ausdehnungslehre* (*The Theory of Linear Extension*), gradually became *the* accepted approach. From vectors, one goes on to mathematical objects called tensors, and these are the tools of relativity theory.

Notation was improved during the latter half of the nineteenth century. In 1881, Josiah Willard Gibbs (1839–1903), professor of mathematical physics at Yale, published for his students a small pamphlet called *The Elements of Vector Analysis*. The Gibbs approach (which is what we have followed in this book) became well known and widely used. Another contributor to the pure vector approach was the English physicist Oliver Heaviside (1850–1925). This approach is found in all modern texts on vector analysis.

Chapter 16
Systems of Linear Equations and Matrices

16-1 Introduction

In this chapter we are concerned primarily with systems of linear equations and their solution by use of matrices and determinants. Although we will first define matrices so that we can use them to define determinants, historically the development was the other way around. Englishman Arthur Cayley (1821–1895) noted that there is a matrix algebra with innumerable applications. We include a brief study of this matrix algebra in this chapter.

Although the work in this chapter is confined to lines in the plane or planes in three-space (dimensions 2 and 3), one can generalize the ideas for n-space, that is, dimension n where $n > 3$.

16-2 Systems of Linear Equations

Systems of linear equations can be interpreted geometrically if the number of variables is two or three. For linear equations in more variables, the same geometric language (borrowed from the plane and from space) is used but without the physical interpretation. One has to *invent higher-dimensional spaces* in which to carry out the discussion.

Consider two linear equations in x and y:

$$\begin{cases} a_1 x + b_1 y = c_1, \\ a_2 x + b_2 y = c_2, \end{cases} \quad (1)$$

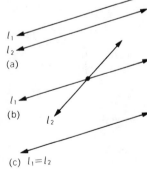

(a)

(b)

(c) $l_1 = l_2$

FIGURE 1

where a_1, b_1, c_1, a_2, b_2, and c_2 are real numbers and not both a_1 and b_1 nor a_2 and b_2 are 0 ($a_1^2 + b_1^2 \neq 0$ and $a_2^2 + b_2^2 \neq 0$). These equations have graphs that are lines l_1 and l_2. Exactly one of the following three situations is possible (see Fig. 1):

(a) l_1 is parallel to l_2. There is no solution of the system (1).

(b) l_1 intersects l_2 in a unique point. There is exactly one solution of the system (1).

(c) $l_1 = l_2$. There are infinitely many solutions of the system (1).

Consider now three linear equations in x, y, and z:

$$a_1 x + b_1 y + c_1 z = d_1,$$
$$a_2 x + b_2 y + c_2 z = d_2, \qquad (2)$$
$$a_3 x + b_3 y + c_3 z = d_3,$$

where the coefficients $a_1, \ldots, d_3$ are real numbers and in each equation not all a_i, b_i, and c_i are 0, $i = 1, 2, 3$ ($a_i^2 + b_i^2 + c_i^2 \neq 0$). These equations have graphs that are planes π_1, π_2, and π_3. Exactly one of the following three situations is possible.

(a) There is no solution of system (2). Either all three planes are parallel or the line of intersection of two of them is parallel to the third plane (Fig. 2a).

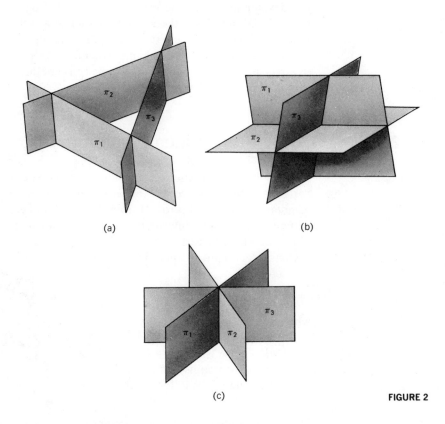

(a)

(b)

(c)

FIGURE 2

(b) There is exactly one solution of system (2). Two of the planes meet in a line that pierces the third plane (Fig. 2b).

(c) There are infinitely many solutions. There is at least one line on all three planes, for if two distinct points were on all planes, the line containing these points would be on all planes (Fig. 2c).

We shall be concerned with algebraic criteria which will distinguish these cases.

Let us first consider the system of two linear equations

$$\begin{cases} a_1x + b_1y = c_1, \\ a_2x + b_2y = c_2, \end{cases} \tag{1}$$

where not both of a_1 and b_1 are zero nor both of a_2 and b_2. The following theorem gives a complete description of the possible solutions of this system.

Theorem 16-1   *System (1) has exactly one solution if and only if $a_1b_2 - a_2b_1 \neq 0$. In this case the solution is*

$$x = \frac{c_1b_2 - c_2b_1}{a_1b_2 - a_2b_1}, \qquad y = \frac{a_1c_2 - a_2c_1}{a_1b_2 - a_2b_1}. \tag{3}$$

If $a_1b_2 - a_2b_1 = 0$, then there is a unique real number $k \neq 0$ such that $a_2 = ka_1$ and $b_2 = kb_1$. There is no solution if $c_2 \neq kc_1$. There are infinitely many solutions if $c_2 = kc_1$.

Proof   We multiply the members of the first equation of (1) by b_2, and the members of the second equation by b_1 and subtract. We obtain

$$(a_1b_2 - a_2b_1)x = c_1b_2 - c_2b_1. \tag{4}$$

In a similar manner, we get

$$(a_1b_2 - a_2b_1)y = a_1c_2 - a_2c_1. \tag{5}$$

Then, if $a_1b_2 - a_2b_1 \neq 0$, equations (3) are obtained from equations (4) and (5). Therefore (3) must be the solution, if there is one. It is easy to check that (3) is a solution. This proves the first half of the theorem.

Suppose now that $a_1b_2 - a_2b_1 = 0$. Then there is a unique real number k such that $a_2 = ka_1$ and $b_2 = kb_1$. If $b_1 \neq 0$ then $a_2 = (b_2/b_1)a_1$, and $b_2 = (b_2/b_1)b_1$. A similar argument holds if $a_1 \neq 0$. See Problem 17. From equations (4) and (5) we see that the system is *inconsistent* (no solution) if either $c_1b_2 - c_2b_1 \neq 0$ or $a_1c_2 - a_2c_1 \neq 0$. If both $c_1b_2 - c_2b_1 = 0$ and $a_1c_2 - a_2c_1 = 0$, then one also has $c_2 = kc_1$. In this case the lines are identical, and there are infinitely many solutions.

If $a_1b_2 - a_2b_1 \neq 0$, *the only solution of the homogeneous* system*

$$\begin{cases} a_1x + b_1y = 0, \\ a_2x + b_2y = 0 \end{cases}$$

is the trivial solution $x = y = 0$.

One could, of course, memorize equations (3) and use those equations as a formula to solve system (1). It will turn out that with determinants (discussed in Section 16–3), one learns without effort formulas (3), along with their generalization to n equations in n variables. Yet neither formulas (3) nor determinants are the most convenient device for solving linear equations. In most cases the easiest and shortest method is by elimination, with which you are already familiar. An example will illustrate the method.

Example

To solve the system

$$\begin{cases} 2x - 3y = \frac{7}{2}, \\ -3x + y = 0, \end{cases} \tag{6}$$

we eliminate one of the variables from one of the equations.

By a sequence of pairs of equivalent equations we reach a system that has an obvious solution. System (6) is equivalent to

$$\begin{cases} 2x - 3y = \frac{7}{2}, \\ -2x + \frac{2}{3}y = 0, \end{cases} \tag{7}$$

by multiplication of the second equation of (6) by $\frac{2}{3}$, and system (7) is equivalent to

$$\begin{cases} 2x - 3y = \frac{7}{2}, \\ - \frac{7}{3}y = \frac{7}{2}, \end{cases} \tag{8}$$

by addition of equations (7) and retaining the first equation. Now system (8) is solved at once. The second equation of (8) gives $y = -\frac{3}{2}$. Substitution of $-\frac{3}{2}$ for y in the first equation of (8) gives $x = -\frac{1}{2}$.

---

*A linear equation is *homogeneous* if the constant term is 0. Then every term is of the first degree in the variables. Every homogeneous equation has the *trivial* solution $x = y = 0$.

Problems

Set A

In Problems 1–6 use the condition of Theorem 16–1 to decide whether the system of equations has a unique solution, no solution (inconsistent), or infinitely many solutions. Sketch each pair of lines.

1. $\begin{cases} x + 2y = 7, \\ 2x + y = 5 \end{cases}$ 2. $\begin{cases} x - 3y = 4, \\ 2x - 6y = 8 \end{cases}$

3. $\begin{cases} 2x - 3y = -1, \\ 6x - 9y = 7 \end{cases}$ 4. $\begin{cases} 3x + y = -1, \\ 3x + y = 2 \end{cases}$

5. $\begin{cases} x - y = 2, \\ 3x + 0 \cdot y = 8 \end{cases}$ 6. $\begin{cases} 8x + 12y = 9, \\ 12x + 16y = -2 \end{cases}$

In Problems 7–10, use the formulas of Theorem 16–1 to find the solution for each system. Sketch each pair of lines.

7. $\begin{cases} x - 2y = 3, \\ 2x + y = 11 \end{cases}$ 8. $\begin{cases} 4x - y = 3, \\ 2x + 3y = -2 \end{cases}$

9. $\begin{cases} x + y = \sqrt{2}, \\ x - y = 3\sqrt{2} \end{cases}$ 10. $\begin{cases} 0.1x + 0.2y = 5, \\ 0.3x - 0.2y = -1 \end{cases}$

In Problems 11–14, use the method of elimination to find the solution for each system.

11. $\begin{cases} 5x - y = 12, \\ 2x + 6y = 24 \end{cases}$ 12. $\begin{cases} 4x + 5y = 4, \\ 4x - 5y = 0 \end{cases}$

13. $\begin{cases} \frac{3}{4}x - \frac{1}{3}y = 2, \\ x + y = -7 \end{cases}$ 14. $\begin{cases} 1.2x - 0.25y = 76, \\ 4x + 3y = 8 \end{cases}$

Set B

15. Describe what happens to the point of intersection of

$$\begin{cases} a_1x + b_1 y = c_1, \\ a_2x + b_2 y = c_2, \end{cases}$$

if a_1/b_1 is nearly equal to a_2/b_2.

16. What happens to the point of intersection of

$$\begin{cases} 2x - 3y = 1, \\ 3x + y = -2 + k, \end{cases}$$

as k varies? Sketch the lines.

Set C

17. If for the system

$$\begin{cases} a_1x + b_1 y = c_1, \\ a_2x + b_2 y = c_2, \end{cases}$$

$a_1 b_2 - a_2 b_1 = 0$ and $a_1 \neq 0$, show that there exists a real number k such that $a_2 = ka_1$ and $b_2 = kb_1$.

18. If $a_1 b_2 - a_2 b_1 \neq 0$ find the solution of

$$\begin{cases} a_1x + b_1 y = c_1, \\ a_2x + b_2 y = c_2 + k. \end{cases}$$

As k varies, what happens to the solution?

19. If in the system

$$\begin{cases} a_1x + b_1 y = c_1, \\ a_2x + b_2 y = c_2, \end{cases}$$

$a_1 b_2 - a_2 b_1 \neq 0$ but is small, what happens as $a_1 b_2 - a_2 b_1$ approaches zero?

Calculator Problem

Solve the systems.

(a) $\begin{cases} 0.9x - 2.1y = 1.2, \\ 0.9x - 2.11y = 1.21 \end{cases}$ (b) $\begin{cases} 0.9x - 2.1y = 1.2, \\ 0.91x - 2.11y = 1.22 \end{cases}$

Sketch a figure for each system.

Matrices and Determinants

The concept of determinant is based on that of matrix. Hence we must first define a matrix.

Definition 16-1 An $m \times n$ *matrix* is a *rectangular array* of m rows and n columns of numbers:

$$\begin{bmatrix} a_{11} & a_{12} & \cdots & a_{1n} \\ a_{21} & a_{22} & \cdots & a_{2n} \\ \vdots & & & \vdots \\ a_{m1} & a_{m2} & \cdots & a_{mn} \end{bmatrix}. \tag{1}$$

The *entries* or *elements* of the matrix are the numbers a_{ij}. A *square matrix* has the same number of rows as columns: $m = n$.

For example, the following are matrices:

$$\begin{bmatrix} a & b \\ c & d \end{bmatrix}, \quad \begin{bmatrix} a & b & c \\ d & e & f \\ g & h & i \end{bmatrix}, \quad \begin{bmatrix} a & b \\ c & d \\ e & f \end{bmatrix}, \quad \begin{bmatrix} a & b & c \\ d & e & f \end{bmatrix}.$$

$$2 \times 2 \qquad\qquad 3 \times 3 \qquad\qquad 3 \times 2 \qquad\qquad 2 \times 3$$

There is an algebra of matrices that is an important part of what is called *linear algebra*. For our present purposes, all that we need is the concept of a rectangular array. Two matrices are *equal* if and only if they have the same number of rows and the same number of columns, and the numbers appearing in the same row and column of the two matrices are equal.

It is possible to define certain useful functions, called *determinant* functions, which map $n \times n$ square matrices into the real numbers. The natural number n is called the *order* of the determinant function. To evaluate a determinant function at a given square matrix is to find the real number associated with the matrix.

We do not use the formal functional notation for determinant functions. We replace the brackets enclosing the array of the matrix by vertical lines. Then, if det is the determinant function, say of order three, we have

$$\det \begin{bmatrix} a & b & c \\ d & e & f \\ g & h & i \end{bmatrix} = \begin{vmatrix} a & b & c \\ d & e & f \\ g & h & i \end{vmatrix}.$$

We need the following definition for determinants of order two.

Definition 16-2 If det is the *determinant* function of order 2, then

$$\det \begin{bmatrix} a_1 & b_1 \\ a_2 & b_2 \end{bmatrix} = \begin{vmatrix} a_1 & b_1 \\ a_2 & b_2 \end{vmatrix} = a_1 b_2 - a_2 b_1.$$

Remarks

1. The real number $(a_1b_2 - a_2b_1)$ is the value of the determinant function det at the matrix
$$\begin{bmatrix} a_1 & b_1 \\ a_2 & b_2 \end{bmatrix}.$$

It is convenient to refer to $(a_1b_2 - a_2b_1)$ as the value of the determinant, and we shall even say that $(a_1b_2 - a_2b_1)$ *is* the determinant although you should realize that we are abusing the language when we do this.

2. the number $(a_1b_2 - a_2b_1)$ is the sum of two terms a_1b_2 and $-a_2b_1$. Observe that each term is plus or minus a product of a number from one row and column and a number from a different row and column. We shall see later that this carries over to determinants of arbitrary order.

3. There is a mnemonic device for Definition 16–2. One forms the products, with the proper signs, according to the arrows of Fig. 3 and takes their sum.

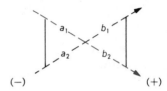

$(-)$ $(+)$

FIGURE 3

Definition 16–2 permits us to restate part of Theorem 16–1 as follows.

Theorem 16–2   *CRAMER'S RULE. The system*

$$a_1x + b_1y = c_1,$$
$$a_2x + b_2y = c_2$$

has the unique solution

$$x = \frac{\begin{vmatrix} c_1 & b_1 \\ c_2 & b_2 \end{vmatrix}}{\begin{vmatrix} a_1 & b_1 \\ a_2 & b_2 \end{vmatrix}}, \qquad y = \frac{\begin{vmatrix} a_1 & c_1 \\ a_2 & c_2 \end{vmatrix}}{\begin{vmatrix} a_1 & b_1 \\ a_2 & b_2 \end{vmatrix}} \qquad\qquad (2)$$

if Δ, *the denominator determinant in (2) is not* 0. *If* $\Delta = 0$, *then either there is no solution or there are infinitely many solutions.*

We note that when the two equations are in the standard form (1) of Section 16–2, the rows of the determinant Δ are the same as the coefficients of x and y. The numerator determinants are obtained by replacing in Δ the coefficients of the variable sought by the constant terms. Equations (2) are known as *Cramer's Rule,* so called after the Swiss mathematician, Gabriel Cramer (1701–1752).

It should be remarked that the solution as given by Cramer's Rule is *not* the way that two linear equations are usually solved. Simple elimination (see Section 16–2) is usually best—and the same applies even to numerical solutions when programmed on a computer.

Example 1 $\begin{vmatrix} -3 & 4 \\ -5 & 8 \end{vmatrix} = (-3)8 - (-5)4 = -24 + 20 = -4$

2   If

$$\begin{vmatrix} x & 2 \\ 3 & (x-1) \end{vmatrix} = 0$$

then by Definition 16–2 we have the quadratic equation

$$x(x-1) - 6 = 0 \qquad \text{or} \qquad x^2 - x - 6 = 0.$$

Hence $(x-3)(x+2) = 0$ and $x = 3$ or $x = -2$. Substituting either of these numbers for x in the determinant equation, we find that both numbers satisfy the equation.

Problems

Set A

Evaluate the determinants.

1. $\begin{vmatrix} 1 & 2 \\ -1 & -1 \end{vmatrix}$

2. $\begin{vmatrix} 7 & -3 \\ -1 & -2 \end{vmatrix}$

3. $\begin{vmatrix} 0.5 & 1.2 \\ -0.6 & 2.1 \end{vmatrix}$

4. $\begin{vmatrix} a & b \\ c & d \end{vmatrix}$

5. $\begin{vmatrix} a + kc & b + kd \\ c & d \end{vmatrix}$

6. $\begin{vmatrix} x & 1 \\ 2 & x-1 \end{vmatrix}$

7. $\begin{vmatrix} x & x \\ x-1 & x+1 \end{vmatrix}$

8. $\begin{vmatrix} \cos\theta & -\sin\theta \\ \sin\theta & \cos\theta \end{vmatrix}$

Solve the equations.

9. $\begin{vmatrix} 3 & 1 \\ x & 2 \end{vmatrix} = 0$

10. $\begin{vmatrix} x-1 & 1 \\ -1 & x-2 \end{vmatrix} = 0$

11. $\begin{vmatrix} x-1 & x-2 \\ x-3 & x \end{vmatrix} = 0$

Solve by using Cramer's Rule.

12. $\begin{cases} 2x + y = 5, \\ x + 3y = 5 \end{cases}$

13. $\begin{cases} 3x + 2y = -11, \\ 2x - 3y = 10 \end{cases}$

14. $\begin{cases} 6x - 9y = 11, \\ 2x - 3y = 7 \end{cases}$

15. $\begin{cases} 2x + 5 = 3y, \\ 1 + y = -2x \end{cases}$

Set B

Solve by using Cramer's Rule, if possible.

16. $\begin{cases} 4x + 12y = 20, \\ 2x + 6y = 10 \end{cases}$

17. $\begin{cases} 3/x - 2/y = 2, \\ 9/x + 4/y = 1 \end{cases}$

18. $\begin{cases} \dfrac{1}{x} + \dfrac{1}{2y} = \dfrac{1}{2}, \\ \dfrac{3}{x} + \dfrac{3}{2y} = 1 \end{cases}$

19. $\begin{cases} 0.4x - 0.1y = 0.5, \\ 1.1x + 2.2y = -1.1 \end{cases}$

20. $\begin{cases} x \tan\theta + y \sec\theta = \sec\theta + \tan\theta, \\ x \sec\theta + y \tan\theta = \tan\theta + \sec\theta \end{cases}$

Set C

21. Solve the inequality

$$\begin{vmatrix} x & x-2 \\ 5 & 10 \end{vmatrix} < 0.$$

22. Show that:

$$\begin{vmatrix} a & b \\ c & d \end{vmatrix} = -\begin{vmatrix} c & d \\ a & b \end{vmatrix} = \begin{vmatrix} a & c \\ b & d \end{vmatrix} = -\begin{vmatrix} c & a \\ d & b \end{vmatrix}.$$

23. State the results of Problem 22 in words. Properties concerning rows and columns of determinants are valid for determinants of any order.

24. Show that

$$\begin{vmatrix} a & b \\ kc & kd \end{vmatrix} = k\begin{vmatrix} a & b \\ c & d \end{vmatrix} = \begin{vmatrix} ka & b \\ kc & d \end{vmatrix}.$$

State the results in words.

Calculator Problem

Use Cramer's Rule to solve the system below. Compute x and y to the nearest thousandth.

$$\begin{cases} 0.4x - 3.1y = 1.5 \\ 2.6x + 0.9y = -4.1 \end{cases}$$

16-4   Third-Order Determinants

We first present the definition.

Definition 16-3

$$\begin{vmatrix} a_1 & b_1 & c_1 \\ a_2 & b_2 & c_2 \\ a_3 & b_3 & c_3 \end{vmatrix} = a_1b_2c_3 + a_2b_3c_1 + a_3b_1c_2 - a_3b_2c_1 - a_1b_3c_2 - a_2b_1c_3.$$

Remarks

1. The determinant is the sum of products each of which has a plus or minus sign. Each product contains a factor from each row and each column. The sign is plus or minus depending on whether or not the number of *inversions on the subscripts is even or odd,* when the product has its factors in the order "*abc*" of the columns.

   The number of *inversions* is the number of times a larger number precedes a smaller number in a sequence of numbers. Thus in "43125" there are five inversions. ("4" precedes "3", "1," and "2," and "3" precedes "1" and "2.") Then, for example, the term $a_3b_2c_1$ in the expansion of the determinant must have a minus sign because in "321" there are three inversions.

2. There is a mnemonic device for Definition 16-3. One forms the products, with the proper signs, according to the arrows of Fig. 4 and takes their sum.

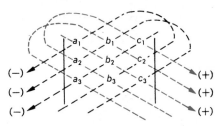

FIGURE 4

Before showing how determinants apply to linear systems in three variables we establish some important theorems that are valid for determinants of any order. Most of the proofs will be left to the reader.

Definition 16-4 The *minor* of an element of a determinant is the determinant of one lower order* that is obtained by deleting the row and column containing that element.

For example, the minor of b_3 in

$$\begin{vmatrix} a_1 & b_1 & c_1 \\ a_2 & b_2 & c_2 \\ a_3 & b_3 & c_3 \end{vmatrix} \quad \text{is} \quad \begin{vmatrix} a_1 & c_1 \\ a_2 & c_2 \end{vmatrix}.$$

The *cofactor* of an element of a determinant is the minor of that element multiplied by 1 or -1, according to whether the sum of the row number and the column number for that element is even or odd.

For example, in the above determinant the element b_3 is in the third row and second column. Since $3 + 2 = 5$ and this sum is odd, the cofactor of b_3 is

$$- \begin{vmatrix} a_1 & c_1 \\ a_2 & c_2 \end{vmatrix}.$$

Theorem 16-3 *A determinant is the sum of the products of the elements of any row (or column) and their corresponding cofactors.*

Example Using the elements of the second row, we have

$$\begin{vmatrix} a_1 & b_1 & c_1 \\ a_2 & b_2 & c_2 \\ a_3 & b_3 & c_3 \end{vmatrix} = -a_2 \begin{vmatrix} b_1 & c_1 \\ b_3 & c_3 \end{vmatrix} + b_2 \begin{vmatrix} a_1 & c_1 \\ a_3 & c_3 \end{vmatrix} - c_2 \begin{vmatrix} a_1 & b_1 \\ a_3 & b_3 \end{vmatrix}. \qquad (1)$$

We can prove that this is correct by computing the right-hand side of (1):

$$-a_2 \begin{vmatrix} b_1 & c_1 \\ b_3 & c_3 \end{vmatrix} + b_2 \begin{vmatrix} a_1 & c_1 \\ a_3 & c_3 \end{vmatrix} - c_2 \begin{vmatrix} a_1 & b_1 \\ a_3 & b_3 \end{vmatrix}$$

$$= -a_2 b_1 c_3 + a_2 b_3 c_1 + a_1 b_2 c_3 - a_3 b_2 c_1 - a_1 b_3 c_2 + a_3 b_1 c_2.$$

---

*The order of a determinant is the number of rows or columns it contains. Hence a determinant of lower order would be one containing fewer rows and columns.

This last expression is the value of the determinant according to Definition 16–3.

Corollary 1 *If a row (or column) of a determinant is multiplied by k, then the determinant is multiplied by k.*

2 *If two adjacent rows (or columns) are interchanged, the determinant is changed in sign.*

Proof The minors of one row are the same as the minors of the other row in the changed determinant. All the cofactors have been changed in sign.

Corollary 3 *If any two rows (or columns) are interchanged, the determinant is changed in sign.*

Proof To interchange any two rows requires an odd number of interchanges of adjacent rows. Apply Corollary 2.

Corollary 4 *If two rows (or columns) of a determinant are the same, the determinant is 0.*

Proof According to Corollary 3, if two rows are interchanged the determinant must change sign. But the interchange of identical rows does not change the value. The only number x such that $x = -x$ is $x = 0$.

Theorem 16–4 *If the elements of any row (or column) are multiplied by the cofactors of any other row (column) and summed, the result is 0.*

For example, referring to the determinants of (1) and using the second row and the cofactors of the first row, we have

$$-a_2 \begin{vmatrix} b_2 & c_2 \\ b_3 & c_3 \end{vmatrix} + b_2 \begin{vmatrix} a_2 & c_2 \\ a_3 & c_3 \end{vmatrix} - c_2 \begin{vmatrix} a_2 & b_2 \\ a_3 & b_3 \end{vmatrix} = 0.$$

[*Proof hint.* Apply Corollary 4 to a determinant that contains two identical rows.]

We are now ready to state, and prove, Cramer's Rule for a third-order system.

Theorem 16-5 *The system*

$$\begin{cases} a_1x + b_1y + c_1z = d_1, \\ a_2x + b_2y + c_2z = d_2, \\ a_3x + b_3y + c_3z = d_3 \end{cases} \tag{2}$$

has the unique solution

$$x = \frac{\begin{vmatrix} d_1 & b_1 & c_1 \\ d_2 & b_2 & c_2 \\ d_3 & b_3 & c_3 \end{vmatrix}}{\begin{vmatrix} a_1 & b_1 & c_1 \\ a_2 & b_2 & c_2 \\ a_3 & b_3 & c_3 \end{vmatrix}}, \quad y = \frac{\begin{vmatrix} a_1 & d_1 & c_1 \\ a_2 & d_2 & c_2 \\ a_3 & d_3 & c_3 \end{vmatrix}}{\begin{vmatrix} a_1 & b_1 & c_1 \\ a_2 & b_2 & c_2 \\ a_3 & b_3 & c_3 \end{vmatrix}}, \quad z = \frac{\begin{vmatrix} a_1 & b_1 & d_1 \\ a_2 & b_2 & d_2 \\ a_3 & b_3 & d_3 \end{vmatrix}}{\begin{vmatrix} a_1 & b_1 & c_1 \\ a_2 & b_2 & c_2 \\ a_3 & b_3 & c_3 \end{vmatrix}}, \tag{3}$$

if the denominator determinant Δ in (3) is not 0. If $\Delta = 0$, then either there is no solution or there are infinitely many solutions.

Proof   Let us denote the cofactors in the determinant Δ of the elements a_i, b_i, c_i by A_i, B_i, C_i, respectively; $i = 1, 2, 3$. We eliminate y and z by multiplying the three equations of (2) by A_1, A_2, and A_3, respectively, and adding. We obtain

$$(a_1A_1 + a_2A_2 + a_3A_3)x + (b_1A_1 + b_2A_2 + b_3A_3)y \\ + (c_1A_1 + c_2A_2 + c_3A_3)z = d_1A_1 + d_2A_2 + d_3A_3.$$

By Theorem 16-4 the coefficients of y and z are 0. The coefficient of x is Δ; hence

$$\Delta x = d_1A_1 + d_2A_2 + d_3A_3. \tag{4}$$

Similarly, we obtain

$$\Delta y = d_1B_1 + d_2B_2 + d_3B_3, \\ \Delta z = d_1C_1 + d_2C_2 + d_3C_3. \tag{5}$$

The right-hand members of equations (4) and (5) are the numerator determinants in (3). Therefore, if $\Delta \neq 0$, the solution to equations (2) must be given by (3). That (3) is actually a solution can be shown by obtaining equations (2) from equations (4) and (5). This is most easily done as follows. To get the first of equations (2) use (4) and (5) to compute $a_1\,\Delta x + b_1\,\Delta y + c_1\,\Delta z$; then (after some rearrangement) by Theorems 16-3 and 16-4 reduce the equality to

$$\Delta(a_1x + b_1y + c_1z) = \Delta d_1.$$

Since $\Delta \neq 0$, we get the first equation. The other equations of (2) are similarly obtained.

If $\Delta = 0$ and not all the right-hand members of (4) and (5) are 0, then there is no solution. If $\Delta = 0$ and all the right-hand members of (4) and (5) are 0, then it can be shown that there are infinitely many solutions, but we omit the proof.

If the homogeneous equations

$$\begin{cases} a_1x + b_1y + c_1z = 0, \\ a_2x + b_2y + c_2z = 0, \\ a_3x + b_3y + c_3z = 0 \end{cases}$$

have a solution different from $x = y = z = 0$, then $\Delta = 0$, and they have infinitely many solutions.

Remark

Cramer's Rule is rarely used to solve specific linear systems. Almost always the method of elimination will prove to be more convenient. The discerning reader may have noted that this is precisely what we did (in a tricky way) in deriving equations (4) and (5).

To illustrate a customary method of elimination, we solve the system of equations (2) and suppose that $a_1 \neq 0$.*

$$\begin{cases} a_1x + b_1y + c_1z = d_1, \\ a_2x + b_2y + c_2z = d_2, \\ a_3x + b_3y + c_3z = d_3. \end{cases} \tag{2}$$

We eliminate x from the second and third equations by subtracting multiples of the first, and obtain

$$\begin{cases} a_1x + b_1y + c_1z = d_1, \\ \left(b_2 - \dfrac{a_2b_1}{a_1}\right)y + \left(c_2 - \dfrac{a_2c_1}{a_1}\right)z = d_2 - \dfrac{a_2d_1}{a_1}, \\ \left(b_3 - \dfrac{a_3b_1}{a_1}\right)y + \left(c_3 - \dfrac{a_3c_1}{a_1}\right)z = d_3 - \dfrac{a_3d_1}{a_1}. \end{cases} \tag{6}$$

System (6) is equivalent to system (2) because one can obtain (2) by adding multiples of the first equation of (6) to the others.

The last two equations of (6) constitute a lower-order system. Then if we eliminate one of the variables, say y, between the equations we obtain a system of the form

$$\begin{cases} a_1x + b_1y + c_1z = d_1, \\ b_2'y + c_2'z = d_2', \\ c_3'z = d_3'. \end{cases}$$

Such a system in *triangular form* is easily solved. From the third equation one gets z. Then y is obtained from the second equation after substitution for z, and finally x is obtained from the first equation.

---

*If not all a_i are 0, we can renumber the equations so that $a_i \neq 0$. If all a_i are 0, then we have three equations in but two unknowns, so either the system is inconsistent or one equation is a linear combination of the others. In the latter case we are really dealing with a lower-order system.

Problems

Set A

Evaluate the determinants.

1. $\begin{vmatrix} 1 & -1 & 1 \\ 2 & 1 & -1 \\ 1 & 2 & 3 \end{vmatrix}$

2. $\begin{vmatrix} 2 & 1 & 3 \\ 1 & 1 & 6 \\ 1 & 2 & 13 \end{vmatrix}$

3. $\begin{vmatrix} -2 & 3 & 7 \\ 4 & -2 & 6 \\ -1 & 3 & 5 \end{vmatrix}$

4. Prove that

$$\begin{vmatrix} a & b & c \\ a & b & c \\ d & e & f \end{vmatrix} = 0 \quad \text{and} \quad \begin{vmatrix} a & a & d \\ b & b & e \\ c & c & f \end{vmatrix} = 0.$$

Solve the following systems, using Cramer's Rule, and also using elimination.

5. $\begin{cases} x + y + z = 1, \\ 3x + 3y - 3z = 2, \\ x - y - z = 0 \end{cases}$

6. $\begin{cases} x - y + 1 = 0, \\ y - z + 2 = 0, \\ x + z + 3 = 0 \end{cases}$

7. $\begin{cases} x - y + 1 = 0, \\ x + z - 6 = 0, \\ y + z - 7 = 0 \end{cases}$

Set B

8. Evaluate the determinant

$$\begin{vmatrix} -1 & 2 & -3 \\ 2 & 1 & -1 \\ 1 & -1 & 2 \end{vmatrix}$$

by cofactors of
(a) the elements of the second row, and
(b) the elements of the third column.

9. Verify Theorem 16–4 for the determinant of Problem 8, using the elements of the third row and the cofactors of the first row.

Solve the following systems of equations using Cramer's rule. Then solve by reducing each to triangular form.

10. $\begin{cases} x + y + z = 1, \\ 3x + 3y - 3z = 2, \\ x - y - z = 0 \end{cases}$

11. $\begin{cases} x - y + 1 = 0, \\ x + z - 6 = 0, \\ y + z - 6 = 0 \end{cases}$

12. $\begin{cases} 2x - 5y - 7z = 18, \\ x + y + 8z = -35, \\ 4x + 6y + z = 13 \end{cases}$

13. $\begin{cases} x + y - z = 2, \\ -x + 2y + 4z = 5, \\ 2x + 5y + z = 9 \end{cases}$

14. $\begin{cases} x + 2y - z = 3, \\ 3x + y - 2z = 4 \end{cases}$

15. $\begin{cases} x - 2y + z = 3, \\ -x + 4y - 3z = 1, \\ 2x - 3y + z = 8 \end{cases}$

Set C

16. Show in two ways that the equation

$$\begin{vmatrix} x & y & 1 \\ x_1 & y_1 & 1 \\ x_2 & y_2 & 1 \end{vmatrix} = 0$$

is an equation of the line through the distinct points (x_1, y_1) and (x_2, y_2). [Hints: (1) There is such a line: $Ax + By + C = 0$. Therefore $Ax_1 + By_1 + C = 0$ and $Ax_2 + By_2 + C = 0$. These three homogeneous equations have a nontrivial solution. Apply the Corollary to Theorem 16–5. (2) The determinant equation is a linear equation in x and y and therefore represents a line. Show that (x_1, y_1) and (x_2, y_2) are on it.]

17. Use the procedure of Problem 16 to find the line through $(1, -2)$ and $(-2, -4)$.

18. Prove that if k times one row (or column) is added to another row (or column), then the determinant is unchanged.

19. The theorem of Problem 18 can be used to get 0's in a determinant array. Thus the determinant

$$\begin{vmatrix} 1 & 2 & 3 \\ 3 & 4 & 6 \\ 3 & 2 & 1 \end{vmatrix} \quad \text{can be changed into} \quad \begin{vmatrix} 1 & 2 & 3 \\ 1 & 0 & 0 \\ 3 & 2 & 1 \end{vmatrix}$$

by adding (-2) times the first row to the second row. The second determinant is easy to expand by cofactors of the second row.

Apply this method to get some 0's in the following determinants. Then evaluate the determinants.

(a) $\begin{vmatrix} 1 & 2 & 3 \\ 4 & 5 & 6 \\ 7 & 8 & 9 \end{vmatrix}$

(b) $\begin{vmatrix} 1 & -1 & 1 \\ -2 & 3 & 2 \\ 1 & 2 & 3 \end{vmatrix}$

(c) $\begin{vmatrix} 1 & 1 & -2 \\ 2 & -1 & 1 \\ 4 & 1 & -2 \end{vmatrix}$

Calculator Problem

Solve the system

$$\begin{cases} 0.2x - 1.5y + 0.8z = 3.4 \\ 2.9x + 7.4y + 1.3z = 12.1 \\ 1.5x + 6.4y - 8.1z = -7.3. \end{cases}$$

Round the values for x, y and z to the nearest thousandth.

16-5   Higher-Order Determinants

To simplify the notation, we formulate the definition of higher-order determinants in terms of fourth-order ones. The extension to orders greater than four will be clear.

Definition 16-5 The *fourth-order determinant*

$$\begin{vmatrix} a_1 & b_1 & c_1 & d_1 \\ a_2 & b_2 & c_2 & d_2 \\ a_3 & b_3 & c_3 & d_3 \\ a_4 & b_4 & c_4 & d_4 \end{vmatrix}$$

is the sum of all products $\pm a_i b_j c_k d_l$ with i, j, k, and l all different. The positive sign is used when the symbol "$ijkl$" has an even number of inversions. The negative sign is used when the number of inversions is odd.

On the basis of this definition it is possible (but not trivial) to prove all of the theorems of Section 16–4. Basic to the development of properties of higher-order determinants are Theorems 16–3 and 16–4. Theorem 16–3 is illustrated by the following example, where we have expanded by cofactors of the second row.

Example

$$\begin{vmatrix} 1 & 2 & 0 & -1 \\ 2 & -1 & 1 & 2 \\ -2 & -3 & -4 & 1 \\ 1 & -1 & 1 & 2 \end{vmatrix} = -2 \begin{vmatrix} 2 & 0 & -1 \\ -3 & -4 & 1 \\ -1 & 1 & 2 \end{vmatrix} + (-1) \begin{vmatrix} 1 & 0 & -1 \\ -2 & -4 & 1 \\ 1 & 1 & 2 \end{vmatrix}$$

$$-(1) \begin{vmatrix} 1 & 2 & -1 \\ -2 & -3 & 1 \\ 1 & -1 & 2 \end{vmatrix} + 2 \begin{vmatrix} 1 & 2 & 0 \\ -2 & -3 & -4 \\ 1 & -1 & 1 \end{vmatrix}$$

$$= -2(-11) + (-1)(-11) + (0) + 2(-11) = 11.$$

Problems

Set A

Evaluate the following.

1. $\begin{vmatrix} 1 & 2 & 3 & 4 \\ 1 & 4 & 10 & 20 \\ 1 & 3 & 6 & 10 \\ 1 & 1 & 1 & 1 \end{vmatrix}$

2. $\begin{vmatrix} 1 & -1 & -1 & -1 \\ -1 & -1 & 1 & -1 \\ -1 & -1 & -1 & 1 \\ -1 & 1 & -1 & 1 \end{vmatrix}$

3. $\begin{vmatrix} 0 & 1 & 2 & 3 \\ -1 & 0 & 4 & 5 \\ -2 & -4 & 0 & 6 \\ -3 & -5 & -6 & 0 \end{vmatrix}$

4. Use the method described in Problem 19, Section 16-4 to evaluate the determinant in Problem 1 above.

Set B

Solve the following systems by use of Cramer's Rule, and also by elimination.

5. $\begin{cases} x + y + z + w = -1, \\ 2x - y + z - 2w = 11, \\ x - y + 2z - w = 9, \\ 3x + y - z + w = -3. \end{cases}$

6. $\begin{cases} x + 2y - z = 8, \\ -w + y + 3z = 3, \\ 4w - x + z = -20, \\ w + 5x - y = 9 \end{cases}$

7. $\begin{cases} w + x + y + z = 0, \\ 2w - x - y + z = 3, \\ w + 2x - 3y - 2z = -11, \\ w + x - y - z = -6 \end{cases}$

8. $\begin{cases} w + x + y + z = 0, \\ x + y + z = -2, \\ y + z = 0, \\ z = 1 \end{cases}$

Set C

9. Use Theorem 16–5 to prove that if the equations

$$a_1 x + b_1 y + c_1 z - d_1 = 0,$$
$$a_2 x + b_2 y + c_2 z - d_2 = 0,$$
$$a_3 x + b_3 y + c_3 z - d_3 = 0,$$
$$a_4 x + b_4 y + c_4 z - d_4 = 0$$

are consistent (that is, have a solution), then

$$\begin{vmatrix} a_1 & b_1 & c_1 & d_1 \\ a_2 & b_2 & c_2 & d_2 \\ a_3 & b_3 & c_3 & d_3 \\ a_4 & b_4 & c_4 & d_4 \end{vmatrix} = 0.$$

10. Show that

$$\begin{vmatrix} 1 & a & (3 + 2a) \\ 1 & b & (3 + 2b) \\ 1 & c & (3 + 2c) \end{vmatrix} = 0.$$

11. Show that

$$\begin{vmatrix} 1 & w & (x + y + z) & a \\ 1 & x & (w + y + z) & b \\ 1 & y & (w + x + z) & c \\ 1 & z & (w + x + y) & d \end{vmatrix} = 0.$$

12. Show that an equation of the plane through the three noncollinear points

$$(x_1, y_1, z_1), \qquad (x_2, y_2, z_2), \qquad (x_3, y_3, z_3)$$

is the determinant equation

$$\begin{vmatrix} x & y & z & 1 \\ x_1 & y_1 & z_1 & 1 \\ x_2 & y_2 & z_2 & 1 \\ x_3 & y_3 & z_3 & 1 \end{vmatrix} = 0.$$

Calculator Problem

Evaluate.

$$\begin{vmatrix} 1.2 & 0.1 & -0.6 & -0.7 \\ 2.4 & 3.5 & -0.4 & 4.1 \\ -0.8 & -1.7 & 1.1 & 3.8 \\ 0.5 & -2.2 & 2.9 & -0.9 \end{vmatrix}$$

16-6   Matrices

In Section 16–3 we defined matrices as rectangular arrays of numbers. Then determinants were defined as functions whose domains are square matrices. In this section and in the following sections of this chapter we present a brief introduction to the algebra of matrices.

First let us review some terminology about matrices. An $m \times n$ matrix is a rectangular array of numbers consisting of m rows and n columns of numbers. Two such arrays are shown in Fig. 5. Two matrices are equal if and only if they have the same number of rows and columns (so they are of the same *order*) and corresponding numbers (entries or elements) in the two matrices are the same.

$$\begin{bmatrix} 2 & -2 & 7 \end{bmatrix}$$
a 1 × 3 matrix

$$\begin{bmatrix} 6 & -1 \\ 3 & 4 \\ 2 & 1 \end{bmatrix}$$
a 3 × 2 matrix

FIGURE 5

It is convenient to use double subscripts to represent the elements of a matrix. Thus, we may denote the element in the ith row the jth column by a_{ij}. Then

$$\begin{bmatrix} a_{11} & a_{12} \ldots a_{1j} & \ldots & a_{1n} \\ a_{21} & a_{22} \ldots a_{2j} & \ldots & a_{2n} \\ \vdots \\ a_{i1} & a_{i2} \ldots a_{ij} & \ldots & a_{in} \\ \vdots \\ a_{m1} & a_{m2} \ldots a_{mj} & \ldots & a_{mn} \end{bmatrix} \begin{matrix} \\ \\ \\ \longleftarrow i\text{th row} \\ \\ \end{matrix}$$

jth column

For brevity we write $A = [a_{ij}]$.

In this section we are concerned with addition of matrices of the same dimensions and multiplication of a matrix by a real number. First we define addition.

Definition 16-6 If A and B are matrices that have the same order, then the *sum* of A and B (written $A + B$) is a matrix of the same order as A and B and whose entries are the sums of the corresponding entries of A and B.

Example 1
$$\begin{bmatrix} 4 & 5 \\ 2 & 8 \end{bmatrix} + \begin{bmatrix} 3 & -1 \\ -2 & 1 \end{bmatrix} = \begin{bmatrix} 7 & 4 \\ 0 & 9 \end{bmatrix}$$

Example 2
$$\begin{bmatrix} a & b & c \\ d & e & f \end{bmatrix} + \begin{bmatrix} g & h & i \\ j & k & l \end{bmatrix} = \begin{bmatrix} a+g & b+h & c+i \\ d+j & e+k & f+l \end{bmatrix}$$

3
$$\begin{bmatrix} 2 & 6 \\ 3 & 9 \end{bmatrix} + \begin{bmatrix} 2 & 6 \\ 3 & 9 \end{bmatrix} = \begin{bmatrix} 2+2 & 6+6 \\ 3+3 & 9+9 \end{bmatrix} = \begin{bmatrix} 2 \cdot 2 & 2 \cdot 6 \\ 2 \cdot 3 & 2 \cdot 9 \end{bmatrix}$$

Note that Example 3 suggests that repeated addition of matrices suggests a kind of multiplication of a matrix by a number.

Definition 16-7 If k is any real number and A is any matrix, then the product $k \cdot A$ or $A \cdot k$ is a matrix whose entries are the products of the entries of A and the factor k.

The real numbers k are often called scalars to distinguish them from vectors and matrices. Then kA is the product of the scalar k and the matrix A.

Example 4 $4 \cdot [1 \quad -1 \quad 2] = [4 \quad -4 \quad 8]$

5 $-2 \cdot \begin{bmatrix} 1 & 2 \\ -1 & -3 \end{bmatrix} = \begin{bmatrix} -2 & -4 \\ 2 & 6 \end{bmatrix}$

6 $k \cdot \begin{bmatrix} a & b \\ c & d \end{bmatrix} = \begin{bmatrix} ka & kb \\ kc & kd \end{bmatrix}$

Definition 16-8 A matrix (of any order) each of whose elements is 0 is called the *zero matrix* (for that order) and is denoted by O.

Example 7
$$\begin{bmatrix} 0 & 0 \\ 0 & 0 \end{bmatrix}, \quad [0 \quad 0 \quad 0] \quad \text{and} \quad \begin{bmatrix} 0 \\ 0 \end{bmatrix}$$

are zero matrices of orders 2×2, 1×3, and 2×1.

It is now possible to prove a few easy theorems about matrix addition and multiplication by scalars. Their proofs are left as exercises.

Theorem 16-6 **PROPERTIES OF MATRIX ADDITION.** *Let A, B, and C be matrices of order m × n.*

(a) $A + B = B + A$.

(b) There is a special matrix O, the zero matrix, such that

$$A + O = O + A = A \quad \text{for all } A.$$

(c) For each matrix A, there exists a matrix $-A = (-1)A$ such that $A + (-A) = O$. The matrix $-A$ is called the additive inverse of A.

(d) $(A + B) + C = A + (B + C)$.

Theorem 16-7 *PROPERTIES OF SCALAR MULTIPLICATION. Let A and B be matrices of order m × n, and let x and y be any real numbers.*

(a) $x(yA) = (xy)A$.
(b) $(x + y)A = xA + yA$.
(c) $x(A + B) = xA + xB$.
(d) $1 \cdot A = A$.
(e) $0 \cdot A = O$.

Problems

Set A

1. How many rows and columns does matrix A have?

$$A = \begin{bmatrix} 2 & 1 & 5 & 0 \\ -2 & 0 & 4 & 4 \\ -3 & 6 & -1 & 2 \end{bmatrix}.$$

2. What is the order of A?

3. What is a_{23} for matrix A of problem 1?

Give the numbers for x and y in each matrix equation.

4. $\begin{bmatrix} x & 1 \\ 1 & y \end{bmatrix} = \begin{bmatrix} -1 & 1 \\ 1 & -1 \end{bmatrix}$ **5.** $\begin{bmatrix} x & 7 \\ y & 4 \end{bmatrix} = \begin{bmatrix} 1 & 7 \\ 0 & 4 \end{bmatrix}$

Find the sums.

6. $\begin{bmatrix} 2 \\ -1 \\ 3 \end{bmatrix} + \begin{bmatrix} 5 \\ 1 \\ -4 \end{bmatrix}$

7. $\begin{bmatrix} 6 & 3 \\ 5 & 8 \\ 0 & -4 \end{bmatrix} + \begin{bmatrix} 1 & 5 \\ -4 & -6 \\ -1 & 5 \end{bmatrix}$

8. $\begin{bmatrix} 5 & -3 \\ -2 & 6 \end{bmatrix} + \begin{bmatrix} -5 & 3 \\ 2 & -6 \end{bmatrix}$

9. $\begin{bmatrix} 5 & 1 & -1 \\ 2 & 1 & 7 \\ 4 & 3 & 4 \end{bmatrix} + \begin{bmatrix} 0 & 0 & 0 \\ 0 & 0 & 0 \\ 0 & 0 & 0 \end{bmatrix}$

10. $[3 \quad -5] + [5 \quad -3]$

11. $\begin{bmatrix} 2 & 1 & 5 \\ 0 & 0 & 0 \\ 2 & 4 & -1 \end{bmatrix} + \begin{bmatrix} -1 & -1 & -4 \\ 0 & 0 & 0 \\ -2 & 2 & -1 \end{bmatrix}$

Find the products.

12. $-2 \cdot \begin{bmatrix} 1 & 3 \\ -2 & 1 \\ 4 & -3 \end{bmatrix}$ **13.** $4 \cdot \begin{bmatrix} 7 \\ 0 \\ 1 \end{bmatrix}$

14. $-1 \cdot \begin{bmatrix} 5 & 1 \\ -1 & -2 \end{bmatrix}$ **15.** $10 \cdot [1 \quad -1 \quad 1]$

Given $A = \begin{bmatrix} 2 & 1 \\ 4 & 3 \end{bmatrix}$, $B = \begin{bmatrix} 1 & 0 \\ 0 & 1 \end{bmatrix}$, and $C = \begin{bmatrix} -1 & 0 \\ -2 & -2 \end{bmatrix}$,

find the matrix that is the result of each of the following operations.

16. $(A + B) + C$ **17.** $2A + C$

18. $B + 3C$ **19.** $-1A + 2C$

20. $(A + 5B) + (-2)C$ **21.** $(A + C) + B$

Set B

22. Show that $\begin{bmatrix} -2 & -3 \\ -5 & 7 \end{bmatrix}$ is the additive inverse of $\begin{bmatrix} 2 & 3 \\ 5 & -7 \end{bmatrix}$.

23. Give the additive inverse of $\begin{bmatrix} 7 & 3 \\ 4 & 5 \end{bmatrix}$.

24. Give the additive inverse of $[2 \quad 3 \quad -4]$.

25. If B is a 2×2 matrix, what are the entries in B?

$$\begin{bmatrix} 6 & -2 \\ 5 & -3 \end{bmatrix} + B = \begin{bmatrix} 0 & 0 \\ 0 & 0 \end{bmatrix}$$

26. Verify that

$$(-6 + 8)\begin{bmatrix} 1 & 2 \\ 3 & 4 \end{bmatrix} = -6\begin{bmatrix} 1 & 2 \\ 3 & 4 \end{bmatrix} + 8\begin{bmatrix} 1 & 2 \\ 3 & 4 \end{bmatrix}.$$

27. Find the matrix X.

$$\begin{bmatrix} 2 & 4 \\ 3 & 1 \end{bmatrix} + X = \begin{bmatrix} 1 & 3 \\ 4 & 1 \end{bmatrix}$$

28. Find the matrix Y if

$$\begin{bmatrix} 3 & 1 & 2 \\ -4 & 1 & 0 \\ 5 & 1 & 4 \end{bmatrix} + Y = \begin{bmatrix} 0 & 0 & 0 \\ 0 & 0 & 0 \\ 0 & 0 & 0 \end{bmatrix}.$$

Set C

Give the numbers for x and y in each matrix equation.

29. $\begin{bmatrix} (x - 2) & 7 \\ (y + 3) & 4 \end{bmatrix} = \begin{bmatrix} 1 & 7 \\ 0 & 4 \end{bmatrix}$

30. $[2 \quad x \quad -5] = [(y - 2) \quad -7 \quad -5]$

31. $[x + y \quad x - y] = [12 \quad 2]$

32. $\begin{bmatrix} (3x + 2) \\ (5y - 1) \end{bmatrix} = \begin{bmatrix} 11 \\ -11 \end{bmatrix}$

Let A, B, and C be the matrices of Problems 16–21. Find the matrix X satisfying each equation.

33. $A + X = C$ **34.** $2B + X = C$

35. $3A + X = B$ **36.** $-4B + X = A$

Let $A = \begin{bmatrix} a & b \\ c & d \end{bmatrix}$, $B = \begin{bmatrix} e & f \\ g & h \end{bmatrix}$, $C = \begin{bmatrix} i & j \\ k & l \end{bmatrix}$.

37. Verify properties (a) through (d) of Theorem 16–6 for this 2×2 case.

38. With the matrices of Problem 37 verify the properties of Theorem 16–7.

39. Prove Theorem 16–6 for $m \times n$ matrices.

40. Prove Theorem 16–7 for $m \times n$ matrices.

Calculator Problem

Find the matrix Y of $-2\begin{bmatrix} 5.61 & -1.43 \\ 3.78 & -2.85 \end{bmatrix} + Y = \begin{bmatrix} 7.09 & 5.93 \\ -6.21 & 0.77 \end{bmatrix}$

16-7   Multiplication of Matrices

Now we consider another binary operation, called matrix multiplication, on certain pairs of matrices. The definition may seem strange and arbitrary, but we give it first and then examine its usefulness.

Definition 16-9 Suppose A is an $m \times n$ matrix and B is an $n \times q$ matrix. Then the *product* of A and B, denoted by AB, is the matrix C of m rows and q columns whose entry in the ith row and jth column is the sum of the products of the elements of the ith row of A and the corresponding elements of the jth column of B.

Thus if $A = [a_{ik}]$ with $i = 1, \ldots, m$ and $k = 1, \ldots, n$, and $B = [b_{kj}]$ with $k = 1, \ldots, n$ and $j = 1, \ldots, q$, then the rows of A and the columns of B have the same number n of entries. Therefore, the following numbers c_{ij} are defined:

$$c_{ij} = a_{i1}b_{1j} + a_{i2}b_{2j} + \cdots + a_{in}b_{nj} = \sum_{k=1}^{n} a_{ik}b_{kj}. \qquad (1)$$

The product AB is equal to C, where $C = [c_{ij}]$ and the c_{ij} are given by equation (1).

Matrix multiplication is briefly described as "row-by-column multiplication."

Example 1
$$\begin{bmatrix} 2 & 6 \\ 1 & 4 \end{bmatrix}\begin{bmatrix} 3 & 5 \\ 4 & 0 \end{bmatrix} = \begin{bmatrix} 2\cdot 3 + 6\cdot 4 & 2\cdot 5 + 6\cdot 0 \\ 1\cdot 3 + 4\cdot 4 & 1\cdot 5 + 4\cdot 0 \end{bmatrix} = \begin{bmatrix} 30 & 10 \\ 19 & 5 \end{bmatrix}$$

2
$$\begin{bmatrix} 1 & -4 & 5 \\ 3 & 0 & 2 \end{bmatrix}\begin{bmatrix} 2 & 1 \\ -1 & 0 \\ 2 & 3 \end{bmatrix}$$

$$= \begin{bmatrix} 1\cdot 2 + (-4)(-1) + 5\cdot 2 & 1\cdot 1 + (-4)\cdot 0 + 5\cdot 3 \\ 3\cdot 2 + 0\cdot(-1) + 2\cdot 2 & 3\cdot 1 + 0\cdot 0 + 2\cdot 3 \end{bmatrix} = \begin{bmatrix} 16 & 16 \\ 10 & 9 \end{bmatrix}$$

3
$$\begin{bmatrix} 1 & -4 & 5 \\ 3 & 0 & 2 \end{bmatrix} \cdot \begin{bmatrix} 1 & 1 & -1 \\ 0 & 2 & 1 \end{bmatrix}$$

is not defined because the number of columns of the first matrix is not equal to the number of rows of the second matrix.

Just as addition of matrices and multiplication by scalars exhibit algebraic properties that are similar to addition and multiplication of real numbers (see Theorems 16–6 and 16–7), so also does matrix multiplication. We now list these properties. Proof of these properties for matrices of low order are left as problems.

Theorem 16-8   *(a) If A, B, and C are $m \times n$, $n \times q$, and $q \times r$ matrices, respectively, then $A(BC) = (AB)C$. Matrix multiplication is associative.*

(b) If A, B, and C are $m \times n$, $n \times q$, and $n \times q$ matrices, respectively, then

$$A(B + C) = AB + AC. \qquad (i)$$

If A, B, C are $q \times r$, $n \times q$, and $n \times q$ matrices, respectively, then

$$(B + C)A = BA + CA. \qquad (ii)$$

Remarks   1. Matrix multiplication is not in general commutative. Usually, $AB \neq BA$ even if both products are defined. (See Problem 10.)

2. Equations (i) and (ii) imply that matrix multiplication is distributive over matrix addition.

One might guess that there should be a matrix that behaves just as 1 does for multiplication. This is indeed the case, but one has a different matrix for each natural number n.

Definition 16-10 For each natural number n, the *identity matrix*, I_n, is the $n \times n$ matrix in which all entries on the main diagonal are 1's and all other entries are 0's.

$$\textit{Example 4} \quad I_2 = \begin{bmatrix} 1 & 0 \\ 0 & 1 \end{bmatrix} \qquad\qquad I_4 = \begin{bmatrix} 1 & 0 & 0 & 0 \\ 0 & 1 & 0 & 0 \\ 0 & 0 & 1 & 0 \\ 0 & 0 & 0 & 1 \end{bmatrix}$$

Theorem 16-9 **If A is an $m \times n$ matrix, then**

$$I_m \cdot A = A, \qquad A \cdot I_n = A.$$

Proofs in special cases are left for the problems.

Problems

Set A

Find the products.

1. $\begin{bmatrix} 1 & 4 \\ 3 & -2 \end{bmatrix}\begin{bmatrix} 2 \\ 3 \end{bmatrix}$ **2.** $\begin{bmatrix} 2 & 6 \\ 4 & 8 \end{bmatrix}\begin{bmatrix} 1 & 0 \\ 0 & 1 \end{bmatrix}$

3. $\begin{bmatrix} 1 & 0 & -1 \end{bmatrix}\begin{bmatrix} 2 & 1 & 4 \\ 2 & 1 & 3 \\ 0 & 2 & 5 \end{bmatrix}$

4. $\begin{bmatrix} 1 & 2 & 3 \end{bmatrix}\begin{bmatrix} 3 \\ 2 \\ 1 \end{bmatrix}$ **5.** $\begin{bmatrix} 2 & 3 \\ 5 & 0 \\ 1 & 2 \end{bmatrix}\begin{bmatrix} 2 & 5 & 1 \\ 3 & 0 & 2 \end{bmatrix}$

6. $\begin{bmatrix} 3 & 2 \\ 6 & 4 \end{bmatrix}\begin{bmatrix} 4 & -2 \\ -6 & 4 \end{bmatrix}$ **7.** $\begin{bmatrix} -4 & -1 \\ -2 & 1 \end{bmatrix}\begin{bmatrix} \frac{1}{2} & \frac{1}{2} \\ 1 & 2 \end{bmatrix}$

8. $\begin{bmatrix} 2 \\ 3 \\ -5 \end{bmatrix}\begin{bmatrix} 1 & 0 & 0 \end{bmatrix}$

Set B

9. Find the products.

(a) $\begin{bmatrix} 0 & 0 \\ 1 & 0 \end{bmatrix}\begin{bmatrix} 0 & 0 \\ 1 & 0 \end{bmatrix}$ (b) $\begin{bmatrix} 2 & 6 \\ 1 & 3 \end{bmatrix}\begin{bmatrix} -9 & -6 \\ 3 & 2 \end{bmatrix}$

In what way are the products different from usual products in algebra?

10. Let $A = \begin{bmatrix} 2 & 3 \\ 5 & -2 \end{bmatrix}$ and $B = \begin{bmatrix} 1 & -1 \\ 4 & 3 \end{bmatrix}$. Find AB and BA. By comparing these products what can you conclude about matrix multiplication?

11. Let $A = \begin{bmatrix} 1 & -1 \\ 2 & 3 \end{bmatrix}$, $B = \begin{bmatrix} 2 & 0 \\ -1 & 4 \end{bmatrix}$, and $C = \begin{bmatrix} 0 & 2 \\ -3 & 5 \end{bmatrix}$. Verify Theorem 16-8 for this special case.

Let $A = \begin{bmatrix} 2 & -2 \\ 3 & 4 \end{bmatrix}$ and $B = \begin{bmatrix} -1 & 0 \\ 2 & -3 \end{bmatrix}$.

Compute the following.

12. A^2, that is, AA **13.** B^2

14. $A + B$ **15.** $A - B$ or $A + (-1)B$

16. $(A + B)(A - B)$ **17.** $A^2 - B^2$

Set C

18. In the algebra of real numbers, if a and b are real, then $(a + b)(a - b) = a^2 - b^2$. Do Problems 16 and 17 show that a similar identity holds for matrices A and B? Explain.

19. If $A = \begin{bmatrix} a_{11} & a_{12} \\ a_{21} & a_{22} \end{bmatrix}$, show that $I_2 A = A I_2 = A$, where I_2 is the 2×2 identity matrix.

20. Suppose A is a 3×3 matrix. Show that $I_3 A = A I_3 = A$.

Let $A = \begin{bmatrix} 1 & 2 \\ 2 & 2 \end{bmatrix}$. Compute the following.

21. $A + 3I_2$ **22.** $A + 2I_2$

23. A^2 **24.** $A^2 + 5A$

25. $A^2 + 5A + 6I_2$ **26.** $(A + 3I_2)(A + 2I_2)$

Calculator Problem

Let $A = \begin{bmatrix} 2.7 & -3.1 & 4.8 \\ -6.5 & 0.9 & -4.7 \end{bmatrix}$ and $B = \begin{bmatrix} 0.5 & -3.7 \\ -1.9 & 0.1 \\ 3.8 & -4.6 \end{bmatrix}$. Compute AB and BA.

16-8   ▪   **Inverses of Matrices**

We have seen in Sections 16-6 and 16-7 that matrices have many of the algebraic properties that are possessed by the real numbers. Now the real numbers have the following special property: If $x \neq 0$, there is a unique real number x^{-1} (the multiplicative inverse of x) such that

$$x^{-1} \cdot x = x \cdot x^{-1} = 1.$$

To discuss whether a similar situation prevails for matrices, we need the following definition.

Definition 16-11 If A and B are $n \times n$ matrices such that $AB = BA = I_n$, where I_n is the identity matrix, then A and B are *multiplicative inverses* of each other. B is called the *multiplicative inverse** of A and is denoted by A^{-1}.

Note that the definition defines inverses only for $n \times n$ or square matrices. Inverses for nonsquare matrices are not defined and we shall see that not every square matrix has a multiplicative inverse.

---

*The inverse, if it exists, is unique. That is, if $BA = AB = I_n$ and $B_1 A = A B_1 = I_n$, then from $AB_1 = I_n$ we get $B(AB_1) = BI_n = B$. But $B(AB_1) = (BA)B_1 = I_n B_1 = B_1$. Thus $B = B_1$.

In this section our purpose is to see how to find inverses of square matrices, when they exist. Suppose

$$A = \begin{bmatrix} a & b \\ c & d \end{bmatrix}.$$

Let us try to find A^{-1}. We must find the entries of a matrix

$$A^{-1} = \begin{bmatrix} w & x \\ y & z \end{bmatrix}$$

such that

$$\begin{bmatrix} a & b \\ c & d \end{bmatrix}\begin{bmatrix} w & x \\ y & z \end{bmatrix} = \begin{bmatrix} 1 & 0 \\ 0 & 1 \end{bmatrix}.$$

Therefore,

$$\begin{matrix} aw + by = 1, \\ cw + dy = 0 \end{matrix} \quad \text{and} \quad \begin{matrix} ax + bz = 0, \\ cx + dz = 1 \end{matrix}$$

must hold. Why?

If

$$\det \begin{bmatrix} a & b \\ c & d \end{bmatrix} = ad - bc \neq 0,$$

the equations above have the unique solutions

$$w = \frac{d}{\begin{vmatrix} a & b \\ c & d \end{vmatrix}}, \; x = \frac{-b}{\begin{vmatrix} a & b \\ c & d \end{vmatrix}}, \; y = \frac{-c}{\begin{vmatrix} a & b \\ c & d \end{vmatrix}}, \; \text{and} \; z = \frac{a}{\begin{vmatrix} a & b \\ c & d \end{vmatrix}}.$$

If we set

$$\begin{vmatrix} a & b \\ c & d \end{vmatrix} = \det A$$

we see that the matrix A has an inverse, provided $\det A \neq 0$, and that it is

$$\frac{1}{\det A} \cdot \begin{bmatrix} d & -b \\ -c & a \end{bmatrix}.$$

Thus we have the following theorem.

Theorem 16-10 *If $ad - bc \neq 0$, then*

$$\begin{bmatrix} a & b \\ c & d \end{bmatrix} \quad and \quad \frac{1}{ad - bc}\begin{bmatrix} d & -b \\ -c & a \end{bmatrix}$$

are inverses of each other.

Example 1 Find the inverse of

$$A = \begin{bmatrix} 2 & -1 \\ 1 & 1 \end{bmatrix}.$$

Solution.

$$\det A = \begin{vmatrix} 2 & -1 \\ 1 & 1 \end{vmatrix} = 3.$$

Therefore

$$A^{-1} = \frac{1}{3} \begin{bmatrix} 1 & 1 \\ -1 & 2 \end{bmatrix} = \begin{bmatrix} \frac{1}{3} & \frac{1}{3} \\ -\frac{1}{3} & \frac{2}{3} \end{bmatrix}.$$

As a check we can multiply:

$$A \cdot A^{-1} = \begin{bmatrix} 2 & -1 \\ 1 & 1 \end{bmatrix} \begin{bmatrix} \frac{1}{3} & \frac{1}{3} \\ -\frac{1}{3} & \frac{2}{3} \end{bmatrix} = \begin{bmatrix} 1 & 0 \\ 0 & 1 \end{bmatrix} = A^{-1}A.$$

Inverses of 3×3 matrices can be found by a method similar to that used for 2×2 determinants. We shall not do that here. Instead, we will simply give the method used to find A^{-1} and state a theorem.

In computing the inverse of a square matrix A it is convenient to calculate a matrix called the *adjoint* of A, adj A. The *row elements* of adj A are the *cofactors* (signed minors) of the corresponding elements in the *columns* of A.

Example 2

$$A = \begin{bmatrix} 1 & 0 & 1 \\ 2 & 1 & 3 \\ 1 & 4 & 0 \end{bmatrix}, \qquad \text{adj } A = \begin{bmatrix} -12 & 4 & -1 \\ 3 & -1 & -1 \\ 7 & -4 & 1 \end{bmatrix}.$$

Verify that the elements of the first row of adj A are the cofactors of the corresponding elements in the first column of A, and make a similar check for the second and third rows of adj A.

Definition 16–12 If

$$A = \begin{bmatrix} a_1 & b_1 & c_1 \\ a_2 & b_2 & c_2 \\ a_3 & b_3 & c_3 \end{bmatrix}$$

and A_i, B_i, and C_i denote the cofactors of the a_i, b_i, and c_i, then the *adjoint of A* (adj A) is

$$\begin{bmatrix} A_1 & A_2 & A_3 \\ B_1 & B_2 & B_3 \\ C_1 & C_2 & C_3 \end{bmatrix}.$$

The following theorem shows how the adjoint of A and A^{-1} are related.

Theorem 16–11* *For any* 3 × 3 *matrix A, A*(adj *A*) = det *A* · *I, and* (adj *A*)*A* = det *A* · *I. Thus if* det *A* ≠ 0,

$$A^{-1} = \frac{1}{\det A} \text{adj } A.$$

Remark   If det $A = 0$, there can be no inverse.

Example 3 To find the inverse of

$$A = \begin{bmatrix} 2 & 4 & 1 \\ 1 & 2 & 3 \\ 2 & -1 & 1 \end{bmatrix},$$

we have

$$\det A = 25 \quad \text{and} \quad \text{adj } A = \begin{bmatrix} 5 & -5 & 10 \\ 5 & 0 & -5 \\ -5 & 10 & 0 \end{bmatrix}.$$

Therefore

$$A^{-1} = \frac{1}{25} \begin{bmatrix} 5 & -5 & 10 \\ 5 & 0 & -5 \\ -5 & 10 & 0 \end{bmatrix} = \begin{bmatrix} \frac{1}{5} & -\frac{1}{5} & \frac{2}{5} \\ \frac{1}{5} & 0 & -\frac{1}{5} \\ -\frac{1}{5} & \frac{2}{5} & 0 \end{bmatrix}.$$

As a check one should multiply $A \cdot A^{-1}$.

Problems

Set A

Which of these 2 × 2 matrices have inverses?

1. $\begin{bmatrix} 1 & 3 \\ 3 & 1 \end{bmatrix}$ **2.** $\begin{bmatrix} 2 & 4 \\ 1 & 2 \end{bmatrix}$

3. $\begin{bmatrix} 6 & -8 \\ -3 & 4 \end{bmatrix}$ **4.** $\begin{bmatrix} 1 & 0 \\ 0 & 1 \end{bmatrix}$

Compute the inverse of each matrix.

5. $\begin{bmatrix} 3 & 2 \\ 4 & 3 \end{bmatrix}$ **6.** $\begin{bmatrix} 3 & 1 \\ 4 & 2 \end{bmatrix}$

7. $\begin{bmatrix} -3 & 4 \\ -6 & 6 \end{bmatrix}$ **8.** $\begin{bmatrix} -5 & -2 \\ -3 & 1 \end{bmatrix}$

9. Find the adjoint of

$$\begin{bmatrix} 2 & -4 & -1 \\ 1 & 0 & 3 \\ 3 & 2 & 5 \end{bmatrix}.$$

Set B

Let $A = \begin{bmatrix} 2 & 1 & 0 \\ 1 & 0 & 3 \\ 3 & 1 & 2 \end{bmatrix}$. Find

10. det A.   **11.** adj A.   **12.** A^{-1}.

---

*A similar theorem is valid for square matrices of order *n*.

Compute the inverse of each matrix.

13. $\begin{bmatrix} 1 & 3 & -1 \\ 2 & 4 & 0 \\ -1 & 2 & 1 \end{bmatrix}$ **14.** $\begin{bmatrix} 4 & -4 & 2 \\ 1 & 0 & 0 \\ 3 & -3 & 1 \end{bmatrix}$

15. Solve the matrix equation

$$\begin{bmatrix} -1 & -1 \\ 4 & 3 \end{bmatrix} \begin{bmatrix} x \\ y \end{bmatrix} = \begin{bmatrix} 5 \\ -1 \end{bmatrix}$$

by multiplying both sides of the equation by the inverse of

$$\begin{bmatrix} -1 & -1 \\ 4 & 3 \end{bmatrix}.$$

Set C

16. Prove Theorem 16–11.

17. Explain why only square matrices have inverses defined.

18. Show that for every real number k the matrices

$$\begin{bmatrix} 1 & 0 & 0 \\ 0 & 1 & 0 \\ k & 0 & 1 \end{bmatrix} \quad \text{and} \quad \begin{bmatrix} 1 & 0 & 0 \\ 0 & 1 & 0 \\ -k & 0 & 1 \end{bmatrix}$$

are inverses of each other.

19. Prove that if A has an inverse, then $(A^{-1})^{-1} = A$.

20. Show that the zero matrix, O, has no inverse.

21. Inverses of 4×4 matrices are found in the same way as those of 3×3 matrices. Find the inverse of

$$\begin{bmatrix} 1 & 2 & 0 & 1 \\ 0 & 1 & -1 & 2 \\ 1 & 2 & 1 & 2 \\ -1 & 2 & 2 & 0 \end{bmatrix}.$$

Calculator Problem

Let $A = \begin{bmatrix} 0.1 & 0.4 & -0.7 \\ -0.2 & 0.5 & 0.8 \\ -0.3 & 0.6 & 0.9 \end{bmatrix}$. Compute A^{-1} if it exists.

16-9   Matrices and Linear Equations

In this section we observe that a system of two (or three) linear equations in two (or three) unknowns can be written as a single matrix equation. Then we shall see how to solve the matrix equation and so solve the original linear system. First an example.

Example 1 Consider the pair of linear equations

$$\begin{cases} 2x + 3y = 5, \\ 4x + 5y = 7, \end{cases} \tag{1}$$

and the matrices

$$A = \begin{bmatrix} 2 & 3 \\ 4 & 5 \end{bmatrix}, \quad X = \begin{bmatrix} x \\ y \end{bmatrix}, \quad B = \begin{bmatrix} 5 \\ 7 \end{bmatrix}.$$

Then

$$AX = \begin{bmatrix} 2 & 3 \\ 4 & 5 \end{bmatrix} \begin{bmatrix} x \\ y \end{bmatrix} = \begin{bmatrix} 2x + 3y \\ 4x + 5y \end{bmatrix}.$$

The situation of the example is quite general. Any system of linear equations is equivalent to a single matrix equation, but we restrict our attention here to systems with two or three unknowns and the same number of equations as unknowns. For two unknowns the general situation should be clear from the example. For three unknowns we state the facts as a theorem.

Theorem 16-12   *If*

$$A = \begin{bmatrix} a_1 & b_1 & c_1 \\ a_2 & b_2 & c_2 \\ a_3 & b_3 & c_3 \end{bmatrix}, \qquad X = \begin{bmatrix} x \\ y \\ z \end{bmatrix}, \qquad B = \begin{bmatrix} d_1 \\ d_2 \\ d_3 \end{bmatrix},$$

then the equation $AX = B$ *is satisfied by* X *if and only if* x, y *and* z *satisfy the system*

$$\begin{cases} a_1x + b_1y + c_1z = d_1, \\ a_2x + b_2y + c_2z = d_2, \\ a_3x + b_3y + c_3z = d_3. \end{cases}$$

A proof is left as a problem.

We now, finally, show how matrix inverses can be used to solve systems of linear equations. For simplicity we confine our considerations to three equations in three unknowns.

The system

$$\begin{cases} a_1x + b_1y + c_1z = d_1, \\ a_2x + b_2y + c_2z = d_2, \\ a_3x + b_3y + c_3z = d_3 \end{cases}$$

is equivalent to the matrix equation $AX = D$ with

$$A = \begin{bmatrix} a_1 & b_1 & c_1 \\ a_2 & b_2 & c_2 \\ a_3 & b_3 & c_3 \end{bmatrix}, \qquad X = \begin{bmatrix} x \\ y \\ z \end{bmatrix}, \qquad D = \begin{bmatrix} d_1 \\ d_2 \\ d_3 \end{bmatrix}.$$

Then, if $\det A \neq 0$, we have

$$\begin{aligned} AX &= D, & \\ A^{-1} \cdot (AX) &= A^{-1}D, & \text{(Why?)} \\ (A^{-1} \cdot A)X &= A^{-1}D, & \text{(Why?)} \\ I_3 X &= A^{-1}D, & \text{(Why?)} \\ X &= A^{-1}D. & \text{(Why?)} \end{aligned}$$

Example 2   Use matrices to solve the system of equations

$$\begin{cases} 2x + y - 2z = 2, \\ x + 2y + 5z = 4, \\ x - y + z = 6. \end{cases}$$

Solution. The system has the matrix form

$$\begin{bmatrix} 2 & 1 & -2 \\ 1 & 2 & 5 \\ 1 & -1 & 1 \end{bmatrix} \begin{bmatrix} x \\ y \\ z \end{bmatrix} = \begin{bmatrix} 2 \\ 4 \\ 6 \end{bmatrix}.$$

The matrix coefficient of

$$\begin{bmatrix} x \\ y \\ z \end{bmatrix}$$

has an inverse of

$$\frac{1}{24} \begin{bmatrix} 7 & 1 & 9 \\ 4 & 4 & -12 \\ -3 & 3 & 3 \end{bmatrix}.$$

Therefore

$$\begin{bmatrix} x \\ y \\ z \end{bmatrix} = \frac{1}{24} \begin{bmatrix} 7 & 1 & 9 \\ 4 & 4 & -12 \\ -3 & 3 & 3 \end{bmatrix} \begin{bmatrix} 2 \\ 4 \\ 6 \end{bmatrix},$$

$$\begin{bmatrix} x \\ y \\ z \end{bmatrix} = \frac{1}{24} \begin{bmatrix} 72 \\ -48 \\ 24 \end{bmatrix} = \begin{bmatrix} 3 \\ -2 \\ 1 \end{bmatrix}.$$

Hence $x = 3$, $y = -2$, and $z = 1$.

Problems

Set A

1. Write a single matrix equation equivalent to the system

$$\begin{cases} x - y = 2, \\ 2x + y = 4. \end{cases}$$

2. If $A = \begin{bmatrix} 2 & -3 \\ 0 & 1 \end{bmatrix}$, $X = \begin{bmatrix} x \\ y \end{bmatrix}$, and $B = \begin{bmatrix} -2 \\ -3 \end{bmatrix}$,

what system of linear equations is equivalent to $AX = B$?

3. Write a single matrix equation equivalent to the system

$$\begin{cases} 2x - y = 3, \\ x + y + z = 4, \\ x - 2z = 1. \end{cases}$$

4. What system of linear equations is implied by the matrix equation

$$\begin{bmatrix} 1 & 2 \\ 3 & -2 \end{bmatrix} \begin{bmatrix} x \\ y \end{bmatrix} = \begin{bmatrix} 5 \\ -1 \end{bmatrix}?$$

Give the linear system that is equivalent to the matrix equation.

5. $\begin{bmatrix} 2 & 1 & -2 \\ 1 & 2 & 5 \\ 1 & 1 & 1 \end{bmatrix}\begin{bmatrix} x \\ y \\ z \end{bmatrix} = \begin{bmatrix} 2 \\ 4 \\ 2 \end{bmatrix}$

6. $\begin{bmatrix} 2 & 3 & -2 \\ 1 & 0 & 1 \\ 0 & 2 & 2 \end{bmatrix}\begin{bmatrix} u \\ v \\ w \end{bmatrix} = \begin{bmatrix} 3 \\ 0 \\ 2 \end{bmatrix}$

Solve each system of equations using matrices.

7. $\begin{cases} 2x + y = 11, \\ x - y = 4 \end{cases}$

8. $\begin{cases} 3x + 5y = -1, \\ x + 4y = 9 \end{cases}$

9. $\begin{cases} x - 3y = -25 \\ 2x + 6y = 10 \end{cases}$

10. $\begin{cases} 2x - 7y = 31, \\ -8x + 3y = 1 \end{cases}$

11. $\begin{cases} x + y + z = 2, \\ x - 2y - z = 1, \\ 3x + y + 4z = 3 \end{cases}$

12. $\begin{cases} x - y + 2z = -2, \\ 3x + 2y - z = 8, \\ 4x + y + 3z = 2 \end{cases}$

Set B

Find the numbers x and y in each matrix equation.

13. $\begin{bmatrix} 2 & 1 \\ 1 & -1 \end{bmatrix}\begin{bmatrix} x \\ y \end{bmatrix} = \begin{bmatrix} 2 \\ 7 \end{bmatrix}$

14. $\begin{bmatrix} 1 & 1 \\ 5 & -1 \end{bmatrix}\begin{bmatrix} x \\ y \end{bmatrix} = \begin{bmatrix} 0 \\ 36 \end{bmatrix}$

Find the numbers x, y and z in each matrix equation.

15. $\begin{bmatrix} 1 & 1 & 1 \\ 2 & -1 & 5 \\ -1 & 2 & -1 \end{bmatrix}\begin{bmatrix} x \\ y \\ z \end{bmatrix} = \begin{bmatrix} 2 \\ -5 \\ 19 \end{bmatrix}$

16. $\begin{bmatrix} 2 & 2 & -1 \\ 1 & -1 & -1 \\ 3 & 1 & 1 \end{bmatrix}\begin{bmatrix} x \\ y \\ z \end{bmatrix} = \begin{bmatrix} 18 \\ 2 \\ 2 \end{bmatrix}$

Set C

17. Solve the matrix equation for $X = \begin{bmatrix} x & z \\ y & w \end{bmatrix}$ given

$$X \cdot \begin{bmatrix} 3 & 1 \\ 2 & 1 \end{bmatrix} = \begin{bmatrix} 1 & 0 \\ 0 & 1 \end{bmatrix}.$$

18. What second-degree algebraic equation is given by this matrix equation?

$$\left([x \ \ y] \begin{bmatrix} 5 & 2 \\ 2 & 2 \end{bmatrix} \right)\begin{bmatrix} x \\ y \end{bmatrix} = [9].$$

19. Prove Theorem 16–12.

Calculator Problem

Find approximate values of x and y in the matrix equation

$$\begin{bmatrix} \sqrt{2} & -\sqrt{3} \\ -\sqrt{5} & \sqrt{6} \end{bmatrix}\begin{bmatrix} x \\ y \end{bmatrix} = \begin{bmatrix} \sqrt{7} \\ \sqrt{8} \end{bmatrix}.$$

Summary

The main emphasis in this chapter has been on the solution of systems of linear equations in two and three unknowns. Three different methods were discussed:

    (a) Elimination of successive variables.
    (b) Use of determinants using Cramer's Rule.
    (c) Use of matrix inverses.

Some highlights of the chapter are the following.

1. A system of simultaneous linear equations may have

    (a) a unique solution,
    (b) no solution (an inconsistent system),
    (c) infinitely many solutions.

2. A system of two (or three) simultaneous equations in two (or three) unknowns has a unique solution if and only if the determinant of the system is not 0.

3. Matrices of the same order may be added by adding corresponding entries.

4. Matrices may be multiplied by a real number (a scalar) by multiplying each entry by the real number.

5. The zero matrix, O, has 0 as every entry.

6. Each matrix has an additive inverse.

7. Addition of matrices is commutative and associative.

8. If A is an $m \times n$ matrix and B is an $n \times q$ matrix, then AB is an $m \times q$ matrix obtained by the "row-by-column" rule of multiplication.

9. Matrix multiplication, even when it is defined, is not necessarily commutative.

10. If a square matrix has a non-zero determinant, we can find the multiplicative inverse of the matrix.

Chapter 16   Test

16–2   For each pair of equations use the condition of Theorem 16–1 to tell whether the system of equations has a unique solution, many solutions or no solutions. Sketch the pair of lines.

1. $\begin{cases} 3x - 4 = 1. \\ 12x - 4y = 4 \end{cases}$ 2. $\begin{cases} x + y = 7, \\ x - 2y = -2 \end{cases}$ 3. $\begin{cases} 2x - 4y = 6, \\ x - 2y = -6 \end{cases}$

16–3   Evaluate each determinant.

4. $\begin{vmatrix} -2 & 1 \\ 5 & -3 \end{vmatrix}$ 5. $\begin{vmatrix} 1 & 2 \\ 2 & -2 \end{vmatrix}$

Solve using Cramer's Rule.

6. $\begin{cases} 5x - y = 2, \\ x + y = 4 \end{cases}$ 7. $\begin{cases} 2x + 3y = -2, \\ x + y = 0 \end{cases}$

16-4   **8.** Evaluate.

$$\begin{vmatrix} 1 & 2 & -2 \\ 2 & -2 & -4 \\ 1 & 0 & -2 \end{vmatrix}$$

9. Solve using Cramer's Rule.

$$\begin{cases} x + y - z = 1, \\ x + 2y + z = 4, \\ x - y - z = -1 \end{cases}$$

16-5   **10.** Evaluate the determinant.

$$\begin{vmatrix} 1 & -2 & 2 & 3 \\ 3 & 1 & -1 & 2 \\ -1 & 1 & 2 & -2 \\ 3 & 2 & 1 & 1 \end{vmatrix}$$

11. Solve the system of equations by any method.

$$\begin{cases} w + x + y + z = 5, \\ 3w - x + 2y + 4z = -1, \\ w + 2x + 3y - z = 2, \\ 2w + 2x - y + z = 15 \end{cases}$$

16-6   Find the sum of the matrices.

12. $\begin{bmatrix} 2 & 5 \\ -3 & 1 \end{bmatrix} + \begin{bmatrix} 1 & -3 \\ 2 & 1 \end{bmatrix}$

13. $\begin{bmatrix} 1 & 5 \\ 3 & 3 \\ 5 & 1 \end{bmatrix} + \begin{bmatrix} 2 & 1 \\ -3 & 2 \\ -4 & 3 \end{bmatrix}$

16-7   Find the product of the matrices.

14. $\begin{bmatrix} 1 & 3 \\ 2 & 4 \end{bmatrix} \begin{bmatrix} 1 & 1 & 2 \\ 2 & 3 & 2 \end{bmatrix}$

15.

$\begin{bmatrix} 2 & -2 & 1 \end{bmatrix} \begin{bmatrix} 3 \\ 0 \\ -1 \end{bmatrix}$

16. Which matrix is the 2×2 identity matrix?

(a) $\begin{bmatrix} 0 & 0 \\ 0 & 0 \end{bmatrix}$ (b) $\begin{bmatrix} 1 & 1 \\ 1 & 1 \end{bmatrix}$ (c) $\begin{bmatrix} 1 & 0 \\ 0 & 1 \end{bmatrix}$ (d) $\begin{bmatrix} 0 & 1 \\ 1 & 0 \end{bmatrix}$

16-8   **17.** Find the inverse of $\begin{bmatrix} 3 & 4 \\ 2 & 3 \end{bmatrix}$ if it exists.

18. Find the inverse of

$$\begin{bmatrix} 2 & 1 & 3 \\ -2 & 1 & 1 \\ 1 & -1 & -1 \end{bmatrix}$$

if it exists.

16-9   **19.** What system of linear equations does this matrix equation imply?

$$\begin{bmatrix} 1 & -1 & 2 \\ 2 & 2 & -1 \\ 1 & 1 & 3 \end{bmatrix} \begin{bmatrix} x \\ y \\ z \end{bmatrix} = \begin{bmatrix} 7 \\ -2 \\ 4 \end{bmatrix}$$

20. Solve the system of Problem 19.

Chapter 17
Circles, Cylinders, and Spheres

17-1   Introduction

Rectilinear figures, namely lines and planes, are the simplest of all geometric figures. Circles, spheres, and cylinders are, perhaps, the next simplest. In this chapter we shall obtain equations for these latter figures and examine some of their simpler properties.

17-2   Circles

In this section we shall always consider figures in a fixed coordinate plane with coordinates x and y. Recall that a circle is the set of all points in a plane at a fixed distance, called the *radius,* from a fixed point, called the *center.*

An equation of a circle is an equation in x and y that is satisfied by the coordinates of a point if and only if the point is on the circle.

Theorem 17-1   **An equation of a circle with radius r and center at (h, k) is**

$$(x - h)^2 + (y - k)^2 = r^2. \qquad \textbf{(1)}$$

The proof is left to the student. (See Fig. 1.)

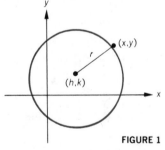

FIGURE 1

Because any equation equivalent to equation (1) is also an equation of the circle, it is convenient to recognize some of these equivalent equations. The most common variant of equation (1) is the equation that results from expanding the squares in (1) and collecting the constant terms. If

$$(x - h)^2 + (y - k)^2 = r^2,$$

then $x^2 - 2hx + h^2 + y^2 - 2ky + k^2 = r^2$, or

$$x^2 + y^2 - 2hx - 2ky + (h^2 + k^2 - r^2) = 0.$$

Theorem 17-2　*The graph of the equation $x^2 + y^2 + ax + by + c = 0$ is*

(a) a circle if

$$\frac{a^2}{4} + \frac{b^2}{4} - c > 0,$$

(b) a point if

$$\frac{a^2}{4} + \frac{b^2}{4} - c = 0,$$

(c) empty if

$$\frac{a^2}{4} + \frac{b^2}{4} - c < 0.$$

Proof　By completing the squares in x and y, the equation is equivalent to

$$\left(x + \frac{a}{2}\right)^2 + \left(y + \frac{b}{2}\right)^2 = \frac{a^2}{4} + \frac{b^2}{4} - c.$$

Therefore, if

$$\frac{a^2}{4} + \frac{b^2}{4} - c > 0,$$

the graph is a circle with center at $(-a/2, -b/2)$ and radius

$$\sqrt{\frac{a^2}{4} + \frac{b^2}{4} - c}.$$

The other assertions of the theorem should be obvious. When

$$\frac{a^2}{4} + \frac{b^2}{4} - c = 0,$$

we often speak of a circle of zero radius, or a *degenerate circle*. And when

$$\frac{a^2}{4} + \frac{b^2}{4} - c < 0,$$

the term *imaginary circle* is sometimes used.

Example 1　Find the center and radius, and sketch the circle

$$x^2 + y^2 + x - 4y - \tfrac{7}{4} = 0.$$

Solution. We have

$$x^2 + x + y^2 - 4y = \tfrac{7}{4},$$
$$(x + \tfrac{1}{2})^2 + (y - 2)^2 = \tfrac{7}{4} + \tfrac{1}{4} + 4,$$
$$(x + \tfrac{1}{2})^2 + (y - 2)^2 = 6.$$

Hence the center is at $(-\tfrac{1}{2}, 2)$, and the radius is $\sqrt{6}$ (Fig. 2).

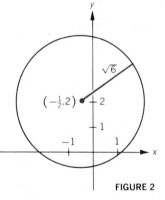

FIGURE 2

Example 2 Find an equation of the circle passing through

$$(9, -7), (-3, -1), \text{ and } (6, 2).$$

Solution. There are at least two ways of proceeding.

Method 1. The circle has an equation

$$x^2 + y^2 + ax + by + c = 0.$$

We must determine the numbers a, b, and c.

The requirement that the circle pass through the three given points leads to three linear equations in a, b, and c.

$$9^2 + (-7)^2 + 9a + (-7)b + c = 0, \tag{2}$$
$$(-3)^2 + (-1)^2 + (-3)a + (-1)b + c = 0, \tag{3}$$
$$6^2 + 2^2 + 6a + 2b + c = 0. \tag{4}$$

Equivalent equations are

$$9a - 7b + c = -130, \tag{2'}$$
$$-3a - b + c = -10, \tag{3'}$$
$$6a + 2b + c = -40. \tag{4'}$$

Solving this system of equations for a, b, and c, we find that

$$a = -6, \, b = 8, \text{ and } c = -20.$$

Therefore an equation of the circle is

$$x^2 + y^2 - 6x + 8y - 20 = 0.$$

This method has the disadvantage that we must do more work to find the center and radius of the circle.

Method 2. This method is more geometric in character. It depends on the geometric fact that the center of the circle is at the intersection of the perpendicular bisectors of segments joining the three given points. It suffices to use only two of those perpendicular bisectors.

As we can see from Fig. 3, the slope of l is

$$\frac{-1 + 7}{-3 - 9} = \frac{6}{-12} = -\frac{1}{2}$$

and the slope of n is

$$\frac{2 + 7}{6 - 9} = \frac{9}{-3} = -3.$$

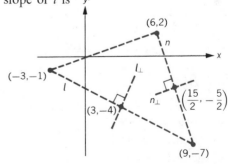

FIGURE 3

Therefore, the slopes of the perpendicular bisectors $l_\perp$ and $n_\perp$ are 2 and $\frac{1}{3}$, respectively. Therefore, the equations of these lines are

$$l_\perp: \quad y + 4 = 2(x - 3) \qquad \text{or} \qquad 2x - y = 10,$$
$$n_\perp: \quad y + \tfrac{5}{2} = \tfrac{1}{3}(x - \tfrac{15}{2}) \qquad \text{or} \qquad x - 3y = 15.$$

Solving these two simultaneous equations we obtain $x = 3$ and $y = -4$. Hence, the center of the circle is $(3, -4)$. (Note that since this is a right triangle, the center is also the midpoint of the hypotenuse.) The radius is $r = \sqrt{[3 - (-3)]^2 + [-4 - (-1)]^2} = \sqrt{45} = 3\sqrt{5}$. An equation of the circle is $(x - 3)^2 + (y + 4)^2 = 45$ or $x^2 + y^2 - 6x + 8y = 20$.

Problems

Set A

Find equations of the circles with the given centers and radii.

1. $(-1, 2)$, $r = \sqrt{2}$
2. $(-\sqrt{2}, -2)$, $r = \sqrt{6}$
3. $(-\pi, 3)$, $r = 3$
4. $(10, -10)$, $r = \frac{1}{2}$
5. $(0, 0)$, $r = a$

Express each equation in the form $(x - h)^2 + (y - k)^2 = r^2$. Give the center and radius of the circle for each equation.

6. $x^2 + y^2 = 6x - 6y$
7. $x^2 + y^2 - 2x + 8y + 16 = 0$
8. $x^2 + y^2 - 3x + 4y - 5 = 0$
9. $2x^2 + 2y^2 + 10x - 5 = 0$
10. $3x^2 + 3y^2 - 2x - 6y = 2$
11. $x^2 + y^2 - 5x - 7y + 20 = 0$

Set B

Find the center and radius of the following circles, and sketch each figure.

12. The circle through $(-8, -4)$, $(8, 8)$, $(5, 9)$
13. The circle through $(-4, -2)$, $(0, 6)$, $(3, -3)$
14. The circle through $(6, 0)$, $(0, 6)$ and $(6, 6)$

Find the center and radius of the following circles.

15. The circle through $(3, 1)$ and touching the x-axis at $(0, 0)$
16. The circle with center on the line $x + 3y = 4$ and passing through $(-2, 2)$ and $(6, 6)$
17. The circle with center on the line $y = -x$, radius 4, and passing through the origin
18. The circle touching the lines $x = 2$ and $x = 12$ and passing through $(4, 0)$

Find an equation of the following circles.

19. The circle with center $(-2, -3)$ and passing through $(2, -6)$
20. The circle which is concentric with the circle $x^2 + y^2 - 2x - 2y = 2$ but which has a radius of 10

Set C

21. Find an equation of the line tangent at $(4, -1)$ to the circle whose equation is $x^2 + y^2 + 4x - 4y = 37$.
22. Find and sketch the points of intersection of the two circles

$$x^2 + y^2 + 6x - 2y = 6,$$
$$x^2 + y^2 - 2x - 6y + 6 = 0.$$

23. Show that the circle $x^2 + y^2 + 2x + 4y = 0$ is tangent to the line $2x + y = 1$ by showing that the line and circle meet in one point.

24. Show that the set of points whose distance from $(0, 0)$ is twice their distance from $(12, 0)$ is a circle. Find its center and radius.

25. Show that the line $x + y = 1$ passes through the points of intersection of the two circles

$$x^2 + y^2 - 6x + 4 = 0,$$
$$x^2 + y^2 - 3x + 3y + 1 = 0.$$

26. Find the equation of the line that passes through the points of intersection of the two circles

$$x^2 + y^2 - 2x + 4y + 4 = 0,$$
$$x^2 + y^2 - x + 6y + 5 = 0.$$

[*Hint:* There is a short cut.]

27. What is the graph of

$$x^2 + y^2 + 4x - 2y = 4, \ x \geq 0 \text{ and } y \geq 0?$$

28. Find the length of the line segment from the point $(10, 2)$ to a point of tangency of a line from $(10, 2)$ to the circle $x^2 + y^2 - 6x + 2y - 12 = 0$.

29. Show that if the distinct circles

$$x^2 + y^2 + ax + by + c = 0$$

and

$$x^2 + y^2 + Ax + By + C = 0$$

intersect at P_1 and $P_2 \neq P_1$, then an equation of the line through P_1 and P_2 is $(a - A)x + (b - B)y + (c - C) = 0$.

30. Find the distance measured along a tangent line from $(3, -2)$ to the circle $(x + 1)^2 + (y - 2)^2 = 4$.

31. If (x', y') is exterior to the circle $(x - h)^2 + (y - k)^2 = r^2$, and if (x_1, y_1) is a point on the circle such that the line through (x_1, y_1) and (x', y') is tangent to the circle, show that the distance L from (x_1, y_1) to (x', y') is given by $L^2 = (x' - h)^2 + (y' - k)^2 - r^2$.

32. Show that equations of the two lines with slope m that are tangent to the circle of radius r with center at the origin are $y = mx \pm r\sqrt{1 + m^2}$.

33. Determine k such that the line $x - 2y = k$ will be tangent to the circle $x^2 + y^2 - 4x - 2y + 1 = 0$. [*Hint:* Apply the discriminant condition for equal roots of a quadratic equation.] Then sketch the graph as a check on your computation. Finally, do the problem in another way.

Describe geometrically the set of points in a plane satisfying

$$\alpha(x^2 + y^2 - 16) + \beta(x^2 + y^2 - 6x - 4y - 12) = 0$$

given that

34. $\alpha = 0$ 35. $\beta = 0$

36. $\alpha = -\beta \neq 0$ 37. $\beta = 2\alpha$

Calculator Problem

Find the center of the circle through the points $(-5.2, 1.4)$, $(3.7, 4.5)$ and $(-2.8, -6.1)$. Find the radius of the circle.

Cylinders

The graph of all points in a plane, with coordinates (x, y), satisfying the equation

$$(x - h)^2 + (y - k)^2 = r^2 \qquad (1)$$

is a circle.

Let us now consider the same equation but ask a question:

What is the set of all points in space whose coordinates (x, y, z) satisfy equation (1)?

The question may at first seem strange because z does not occur in equation (1). But it is this fact that makes the graphing problem in space particularly simple. *If x and y satisfy (1), then x, y, and z satisfy (1) regardless of what z is.*

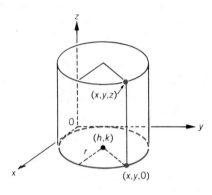

FIGURE 4

Part of the graph in space of equation (1) is shown in Fig. 4. The xy-plane consists of all points whose z-coordinate is 0. If $(x, y, 0)$ is on the circle given by (1), then (x, y, z) is on the right circular cylinder that has this circle as a base or cross section.

Example 1   Graph the portion of the cylinder $x^2 + y^2 = 4$ that is in the first octant and between the planes $z = 0$ and $z = 1$.

Solution. In the xy-plane we have a circle of radius 2 with center at the origin. The graph in space is a right circular cylinder erected on this circle as base. The desired portion is shown in Fig. 5.

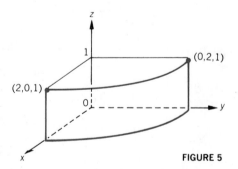

FIGURE 5

From this example it may be expected that cylinders, in general, will have simpler equations than many other surfaces—but what is a cylinder?

Definition 17-1 Suppose that C is a curve* in space, and let l be a line through a point of C. Consider the set of all points on all lines that are parallel to l and contain a point of C. This set of points is called a *cylinder with directrix C*. The line l and the lines parallel to l on the cylinder are called *generators* of the cylinder (Fig. 6).

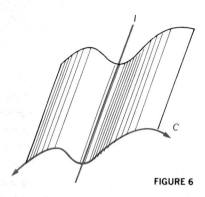

FIGURE 6

It should be noted that the curve C need not be a circle; neither need the curve C lie on a plane, nor, if it does, need the line be perpendicular to the plane. However, if the directrix is in a coordinate plane and the generators are perpendicular to that plane, then the cylinder has an equation which is particularly simple.

Example 2 Find an equation of the cylinder whose directrix is the circle in the xz-plane with center at $(1, 0, 2)$ and radius $\sqrt{5}$ and whose generators are parallel to the y-axis. Sketch the portion of the cylinder between the planes $y = 0$ and $y = 4$ (Fig. 7).

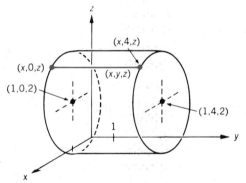

FIGURE 7

Solution. The directrix circle in the xz-plane has an equation

$$(x - 1)^2 + (z - 2)^2 = 5.$$

The same equation is an equation of the cylinder.

_____

*We shall return to curves in Chapter 20 and give there a precise description. At present, we assume that you know intuitively what a curve is.

Example 3   Sketch the set of all points (x, y, z) whose coordinates satisfy the equation $x^2 = y$. Show that this set is a cylinder.

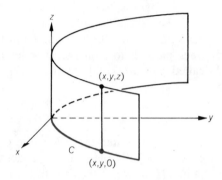

FIGURE 8

Solution. The graph of $x^2 = y$, in the xy-plane, is the curve C of Fig. 8. If $(x, y, 0)$ is on C, then (x, y, z) satisfies the same equation. In other words, all points on a line through $(x, y, 0)$ and parallel to the z-axis are also in the set. Therefore, the graph is a cylinder. It is called a *parabolic* cylinder because a parabola is a directrix.

Problems

Set A

Sketch the portions of the cylinders as described.

1. $x^2 + y^2 - 4x = 0$, $y \geq 0$, $0 \leq z \leq 1$
2. $y^2 + z^2 = 9$, $y \geq 0$, $z \geq 0$, $0 \leq x \leq 2$
3. $x^2 = 4 - z$, $x \geq 0$, $z \geq 0$, $0 \leq y \leq 3$
4. $(x - 3)^2 + (y - 3)^2 = 4$, $0 \leq z \leq 1$
5. $xy = 1$, $0 \leq x \leq 2$, $0 \leq z \leq 2$
6. $3x + 4y = 12$, $x \geq 0$, $0 \leq z \leq 2$

Set B

7. Find an equation of a cylinder whose directrix is a circle in the xy-plane with center at $(2, 4, 0)$ and radius of 2 and whose generators are parallel to the z-axis. Sketch the portion of the cylinder between the planes $z = 0$ and $z = 4$.

8. The directrix of a cylinder is a circle in the xz-plane with generators perpendicular to that plane. The directrix is tangent to the x-axis at $x = 3$ and is tangent to the z-axis at $z = 3$. Find an equation of the cylinder. Sketch the portion of the cylinder between the xz-plane and the plane $y = 5$.

9. Sketch the portion of the cylinder $x^2 = z$ that lies between the planes, $y = 0$, $y = -4$ and $z = 9$.

10. The directrix of a cylinder is in the xy-plane and is given by the equation $x = \sin y$, $0 \leq y \leq 2\pi$. Graph the portion of the cylinder that lies between the planes $z = 0$ and $z = 2$.

Set C

11. Sketch the cylinder whose equation is
$|x| + |y| = 1$.

Sketch the part of the curve of intersection that is in the first octant of the pairs of cylinders.

12. $2x = y$, $x^2 + z^2 = 4$

13. $x + y = 7$, $x^2 + y^2 = 25$

14. $x^2 + y^2 = 9$, $x^2 + z^2 = 4$

15. $x^2 = 4y$, $y^2 + z^2 = 1$

16. The directrix of a cylinder is

$$x^2 + y^2 - 6x - 6y + 9 = 0.$$

A generator of the cylinder is the line $y = z + 3$ in the yz-plane. Sketch that portion of the cylinder between the planes $z = 0$ and $z = 4$.

17. Sketch a picture of the set of points in the first octant satisfying $y^2 + z^2 \geq 9$, $y^2 + z^2 \leq 16$, and $x \leq 4$.

Calculator Problem

An equation of a right circular cylinder is $(x - 3)^2 + (y - 4)^2 = 4$. What is the shortest distance from point $A = (3, 2, 0)$ on the cylinder to point $B = (3, 6, 8)$ on the cylinder *along the surface of the cylinder*? [*Hint:* Think of cutting the cylinder along a generator through A and unrolling the cylinder to form a rectangle.]

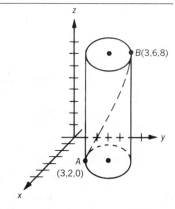

17-4   Spheres

The space analog of a circle is a sphere. It is the set of all points P in space at a fixed distance from a point called the center of the sphere. Theorems analogous to Theorems 17–1 and 17–2 can be proved for spheres, and in much the same way.

Theorem 17-3   *An equation of a sphere with radius r and center at (h, k, p) is*

$$(x - h)^2 + (y - k)^2 + (z - p)^2 = r^2.$$

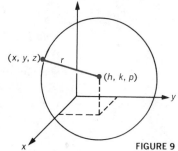

FIGURE 9

Theorem 17-4   *The graph of the equation*

$$x^2 + y^2 + z^2 + ax + by + cz + d = 0$$

(a) is a sphere if

$$\frac{a^2}{4} + \frac{b^2}{4} + \frac{c^2}{4} - d > 0,$$

(b) is a point if

$$\frac{a^2}{4} + \frac{b^2}{4} + \frac{c^2}{4} - d = 0,$$

(c) is empty if

$$\frac{a^2}{4} + \frac{b^2}{4} + \frac{c^2}{4} - d < 0.$$

Remark   In sketching a sphere, it is usually convenient to sketch one or two of the great circles of the sphere that are intersections of the sphere with planes parallel to coordinate planes. Furthermore, because of the symmetry of the sphere it often suffices to sketch only one-eighth of the sphere.

Example 1   Find an equation of the sphere with center at $(1, 2, 1)$ and radius 2.

Solution. The point (x, y, z) is on the sphere if and only if $(x - 1)^2 + (y - 2)^2 + (z - 1)^2 = 4$ or, equivalently, if and only if $x^2 + y^2 + z^2 - 2x - 4y - 2z + 2 = 0$.
   A sketch of one-eighth of the sphere is shown in Fig. 10.

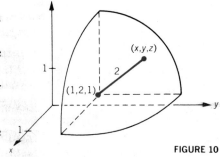

FIGURE 10

Example 2   Find center and radius and sketch the sphere that has an equation

$$4x^2 + 4y^2 + 4z^2 - 8x + 4y + 8z = 27.$$

Solution. This equation is equivalent to $x^2 + y^2 + z^2 - 2x + y + 2z = \frac{27}{4}$, which, in turn, is equivalent to $(x - 1)^2 + (y + \frac{1}{2})^2 + (z + 1)^2 = 9$. This last equation is that of a sphere with center at $(1, -\frac{1}{2}, -1)$ and radius 3.

Problems

Set A

Find equations of the following spheres and sketch one-eighth of each sphere.

1. Center $(2, 1, 0)$, radius 2
2. Center $(1, 1, -1)$, radius $\frac{1}{2}$
3. Center $(-4, 2, -3)$, radius 5
4. Center $(0, 0, 0)$, radius a
5. Center $(-1, 2, -2)$ and passing through $(0, 0, 0)$
6. Center $(3, 2, 4)$ and tangent to the xy-plane

Find the center and radius and sketch a portion of each of the following spheres.

7. $x^2 + y^2 + z^2 - x - y - z = \frac{9}{4}$
8. $2x^2 + 2y^2 + 2z^2 - 9z = 1$
9. $x^2 + y^2 + z^2 - 20x - 20y + 199 = 0$
10. $x^2 + y^2 + z^2 - 2ay = 0$ if $a > 0$. Sketch the portion for which $x > 0$ and $z > 0$.

Set B

Use Theorem 17-4 to tell if the equation is a sphere, a point, or empty. Give the center and radius for each sphere.

11. $x^2 + y^2 + z^2 - 4x + 2y + z + 12 = 0$
12. $x^2 + y^2 + z^2 - x + 8y - 2z - 6 = 0$
13. $x^2 + y^2 + z^2 + 6x - 2y - 10z + 35 = 0$
14. $x^2 + y^2 + z^2 - 14x - 8y - 10z + 89 = 0$
15. The plane $y = 2$ intersects the sphere

$$x^2 + y^2 + z^2 + 2y - 2z = 14$$

in a circle. Find an equation of the cylinder that has this circle as directrix and whose generators are parallel to the y-axis. Sketch the figure.

Set C

16. Show that the point $(-2, -3, 2)$ is on the sphere whose equation is $x^2 + y^2 + z^2 = 17$. What are the direction cosines of the ray from the origin through $(-2, -3, 2)$? Write parametric equations of the line that passes through $(-2, -3, 2)$ and the origin.

17. A ray has direction cosines $\frac{1}{2}$, $-\frac{1}{2}$, and $-1/\sqrt{2}$ and emanates from the center of the sphere with an equation

$$x^2 + y^2 + z^2 - 2x + 2y = 6.$$

Find the point where the ray intersects the sphere.

18. Show that the plane $3x - y - 3 = 0$ is tangent to the sphere

$$x^2 + y^2 + z^2 + 4x - 2y - 4z = 1.$$

Sketch the plane and the sphere.

19. What are the coordinates of the point of tangency of the plane and the sphere of Problem 18?

20. A ray from the center of the sphere

$$x^2 + y^2 + z^2 + 2x - 6y + 1 = 0$$

passes through the point $P = (2, 0, 3)$. Find an equation of the plane tangent to the sphere at the point where the ray pierces the sphere.

Calculator Problem

The sphere $x^2 + y^2 + z^2 - 8x - 8y - 6z + 25 = 0$ is tangent to the sphere $x^2 + y^2 + z^2 - 8x - 24y - 18z + 205 = 0$. Find the coordinates of the point of tangency.

Summary

In this chapter we have used analytic geometry to study some familiar geometric figures. You should be able to recognize circles, cylinders with axes parallel to the coordinate axes, and spheres from their equations, and sketch the graphs of these figures.

1. $$(x - h)^2 + (y - k)^2 = r^2$$

is an equation of a circle in the xy-plane with center at (h, k) and radius r.

2. The set of all points (x, y, z) in space satisfying equation (1) is a right circular cylinder having as directrix the circle

$$(x - h)^2 + (y - k)^2 = r^2.$$

3. $$(x - h)^2 + (y - k)^2 + (z - p)^2 = r^2$$

is an equation of a sphere with center at (h, k, p) and radius r.

Chapter 17   Test

17-2   State the conditions for which the graph of $x^2 + y^2 + ax + by + c = 0$ will be one of the following.

    1. A circle   **2.** A point   **3.** An imaginary circle

Determine the center and radius of the following circles.

    4. $x^2 + y^2 - 7x + 8y = \frac{9}{2}$

    5. $x^2 + y^2 + x - y - 2 = 0$

    6. $x^2 + y^2 - 6x = 0$

    7. Write an equation of the circle that contains the points $(3, 1)$, $(-2, 4)$, and $(0, -4)$.

    8. A circle has radius 5 and is tangent to the positive x- and y-axes. What is an equation of the circle?

17-3   Sketch pictures of the following cylinders.

    9. $x^2 + y^2 - 2x - 3 = 0$, $0 \leq z \leq 3$

    10. $y^2 + z^2 = 16$, $z \geq 0$, $0 \leq x \leq 4$

    11. $y^2 + z^2 - 4y - 4z + 4 = 0$, $0 \leq x \leq 5$

    12. Sketch the cylinder $xy = 12$, where $x > 0$, $y > 0$ and between the planes $z = 0$ and $z = 4$.

17-4   Determine the center and radius of the following spheres and sketch one-eighth of the sphere.

    13. $x^2 + y^2 + z^2 + 8x + 2y = 8$ **14.** $x^2 + y^2 + z^2 - 3x + 4y - 6z = 1$

    15. The plane $z = 2$ intersects the sphere $x^2 + y^2 + z^2 - 2x - 4y - 6z + 5 = 0$ in a circle. Determine the radius of the circle.

Historical Note

Maria Agnesi
(1718–1799)

Several women have made contributions to mathematics. Maria Agnesi (1718–1799) wrote one of the first comprehensive textbooks on calculus, *Analytical Institutions*. Representing ten years of work, the two-volume book included the methods of both Newton and Leibniz. Among the topics discussed were analysis of finite quantities, conics, and differential and integral calculus.

Maria Agnesi's name is most widely known in association with one of the curves she discussed, the curve with the equation $x^2y = 4a^2(2a - y)$ (See page 466). This curve was named "The Witch of Agnesi" by a man who mistranslated the verb "versiera" into "witch" instead of "to turn."

Sophie Germain (1776–1831) was the first woman to do original math research. Her main interests were number theory and the theory of surfaces. Her work in number theory included a proof of Fermat's Last Theorem—that the equation $x^n + y^n = z^n$ is unsolvable over the integers when n is an odd prime number less than 100. For her research in applied mathematics she received a Grand Prize from the French Academy of Sciences in 1816.

Sophie Germain became a noted mathematician through persistence. As a child she was forbidden to study mathematics by her parents, but she would study with hidden candles at night. Denied admittance to the French Academy because she was a woman, she obtained lecture notes through friends and studied them by herself. So that she would not be ignored or ridiculed, she used a man's name and corresponded with two prominent mathematicians, Lagrange and Gauss. She impressed both men with her understanding and insights into difficult mathematics.

Two other women noted for their works in mathematics are Emilie du Châtelet (1706–1749), who wrote a translation and analysis of Newton's *Principia;* and Emmy Noether (1882–1935), who contributed significantly to the field of abstract algebra.

Chapter 18
Conics

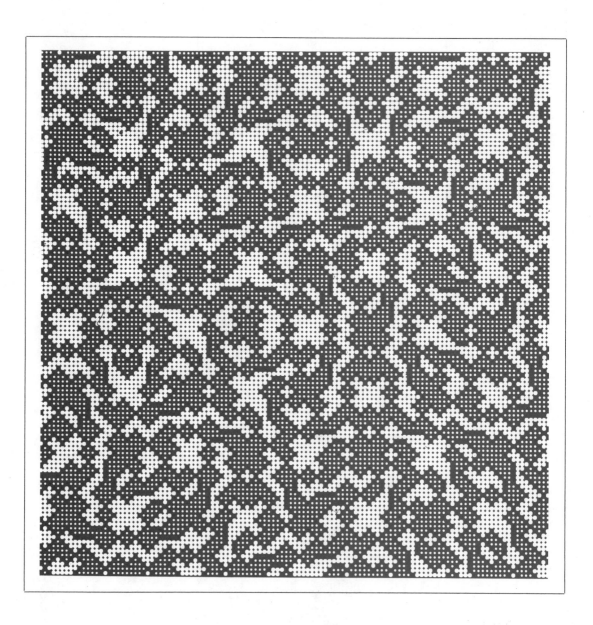

18-1   Introduction

We have seen that a first-degree (linear) equation in x and y has a graph that is a straight line; and conversely that every straight line in the plane has such an equation. It is reasonable, therefore, to ask, "What kind of graphs do second-degree equations have?" We shall see, in this chapter, that graphs of second-degree equations are the curves called *conic sections*.

These curves, the conic sections, were extensively studied by the ancient Greeks, and especially by Apollonius (third century B.C.). The Greeks considered the conics to be the curves of intersection of a plane and a right circular cone (see Fig. 1), and studied them in a purely geometric way.

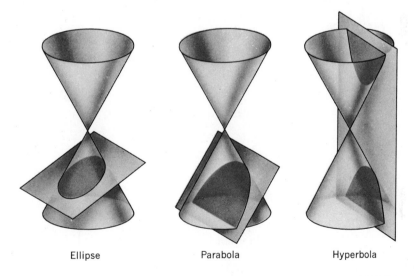

Ellipse   Parabola   Hyperbola

FIGURE 1

We shall see that all these conic sections have equations that are of the second degree in the rectangular coordinates x and y. And we shall see how to recognize the curve quickly from its equation. Finally, we shall see that every second-degree equation that has a graph consisting of more than one point and that cannot be factored into a product of two linear equations, must be an equation of one of the conic sections.

The Conic Sections

There are two common definitions of these curves. We shall choose the one that clearly includes all three types (ellipse, parabola, hyperbola) in a single family of curves. (Fig. 2.)

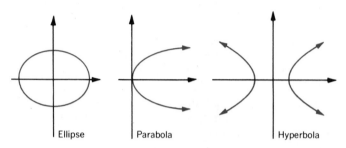

Ellipse   Parabola   Hyperbola

FIGURE 2

Definition 18-1 Let l be a given line, called the *directrix,* and F be a given point, not on l, called the *focus.* Let e be a given positive number, called the *eccentricity.* Let ζ be the set of all points P such that the ratio of the distance $|PF|$ (from P to the focus F) to the distance $|PM|$ (from P to the directrix l) is e. The point set ζ is called a *conic.*

The conic ζ is $\begin{cases} \text{an } \textit{ellipse} & \text{if } e < 1, \\ \text{a } \textit{parabola} & \text{if } e = 1, \\ \text{a } \textit{hyperbola} & \text{if } e > 1. \end{cases}$

Thus P is on the conic (see Fig. 3) if and only if

$$\frac{|PF|}{|PM|} = e. \qquad (1)$$

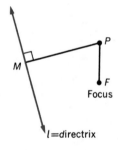

l=directrix

FIGURE 3

Example Let us suppose that F and l are as shown in Fig. 4 and that $e = \frac{1}{2}$.

By trial, one can approximately locate points P_1, P_2, P_3, and P_4 on the conic. The conic is an ellipse. It appears that the ellipse has the same shape at both ends. We shall see later that this is so.

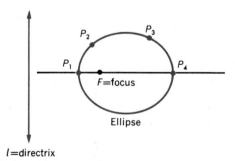

l=directrix

FIGURE 4

Problems

Set A

In each problem, F is the focus, P is a point on a conic and PM is the distance from P to the directrix. (See Fig. 3.) Find the eccentricity e and tell which conic is illustrated.

1. $F = (0, 2)$, $P = (4, 2)$, $|PM| = 4$
2. $F = (4, 0)$, $P = (3, 2)$, $|PM| = 3$
3. $F = (2, 0)$, $P = (2, 5)$, $|PM| = 2$
4. $F = (5, 0)$, $P = (5, \frac{9}{4})$, $|PM| = \frac{9}{5}$
5. $F = (2, 2)$, $P = (1, 3)$, $|PM| = \sqrt{2}$
6. $F = (3, 0)$, $P = (2, \sqrt{3})$, $|PM| = 4$

Set B

7. The directrix of a parabola is $y = -2$. The focus is at $(0, 2)$. Graph several points that are on the parabola and then sketch the curve.

Use the distance formula to show that each point below is the same distance from the directrix $y = -2$ in Problem 7 as it is from the focus $(0, 2)$.

8. $(0, 0)$
9. $(4, 2)$
10. $(-4, 2)$
11. $(2\sqrt{2}, 1)$
12. $(-2\sqrt{2}, 1)$
13. $(2, \frac{1}{2})$
14. $(-2, \frac{1}{2})$
15. $(\pm a, a^2/8)$

Set C

16. Draw a directrix l and choose a point F as a focus. Plot many points on the ellipse with eccentricity $\frac{1}{2}$. Then draw circles C_r of different radii r with center F. For each radius r draw a line l_r parallel to l and at a distance $2r$ from l. Points where the circle C_r meets l_r will be on the ellipse. Why? How large must r be for this construction to yield points of the conic? Can r be too large?

17. Draw a directrix and choose a point as a focus. Draw several points on the hyperbola with eccentricity $\frac{3}{2}$ and your focus and directrix. Draw circles C_r with radius r and center at the focus. Draw lines l_r parallel to the directrix and at distance $\frac{2}{3}r$ from it. What are points of intersection of C_r and l_r? How large must r be for C_r and l_r to intersect? Can r be too large? Can lines l_r that are on the side of the directrix opposite to the focus meet C_r?

18. A parabola has focus at $(1, 0)$ and as directrix the line with the equation $x = -1$. Find an equation satisfied by the coordinates of all points (x, y) on the parabola.

19. Show that any conic has an equation of the second degree in x and y. [*Hint:* Suppose that the directrix is the line $ax + by + c = 0$ and that the focus is at (h, k). Then use equation (1) of Definition 18–1.]

Calculator Problem

The focus F of a conic is at $(3.75, 1.29)$. A point P of the conic is at $(-2.98, 5.23)$. Point M is the point on the directrix such that $\overline{PM}$ is perpendicular to the directrix. M has coordinates $(8.80, 9.26)$. Calculate the eccentricity of the conic, $e = |PF|/|PM|$, and tell which kind of conic is represented.

The Parabola

If the focus and directrix of a parabola are placed conveniently with respect to the coordinate axes, then the equation of the parabola will be especially simple.

Let us suppose that the focus is at $(c, 0)$, and that the directrix has an equation $x = -c$, as in Fig. 5.

Then the point $P(x, y)$ is on the parabola if and only if

$$|PF| = |PM|e, \quad \text{but} \quad e = 1,$$

or

$$\sqrt{(x - c)^2 + y^2} = |x + c|. \quad (1)$$

Equation (1) is equivalent to the following equations:

$$(x - c)^2 + y^2 = (x + c)^2,$$
$$y^2 = 4cx. \quad (2)$$

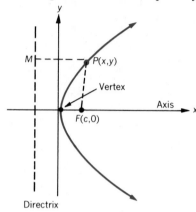

FIGURE 5

The point $(0, 0)$ satisfies equation (2) and is therefore a point on the parabola. It is midway between the focus and directrix and is called the *vertex*.

Equation (2) is the *standard form* for a parabola with its vertex at the origin and its axis along the x-axis. (The *axis* of a parabola is the line through the focus perpendicular to the directrix.) *It is to be emphasized that all points (x, y) on the parabola satisfy (2), and conversely if x and y satisfy (2), then the point (x, y) is on the parabola.*

Several observations can be made from equation (2).

(a) The parabola is *symmetric* with respect to its axis. If (x, y) is on the parabola, so is $(x, -y)$, because then $y^2 = (-y)^2 = 4cx$.

(b) The derivation of equation (2) is valid when c is either positive or negative. Figure 5 shows the parabola for $c > 0$. For $c < 0$, the focus would be to the left of the origin and the parabola would "open" to the left.

(c) If the parabola has its focus on the y-axis and its directrix parallel to the x-axis, then it appears as shown in Fig. 6 and has the standard equation $x^2 = 4cy$.

(d) If the vertex is at a point (h, k) other than the origin and the directrix is parallel to the y-axis, then the focus is at $(h + c, k)$ and the directrix is $x = h - c$. (See Fig. 7.)

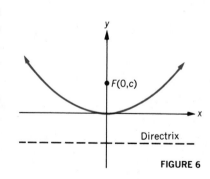

FIGURE 6

Just as before, an equation of the parabola is

$$\sqrt{(x - h - c)^2 + (y - k)^2} = |x - h + c|,$$

which is easily seen to be equivalent to

$$(y - k)^2 = 4c(x - h). \qquad (3)$$

Equation (3) is the standard form for a parabola with vertex at (h, k) and axis parallel to the x-axis. If the axis were parallel to the y-axis, the standard form would be

$$(x - h)^2 = 4c(y - k). \qquad (4)$$

We summarize these results in the following theorem.

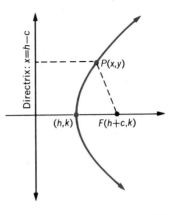

Directrix: $x=h-c$

$P(x,y)$

(h,k) $F(h+c,k)$

FIGURE 7

Theorem 18-1   *The following equations have graphs that are parabolas.*

$y^2 = 4cx.$ *The vertex is (0, 0) and the focus is at (c, 0). The graph is symmetric with the x-axis.*

$x^2 = 4cy.$ *The vertex is (0, 0) and the focus is at (0, c). The graph is symmetric with the y-axis.*

$(y - k)^2 = 4c(x - h).$ *The vertex is (h, k), the focus is at (c + h, k) and the axis of the graph is parallel to the x-axis.*

$(x - h)^2 = 4c(y - k).$ *The vertex is (h, k), the focus is at (h, c + k) and the axis of the graph is parallel to the y-axis.*

Example 1   Sketch the parabola whose equation is $y^2 = -6x$. Find its focus and directrix.

Solution. Comparing $y^2 = -6x$ with the standard form $y^2 = 4cx$, we see that

$$4c = -6 \quad \text{and} \quad c = -\tfrac{3}{2}.$$

The focus is at $(-\tfrac{3}{2}, 0)$ and the directrix is the line $x = \tfrac{3}{2}$. The parabola is sketched in Fig. 8. Observe that the segment $\overline{AB}$ through the focus has a length $|AB| = 6 = |4c|$. Note that the segment corresponding to $\overline{AB}$ in a parabola always has a length of $4|c|$. $\overline{AB}$ is called the *latus rectum* of the parabola.

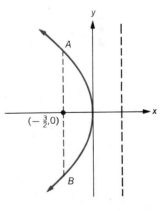

$(-\tfrac{3}{2}, 0)$

A

B

FIGURE 8

Example 2   Find the standard form for the parabola with the equation $x^2 + 2x + 6y - 11 = 0$. Find its vertex, focus, and equation of directrix, and sketch the figure.

Solution. The equation is equivalent to

$$x^2 + 2x = -6y + 11, \qquad (x + 1)^2 = -6(y - 2).$$

This last is in the standard form (4). Therefore the vertex is at $(-1, 2)$, with the parabola opening down. We have $4c = -6$, where $c = -\frac{3}{2}$. The focus is at $(-1, \frac{1}{2})$, and an equation of the directrix is $y = \frac{7}{2}$. (See Fig. 9.)

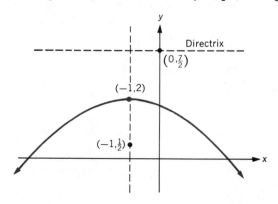

FIGURE 9

Parabolas have a focusing property that has many practical applications. Light rays parallel to the axis of a parabolic surface, such as a parabolic mirror used in reflecting telescopes, will be reflected to the focal point of the parabola. This reflecting property is used in the design of radar transmitters, automobile headlights, and other applications. (Fig. 10.)

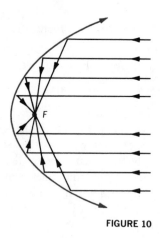

FIGURE 10

444   Conics

Problems

Set A

1. Sketch, on the same coordinate system, the parabolas $x^2 = 4cy$ for $c = \frac{1}{4}, \frac{1}{2}, 1, 2,$ and 4.

Find the focus and equation of the directrix, and sketch each of the following parabolas.

2. $y^2 = 6x$ 3. $y^2 = -6x$

4. $x^2 = \frac{1}{2}y$ 5. $x^2 = -2y$

Find vertex, focus, and equation of directrix, and sketch each of the following parabolas.

6. $3x^2 = 8y - 16$ 7. $y^2 + 4y = 4x$

8. $y^2 - 4y - 2x - 8 = 0$

9. $3x^2 + 4y = 12$

Set B

10. A parabola has its vertex at the origin, its axis parallel to the y-axis, and passes through $(-1, 3)$. Find its equation and sketch the parabola.

Use the definition of a parabola to find equations of the following parabolas.

11. Focus at $(4, 3)$, directrix $x + 2 = 0$

12. Focus at $(-1, 1)$, directrix $2y = 5$

13. Focus at $(-4, -2)$, directrix $x = 2$

14. Focus at $(5, 0)$, directrix $y - 4 = 0$

Set C

Find the points of intersection of each of the following pairs of curves and sketch the curves.

15. $x = 3y - y^2$,   16. $x^2 - y - 2 = 0$,
     $x - 2y + 2 = 0$ $y - x = 0$

17. $y^2 - 2y + 3x = 3$,
     $y^2 = 3x + 1$

18. $y^2 - 4y - 6x + 24 = 0$,
     $x^2 - 4x - 2y = 0$

For Problems 19 through 23 refer to the parabola $x^2 = 4cy$ shown in the figure.

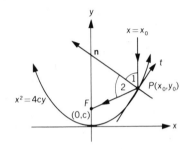

19. What is the slope of the tangent t at point (x_0, y_0)?

20. Show that $x_0 x - 2cy - 2cy_0 = 0$ is an equation of the tangent line through (x_0, y_0). [*Hint:* Observe that $x_0^2 = 4cy_0$.]

21. Find the equation of the normal $\mathbf{n}$ to the tangent through (x_0, y_0).

22. Find the equation of the line through P and the focal point F.

23. Show that $\cos \angle 1 = \cos \angle 2$ in the figure.

Calculator Problem

Find the measures of angles 1 and 2 for the figure for Problems 19–23 if $x^2 = 8y$ and $P = (x_0, y_0) = (4, 2)$.

The Ellipse

Like the parabola, the ellipse also has a very simple equation if the focus and directrix are suitably placed with respect to the axes. However, for the ellipse, this "conveniently chosen" coordinate system is much less obvious. Let us anticipate how things will work out in order to justify our choice of the coordinate system. From the example of Section 18–2 and Fig. 4 we may expect the ellipse to have "the same shape at both ends." So there should be two foci F_1 and F_2, and two points V_1 and V_2 on the ellipse and on the line through the foci. Let us choose the origin midway between the foci, and the line through the foci as the x-axis. Then we may give coordinates to F_1, F_2, V_1, and V_2, as shown in Fig. 11. If the directrix is at a distance d from the origin, then it has an equation $x = d$. Consider the relation of V_1 and V_2 of the ellipse, to F_1 and the directrix; by Definition 18–1 we have

$$\frac{|V_1F_1|}{|V_1M|} = e = \frac{|V_2F_1|}{|V_2M|},$$

$$\frac{|c - a|}{|d - a|} = e = \frac{|c - (-a)|}{|d - (-a)|}.$$

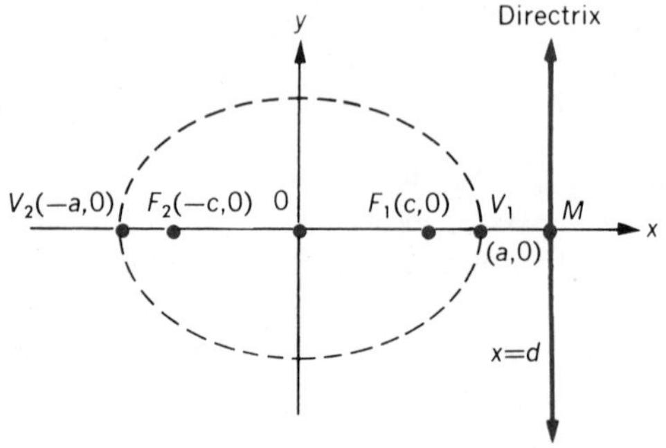

Since

$$-a < -c < 0 < c < a < d,$$

it follows that

$$\frac{a - c}{d - a} = e = \frac{a + c}{d + a},$$

and hence

$$a - c = de - ae, \quad \text{and} \quad a + c = de + ae.$$

Solving these simultaneous equations, we obtain

$$c = ae \quad \text{and} \quad a = de \quad \text{or} \quad d = \frac{c}{e^2}.$$

These last equations show where we should locate the focus and directrix in order to get a simple equation for the ellipse.

We have now arrived at a choice for the location of the ellipse with respect to the axes. Let us see how this works out. Accordingly, suppose that the focus is at $(c, 0)$, $c > 0$, and that the directrix has the equation

$$x = \frac{c}{e^2},$$

(see Fig. 12) where e is the eccentricity and, of course, $e < 1$. Then $P(x, y)$ is on the ellipse if and only if $|PF| = |PM|e$:

$$\sqrt{(x - c)^2 + y^2} = \left| \frac{c}{e^2} - x \right| e. \tag{1}$$

FIGURE 11

This equation is equivalent to the following equations:

$$(x - c)^2 + y^2 = \left(\frac{c}{e^2} - x\right)^2 e^2,$$

$$x^2 - 2cx + c^2 + y^2 = \frac{c^2}{e^2} - 2cx + e^2 x^2,$$

$$x^2(1 - e^2) + y^2 = \frac{c^2(1 - e^2)}{e^2},$$

$$\frac{x^2}{\dfrac{c^2}{e^2}} + \frac{y^2}{\dfrac{c^2(1 - e^2)}{e^2}} = 1.$$

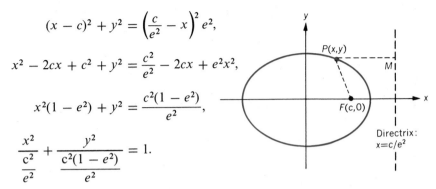

FIGURE 12

Let us now introduce new positive constants a and b such that

$$a^2 = \frac{c^2}{e^2}, \qquad b^2 = \frac{c^2(1 - e^2)}{e^2}. \tag{2}$$

Then the equation of the ellipse assumes the *standard form,*

$$\frac{x^2}{a^2} + \frac{y^2}{b^2} = 1. \tag{3}$$

Solving the first equation of (2) for c^2 and substituting in the second, we get $b^2 = a^2 - a^2 e^2$. From a second substitution in the last equation, we find that $a^2 = b^2 + c^2$.

If a point (x, y) is on the ellipse, then x and y satisfy equation (3), and conversely, if x and y satisfy (3), then the point (x, y) is on the ellipse.

The points $(-a, 0)$ and $(a, 0)$ are *vertices* of the ellipse and the ends of the *major axis,* so that a is the length of the semimajor axis. Likewise, the points $(0, b)$ and $(0, -b)$ are *vertices* and the ends of the *minor axis* of the ellipse, so that b is the length of the semiminor axis. We observe that $b < a$. The origin is the *center* of the ellipse.

A number of observations can be made from equation (3).

(a) As we surmised earlier, the ellipse is *symmetric* with respect to both coordinate axes. If (x, y) is on the ellipse, so are $(x, -y)$, $(-x, y)$, and $(-x, -y)$. The two "ends" of the ellipse look alike.

(b) As a consequence of this symmetry, there must be another directrix at the other end of the ellipse. The equation of this second directrix would be $x = d' = -c/e^2$. Equation (3) could also be derived by choosing F_2 (or $c < 0$) and the directrix at $-c/e^2$. The ellipse with its two foci and directrices is shown in Fig. 13.

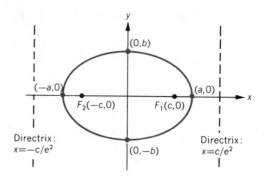

FIGURE 13

(c) If the ellipse has its foci on the y-axis, the standard equation of the ellipse is

$$\frac{x^2}{b^2} + \frac{y^2}{a^2} = 1,$$

where a and b are the semiaxes.

(d) If the center of the ellipse is at the point (h, k) and the two foci are at $(h + c, k)$ and $(h - c, k)$, then an equation of the ellipse is

$$\sqrt{(x - h - c)^2 + (y - k)^2} = \left| h + \frac{c}{e^2} - x \right| e,$$

which can be shown to be equivalent to

$$\frac{(x - h)^2}{a^2} + \frac{(y - k)^2}{b^2} = 1. \tag{4}$$

Equation (4) is the standard form for an ellipse with center at (h, k) and major axis parallel to the x-axis. If the major axis were parallel to the y-axis, a and b would be interchanged in the equation.

Theorem 18–2 summarizes our results.

Theorem 18–2   *The standard equation of an ellipse is*

(a) $\dfrac{x^2}{a^2} + \dfrac{y^2}{b^2} = 1$ *with foci on the x-axis and center at the origin,*

(b) $\dfrac{x^2}{b^2} + \dfrac{y^2}{a^2} = 1$ *with foci on the y-axis and center at the origin,*

(c) $\dfrac{(x - h)^2}{a^2} + \dfrac{(y - k)^2}{b^2} = 1$ *with center (h, k) and foci on a line parallel to the x-axis,*

448   Conics

(d) $\dfrac{(x-h)^2}{b^2} + \dfrac{(y-k)^2}{a^2} = 1$ *with center (h, k) and foci on a line parallel to the y-axis.*

Example 1 Graph the ellipse having an equation $4x^2 + 3y^2 = 48$, and find its foci, eccentricity, and the equations of its directrices.

Solution. Dividing both sides of the equation by 48, we get the standard form

$$\frac{x^2}{12} + \frac{y^2}{16} = 1.$$

Then $a = 4$, $b = \sqrt{12} = 2\sqrt{3}$, and the major axis is along the y-axis. (See Fig. 14.)

From equations (2), $a^2 = b^2 + c^2$, or $16 = 12 + c^2$, and $c = 2$. Therefore the foci are at $(0, \pm 2)$. The eccentricity is obtained from equations (2):

$$e = \frac{c}{a} = \frac{2}{4} = \frac{1}{2}.$$

Therefore,

$$\frac{c}{e^2} = \frac{2}{(\frac{1}{2})^2} = 8$$

and the directrices have equations $y = \pm 8$.

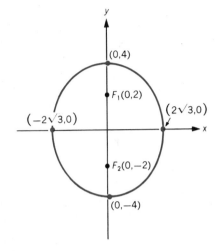

FIGURE 14

2   An ellipse has its center at $(-2, 3)$ and semiaxes of lengths 2 and 1, with the major axis parallel to the x-axis. Find the standard form of the equation of the ellipse, its foci, and sketch the curve.

Solution. In this case, $a = 2$ and $b = 1$; therefore, the standard form is

$$\frac{(x+2)^2}{4} + \frac{(y-3)^2}{1} = 1. \quad (5)$$

From $a^2 = b^2 + c^2$ we obtain $4 = 1 + c^2$ and $c = \sqrt{3}$. The foci are $(-2 \pm \sqrt{3}, 3)$. (See Fig. 15.)

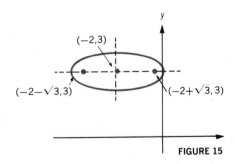

FIGURE 15

Remark

Another form of an equation of the ellipse is obtained if we expand $(x + 2)^2$ and $(y - 3)^2$ in (5) and clear of fractions. We then have

$$x^2 + 4y^2 + 4x - 24y + 36 = 0, \qquad (6)$$

which is also an equation of the ellipse. Had we been given (6) we would have completed the squares on the x- and y-terms to obtain the standard form (5). (See the next example.)

Example 3

Show that the graph of $3x^2 + y^2 - 12x + 2y + 4 = 0$ is an ellipse. Find its center, foci, eccentricity, and sketch the ellipse.

Solution. We rewrite the equation as

$$3(x^2 - 4x \quad) + (y^2 + 2y \quad) = -4,$$

and complete the squares of the terms in parentheses to obtain

$$3(x - 2)^2 + (y + 1)^2 = 9,$$

which is equivalent to

$$\frac{(x - 2)^2}{3} + \frac{(y + 1)^2}{9} = 1.$$

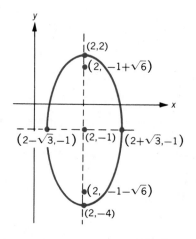

FIGURE 16

This last equation is the standard form for the ellipse with semiaxes $a = 3$, $b = \sqrt{3}$, and center at $(2, -1)$. (See Fig. 16.) Then $c^2 = 9 - 3$ and $c = \sqrt{6}$. The eccentricity is $e = c/a = \sqrt{6}/3$.

Remark

An ellipse, as we have defined it, is never a circle. Yet it is clear that when b is close to a, the ellipse is very nearly a circle. If b is close to a, then $c = \sqrt{a^2 - b^2}$ is very nearly 0, and the eccentricity $e = c/a$ is also nearly 0. The directrices $x = \pm c/e^2 = \pm a^2/c$ recede farther and farther from the center as b approaches a. (See Fig. 17.)

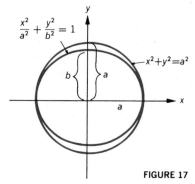

FIGURE 17

By agreement we shall say that a circle is a special ellipse with *eccentricity zero*, even though the circle does not satisfy the definition of an ellipse. The two foci then coincide with the center of the circle and there are no directrices.

Problems

Set A

Sketch the following ellipses. Find the eccentricity, foci, and equations of directrices of each.

1. $\dfrac{x^2}{9} + \dfrac{y^2}{4} = 1$ **2.** $\dfrac{x^2}{16} + \dfrac{y^2}{36} = 1$

3. $x^2 + 4y^2 = 25$ **4.** $5x^2 + y^2 = 80$

5. $4x^2 + 4y^2 = 25$ **6.** $2x^2 + y^2 = 16$

Write each equation in the standard form of an ellipse. Sketch the ellipses and give the foci.

7. $9x^2 + 16y^2 - 18x - 64y = 71$

8. $9x^2 + 5y^2 + 36x - 30y + 36 = 0$

9. $25x^2 + 9y^2 + 150x + 18y + 9 = 0$

10. $9x^2 + y^2 - 8y + 7 = 0$

11. $2x^2 + y^2 + 12x + 4y = 0$

12. $25x^2 + 4y^2 + 200x = 0$

Set B

Write the equations of each of the following ellipses and sketch the curves.

13. Foci at $(\pm\sqrt{3}, 0)$ and semimajor axis $\sqrt{6}$

14. Vertices at $(\pm 3, 0)$ and $(0, \pm 2)$

15. Center at $(0, 0)$, eccentricity $1/\sqrt{2}$, and semiminor axis along the x-axis and 2 units long

16. Foci at $(0, \pm 5)$ and eccentricity $\sqrt{5}/4$.

17. Major axis 8 units long and foci at $(0, 2)$ and $(6, 2)$

18. Eccentricity $1/\sqrt{2}$ and foci at $(-1, -2 \pm 2\sqrt{2})$

19. Minor axis 10 units long and parallel to the y-axis, with eccentricity $\frac{2}{3}$ and center $(1, 1)$

20. Foci at $(4, 1)$ and $(0, 1)$ and eccentricity $\frac{2}{3}$

21. Major axis 10 units long and foci at $(1, 4)$ and $(1, 0)$

22. Minor axis 8 units long and parallel to the x-axis, with center at $(-2, 3)$ and eccentricity $\frac{3}{4}$

23. Foci at $(\pm 2\sqrt{5}, 0)$ and passes through $(-3\sqrt{2}, 2\sqrt{2})$.

Find the points of intersection of the following pairs of curves and sketch each pair of curves.

24. $x^2 + 3y^2 = 52$,
    $x^2 = 3y + 16$

25. $3x^2 + y^2 = 16$,
    $3x + y = 1$

26. $2x^2 + y^2 = 18$,
    $x^2 + 5y^2 = 45$

27. $x^2 + 2y^2 = 9$,
    $x^2 + y^2 - 4x = 1$

Set C

28. Find an equation of a parabola with vertex at the origin and focus at a focus of the ellipse

$$x^2 + 5y^2 = 10.$$

Show that the graphs of the following equations either consist of one point or are the empty set.

29. $3x^2 + y^2 = 0$

30. $4x^2 + y^2 - 16x - 2y + 17 = 0$

31. $4x^2 + y^2 - 16x - 2y + 18 = 0$

32. A rod 6 units long moves so that its ends are on two perpendicular lines. (See figure.) Show that a point P two units from one end describes an ellipse.

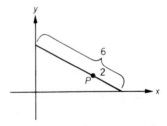

Find the points of intersection of the graphs of the following pairs of equations and sketch the graphs.

33. $9x^2 + y^2 - 18x - 4y - 72 = 0$,
    $y - 3x = 6$

34. $x^2 + 2y^2 = 4$,
    $x^2 + 3y^2 - 2x = 0$

35. $25x^2 + 12y^2 + 50x - 48y = 27$,
    $4y^2 - 4y = 5x + 3$

36. $x^2 + y^2 + 6x + 4y = 0$,
    $2y^2 + 8y - 9x = 19$

37. $x^2 + y^2 - 6x + 4 = 0,$
   $2x - y = 1$

38. $y^2 - 5x + 10 = 0,$
   $y^2 + 5x - 10 = 0$

39. $x^2 - 4x - 8y + 12 = 0,$
   $x^2 - 4x + 8y - 20 = 0$

40. $3x^2 + 4y^2 - 48 = 0,$
   $3x^2 + 4y^2 - 8y - 44 = 0$

41. The ellipse has several properties that serve to characterize it. One of these is the following, which is sometimes used as the definition: *If P is on an ellipse with foci F_1 and F_2, then*

$|PF_1| + |PF_2|$ *is a constant, and conversely.*

Prove that if $P = (x, y)$ is on the ellipse $b^2x^2 + a^2y^2 = a^2b^2$ with foci $F_1 = (c, 0)$ and $F_2 = (-c, 0)$, then

$$|PF_1| + |PF_2| = 2a.$$

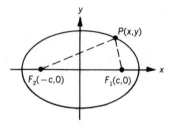

Calculator Problem

Verify the result of Problem 41 for the ellipse

$$\frac{(x - 3)^2}{25} + \frac{(y + 2)^2}{9} = 1 \quad \text{using} \quad P = \left(\frac{9 - 5\sqrt{5}}{3}, 0\right).$$

Find another point on the ellipse and verify the relation again.

18-5   # The Hyperbola

We choose the focus and directrix such that they are conveniently located with respect to the axes. Our choice of location is formally identical with the one we made for the ellipse.

Accordingly, let us suppose that the focus is at $(c, 0)$, where $c \neq 0$ ($c > 0$ in Fig. 18). Let us further suppose that the directrix is

$$x = \frac{c}{e^2},$$

where e is the eccentricity and, of course, $e > 1$.

Then $P(x, y)$ is on the hyperbola if and only if $|PF| = |PM|e$, or

$$\sqrt{(x - c)^2 + y^2} = \left|\frac{c}{e^2} - x\right| e. \quad (1)$$

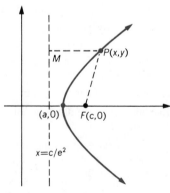

FIGURE 18

This equation is formally the same as equation (1) of Section 18–4, and so by the same algebraic steps is equivalent to

$$\frac{x^2}{\dfrac{c^2}{e^2}} + \frac{y^2}{\dfrac{c^2}{e^2}(1 - e^2)} = 1.$$

But for the hyperbola $e > 1$, so the factor $(1 - e^2)$ in the denominator of the second fraction is a negative number. Therefore we substitute $-(e^2 - 1)$ for $(1 - e^2)$ and rewrite the equation above in the more useful form

$$\frac{x^2}{\dfrac{c^2}{e^2}} - \frac{y^2}{\dfrac{c^2}{e^2}(e^2 - 1)} = 1.$$

As for the ellipse, we introduce new positive constants a and b according to

$$a^2 = \frac{c^2}{e^2}, \qquad b^2 = \frac{c^2}{e^2}(e^2 - 1) = c^2 - a^2,$$

so that

$$c^2 = a^2 + b^2. \tag{2}$$

Unlike the ellipse, the hyperbola may have $a > b$ or $b > a$, or even $a = b$, since $c^2 = a^2 + b^2$. The equation of the hyperbola then assumes the *standard form*

$$\frac{x^2}{a^2} - \frac{y^2}{b^2} = 1. \tag{3}$$

If a point (x, y) is on the hyperbola, then x and y satisfy (3), and conversely, if x and y satisfy (3), then the point (x, y) is on the hyperbola. The points $(a, 0)$ and $(-a, 0)$ are the *vertices* of the hyperbola. The number a is the length of the *semitransverse axis*. The number b is the length of the *semiconjugate axis*. (Geometric interpretations for a and b are given below.) The *center* of the hyperbola is at $(0, 0)$.

A number of observations can be made from equation (3).

(a) The hyperbola is *symmetric* with respect to the coordinate axes, which are called the *axes* of the hyperbola, and has its center at $(0, 0)$.

(b) From observation (a) we see that there must be a second focus and directrix. This fact may also be seen by observing that equations (1), (2), and (3) are not dependent on the sign of c. Figure 18 shows the focus and directrix when $c > 0$.

(c) If the hyperbola has its foci on the y-axis, the standard form of the equation is

$$\frac{y^2}{a^2} - \frac{x^2}{b^2} = 1.$$

(d) If we solve (3) for y, we obtain

$$y = \pm \frac{b}{a} \sqrt{x^2 - a^2}, \tag{4}$$

from which we see that x^2 must be greater than or equal to a^2, and that the hyperbola does not meet the y-axis.

From equation (4) we can also see that there are two straight lines, called *asymptotes,* that are intimately related to the hyperbola. From (4) we have

$$y = \pm \frac{b|x|}{a} \sqrt{1 - \frac{a^2}{x^2}} \qquad \text{if} \qquad |x| > a.$$

This last equation suggests that for large $|x|$, and therefore small a^2/x^2, the hyperbola should be very near the straight lines

$$y = \pm \frac{bx}{a}.$$

That this is indeed the case can be shown as follows (where, because of symmetry, we may restrict ourselves to the first quadrant):

$$y_{\text{line}} - y_{\text{hyperbola}} = \frac{b}{a} x - \frac{b}{a} \sqrt{x^2 - a^2}$$

$$= \frac{b}{a} (x - \sqrt{x^2 - a^2})$$

$$= \frac{b}{a} \frac{(x - \sqrt{x^2 - a^2})(x + \sqrt{x^2 - a^2})}{x + \sqrt{x^2 - a^2}}$$

$$= \frac{ab}{x + \sqrt{x^2 + a^2}}.$$

When x is very large, this last fraction represents a small number. Therefore the ordinate on the line is very near the corresponding ordinate on the hyperbola if x is very large.

Such a line is called an *asymptote.* That is, *an asymptote is a line that a curve approaches as a point on the curve "recedes to infinity."* An asymptote is *not* a part of the hyperbola.

A hyperbola with both foci, both directrices, and asymptotes is shown in Fig. 19.

We note that the asymptotes are very helpful in drawing the hyperbola. The asymptotes are easy to draw if one constructs the dotted rectangle of dimensions $2a$ and $2b$ shown in Fig. 19. We see that, geometrically, a and b

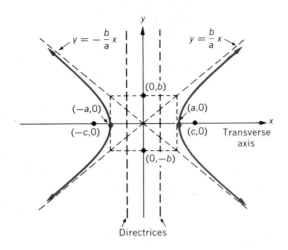

FIGURE 19

are equal to half the respective measures of this rectangle. The axis of the hyperbola containing the two foci is called the *transverse* axis.

(e) If the center of the hyperbola is at (h, k) and the two foci are at $(h \pm c, k)$, then an equation of the hyperbola is

$$\sqrt{(x - h - c)^2 + (y - k)^2} = \left| h + \frac{c}{e^2} - x \right| e,$$

which is equivalent to

$$\frac{(x - h)^2}{a^2} - \frac{(y - k)^2}{b^2} = 1. \tag{5}$$

Equation (5) is the standard form for a hyperbola with center at (h, k) and transverse axis parallel to the x-axis. If the transverse axis were parallel to the y-axis, the equation would be

$$\frac{(y - k)^2}{a^2} - \frac{(x - h)^2}{b^2} = 1.$$

We collect these results in Theorem 18–3.

Theorem 18-3   *The standard forms for an equation of a hyperbola with center at the origin are*

$$\frac{x^2}{a^2} - \frac{y^2}{b^2} = 1 \quad or \quad \frac{y^2}{a^2} - \frac{x^2}{b^2} = 1.$$

If the center is at (h, k) the standard forms are

$$\frac{(x - h)^2}{a^2} - \frac{(y - k)^2}{b^2} = 1 \quad or \quad \frac{(y - k)^2}{a^2} - \frac{(x - h)^2}{b^2} = 1.$$

Example 1   Graph the hyperbola having an equation $8x^2 - 3y^2 = 48$, and find its foci, the equations of its directrices and asymptotes, and its eccentricity.

Solution. Dividing both sides of the equation by 48, we get the standard form

$$\frac{x^2}{6} - \frac{y^2}{16} = 1.$$

Therefore (see Fig. 20),

$$a = \sqrt{6},\ b = 4,$$
$$c = \sqrt{6 + 16} = \sqrt{22}.$$

The foci are at $(\pm\sqrt{22}, 0)$. The eccentricity is

$$e = \sqrt{\tfrac{22}{6}} = \sqrt{\tfrac{11}{3}}.$$

The directrices are

$$x = \pm\frac{c}{e^2} = \pm\frac{3\sqrt{22}}{11}.$$

The asymptotes are

$$y = \pm\frac{4}{\sqrt{6}}x.$$

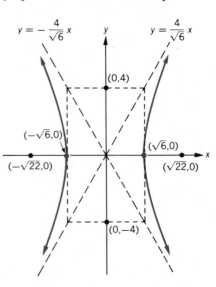

FIGURE 20

2   Find the standard form for the equation of the hyperbola with center at $(-2, 3)$, transverse axis parallel to the y-axis, and semiaxes of lengths a and b equal to 4 and 2, respectively. What are the equations of the asymptotes? Sketch the hyperbola and its asymptotes.

Solution. Since $c^2 = a^2 + b^2$, we have $c = \sqrt{20} = 2\sqrt{5}$. The foci are at $(-2, 3 \pm 2\sqrt{5})$. (See Fig. 21.) The vertices are at $(-2, 7)$ and $(-2, -1)$. The asymptotes have slopes ± 2 and pass through the center. Their equations are

$$y - 3 = \pm 2(x + 2).$$

The equation of the hyperbola is

$$\frac{(y - 3)^2}{16} - \frac{(x + 2)^2}{4} = 1,$$

which is equivalent to $y^2 - 4x^2 - 16x - 6y = 23$.

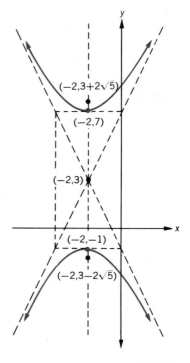

FIGURE 21

Example 3   Show that the graph of $-4x^2 + 9y^2 + 36y + 8x + 68 = 0$ is a hyperbola, find its center, the equations of its asymptotes, and make a sketch.

Solution. Completing the squares on the x- and y-terms, we have

$$-4(x^2 - 2x + 1) + 9(y^2 + 4y + 4) = -68 - 4 + 36 = -36.$$

Dividing through by -36, we obtain the equivalent equation and standard form

$$\frac{(x-1)^2}{9} - \frac{(y+2)^2}{4} = 1,$$

which is recognized as the equation of a hyperbola with center at $(1, -2)$ and axis parallel to the x-axis. We have $a = 3$, $b = 2$, and asymptotes with equations $y + 2 = \pm\frac{2}{3}(x - 1)$. (See Fig. 22.)

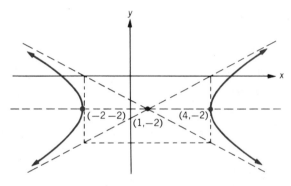

FIGURE 22

Problems

Set A

Sketch the following hyperbolas. Find the eccentricity, foci, and the equations of the asymptotes of each.

1. $16x^2 - 9y^2 = 144$
2. $4x^2 - 5y^2 + 20 = 0$
3. $2x^2 - y^2 = 8$
4. $10x^2 - 16y^2 + 25 = 0$

Sketch the following hyperbolas. For each find its center, foci, eccentricity, and the equations of its asymptotes.

5. $9x^2 - 16y^2 - 18x - 64y = 19$
6. $9x^2 - 5y^2 + 36x + 30y + 36 = 0$

7. $25x^2 - 9y^2 + 150x + 18y = 9$
8. $9x^2 - y^2 + 8y = 7$
9. $y^2 - 2x^2 + 12x + 4y = -4$
10. $9x^2 - 4y^2 + 72x + 24y + 72 = 0$

Set B

Write equations of each of the following hyperbolas and sketch them.

11. Foci at $(\pm\sqrt{3}, 0)$ and semitransverse axis $\sqrt{2}$
12. Center at $(0, 0)$, eccentricity $\sqrt{2}$, and semiconjugate axis 2 units long along the x-axis

13. Vertices at $(\pm 3, 0)$ and asymptotes with slopes $\pm\frac{1}{3}$

14. Foci at $(0, \pm 5)$ and eccentricity $\frac{5}{4}$

15. Asymptotes with slope $\pm\frac{5}{2}$, center at $(-2, 3)$, and transverse axis parallel to the x-axis

16. Vertices at $(-3, 1)$ and $(-3, -3)$, asymptotes with slopes ± 1

17. Transverse axis 8 units long and foci at $(-2, 2)$ and $(8, 2)$

18. Eccentricity $\sqrt{2}$ and foci at $(-1, -2 \pm 2\sqrt{2})$

19. Semiconjugate axis 5, with eccentricity $\frac{3}{2}$, center at $(1, 1)$, and transverse axis parallel to the x-axis

20. Foci at $(0, \pm 2\sqrt{5})$ and passes through $(-2\sqrt{6}, 4\sqrt{3})$

Set C

Find the points of intersection of the following pairs of curves and sketch each pair.

21. $3x^2 + 2y^2 = 8,$
    $x^2 - y^2 = 1$

22. $x^2 - y^2 = 1,$
    $y = 2x + 1$

23. $x^2 - 2y^2 = 2,$
    $y^2 = x$

24. $3y^2 - 4x^2 = 12,$
    $2x = (2\sqrt{6} + 3)y - 8\sqrt{6} - 18$

25. $x^2 + 10y^2 - 16x - 20y - 18 = 0,$
    $x^2 - 4y^2 - 16x - 20y - 4 = 0$

26. $y^2 - 4x^2 + 2y - 8x - 6 = 0,$
    $3x - y + 2 = 0$

27. The hyperbola has several properties that serve to characterize it. One of these is sometimes used as the definition, namely: *If P is on a hyperbola with foci F_1 and F_2, then*

$$|PF_2| - |PF_1| = \pm 2a$$

(depending on which branch P lies), and conversely.

Show that if $P(x, y)$ is on the right-hand branch of the hyperbola of Fig. 19 then $|PF_2| - |PF_1| = 2a$ if $F_1 = (c, 0)$ and $F_2 = (-c, 0)$.

28. Sketch the pair of hyperbolas given on the same axis:

$$\frac{x^2}{9} - \frac{y^2}{4} = 1$$

and

$$\frac{y^2}{4} - \frac{x^2}{9} = 1.$$

What are equations of the asymptotes of the hyperbolas? Two hyperbolas in which the transverse axis of either one is the conjugate axis of the other are called *conjugate hyperbolas*. Conjugate hyperbolas have the same asymptotes.

Calculator Problem

Verify the relation given in Problem 27 for the hyperbola

$$\frac{(x - 5)^2}{9} - \frac{(y - 3)^2}{1} = 1$$

and point P on the hyperbola where $P = (5 + 3\sqrt{5}, 1)$.
Find another point on the hyperbola and verify the relation again.

18-6 Degenerate Conics

In the preceding sections we have seen that the conics, ellipses, parabolas, and hyperbolas (with axes parallel to the coordinate axes) have equations that are of the second degree in x and y. In this and the following section we shall complete our study of what the graphs of second-degree equations in x and y can be. We shall see that except for *degenerate cases,* these graphs are always conics. In this section we investigate these degenerate cases by a study of examples.

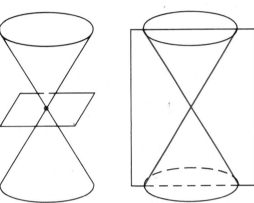

FIGURE 23

From Fig. 23 we see that there are intersections of a plane with a cone that are not ellipses, parabolas or hyperbolas. If the plane passes through the vertex of the cone it can intersect the cone in a point or it may intersect the cone in two intersecting straight lines. Thus there are other sections of a cone than the ones we have studied thus far.

If a plane intersects a cone at a point or in two intersecting straight lines, then we usually call these cases *degenerate conics.*

Example 1 The equation $x^2 + 2y^2 = 0$ has a graph consisting of only one point.

2 The equation $x^2 + 2y^2 + 1 = 0$ has an empty graph.

3 Sometimes it is not easy to recognize the types shown in Examples 1 and 2; they may be disguised as shown here. The equation

$$x^2 + 2y^2 - 4x + 8y + 13 = 0$$

becomes, on completion of the squares on x and y,

$$(x - 2)^2 + 2(y + 2)^2 + 1 = 0.$$

The graph of this equation is empty. Sometimes the graph is described as being *imaginary*. This means that the only numbers x and y that satisfy the equation are complex numbers with at least one of them having a nonzero imaginary part.

These examples illustrate one type of degeneracy of second-degree equations. The examples below illustrate the other type of degeneracy.

Example 4 Sketch the graph of $x^2 - xy - 2y^2 - x + 11y - 12 = 0$.

Solution. The polynomial happens to factor, so the equation is

$$x^2 - xy - 2y^2 - x + 11y - 12 = (x - 2y + 3)(x + y - 4) = 0.$$

Therefore its graph is the union of the graphs of $x - 2y + 3 = 0$ and $x + y - 4 = 0$. It is shown in Fig. 24.

The student may very well wonder how one is to determine whether or not a given equation factors. Inspection of the quadratic terms will usually show how to proceed. Thus in the above example, the quadratic terms alone factor: $x^2 - xy - 2y^2 = (x - 2y)(x + y)$. It remains then to see whether there are suitable choices of a and b for which we can have

$$x^2 - xy - 2y^2 - x + 11y - 12 = (x - 2y + a)(x + y + b).$$

A few trials will usually decide the issue.

However, if there is *no xy-term* in the equation, then simple completion of the squares on x and y will show whether or not the equation factors. The next example illustrates this case.

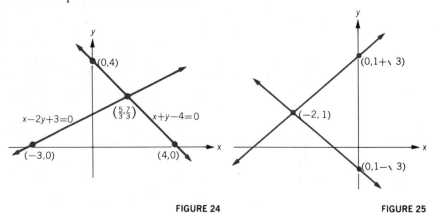

FIGURE 24   FIGURE 25

Example 5 The equation $3x^2 - 4y^2 + 12x + 8y + 8 = 0$ becomes, after completion of the squares,

$$3(x + 2)^2 - 4(y - 1)^2 = 0.$$

The left-hand member of this last equation is the difference of two squares and it factors as the product of a sum and a difference:

$$[\sqrt{3}(x + 2) + 2(y - 1)] \times [\sqrt{3}(x + 2) - 2(y - 1)] = 0.$$

The graph of the equation is the union of the graphs of

$$\sqrt{3}(x + 2) + 2(y - 1) = 0, \quad \text{and} \quad \sqrt{3}(x + 2) - 2(y - 1) = 0,$$

and is shown in Fig. 25.

Problems

Set A

1. The graph of $x^2 - y^2 = 0$ is the union of two intersecting lines. What are the equations of the lines? Sketch the graph.

2. The graph of $x^2 + 4y^2 - 4x - 8y + 8 = 0$ consists of a single point. Complete the squares in x and y and determine the coordinates of the point.

3. Explain why $x^2 + 2y^2 + 1 = 0$ has an empty graph.

4. Find two linear factors of

$$x^2 - 6y^2 + xy - 3x + 11y - 4 = 0.$$

Graph the two resulting lines.

Set B

Identify and sketch the following degenerate conics.

5. $3x^2 + 4y^2 = 0$

6. $3x^2 + 4y^2 + 6x + 4y + 5 = 0$

7. $x^2 - 4y^2 = 0$

8. $x^2 - 4y^2 + 2x + 4y = 0$

9. $2x^2 - 3y^2 + 3y - \frac{3}{4} = 0$

10. $xy = 0$

11. $y^2 = 2xy$

12. $x^2 + 2xy + y^2 - 2x - 2y + 1 = 0$

13. $x^2 + 2xy + y^2 + x + y = 0$

Set C

14. Show that the graph of $Ax^2 + By^2 + Cx + Dy + E = 0$ consists of two intersecting straight lines if

$$AB < 0 \quad \text{and} \quad E = \frac{C^2}{4A} + \frac{D^2}{4B}.$$

(Without loss of generality you may assume that $A > 0$ and $B < 0$. Why?)

Calculator Problem

The mirror in the Hale telescope of Palomar Observatory has a parabolic cross section and is 5.08 m in diameter. The focal point is 13.97 m from the mirror center.

Write an equation for the parabola. Find the depth d in the figure to which the mirror is ground.

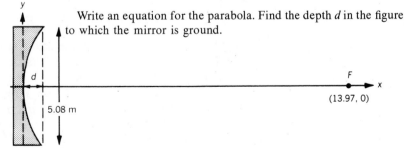

From the last section we see that if there is no xy-term, then by completing the square it is easy to determine whether or not the conic is degenerate. If the conic given by

$$Ax^2 + Cy^2 + Dx + Ey + F = 0 \qquad (A^2 + C^2 \neq 0)$$

is not degenerate, then from the preceding sections if follows that after completing the squares we obtain the equation of an ellipse, parabola, or hyperbola in standard form—and the type of graph obtained depends only on the signs of A and C. (Remember that we call a circle a special ellipse.) Our present state of knowledge is summarized in the following theorem.

Theorem 18-4 *If the graph of*

$$Ax^2 + Cy^2 + Dx + Ey + F = 0$$

is not degenerate, and not both A and C are 0, then the graph is

(a) *an ellipse if $AC > 0$,*

(b) *a parabola if $AC = 0$,*

(c) *a hyperbola if $AC < 0$.*

Example 1   Consider the equation $2x^2 - 9y^2 + 4x + 18y + 1 = 0$. Assuming that its graph is not degenerate, we see that Theorem 18-4(c) applies, $AC = -18 < 0$, and we must have a hyperbola. It is easy to verify that this is indeed the case. We obtain

$$2(x + 1)^2 - 9(y - 1)^2 = -1 + 2 - 9 = -8,$$

and a standard form for a hyperbola,

$$\frac{(y - 1)^2}{\frac{8}{9}} - \frac{(x + 1)^2}{4} = 1.$$

We turn now to the general quadratic equation in x and y:

$$Ax^2 + Bxy + Cy^2 + Dx + Ey + F = 0, \tag{1}$$

where not all of A, B, and C are 0. In the next chapter we shall see that the xy-term in (1) can be eliminated by rotation of the axes through a suitably selected angle θ. In other words, if a second coordinate system were chosen, with axes x', y' as indicated in Fig. 26, then in terms of the new coordinates equation (1) would become the equivalent equation

$$A'x'^2 + C'y'^2 + D'x' + E'y' + F' = 0, \tag{2}$$

(note that $B' = 0$ for the special value of θ), where the coefficients $A', \ldots, F'$ can be found in terms of $A, \ldots, F$, and θ. We see therefore that equation (1) must represent a conic, degenerate or not.

When this transformation to the $x'y'$-coordinate system is carried out (and we shall do this in the next chapter), it is an easy calculation to show that

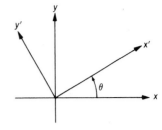

FIGURE 26

$$B^2 - 4AC = B'^2 - 4A'C',$$

no matter through what angle θ the axes may be rotated. In other words, $B^2 - 4AC$ remains *invariant* under rotation of coordinate axes. Because, the graph of equation (2) is readily identified by application of Theorem 18–4 we are able to distinguish the graph of (1) with little effort.

We state our conclusions as follows.

Theorem 18–5 *If not all of A, B, and C are 0, and if the graph of*

$$Ax^2 + Bxy + Cy^2 + Dx + Ey + F = 0,$$

is not degenerate, then the graph is

(a) an ellipse if $B^2 - 4AC < 0$,

(b) a parabola if $B^2 - 4AC = 0$,

(c) a hyperbola if $B^2 - 4AC > 0$.

Armed with knowledge of this theorem, one can make a rather good sketch of the graph of a second-degree equation without bothering to remove the xy-term. The following example may serve to illustrate the method.

Example 2 Consider the equation $4x^2 + 3xy + y^2 - 12 = 0$.

Here $A = 4$, $B = 3$, $C = 1$, and $B^2 - 4AC = 9 - 16 = -7 < 0$. Therefore the graph, if not degenerate, is an ellipse.

Let us try to sketch the graph directly. First we observe that the given equation is quadratic in y and hence can easily be solved for y by the quadratic formula

$$y^2 + 3xy + (4x^2 - 12) = 0,$$

$$y = \frac{-3x \pm \sqrt{9x^2 - 4(4x^2 - 12)}}{2}$$

$$= -\frac{3x}{2} \pm \frac{\sqrt{48 - 7x^2}}{2}.$$

From this last equation we see that $|x|$ cannot exceed $\sqrt{\frac{48}{7}}$. Therefore the graph is confined to a bounded portion of the plane and must be an ellipse. (See Fig. 27.) The points of the ellipse must lie above, on, and below the line $y = -\frac{3}{2}x$.

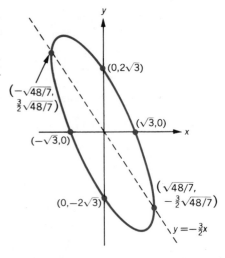

FIGURE 27

Problems

Set A

Assume that the graphs of the following conics are not degenerate. In each case use Theorem 18–5 to predict the type of conic.

1. $x^2 - xy + y^2 + x + y = 0$
2. $x^2 - xy - y^2 + x + y = 0$
3. $x^2 + 2xy + y^2 + x - y = 0$
4. $17x^2 + 12xy + 8y^2 - 60x + 24y - 12 = 0$
5. $xy - 7 = 0$
6. $xy - x - 1 = 0$

Set B

Using Theorem 18–5, determine the kinds of graphs described by the following equations. Then sketch the graph of each by solving for y and plotting a few points.

7. $5x^2 - 4xy + 4y^2 = 12$

8. $3x^2 + 4xy - 4y^2 - 12 = 0$
9. $x^2 - 4xy + 4y^2 - 4x + 8 = 0$
10. $xy + y + x = 0$

Set C

11. A conic has focus $(1, 1)$, directrix $x + y + 1 = 0$, and eccentricity $\sqrt{2}$. Use Definition 18–1 to find a second-degree equation of the conic. Verify that Theorem 18–5 predicts the correct type of conic.

12. A parabola has its focus at $(4, 1)$ and its directrix $2x - y + 3 = 0$. Use Definition 18–1 to find an equation of the parabola. Verify that Theorem 18–5 predicts the correct type of conic.

Calculator Problem

Solve $4x^2 + 3xy - y^2 = 12$ for y in terms of x. Then find several points on the conic given by the equation. Can you determine the kind of conic without using Theorem 18–5?

Higher-Degree Curves

At this point our position is such that we can predict the kinds of graphs of the following equations:

$$Ax + By + C = 0,$$
$$Ax^2 + Bxy + Cy^2 + Dx + Ey + F = 0.$$

We can also sketch the graphs of such equations fairly quickly. It therefore is natural to wonder about the graphs of equations obtained from polynomials of degree three or more in x and y, for example *cubic* curves that have equations of the form

$$Ax^3 + Bx^2y + Cxy^2 + Dy^3 + Ex^2 + Fxy + Gy^2 + Hx + Iy + J = 0.$$

Such curves are called *algebraic curves,* and the classification of the kinds one can obtain is part of *algebraic geometry*. We cannot go into these questions here, partly for lack of space, but also because more advanced methods are needed for such a study. Nevertheless, a few of these curves are quite easy to graph by the methods we have at our disposal. If the algebraic equation is either linear or quadratic in y, then it is easy to solve for y, and the graph can usually be sketched after a few points have been plotted. Consider the following examples.

Example 1   Sketch the graph of $y^2 = x(x - 1)^2$.

Solution. We observe that the graph is symmetric with respect to the x-axis because if x and y satisfy the equation, so do x and $-y$. We also observe that we must have $x \geq 0$, for otherwise y could not be a real number. The graph is shown in Fig. 28.

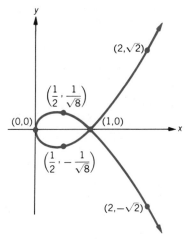

FIGURE 28

Example 2 Sketch the graph of $x^2y - x^2 - y = 0$.

Solution. This equation is also a cubic (of degree three) because of the x^2y-term. It is of the first degree in y, and

$$y = \frac{x^2}{(x^2 - 1)}.$$

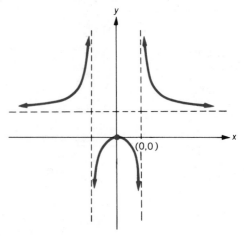

The graph is symmetric with respect to the y-axis. This curve has asymptotes just as a hyperbola does. We observe that as $|x| \to 1$, $y \to \pm\infty$, depending on whether $|x| > 1$ or $|x| < 1$. Furthermore, as $|x|$ becomes infinite, y approaches 1. The graph is shown in Fig. 29.

FIGURE 29

Problems

Set A

Sketch the graphs of the following equations.

1. $x^3y = 4$
2. $x^2 = y^3 - 1$
3. $y^2 = 2x(x - 2)^2$
4. $x^2y = 4(2 - y)$

12. $y = x(x + 1)^2(x - 4)^3$

13. $y = \dfrac{(x - 1)(x + 3)}{(x - 2)^2(x + 4)^3}$

Set B

Sketch the graphs of the following equations.

5. $x^2y = 4a^2(2a - y)$, $a > 0$
   (the Witch of Agnesi)
6. $y^2 = ax^3$, $a > 0$ (a semicubical parabola)
7. $y^2 = x^2(x - 1)$
   (a curve with an isolated point)
8. $y^2 = x(x - 1)(x - 2)$
9. $y = (x - 1)(x - 2)(x - 3)$
10. $y = \dfrac{(x - 1)(x - 3)}{x - 2}$
11. $y = \dfrac{x - 1}{(x - 2)(x - 3)}$

Set C

Sketch the graphs of the following equations.

14. $y^2 = \dfrac{(x - 1)^2(x + 3)}{(x - 2)^2(x + 4)^5}$

15. $y = \dfrac{(x + 2)^2(x + 1)}{(x^2 - 4)(x^2 - 9)}$

16. $y^2 = \dfrac{x^2(x - 5)(x + 5)^2}{(x^2 - 9x + 20)^2(x^2 + 5x + 4)}$

17. $(x^2 + y^2)^2 = a^2(x^2 - y^2)$ (a lemniscate)

18. $x^3 + y^3 = 3axy$, $a > 0$ (the folium of Descartes)

Calculator Problem

An approximate equation for the elliptical orbit of the earth around the sun is

$$\frac{x^2}{(149{,}604{,}500 \text{ km})^2} + \frac{y^2}{(149{,}583{,}600 \text{ km})^2} = 1.$$

Calculate the following.

(a) The eccentricity of the orbit
(b) The minimum distance from the earth to the sun
(c) The maximum distance from the earth to the sun

18-9 Quadric Surfaces

Thus far we have considered curves in the *plane,* and mainly curves represented by second-degree equations in x and y. One generalization was suggested in Section 18–8, where we briefly mentioned curves represented by algebraic equations of higher degree.

A different generalization is to consider the graphs of second-degree equations in *three* variables:

$$Ax^2 + By^2 + Cz^2 + Dxy + Eyz + Fzx + Gx + Hy + Iz + J = 0. \quad (1)$$

The graphs of such equations are called *quadric surfaces.* (A general discussion of surfaces will be found in the final chapter.) A complete description of these surfaces would take us too far afield, and so we shall content ourselves with sketching a few examples. In Fig. 30 the nondegenerate quadric surfaces are shown along with the equations they have when the axes are conveniently chosen.

Actually, the ideas of this section were anticipated in the preceding chapter, where cylinders and spheres were discussed. The method we follow is that of examining the intersections of these surfaces with planes parallel to the coordinate planes. These sections will be conics and therefore easy for us to sketch. When a few of these sections have been drawn, the appearance of the surface will usually be clear.

Example 1 Sketch the quadric surface whose equation is $2x^2 + y^2 = z$.

Solution. First we examine the *traces* of this surface in the coordinate planes. They are

xy-trace: $2x^2 + y^2 = 0$, $z = 0$ (the trace is a point),
yz-trace: $y^2 = z$, $x = 0$ (the trace is a parabola),
zx-trace: $2x^2 = z$, $y = 0$ (the trace is a parabola).

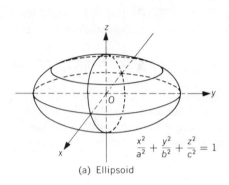

$$\frac{x^2}{a^2} + \frac{y^2}{b^2} + \frac{z^2}{c^2} = 1$$

(a) Ellipsoid

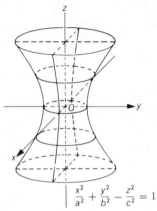

$$\frac{x^2}{a^2} + \frac{y^2}{b^2} - \frac{z^2}{c^2} = 1$$

(b) Hyperboloid of one sheet

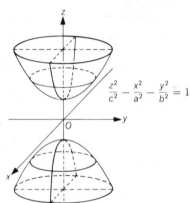

$$\frac{z^2}{c^2} - \frac{x^2}{a^2} - \frac{y^2}{b^2} = 1$$

(c) Hyperboloid of two sheets

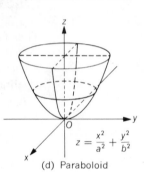

$$z = \frac{x^2}{a^2} + \frac{y^2}{b^2}$$

(d) Paraboloid

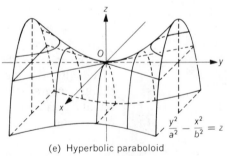

$$\frac{y^2}{a^2} - \frac{x^2}{b^2} = z$$

(e) Hyperbolic paraboloid

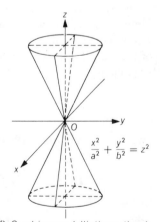

$$\frac{x^2}{a^2} + \frac{y^2}{b^2} = z^2$$

(f) Quadric cone (elliptic sections)

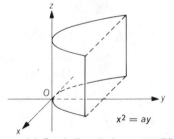

$$x^2 = ay$$

(g) Parabolic cylinder **FIGURE 30**

The parabolic traces (half of each) are shown in color in Fig. 31.

Let us consider the intersections of the surface with planes $z = c$ where c is a constant. These curves are ellipses for all positive c. Two are shown in Fig. 31. Actually only one-fourth of the quadric is shown in Fig. 31. The full surface is shown in Fig. 30(d).

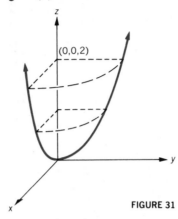

FIGURE 31

Example 2   Sketch the graph of $2x^2 - y^2 + z^2 = 4$.

Solution. The traces in the coordinate planes are

$$xy\text{-trace:} \quad 2x^2 - y^2 = 4, \quad z = 0 \quad \text{(a hyperbola)},$$
$$yz\text{-trace:} \quad -y^2 + z^2 = 4, \quad x = 0 \quad \text{(a hyperbola)},$$
$$zx\text{-trace:} \quad 2x^2 + z^2 = 4, \quad y = 0 \quad \text{(an ellipse)}.$$

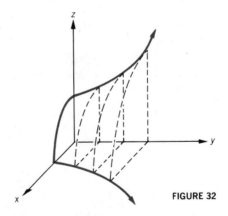

FIGURE 32

Parts of these traces are drawn as solid lines in Fig. 32. To make the surface "stand out" we slice it by planes parallel to one of the coordinate planes. Which plane to use is dictated by ease in drawing the sections. Since all sections determined by the planes $y = c$ are ellipses and therefore easy to draw, we shall use these planes. Parts of these ellipses are drawn as dashed lines for $c = 1, 2, 3$ in Fig. 32.

Problems

Set A

In each of the following quadrics, sketch the traces in the coordinate planes and sections produced by several planes parallel to the coordinate plane.

1. $x^2 + 2y^2 + 3z^2 = 6$

2. $x^2 + 2y^2 - 3z^2 = 6$

3. $-x^2 + 2y^2 - 3z^2 = 6$

4. $x^2 - y^2 + z^2 = 0$

5. $x^2 + z^2 - y = 0$

6. $y^2 - x^2 = z$

7. $(x + z - 1)(x - y) = 0$

8. $x^2 + 2y^2 = 6$ 9. $y^2 = 4x$

Set B

For the following quadrics, first complete the squares on the appropriate variables, and then sketch each surface. Identify the kind of quadric by reference to Fig. 30.

10. $x^2 + y^2 + z^2 - 4z = 0$

11. $x^2 + 2y^2 + 3z^2 - 2x - 8y + 3 = 0$

12. $x^2 + y^2 - z^2 - 2x - 4y + 1 = 0$

13. $y^2 + 4x - 4y + 8 = 0$

14. $x^2 + y^2 - 3z^2 - 2x - 2y + 6z - 1 = 0$

15. $-3x^2 - 2y^2 - 6x - 4y + 6z + 1 = 0$

Set C

16. Sketch the quadric $xz = y^2$.

17. Show that sections of the general quadric surface of equation (1) of this section made by planes parallel to the coordinate planes are conic sections.

Calculator Problem

The formula $C_n = C_0(1 + r)^n$ is an "inflation formula" by which one can compute the cost of articles in future years based on a constant yearly percentage rate of inflation. In the formula

$$C_0 = \text{present day cost of an article}$$
$$r = \text{yearly inflation rate}$$
$$n = \text{number of years}$$
$$C_n = \text{cost of the article } n \text{ years from now}$$

Use this formula to solve these problems.

(a) Find the cost of a 25¢ candy bar 20 years from now if the inflation rate is 10%.

(b) Find the cost of a $6000 automobile 36 years from now if the yearly inflation rate is 12%.

(c) Find the cost of a home that presently sells for $60,000 twenty-five years from now if the inflation rate is 9%.

Find the number of years it takes for an article to double in cost if the inflation rate is

(d) 2%   (e) 8%   (f) 10%   (g) 20%

Summary

The emphasis of this chapter has been on the graphs of second-degree equations. These graphs are called *conic* sections.

The principal nondegenerate conic sections are the parabola, ellipse, and hyperbola. Definition 18–1, which defines the conic sections, is of primary importance. The eccentricity e of a conic tells us the kind of conic we are considering. Thus, if (a) $e < 1$, the conic is an ellipse, (b) $e = 1$, the conic is a parabola, or (c) $e > 1$, the conic is a hyperbola.

If the focus and directrix of one of the conic sections is suitably placed with respect to the coordinate axes, then an equation of the conic is quite simple.

1. $y^2 = 4cx.$ Parabola with vertex at the origin and axis along the x-axis; c is the focus.

2. $\dfrac{x^2}{a^2} + \dfrac{y^2}{b^2} = 1.$ Ellipse with *semimajor axis* a and *semiminor axis* b. $a^2 = b^2 + c^2$. The foci are at $(c, 0)$ and $(-c, 0)$, $e = (c/a) < 1$.

3. $\dfrac{x^2}{a^2} - \dfrac{y^2}{b^2} = 1.$ Hyperbola with *semitransverse axis* of length a and *semiconjugate axis* of length b. The foci are at $(\pm c, 0)$, where $c^2 = a^2 + b^2$. Equations of the *asymptotes* are $y = \pm(b/a)x$.

4. The graph of the equation

$$Ax^2 + Cy^2 + Dx + Ey + F = 0,$$

if not degenerate, is .

(a) an ellipse   if $AC > 0$,
(b) a parabola   if $AC = 0$,
(c) a hyperbola   if $AC < 0$.

5. The graph of the equation

$$Ax^2 + Bxy + Cy^2 + Dx + Ey + F = 0,$$

if not degenerate, is

(a) an ellipse   if $B^2 - 4AC < 0$,
(b) a parabola   if $B^2 - 4AC = 0$,
(c) a hyperbola   if $B^2 - 4AC > 0$.

In addition to the conic sections we considered a few *algebraic curves* of degree greater than two. Our method of graphing such higher-degree equations was that of plotting enough points to visualize the shape of the curve.

Finally, we extended the idea of conic sections to space by considering equations of the form

$$Ax^2 + By^2 + Cz^2 + Dxy + Eyz + Fzx + Gx + Hy + Iz + J = 0.$$

The method of plotting the *quadric surfaces* given by this equation was to examine the traces of the surface in planes parallel to the coordinate planes.

Chapter 18   Test

18-2   Identify the kind of conic given the eccentricity e.

1. $e > 1$ 2. $e = 1$ 3. $e < 1$

18-3   4. Find an equation of a parabola if the focus is at $(1, -2)$ and the directrix is $y = 4$.

5. Find an equation of a parabola if the vertex is $(2, 2)$ and the focus is $(4, 2)$.

6. Find the focus and an equation of the directrix of the parabola with the equation $y^2 + 2y - 6x + 13 = 0$. Sketch the parabola.

18-4   7. Find the length of the semimajor axis and the eccentricity of the ellipse $x^2 + 9y^2 = 144$.

8. An ellipse has eccentricity $e = \sqrt{3}/2$ and foci $(\pm 2\sqrt{3}, 0)$. Write an equation of the ellipse.

9. Find the center and foci of the ellipse $9x^2 + 25y^2 - 90x + 100y + 100 = 0$. Sketch the conic.

18-5   10. Sketch the hyperbola

$$\frac{x^2}{9} - \frac{y^2}{4} = 1.$$

Find the eccentricity, foci, and equations of the asymptotes.

11. Sketch the hyperbola $9y^2 - 4x^2 - 54y + 16x + 29 = 0$. Give the center and the equations of the asymptotes.

12. Find the points of intersection of the graphs of the following pair of equations. Check by sketching the graphs of the equations.

$$\frac{x^2}{25} + \frac{y^2}{9} = 1, \qquad \frac{x^2}{25} - \frac{y^2}{9} = 1$$

18-6   13. The equation $x^2 - 2xy + y^2 - 9 = 0$ represents a degenerate conic which has two linear factors. Find the factors and sketch the graph.

14. Describe the degenerate conic given by the equation $x^2 + y^2 + 6x - 2y + 10 = 0$.

18-7   Find $B^2 - 4AC$ for each equation given, then tell which conic the given equation represents.

15. $2x^2 + 3xy + y^2 - x + 6y + 7 = 0$

16. $x^2 - 6xy + 9y^2 + 10 - y + 1 = 0$

18-8   Sketch each curve.

17. $y^2(x - 1)^2 = 1$ 18. $y = (x - 3)(x - 1)(x + 2)$

18-9   Sketch a portion of each of the following quadric surfaces by considering traces of the surface in planes parallel to the coordinate planes.

19. $y^2 - 6y - 4x + 17 = 0$ 20. $9x^2 + y^2 + 9z^2 = 9$

Historical Note

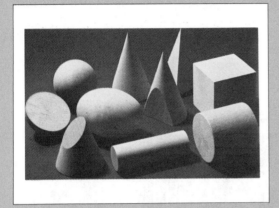

Why do we study the conics? There are several reasons. First, these curves are encountered with astonishing frequency in all sorts of real problems. For example, because of gravitational attraction, described in Newton's law, the path of a planet around the sun is an ellipse, except for the slight disturbing effect of the other planets. Second, next to straight lines, the conics are the simplest curves in the plane; they have equations of the second degree in x and y. Third, the conics are interesting in themselves for the variety of surprising properties that they possess.

Apart from these mathematical reasons, there is also the influence of the past. The conics have attracted mathematicians for 2000 years. As in so many fields, we are indebted to the ancient Greeks, who developed an extensive theory of the conics. A great part of that theory is the work of one man, *Apollonius of Perga* (262?–200? B.C.). He was one of the three great geometers of the third century B.C., the other two being Euclid and Archimedes. In his book *Conic Sections,* Appollonius systematized and vastly extended the work of earlier writers. The approximately 400 propositions of the book include much more mate-rial than has been mentioned in this brief chapter.

Before Apollonius, the definitions of the conics were based on the requirement that the sectioning plane be perpendicular to a generator of the cone. Hence one obtained the three kinds of conics by making the vertex angle of the cone acute, right, or obtuse (see Fig. 33).

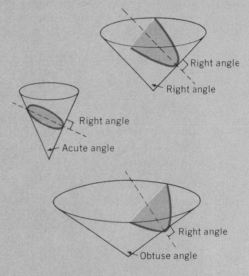

FIGURE 33

Note that since this construction used only one nappe, or half of the complete cone, only half of the hyperbola was obtained. Apollonius obtained all the conics from a single, complete cone (using both nappes) by permitting the sectioning plane to cut a generator at any angle.

Apollonius also gave us the names *ellipse, parabola,* and *hyperbola.* To catch the spirit of his writing we shall paraphrase his terminology with respect to eccentricity. He said that a conic suffers *ellipsis* if the eccentricity *falls short* of 1, *parabole* if the eccentricity is *precisely* 1, or *hyperbole* if the eccentricity *exceeds* 1.

Chapter 19
Other Coordinate Systems

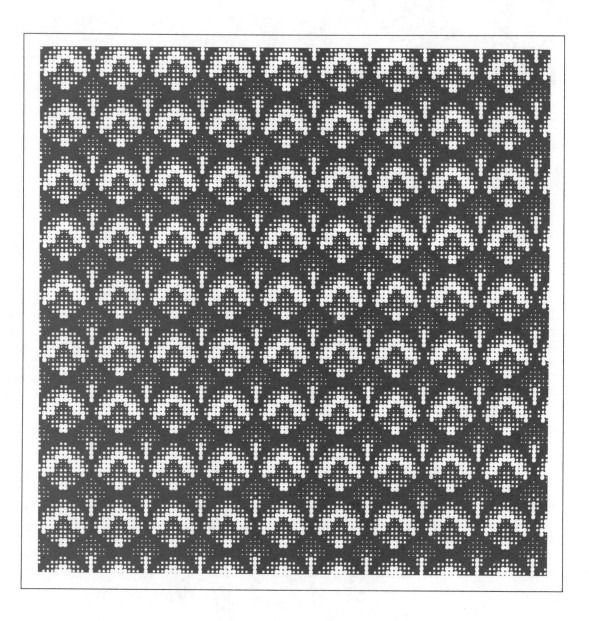

19-1   Introduction

What is a coordinate system in the plane? On reflection one sees that *a coordinate system is a mapping* that associates with each point *P* an ordered pair of numbers called the coordinates of *P*:

$$P \rightarrow \text{(first coordinate, second coordinate)}.$$

Let us suppose that we have, in a region, two families of curves labeled *A, B, C, ...* and *a, b, c, ...*, as in Fig. 1. And let us further suppose that each point of the region is on exactly one curve of each family. Then the two families of curves give a coordinate system in the region. Each point of the region has associated with it a unique ordered pair of numbers, for example, (*C, b*).

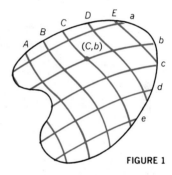

FIGURE 1

In the preceding chapters we have concerned ourselves with rectangular coordinates, but clearly there are infinitely many kinds of coordinate systems because of the infinite variety of curve families we can choose. In this chapter we shall investigate some of the more important of these nonrectangular coordinate systems.

19-2   Translation of Axes

We first study the relations between the different rectangular coordinate systems that can be chosen.

Let us suppose that we have two rectangular coordinate systems in the plane, with origins at *O* and *O'*, and with the first and second coordinate axes parallel in the two systems, as in Fig. 2.

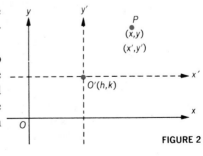

FIGURE 2

Then the point P in the plane has two sets of coordinates, x, y and x', y' with respect to the two sets of coordinate axes. We say that the origin of the xy-coordinate system has been *translated* to the point O'.

If the coordinates of O' are (h, k) with respect to the old axes, then how are the coordinates (x, y) and (x', y') related? An easy geometric argument will show that for all real numbers h and k,

$$\begin{aligned} x' &= x - h, \\ y' &= y - k. \end{aligned} \tag{1}$$

Equations (1) are called the *translation equations*.

An equation in x and y may become considerably simpler if the origin O is translated to a properly selected point O'.

Example   Find an equation of the conic

$$2x^2 + 3y^2 - 4x + 9y = \tfrac{13}{4}$$

after the origin has been translated to the point $(1, -\tfrac{3}{2})$. (See Fig. 3.)

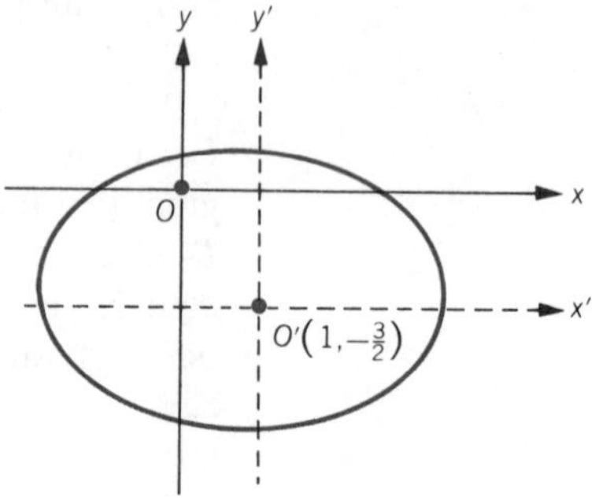

Solution.   Since $O' = (1, -\tfrac{3}{2})$, we have $h = 1$ and $k = -\tfrac{3}{2}$. The translation equations are

$$\begin{aligned} x' &= x - 1, \\ y' &= y + \tfrac{3}{2}, \end{aligned}$$

FIGURE 3

where $x = x' + 1$ and $y = y' - \tfrac{3}{2}$. Substitution of these for x and y in the given equation results in

$$2(x' + 1)^2 + 3(y' - \tfrac{3}{2})^2 - 4(x' + 1) + 9(y' - \tfrac{3}{2}) = \tfrac{13}{4}.$$

This equation reduces to

$$2x'^2 + 3y'^2 = 12, \tag{2}$$

which is an ellipse with center at O' and semiaxes $\sqrt{6}$ and 2.

When we complete the squares in the original equation, we are led automatically to the proper point O' to which we should translate the origin:

$$2(x^2 - 2x \quad) + 3(y^2 + 3y \quad) = \tfrac{13}{4},$$

$$2(x - 1)^2 + 3(y + \tfrac{3}{2})^2 = \tfrac{13}{4} + 2 + \tfrac{27}{4},$$

or

$$2(x - 1)^2 + 3(y + \tfrac{3}{2})^2 = 12.$$

This last equation is our previous equation (2) with $x' = x - 1$ and $y' = y + \tfrac{3}{2}$.

Problems

Set A

Give the new coordinates of the points below if the origin is translated to the point $(-2, 3)$.

1. $(4, 2)$ **2.** $(-1, -1)$ **3.** $(0, 0)$

4. $(-5, 4)$ **5.** $(3, 0)$ **6.** (a, b)

7. Transform the equation $x - y + 3 = 0$ by translating the origin to the point $(2, 5)$. Sketch the graph.

8. Transform the equation $x^2 - 6x - 8y - 31 = 0$ by translating the origin to $(3, -5)$. Sketch the graph.

9. Transform the equation $4x^2 - 9y^2 - 16x - 18y = 18$ by translating the origin to the point $(2, -1)$. Then sketch the graph.

Set B

10. When the origin was translated to the point $(-3, 1)$, the equation for an ellipse was $x'^2 + 9y'^2 = 1$. What was the original equation in x and y?

11. Transform the equation $4x^2 + y^2 - 24x + 4y + 24 = 0$ by translating the origin to the point (h, k). Determine h and k so that the x'- and y'-terms are absent. Complete the squares in the original equation. How do you interpret your result?

12. Transform the equation $y^2 - 6y - 2x + 7 = 0$ by translating the origin to the point (h, k). Determine h and k so that the y'-term and the constant terms are absent.

Set C

13. Prove that the formula for the slope of the line through (x_1, y_1) and (x_2, y_2) remains valid after translation of axes. [*Hint:* Translate the origin to the point (h, k).]

Calculator Problem

Transform the equation $x^2 + y^2 - 3.7x + 7.9y = 0.13$ by translating the origin to the point (h, k). Determine h and k so the x'-term and y'-term are absent.

19-3   Rotation of Axes

In addition to a translation of the origin, two rectangular coordinate systems can also be related by a *rotation of axes,* as indicated in Fig. 4. The positive x'-axis meets the unit circle in a point $W(\theta)$, where W denotes the wrapping function. Then the positive y'-axis meets the unit circle at the point $W(\theta + \pi/2)$.

A point P has two sets of coordinates (x, y) and (x', y'). The relation

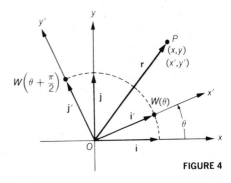

FIGURE 4

between these coordinates is easily obtained by examining the position vector $\overrightarrow{OP} = \mathbf{r}$ in the two coordinate systems. Let $\mathbf{i}, \mathbf{j}$ and $\mathbf{i}', \mathbf{j}'$ be the unit vectors along the axes in the two systems. Then

$$\mathbf{r} = x\mathbf{i} + y\mathbf{j} = x'\mathbf{i}' + y'\mathbf{j}'.$$

Because $\mathbf{r} \cdot \mathbf{i} = x$ and $\mathbf{r} \cdot \mathbf{j} = y$, we have

$$x = \mathbf{r} \cdot \mathbf{i} = (x'\mathbf{i}' + y'\mathbf{j}') \cdot \mathbf{i} \quad \text{and} \quad y = \mathbf{r} \cdot \mathbf{j} = (x'\mathbf{i}' + y'\mathbf{j}') \cdot \mathbf{j}.$$

Finally, we get

$$x = x'(\mathbf{i}' \cdot \mathbf{i}) + y'(\mathbf{j}' \cdot \mathbf{i}), \qquad y = x'(\mathbf{i}' \cdot \mathbf{j}) + y'(\mathbf{j}' \cdot \mathbf{j}), \tag{1}$$

and all that remains is to find the dot products in (1). Clearly,

$$\mathbf{i}' \cdot \mathbf{i} = \mathbf{j}' \cdot \mathbf{j} = \cos\theta,$$

$$\mathbf{i}' \cdot \mathbf{j} = \cos(\pi/2 - \theta) = \sin\theta,$$

$$\mathbf{j}' \cdot \mathbf{i} = \cos(\pi/2 + \theta) = -\sin\theta.$$

Therefore, *the equations for rotation of axes through an angle of measure θ are*

$$x = x'\cos\theta - y'\sin\theta, \qquad y = x'\sin\theta + y'\cos\theta. \tag{2}$$

Formulas for x' and y' in terms of x and y can be found by solving the linear equations (2) for x' and y'. (See Problem 9 below.)

It may happen that after rotation of axes through a suitably chosen angle, the equation of a curve takes a simpler form. An important instance of this is given in the following theorem.

Theorem 19-1   *The general quadratic in x and y,*

$$Ax^2 + Bxy + Cy^2 + Dx + Ey + F = 0, \tag{3}$$

can be transformed into

$$A'x'^2 + C'y'^2 + D'x' + E'y' + F = 0 \tag{4}$$

by rotation of the axes through an angle of measure θ such that

$$\tan 2\theta = \frac{B}{A - C} \quad \textit{if } A \neq C,$$

or by rotation through

$$\theta = \frac{\pi}{4} \quad \textit{if } A = C.$$

Proof   We use the equations for rotation (2) and substitute these expressions for x and y in the general quadratic. We obtain

$$A(x' \cos \theta - y' \sin \theta)^2 + B(x' \cos \theta - y' \sin \theta)(x' \sin \theta + y' \cos \theta)$$
$$+ C(x' \sin \theta + y' \cos \theta)^2 + D(x' \cos \theta - y' \sin \theta)$$
$$+ E(x' \sin \theta + y' \cos \theta) + F = 0.$$

After carrying out the multiplications and collecting terms containing x'^2, $x'y'$, y'^2, x', and y', we obtain

$$(A \cos^2 \theta + B \sin \theta \cos \theta + C \sin^2 \theta)x'^2$$
$$+ [-2A \sin \theta \cos \theta + B(\cos^2 \theta - \sin^2 \theta) + 2C \sin \theta \cos \theta]x'y'$$
$$+ (A \sin^2 \theta - B \sin \theta \cos \theta + C \cos^2 \theta)y'^2$$
$$+ (D \cos \theta + E \sin \theta)x' + (E \cos \theta - D \sin \theta)y' + F = 0. \quad (5)$$

This last equation has the same graph in the plane as does the original equation. It has the form

$$A'x'^2 + B'x'y' + C'y'^2 + D'x' + E'y' + F = 0, \quad (6)$$

where A', B', C', D', and E' can be obtained from equation (5) in terms of A, B, C, D, and E and functions of θ. The $x'y'$-term will be absent from (6) if

$$B' = -2A \sin \theta \cos \theta + B(\cos^2 \theta - \sin^2 \theta) + 2C \sin \theta \cos \theta = 0. \quad (7)$$

This is a trigonometric equation that is relatively easy to solve. Recall that $\sin 2\theta = 2 \sin \theta \cos \theta$ and $\cos 2\theta = \cos^2 \theta - \sin^2 \theta$. Then equation (7) becomes

$$B \cos 2\theta + (C - A) \sin 2\theta = 0,$$

so that

$$\tan 2\theta = \frac{B}{A - C} \quad \text{if} \quad A \neq C.$$

However, if $A = C$, then $\cos 2\theta = 0$, and $\theta = \pi/4$ will satisfy the equation. This completes the proof.

Example Rotate the axes to remove the xy-term from the equation $34x^2 - 24xy + 41y^2 = 200$, and sketch the graph.

Solution. If θ is the measure of the angle of Theorem 19–1, then

$$\tan 2\theta = \frac{-24}{34 - 41} = \frac{24}{7}.$$

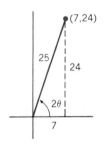

We may therefore choose 2θ in the first quadrant, as has been done in Fig. 5. Then $\cos 2\theta = \frac{7}{25}$, and

$$\sin \theta = \sqrt{\frac{1 - \cos 2\theta}{2}} = \sqrt{\frac{1 - \frac{7}{25}}{2}} = \frac{3}{5},$$

$$\cos \theta = \sqrt{\frac{1 + \cos 2\theta}{2}} = \sqrt{\frac{1 + \frac{7}{25}}{2}} = \frac{4}{5}.$$

FIGURE 5

The equations of the transformation are therefore

$$x = \tfrac{4}{5}x' - \tfrac{3}{5}y' = \frac{4x' - 3y'}{5},$$

$$y = \tfrac{3}{5}x' + \tfrac{4}{5}y' = \frac{3x' + 4y'}{5}.$$

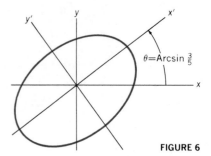

FIGURE 6

Substitution in the original equation yields

$$34(4x' - 3y')^2 - 24(4x' - 3y')(3x' + 4y') + 41(3x' + 4y')^2 = 200(25).$$

This equation simplifies to $x'^2 + 2y'^2 = 8$, and its graph is the ellipse of Fig. 6.

In Chapter 18 we used, without proof, the result of the following theorem, for which we can now give a straightforward, though long, proof by reference to equations (5) and (6).

Theorem 19–2 *For arbitrary rotations of the axes [and in the notation of equations (5) and (6)],*

$$B^2 - 4AC = B'^2 - 4A'C'.$$

To show that the relation given in Theorem 19–2 holds for the example above we must be certain that the original equation and the equation obtained after rotation of axes have the same constant term, F, in the notation of Theorem 19–1. We have

$$34x^2 - 24xy + 41y^2 = 200$$

so that $A = 34$, $B = -24$, $C = 41$ and $F = -200$. This equation was transformed by the rotation to

$$x'^2 + 2y'^2 - 8 = 0.$$

Multiplying both sides of this equation by 25 to get the same constant term as in the previous equation we have

$$25x'^2 + 50y'^2 - 200 = 0.$$

Therefore, $A' = 25$, $B' = 0$, $C' = 50$ and $F = -200$. Now, $B^2 - 4AC = B'^2 - 4A'C'$ or

$$(-24)^2 - 4(34)(41) = 0^2 - 4(25)(50) = -5000.$$

Problems

Set A

Rotate the axes through a positive acute angle to remove the xy-term from each of the following equations. Sketch the graph showing both sets of axes.

1. $xy = 4$
2. $3x^2 - 4xy + 8x - 3y - 1 = 0$
3. $4x^2 - 24xy + 11y^2 = 0$
4. $x^2 - 2xy + y^2 + 2x + 4y - 4 = 0$
5. $17x^2 + 12xy + 8y^2 = 20$
6. $21x^2 + 10\sqrt{3}\,xy + 31y^2 = 144$
7. Verify Theorem 19-2 for the equations in Problems 1-6.
8. The axes are rotated through an angle of $\pi/6$. What is the equation of the line $x - 3y = 0$ in terms of the new coordinates x' and y'?

Set B

9. Solve equations (2) for x', y' in terms of x and y. Show that the same result can be obtained as a rotation from x', y'-axes to x, y-axes.
10. After the axes had been rotated through an angle of $\pi/6$, the equation of an ellipse was

$$\frac{x'^2}{25} + \frac{y'^2}{4} = 1.$$

What was the original equation? [*Hint:* Use the results of Problem 9.]

11. Using the notation of equations (5) and (6), solve for A', B', and C', and prove Theorem 19-2.
12. Show that in Theorem 19-1 we may always choose θ so that $0 < \theta < \pi/2$ if B is not already 0.
13. Are there any equations of the form of equation (3) for which a rotation of $90°$ will remove the xy-term? Explain.

Set C

14. Show that the graph of

$$Ax^2 + Bxy + Cy^2 + F = 0$$

is a hyperbola if $AC < 0$ and $F \neq 0$.
15. Given two points $P(x_1, y_1)$ and $P(x_2, y_2)$, prove that the distance $|P_1 P_2|$ is invariant under rotation of axes by showing that the distance formula gives the same number in both coordinate systems.
16. Show that if $x' = ax + by$, $y' = -bx + ay$, and $a^2 + b^2 = 1$, then the equations give a rotation.

Calculator Problem

Rotate the axes through an appropriate angle to remove the xy-term from the equation of the parabola

$$x^2 + 2xy + y^2 - 4x + 6y - 8 = 0.$$

Then complete the square of the x'-terms to give a translation to x'', y''-axes. Sketch the three coordinate axes and the graph of the parabola.

Polar Coordinates

As we suggested in Section 19–1, there are infinitely many coordinate systems. Among the nonrectangular ones the most important are the *polar coordinate systems* in a plane, which we now define.

We will *choose* a point O in the plane, which will be called the *pole*, and a ray emanating from O, called the *polar axis*. The unit circle with center at O meets the polar axis at a point A. (See Fig. 7.) We next *choose* a positive sense around the unit circle and map the real numbers on the circle by the standard map W with $W(0) = A$. Each point Q on the unit circle then corresponds to infinitely many real numbers, $Q = W(\theta + 2k\pi)$, where $k = 0, \pm 1, \pm 2, \ldots$.

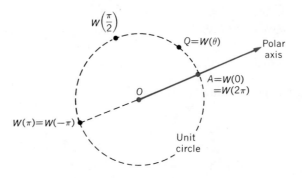

FIGURE 7

Let us consider any point $P \neq O$ in the plane. The ray from O through P meets the unit circle in a point $Q = W(\theta)$, where θ is a real number. We suppose that P is at a distance r from the pole. Then the pair of numbers (r, θ) uniquely determine the point P in the plane. With this notation, we can give the definition of polar coordinates.

Definition 19–1 With the above notation (shown in Fig. 8), the ordered pairs of numbers

$$(r, \theta + 2k\pi), \qquad k = 0, \pm 1, \ldots,$$

are polar coordinates of P. If $P = O$, then $r = 0$ and θ is arbitrary.

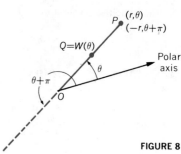

FIGURE 8

We shall also permit negative values for r. If r is negative, we simply measure distance along the ray *oppositely* directed to the ray through O and $W(\theta)$. (See Fig. 8.)

Some points with some of their polar coordinates are shown in Fig. 9.

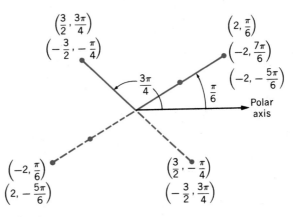

FIGURE 9

Remarks

1. Even when the pole and polar axis are fixed, *there are infinitely many polar coordinates for each point*. However, given an ordered pair (r, θ), of real numbers, there is a unique point that has these numbers as polar coordinates.

2. Consider the $r\theta$-plane, where r and θ are now rectangular coordinates. The shaded portion of Fig. 10(a) maps onto the whole plane with r and θ as polar coordinates, as indicated in Fig. 10(b).

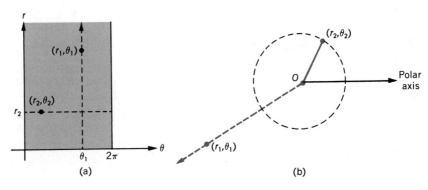

(a)   (b)

FIGURE 10

The vertical ray of Fig. 10(a) maps onto the dashed ray from the pole in Fig. 10(b).

The horizontal segment in Fig. 10(a) maps onto the circle in Fig. 10(b).

3. We have used polar coordinates previously in writing the polar form of a complex number. Recall that polar coordinates (r, θ) determine the complex number $z = x + iy = r(\cos \theta + i \sin \theta)$ where $r = \sqrt{x^2 + y^2}$.

Problems

Set A

Plot the points with the following polar coordinates.

1. $(4, \pi/3)$, $(-4, -2\pi/3)$, $(-4, 4\pi/3)$, $(-4, \pi/3)$, $(4, -2\pi/3)$

2. $(\frac{1}{2}, 5\pi/4)$, $(-\frac{1}{2}, -\pi/4)$, $(\frac{1}{2}, 13\pi/4)$, $(\frac{1}{2}, -\pi/4)$

3. $(2, 1)$, $(-2, \pi + 1)$, $(-2, 1)$, $(-2, -1)$, $(-2, 1 - \pi)$, $(2, 1 - \pi)$

4. $(-3, \pi/2)$, $(-3, \pi)$, $(-3, 3\pi/2)$, $(-3, 0)$

Find three other pairs of polar coordinates for each of the points with the following polar coordinates.

5. $(3, \pi/3)$ **6.** $(2, \frac{1}{2})$

7. $(-1, -\pi/4)$ **8.** (π, π)

9. $(-1, \pi/2)$ **10.** $(-4, \pi/6)$

Set B

11. What is the graph of the set of points whose polar coordinates are $(r, \pi/4)$ where r is any real number? Sketch the graph.

12. Sketch the graph of all points whose polar coordinates are $(1, \theta)$ where θ is any real number.

Set C

Sketch the graphs of the following polar equations. In other words, sketch the set of points $P(r, \theta)$ whose coordinates satisfy the equations below.

13. $r = 3$ **14.** $r = -3$

15. $\theta = 5\pi/6$ **16.** $\theta = 5\pi/6$ and $r > 0$

17. $\cos \theta = 1/r$

Calculator Problem

Graph the set of points whose polar coordinates are $(\tan \theta, \theta)$ where θ is any real number except odd multiples of $\pi/2$.

19-5   Curves in Polar Coordinates

Just as certain curves have simple equations in rectangular coordinates (for example, lines and conics), so will some curves have simple equations in polar coordinates. However, a new variety of curves comes to our attention, and equations with familiar graphs in rectangular coordinates will now have different graphs in polar coordinates. Since many of our examples involve the circular functions, it will be very helpful if the variations of the circular functions are kept in mind.

Remark

Observe that the graphs of the same equation, $r = f(\theta)$, are quite different, depending on whether r and θ are polar coordinates or rectangular coordinates. Whenever the graph of $r = f(\theta)$ is known for either rectangular or polar coordinates, it may be helpful to use it to help with the drawing of the other.

Example 1

Sketch the graph of $r = a\cos\theta$.

Solution. We first observe that the cosine has period 2π, and hence we may restrict our attention to the interval $0 \le \theta \le 2\pi$. Moreover, the cosine is an even function, so the full graph can be inferred from the graph for $0 \le \theta \le \pi$. We make a small table of r versus θ.

θ	0	$\pi/4$	$\pi/2$	$3\pi/4$	π	$5\pi/4$	$3\pi/2$	$7\pi/4$	2π
r	a	$a\sqrt{2}/2$	0	$-a\sqrt{2}/2$	$-a$	$-a\sqrt{2}/2$	0	$a\sqrt{2}/2$	a

Figure 11(a) shows the graph of $0 \le \theta \le \pi$ in polar coordinates. The arrowheads indicate how the point (r, θ) moves as θ increases from 0 to π. For $\pi \le \theta \le 2\pi$, the same points are obtained, although not the same coordinates. The graph appears to be a circle. We shall see in the next section that it actually is.

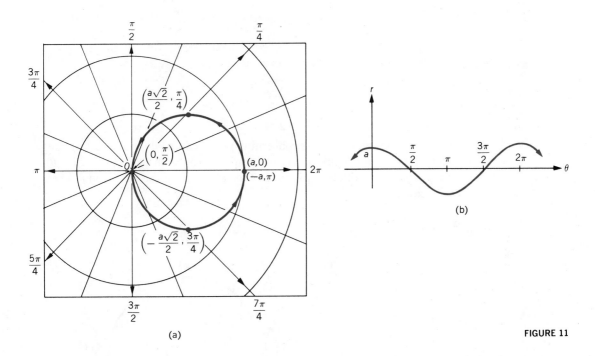

(a)

(b)

FIGURE 11

Note that the graph of $r = a\cos\theta$ in rectangular coordinates is the cosine wave of Fig. 11(b). From this graph the polar graph of the equation is quickly sketched.

Example 2

Sketch the graph of $r = 1 + \cos\theta$.

Solution. In this example, we observe that $r \geq 0$ for all θ. As in Example 1, the periodicity of the cosine permits us to restrict θ to the interval $0 \leq \theta \leq 2\pi$. Because the cosine is even, the graph for $\pi \leq \theta \leq 2\pi$ can be inferred from the graph for $0 \leq \theta \leq \pi$. The graph, shown in Fig. 12(a), is called a *cardioid*. The solid curve is $0 \leq \theta \leq \pi$. The dashed curve is the graph of $\pi \leq \theta \leq 2\pi$.

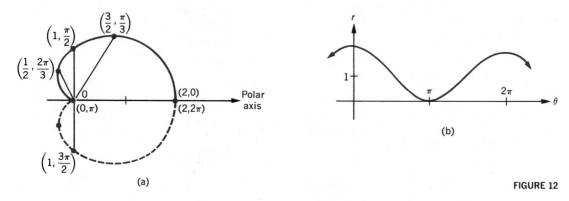

(a)

(b)

FIGURE 12

Note that the graph of $r = 1 + \cos\theta$ in rectangular coordinates is the wave of Fig. 12(b). Obviously r is never negative.

Example 3

Sketch the graph of $r = 1 + 2\cos\theta$.

Solution. The same remarks concerning periodicity and the interesting range on θ can be made as in Examples 1 and 2. The graph of $r = 1 + 2\cos\theta$ in rectangular coordinates appears in Fig. 13(a). Note the range on θ when r is negative.

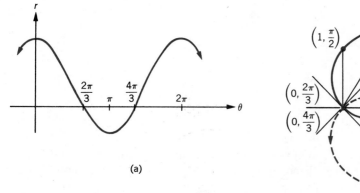

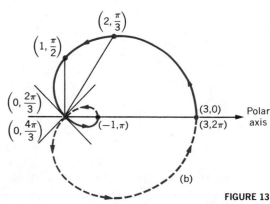

(a)

(b)

FIGURE 13

The graph in polar coordinates for $0 \leq \theta \leq \pi$ is shown in Fig. 13(b) as a solid curve. The graph for $\pi \leq \theta \leq 2\pi$ is shown dashed. The arrows indicate how the curve is traversed as θ increases from 0 to 2π. We observe that for $0 \leq \theta \leq 2\pi/3$, r is nonnegative. But for $2\pi/3 < \theta \leq \pi$, r is negative, and the lower part of the loop to the right of the pole is obtained. The curve is called a *limaçon*.

Example 4   Sketch the graph of $r = \theta$.

Solution. In this case, there is no periodicity, and r simply increases with θ. The graph for positive θ is shown as the solid curve in Fig. 14. The graph for negative θ is shown dashed. The curve is a *spiral of Archimedes*.

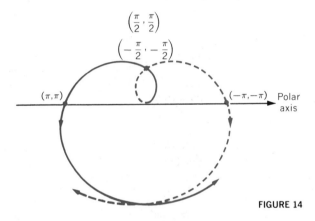

FIGURE 14

Example 5   Sketch the graph of $r = a \cos 2\theta$, $a > 0$.

Solution. This interesting curve (a four-leaved rose) is shown in Fig. 15. The graph for $0 \leq \theta \leq \pi$ is shown as a solid curve. That for $\pi \leq \theta \leq 2\pi$ is shown dashed. For $\pi/4 < \theta < 3\pi/4$, r is negative, and we get the bottom petal on the rose.

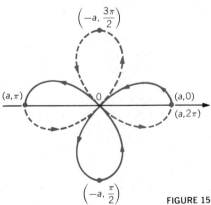

FIGURE 15

A selection of other interesting polar curves is shown in Fig. 16.

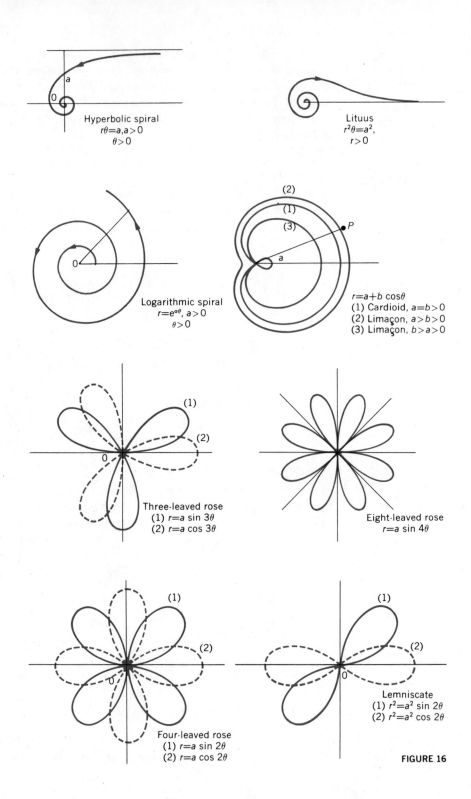

Hyperbolic spiral
$r\theta = a, a > 0$
$\theta > 0$

Lituus
$r^2\theta = a^2,$
$r > 0$

Logarithmic spiral
$r = e^{a\theta}, a > 0$
$\theta > 0$

P

$r = a + b\cos\theta$
(1) Cardioid, $a = b > 0$
(2) Limaçon, $a > b > 0$
(3) Limaçon, $b > a > 0$

(1)
(2)
Three-leaved rose
(1) $r = a\sin 3\theta$
(2) $r = a\cos 3\theta$

Eight-leaved rose
$r = a\sin 4\theta$

(1)
(2)
Four-leaved rose
(1) $r = a\sin 2\theta$
(2) $r = a\cos 2\theta$

(1)
(2)
Lemniscate
(1) $r^2 = a^2\sin 2\theta$
(2) $r^2 = a^2\cos 2\theta$

FIGURE 16

Problems

Set A

Sketch the graphs of the following equations in polar coordinates.

1. $r = 3 \sin \theta$ **2.** $r = 2 \cos \theta$

3. $r = 1 + \sin \theta$ **4.** $r = 1 - \sin \theta$

5. $r = 1 - \sqrt{2} \cos \theta$ **6.** $r = 2 + \cos \theta$

7. $r = 1/\sin \theta$ **8.** $r = 1/\sin (\theta - \pi/3)$

Set B

Sketch the graphs of the following equations in polar coordinates.

9. $r = a \sin 2\theta$ **10.** $r = a \cos 3\theta$

11. $r = a \cos 4\theta$ **12.** $r = 1/\theta^2, \; \theta > 0$

13. $r^2 = a^2 \sin 2\theta$ **14.** $r^2 = a^2 \sec 2\theta$

15. $r^2 = a^2 \cos 3\theta$ **16.** $r = a \cos^2 \theta, \; a > 0$

Set C

17. What is the graph of $r = \sin^2 \theta + \cos^2 \theta$?

18. Sketch the graph of $r = a \sin 5\theta$.

19. The limaçon of Example 3 can be used to trisect angles. Let A be a given acute angle of measure α placed with respect to the limaçon, $r = 1 + 2 \cos \theta$, as in the figure. The unit circle with center at A has a polar equation $r = 2 \cos \theta$. Referring to the figure, explain why the following statements are true.

(a) $\angle AOB \cong \angle OBA$
(b) $\alpha + \beta = 2\theta$
(c) $|BC| = 1$
(d) $\angle BAC \cong \angle BCA$
(e) $\theta = 2\beta$
(f) Therefore $\alpha = 3\beta$, and $\angle BAC$ is the desired trisection of $\angle CAD$.

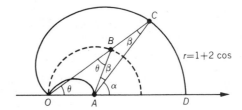

Calculator Problem

Sketch the graph of

$$r = \frac{12}{\sqrt{16 \sin^2 \theta + 9 \cos^2 \theta}}$$

by plotting enough points. What is a rectangular equation of the curve?

Polar and Rectangular Coordinates

There are infinitely many polar coordinate systems, differing by the choices made for pole and polar axis. Likewise, there are infinitely many rectangular coordinate systems with different origins and axes. Relations between arbitrary polar and rectangular coordinate systems could be quite complicated. However, if the pole and the origin coincide, if the positive x-axis is the polar axis, and if the unit circle with center O is oriented in the same way in both systems, then the two coordinate systems are simply related. (See Fig. 17.) In this section we shall assume that the two systems are so related. It is clear from the figure that

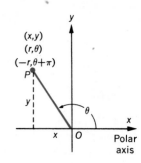

$$x = r \cos \theta, \qquad y = r \sin \theta,$$

and (1)

$$r^2 = x^2 + y^2.$$

FIGURE 17

Equations (1) are satisfied by the polar coordinates (r, θ), or by $(r, \theta + 2k\pi)$, or by $(-r, \theta + (2k + 1)\pi)$, where k is an integer. This is the case because

$$\cos (\theta + \pi) = -\cos \theta \qquad \text{and} \qquad \sin (\theta + \pi) = -\sin \theta.$$

Equations (1) permit us to find a polar equation of a curve from a rectangular equation.

Example 1   Find a polar equation of the circle $x^2 + y^2 - ax = 0$.

Solution. From equations (1) we have

$$r^2 \cos^2 \theta + r^2 \sin^2 \theta - ar \cos \theta = 0$$

or

$$r^2 - ar \cos \theta = r(r - a \cos \theta) = 0.$$

The last equation is satisfied if either $r = 0$ (the pole) or $r - a \cos \theta = 0$. Because the graph of $r - a \cos \theta = 0$ contains the pole ($r = 0$ at $\theta = \pi/2$) (see Fig. 18), we *do not omit any point of the graph by neglecting the factor r*. Therefore, an equation of the circle in polar coordinates is

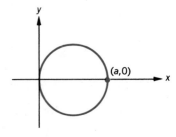

$$r = a \cos \theta.$$

Equations (1) can be solved for r and θ. We have

FIGURE 18

$$x^2 + y^2 = r^2 \cos^2 \theta + r^2 \sin^2 \theta = r^2,$$

$$\frac{y}{x} = \frac{\sin \theta}{\cos \theta} = \tan \theta,$$

and therefore

$$r = \pm\sqrt{x^2 + y^2}, \qquad \theta = \arctan \frac{y}{x}. \tag{2}$$

Note that we do not select the principal value of the inverse tangent. *Any* θ such that $\tan \theta = y/x$ will suffice *if* we select a suitable sign for r, so that (r, θ) is in the same quadrant as (x, y).

Example 2 Find a rectangular equation of the curve with the polar equation $r \cos \theta = a$.

Solution. Since $x = r \cos \theta$, the graph is the straight line with equation $x = a$ (Fig. 19a).

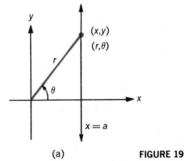

(a)   FIGURE 19

Similarly, the equation $r \cos (\theta - \alpha) = a$ is equivalent to $r \cos \theta \cos \alpha + r \sin \theta \sin \alpha = a$, or the straight-line equation (Fig. 19b) $x \cos \alpha + y \sin \alpha = a$.

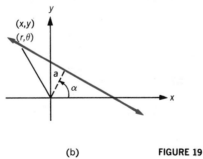

(b)   FIGURE 19

We note that the dot product of **r** and the unit position vector $\cos \alpha \mathbf{i} + \sin \alpha \mathbf{j}$ is equal to a:

$$\mathbf{r} \cdot (\cos \alpha \, \mathbf{i} + \sin \alpha \, \mathbf{j}) = a.$$

Problems

Set A

Find the rectangular coordinates of the points with the given polar coordinates.

1. $(3, \pi/6)$ 2. $(4, -5\pi/6)$

3. $(-4, -5\pi/4)$ 4. $(-5, \pi/2)$

5. $(\sqrt{3}, -\pi/3)$ 6. $(2, 2)$

Find polar coordinates of the points with rectangular coordinates.

7. $(5, 5)$ 8. $(-3, 4)$

9. $(-2, -2)$ 10. $(2, -2\sqrt{3})$

11. $(\frac{3}{5}, \frac{4}{5})$ 12. $(3 \sin 4, 3 \cos 4)$

Find polar equations of the following curves and sketch them.

13. $x^2 + y^2 = a^2$ 14. $x + 5 = 0$

15. $x + y = 2$ 16. $x^2 + y^2 = 4y$

17. $(x^2 + y^2)^2 = a^2(x^2 - y^2)$

18. $xy = 1$

Find rectangular equations of the curves with the following polar equations and sketch them.

19. $r = a \sin \theta$ 20. $r = 4$

21. $r = 1/(1 - \cos \theta)$ 22. $r^2 = a^2 \sin 2\theta$

23. $r = \tan \theta$ 24. $r^2 = \tan \theta \sec^2 \theta$

Set B

Find polar equations of the following curves and sketch them.

25. $(x^2 + y^2)^3 = a^2(x^2 - y^2)^2$

26. $y = b$

27. $x \cos \gamma + y \sin \gamma = p$

28. $4x^2 + 3y^2 - 2y - 1 = 0$

29. $y^2 = x^3$

30. $x^2 + 4y^2 = 4$

Find rectangular equations of each curve and sketch them.

31. $r = a \sin 2\theta$ 32. $r = \cos \theta - \sin \theta$

33. $r = \theta$ 34. $r = \tan \frac{1}{2}\theta$

Set C

35. Show that the distance between the points (r_1, θ_1) and (r_2, θ_2) is

$$d = \sqrt{r_1^2 + r_2^2 - 2r_1 r_2 \cos(\theta_1 - \theta_2)}.$$

36. Prove that a straight line not passing through the origin has an equation of the form $r(A \cos \theta + B \sin \theta) = 1$. If the line passes through the origin, what is the form of a polar equation for it?

37. Find a rectangular equation of the line through the points P_1 and P_2 if the polar coordinates of these points are $P_1 = (4, \pi/2)$ and $P_2 = (4\sqrt{2}, -\pi/4)$.

Calculator Problem

Calculate the distance between the points P_1 and P_2 of Problem 37 in two ways.

(a) Use the formula given in Problem 35.

(b) Find the rectangular coordinates of the points and then use the distance formula for the rectangular coordinate plane.

To find the intersections of curves given in rectangular coordinates, one simply solves the two simultaneous equations, because we know that a point is on both curves if and only if its (unique) coordinates satisfy both equations.

To find the intersection of curves with polar equations, more care must be taken because a point has many sets of polar coordinates. Thus on one curve, the point may be given by one pair of coordinates while on the other curve, it is given by a different pair. Naturally, solution of the two simultaneous polar equations (if any solution exists) will yield points on both curves, but it may not give all of them. The procedure we shall follow is to

(a) solve the two polar equations, and

(b) graph the two equations to see whether all points of intersection have been obtained.

Example   Find the points of intersection of the circle $r = \sin \theta$ and the cardioid $r = 1 - \sin \theta$.

Solution. Eliminating θ between the two equations gives $r = 1 - r$ and $r = \frac{1}{2}$, so $\sin \theta = \frac{1}{2}$ and $\theta = \pi/6$ or $5\pi/6$. The two points of intersection so obtained are shown in Fig. 20. Furthermore, we see from the figure that the curves also intersect at the pole. As a point of the circle, the pole has coordinates $(0, 0)$, $(0, \pi)$, $(0, 2\pi)$, and as a point of the cardioid, it has coordinates $(0, \pi/2)$. We may visualize this situation by thinking of two ships, both starting at P and sailing along the two curves to O. They pass through O at different times because their paths from their starting point to O are different. One would go from P to O directly; the other would go from P to R to S and then to O.

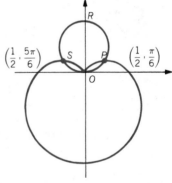

FIGURE 20

Problems

Set A

Find the points of intersection of the pairs of curves with the following polar equations. Sketch each pair.

1. $r = 3, r = 3 + 2 \cos \theta$ **2.** $r = 2, r = 2 \sin 2\theta$

3. $r = \sin \theta, r = \cos 2\theta$ **4.** $r = \cos \theta, r = \sin 2\theta$

5. $r = \sin 2\theta, r = \cos 2\theta$ **6.** $r = 2, r^2 = 8 \cos 2\theta$

Set B

Find the points of intersections of the pairs of curves. Sketch the curves.

7. $r = 2, r = \sec^2 \frac{1}{2}\theta$

8. $r^2 = a^2 \cos 2\theta, r^2 = a^2 \sin 2\theta$

9. $r^2 = \sin 2\theta, r = \sin \theta$

10. $r = \cos\theta, \ r = 1 + \cos\theta$

11. $r = 1 - \sin\theta, \ r = \cos 2\theta$

12. $r^2 = \cos 2\theta, \ r^2 = \sin 2\theta$

Set C

13. Find the point of intersection of the pair of lines whose polar equations are

$$r = \frac{-1}{\sin\theta + \cos\theta}$$

and

$$r = \frac{2}{3\sin\theta - 2\cos\theta}.$$

14. Find rectangular equations of the lines in Problem 13. Solve the simultaneous equations and obtain the point of intersection in rectangular coordinates.

15. Show, by an example, that even though (r_0, θ_0) may satisfy the equation of a polar curve, other coordinates for the same point, $(r_0, \theta_0 + 2k\pi)$ or $(-r_0, \theta_0 + k\pi)$, may not satisfy the equation.

Calculator Problem

Sketch the curve $r^2 = 16 \sin\frac{1}{2}\theta$. Use increments of $\pi/12$ ($15°$) for θ.

19-8   Conics

Equations of conics in polar coordinates are quite simple if the focus is at the pole and the directrix is perpendicular to the polar axis. The polar form of an equation of a conic is often used in calculation of orbits of planets or satellites.

Let us suppose that the focus and directrix of a conic are as in Fig. 21. Then P is on the conic of eccentricity e if and only if $|PF| = |PM|e$. Since $|PF| = r$ and $|PM| = p + r\cos\theta$, we have $r = (p + r\cos\theta)e$ or

$$r = \frac{pe}{1 - e\cos\theta}. \tag{1}$$

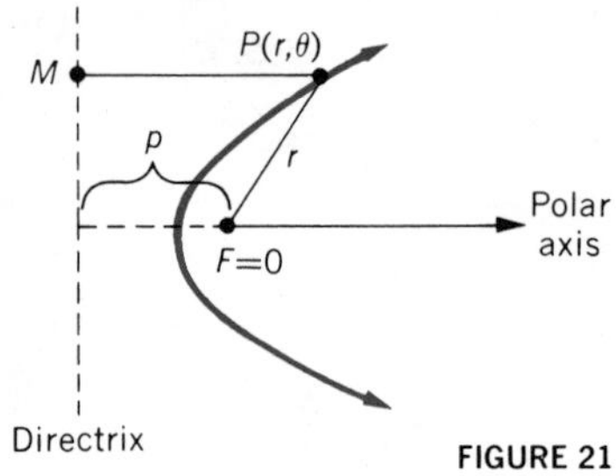

FIGURE 21

Equation (1) can be used to quickly sketch the conic, as the following example shows.

Example   Sketch the curve with the equation

$$r = \frac{4}{2 - \cos\theta}.$$

Solution. The equation, as it stands, is not in the standard form (1). Dividing numerator and denominator of the fraction by 2 gives

$$r = \frac{2}{1 - \frac{1}{2}\cos\theta},$$

which is the equation of a conic with eccentricity $\frac{1}{2}$.

Recall that when $e < 1$, the conic is an ellipse; when $e = 1$, the conic is a parabola; and when $e > 1$, the conic is a hyperbola. In this example, since $e < 1$, we have an ellipse. From (1) we see that the distance from focus to directrix is $p = 4$. The ellipse is shown in Fig. 22.

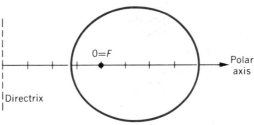

FIGURE 22

Problems

Set A

Sketch the following conics.

1. $r = \dfrac{2}{3 - 2\cos\theta}$ **2.** $r = \dfrac{1}{1 - \cos\theta}$

3. $r = \dfrac{4}{1 - 2\cos\theta}$ **4.** $r = \dfrac{9}{10 - 9\cos\theta}$

Set B

5. Find the equation of the conic if the directrix is perpendicular to the polar axis and a distance p to the right of the pole.

6. Find the equation of the conic if the directrix is parallel to the polar axis and a distance p above it.

7. Show that $r = 2p\sec^2\frac{1}{2}\theta$ represents a parabola.

Set C

8. Find an equation, in standard rectangular coordinates, for the ellipse whose equation in polar form is

$$r = \frac{4}{2 - \cos\theta}.$$

9. Find the equation of the conic if the directrix is at a distance p from the pole and is inclined, as shown in the figure below.

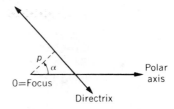

10. A *reciprocal transformation* is defined as follows. (See the figure.) The point P' is the transform of the point P if

$$|OP'| = \frac{1}{|OP|}.$$

The reciprocal transformation maps, one-to-one, the exterior of the unit circle onto the interior (except for the center).

Show that a conic with focus at the pole is transformed into a limaçon or cardioid by a reciprocal transformation.

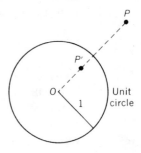

Calculator Problem

What are the polar coordinates of the point nearest the pole of the conic

$$r = \frac{8}{10 - 7\cos\theta}?$$

[*Hint:* Find the minimum value of r. Sketch a graph.]

19-9   Cylindrical Coordinates

We turn now to nonrectangular coordinate systems in space. Two of these systems are of major importance, and we shall examine them briefly in this and the next section. As with rectangular and polar coordinates in a plane, there are infinitely many choices for the placement of these new systems. In these sections, we shall place them in the simple *standard* position with respect to a rectangular system. We are concerned primarily with two aspects:

(1) the surfaces that are the graphs of very simple equations, and
(2) the relations between the new coordinates and the rectangular coordinates for space.

The *cylindrical* and rectangular systems are shown in Fig. 23. We choose polar coordinates in the xy-plane (with the two systems related as in Section 19-7). The segment $\overline{PQ}$ is parallel to the z-axis. The third coordinate is the rectangular z-coordinate. *The cylindrical coordinates of P are (r, θ, z).*

The two coordinate systems are related by

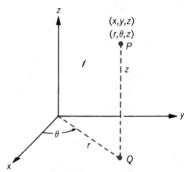

FIGURE 23

$$x = r \cos \theta,$$
$$y = r \sin \theta,$$
$$z = z;$$

or

$$r = \pm \sqrt{x^2 + y^2},$$
$$\theta = \arctan \frac{y}{x},$$
$$z = z.$$

(1)

As with polar coordinates, the choice of $\theta = \arctan(y/x)$ will dictate which sign to use for $r = \pm \sqrt{x^2 + y^2}$.

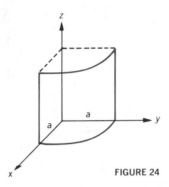

FIGURE 24

Example 1   The graph of the equation $r = a$ is the right circular cylinder of radius a with its axis along the z-axis. A portion of the cylinder is sketched in Fig. 24.

2   The graph of $\theta = \pi/4$ is a plane perpendicular to the xy-plane and whose trace in the xy-plane makes an angle of $\pi/4$ with the positive x-axis. (Fig. 25.)

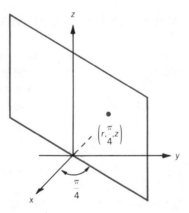

FIGURE 25

It is rather clear that physical problems involving axial symmetry might be conveniently described in terms of cylindrical coordinates. Some examples are the flow of fluids in straight pipes, heat transfer in long tubes, and the magnetic fields surrounding long straight wires.

Problems

Set A

Sketch the surfaces having the following equations in cylindrical coordinates. Where convenient, change to rectangular coordinates.

1. $\theta = \pi/6$ **2.** $r^2 + z^2 = 1$

3. $r = z$ **4.** $r = 2a \sin \theta$

5. $z = 1$ **6.** $r = 1 + \cos \theta$

7. $r = 2$ **8.** $r = \sin \theta + \cos \theta$

9. $r = \sin \theta - \cos \theta$

Set B

Sketch the surfaces having the equation given.

10. $r^2 - 3r + 2 = 0$ **11.** $r = e^\theta$

12. $r + z = 1$

13. $8\theta^2 - 6\pi\theta + \pi^2 = 0$

14. Express the equation $r^2 + z^2 = 16$ in rectangular coordinates. What is the graph of the equation?

Set C

15. Derive a formula in cylindrical coordinates for the distance between two points.

16. The points P_1 and P_2 are on the cylinder $r = 6$. Find the distance between P_1 and P_2 if $P_1 = (6, \pi/3, 4)$ and $P_2 = (6, 3\pi/2, 10)$.

17. Show that the graph of $r = c \sec^2 \frac{1}{2}\theta$ is a parabolic cylinder.

Calculator Problem

Sketch a graph of the hyperbolic spiral

$$r = \frac{2}{\theta}, \quad \theta \neq 0.$$

19-10   Spherical Coordinates

The *spherical* and rectangular coordinate systems are shown in Fig. 26. The point P is projected by a line parallel to the z-axis into a point R in the xy-plane. Suppose that r, θ are polar coordinates of R. If the position vector, $\overrightarrow{OP}$, makes an angle of measure φ with the positive z-axis, and if

$$|\overrightarrow{OP}| = \rho,$$

then *the spherical coordinates of P are* (ρ, θ, φ).

From the definitions one has

$$0 \leq \varphi \leq \pi \quad \text{and} \quad \rho \geq 0,$$
$$r = \rho \sin \varphi \quad \text{and} \quad r^2 + z^2 = \rho^2.$$

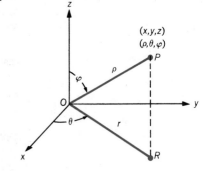

FIGURE 26

Thus the two coordinate systems are related by

$$x = r \cos \theta = \rho \sin \varphi \cos \theta,$$
$$y = r \sin \theta = \rho \sin \varphi \sin \theta,$$
$$z = \rho \cos \varphi.$$

(1)

If these equations are solved for ρ, θ, φ, one obtains

$$\rho = \sqrt{x^2 + y^2 + z^2},$$

$$\theta = \arctan \frac{y}{x},$$

(2)

$$\varphi = \text{Arccos} \frac{z}{\sqrt{x^2 + y^2 + z^2}}.$$

Example 1   The graph of the equation $\rho = a$ is the sphere of radius a with center at the origin. One-eighth of the sphere is shown in Fig. 27.

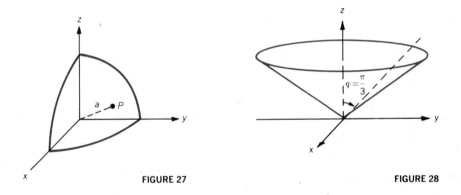

FIGURE 27   FIGURE 28

2   The rectangular equation of the surface whose equation in spherical coordinates is $\varphi = \pi/3$ is found by setting

$$\frac{\pi}{3} = \text{Arccos} \frac{z}{\sqrt{x^2 + y^2 + z^2}}.$$

Since $\cos \pi/3 = \frac{1}{2}$ we have

$$\frac{1}{2} = \frac{z}{\sqrt{x^2 + y^2 + z^2}} \qquad \text{or} \qquad x^2 + y^2 - 3z^2 = 0.$$

The graph is a circular cone with the z-axis as its line of symmetry. A portion of the graph is shown in Figure 28.

Problems

Set A

Give the rectangular coordinates for points with the following spherical coordinates.

1. $(3, \pi/2, \pi/2)$ **2.** $(4, \pi/6, \pi)$

3. $(1, \pi/4, \pi/4)$ **4.** $(8, 2\pi/3, \pi/3)$

5. $(5, -5\pi/6, \pi/2)$ **6.** $(10, 7\pi/6, 3\pi/4)$

Sketch the surfaces having the following equations in spherical coordinates.

7. $\rho = 4$ and $\varphi \geq \dfrac{\pi}{2}$ **8.** $\rho = 4$ and $\varphi \leq \dfrac{\pi}{2}$

9. $\varphi = \dfrac{\pi}{6}$ **10.** $\theta = \dfrac{\pi}{4}$

11. $\rho \sin \varphi = a > 0$

12. $\rho^2 \sin^2 \varphi \cos^2 \theta + \rho^2 \cos^2 \varphi = 1$. [*Hint:* Change to rectangular coordinates.]

13. $\rho \cos \varphi = a$

Set B

Obtain equations in spherical coordinates for these surfaces in rectangular coordinates.

14. $z = 2$ **15.** $x = a$

16. $x^2 + y^2 = a^2$ **17.** $x = y$

18. Give the spherical coordinates of a point P if the position vector to point P is
$$3\mathbf{i} - 2\mathbf{j} + 6\mathbf{k}.$$

19. Give the rectangular coordinates of a point with spherical coordinates $(5, \mathrm{Tan}^{-1} -\frac{1}{2}, \mathrm{Cos}^{-1} \sqrt{5}/5)$.

Set C

20. If the earth is a sphere and spherical coordinates are chosen with origin at the center, the z-axis toward the North Pole, and the plane $\theta = 0$ through Greenwich, England, what are the relations between θ and φ and longitude and latitude?

21. Derive a formula for the distance between two points in spherical coordinates.

Calculator Problem

Find the distance between the points $P_1 (4, \pi/4, \pi/3)$ and $P_2 (4, -\pi/3, \pi/3)$ which lie on the sphere $\rho = 4$.

Find the shortest distance between P_1 and P_2 *along the surface of the sphere.*

19-11　　Other Coordinates

As would be expected, we have come nowhere near exhausting the variety of possible coordinate systems for a plane or space. In this section we give some examples that may suggest the possibilities.

Example 1　(*Parabolic coordinates*) Consider the two families of parabolas, where $\lambda > 0$, $\mu > 0$:

$$\begin{aligned} y^2 &= 4\lambda(x + \lambda), \\ y^2 &= -4\mu(x - \mu). \end{aligned} \quad (1)$$

Through each point of the plane there is exactly one parabola of each family. The parabolas (the upper half) of the λ-family are drawn as solid lines in Fig. 29.

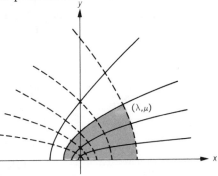

FIGURE 29

Those of the μ-family are represented by the dashed lines. Points symmetrically located with respect to the x-axis will lie on the same two parabolas. This is why we restrict our attention to the upper half-plane.

The two numbers, λ and μ (*parabolic coordinates*), establish a coordinate system for the upper half-plane. The first quadrant of the $\lambda\mu$-plane is mapped one-to-one on the upper half of the xy-plane. The shaded region of Fig. 29 corresponds to the shaded region of Fig. 30.

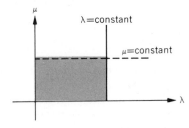

FIGURE 30

2　What are the rectangular coordinates of a point whose parabolic coordinates are $(2, 3)$?

Solution. It is given that $\lambda = 2$ and $\mu = 3$. Substituting these values in equations (1) we have

$$\begin{aligned} y^2 &= 4 \cdot 2(x + 2), \\ y^2 &= -4 \cdot 3(x - 3). \end{aligned}$$

Solving these equations simultaneously, we find

$$\begin{aligned} 8x + 16 &= -12x + 36, \\ 20x &= 20, \\ x &= 1. \end{aligned}$$

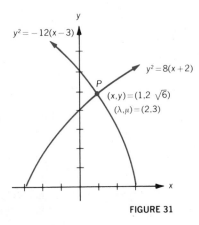

FIGURE 31

Therefore

$$y^2 = 8(1 + 2),$$
$$y^2 = 24,$$
$$y = 2\sqrt{6}.$$

The point with parabolic coordinates (2, 3) is point P, the intersection in the upper plane of the two parabolas (Fig. 31). The rectangular coordinates of P are $(1, 2\sqrt{6})$.

Problems

Set A

Find the rectangular coordinates of points whose parabolic coordinates (λ, μ) are given below.

1. (1, 1)   2. (3, 4)

3. (2, 1)   4. (5, 1)

Find the parabolic coordinates of points whose rectangular coordinates (x, y) are given below.

5. (2, 2)   6. (4, 3)

7. (−3, 2)   8. (−5, 4)

Set B

9. The parabolic coordinates of a point are (1, 2). Sketch a graph in the xy-plane showing the two parabolas on which the point lies. Show the rectangular coordinates of the point.

10. Suppose that in equations (1) of this section $\lambda = \mu$. Show that this implies that the rectangular coordinates of the point whose parabolic coordinates are (λ, λ) are $(0, 2\lambda)$.

Set C

11. Show that all parabolas of Example 1 have focus at the origin. Hence we can say that we have families of *confocal* (having the same foci) *conics*.

12. Draw several members of each of the following families:

$$\frac{x^2}{\lambda - b^2} + \frac{y^2}{\lambda - a^2} = 1,$$

where

$$a^2 > b^2 \quad \text{and} \quad \lambda > a^2 \qquad \text{(ellipses)},$$

and

$$\frac{x^2}{\mu - b^2} - \frac{y^2}{a^2 - \mu} = 1,$$

where

$$b^2 < \mu < a^2 \qquad \text{(hyperbolas)}.$$

Show that

(a) all ellipses and the hyperbolas have the same foci,

(b) the (elliptic) coordinates λ and μ establish a coordinate system for the first quadrant of the xy-plane.

Calculator Problem

Find the foci of the ellipse and hyperbola

$$\frac{x^2}{\lambda - 9} + \frac{y^2}{\lambda - 16} = 1 \quad \text{and} \quad \frac{x^2}{\mu - 9} - \frac{y^2}{16 - \mu} = 1.$$

Find the rectangular coordinates of the point in the first quadrant whose elliptic coordinates (λ, μ) are (25, 10). Sketch a graph of the conics in the xy-plane to show this point.

Summary

There are infinitely many ways of setting up a coordinate system for the plane, space, or portions of either. The most important ones are the following.

1. Different rectangular coordinates related by:
   (a) Translation of axes: $x' = x - h, \quad y' = y - k$.

   If a second-degree equation does not contain an xy-term, we can find a convenient point to translate the origin to by completing the squares.
   (b) Rotation of axes: $x' = x \cos \theta + y \sin \theta$,
   $$y' = -x \sin \theta + y \cos \theta.$$

   The xy-term can be removed from

   $$Ax^2 + Bxy + Cy^2 + Dx + Ey + F = 0$$

   by rotating axes through an angle θ given by

   $$\tan 2\theta = \frac{B}{A - C}.$$

2. A point in the plane has infinitely many polar coordinates. If rectangular axes are placed in the standard position with respect to the polar axis, the two coordinate systems are connected by

   $$\left. \begin{aligned} x &= r \cos \theta, \\ y &= r \sin \theta, \end{aligned} \right\} \quad \text{or} \quad \left\{ \begin{aligned} r &= \pm \sqrt{x^2 + y^2}, \\ \theta &= \arctan \frac{y}{x}. \end{aligned} \right.$$

   Simple polar equations give a variety of new curves. When finding intersections of curves given by polar equations, we must be careful to get all points of intersection.

3. Cylindrical coordinates are simply related to rectangular coordinates if the two sets of axes are suitably placed.

   $$\left. \begin{aligned} x &= r \cos \theta, \\ y &= r \sin \theta, \\ z &= z, \end{aligned} \right\} \quad \text{or} \quad \left\{ \begin{aligned} r &= \pm \sqrt{x^2 + y^2}, \\ \theta &= \arctan \frac{y}{x}, \\ z &= z. \end{aligned} \right.$$

4. Spherical coordinates are simply related to rectangular coordinates if the two sets of axes are suitably placed.

   $$\left. \begin{aligned} x &= \rho \sin \varphi \cos \theta, \\ y &= \rho \sin \varphi \sin \theta, \\ z &= \rho \cos \varphi, \end{aligned} \right\} \quad \text{or} \quad \left\{ \begin{aligned} \rho &= \sqrt{x^2 + y^2 + z^2}, \\ \theta &= \arctan \frac{y}{x}, \\ \varphi &= \text{Arccos} \frac{z}{\sqrt{x^2 + y^2 + z^2}}. \end{aligned} \right.$$

Chapter 19 Test

19–2   1. The origin is translated to the point $(-3, 3)$. What are the new coordinates of the point $(-7, -5)$?

Where should the origin be translated to in order to remove the x- and y-terms from the equations? Sketch each graph.

2. $4x^2 + 3y^2 + 16x - 6y + 12 = 0$

3. $2x^2 - y^2 + 12x - 8y + 5 = 0$

19–3   4. The axes are rotated through $\pi/6$. If the new coordinates of a point are $(\sqrt{3}, 2)$, what were the original coordinates?

Rotate the axes to remove the xy-term from each of the following equations, and sketch each curve.

5. $3x^2 + 12xy - 2y^2 + 84 = 0$

6. $3x^2 + 2\sqrt{3}\,xy + y^2 - 8x + 8\sqrt{3}\,y = 0$

19–4   7. Two of the following three pairs of polar coordinates name the same point. Which two are the same point?

(a) $(4, \pi/4)$ (b) $(4, -\pi/4)$ (c) $(-4, 5\pi/4)$

19–5   Sketch the graphs of the following equations in polar coordinates.

8. $r = 5\cos 2\theta$ 9. $r = a\cos\theta,\ a < 0$

10. $r^2 = 16\cos 2\theta$ 11. $r = 2/(1 - \cos\theta)$

19–6   12. The polar coordinates of a point are $(6, \pi/3)$. What are the rectangular coordinates of the point?

Find rectangular equations of, and sketch, each of the curves whose equations in polar coordinates are

13. $r = a\cos\theta + a\sin\theta$.   14. $r^2 = a^2\cos 2\theta$.

Find polar equations of, and sketch, the curves whose rectangular equations are

15. $x^3 + xy^2 = y$.   16. $3x^2 - y^2 - 12x + 9 = 0$.

19–7   Find the points of intersection of the following curves given by their polar equations. Sketch each graph.

17. $r = 2\sin\theta,\ r = 2\cos 2\theta$ 18. $r = 1 + \cos\theta,\ r = 3\cos\theta$

19–8   19. Which conic is given by the polar equation

$$r = \frac{6}{3 - 2\cos\theta}?$$

Sketch the graph.

19–9   Sketch the surfaces whose equations in cylindrical coordinates are

20. $r = 6\cos\theta$.   21. $r = 2z$.

19–10   Sketch the surfaces whose equations in spherical coordinates are

22. $\rho = 2,\ \pi/4 \le \theta \le \pi/2$.   23. $\rho\cos\varphi = 3$.

Historical Note

Jakob Bernoulli
(1654–1705)

In a sense, a variety of coordinate systems have been with us since ancient times. Latitude and longitude on the celestial sphere, as used by the ancient astronomers, have a close connection with spherical coordinates. However, with the exception of Descartes' invention (and he used only cartesian coordinates), there are no great landmarks in the theory of coordinate systems until modern times. Gradually, new coordinate systems appeared in order to help solve special problems.

Polar coordinates were introduced by the Swiss Jakob Bernoulli (1654–1705) of the distinguished Bernoulli family of mathematicians. Initially, polar coordinates were applied chiefly to spirals, but Jakob Bernoulli also made use of them in other situations.

No new coordinate systems were conceived until the end of the eighteenth century, and it was only in the nineteenth century, after analysis and physics had become sufficiently sophisticated, that mathematicians developed a systematic notion of general coordinate systems. Highly instrumental in the development of a general point of view was the work of Karl Friedrich Gauss (1777–1855) on the curvature of surfaces. The Gaussian point of view was generalized by Georg Friedrich Bernhard Riemann (1826–1866), who founded n-dimensional differential geometry. In this discipline the properties of n-dimensional space are studied in terms of the n coordinates, $x_1, \ldots, x_n$, of a point. The fundamental work of Riemann was highly developed by a number of geometers and was later found to be the natural mathematical language needed for the theory of relativity.

A book by the engineer G. Lamé, published in 1859, contains material on curvilinear coordinates. In this book are found numerous applications to problems of physics. Today the theory of general coordinate systems is taught to most engineering students.

Chapter 20
Parametric Representation
of Curves and Surfaces

20-1 Introduction

What is a curve? What is a surface? These are questions we propose to answer by giving natural, intuitively satisfying, *definitions*.

A definition of curve that might be given by the non-mathematician is as follows:

"A curve is a bent (and/or stretched or compressed) line." (See Fig. 1.)

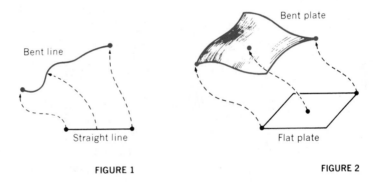

FIGURE 1

FIGURE 2

In the same spirit a definition of a surface might be:

A surface is a bent (and/or stretched or compressed) flat plate." (See Fig. 2.)

These tentative, and as yet vague, definitions will be made precise in the sections to follow.

It should be noted that a set of points that is a "bent and stretched" line could be obtained by bending and stretching many different ways. In other words, there is no one single way of bending and stretching a line to give a curve.

When we "bend and stretch" a line to get a curve, we naturally do not permit the line to be broken and then bent or stretched in piecemeal fashion. This will be reflected later in our requirement that the functions that define a curve, or surface, be continuous.

A final geometric illustration of a curve (and a most important one in physics) is the following: Imagine a particle moving continuously in such

507

a manner that at each instant of time t, after an initial time t_0, the particle is at the point P_t. (See Fig. 3.) The set of points occupied by the moving particle is a curve because it is simply the image in space of an interval of the time axis. Time has been "bent and stretched" into a curve in space.

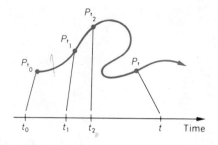

FIGURE 3

20-2   Parametric Curves

In accordance with the intuitive ideas of the preceding section, we shall make a precise definition of a parametrized curve.

Definition 20-1   A *parametrized curve* is a *continuous function* from an interval of the real numbers into space (or into the plane if we are concerned with plane curves).

This definition implies that the three coordinates that fix a point in space are continuous functions on the given interval. A variable that represents a real number in the domain of a function is called a *parameter*.

A line can be parametrized, as in Fig. 3, by the coordinates on a line. That is, the coordinates t_0, t_1, t_2, etc., of the time line can be used to locate the position of a point $P(x, y, z)$ in space. Therefore, when we "bend and stretch" a line into space, we have a mapping of an interval of real numbers into space.

Thus, if rectangular coordinates are used to locate the point, and if the interval of the real line on which the mapping is defined is $a \le t \le b$, then a parametrized curve is given by the equations

$$\left. \begin{array}{l} x = f(t), \\ y = g(t), \\ z = h(t), \end{array} \right\} \quad \text{for} \quad a \le t \le b, \tag{1}$$

where the functions f, g, and h are *continuous*. The variable t is the *parameter*. Equations (1) are *parametric equations* of the parametrized curve.

Remarks

1. One need not be restricted to rectangular coordinates.

2. Most of our examples will be plane curves given by $x = f(t)$ and $y = g(t)$, where f and g are very simple functions.

3. The domain of the parameter may be the whole real line, in which case $-\infty < t < \infty$.

4. In this section our technique for drawing parametrized curves will be to make a table of values of the coordinates versus the parameter. After these points are plotted, it will then be clear how to draw the curve.

5. We have already met with parametrized curves in Chapters 11 and 13, where we discussed parametric equations of lines:

$$\left.\begin{array}{l} x = x_0 + c_1 d, \\ y = y_0 + c_2 d, \\ z = z_0 + c_3 d, \end{array}\right\} \quad \text{for} \quad -\infty < d < +\infty.$$

Example 1   Sketch the parametrized curve

$$\left.\begin{array}{l} x = t, \\ y = t^2, \end{array}\right\} \quad \text{for} \quad -\infty < t < \infty.$$

Solution.

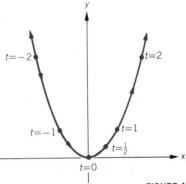

t	0	± 1	± 2	$\pm\frac{1}{2}$	$\pm\frac{3}{2}$
x	0	± 1	± 2	$\pm\frac{1}{2}$	$\pm\frac{3}{2}$
y	0	1	4	$\frac{1}{4}$	$\frac{9}{4}$

FIGURE 4

The points on the curve corresponding to some of the values of t are shown in Fig. 4. The arrowheads on the curve indicate the direction of increasing t.

2   If W is the wrapping function, then W makes the unit circle a parametrized curve. The parametric equations are

$$\left.\begin{array}{l} x = \cos\theta, \\ y = \sin\theta, \end{array}\right\} \quad -\infty < \theta < \infty.$$

Observe that we also have the polar parametric representation of the unit circle:

$$\left.\begin{array}{l} r = 1, \\ \theta = \theta, \end{array}\right\} \quad -\infty < \theta < \infty.$$

(See Fig. 5.)

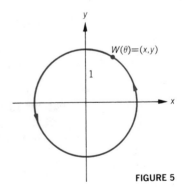

FIGURE 5

Example 3   Consider the parametrized curve

$$\left.\begin{array}{l} x = 2^t, \\ y = 2^{-t}, \end{array}\right\} \quad -\infty < t < \infty.$$

The curve with some parameter values is shown in Fig. 6(a).

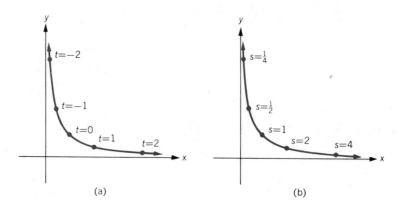

(a)   (b)

FIGURE 6

The same set of points can be parametrized in other ways. For example, the equations

$$\left.\begin{array}{l} x = s, \\ y = \dfrac{1}{s}, \end{array}\right\} \quad 0 < s < \infty,$$

also give the same set of points. Observe how the parameter values in this case are spread along the curve in Fig. 6(b).

4   The equations

$$\left.\begin{array}{l} x = 1 + t, \\ y = 1 - t, \\ z = 2 + t, \end{array}\right\} \quad \infty \le t \le \infty,$$

parametrize a set of points in space. A sketch for some values of t gives the line shown in Fig. 7.

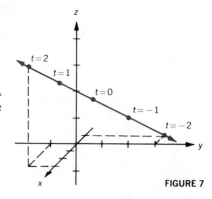

FIGURE 7

Problems

Set A

Sketch the following parametrized curves by plotting enough points to see where the graphs go. On each graph mark some points with their parameter values.

1. $x = s^2$, $y = s$, $\quad -\infty < s \leq 0$

2. $x = 1/(t+1)$, $y = t+2$, $\quad 0 \leq t < \infty$

3. $x = \sin t$, $y = \tan t$, $\quad 0 \leq t < \pi/2$

4. $x = 1/(t^2+1)$, $y = t$, $\quad -\infty < t < \infty$

5. $x = 2\sin t$, $y = 3\cos t$, $\quad -\infty < t < \infty$

6. $x = 2 + 3\cos t$, $y = 4 + 3\sin t$,
   $\quad -\infty < t < \infty$

7. $x = \sin t$, $y = \cos 2t$, $\quad -\infty < t < \infty$

8. $x = \sin t$, $y = 2\sin t$, $\quad -\infty < t < \infty$

Set B

Sketch the graphs of the following parametrized curves in space.

9. $x = 1 - t$. $y = t$, $z = 1$, $\quad 0 \leq t \leq 1$

10. $x = 1 - t$, $y = t$, $z = t^2$, $\quad 0 \leq t \leq 1$

11. $x = \cos t$, $y = \sin t$, $z = 1$, $\quad 0 \leq t \leq 2\pi$

12. $x = \cos t$, $y = \sin t$, $z = \frac{1}{3}t$, $\quad 0 \leq t \leq 2\pi$

13. Sketch the graph of

$$\left. \begin{array}{l} x = 2 + t, \\ y = -2 - 2t, \\ z = -t, \end{array} \right\} \quad -\infty < t < \infty.$$

What geometric significance does t have?

Set C

14. Suppose that f is a continuous function with domain the interval $[a, b]$. Show that the graph of $y = f(x)$, $a \leq x \leq b$, can be parametrized in a natural way. This will prove that our earlier language, when we referred to the graph of f as a curve, is now consistent with our present definition of a curve.

15. Suppose that $x = f(t)$, $y = g(t)$, and $a \leq t \leq b$, are parametric equations of a curve. Suppose also that $t = \varphi(s)$, for $c \leq s \leq d$, is a continuous mapping of the interval $[c, d]$ *onto* the interval $[a, b]$. Show that $x = f(\varphi(s))$, $y = g(\varphi(s))$, $c \leq s \leq d$, is a new parametrization of the same set of points. Hence you may conclude that there are infinitely many parametrizations of a given parametrized set of points.

Calculator Problem

Sketch the parameterized curve

$$\left. \begin{array}{l} x = 4\cos t, \\ y = -4\sin t, \\ z = 4\sin t. \end{array} \right\} \quad 0 \leq t \leq 2\pi.$$

Identify the curve.

20-3   Elimination of the Parameter

Parametric equations of a plane curve may not have a form that permits one to recognize the curve at a glance. In previous chapters we have regarded curves as graphs of equations in rectangular (or polar) coordinates, and we have developed some skill in recognizing at once some of these curves from their equations. Therefore, in drawing parametrized curves it will frequently help to *eliminate the parameter*. This will result in a rectangular (or polar) equation which we can perhaps recognize. But *one must be careful because the parametrized curve may not be all of the graph of the rectangular (or polar) equation.* Examples will illustrate this idea.

Example 1   Graph the parametrized curve

$$\left. \begin{array}{l} x = \cos^2 t, \\ y = \sin^2 t, \end{array} \right\} \quad -\infty < t < \infty.$$

Solution. If the point (x, y) is on the parametrized curve, then

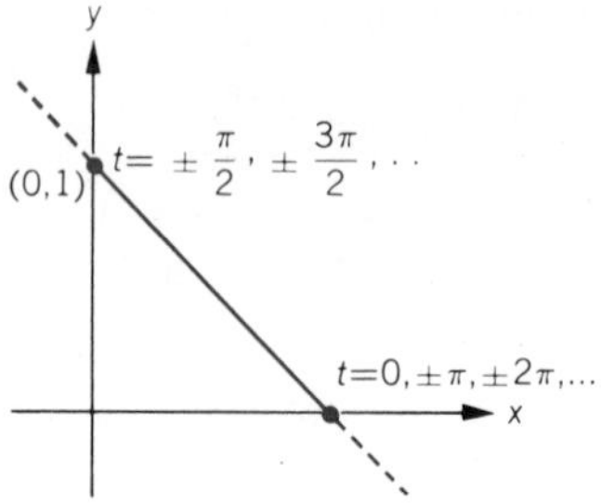

$$x + y = \cos^2 t + \sin^2 t = 1.$$

Therefore the point (x, y) is on the straight line $x + y = 1$. (See Fig. 8.) But the parametrized curve cannot be all of this line because x and y on the parametrized curve must be between 0 and 1. Clearly the point (x, y) on the parametrized curve moves back and forth on the line between $(1, 0)$ and $(0, 1)$ as t increases.

FIGURE 8

2   Let us assume that the earth is flat, that there is no air resistance, and that the only force acting on a projectile is the force of gravity. It is shown in physics that a projectile fired at an angle of elevation α with the horizontal will trace a path given by the parametric equations

$$\begin{cases} x = v_0 t \cos \alpha, \\ y = v_0 t \sin \alpha - \frac{1}{2} g t^2. \end{cases}$$

These equations are based on the assumptions that the axes are chosen as in Fig. 9, that t is the time in seconds from the instant of firing, g is the acceleration of gravity (say, in meters per second per second), and v_0 is the initial velocity (in meters per second).

If we eliminate t by solving for t in terms of x and substitute in the equation for y, we obtain

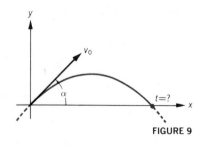

FIGURE 9

512   Parametric Representation

$$y = x \tan \alpha - \frac{g}{2v_0^2 \cos^2 \alpha} x^2,$$

which is recognized as the equation of a parabola. Clearly, not all of the parabola is the path, or trajectory, of the projectile. The projectile begins its motion at $t = 0$. It is also clear that when the projectile strikes the earth, there is an end to the parabolic path.

Problems

Set A

Eliminate the parameter, identify the curve if possible, and sketch it. Show how a point on the parametrized curve moves as the parameter increases.

1. $x = 2 + \sin \theta$, $y = \cos \theta$, $\quad -\infty < \theta < \infty$

2. $x = 2 + t$, $y = 1 - t$, $\quad 0 \le t < \infty$

3. $x = 1 - t^2$, $y = 1 + t^2$, $\quad -\infty < t < \infty$

4. $x = 4 \cos s$, $y = 3 \sin s$, $\quad -\infty < s < \infty$

5. $x = 3 \sin \theta - 1$, $y = 2 \cos \theta + 1$, $\quad -\infty < \theta < \infty$

6. $r = 1 + 2 \cos t^2$, $\theta = t^2$, $\quad -\infty < t < \infty$ (polar coordinates)

7. $x = \tan \theta$, $y = \sec^2 \theta$, $\quad -\pi/2 < \theta < \pi/2$

8. $x = u + 1/u$, $y = u - 1/u$, $\quad 0 < u < \infty$

9. $x = \cos^2 \theta - 1$, $y = \cos \theta - 1$, $\quad -\infty < \theta < \infty$

10. $r = 2\sqrt{\cos t}$, $\theta = \frac{1}{2}t$, $\quad -\pi/2 \le t \le \pi/2$ (polar coordinates)

Set B

11. Show that $x = A \cos t + B \sin t$, and $y = A \sin t - B \cos t$ are parametric equations of a circle. Find its center and radius and show how a point moves on the circle as t increases from 0 to ∞.

12. At what instant and where does the projectile of Example 2 above reach the earth? What is the maximum height of the projectile?

13. Show that the parametric equations $x = h + a \cos \theta$ and $y = k + b \sin \theta$, $-\infty < \theta < \infty$, represent an ellipse.

Set C

14. Show that the parametric equations
$$x = \frac{at}{1 + t^2},$$
$$y = \frac{a}{1 + t^2},$$
$\quad -\infty < t < \infty$ and $a > 0$,

represent almost a full circle.

15. The *folium of Descartes* is given by the parametric equations
$$x = \frac{3t^2}{1 + t^3},$$
$$y = \frac{3t}{1 + t^3},$$
$\quad t \ne -1.$

(a) Sketch the curve.
(b) Show that its rectangular equation is $x^3 + y^3 - 3xy = 0$.
(c) Show that $x + y + 1 = 0$ is an asymptote. [*Hint:* Show that when t is near -1, then $x + y + 1$ is near 0.]

Calculator Problem

A baseball hit from home plate toward the right field wall traveled a path given by the parametric equations

$$x = 40t,$$
$$y = 15t - 4.9t^2, \qquad t \geq 0.$$

The parameter t represents the time in seconds from $t = 0$, and x and y are distances in meters.

(a) Sketch a graph of the path of the ball from $t = 0$ to $t = 3$. Use 0.5 second intervals.

(b) If the right field wall is 100 m from home plate, will the ball reach the wall on the fly?

(c) What is the time in seconds that the ball will be in the air until hitting the ground?

(d) What is the horizontal distance (x-distance) the ball will travel in the air before hitting the ground?

(e) What is the greatest height that the ball will reach?

(f) If the right field wall was 3 m in height, how far above the wall was the ball as it passed over it?

20–4   On the Parametrization of Curves

We have defined *parametrized curves,* and we have seen that they can be parametrized in different ways. We have not yet defined what we mean by *curve,* without any qualifying adjective. We now fill this gap in our set of mathematical concepts.

Definition 20–2 A set C of points in space is a *curve* if this set can be parametrized.

In other words, C is a curve if there are continuous functions f, g, and h such that the points (x, y, z) of C are given by

$$x = f(t), \qquad y = g(t), \qquad z = h(t),$$

for numbers t in an interval $a \leq t \leq b$.

Remarks

1. We have seen many examples of sets that can be parametrized. In this section we shall see other examples in which the parameter can be chosen in a quite natural way.

2. According to Definitions 20–1 and 20–2 curves can be exceedingly complicated. The single requirement of continuity of the functions f, g, and h is not enough to prevent rather strange sets from being curves. (See the

Historical Note at the end of this chapter.) However, *if f, g, and h are elementary functions,* then we always get sets of points which it seems natural to call curves. The surprising cases do not occur.

3. The union of two curves (see Fig. 10), with non-empty intersection, is also a curve. In other words, the combined set can be parametrized. The next example suggests why this is the case.

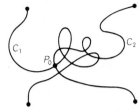

FIGURE 10

Example 1   Let C be the union of two segments, one on each of the x- and y-axes, as shown in Fig. 11(a). We shall parametrize C so that it is the continuous image of the interval $0 \leq t \leq 1$.

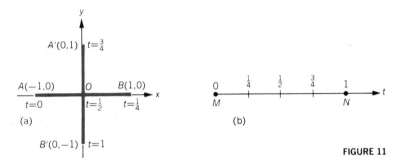

(a)

(b)

FIGURE 11

Divide the unit interval $\overline{MN}$ of the t-axis into fourths. (See Fig. 11b.) We shall map successive fourths of $\overline{MN}$ into $\overline{AB}$, $\overline{BO}$, $\overline{OA'}$, and $\overline{A'B'}$ in that order. Let

$$
\begin{array}{llll}
x = -1 + 8t, & y = 0 & \text{if} \ \ 0 \leq t \leq \tfrac{1}{4}, \\
x = 2 - 4t, & y = 0 & \text{if} \ \ \tfrac{1}{4} \leq t \leq \tfrac{1}{2}, \\
x = 0, & y = -2 + 4t & \text{if} \ \ \tfrac{1}{2} \leq t \leq \tfrac{3}{4}, \\
x = 0, & y = 7 - 8t & \text{if} \ \ \tfrac{3}{4} \leq t \leq 1.
\end{array}
$$

These equations give a parametrization of C because x and y are continuous functions of t. In each of the subintervals, the continuity is clear because the functions are linear functions of t. At the ends of the intervals, that is, at $t = \tfrac{1}{4}, \tfrac{1}{2}$, and $\tfrac{3}{4}$, the values of x and y given by the two formulas agree.

2   Consider two circles of radii a and $b < a$ with center at the origin. (See Fig. 12). Let A and B be the points at which a ray from O meets these circles. Let P be the intersection of the vertical and horizontal lines through A and B, respectively.

   Let C be the set of all such points P. Each point of C is on a unique ray from the origin. Therefore, if we parametrize these rays, we will obtain a parametrization of C.

Let (a, θ) and (b, θ) be polar coordinates of A and B respectively. Then to each real number θ there is a unique ray from O. If the rectangular coordinates of P are x and y, then

$$\left.\begin{array}{l} x = a \cos \theta, \\ y = b \sin \theta, \end{array}\right\} \qquad -\infty < \theta < \infty. \quad (1)$$

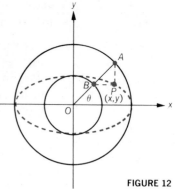

Equations (1) parametrize C because $a \cos \theta$ and $b \sin \theta$ are continuous functions of θ. They are seen to be parametric equations of an ellipse because

$$\frac{x^2}{a^2} + \frac{y^2}{b^2} = \cos^2 \theta + \sin^2 \theta = 1.$$

FIGURE 12

Example 3   Imagine a circle of radius a rolling on a horizontal line with one point P marked on the circle. The set of points described by the moving point P is called a *cycloid*.

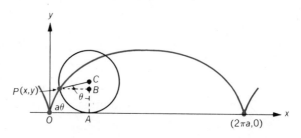

FIGURE 13

We shall parametrize the cycloid. We first choose axes so that the circle rolls along the x-axis and one point of contact of P with the x-axis is at the origin. (See Fig. 13.) We select as our parameter the angle θ through which the circle has rotated since P coincided with O. It is convenient to use vectors. We have

$$\overrightarrow{OP} = \overrightarrow{OA} + \overrightarrow{AC} + \overrightarrow{CP},$$

where

$$\overrightarrow{OP} = x\mathbf{i} + y\mathbf{j},$$
$$\overrightarrow{OA} = a\theta\mathbf{i},$$
$$\overrightarrow{AC} = a\mathbf{j},$$
$$\overrightarrow{CP} = -a \sin \theta \mathbf{i} - a \cos \theta \mathbf{j}.$$

Then

$$x\mathbf{i} + y\mathbf{j} = (a\theta - a \sin \theta)\mathbf{i} + (a - a \cos \theta)\mathbf{j},$$

and, equating components, we have

$$x = a\theta - a\sin\theta,$$
$$y = a - a\cos\theta.$$

These equations are valid for all θ, and give x and y as continuous functions of θ. Thus the cycloid is parametrized by

$$x = a(\theta - \sin\theta),$$
$$y = a(1 - \cos\theta).$$

Problems

Set A

Given the following rectangular equations, make the suggested substitution (t is the parameter) and so parametrize the graph of each equation.

1. $2x + y = 4$. Let $x = \frac{1}{2}t$.

2. $y = \sqrt{x} - 1$. Let $x = t^2$.

3. $y \log x = 2$. Let $x = 10^t$.

4. $y = \sqrt{1 - x^2}$. Let $x = \cos t$.

5. $9x^2 + y^2 = 1$. Let $y = \sin t$.

6. $x^2y + xy + 1 = 0$. Let $x = t$.

7. $y = f(x)$. Let $x = t$.

8. $x^{2/3} + y^{2/3} = a^{2/3}$. Let $y = a\sin^3 t$, $a > 0$.

9. $(x + 2)^2 + 4(y - 3)^2 = 16$.
   Let $y = 3 + 2\cos t$.

10. $x^2 - y^2 = a^2$. Let $x = a\sec t$.

Set B

Parametrize, in some way, the graphs of the following equations.

11. $(x - 1)^2 + 2(y + 2)^2 = 4$

12. $xy^2 = x + y$

13. $y(a^2 + x^2) = 2ax$

14. $x^3 + y^3 = a^3$

15. Consider the family of lines $y = mx + b$, where m is the parameter and b is fixed and not 0. Each of these lines meets (if $m \neq 0$) the x-axis at a point A. If $B = (0, b)$, parametrize in terms of m the set of midpoints of the segments $\overline{AB}$.

16. Parametrize the unit circle in terms of the slope m of a line through $(-1, 0)$. (See figure.)

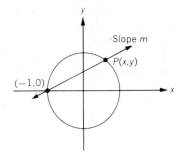

17. Use the result of Problem 16 to generate Pythagorean triples, that is, *whole* numbers r, s, t such that $r^2 + s^2 = t^2$. [*Hint:* Let $m = p/q$, where $p < q$ and p and q are relatively prime integers.]

Show how to parametrize the following curves C with the parameter t in the interval $[0, 1]$. (There are many answers.)

18.

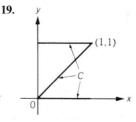

(1,1)

C

19.

(1,1)

C

20.

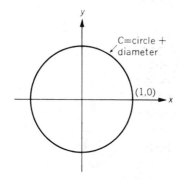

C=circle + diameter

(1,0)

Set C

21. The curve called the *Witch of Agnesi* is obtained as suggested in the figure below. A ray from O in the upper half-plane meets the circle $r = a \sin \theta$ (polar coordinates) in a point A, and the line $y = a$ in a point B. The point P on the Witch has the x-coordinate of B and the y-coordinate of A. Parametrize the Witch with θ, the polar angle, as parameter. Sketch the curve and find a rectangular equation of it.

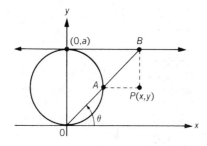

(0,a)   B

A

P(x,y)

θ

0

22. Parametrize the ellipse $x^2/a^2 + y^2/b^2 = 1$ in terms of the parameter m which is equal to the slope of the line through $(-a, 0)$. (See the figure below.) Do you get all of the ellipse?

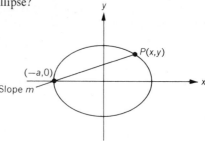

P(x,y)

(−a,0)

Slope m

23. Find a rectangular equation for the cycloid.

24. If a cycloid is generated by a rolling circle with its center below the x-axis, what are parametric equations of it?

25. The *hypocycloids* are generated by a small circle rolling inside a larger circle. They are curves generated by a point P fixed on the small circle. Use the notation and axes of the figure to parametrize the *hypocycloid of four cusps* that is obtained when $4b = a$, and $P = (a, 0)$ when $\theta = 0$. Using vectors, show that $x = a \cos^3 \varphi$ and $y = a \sin^3 \varphi$. Note that $\overrightarrow{OP} = \overrightarrow{OC} + \overrightarrow{CP}$ and $\varphi = \frac{1}{4}\theta$.

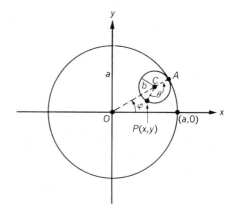

a

b C   A

θ

φ

0   (a,0)

P(x,y)

26. Show that if for a hypocycloid (see Problem 25) the ratio of the radii, a/b, is an irrational number, then the curve never "closes up" or repeats itself.

27. The *prolate cycloid* is generated by a point P fixed with respect to a circle rolling on a line, where the distance P from the center of the circle, b, is greater than the radius, a, of the circle. Choose axes and parameter as in Example 3, p. 516. Show that parametric equations of the prolate cycloid are $x = a\theta - b\sin\theta$ and $y = a - b\cos\theta$. Sketch the curve. [*Hint:* Use vectors. Note that $\overrightarrow{CP} = -b\sin\theta\,\mathbf{i} - b\cos\theta\,\mathbf{j}$.]

28. The *curtate cycloid* is generated similarly to the prolate cycloid in Problem 27 but with $b < a$. Find parametric equations for the curtate cycloid and sketch.

29. The *epicycloids* are generated by a point P on a small circle that rolls on the outside of a larger circle. If the radii are a and $b < a$, and if P is at $(a, 0)$ when $\theta = 0$ (see the figure below), show that the parametric equations of the epicycloid are

$$x = (a + b)\cos\varphi - b\cos\frac{a + b}{b}\varphi,$$

$$y = (a + b)\sin\varphi - b\sin\frac{a + b}{b}\varphi.$$

[*Hint:* $\overrightarrow{OP} = \overrightarrow{OC} + \overrightarrow{CP}$ and $b\theta = a\varphi$.]

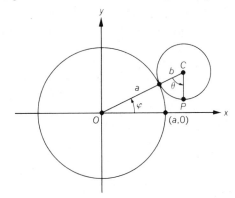

30. A string (zero thickness) is wrapped round a circle and then unwrapped keeping the string taut. (See the figure below for notation and choice of axes.) The set of points occupied by the end of the string is called an *involute* of the circle. Show that parametric equations of the involute are

$$x = a(\cos\theta + \theta\sin\theta),$$
$$y = a(\sin\theta - \theta\cos\theta).$$

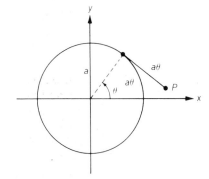

31. Show that the three sets of parametric equations

$$\left.\begin{array}{l} x = \cos^4 t, \\ y = \sin^4 t, \end{array}\right\} \quad \left.\begin{array}{l} x = \sec^4 t, \\ y = \tan^4 t, \end{array}\right\} \quad \left.\begin{array}{l} x = \tan^4 t, \\ y = \sec^4 t \end{array}\right\}$$

represent different arcs of the same parabola. [*Hint:* Show that in the three cases $x^{1/2} + y^{1/2} = 1$, $x^{1/2} - y^{1/2} = 1$, and $-x^{1/2} + y^{1/2} = 1$, respectively. Then show that each is a part of the parabola

$$x^2 - 2xy + y^2 - 2x - 2y + 1 = 0.]$$

32. The *folium of Descartes* has the rectangular equation $x^3 + y^3 - 3axy = 0$, $a > 0$. Find parametric equations of the curve by letting $y = mx$ and solving for x and y in terms of the parameter m. Sketch the curve. Show that the line $x + y + a = 0$ is an asymptote by showing that as m approaches -1, both x and y become infinite while $x + y + a$ is a very small number.

33. The *conchoid of Nicomedes** is generated as suggested by the accompanying figure. The point B is at $(0, -b)$ and $a > b > 0$. A directed line through B makes an angle of measure θ (measured positively clockwise) with the y-axis, and meets the axis at a point C. Along the directed line choose the point P at a distance a from C. The set of all such points P (except for θ, an odd multiple of $\pi/2$) is the conchoid. Obtain parametric equations for the conchoid in terms of the parameter θ. Find a rectangular equation of it. [*Hint:* Note the position vector $\overrightarrow{OP} = \overrightarrow{OC} + \overrightarrow{CP}$.]

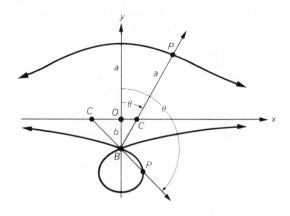

Calculator Problem

A plane curve C is parametrized by the equations below so that it is the continuous image of the interval $0 \le t \le 1$.

$$
\begin{array}{lll}
x = 4t - 1, & y = 4t & \text{if } 0 \le t \le 0.25 \\
x = 4t - 1, & y = -4t + 2 & \text{if } 0.25 \le t \le 0.50 \\
x = -4t + 3, & y = -4t + 2 & \text{if } 0.50 \le t \le 0.75 \\
x = -4t + 3, & y = 4t - 4 & \text{if } 0.75 \le t \le 1
\end{array}
$$

Sketch a graph of C.

20–5   Surfaces

We now give definitions for surfaces and parametric surfaces which are similar to those definitions we gave for curves. Our development of these ideas will be quite brief.

First we must decide what set, in parameter space, is to replace the parameter interval that we used for curves. In Section 20–1 we regarded a surface as a "bent plate." We must now decide what "plates" to use.

As shown in Fig. 14, we let C be a simple closed curve (a bent circle) in the uv-plane (the plane of the parameters). We will call R the interior of C. (We shall also allow R to be the whole plane.) Such regions, with or without their boundaries, will be our "plates."

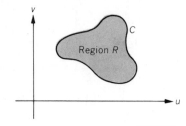

FIGURE 14

---

*See Thomas L. Heath, *Euclid's Elements*, p. 160.

Definition 20-3 A *parametrized surface* is *the image of a continuous function* from a region R in a *uv*-plane into space. The variables u and v are *parameters*.

Thus, if rectangular coordinates are used to locate points, the parametrized surface is given by*

$$\left.\begin{array}{l} x = f(u, v), \\ y = g(u, v), \\ z = h(u, v), \end{array}\right\} \quad \text{for } (u, v) \text{ in } R, \tag{1}$$

where f, g, h are continuous real-valued functions.

Definition 20-4 A set S of points in space is a *surface* if this set can be parametrized.

In other words, S is a surface if a region R and continuous real functions f, g, and h, with domain R can be found, such that S is the graph of equations (1).

We shall be interested in only the simplest examples.

Example 1 The plane $z = 2 - 2x - y$ (see Fig. 15) can be parametrized by

$$x = u,$$
$$y = v,$$
$$z = 2 - 2u - v,$$

where u and v are arbitrary real numbers. The region R of parameter space is the whole *uv*-plane.

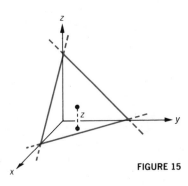

FIGURE 15

---

*The symbol "$f(u, v)$" is standard functional notation for the value of the function f (of two variables) corresponding to the values u and v.

Example 2   Consider the upper half of the ellipsoid $2x^2 + y^2 + 4z^2 = 8$. (See Fig. 16.) This set of points is parametrized by

$$x = u,$$
$$y = v,$$
$$z = \tfrac{1}{2}\sqrt{8 - 2u^2 - v^2}.$$

The region R of the parameters is the ellipse $2u^2 + v^2 = 8$ plus its interior.

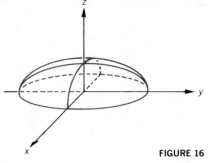

FIGURE 16

3   The sphere with center at the origin and radius a (Fig. 17a) is parametrized by spherical coordinates:

$$x = a \sin \varphi \cos \theta,$$
$$y = a \sin \varphi \sin \theta,$$
$$z = a \cos \varphi.$$

The region R of parameter space is the rectangle (Fig. 17b) $0 \leq \theta \leq 2\pi$, $0 \leq \varphi \leq \pi$.

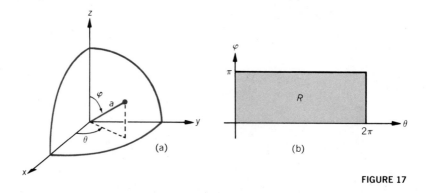

(a)   (b)

FIGURE 17

Problems

Set A

1. A plane is parametrized by $x = u$, $y = 3v$ and $z = 6 - u + 9v$. Find a rectangular equation of the plane by eliminating the parameters u and v.

2. Parametrize the plane $2x - 4y + z = 10$ by letting $x = \tfrac{1}{2}u$ and $y = \tfrac{1}{4}v$. What is z in terms of u and v?

3. Show that

$$\left.\begin{array}{l} x = 2 + 4 \sin \varphi \cos \theta, \\ y = 3 + 4 \sin \varphi \cos \theta, \\ z = 4 + 4 \cos \varphi, \end{array}\right\} \quad \begin{array}{l} 0 \leq \theta \leq 2\pi, \\ 0 \leq \varphi < \pi, \end{array}$$

are parametric equations of a sphere with center at $(2, 3, 4)$ and radius 4.

Set B

4. Parametrize the hemisphere

$$x^2 + y^2 + z^2 = a^2, \quad y \geq 0,$$

by solving for y. What is the region R of parameter space? Sketch the surface.

5. Parametrize the cylinder $x^2 + y^2 = a^2$ by using cylindrical coordinates. What is the parameter region R? Sketch the cylinder.

6. Parametrize the paraboloid $z = x^2 + y^2$. What is R? Sketch the surface.

7. Sketch the portion of a cone, $x^2 + y^2 = z^2$, if $z \leq 0$. Parametrize this cone. Use cylindrical coordinates.

Set C

8. Parametrize the surface $z = \sin y$ and sketch the surface.

9. Suppose in Definition 20–3 that the three functions f, g, and h are constant functions. We say that the surface is degenerate. What surface is it?

Suppose that only two of the three functions f, g, and h are constant. In what way is the surface "degenerate"?

Suppose that only one of the three functions f, g, and h is a constant. Must the surface be degenerate in some way?

Calculator Problem

What can you use to find

$$\sqrt{\frac{38,424,771 \times 9}{11}}$$

without using a calculator? (Find the answer with a calculator, then turn the answer upside down.)

Summary

In this chapter we have finally defined precisely the meaning of *curve* and *surface*. The sequence of ideas is as follows.

1. A *parametrized curve* is a continuous mapping (a continuous function) from an interval of real numbers into space.

2. A *curve* is a set of points that can be parametrized. There are infinitely many ways to parametrize a curve.

3. A rectangular equation of a parametrized plane curve is obtained by eliminating the parameter between the two parametric equations.

4. A *parametrized surface* is a continuous mapping from a plane region into space. Coordinates in the plane region are parameters.

5. A *surface* is a set of points that can be parametrized to give a parametrized surface.

Chapter 20   Test

20-2   Sketch the plane curves given by the following parametric equations.

1. $x = t$, $y = t + 2$, $-\infty \leq t \leq \infty$
2. $x = 4\cos\theta$, $y = 4\sin\theta$, $0 \leq \theta \leq 2\pi$
3. $x = 4t$, $y = 1/t$, $t \neq 0$
4. $y = t$, $x = \dfrac{t^2 + 4}{4}$, $-\infty \leq t \leq \infty$
5. Graph the set of points (x, y, z) in space given by $x = t$, $y = 2 - t$ and $z = 3 + t$, where $-2 \leq t \leq 2$.

20-3   Eliminate the parameter from the equations. Then sketch a graph of the curve.

6. $x = 1 + 2\sqrt{\mu}$, $y = \mu$, $0 \leq \mu < \infty$
7. $x = 2\sin^2 t$ $y = 3\cos^2 t$, $-\infty < t < \infty$
8. $x = 1 - \cos t$, $y = 2 - 2\sin t$, $-\pi/2 \leq t \leq \pi/2$
9. $x = \tan\theta$, $y = \cot\theta$, $\pi/2 < \theta < \pi$
10. $x = a\sec\theta$, $y = b\tan\theta$, $-\pi/2 < \theta < \pi/2$

20-4   Parametrize each curve by making the suggested substitution.

11. $4x - 2y = 7$. Let $x = 4t$.
12. $x^2 - y^2 = 1$. Let $y = \tan\theta$.
13. $xy^2 = 4$. Let $y = t$.
14. $x + xy^2 = 1$. Let $y = t$.

20-5   15. Parametric equations of a plane are

$$x = u, \quad y = 2v \quad \text{and} \quad z = 8 - 3u + 4v.$$

What is a rectangular equation of the plane?

16. Sketch the parametrized curve

$$x = 4\cos t, \quad y = 4\sin t, \quad z = 2, \quad 0 \leq t \leq 2\pi.$$

17. Sketch the parametrized curve

$$x = 4\cos t, \quad y = 4\sin t, \quad z = t, \quad 0 \leq t \leq 2\pi.$$

Historical Note

Giuseppi Peano
(1858–1922)

The notion of a parametrized curve is as old as the idea of curve itself. From the beginning, geometers have imagined the path of a moving point—a natural parametrization with time as the parameter.

A vast literature exists about curves of special kinds: cubic curves, quartic curves, algebraic curves, polar curves, etc. There was no attempt, on the part of the earlier writers, to look for "the most general curve."

However, during the years 1874–1895, George Cantor (1845–1918) published a series of papers on the general *theory of sets*. One effect of Cantor's work was that mathematicians began to look for *very general,* yet quite precise, formulations of mathematical concepts, and thus the notion of curve came under close scrutiny. Camille Jordan (1838–1922) suggested that a curve was a "continuous line"—which is essentially the definition of parametrized curve given in this book. At this period, toward the end of the nineteenth century, it was not known how peculiar a continuous line might be. Jordan himself raised the

question as to whether a continuous line might possibly fill up an area. This question, which at first hearing sounds absurd, was answered in 1890 in the affirmative by Giuseppi Peano (1858–1922). He gave an example of a continuous line (parametrized curve) that *fills up a square!*

Specifically, Peano showed that there are continuous real functions, f and g, such that the curve defined by

$$x = f(t),$$
$$\qquad\qquad 0 \le t \le 1, \qquad (1)$$
$$y = g(t),$$

maps the unit interval [0, 1] on the whole unit square, as indicated in Fig. 18. *Every* point of

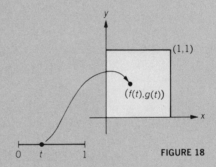

FIGURE 18

the square, as well as every point in the interior of the square, is the image of at least one point, t, in the interval [0, 1].

This astonishing discovery by Peano made it clear that if the concept "curve" were not to include such astonishing examples, then, in addition to continuity, other restrictions would have to be imposed on the functions f and g of equation (1). (Note that the functions f and g of the Peano example must be very "wiggly" in order for the points $(f(t), g(t))$ to fill out the square.)

The definition of a curve in this book relates to elementary functions and does not lead to curves like the Peano example.

APPENDIX

A-1   Common Logarithm Tables

Every positive number N may be written uniquely in scientific notation $N = 10^k x$, where k is an integer and $1 \leq x < 10$. For example,

$$103 = 10^2(1.03), \qquad 0.00345 = 10^{-3}(3.45),$$
$$25 = 10^1(2.5), \qquad 1000 = 10^3 \cdot 1,$$
$$9960 = 10^3(9.960), \qquad 3.2 = 10^0 \cdot 3.2.$$

Now, when N is written in this form,

$$\log N = \log(10^k \cdot x) = \log 10^k + \log x = k + \log x.$$

Example 1 $\log 103 = \log 10^2 \cdot 1.03 = \log 10^2 + \log 1.03 = 2 + \log 1.03$

2 $\log 0.00345 = \log 10^{-3} \cdot 3.45 = \log 10^{-3} + \log 3.45 = -3 + \log 3.45$

Hence, except for the integer k, the logarithm of N is determined by $\log x$ alone. Thus a table of logarithms need list only those logarithms of numbers between 1 and 10.

Definition A-1   If $N = 10^k x$, where $1 \leq x < 10$, then the integer k is called the *characteristic* of $\log N$. The number $\log x$ is called the *mantissa** of $\log N$.

The characteristic of the logarithm of a number can be found by counting the number of places the decimal point must be moved in order to get a number between 1 and 10. If the decimal point is moved to the left, the characteristic is a positive integer; if the decimal is moved to the right, it is a negative integer. For example,

$$N = 23.72 \qquad \text{characteristic is } 1,$$
$$N = 0.00236, \qquad \text{characteristic is } -3,$$
$$N = 476.2, \qquad \text{characteristic is } 2.$$

Most computation will be simpler if each negative characteristic is written as the difference of two positive integers one of which is 10, 20, 30, etc. For example,

$$-1 = 9 - 10, \qquad -5 = 5 - 10, \qquad -2 = 8 - 10.$$

Using this idea, we can write

$$\log 0.2 = -1 + 0.3010 = 9.3010 - 10,$$
$$\log 0.05 = -2 + 0.6990 = 8.6990 - 10,$$
$$\log 0.00003 = -5 + 0.4771 = 5.4771 - 10.$$

---

*This is a strange word derived from an Etruscan root. It is due to the English mathematician John Wallis, who presented it in his *Algebra* of 1685.

With this agreement, we shall now write our logarithms in a more natural manner—not separating characteristic and mantissa unless the characteristic is negative. For example,

$$\log 20 = 1.3010,$$
$$\log 0.0002 = 6.3010 - 10.$$

Because all mantissas are numbers between 0 and 1, the decimal point is not written in the table. In Table I after the appendix, the first digits of N are in the left-hand column. The last digit of N is at the top of the page. The process for finding the mantissa in cases where there is a fourth digit not equal to 0 is explained in the next section. From the table, you should see that

$\log 3.59 = 0.5551,$	$\log 7.01 = 0.8457,$
$\log 359 = 2.5551,$	$\log 7010 = 3.8457,$
$\log 0.000359 = 6.5551 - 10,$	$\log 0.701 = 9.8457 - 10.$

Problems

Write each number as $10^k \cdot x$, where $1 \le x < 10$, and determine the characteristic of its common logarithm.

1. 0.2   **2.** 0.002   **3.** 200

4. 3.5   **5.** 10^{-17} **6.** 37.63

7. 157   **8.** 0.157   **9.** 0.1005

10. 10^{23} **11.** 6.91   **12.** 0.000845

Find the logarithms of the following numbers.

13. 105.0   **14.** 0.0909   **15.** 0.00873

16. 86.9   **17.** 45.7   **18.** 0.508

19. 0.0000007   **20.** 1.7×10^{-17} **21.** 68,700

22. 0.00103   **23.** 0.000205   **24.** 0.0000449

Find the numbers whose logarithms are the following.

25. $9.9455 - 10$ **26.** $8.8000 - 10$

27. $7.6503 - 10$ **28.** 1.6599

29. 2.2201   **30.** $4.4048 - 10$

31. $1.6972 - 10$ **32.** $9.9009 - 10$

33. $7.5809 - 10$ **34.** 7.8745

35. $3.9805 - 10$ **36.** 2.1335

Find logarithms of the following numbers.

37. 2.43×10^6 **38.** 6.07×10^{10}

39. 8.11×10^{-3} **40.** 3.07×10^{-9}

41. 1.13×10^{-4} **42.** 6.25×10^5

A-2   Interpolation; Computation with Logarithms

In this section we discuss first the method of finding the logarithms of numbers with more than three significant digits, called *interpolation*.

In any short interval of the x-axis, the graph of $\log x$ is nearly straight. Thus, in Fig. A–1 the graph between 2 and 3 is not bent much, and we can approximate the graph roughly by the dashed straight line.

Example 1

Find log 2.563.

Solution. From the table,

$$\log 2.57 = 0.4099,$$
$$\underline{\log 2.56 = 0.4082,}$$
$$\text{difference} = 0.0017.$$

Then log 2.563 should be approximately $\frac{3}{10}$ of this difference more than log 2.56. This is $\log 2.563 = \log 2.56 + 0.3(0.0017)$ $= 0.4082 + 0.0005$, or $\log 2.563 = 0.4087$.

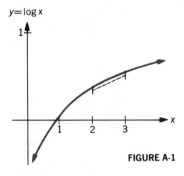

FIGURE A-1

It is sometimes necessary to use interpolation in finding the antilogarithm of a number.

Example 2

Find antilog 0.7130.

Solution. From the table,

$$\text{antilog } 0.7126 = 5.16,$$
$$\text{antilog } 0.7135 = 5.17.$$

The difference of 0.7135 and 0.7126 is 0.0009, while the difference of 0.7130 and 0.7126 is 0.0004. Thus the antilog 0.7130 should be 5.16 plus about $\frac{4}{9}$ of the difference between 5.16 and 5.17; hence

$$\text{antilog } 0.7130 = 5.160 + 0.004 = 5.164.$$

We can now use logarithms for computation.

Example 3

Using logarithms, compute (45.32)(0.7836).

Solution. If $N = (45.32)(0.7836)$, then $\log N = \log 45.32 + \log 0.7836$.

$$\log 45.32 = 1.6563,$$
$$\log 0.7836 = \underline{9.8941 - 10,}$$
$$\log N = 1.5504,$$
$$N = \text{antilog } 1.5504 = 35.52.$$

4

Find $\sqrt[5]{472.5}$.

Solution. If $N = \sqrt[5]{472.5} = (472.5)^{1/5}$, then $\log N = \frac{1}{5}\log 472.5$.

$$\log 472.5 = 2.6744,$$
$$\log N = 0.5349,$$
$$N = 3.427.$$

Interpolation can also be used with the trigonometric tables to obtain greater accuracy. The procedure is the same as the one used with logarithm tables. In interpolating values of the cosine and cotangent functions, however, there is a slight difference.

Example 5   Find cos 69.72°

Solution.

$\cos 69.7° = 0.3469$ Therefore,
$\cos 69.72° = \quad ?$ $\cos 69.72 = 0.3469 - \frac{2}{10}(0.0016)$
$\cos 69.8° = \underline{0.3453}$ $= 0.3469 - 0.0003$
difference $= 0.0016$ $= 0.3466$

Notice that the interpolated amount is subtracted from cos 69.7° because the cosine is decreasing.

Problems

Find the logarithms of the following numbers.

1. 482.4   **2.** 0.3456   **3.** 0.008722

4. 10.17   **5.** 59,170   **6.** 0.07777

7. 135,400   **8.** 0.001234   **9.** 2003

10. 12.76   **11.** 0.9872   **12.** 0.0009124

13. 0.6037   **14.** 538.8   **15.** 1.259

Find the antilogarithms of the following.

16. 1.6734   **17.** 9.7366 − 10

18. 8.9550 − 10   **19.** 0.8350

20. 7.1234 − 10   **21.** 3.4569

22. 1.6860   **23.** 2.8964

24. 5.8211 − 10   **25.** 4.9793

26. 3.8940 − 10   **27.** 9.8020 − 10

28. 4.7570 − 20   **29.** 0.9505

30. 8.0092 − 10

Compute by logarithms, giving the answers to three significant figures.

31. 3.44 × 272   **32.** 9.21 × 326

33. 72.8 ÷ 3.62   **34.** 603 ÷ 373

35. $\sqrt{870}$ **36.** 305 ÷ 2.34

37. 84 × 92   **38.** 91 × 172

39. 200 × 612   **40.** $\sqrt[3]{94}$

41. 4.58 ÷ 76   **42.** 100 ÷ 53

43. 4 × 3.16   **44.** 27 × 0.093

45. $(24.3)(5.78)^3$ **46.** $\sqrt{(1771)(0.687)}$

47. $\dfrac{7.48}{0.0553}(9.96)$ **48.** $(3.14)^7 ÷ (284)$

49. $(\sqrt{2793})^3$ **50.** $\sqrt[3]{89.5} \cdot \sqrt{258}$

Interpolate to find approximate values of the following.

51. cos 59.62°   **52.** sin 28.28°

53. tan 41.84°   **54.** cot 61.15°

55. sin 126.59°   **56.** cos 99.28°

57. tan 98.08°   **58.** cot 162.33°

59. sin 212.33°   **60.** cos 261.47°

61. tan 310.48°   **62.** cos 278.75°

For each of the following find A to the nearest hundredth such that $0 < A < 90$.

63. sin $A° = 0.7777$ **64.** cos $A° = 0.7444$

65. tan $A° = 1.1000$ **66.** cot $A° = 1.2000$

67. cos $A° = 0.9922$ **68.** sin $A° = 0.0400$

69. tan $A° = 0.0400$ **70.** cos $A° = 0.0200$

71. sin $A° = 0.0900$ **72.** cos $A° = 0.9000$

73. cot $A° = 0.6956$ **74.** tan $A° = 1.3000$

TABLE I
Four-Place Logarithms of Numbers

N	0	1	2	3	4	5	6	7	8	9
10	0000	0043	0086	0128	0170	0212	0253	0294	0334	0374
11	0414	0453	0492	0531	0569	0607	0645	0682	0719	0755
12	0792	0828	0864	0899	0934	0969	1004	1038	1072	1106
13	1139	1173	1206	1239	1271	1303	1335	1367	1399	1430
14	1461	1492	1523	1553	1584	1614	1644	1673	1703	1732
15	1761	1790	1818	1847	1875	1903	1931	1959	1987	2014
16	2041	2068	2095	2122	2148	2175	2201	2227	2253	2279
17	2304	2330	2355	2380	2405	2430	2455	2480	2504	2529
18	2553	2577	2601	2625	2648	2672	2695	2718	2742	2765
19	2788	2810	2833	2856	2878	2900	2923	2945	2967	2989
20	3010	3032	3054	3075	3096	3118	3139	3160	3181	3201
21	3222	3243	3263	3284	3304	3324	3345	3365	3385	3404
22	3424	3444	3464	3483	3502	3522	3541	3560	3579	3598
23	3617	3636	3655	3674	3692	3711	3729	3747	3766	3784
24	3802	3820	3838	3856	3874	3892	3909	3927	3945	3962
25	3979	3997	4014	4031	4048	4065	4082	4099	4116	4133
26	4150	4166	4183	4200	4216	4232	4249	4265	4281	4298
27	4314	4330	4346	4362	4378	4393	4409	4425	4440	4456
28	4472	4487	4502	4518	4533	4548	4564	4579	4594	4609
29	4624	4639	4654	4669	4683	4698	4713	4728	4742	4757
30	4771	4786	4800	4814	4829	4843	4857	4871	4886	4900
31	4914	4928	4942	4955	4969	4983	4997	5011	5024	5038
32	5051	5065	5079	5092	5105	5119	5132	5145	5159	5172
33	5185	5198	5211	5224	5237	5250	5263	5276	5289	5302
34	5315	5328	5340	5353	5366	5378	5391	5403	5416	5428
35	5441	5453	5465	5478	5490	5502	5514	5527	5539	5551
36	5563	5575	5587	5599	5611	5623	5635	5647	5658	5670
37	5682	5694	5705	5717	5729	5740	5752	5763	5775	5786
38	5798	5809	5821	5832	5843	5855	5866	5877	5888	5899
39	5911	5922	5933	5944	5955	5966	5977	5988	5999	6010
40	6021	6031	6042	6053	6064	6075	6085	6096	6107	6117
41	6128	6138	6149	6160	6170	6180	6191	6201	6212	6222
42	6232	6243	6253	6263	6274	6284	6294	6304	6314	6325
43	6335	6345	6355	6365	6375	6385	6395	6405	6415	6425
44	6435	6444	6454	6464	6474	6484	6493	6503	6513	6522
45	6532	6542	6551	6561	6571	6580	6590	6599	6609	6618
46	6628	6637	6646	6656	6665	6675	6684	6693	6702	6712
47	6721	6730	6739	6749	6758	6767	6776	6785	6794	6803
48	6812	6821	6830	6839	6848	6857	6866	6875	6884	6893
49	6902	6911	6920	6928	6937	6946	6955	6964	6972	6981
50	6990	6998	7007	7016	7024	7033	7042	7050	7059	7067
51	7076	7084	7093	7101	7110	7118	7126	7135	7143	7152
52	7160	7168	7177	7185	7193	7202	7210	7218	7226	7235
53	7243	7251	7259	7267	7275	7284	7292	7300	7308	7316
54	7324	7332	7340	7348	7356	7364	7372	7380	7388	7396

(Continued)

TABLE I
Four-Place Logarithms of Numbers

N	0	1	2	3	4	5	6	7	8	9
55	7404	7412	7419	7427	7435	7443	7451	7459	7466	7474
56	7482	7490	7497	7505	7513	7520	7528	7536	7543	7551
57	7559	7566	7574	7582	7589	7579	7604	7612	7619	7627
58	7634	7642	7649	7657	7664	7672	7679	7686	7694	7701
59	7709	7716	7723	7731	7738	7745	7752	7760	7767	7774
60	7782	7789	7796	7803	7810	7818	7825	7832	7839	7846
61	7853	7860	7868	7875	7882	7889	7896	7903	7910	7917
62	7924	7931	7938	7945	7952	7959	7966	7973	7980	7987
63	7993	8000	8007	8014	8021	8028	8035	8041	8048	8055
64	8062	8069	8075	8082	8089	8096	8102	8109	8116	8122
65	8129	8136	8142	8149	8156	8162	8169	8176	8182	8189
66	8195	8202	8209	8215	8222	8228	8235	8241	8248	8254
67	8261	8267	8274	8280	8287	8293	8299	8306	8312	8319
68	8325	8331	8338	8344	8351	8357	8363	8370	8376	8382
69	8388	8395	8401	8407	8414	8420	8426	8432	8439	8445
70	8451	8457	8463	8470	8476	8482	8488	8494	8500	8506
71	8513	8519	8525	8531	8537	8543	8549	8555	8561	8567
72	8573	8579	8585	8591	8597	8603	8609	8615	8621	8627
73	8633	8639	8645	8651	8657	8663	8669	8675	8681	8686
74	8692	8698	8704	8710	8716	8722	8727	8733	8739	8745
75	8751	8756	8762	8768	8774	8779	8785	8791	8797	8802
76	8808	8814	8820	8825	8831	8837	8842	8848	8854	8859
77	8865	8871	8876	8882	8887	8893	8899	8904	8910	8915
78	8921	8927	8932	8938	8943	8949	8954	8960	8965	8971
79	8976	8982	8987	8993	8998	9004	9009	9015	9020	9025
80	9031	9036	9042	9047	9053	9058	9063	9069	9074	9079
81	9085	9090	9096	9101	9106	9112	9117	9122	9128	9133
82	9138	9143	9149	9154	9159	9165	9170	9175	9180	9186
83	9191	9196	9201	9206	9212	9217	9222	9227	9232	9238
84	9243	9248	9253	9258	9263	9269	9274	9279	9284	9289
85	9294	9299	9304	9309	9315	9320	9325	9330	9335	9340
86	9345	9350	9355	9360	9365	9370	9375	9380	9385	9390
87	9395	9400	9405	9410	9415	9420	9425	9430	9435	9440
88	9445	9450	9455	9460	9465	9469	9474	9479	9484	9489
89	9494	9499	9504	9509	9513	9518	9523	9528	9533	9538
90	9542	9547	9552	9557	9562	9566	9571	9576	9581	9586
91	9590	9595	9600	9605	9609	9614	9619	9624	9628	9633
92	9638	9643	9647	9652	9657	9661	9666	9671	9675	9680
93	9685	9689	9694	9699	9703	9708	9713	9717	9722	9727
94	9731	9736	9741	9745	9750	9754	9759	9763	9768	9773
95	9777	9782	9786	9791	9795	9800	9805	9809	9814	9818
96	9823	9827	9832	9836	9841	9845	9850	9854	9859	9863
97	9868	9872	9877	9881	9886	9890	9894	9899	9903	9908
98	9912	9917	9921	9926	9930	9934	9939	9943	9948	9952
99	9956	9961	9965	9969	9974	9978	9983	9987	9991	9996

TABLE II
Trigonometric Functions

Deg.	Sin	*Tan	*Cot	Cos	Deg.	Deg.	Sin	Tan	Cot	Cos	Deg.
0.0	0.00000	0.00000	∞	1.0000	**90.0**	**4.0**	0.06976	0.06993	14.301	0.9976	**86.0**
.1	.00175	.00175	573.0	1.0000	89.9	.1	.07150	.07168	13.951	.9974	85.9
.2	.00349	.00349	286.5	1.0000	.8	.2	.07324	.07344	13.617	.9973	.8
.3	.00524	.00524	191.0	1.0000	.7	.3	.07498	.07519	13.300	.9972	.7
.4	.00698	.00698	143.24	1.0000	.6	.4	.07672	.07695	12.996	.9971	.6
.5	.00873	.00873	114.59	1.0000	.5	.5	.07846	.07870	12.706	.9969	.5
.6	.01047	.01047	95.49	0.9999	.4	.6	.08020	.08046	12.429	.9968	.4
.7	.01222	.01222	81.85	.9999	.3	.7	.08194	.08221	12.163	.9966	.3
.8	.01396	.01396	71.62	.9999	.2	.8	.08368	.08397	11.909	.9965	.2
.9	.01571	.01571	63.66	.9999	89.1	.9	.08542	.08573	11.664	.9963	85.1
1.0	0.01745	0.01746	57.29	0.9998	**89.0**	**5.0**	0.08716	0.08749	11.430	0.9962	**85.0**
.1	.01920	.01920	52.08	.9998	88.9	.1	.08889	.08925	11.205	.9960	84.9
.2	.02094	.02095	47.74	.9998	.8	.2	.09063	.09101	10.988	.9959	.8
.3	.02269	.02269	44.07	.9997	.7	.3	.09237	.09277	10.780	.9957	.7
.4	.02443	.02444	40.92	.9997	.6	.4	.09411	.09453	10.579	.9956	.6
.5	.02618	.02619	38.19	.9997	.5	.5	.09585	.09629	10.385	.9954	.5
.6	.02792	.02793	35.80	.9996	.4	.6	.09758	.09805	10.199	.9952	.4
.7	.02967	.02968	33.69	.9996	.3	.7	.09932	.09981	10.019	.9951	.3
.8	.03141	.03143	31.82	.9995	.2	.8	.10106	.10158	9.845	.9949	.2
.9	.03316	.03317	30.14	.9995	88.1	.9	.10279	.10334	9.677	.9947	84.1
2.0	0.03490	0.03492	28.64	0.9994	**88.0**	**6.0**	0.10453	0.10510	9.514	0.9945	**84.0**
.1	.03664	.03667	27.27	.9993	87.9	.1	.10626	.10687	9.357	.9943	83.9
.2	.03839	.03842	26.03	.9993	.8	.2	.10800	.10863	9.205	.9942	.8
.3	.04013	.04016	24.90	.9992	.7	.3	.10973	.11040	9.058	.9940	.7
.4	.04188	.04191	23.86	.9991	.6	.4	.11147	.11217	8.915	.9938	.6
.5	.04362	.04366	22.90	.9990	.5	.5	.11320	.11394	8.777	.9936	.5
.6	.04536	.04541	22.02	.9990	.4	.6	.11494	.11570	8.643	.9934	.4
.7	.04711	.04716	21.20	.9989	.3	.7	.11667	.11747	8.513	.9932	.3
.8	.04885	.04891	20.45	.9988	.2	.8	.11840	.11924	8.386	.9930	.2
.9	.05059	.05066	19.74	.9987	87.1	.9	.12014	.12101	8.264	.9928	83.1
3.0	0.05234	0.05241	19.081	0.9986	**87.0**	**7.0**	0.12187	0.12278	8.144	0.9925	**83.0**
.1	.05408	.05416	18.464	.9985	86.9	.1	.12360	.12456	8.028	.9923	82.9
.2	.05582	.05591	17.886	.9984	.8	.2	.12533	.12633	7.916	.9921	.8
.3	.05756	.05766	17.343	.9983	.7	.3	.12706	.12810	7.806	.9919	.7
.4	.05931	.05941	16.832	.9982	.6	.4	.12880	.12988	7.700	.9917	.6
.5	.06105	.06116	16.350	.9981	.5	.5	.13053	.13165	7.596	.9914	.5
.6	.06279	.06291	15.895	.9980	.4	.6	.13226	.13343	7.495	.9912	.4
.7	.06453	.06467	15.464	.9979	.3	.7	.13399	.13521	7.396	.9910	.3
.8	.06627	.06642	15.056	.9978	.2	.8	.13572	.13698	7.300	.9907	.2
.9	.06802	.06817	14.669	.9977	86.1	.9	.13744	.13876	7.207	.9905	82.1
Deg.	Cos	*Cot	*Tan	Sin	Deg.	Deg.	Cos	Cot	Tan	Sin	Deg.

*Interpolation in this section of the table is inaccurate.

(Continued)

TABLE II
Trigonometric Functions

Deg.	Sin	Tan	Cot	Cos	Deg.	Deg.	Sin	Tan	Cot	Cos	Deg.
8.0	0.13917	0.14054	7.115	0.9903	**82.0**	**12.0**	0.2079	0.2126	4.705	0.9781	**78.0**
.1	.14090	.14232	7.026	.9900	81.9	.1	.2096	.2144	4.665	.9778	77.9
.2	.14263	.14410	6.940	.9898	.8	.2	.2113	.2162	4.625	.9774	.8
.3	.14436	.14588	6.855	.9895	.7	.3	.2130	.2180	4.586	.9770	.7
.4	.14608	.14767	6.772	.9893	.6	.4	.2147	.2199	4.548	.9767	.6
.5	.14781	.14945	6.691	.9890	.5	.5	.2164	.2217	4.511	.9763	.5
.6	.14954	.15124	6.612	.9888	.4	.6	.2181	.2235	4.474	.9759	.4
.7	.15126	.15302	6.535	.9885	.3	.7	.2198	.2254	4.437	.9755	.3
.8	.15299	.15481	6.460	.9882	.2	.8	.2215	.2272	4.402	.9751	.2
.9	.15471	.15660	6.386	.9880	81.1	.9	.2233	.2290	4.366	.9748	77.1
9.0	0.15643	0.15838	6.314	0.9877	**81.0**	**13.0**	0.2250	0.2309	4.331	0.9744	**77.0**
.1	.15816	.16017	6.243	.9874	80.9	.1	.2267	.2327	4.297	.9740	76.9
.2	.15988	.16196	6.174	.9871	.8	.2	.2284	.2345	4.264	.9736	.8
.3	.16160	.16376	6.107	.9869	.7	.3	.2300	.2364	4.230	.9732	.7
.4	.16333	.16555	6.041	.9866	.6	.4	.2317	.2382	4.198	.9728	.6
.5	.16505	.16734	5.976	.9863	.5	.5	.2334	.2401	4.165	.9724	.5
.6	.16677	.16914	5.912	.9860	.4	.6	.2351	.2419	4.134	.9720	.4
.7	.16849	.17093	5.850	.9857	.3	.7	.2368	.2438	4.102	.9715	.3
.8	.17021	.17273	5.789	.9854	.2	.8	.2385	.2456	4.071	.9711	.2
.9	.17193	.17453	5.730	.9851	80.1	.9	.2402	.2475	4.041	.9707	76.1
10.0	0.1736	0.1763	5.671	0.9848	**80.0**	**14.0**	0.2419	0.2493	4.011	0.9703	**76.0**
.1	.1754	.1781	5.614	.9845	79.9	.1	.2436	.2512	3.981	.9699	75.9
.2	.1771	.1799	5.558	.9842	.8	.2	.2453	.2530	3.952	.9694	.8
.3	.1788	.1817	5.503	.9839	.7	.3	.2470	.2549	3.923	.9690	.7
.4	.1805	.1835	5.449	.9836	.6	.4	.2487	.2568	3.895	.9686	.6
.5	.1822	.1853	5.396	.9833	.5	.5	.2504	.2586	3.867	.9681	.5
.6	.1840	.1871	5.343	.9829	.4	.6	.2521	.2605	3.839	.9677	.4
.7	.1857	.1890	5.292	.9826	.3	.7	.2538	.2623	3.812	.9673	.3
.8	.1874	.1908	5.242	.9823	.2	.8	.2554	.2642	3.785	.9668	.2
.9	.1891	.1926	5.193	.9820	79.1	.9	.2571	.2661	3.758	.9664	75.1
11.0	0.1908	0.1944	5.145	0.9816	**79.0**	**15.0**	0.2588	0.2679	3.732	0.9659	**75.0**
.1	.1925	.1962	5.097	.9813	78.9	.1	.2605	.2698	3.706	.9655	74.9
.2	.1942	.1980	5.050	.9810	.8	.2	.2622	.2717	3.681	.9650	.8
.3	.1959	.1998	5.005	.9806	.7	.3	.2639	.2736	3.655	.9646	.7
.4	.1977	.2016	4.959	.9803	.6	.4	.2656	.2754	3.630	.9641	.6
.5	.1994	.2035	4.915	.9799	.5	.5	.2672	.2773	3.606	.9636	.5
.6	.2011	.2053	4.872	.9796	.4	.6	.2689	.2792	3.582	.9632	.4
.7	.2028	.2071	4.829	.9792	.3	.7	.2706	.2811	3.558	.9627	.3
.8	.2045	.2089	4.787	.9789	.2	.8	.2723	.2830	3.534	.9622	.2
.9	.2062	.2107	4.745	.9785	78.1	.9	.2740	.2849	3.511	.9617	74.1
Deg.	Cos	Cot	Tan	Sin	Deg.	Deg.	Cos	Cot	Tan	Sin	Deg.

(Continued)

TABLE II
Trigonometric Functions

Deg.	Sin	Tan	Cot	Cos	Deg.	Deg.	Sin	Tan	Cot	Cos	Deg.
16.0	0.2756	0.2867	3.487	0.9613	**74.0**	**20.0**	0.3420	0.3640	2.747	0.9397	**70.0**
.1	.2773	.2886	3.465	.9608	73.9	.1	.3437	.3659	2.733	.9391	69.9
.2	.2790	.2905	3.442	.9603	.8	.2	.3453	.3679	2.718	.9385	.8
.3	.2807	.2924	3.420	.9598	.7	.3	.3469	.3699	2.703	.9379	.7
.4	.2823	.2943	3.398	.9593	.6	.4	.3486	.3719	2.689	.9373	.6
.5	.2840	.2962	3.376	.9588	.5	.5	.3502	.3739	2.675	.9367	.5
.6	.2857	.2981	3.354	.9583	.4	.6	.3518	.3759	2.660	.9361	.4
.7	.2874	.3000	3.333	.9578	.3	.7	.3535	.3779	2.646	.9354	.3
.8	.2890	.3019	3.312	.9573	.2	.8	.3551	.3799	2.633	.9348	.2
.9	.2907	.3038	3.291	.9568	73.1	.9	.3567	.3819	2.619	.9342	69.1
17.0	0.2924	0.3057	3.271	0.9563	**73.0**	**21.0**	0.3584	0.3839	2.605	0.9336	**69.0**
.1	.2940	.3076	3.251	.9558	72.9	.1	.3600	.3859	2.592	.9330	68.9
.2	.2957	.3096	3.230	.9553	.8	.2	.3616	.3879	2.578	.9323	.8
.3	.2974	.3115	3.211	.9548	.7	.3	.3633	.3899	2.565	.9317	.7
.4	.2990	.3134	3.191	.9542	.6	.4	.3649	.3919	2.552	.9311	.6
.5	.3007	.3153	3.172	.9537	.5	.5	.3665	.3939	2.539	.9304	.5
.6	.3024	.3172	3.152	.9532	.4	.6	.3681	.3959	2.526	.9298	.4
.7	.3040	.3191	3.133	.9527	.3	.7	.3697	.3979	2.513	.9291	.3
.8	.3057	.3211	3.115	.9521	.2	.8	.3714	.4000	2.500	.9285	.2
.9	.3074	.3230	3.096	.9516	72.1	.9	.3730	.4020	2.488	.9278	68.1
18.0	0.3090	0.3249	3.078	0.9511	**72.0**	**22.0**	0.3746	0.4040	2.475	0.9272	**68.0**
.1	.3107	.3269	3.060	.9505	71.9	.1	.3762	.4061	2.463	.9265	67.9
.2	.3123	.3288	3.042	.9500	.8	.2	.3778	.4081	2.450	.9259	.8
.3	.3140	.3307	3.024	.9494	.7	.3	.3795	.4101	2.438	.9252	.7
.4	.3156	.3327	3.006	.9489	.6	.4	.3811	.4122	2.426	.9245	.6
.5	.3173	.3346	2.989	.9483	.5	.5	.3827	.4142	2.414	.9239	.5
.6	.3190	.3365	2.971	.9478	.4	.6	.3843	.4163	2.402	.9232	.4
.7	.3206	.3385	2.954	.9472	.3	.7	.3859	.4183	2.391	.9225	.3
.8	.3223	.3404	2.937	.9466	.2	.8	.3875	.4204	2.379	.9219	.2
.9	.3239	.3424	2.921	.9461	71.1	.9	.3891	.4224	2.367	.9212	67.1
19.0	0.3256	0.3443	2.904	0.9455	**71.0**	**23.0**	0.3907	0.4245	2.356	0.9205	**67.0**
.1	.3272	.3463	2.888	.9449	70.9	.1	.3923	.4265	2.344	.9198	66.9
.2	.3289	.3482	2.872	.9444	.8	.2	.3939	.4286	2.333	.9191	.8
.3	.3305	.3502	2.856	.9438	.7	.3	.3955	.4307	2.322	.9184	.7
.4	.3322	.3522	2.840	.9432	.6	.4	.3971	.4327	2.311	.9178	.6
.5	.3338	.3541	2.824	.9426	.5	.5	.3987	.4348	2.300	.9171	.5
.6	.3355	.3561	2.808	.9421	.4	.6	.4003	.4369	2.289	.9164	.4
.7	.3371	.3581	2.793	.9415	.3	.7	.4019	.4390	2.278	.9157	.3
.8	.3387	.3600	2.778	.9409	.2	.8	.4035	.4411	2.267	.9150	.2
.9	.3404	.3620	2.762	.9403	70.1	.9	.4051	.4431	2.257	.9143	66.1
Deg.	Cos	Cot	Tan	Sin	Deg.	Deg.	Cos	Cot	Tan	Sin	Deg.

(Continued)

Tables

TABLE II
Trigonometric Functions

Deg.	Sin	Tan	Cot	Cos	Deg.		Deg.	Sin	Tan	Cot	Cos	Deg.
24.0	0.4067	0.4452	2.246	0.9135	**66.0**		**28.0**	0.4695	0.5317	1.881	0.8829	**62.0**
.1	.4083	.4473	2.236	.9128	65.9		.1	.4710	.5340	1.873	.8821	61.9
.2	.4099	.4494	2.225	.9121	.8		.2	.4726	.5362	1.865	.8813	.8
.3	.4115	.4515	2.215	.9114	.7		.3	.4741	.5384	1.857	.8805	.7
.4	.4131	.4536	2.204	.9107	.6		.4	.4756	.5407	1.849	.8796	.6
.5	.4147	.4557	2.194	.9100	.5		.5	.4772	.5430	1.842	.8788	.5
.6	.4163	.4578	2.184	.9092	.4		.6	.4787	.5452	1.834	.8780	.4
.7	.4179	.4599	2.174	.9085	.3		.7	.4802	.5475	1.827	.8771	.3
.8	.4195	.4621	2.164	.9078	.2		.8	.4818	.5498	1.819	.8763	.2
.9	.4210	.4642	2.154	.9070	65.1		.9	.4833	.5520	1.811	.8755	61.1
25.0	0.4226	0.4663	2.145	0.9063	**65.0**		**29.0**	0.4848	0.5543	1.804	0.8746	**61.0**
.1	.4242	.4684	2.135	.9056	64.9		.1	.4863	.5566	1.797	.8738	60.9
.2	.4258	.4706	2.125	.9048	.8		.2	.4879	.5589	1.789	.8729	.8
.3	.4274	.4727	2.116	.9041	.7		.3	.4894	.5612	1.782	.8721	.7
.4	.4289	.4748	2.106	.9033	.6		.4	.4909	.5635	1.775	.8712	.6
.5	.4305	.4770	2.097	.9026	.5		.5	.4924	.5658	1.767	.8704	.5
.6	.4321	.4791	2.087	.9018	.4		.6	.4939	.5681	1.760	.8695	.4
.7	.4337	.4813	2.078	.9011	.3		.7	.4955	.5704	1.753	.8686	.3
.8	.4352	.4834	2.069	.9003	.2		.8	.4970	.5727	1.746	.8678	.2
.9	.4368	.4856	2.059	.8996	64.1		.9	.4985	.5750	1.739	.8669	60.1
26.0	0.4384	0.4877	2.050	0.8988	**64.0**		**30.0**	0.5000	0.5774	1.7321	0.8660	**60.0**
.1	.4399	.4899	2.041	.8980	63.9		.1	.5015	.5797	1.7251	.8652	59.9
.2	.4415	.4921	2.032	.8973	.8		.2	.5030	.5820	1.7182	.8643	.8
.3	.4431	.4942	2.023	.8965	.7		.3	.5045	.5844	1.7113	.8634	.7
.4	.4446	.4964	2.014	.8957	.6		.4	.5060	.5867	1.7045	.8625	.6
.5	.4462	.4986	2.006	.8949	.5		.5	.5075	.5890	1.6977	.8616	.5
.6	.4478	.5008	1.997	.8942	.4		.6	.5090	.5914	1.6909	.8607	.4
.7	.4493	.5029	1.988	.8934	.3		.7	.5105	.5938	1.6842	.8599	.3
.8	.4509	.5051	1.980	.8926	.2		.8	.5120	.5961	1.6775	.8590	.2
.9	.4524	.5073	1.971	.8918	63.1		.9	.5135	.5985	1.6709	.8581	59.1
27.0	0.4540	0.5095	1.963	0.8910	**63.0**		**31.0**	0.5150	0.6009	1.6643	0.8572	**59.0**
.1	.4555	.5117	1.954	.8902	62.9		.1	.5165	.6032	1.6577	.8563	58.9
.2	.4571	.5139	1.946	.8894	.8		.2	.5180	.6056	1.6512	.8554	.8
.3	.4586	.5161	1.937	.8886	.7		.3	.5195	.6080	1.6447	.8545	.7
.4	.4602	.5184	1.929	.8878	.6		.4	.5210	.6104	1.6383	.8536	.6
.5	.4617	.5206	1.921	.8870	.5		.5	.5225	.6128	1.6319	.8526	.5
.6	.4633	.5228	1.913	.8862	.4		.6	.5240	.6152	1.6255	.8517	.4
.7	.4648	.5250	1.905	.8854	.3		.7	.5255	.6176	1.6191	.8508	.3
.8	.4664	.5272	1.897	.8846	.2		.8	.5270	.6200	1.6128	.8499	.2
.9	.4679	.5295	1.889	.8838	62.1		.9	.5284	.6224	1.6066	.8490	58.1
Deg.	Cos	Cot	Tan	Sin	Deg.		Deg.	Cos	Cot	Tan	Sin	Deg.

(Continued)

TABLE II
Trigonometric Functions

Deg.	Sin	Tan	Cot	Cos	Deg.	Deg.	Sin	Tan	Cot	Cos	Deg.
32.0	0.5299	0.6249	1.6003	0.8480	**58.0**	**36.0**	0.5878	0.7265	1.3764	0.8090	**54.0**
.1	.5314	.6273	1.5941	.8471	57.9	.1	.5892	.7292	1.3713	.8080	53.9
.2	.5329	.6297	1.5880	.8462	.8	.2	.5906	.7319	1.3663	.8070	.8
.3	.5344	.6322	1.5818	.8453	.7	.3	.5920	.7346	1.3613	.8059	.7
.4	.5358	.6346	1.5757	.8443	.6	.4	.5934	.7373	1.3564	.8049	.6
.5	.5373	.6371	1.5697	.8434	.5	.5	.5948	.7400	1.3514	.8039	.5
.6	.5388	.6395	1.5637	.8425	.4	.6	.5962	.7427	1.3465	.8028	.4
.7	.5402	.6420	1.5577	.8415	.3	.7	.5976	.7454	1.3416	.8018	.3
.8	.5417	.6445	1.5517	.8406	.2	.8	.5990	.7481	1.3367	.8007	.2
.9	.5432	.6469	1.5458	.8396	57.1	.9	.6004	.7508	1.3319	.7997	53.1
33.0	0.5446	0.6494	1.5399	0.8387	**57.0**	**37.0**	0.6018	0.7536	1.3270	0.7986	**53.0**
.1	.5461	.6519	1.5340	.8377	56.9	.1	.6032	.7563	1.3222	.7976	52.9
.2	.5476	.6544	1.5282	.8368	.8	.2	.6046	.7590	1.3175	.7965	.8
.3	.5490	.6569	1.5224	.8358	.7	.3	.6060	.7618	1.3127	.7955	.7
.4	.5505	.6594	1.5166	.8348	.6	.4	.6074	.7646	1.3079	.7944	.6
.5	.5519	.6619	1.5108	.8339	.5	.5	.6088	.7673	1.3032	.7934	.5
.6	.5534	.6644	1.5051	.8329	.4	.6	.6101	.7701	1.2985	.7923	.4
.7	.5548	.6669	1.4994	.8320	.3	.7	.6115	.7729	1.2938	.7912	.3
.8	.5563	.6694	1.4938	.8310	.2	.8	.6129	.7757	1.2892	.7902	.2
.9	.5577	.6720	1.4882	.8300	56.1	.9	.6143	.7785	1.2846	.7891	52.1
34.0	0.5592	0.6745	1.4826	0.8290	**56.0**	**38.0**	0.6157	0.7813	1.2799	0.7880	**52.0**
.1	.5606	.6771	1.4770	.8281	55.9	.1	.6170	.7841	1.2753	.7869	51.9
.2	.5621	.6796	1.4715	.8271	.8	.2	.6184	.7869	1.2708	.7859	.8
.3	.5635	.6822	1.4659	.8261	.7	.3	.6198	.7898	1.2662	.7848	.7
.4	.5650	.6847	1.4605	.8251	.6	.4	.6211	.7926	1.2617	.7837	.6
.5	.5664	.6873	1.4550	.8241	.5	.5	.6225	.7954	1.2572	.7826	.5
.6	.5678	.6899	1.4496	.8231	.4	.6	.6239	.7983	1.2527	.7815	.4
.7	.5693	.6924	1.4442	.8221	.3	.7	.6252	.8012	1.2482	.7804	.3
.8	.5707	.6950	1.4388	.8211	.2	.8	.6266	.8040	1.2437	.7793	.2
.9	.5721	.6976	1.4335	.8202	55.1	.9	.6280	.8069	1.2393	.7782	51.1
35.0	0.5736	0.7002	1.4281	0.8192	**55.0**	**39.0**	0.6293	0.8098	1.2349	0.7771	**51.0**
.1	.5750	.7028	1.4229	.8181	54.9	.1	.6307	.8127	1.2305	.7760	50.9
.2	.5764	.7054	1.4176	.8171	.8	.2	.6320	.8156	1.2261	.7749	.8
.3	.5779	.7080	1.4124	.8161	.7	.3	.6334	.8185	1.2218	.7738	.7
.4	.5793	.7107	1.4071	.8151	.6	.4	.6347	.8214	1.2174	.7727	.6
.5	.5807	.7133	1.4019	.8141	.5	.5	.6361	.8243	1.2131	.7716	.5
.6	.5821	.7159	1.3968	.8131	.4	.6	.6374	.8273	1.2088	.7705	.4
.7	.5835	.7186	1.3916	.8121	.3	.7	.6388	.8302	1.2045	.7694	.3
.8	.5850	.7212	1.3865	.8111	.2	.8	.6401	.8332	1.2002	.7683	.2
.9	.5864	.7239	1.3814	.8100	54.1	.9	.6414	.8361	1.1960	.7672	50.1
Deg.	Cos	Cot	Tan	Sin	Deg.	Deg.	Cos	Cot	Tan	Sin	Deg.

(Continued)

TABLE II
Trigonometric Functions

Deg.	Sin	Tan	Cot	Cos	Deg.
40.0	0.6428	0.8391	1.1918	0.7660	**50.0**
.1	.6441	.8421	1.1875	.7649	49.9
.2	.6455	.8451	1.1833	.7638	.8
.3	.6468	.8481	1.1792	.7627	.7
.4	.6481	.8511	1.1750	.7615	.6
.5	0.6494	0.8541	1.1708	0.7604	.5
.6	.6508	.8571	1.1667	.7593	.4
.7	.6521	.8601	1.1626	.7581	.3
.8	.6534	.8632	1.1585	.7570	.2
.9	.6547	.8662	1.1544	.7559	49.1
41.0	0.6561	0.8693	1.1504	0.7547	**49.0**
.1	.6574	.8724	1.1463	.7536	48.9
.2	.6587	.8754	1.1423	.7524	.8
.3	.6600	.8785	1.1383	.7513	.7
.4	.6613	.8816	1.1343	.7501	.6
.5	.6626	.8847	1.1303	.7490	.5
.6	.6639	.8878	1.1263	.7478	.4
.7	.6652	.8910	1.1224	.7466	.3
.8	.6665	.8941	1.1184	.7455	.2
.9	.6678	.8972	1.1145	.7443	48.1
42.0	0.6691	0.9004	1.1106	0.7431	**48.0**
.1	.6704	.9036	1.1067	.7420	47.9
.2	.6717	.9067	1.1028	.7408	.8
.3	.6730	.9099	1.0990	.7396	.7
.4	.6743	.9131	1.0951	.7385	.6

Deg.	Cos	Cot	Tan	Sin	Deg.

Deg.	Sin	Tan	Cot	Cos	Deg.
42.5	.6756	.9163	1.0913	.7373	**47.5**
.6	.6769	.9195	1.0875	.7361	.4
.7	.6782	.9228	1.0837	.7349	.3
.8	.6794	.9260	1.0799	.7337	.2
.9	.6807	.9293	1.0761	.7325	47.1
43.0	0.6820	0.9325	1.0724	0.7314	**47.0**
.1	.6833	.9358	1.0686	.7302	46.9
.2	.6845	.9391	1.0649	.7290	.8
.3	.6858	.9424	1.0612	.7278	.7
.4	.6871	.9457	1.0575	.7266	.6
.5	.6884	.9490	1.0538	.7254	.5
.6	.6896	.9523	1.0501	.7242	.4
.7	.6909	.9556	1.0464	.7230	.3
.8	.6921	.9590	1.0428	.7218	.2
.9	.6934	.9623	1.0392	.7206	46.1
44.0	0.6947	0.9657	1.0355	0.7193	**46.0**
.1	.6959	.9691	1.0319	.7181	45.9
.2	.6972	.9725	1.0283	.7169	.8
.3	.6984	.9759	1.0247	.7157	.7
.4	.6997	.9793	1.0212	.7145	.6
.5	.7009	.9827	1.0176	.7133	.5
.6	.7022	.9861	1.0141	.7120	.4
.7	.7034	.9896	1.0105	.7108	.3
.8	.7046	.9930	1.0070	.7096	.2
.9	.7059	.9965	1.0035	.7083	45.1
45.0	0.7071	1.0000	1.0000	0.7071	**45.0**

Deg.	Cos	Cot	Tan	Sin	Deg.

TABLE III
Powers and Roots

No.	Sq.	Sq. Root	Cube	Cube Root	No.	Sq.	Sq. Root	Cube	Cube Root
1	1	1.000	1	1.000	51	2,601	7.141	132,651	3.708
2	4	1.414	8	1.260	52	2,704	7.211	140,608	3.733
3	9	1.732	27	1.442	53	2,809	7.280	148,877	3.756
4	16	2.000	64	1.587	54	2,916	7.348	157,464	3.780
5	25	2.236	125	1.710	55	3,025	7.416	166,375	3.803
6	36	2.449	216	1.817	56	3,136	7.483	175,616	3.826
7	49	2.646	343	1.913	57	3,249	7.550	185,193	3.849
8	64	2.828	512	2.000	58	3,364	7.616	195,112	3.871
9	81	3.000	729	2.080	59	3,481	7.681	205,379	3.893
10	100	3.162	1,000	2.154	60	3,600	7.746	216,000	3.915
11	121	3.317	1,331	2.224	61	3,721	7.810	226,981	3.936
12	144	3.464	1,178	2.289	62	3,844	7.874	238,328	3.958
13	169	3.606	2,197	2.351	63	3,969	7.937	250,047	3.979
14	196	3.742	2,744	2.410	64	4,096	8.000	262,144	4.000
15	225	3.873	3,375	2.466	65	4,225	8.062	274,625	4.021
16	256	4.000	4,096	2.520	66	4,356	8.124	287,496	4.041
17	289	4.123	4,913	2.571	67	4,489	8.185	300,763	4.062
18	324	4.243	5,832	2.621	68	4,624	8.246	314,432	4.082
19	361	4.359	6,859	2.668	69	4,761	8.307	328,509	4.102
20	400	4.472	8,000	2.714	70	4,900	8.367	343,000	4.121
21	441	4.583	9,261	2.759	71	5,041	8.426	357,911	4.141
22	484	4.690	10,648	2.802	72	5,184	8.485	373,248	4.160
23	529	4.796	12,167	2.844	73	5,329	8.544	389,017	4.179
24	576	4.899	13,824	2.884	74	5,476	8.602	405,224	4.198
25	625	5.000	15,625	2.924	75	5,625	8.660	421,875	4.217
26	676	5.099	17,576	2.962	76	5,776	8.718	438,976	4.236
27	729	5.196	19,683	3.000	77	5,929	8.775	456,533	4.254
28	784	5.292	21,952	3.037	78	6,084	8.832	474,552	4.273
29	841	5.385	24,389	3.072	79	6,241	8.888	493,039	4.291
30	900	5.477	27,000	3.107	80	6,400	8.944	512,000	4.309
31	961	5.568	29,791	3.141	81	6,561	9.000	531,441	4.327
32	1,024	5.657	32,768	3.175	82	6,724	9.055	551,368	4.344
33	1,089	5.745	35,937	3.208	83	6,889	9.110	571,787	4.362
34	1,156	5.831	39,304	3.240	84	7,056	9.165	592,704	4.380
35	1,225	5.916	42,875	3.271	85	7,225	9.220	614,125	4.397
36	1,296	6.000	46,656	3.302	86	7,396	9.274	636,056	4.414
37	1,369	6.083	50,653	3.332	87	7,569	9.327	658,503	4.431
38	1,444	6.164	54,872	3.362	88	7,744	9.381	681,472	4.448
39	1,521	6.245	59,319	3.391	89	7,921	9.434	704,969	4.465
40	1,600	6.325	64,000	3.420	90	8,100	9.487	729,000	4.481
41	1,681	6.403	68,921	3.448	91	8,281	9.539	753,571	4.498
42	1,764	6.481	74,088	3.476	92	8,464	9.952	778,688	4.514
43	1,849	6.557	79,507	3.503	93	8,649	9.644	804,357	4.531
44	1,936	6.633	85,184	3.530	94	8,836	9.695	830,584	4.547
45	2,025	6.708	91,125	3.557	95	9,025	9.747	857,375	4.563
46	2,116	6.782	97,336	3.583	96	9,216	9.798	884,736	4.579
47	2,209	6.856	103,823	3.609	97	9,409	9.849	912,673	4.595
48	2,304	6.928	110,592	3.634	98	9,604	9.899	941,192	4.610
49	2,401	7.000	117,649	3.659	99	9,801	9.950	970,299	4.626
50	2,500	7.071	125,000	3.684	100	10,000	10.000	1,000,000	4.642

TABLE IV
Exponential Functions, Base e

x	e^x	e^{-x}	x	e^x	e^{-x}
0.00	1.0000	1.0000	2.5	12.182	0.0821
0.05	1.0513	0.9512	2.6	13.464	0.0743
0.10	1.1052	0.9048	2.7	14.880	0.0672
0.15	1.1618	0.8607	2.8	16.445	0.0608
0.20	1.2214	0.8187	2.9	18.174	0.0550
0.25	1.2840	0.7788	3.0	20.086	0.0498
0.30	1.3499	0.7408	3.1	22.198	0.0450
0.35	1.4191	0.7047	3.2	24.533	0.0408
0.40	1.4918	0.6703	3.3	27.113	0.0369
0.45	1.5683	0.6376	3.4	29.964	0.0334
0.50	1.6487	0.6065	3.5	33.115	0.0302
0.55	1.7333	0.5769	3.6	36.598	0.0273
0.60	1.8221	0.5488	3.7	40.447	0.0247
0.65	1.9155	0.5220	3.8	44.701	0.0224
0.70	2.0138	0.4966	3.9	49.402	0.0202
0.75	2.1170	0.4724	4.0	54.598	0.0183
0.80	2.2255	0.4493	4.1	60.340	0.0166
0.85	2.3396	0.4274	4.2	66.686	0.0150
0.90	2.4596	0.4066	4.3	73.700	0.0136
0.95	2.5857	0.3867	4.4	81.451	0.0123
1.0	2.7183	0.3689	4.5	90.017	0.0111
1.1	3.0042	0.3329	4.6	99.484	0.0101
1.2	3.3201	0.3012	4.7	109.95	0.0091
1.3	3.6693	0.2725	4.8	121.51	0.0082
1.4	4.0552	0.2466	4.9	134.29	0.0074
1.5	4.4817	0.2231	5	148.41	0.0067
1.6	4.9530	0.2019	6	403.43	0.0025
1.7	5.4739	0.1827	7	1096.6	0.0009
1.8	6.0496	0.1653	8	2981.0	0.0003
1.9	6.6859	0.1496	9	8103.1	0.0001
2.0	7.3891	0.1353	10	22026	0.00005
2.1	8.1662	0.1225			
2.2	9.0250	0.1108			
2.3	9.9742	0.1003			
2.4	11.023	0.0907			

List of Formulas

Analytic Geometry

Basic formulas

1. The distance between two points:

$$|d| = \sqrt{(x_2 - x_1)^2 + (y_2 - y_1)^2 + (z_2 - z_1)^2}.$$

2. Direction cosines of a line: If d is the directed distance from (x_0, y_0, z_0) to (x_1, y_1, z_1), then the line containing these points has direction cosines

$$c_1 = \frac{x_1 - x_0}{d}, \qquad c_2 = \frac{y_1 - y_0}{d}, \qquad c_3 = \frac{z_1 - z_0}{d}.$$

3. Rectangular equation of a plane: Every plane has an equation of the form

$$Ax + By + Cz + D = 0,$$

where not all of the real numbers A, B, and C are zero.

Equations of straight line

1. Point slope form: $y - y_1 = m(x - x_1)$, where m is the slope.
2. Slope-intercept form: $y = mx + b$, where m is the slope and b is the y-intercept.
3. General linear form: $Ax + By = C$, where not both of the real numbers A and B are zero.
4. Parametric equations of a line:

$$x = x_0 + c_1 d, \qquad y = y_0 + c_2 d, \qquad z = z_0 + c_3 d,$$

where d is the parameter and is the directed distance along the line.

Circle

$(x - h)^2 + (y - k)^2 = r^2$; center at (h, k) and radius r.

Right circular cylinder

The set of all points (x, y, z) in space satisfying $(x - h)^2 + (y - k)^2 = r^2$.

Sphere

$(x - h)^2 + (y - k)^2 + (z - p)^2 = r^2$; center at (h, k, p) and radius r.

Conic sections

1. Eccentricity e: $e < 1$,   the conic is an ellipse,
$e = 1$,   the conic is a parabola,
$e > 1$,   the conic is a hyperbola.

2. Equations:
   (a) $y^2 = 4cx$ Parabola with vertex at the origin and axis along the x-axis; c is the focus.

(b) $\dfrac{x^2}{a^2} + \dfrac{y^2}{b^2} = 1$ Ellipse with *semimajor axis a* and *semiminor axis b*. $a^2 = b^2 + c^2$. The foci are at $(c, 0)$ and $(-c, 0)$. $e = (c/a) < 1$.

(c) $\dfrac{x^2}{a^2} - \dfrac{y^2}{b^2} = 1$ Hyperbola with *semitransverse axis* of length a and *semiconjugate axis* of length b. The foci are at $(\pm c, 0)$, where $c^2 = a^2 + b^2$. *Asymptotes* have equations $y = \pm (b/a)x$.

Angles, Lines, Planes and Vectors

1. The cosine of the angle between the vectors $\mathbf{a} = a_1\mathbf{i} + a_2\mathbf{j} + a_3\mathbf{k}$ and $\mathbf{b} = b_1\mathbf{i} + b_2\mathbf{j} + b_3\mathbf{k}$:

$$\cos\theta = \frac{a_1b_1 + a_2b_2 + a_3b_3}{|\mathbf{a}| \cdot |\mathbf{b}|}.$$

2. The scalar product of $\mathbf{a}$ and $\mathbf{b}$: $\mathbf{a} \cdot \mathbf{b} = |\mathbf{a}| \cdot |\mathbf{b}| \cos\theta$, where θ is the measure of the angle between $\mathbf{a}$ and $\mathbf{b}$.

3. The distance p from the origin to the line is

$$p = \frac{|c|}{\sqrt{a^2 + b^2}}.$$

4. The distance p from the origin to the plane is

$$p = \frac{|D|}{\sqrt{A^2 + B^2 + C^2}}.$$

5. The cross product of vectors: If

$$\mathbf{a} = a_1\mathbf{i} + a_2\mathbf{j} + a_3\mathbf{k} \qquad \text{and} \qquad \mathbf{b} = b_1\mathbf{i} + b_2\mathbf{j} + b_3\mathbf{k},$$

then

$$\mathbf{a} \times \mathbf{b} = (a_2b_3 - a_3b_2)\mathbf{i} + (a_3b_1 - a_1b_3)\mathbf{j} + (a_1b_2 - a_2b_1)\mathbf{k}.$$

Series, Combinations, Permutations

1. The sum of an arithmetic series having n terms and first term a is

$$A_n = n\left(\frac{a + a_n}{2}\right).$$

2. The sum of a geometric series having n terms, first term a and common ratio r is

$$G_n = \frac{a - ar^n}{1 - r}.$$

3. The permutation of n objects r at a time is

$$P(n, r) = \frac{n!}{(n - r)!}.$$

4. The combination of n objects taken r at a time is

$$C(n, r) = \frac{n!}{r!(n - r)!}.$$

List of Symbols

Symbols	Meaning
N	The set of natural numbers
R	The set of real numbers
P_x	The point on the line corresponding to the real number x
$|P_x P'_x|$	The distance between P_x and $P'_x = |x - x'|$
$|AB|$	The distance between A and B
$P_x P'_x$	The directed distance from P_x to $P'_x = x' - x$
$\left.\begin{array}{l}(x, y) \\ P(x, y)\end{array}\right\}$	The point with rectangular coordinates x and y
$|x|$	The absolute value of x
lub S	The least upper bound of the set S
$\left.\begin{array}{l}f: X \to Y \\ f: x \to y \\ X \xrightarrow{f} Y \\ x \to y \\ x \to f(x)\end{array}\right\}$	Notations for a function f
Id	Identity function
$\left.\begin{array}{l}f \circ g \\ f(g)\end{array}\right\}$	The composition of two functions f and g
f^{-1}	The inverse function to the function f
$\langle a, b \rangle$	Open interval
$\left.\begin{array}{l}[a, b\rangle \\ \langle a, b]\end{array}\right.$	Half-open intervals
$[a, b]$	Closed interval
$\pm\infty$	Plus, or minus, infinity
e	The base for natural logarithms

Symbols	Meaning
$\log_a$	The logarithm function with base a
$m(\angle AOB)$	The measure, in radians, of angle AOB, or where evident, also the measure in degrees
$\cong$	Is congruent to
W	The wrapping function, or standard map, from R to the unit circle
$\{a_n\}$	A sequence
Σ	A summation
$n!$	$n(n - 1)(n - 2) \ldots$
$\left.\begin{array}{l}P(n, r) \\ {}_nP_r\end{array}\right\}$	The number of permutations of n objects r at a time
$\left.\begin{array}{l}C(n, r) \\ {}_nC_r \\ \binom{n}{r}\end{array}\right\}$	The number of combinations of n objects r at a time
m	Slope
f'	The derivative of f
Δx	The change in, or increment of, x
α, β, γ	Direction angles
c_1, c_2, c_3	Direction cosines
(A, B)	The arrow from A to B
$\left.\begin{array}{l}\mathbf{a, b, v} \\ \overrightarrow{AB}\end{array}\right\}$	Vectors
$\mathbf{0}$	Null vector
$\mathbf{i, j, k}$	Unit basis vectors
$\left.\begin{array}{l}|\mathbf{a}| \\ |\overrightarrow{AB}|\end{array}\right\}$	The magnitude of the vector

Symbols	Meaning	Symbols	Meaning
$\bar{x} = a - bi$	The complex conjugate of $x = a + bi$	$\begin{vmatrix} a_{11} & a_{12} \\ a_{21} & a_{22} \end{vmatrix}$	A determinant
$\mathbf{u} \cdot \mathbf{v}$	The dot product of $\mathbf{u}$ and $\mathbf{v}$	O	The zero matrix
$\mathbf{n}$	The unit normal	I_n	The identity matrix
$\mathbf{a} \times \mathbf{b}$	The vector product of $\mathbf{a}$ and $\mathbf{b}$	(r, θ)	Polar coordinates
		(r, θ, z)	Cylindrical coordinates
$\begin{bmatrix} a_{11} & a_{12} \\ a_{21} & a_{22} \end{bmatrix}$	A matrix	(r, θ, φ)	Spherical coordinates

Greek Alphabet

Letters		Names	Letters		Names
A	α	Alpha	N	ν	Nu
B	β	Beta	Ξ	ξ	Xi
Γ	γ	Gamma	O	o	Omicron
Δ	δ	Delta	Π	π	Pi
E	ε	Epsilon	P	ρ	Rho
Z	ζ	Zeta	Σ	σ	Sigma
H	η	Eta	T	τ	Tau
Θ	θ	Theta	Υ	υ	Upsilon
I	i	Iota	Φ	φ	Phi
K	κ	Kappa	X	χ	Chi
Λ	λ	Lambda	Ψ	ψ	Psi
M	μ	Mu	Ω	ω	Omega

Index

Answer Section

Answers are given for most odd-numbered problems and calculator problems. Answers are not included for Chapter Tests.

CHAPTER 1

Section 1-2, page 4

1. The Commutative Principle for Multiplication   **3.** The Distributive Principle   **5.** Inverse Element for Multiplication
7. $6x^2 - 15x$ **9.** $6x^2 + 13x + 5$ **11.** 3   **13.** $1/\sqrt{3}$ or $\sqrt{3}/3$ **15.** 9   **17.** 0.3   **19.** $-x$ **21.** $x < -5$ **23.** $y < -5$ **25.** $x > 3$ or $x < 1$ **27.** $x = 5$ or $x = -5$ **29.** $-9 < x < 11$ **31.** $1 \leqslant x \leqslant 3$ **33.** The least upper bound of S is equal to 1.   **35.** Since $x < y$ and $-z > 0$, then $-xz < -yz$. By the additive property, $yz - xz < 0$ and $yz < xz$. Therefore, $xz > yz$.
37. Yes. Use Problem 36 to show that $|xy|^2 = |x|^2|y|^2$.
Calculator Problem.   **(g)** $(2.65)^2 = 7.0225$ so $x \leqslant (2.65)^2$ for all x in S **(h)** Answers may vary.   **(i)** lub $S = \sqrt{7}$

Section 1-3, page 7

1. 4   **3.** 8   **5.** 10   **7.** 9   **9.** -5 **11.** -7.1 **13-27.** The graph consists of the set of all points: **13.** to the right of 2/3.
15. except those between 0 and 1, not including the endpoints.
17. between 0 and 1.   **19.** except those between 0 and 1, not including the endpoints.   **21.** except those between -1 and 1.
23. -4 and 8.   **25.** except those between -4 and 8, not including the endpoints.   **27.** between -1 and 1.   **29.** If $|AC| = |BD|$, then $|c - a| = |d - b|$. Hence $c - a = d - b$ or $c - a = -(d - b)$. Therefore, $d = b + (c - a)$ or $d = b - (c - a)$.
31. Since $|10 - 6| = |14 - 10|$, C is equidistant from A and B.
33. 7 or -11 **35.** If $|x - a| < 3$, then $x - a < 3$ or $-(x - a) < 3$. $-(x - a) < 3 \rightarrow x - a > -3$. Hence, $-3 < x - a < 3$. Adding a we have $a - 3 < x < a + 3$.   **37.** Since the result of Problem 36 holds for all real numbers x, y, and z, then it must hold for the case of $z = 0$ and $y = -y$. Making these substitutions gives the desired result, $|x + y| \leqslant |x| + |y|$.
Calculator Problem.   **(a)** $n = 1, x = 2; n = 2, x = 2.25; n = 3$, $x = 2.3703704; n = 4, x = 2.4414063; n = 5, x = 2.48832; n = 6$, $x = 2.5216264; n = 7, x = 2.5464997; n = 8, x = 2.5657845$; $n = 9, x = 2.5811748; n = 10, x = 2.5937425; n = 10^2, x = $ $2.7048138; n = 10^3, x = 2.7169236; n = 10^4, x = 2.7181459$
(b) 2.719 (Answers may vary.)

Section 1-4, page 10

13. II   **15.** III   **17.** II   **19.** $(-2, 0)$ **21.** x-coordinate is zero, y-coordinate is negative.   **23.** x-coordinate is -2. A line parallel to the y-axis and two units to the left of the y-axis. The y-axis. A line parallel to the y-axis and π units to the right of the

y-axis.   **25.** Quadrant I consists of all points of the plane whose coordinates (x, y) are such that $x > 0$ and $y > 0$. Quadrant II: $x < 0$ and $y > 0$. Quadrant III: $x < 0$ and $y < 0$. Quadrant IV: $x > 0$ and $y < 0$.   **27.** The distance between the points is the absolute value of the difference of their second coordinates, $|y_2 - y_1|$.   **29.** All the points in the plane except those on the y-axis.   **31.** The graph is the set of points in the exterior of the square with vertices $(1, 1)$, $(-1, 1)$, $(-1, -1)$, and $(1, -1)$. The second graph consists of the points in the interior of this square.
Calculator Problem.   355/113

Section 1-5, page 12

1. 5   **3.** 10   **5.** $\sqrt{2}$ **7.** 1   **9.** $\sqrt{a^2 + b^2}$ **11.** Use the converse of the Pythagorean Theorem.   **13.** $y = 1 \pm \sqrt{7}$
15. The point $(3, \sqrt{7})$ is 4 units from $(0, 0)$. Hence, by the definition of the circle, it is a point on the circle.   **17.** $|AB| = 2\sqrt{17}$ **19.** Distance $= \sqrt{(x_1 - x_1)^2 + (y_1 - y_2)^2} = \sqrt{(y_1 - y_2)^2} = |y_1 - y_2|$ **21.** Show that the triangle whose vertices are $(r, 0)$, $(-r, 0)$, and (x, y) is a right triangle. You will have shown that an angle inscribed in a semicircle is a right angle.
Calculator Problem. $\sqrt{40} + \sqrt{37} + \sqrt{41} \doteq 18.81$

CHAPTER 2

Section 2-2, page 19

1. Yes   **3.** Yes   **5.** No   **7.** No   **9.** The domain is the set of integers from -3 to 3 inclusive. The range is the set of integers 0 to 3 inclusive. The image of -2 is 2, and the image of 2 is 2.   **11-15.** Figures 11 and 15 are graphs of functions on X into Y with domain R. The graph of Figure 11 has range R. The graph of Figure 13 is not a function.   **17.** Yes. If t is the time of day and l is length, then for each value of t there is exactly one value for l.   **19.** $-1, 11, -16, -4$ **21.** A function on X into Y.   **23.** Not a function.   **25.** Let x be the number of ounces and k be the cost per ounce. Then $f(x) = k[1 + x]$, where $[\ ]$ denotes the greatest integer function. The domain is the set of positive real numbers. The range is the set of positive integers.   **27.** If x is the length of the edge of a cube, then $V = f(x) = x^3$.
Calculator Problem. $\sqrt{2} - \sqrt[4]{3} = 0.09813955 \ldots \ldots f(1) = 0$, $f(2) = 1, f(3) = 0, f(4) = 1, f(5) = 1, f(6) = 1, f(7) = 1$. The range of f is $\{0, 1\}$.

Section 2-3, page 23

1. 1   **3.** –11   **5.** –43   **7.** 4   **9.** 1   **11.** 1   **13.** 31
15. 1.75
17.

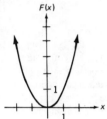

19.

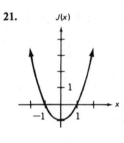

21.

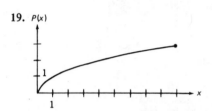

23. A is probably not a constant function because the students' ages are probably not all the same number of years.
25. The graphs are the same except at $x = 1$. $f(x)$ does not exist at $x = 1$.   **27.** $\mathrm{Id}(1 + \sqrt{2}) = 1 + \sqrt{2}$ **29.** A semicircle with center at $(0, 0)$ containing $(-2, 0)$, $(0, 2)$, $(2, 0)$.

31.

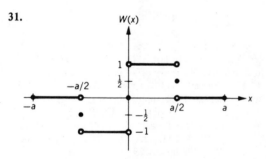

33. The graph is a parabola with its vertex at $(10^{10}, 1)$ and containing the points $(10^{10} + 1, 2)$ and $(10^{10} - 1, 2)$.
Calculator Problem.   Negative for (a), (b), (e), (f), (g). Positive for (c), (d), (h).   **(i)** $\sqrt[3]{2} = 1.259921$

Section 2-4, page 27

1.

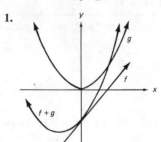

3.

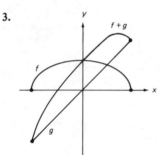

5.

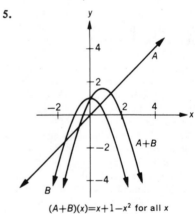

$(A+B)(x)=x+1-x^2$ for all x

7.

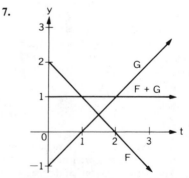

$(F + G)(t) = 1$ for all t, such that $t \geqslant 0$

9.

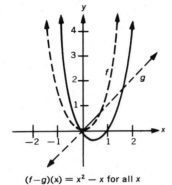

$(f-g)(x) = x^2 - x$ for all x

11.

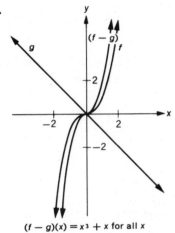

$(f-g)(x) = x^3 + x$ for all x

13.

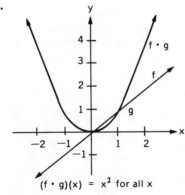

$(f \cdot g)(x) = x^2$ for all x

15.

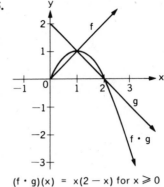

$(f \cdot g)(x) = x(2-x)$ for $x \geqslant 0$

17.

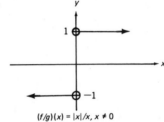

$(f/g)(x) = |x|/x, \; x \neq 0$

19. If f and g are functions with domains X_1 and X_2 respectively such that $X_1 \cap X_2 = X$ and X is not the empty set, then $f \cdot g$ is a function with domain X and $(f \cdot g)(x) = f(x) \cdot g(x)$, for $x \in X$.   **21.** Yes; each height in cm is a number, and the two numbers $f(x)$ and $g(x)$ can be added.

23.

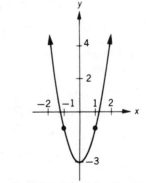

$(f \cdot g + h)(x) = 2x^2 - 3$ for all real x

Calculator Problem. $1^3 + 2^3 + 3^3 + \ldots + n^3 = \left[\frac{1}{2}n(n+1)\right]^2$

Section 2-5, page 30

1. −1   **3.** −3   **5.** 15   **7.** 197   **9.** $(f \circ g)(x) = x$ for all x
11. $(f \circ g)(x) = 1/(x^2 + 1)$ for all x **13.** $(f \circ g)(x) = x$ for $x \neq 0$
15. $(f \circ g)(x) = 17$ for all x **17.** $(f \circ g)(x) = x$ for $x \geq 2$
19. $p(q(x)) = x^2 − 2x + 2$, $q(p(x)) = x^2$ **21.** $f = G \circ F$ where,
for all x, $F(x) = 1 + x$ and $G(x) = 2x^2 − 3$.   **23.** $H = F \circ G$,
where $F(x) = \sqrt{x + 3}$ for $x \geq −3$, and $G(x) = \sqrt{x^2 + 2}$ for all x.
25. $(\text{Id} \circ f)(x) = \text{Id}(f(x)) = f(x); (f \circ \text{Id})(x) = f(\text{Id}(x)) = f(x)$.
27. $f(x) = (x − 1)/2$, for all x. Yes.
Calculator Problem.

$$x_1 = 1.618, x_2 = −0.618$$

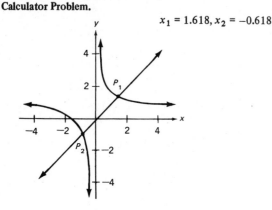

Section 2-6, page 34

1, 3. The graph of the inverse function is obtained by reflecting
the function in the line $y = x$.   **5.** No inverse.   **7.** 1 and 3; 4
and 6.   **9.** $[g^{-1} \circ g](1) = 1$ **11.** The function has an inverse
because no two ordered pairs have the same second element.
The domain of f^{-1} is $\{2, 3, 5, 7\}$ and the range is $\{1, 2, 3, 4\}$.
13. $f^{-1}(x) = x − 2$ **15.** $f^{-1}(x) = x/3$ **17.** $f^{-1}(x) =$
$(x − 1)/2$ **19.** $f^{-1}(x) = 3 − x$ **21.** $f^{-1}(x) = (1 − x)/x$, for
$x \neq 0$ **23.** $f^{-1}(x) = x^2 − 2$, for $x > 0$ **25.** For the given
domain, $−4 \leq x \leq 4$, the range is $0 \leq f(x) \leq 4$. The <u>inverse</u> function cannot have domain $−4 \leq f^{-1}(x) \leq 4$ since $\sqrt{16 − x^2}$ cannot be negative. If the domain of f were restricted to $0 \leq x \leq 4$,
then the function would have an inverse.
27.

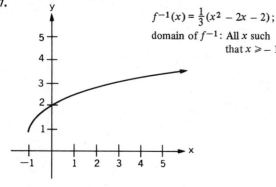

$f^{-1}(x) = \frac{1}{3}(x^2 − 2x − 2)$;

domain of f^{-1}: All x such
that $x \geq −1$

29. $f^{-1}(x) = \sqrt{(1/2)(\sqrt{1 + 4x} − 1)}$; domain of f^{-1}: All x
such that $x \geq 0$

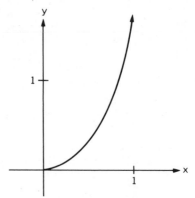

31. From the definition of "inverse," for each x in the domain
of f, $f(x) = r$ if and only if $f^{-1}(r) = x$, where r belongs to the
domain of f^{-1}. Hence, since f^{-1} is one-to-one, $f^{-1}(f(x)) =$
$f^{-1}(r) = x$ and $f(f^{-1}(r)) = f(x) = r$.
33.

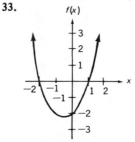

f would have an inverse if the

domain were $x \geq −\frac{1}{2}$ or $x \leq −\frac{1}{2}$

Calculator Problem. $f(4) = 53, f(5) = 61, f(6) = 71$. The
values are all prime numbers for $x < 41$. $f(41) = 1681 = 41^2$.

Section 2-7, page 37

1. Decreasing   **3.** Decreasing   **5-11.** The graph is the set of
all points between: **5.** 0 and 1, including 0.   **7.** −4 and 2, including −4 and 2.   **9.** 0 and 1/2, including 1/2.   **11.** π and 4,
including 4.   **13.** Bounded   **15.** Bounded below   **17.** Increasing
19. Bounded

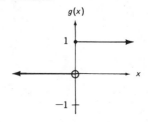

21. Bounded

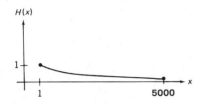

23. Bounded

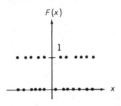

25. Suppose $x_1 < x_2$. Then, $f(x_1) - f(x_2) = 2(x_1 - x_2) < 0$.
27. Suppose $x_1 < x_2$. Then, $1/x_1 - 1/x_2 = (x_2 - x_1)/(x_1 x_2)$ > 0. **29.** Because g is increasing and $1 < 2$ we must have $g(1)$ $< g(2)$. Since $g(1) = 3$, then $g(2) > 3$ so that $g(2) \neq 0$.
31. Bounded below

Calculator Problem. $f(x) = (x^3 - x^2 + x - 1)/x^3$; $f(1) = 0$, $f(1.1) = 0.16604050$, $f(1.3) = 0.367319$, $f(1.5) = 0.4814814$, $f(1.7) = 0.5542438$, $f(1.9) = 0.6048986$, $f(2) = 0.625$.

Section 2-8, page 41

1. (a) Yes   (b) $<c, b]$ (c) $[a, c>$ (d) No. F is discontinuous at c.
3. Continuous

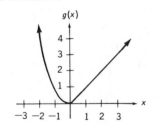

5. Continuous

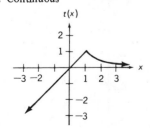

7. $f(-1) = -3, f(-2) = 3$; yes   **9.** Answers will vary.
11. Yes.

13. The zeros of f are $1/2$, $3/2$, and $-3/2$.

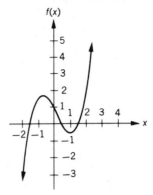

15. Since f is continuous on the closed interval $[1, 2]$, there exists at least one positive real number x in $< 1, 2 >$ such that $f(x) = 2$, by the Intermediate Value Theorem. This means that $\sqrt{2}$ exists.   **17.** Prove the contrapositive: If $\sqrt{x_1} \geq \sqrt{x_2}$, then $x_1 \geq x_2$. To show that f is unbounded suppose, to the contrary, that there is some positive number N such that for all x in the domain of f, $f(x) = \sqrt{x} < N$.
Calculator Problem. $f(0) = 1$. $f(1) = -1$. Hence $f(x) = 0$ in $< 0, 1 >$ for some x. $f(0.6) = 0.0496$. $f(0.7) = -0.2299$. Hence $x = 0.6$ to the nearest tenth.

CHAPTER 3

Section 3-2, page 47

1. $3x - 2$ **3.** $3x^2 - 2x - 6$ **5.** $7, 0, 2, -1, 0, -7$; Five, 7
7. 5; Zero, 5   **9.** a, b, c; Two, a (provided $a \neq 0$)   **11.** $a, 0$, b, c; Three, a (provided $a \neq 0$)   **13.** $5x^2 + 2x - 1$ **15.** $x^2 + 5$
17. $2x^4 - x^3 - x^2 + 3x + 5$ **19.** $(2)^2 + 2 - 6 = 0$; $(-3)^2 + (-3) - 6 = 0$ **21.** $p(-1) = -1 + 1 - 1 + 1 = 0$
23. $a = 2, b = -7/2, c = \sqrt{5}$ or $c = -\sqrt{5}$ **25.** $b = 1$
27. a, b, c **29.** c **31.** $r = 2, s = -3, t = 4$
Calculator Problem.

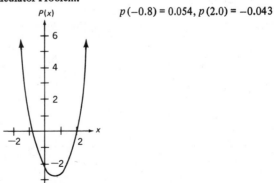

$p(-0.8) = 0.054, p(2.0) = -0.043$

Section 3-3, page 50

1. The graph is the graph of f (Section 2-4, Problem 9) translated upward one-half unit.   **3.** See the graph of f (Section 2-4, Problem 11).

5.

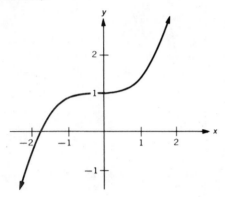

7.

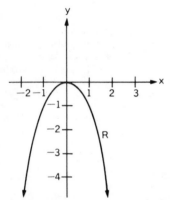

9. The graph is a line with intercepts $(0, 1)$ and $(2, 0)$.
11. The graph is the graph of f (Problem 5 of this section) translated downward two units.   **13.** The graph is the graph of f (Section 2-4, Problem 9) reflected in the x-axis, and translated to the left one-half unit and downward three-fourths units.
15. $f(-1) = f(0) = f(1) = 0$

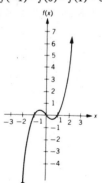

17. $g(1) = g(2) = g(3) = 0.$
The graph is similar to
Problem 15 translated to
the right two units.

19. $T(-2) = T(-1) =$
$T(1) = T(0) = T(2) = 0$

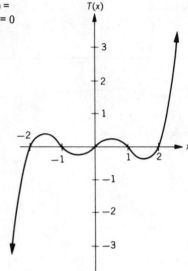

21.

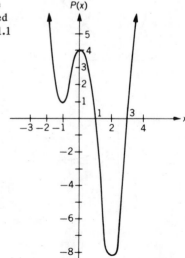

23. The graph of ax^n is the reflection in the x-axis of the graph of $-ax^n$. If $a > 0$ and n is odd, as x increases so does ax^n. If n is even, then ax^n increases and decreases, for increasing positive values and increasing negative values, respectively.

25. The zeros of the polynomial, estimated from the graph, are 1.1 and 2.9.

27.

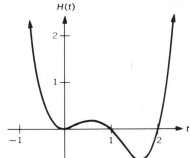

29.

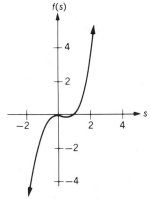

31.

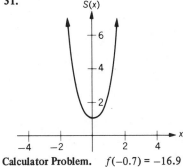

Calculator Problem. $f(-0.7) = -16.9$

33. The graph is the same as f (Section 2-4, Problem 10) translated two units to the right and four units upward. The minimum value of $f(x) = (x - 2)^2 + 4$ is 4 and the lowest point is $(2, 4)$.

Section 3-4, page 53

1. $Q(x) = 3x - 5, R = 0$ **3.** $Q(x) = 3x + 1, R = 0$ **5.** $Q(x) = (2/3)x^2 + x, R(x) = x + 1$ **7.** $Q(x) = x^2 + 3x + 2, R = 3$ **9.** $Q(x) = x^2 + 2x + 4, R = 0$ **11.** $Q(x) = (2/3)x^2 + (7/9)x - (7/27), R(x) = (34/27)x + 1$ **13.** $Q(y) = y^3 - y^2 + y - 1, R = -15$ **15.** $Q(y) = y^2 - y, R(y) = y - 16$ **17.** $Q(x) = x^2 - 6x - 4, R(x) = -9x - 9$ **19.** $Q(z) = z^2 + z + 1, R = 0$ **21.** $Q(x) = ax + b, R = 0$ **23.** Yes **25.** $k = -13$ **27.** There are various answers. For example, if $P(x) = x^2 + 2x + 5, D(x) = x + 1, Q(x) = x, R(x) = x + 5$ and $S(x) = 4$, then $P = Q \cdot D + R$ and $P = D \cdot D + S$.

Calculator Problem. $(26.51988 - 13.68488)/3.98688 = 6.6517879$

Section 3-5, page 55

1. $Q(x) = x^2 + 1, R = 0$ **3.** $Q(x) = x^2 + 4x - 2, R = 6$ **5.** $Q(x) = x^4 - x^3 - x^2 - 5x - 5, R = -3$ **7.** $Q(x) = 4x^3 + 2x^2 + 3x + 3/2, R = -1/4$ **9.** $Q(x) = 3x^3 - 2x^2 - 3x + 2, R = 0$ **11.** $Q(x) = x^2 + 6x + 16, R = 50$ **13.** $Q(x) = 2x - 6, R = 3$ **15.** $Q(x) = x^4 + x^2 + 1, R = 0$ **17.** $Q(x) = -x^4 + 13x^3 - 78x^2 + 470x - 2820, R = 16,915$ **19.** $Q(x) = 7x^2 - 7x + 7, R = 0$ **21.** $t = -7$ **23.** $Q(x) = x^2 + (1/2)x - (1/4), R = 0$

Calculator Problem. $Q(x) = 1.8x^2 - 2.64x - 6.348, R = 0$

Section 3-6, page 58

1. 13 **3.** 0 **5.** 1121 **7.** 86 **9.** $P(-4) = 0$, yes
11. $P(2) = 0$, yes **13.** $(z - 2)$ is a factor of $P(z) = z^5 - 32$ because $P(2) = 0$. **15. (a)** 0 **(b)** -20 **(c)** 0 **(d)** -8
(e) 0 **(f)** 120 **(g)** $(x - 1), (x - 3), (x + 2)$
17. (a) $(x - 1), (x - 2), (x + 3)$ **(b)** $(x^2 - 3x + 2)$ or $(x^2 + 2x - 3)$ or $(x^2 + x - 6)$ **(c)** $P(x) = 5x^3 - 35x + 30$
19. $x + 2, x - 1$, and $x - 4$ are approximations to the factors of P.

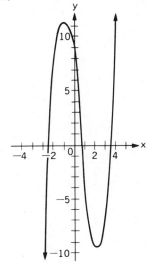

21. (a) $x = (-1 \pm \sqrt{5})/2$ **(b)** $(-1 - \sqrt{5})/2, (-1 + \sqrt{5})/2$
(c) $(x + (1 - \sqrt{5})/2)(x + (1 + \sqrt{5})/2)$ **23.** $(x - a)$ is a factor of $x^4 + x^2 + 1$ if and only if $a^4 + a^2 + 1 = 0$. But, for a real, $a^4 + a^2 + 1 \neq 0$. **25. (a)** $\pm 1, \pm 1/2, \pm 1/3, \pm 1/6$ **(b)** $-1/2, 1/3$ **27.** $2, -3$

Calculator Problem.

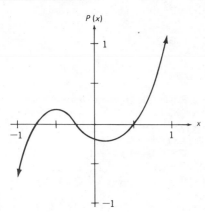

3.

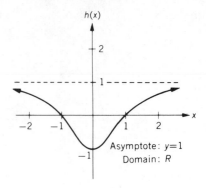

Asymptote: $y=1$
Domain: R

5.

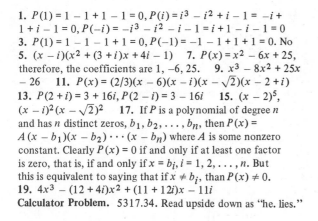

Asymptotes:
$y=0, x=\pm 1$
Domain: all real x,
such that $x \neq \pm 1$

Section 3-7, page 61

1. $P(1) = 1 - 1 + 1 - 1 = 0, P(i) = i^3 - i^2 + i - 1 = -i +$
$1 + i - 1 = 0, P(-i) = -i^3 - i^2 - i - 1 = i + 1 - i - 1 = 0$
3. $P(1) = 1 - 1 - 1 + 1 = 0, P(-1) = -1 - 1 + 1 + 1 = 0.$ No
5. $(x - i)(x^2 + (3 + i)x + 4i - 1)$ **7.** $P(x) = x^2 - 6x + 25,$
therefore, the coefficients are 1, -6, 25.   **9.** $x^3 - 8x^2 + 25x$
$- 26$ **11.** $P(x) = (2/3)(x - 6)(x - i)(x - \sqrt{2})(x - 2 + i)$
13. $P(2 + i) = 3 + 16i, P(2 - i) = 3 - 16i$ **15.** $(x - 2)^5,$
$(x - i)^2(x - \sqrt{2})^2$ **17.** If P is a polynomial of degree n
and has n distinct zeros, $b_1, b_2, \ldots, b_n$, then $P(x) =$
$A(x - b_1)(x - b_2) \cdots (x - b_n)$ where A is some nonzero
constant. Clearly $P(x) = 0$ if and only if at least one factor
is zero, that is, if and only if $x = b_i, i = 1, 2, \ldots, n$. But
this is equivalent to saying that if $x \neq b_i$, than $P(x) \neq 0$.
19. $4x^3 - (12 + 4i)x^2 + (11 + 12i)x - 11i$
Calculator Problem.   5317.34. Read upside down as "he. lies."

7.

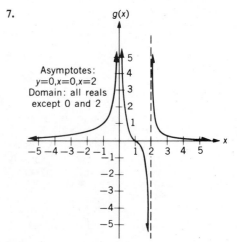

Asymptotes:
$y=0, x=0, x=2$
Domain: all reals
except 0 and 2

Section 3-8, page 66

1.

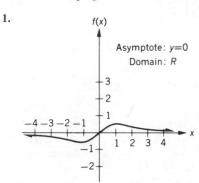

Asymptote: $y=0$
Domain: R

9.

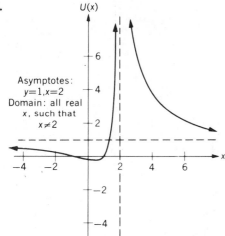
U(x)

Asymptotes:
$y=1, x=2$
Domain: all real
x, such that
$x \neq 2$

3.

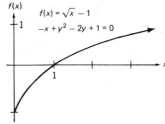
f(x)

$f(x) = \sqrt{x} - 1$
$-x + y^2 - 2y + 1 = 0$

5.

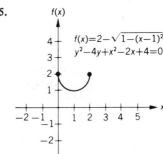
f(x)

$f(x) = 2 - \sqrt{1 - (x-1)^2}$
$y^2 - 4y + x^2 - 2x + 4 = 0$

11. 1 is an odd function. 2-6 are even functions. 7-10 are neither odd nor even. **13.** The lines $y = x$ and $x = 0$ are asymptotes of t. **15.** No. $x^2 - 1$ and $x + 1$ have the common factor $x + 1$, so $(x^2 - 1)/(x + 1) = x - 1$ for $x \neq -1$.
17. $f(x) = x^{10}/(x^{12} + 17) = (1/x^2)/[1 + (17/x^{12})]$. As $x \to \pm\infty$ $f(x) \to 0/1 = 0$; hence f has a horizontal asymptote, $y = 0$.
19. If F is a rational function, then by definition there are two polynomials P_0 and P_1 with no common nonconstant factors, such that $F(x) = -P_1(x)/P_0(x)$, for all x for which $P_0(x) \neq 0$. Thus, $P_0(x)F(x) + P_1(x) = 0$.
Calculator Problem.

$-0.5, 0.5$

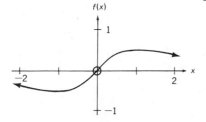
f(x)

7.

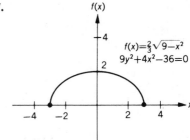
f(x)

$f(x) = \frac{2}{3}\sqrt{9 - x^2}$
$9y^2 + 4x^2 - 36 = 0$

Section 3-9, page 69

1.

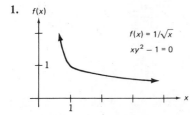
f(x)

$f(x) = 1/\sqrt{x}$
$xy^2 - 1 = 0$

9.

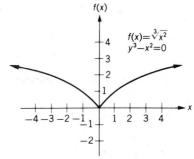
f(x)

$f(x) = \sqrt[3]{x^2}$
$y^3 - x^2 = 0$

11. $y = (1 + \sqrt{x})/2$ or $y = (1 - \sqrt{x})/2$

559

13. $y = \sqrt[3]{1/x^2}$

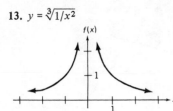

Calculator Problem. $y^3 + 3xy^2 + 3x^2y + x^3 - x = 0$,
Maximum at $x \doteq 0.2$, Minimum at $x \doteq -0.2$

15. By Definition 3-7
17. The function f given
by $f(x) = \sqrt[4]{x}$ satisfies
$y^4 - x = 0$.

29.

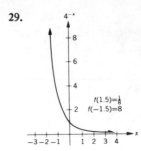

$f(1.5)=\frac{1}{8}$
$f(-1.5)=8$

31. The graph is similar to that
in Problem 27 reflected in the
y-axis, and the second coordinate multiplied by 3. $f(1.5) =$
8.5, $f(-1.5) = 1.1$.
33. (a) 2.0   (b) 7.94
(c) 0.13   (d) 0.50   (e) 1.78
(f) 0.56   (g) 5.62   (h) 0.18
(i) 1.26   (j) 0.79   (k) 0.3
(l) −0.3   (m) 0.48
(n) −0.48   (o) 0.7
(p) −0.7   (q) 0.95
(r) −0.95   (s) 0.51
(t) −0.2

CHAPTER 4

Section 4-2, page 76

1. x^{-3} **3.** y^{-3} **5.** 1   **7.** $3x^{-5}y^3$ **9.** 2^6 **11.** $2x^{-3}y^2$
13. $2^{-5}x^{-10}$ **15.** x^3y^{-3} **17.** 1   **19.** $x^4y^6z^{-4}$ **21.** 1/3
23. 64   **25.** 4   **27.** 9   **29.** 1/128   **31.** 1/32
33. −1/125   **35.** $15/x^3$ **37.** $1/(4y^{1/6})$ **39.** $1/y^{1/2}$
41. $2/(3x^2y)$ **43.** $1/(a^2|b|)$ **45.** $(81/4)x^4y^2$ **47.** 8
49. 1/16   **51.** −3   **53.** −2   **55.** −1/2   **57.** 2/3   **59.** 4
61. 2   **63.** 10   **65.** 16   **67.** 9/4   **69.** 4   **71.** 1/16
73. $x = 2$ and $y = 4$ or $x = 4$ and $y = 2$ **75.** Between 5 and 6
Calculator Problem. $(1/8)^{-3/4} = 8^{3/4}$ and $(1/9)^{-3/4} = 9^{3/4}$, so
$8^{3/4} < x < 9^{3/4}$ and $x = 5$.

Section 4-3, page 79

1. $3^{2.5}$ **3.** $5^{3.7}$ **5.** 2^5 **7.** a^2 **9.** $3^{-4.24}$ **11.** a^{x+y+s}
13. $2^{-0.4}$ **15.** $10^{2.32}$ **17.** 0   **19.** −3   **21.** 3   **23.** 0
25.

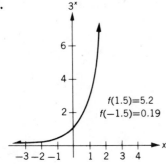

$f(1.5)=5.2$
$f(-1.5)=0.19$

27.

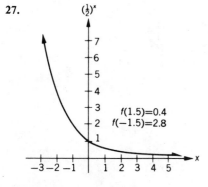

$f(1.5)=0.4$
$f(-1.5)=2.8$

35.

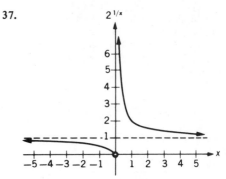

37.

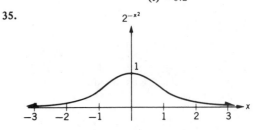

39, 40.

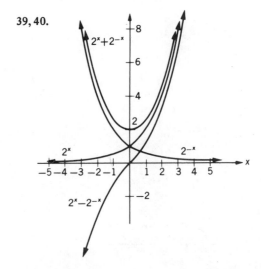

41. The range of f is the set of negative real numbers. f is bounded above by 0 and has the horizontal asymptote, $y = 0$.

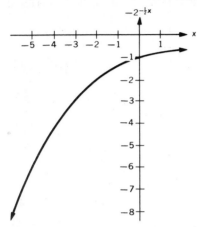

43. $f(x_1 - x_2) = a^{x_1 - x_2} = a^{x_1}/a^{x_2} = f(x_1)/f(x_2)$.
45. Yes. $f = g$ because for each x, $f(x) = 2^{-x} = (1/2)^x = g(x)$.
Calculator Problem. If $x = 0.879$, $3^x = 2.6265736$. If $x = 1.560$, $x^x = 2.0011257$.

Section 4-4, page 82

1. $T = 25$ **3.** $T = 1000$ **5.** 4.096×10^6; 2.815×10^{17} (approximately); 1.329×10^{39} (approximately)   **7.** 17,000 years
9. 279 days   **11.** $N = N_0 \cdot 2^{7/4}$, where N_0 is the number of bacteria present when $t = 0$.   **13.** $A = A_0 2^{-6.29} \times 10^{-4}t$
Calculator Problem. (a) In 1986 it will cost \$1.97   (b) \$9.65

Section 4-5, page 84

1. $\log_2 32 = 5$ **3.** $\log_8 2 = 1/3$ **5.** $\log_{10} 0.01 = -2$
7. $\log_5 1 = 0$ **9.** $\log_{10} 3.162 = 1/2$ **11.** $\log_8 0.125 = -1$
13. $\log_{10} y = x$ **15.** $\log_t v = u$ **17.** $a^0 = 1$ **19.** $10^2 = 100$
21. $10^{0.3010} = 2$ **23.** $10^{-0.301} = 1/2$ **25.** $4^3 = 64$
27. $3/2$ **29.** 0   **31.** -3
33.

N	1/8	1/4	1/2	1	2	4	8
$\log_2 N$	-3	-2	-1	0	1	2	3

35. The logarithm function is continuous and increasing on the half-open interval [1, 10 >. Then $\log_{10} 1 = 0$ and $\log_{10} 10 = 1$. By the definition of an increasing function, if $1 \leqslant x < 10$, then $0 \leqslant \log_{10} x < 1$.   **37.** 100   **39.** 0.1
Calculator Problem. $x = 1.9022706$

Section 4-6, page 87

1. Reflect the graph $f(x) = 10^x$ in the line $y = x$.   **3.** (a) 1.8
(b) 3.2   (c) 5.6   (d) 10   (e) 7.9   (f) 2.5   **5.** 4.893
7. 0.571   **9.** 0.738   **11.** 0.940   **13.** $\log_a 100 = \log_a 10^2$
$= 2 \log_a 10$ **15.** $\log 23.6 = \log 10 + \log 2.36 = 1 + \log 2.36$
17. $\log 0.0236 = \log 0.01 + \log 2.36 = -2 + \log 2.36$
19. $\log_a 1 \cdot x = \log_a 1 + \log_a x = \log_a x$ **21-23.** Reflect the graphs in the line $y = x$.   **21.** 3^x (Section 4-3, Problem 25)
23. 2^{-x} (Section 4-3, Problem 39)

25. $\log_2 \sqrt{x}$

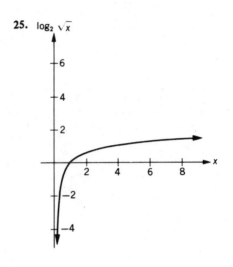

27.

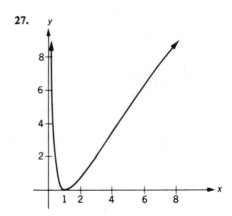

29. Let $\log_a x = u$ so that $a^u = x$. $x^k = (a^u)^k = a^{uk}$, by the Laws of Exponents. Then, by the definition of logarithms, $\log_a x^k = uk = k \cdot \log_a x$.   **31.** Applying Theorem 4-4(a)

twice, it follows that, $\log_a xyz = \log_a xy + \log_a z = \log_a x + \log_a y + \log_a z$.   **33.** $\log_5 9 = (\log 9)(\log_5 10) = \log 9/\log 5 = (0.9542)/(0.6990) = 1.3651$ **35.** $\log_a 1/N = \log_a 1 - \log_a N = 0 - \log_a N = -\log_a N$ **37.** 1   **39.** 3   **41.** Let $g(x) = x^2 + 1, h(x) = 3^x; h(g(x)) = f(x) = 3^{x^2+1}$.   **43.** Let $f(x) = 2^x$ and $g(x) = x^2 + 3x - 3$. Then $g(f(x)) = H(x) = 2^{2x} + 3 \cdot 2^x - 3$.   **45.** Let $g(x) = 10^x$ and $f(x) = 10^x$. Then $f(g(x)) = E(x) = 10^{10^x}$

Calculator Problem.   **(a)** $\log 10 = 1$, $\log (\log 10) = 0$, but $\log (\log (\log 10))$ has no meaning since there is no x such that $10^x = 0$. So the calculator shows "Error."

(b) $\log 2^{\log 2^{\log 2}} = 0.4332587, ((\log 2)^{\log 2})^{\log 2} = 0.8969166$

21.

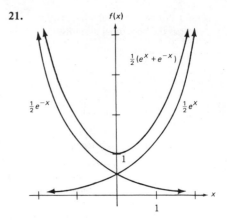

Section 4-7, page 90

1. 3.322   **3.** 3 or −2   **5.** ±1.372   **7.** −6   **9.** 400
11. 16.610   **13.** 1.386   **15.** $x = 7$ **17.** $x = 2.477$ and $y = -0.523$ **19.** About 45°; for t large, the temperature is very near 40°, and for t near zero, the temperature is near 100°.
Calculator Problem.   1980: $\$1.2753 \times 10^{48}$; 1981: $\$1.3518 \times 10^{48}$; 1982: $\$1.4329 \times 10^{48}$; 1983: $\$1.5189 \times 10^{48}$; 1984: $\$1.61 \times 10^{48}$; 1985: $\$1.7066 \times 10^{48}$

23.

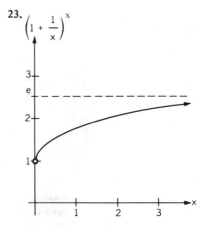

Calculator Problem.   **(a)** 2.7048138   **(b)** 2.7169236
(c) 2.7182818 e is the least upper bound of $f(x)$.

Section 4-8, page 92

1. $\ln 1 = 0$ **3.** $\ln 0.3679 = -1$ **5.** $\ln 3.320 = 1.2$
7. $e^{0.6931} = 2$ **9.** $e^{-0.6931} = 0.5$ **11.** $e^{-2} = 0.1353$
13.

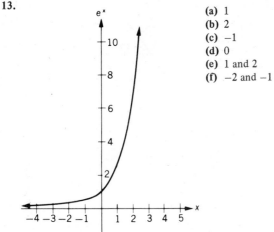

(a) 1
(b) 2
(c) −1
(d) 0
(e) 1 and 2
(f) −2 and −1

15. e **17.** 3   **19.** 1/2

CHAPTER 5

Section 5-2, page 99

1. $5\pi/6$ **3.** $\pi/6$ **5.** $\pi/3$ **7.** $4\pi/9$ **9.** $3\pi/4$ **11.** $\pi/8$
13. 100   **15.** 105   **17.** $216/\pi$ or $\doteq 68.8$ **19.** 150
21. 70   **23.** 54   **25.** $r = 4$ **27.** 16 units   **29.** $\pi/4$
31. $70\pi/3$ **33.** Use a degree-protractor as a guide. Convert degrees to radians.
Calculator Problem.   1,390,350 km

Section 5-3, page 102

1. 4π **3.** $-\pi$ **5.** 1   **7.** $\pi/2$ **9.** $(4k + 1)\pi/2, k$ an integer
Calculator Problem.   All paths are equal! The length is $4\pi = 12.566371 \ldots \ldots$

Section 5-4, page 105

1. π **3.** π **5.** $\pi/6$ **7.** $2\pi/3$ **9.** $5\pi/3$ **11.** $\pi/3$
13.

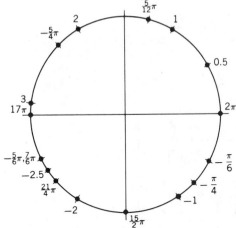

15. $W(-5\pi/4) = W(-5\pi/4 + 2\pi) = W(3\pi/4)$, $W(11\pi/4) =$
$W(11\pi/4 - 2\pi) = W(3\pi/4)$ **17.** $(1/2, \sqrt{3}/2)$ **19.** If $W(\theta) =$
P and $P \neq (1, 0)$ and $P \neq (-1, 0)$, then $W(-\theta) = P'$ where P' is
on the opposite side of the x-axis from P and the x-axis is the
perpendicular bisector of $\overline{PP'}$. If $W(\theta) = P = (1, 0)$, then $W(-\theta)$
$= P' = (-1, 0)$. **21.** *Hint:* Use part (d) of Definition 5-3.
Calculator Problem. Quadrant IV.

Section 5-5, page 107

1. 0 **3.** 1 **5.** $\sqrt{2}/2$ **7.** 0 **9.** 0 **11.** 0 **13.** $\sqrt{2}/2$
15. $1/2$ **17.** $\sqrt{3}/2$ **19.** $1/2$ **21.** $\sqrt{3}/2$ **23.** -1
25. If P lies on a circle of radius r, then the coordinates of P are,
(a) $(r\sqrt{2}/2, r\sqrt{2}/2) = (r \cos \pi/4, r \sin \pi/4)$. **(b)** $(0, r) =$
$(r \cos \pi/2, r \sin \pi/2)$. **(c)** $(r\sqrt{3}/2, r/2) = (r \cos \pi/6, r \sin \pi/6)$.
27. As θ increases from 0 to $\pi/2$, $\sin \theta$ increases from 0 to 1
while $\cos \theta$ decreases from 1 to 0. **29.** $\cos \theta = 0.8$ **31.** Let
$P = W(\theta)$ and let R be the foot of the perpendicular from P to
the x-axis. Let Q be the point such that $Q = W(\pi/2 - \theta)$ and let
S be the foot of the perpendicular from Q to the x-axis. $\triangle OPR$
$\cong \triangle QOS$, where O represents the origin. Therefore, $\overline{OS} \cong \overline{PR}$ and
$\overline{QS} \cong \overline{OR}$. Then if the coordinates of P are (x, y), the coordinates
of Q are (y, x) so that $x = \cos \theta = \sin (\pi/2 - \theta)$. **33.** See Fig.
22 on p. 114.

35.

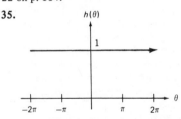

Calculator Problem. $\sin \theta = \pm 0.25$, $\cos \theta = \pm 0.9682458$

Section 5-6, page 110

1. $\tan \theta = 4/3$, $\csc \theta = 5/4$, $\sec \theta = 5/3$, $\cot \theta = 3/4$ **3.** $\tan \theta$
$= 2/3$, $\csc \theta = -\sqrt{13}/2$, $\sec \theta = -\sqrt{13}/3$, $\cot \theta = 3/2$
5. (a) All six functions **(b)** Sine and cosecant
(c) Tangent and cotangent **(d)** Cosine and secant

	θ	sin	cos	tan	cot	sec	csc
7.	0.5	0.48	0.88	0.55	1.8	1.1	2.1
9.	-0.1	-0.1	0.99	-0.1	-10	1.01	-10
11.	2	0.91	-0.41	-2.2	-0.45	-2.4	1.1
13.	20	0.92	0.40	2.3	0.44	2.5	1.09

15. θ is approximately $1/4 + 2\pi k$, where k is an integer, or
about $14° + k \cdot 360°$. **17.** $\cos \theta = x = -2/3$, $\sec \theta = 1/x = -3/2$
19. $\sin \theta = 0.97$, $\tan \theta = -3.9$, $\cot \theta = -0.26$, $\sec \theta = -4$,
$\csc \theta = 1.03$ **21.** $\cot \theta$ **23.** $\sec \theta$
Calculator Problem. **(a)** $\cot 2 = -0.45765755$, $\sec 2 =$
-2.402998, $\csc 2 = 1.0997502$ **(c)** Error **(d)** The calculator
will display a number $>37,000,000$.

Section 5-7, page 112

1. $-1/2$ **3.** 0 **5.** Undefined **7.** $\sqrt{2}/2$ **9.** $1/2$ **11.** 1
13. $-1/2$ **15.** $-\sqrt{3}/2$ **17.** $-1/2$ **19.** -1 **21.** 0
23. $-\sqrt{3}$ **25.** 0 **27.** $\sqrt{3}$ **29.** $\pi/6, 5\pi/6$ **31.** $\pi/2$
33. $3\pi/2$ **35.** $5\pi/6, 7\pi/6$ **37.** $0, \pi$ **39.** $\pi/4, 5\pi/4$
41. $7\pi/6, 11\pi/6$ **43.** $\pi/4, 3\pi/4$ **45.** $\pi/2, 3\pi/2$ **47.** $\pi/2,$
$3\pi/2$ **49.** $\pi/4, 5\pi/4$ **51.** $0, \pi$ **53.** $\pi/3, 5\pi/3$ **55.** $\pi/6,$
$11\pi/6$ **57.** $2\pi/3, 4\pi/3$ **59.** $2\pi/3, 5\pi/3$ **61.** $3\pi/4, 7\pi/4$
63. θ does not exist **65.** $\pi/4, 7\pi/4$ **67.** $5\pi/6, 7\pi/6$
69. $2\pi/3, 4\pi/3$ **71.** $\pi/4, 3\pi/4$ **73.** $0, \pi$ **75.** The standard
map W is such that if θ is any real number, $W(\theta) = W(\theta + 2\pi n)$
where n is an integer. If $W(\theta) = P(x, y)$, then $x = \cos \theta$ by definition of cosine and $\cos \theta = \cos (\theta + 2\pi n)$. **77.** If k is an odd
integer, $W(k\pi - \pi/4) = W(3\pi/4)$. Therefore, $\tan (k\pi - \pi/4) =$
$\tan 3\pi/4 = -1$.
Calculator Problem. 7200 days or about 19.7 years

Section 5-8, page 115

1. Increasing between 0 and $\pi/2$ and between $3\pi/2$ and 2π;
decreasing between $\pi/2$ and $3\pi/2$. **3.** Increasing
5. $[-\infty, \infty]$

7.

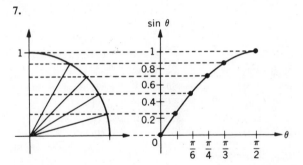

9. Domain: all real numbers except integral multiples of π
Range: all real numbers

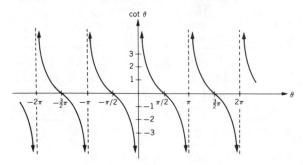

11. The domain of the cosecant is all real numbers except integral multiples of π. No real number between -1 and 1 is in the range of the cosecant, but all other real numbers are in the range.

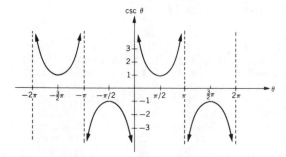

13. In the open interval $< -\pi/2, \pi/2 >$, the tangent is continuous and increasing and assumes every real number as a value in this interval. Thus if y is any real number, there must be some real number x in the interval such that $y = \tan x$. The uniqueness of x is assured by the fact that tangent is increasing in the interval.   **15.** The cosine function is continuous and decreasing in the interval, $[0, \pi]$, and assumes as values all real numbers in $[-1, 1]$. If y is a real number such that $-1 \leqslant y \leqslant 1$, there exists a unique real x in $[0, \pi]$ such that $y = \cos x$.
Calculator Problem. $\sin \theta = 2/\sqrt{5} \doteq 0.89442719$, $\cos \theta = 1/\sqrt{5} \doteq 0.4472136$

Section 5-9, page 118

Each answer states a graph which has similar shape, the interval over which the function will have a full cycle of values, and the amplitude or vertical asymptote.

1. $\sin x$, $[0, 2\pi/3]$, 1 **3.** $\sin x$, $[0, 2\pi/3]$, 2 **5.** $\cos x$, $[0, 4\pi]$, $1/2$ **7.** $\sin x$, $[0, 1]$, $\sqrt{2}$ **9.** $\sin x$, $[0, 4]$, 1
11. $\tan x$, $[0, 2]$, asymptote at 1 **13.** $\sec x$, $[0, 6\pi]$, asymptotes at $3\pi/2$, $9\pi/2$

15.

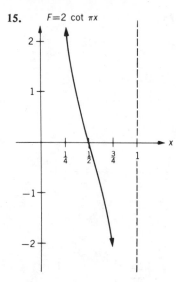

$F = 2 \cot \pi x$

17. $\tan x$, $[0, 3\pi]$, asymptote at $3\pi/2$
19. $\sec x$, $[0, 6]$, asymptotes at $3/2$, $9/2$
21. $\csc x$, $[0, 4]$, asymptotes at 0, 4
23. $y = 3 \sin 2x$
25. $y = 5 \cos (x/3)$
27. $y = (1/2) \cos (x/5)$
29. $y = \sqrt{5} \sin \pi x$

Calculator Problem. As x approaches 0, $f(x)$ is very close to 1. If $f(0)$ were defined to be 1, then the function would be continuous in $[\pi, -\pi]$.

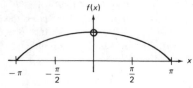

Section 5-10, page 120

1. Periodic. The period is 4.   **3.** Not periodic.   **5.** Not periodic.   **7.** π **9.** $\pi/5$ **11.** 1   **13.** *Hint:* $f(x + 2p) = f((x + p) + p)$ **15.** *Hint:* For θ any real number, it follows from the definition of the standard map W that if $W(\theta) = P(x, y)$, then $W(\theta + \pi) = Q(-x, -y)$; that is Q is diametrically opposite P on the unit circle. Use the definition of the tangent function to show that π is a period of the tangent. You must also show that π is the smallest positive period. The cotangent may be shown to have π as its period by using the relation $\cot \theta = 1/\tan \theta$.   **17.** If f is a periodic function with period p, then $f(x) = f(x + p)$ for every number x in the domain of f. Therefore, $(1/f)(x) = 1/f(x) = 1/f(x + p) = (1/f)(x + p)$ for every real number x such that $f(x) \neq 0$. (Note that if $f(x) \neq 0$ then $f(x + p) \neq 0$.) Thus $1/f$ is periodic with period p.
19. (a) The graph consists of all those points on the line $y = 1$ for which the first coordinate is rational, together with the points on the line $y = -1$ for which the first coordinate is irrational.   **(b)** *Hint:* Use definition of periodic function.
(c) *Hint:* Use indirect proof and the definition of periodic function.   **(d)** There is no smallest positive rational number.
Calculator Problem. $x = 0.7390851$

564

Section 5-11, page 124

1. Graph: $\sqrt{2} \sin (x + \pi/4)$

3.

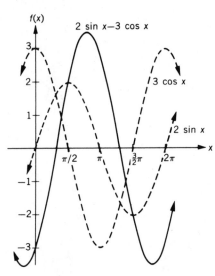

5. 2; 2; (1/4, 0)   **7.** 4π; 4; (4, 0)   **9.** 1; $\sqrt{2}$ **11.** 4π; 3
13. 2000; 10   **15.** $\pi/3$; 3/2   **17.** 1/60; 110; $(-1/180, 0)$
19. 6π; 2; (1, 2)
21.

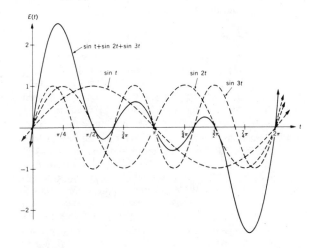

23. Let f and g be periodic functions both with period p. Then by definition of periodic functions, $f(x) = f(x + p)$ and $g(x) = g(x + p)$. By the definition of addition of functions, $(f + g)(x) = f(x) + g(x)$. Therefore, $(f + g)(x) = f(x + p) + g(x + p) = (f + g)(x + p)$. Hence $f + g$ is periodic.

Calculator Problem.

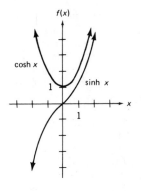

CHAPTER 6

Section 6-2, page 133

1. $-\sin (\pi/4)$ **3.** $-\tan (\pi/4)$ **5.** $-\sin (\pi/3)$ **7.** $\tan (\pi/3)$
9. $\csc (\pi/3)$ **11.** $\cot (\pi/3)$ **13.** $\csc (\pi/3)$ **15.** $\sec (\pi/3)$
17. $\cot (\pi/4)$ **19.** $\tan (\pi/4)$ **21.** $\cos (\pi/2)$
23. $\cos 11\pi/6 = \sqrt{3}/2$; $\cos \pi/6 = \sqrt{3}/2$; $\cos 5\pi/6 = -\sqrt{3}/2$
25-31. Problems 25, 27, and 29 are positive.   **33.** $\sin \theta = 2\sqrt{2}/3$; $\cos \theta = 1/3$; $\tan \theta = 2\sqrt{2}$ **35.** $\sin \theta = -2/\sqrt{5}$; $\cos \theta = -1/\sqrt{5}$; $\tan \theta = 2$
Calculator Problem. $\sin \theta = (-1 + \sqrt{5})/2$, $\theta \doteq 0.666$

Section 6-3, page 135

1. 0.3955   **3.** 0.8421   **5.** 0.9945   **7.** 1.5282   **9.** 0.2470
11. 0.8471   **13.** 12.2°   **15.** 42.0°   **17.** 66.4°   **19.** 80.3°
21. 49.1°   **23.** 49.2°   **25.** 0.8290   **27.** 0.2924
29. -0.4019 **31.** -0.2773 **33.** -0.6858 **35.** 60.4°
37. 45.9°   **39.** 23.5°   **41.** $\sin (\pi - 2)$ **43.** $-\cot (\pi - 2.5)$
45. $-\cos (\pi - 2.9)$ **47.** $-\cot (\pi - 1.83)$
Calculator Problem.   **(a)** 0.54768086   **(b)** 0.57930093
(c) 0.37829518   **(d)** 0.44400975   **(e)** 11.149832
(f) 0.32754773

Section 6-4, page 137

1. 23.8 cm   **3.** 81.6 cm   **5.** 46.0°   **7.** 2.3°   **9.** 190.5 m
11. 1.11 cm   **13.** 76°   **15.** 35.8 m
Calculator Problem. $l = w((1 + \sqrt{5})/2)$, $l/w = (1 + \sqrt{5})/2$; 58.282525°

Section 6-5, page 142

1. $m(\angle B) = 11.8°, m(\angle C) = 150.7°, c = 100.9$ 3. $m(\angle C) = 51.9°, a = 39.6, b = 34.6$ 5. $m(\angle A) = 30.2°, m(\angle B) = 24.2°, b = 10.4$ 7. $b = 22.3, m(\angle A) = 44.3°, m(\angle C) = 75.7°$ 9. $m(\angle A) = 36.9°, m(\angle B) = m(\angle A) = 36.9°, m(\angle C) = 106.2°$ 11. one solution 13. one solution 15. two solutions 17. 3.9 km 19. 7.2 cm 21. Suppose $\triangle ABC$ is a right triangle and $\angle C$ is the right angle. Then, by the Law of Cosines, $c^2 = a^2 + b^2 - 2ab \cos C$. Since $\cos C = 0, c^2 = a^2 + b^2$. 23. Let $\triangle ABC$ be any triangle. Let h be the length of the altitude of the triangle from vertex A. The area of $\triangle ABC = (1/2)ah$. But $h = b \sin C$, so that the area of $\triangle ABC$ is equal to $(1/2)ab \sin C$. 25. Using the Law of Cosines, we have $|AB|^2 = r^2 + r^2 - 2r^2 \cos \theta = r^2[2(1 - \cos \theta)], |AB| = r\sqrt{2(1 - \cos \theta)}$. If $\angle AOB$ is a straight angle, then $\cos \theta = -1$ and $|AB| = 2r$.

27.

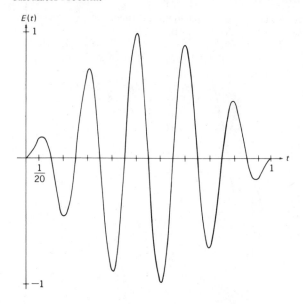

(a) *Hint:* Show that the Law of Sines implies that $(a + b + c)/c = (\sin A + \sin B + \sin C)/\sin C$. If s is the semiperimeter, then $a + b + c = 2s$. Show that $R = (c/2)/\sin C$ by showing that $\angle ACB \cong \angle DOB$ and using the lengths of the sides of $\triangle DOB$.
(b) From the proof in part (a), we have $(c/2)/\sin C = R$. Therefore, $2R = c/(\sin C) = b/(\sin B) = a/(\sin A)$, by multiplication and the Law of Sines.
Calculator Problem. (a) $b = 287.0$ (b) $\sin A = 237.4/372.5, m(\angle A) = 39.6°; b = 287.0$

Section 6-6, page 146

1. $p = 1/2, \nu = 2, \omega = 4\pi, A = 20$ 3. $p = 1/60, \nu = 60, \omega = 120\pi, A = 110$ 5. $p = 2, \nu = 1/2, \omega = \pi, A = 3$ 7. $d = 4 \sin 6\pi t$. The graph is similar to the graph of $\sin x$. It has a period of $1/3$ and an amplitude of 4. 9. $1/6$ 11. $1/2$ second 13. $\theta = 1/10 \sin \pi t$
Calculator Problem. Distance from Dallas to NYC = $19.9° \times 111.12 \text{ km}/1° = 2211.288 \text{ km} \doteq 2210 \text{ km}$

Section 6-8, page 152

1. (a) FM (b) AM 3. No 5. $E(t) = (A_0 + A_1 \sin 2\pi t) \sin 16\pi t$. The graph is similar to the graph in Fig. 6-23. 7. $P = P_0 + A_1 \sin 880\pi t + (1/4)A_1 \sin 1760\pi t + (1/8)A_1 \sin 2640\pi t$

Calculator Problem.

CHAPTER 7

Identities that begin by changing to sine and cosine are not included. The letter k represents an integer in the domain statements throughout the chapter.

Section 7-2, page 161

1. $\theta \neq k\pi$ 3. $t \neq k\pi/2$ 5. $x \neq k\pi$ 7. $z \neq k\pi/2$ 9. $\theta \neq k\pi$ 11. $(1 - \sin x)/\cos x, x \neq (2k + 1)\pi/2$ 13. $((1 - \sin u)/\cos u)^2, u \neq (2k + 1)\pi/2$ 15. $\cos^2 - \sin^2, \theta \neq (2k + 1)\pi/2$ 17. $(\sin \theta + \cos \theta)/(\sin \theta - \cos \theta), \theta \neq k\pi$ or $\theta \neq (4k + 1)\pi/4$ 19. $\sin \theta, \theta \neq k\pi$ 21. $\theta \neq k\pi/2$ 23. $x \neq k\pi/2$ 25. $y \neq k\pi/2$ 27. $A \neq k\pi$ 29. Separate into two fractions; $\theta \neq k\pi$. 31. Factor out $\sin \theta \cos \theta$; all real numbers. 33. Divide numerator and denominator by $\cos^2 \alpha; \alpha \neq k\pi/4$. 35. Express in terms of $\sin \theta$ and $\cos \theta$, find lcd; $\theta \neq k\pi/4$. 37. Factor as difference of two squares; all real numbers. 39. $A \neq k\pi/2$ 41. Express second factor as $\cos^2 z; z \neq (2k + 1)\pi/2$. 43. $\cos \theta = \pm \sqrt{1 - \sin^2 \theta}$; use $-$ in quadrants II and III; use $+$ in quadrants I and IV 45. $\sin \theta = \pm (\tan \theta)/\sqrt{1 + \tan^2 \theta}$; use $+$ in quadrants I and IV; use $-$ in quadrants II and III. 47. $\sin \theta = \pm \sqrt{\sec^2 \theta - 1}/\sec \theta$; use $+$ in quadrants I and III; use $-$ in quadrants II and IV. 49. $\sin x$ 51. $\cos^2 - \sin^2$ 53. $(\sin + \cos)^2/\sin \cos^3$ 55. Use $\sec^2$ for $\tan^2 + 1$; domain $\neq (2k + 1)\pi/2$. 57. Domain $\neq k\pi/2$ 59. Use $\sin^2 - \cos^2$ as numerator; domain $\neq k\pi/2$. 61. Factor out $\sec^2$ term; $A + \sqrt{2}B \neq (2k + 1)\pi/2$. 63. Express as complex fraction in sin and cos; domain $\neq k\pi/2$. 65. Domain $\neq k\pi/2$ 67. Divide each term by $\cos \alpha \cos \beta; \alpha, \beta \neq (2k + 1)\pi/2$.

69. If θ is in quadrants II or IV, $\cos \theta \sqrt{\sec^2\theta - 1} =$
$\cos \theta \sqrt{\tan^2\theta} = \cos \theta |\tan \theta| = \cos \theta |\sin \theta|/|\cos \theta|$. Now we see
that when θ is in quadrant II, $(\cos \theta)/|\cos \theta| = -1$ and $|\sin \theta| =$
$\sin \theta$, so $\cos \theta \sqrt{\sec^2\theta - 1} = -\sin \theta$. When θ is in quadrant IV,
$(\cos \theta)/|\cos \theta| = 1$ and $|\sin \theta| = -\sin \theta$. Hence, in any case
$\cos \theta \sqrt{\sec^2\theta - 1} = -\sin \theta$. **71.** If $y \neq 0$, then $\csc \theta = 1/y$
and $\cot \theta = x/y$, where $W(\theta) = (x, y)$ is a point on the unit circle.
Now if $\csc \theta = \cot \theta$, then $1/y = x/y$ and thus $x = 1$. If $x = 1$,
then $y = 0$ since (x, y) is a point on the unit circle. But neither
function is defined if $y = 0$, so $\csc \theta \neq \cot \theta$ for any real number
θ.
Calculator Problem. $\sin (\cos 1) = 0.5143952 < \cos (\sin 1) =$
0.6663667

Section 7-3, page 166

1. $(\sqrt{2} + \sqrt{6})/4$ **3.** $(-\sqrt{2} + \sqrt{6})/4$ **5.** $(-\sqrt{6} + \sqrt{2})/4$
7. Use $-\beta$ for β, then expand. $(\cos (-\beta) = \cos \beta$ and $\sin (-\beta)$
$= -\sin \beta)$ **9.** Use $-\beta$ for β in $\tan (\alpha + \beta)$ **11.** Use $-\beta$ for β
in $\cot (\alpha + \beta)$ **13.** Apply addition formula and simplify.
15. Apply addition formula and simplify.   **17.** Use the fact
that $\cos \alpha = \sin (\pi/2 - \alpha)$ on second term.   **19.** Form is
$\cos A \cos B + \sin A \sin B$ **21.** Use the addition formulas.
23. Use sin/cos substitution for tan.   **25.** Note that
$\sin (x + y + z) = \sin (x + (y + z))$.   **27.** Form is $\tan (\alpha - \beta)$.
29. Apply addition formulas and multiply.   **31.** *Hint:* Triangles
ABD and BCD are right triangles.
Calculator Problem. $|CD| = 0.9165151$, $|AC| = 0.973212$,
$\alpha + \beta = 1.3388116 = 76.708253°$

Section 7-4, page 170

7. $(2 + 2\sqrt{10})/9$ **9.** $2(\sqrt{2} + \sqrt{5})/3$ **11.** $(4\sqrt{2} + \sqrt{5})/3$
13. *Case 1.* α and β both in quadrant II. $\cos (\alpha + \beta) = -33/65$.
Case 2. α in quadrant II, β in quadrant III. $\cos (\alpha + \beta) = 63/65$.
Case 3. α in quadrant IV, β in quadrant II. $\cos (\alpha + \beta) = 33/65$.
Case 4. α in quadrant IV, β in quadrant III. $\cos (\alpha + \beta) = -63/65$.
15. $\cos \theta$ or $-\cos \theta$ for k an even or odd integer, respectively.
17. $\cot \theta$ **19.** $(\sqrt{2}/2)(\cos \theta + \sin \theta)$
21. $(\sqrt{2}/2)(\sin \theta - \cos \theta)$ **23.** $(1/2)(\sqrt{3} \cos \theta + \sin \theta)$
25. $5 \sin (\theta - \alpha)$, where $\cos \alpha = 3/5$ and $\sin \alpha = 4/5$
27. $\sqrt{10} \sin (\theta + \alpha)$, where $\cos \alpha = \sqrt{3}/\sqrt{10}$ and $\sin \alpha =$
$\sqrt{7}/\sqrt{10}$.   **29.** $\sqrt{A^2 + B^2} \sin (\theta + \alpha)$ **31.** $\sqrt{2} \sin (\theta + \pi/4)$
33. $(u\sqrt{1 - u^2} - v\sqrt{1 - v^2})/(v^2 - u^2)$ **35.** $2 \sin \alpha \cos \alpha$
37. $\sin 1$ **39.** $\theta \neq k\pi/2$ **41.** $\theta \neq k\pi/2$ **43.** Form is
$\sin (3\theta - 2\theta)$; $\theta \neq k\pi/4$ **45.** $\sin 4\theta = \sin 2(2\theta)$; domain all
real numbers   **47.** Add 1 to each term and subtract 3 at the
end of left-hand side. Use tan addition formula on each of the
new terms. $\theta \neq (2k + 1)\pi/2$ or $\theta \neq (3k + 1)\pi/6$
Calculator Problem.   **(a)** $F(1.2) = \sqrt{5} \sin 1.2 + \sqrt{3} \cos 1.2 =$
2.7117247 **(b)** $F(\theta) = \sqrt{8}(\sin (\theta + \alpha))$, $\alpha = 0.659058$,
$F(1.2) = \sqrt{8}(\sin (1.2 + 0.659058)) = 2.7117247$

Section 7-5, page 173

1. $\mp120/169, -119/169, \pm120/119$ **3.** $-4\sqrt{5}/9, 1/9, -4\sqrt{5}$
5. $2\sqrt{2}/3, 1/3, 2\sqrt{2}$ **7.** $-2a\sqrt{1 - a^2}, 1 - 2a^2$,
$-2a\sqrt{1 - a^2}/(1 - 2a^2)$ **9.** $(1/2)\sqrt{2 - \sqrt{3}}$ **11.** Using formulas (4) or (5), $\tan \pi/12 = 2 - \sqrt{3}$.   **15.** $\sin (x/2) =$
$(1 + \sqrt{7})/4$, $\cos (x/2) = (\sqrt{7} - 1)/4$, $\tan (x/2) = (\sqrt{7} + 4)/3$,
$\cot (x/2) = (4 - \sqrt{7})/3$, $\sec (x/2) = 2(\sqrt{7} + 1)/3$, $\csc (x/2) =$
$2(\sqrt{7} - 1)/3$ **17.** Use sin/cos for tan and multiply by
$\cos (x/2)/\cos (x/2)$.   **19.** $\sin 3x = 3 \sin x - 4 \sin^3 x$ **23.** Use
fact that $\tan \pi/4 = 1$ before substituting sin/cos.   **25.** Use sub-
stitutions for $\cos 3x$ and $\sin 3x$ from Problems 18 and 19.
29. Use $\sin = 1/\csc$ and multiply fraction by csc/csc.   **31.** Find
lcd of fractions.   **37.** *Hint:* $\sin A + \sin B =$
$2 \sin (A/2 + B/2) \cos (A/2 - B/2)$. However, $(A + B)/2 =$
$\pi/2 - C/2$, so $\sin (A/2 + B/2) = \cos C/2$.
Calculator Problem. $\sin A + \sin B + \sin C = 0.8090169 + 0.5 +$
$0.9945218 = 2.3035387$. $4 \cos (A/2) \cos (B/2) \cos (C/2) =$
$4(0.8910065)(0.9659258)(0.6691306) = 2.3035387$

Section 7-6, page 179

1. $3(\cos 0 + i \sin 0)$ **3.** $2(\cos 7\pi/6 + i \sin 7\pi/6)$
5. $\sqrt{2}(\cos 5\pi/4 + i \sin 5\pi/4)$ **7.** $-\sqrt{2} + \sqrt{2}i$
9. $-2 - 2\sqrt{3}i$ **11.** $-\sqrt{3}/2 + (1/2)i$ **13.** 2   **15.** $-1 + i$
17. 4   **19.** $-2 - 2\sqrt{3}i$ **21.** $16i$ **23.** 1   **25.** $\sqrt{2} - \sqrt{2}i$
27. $1, -1/2 + (\sqrt{3}/2)i, -1/2 - (\sqrt{3}/2)i$ **29.** $\sqrt{3}/2 + (1/2)i$,
$-\sqrt{3}/2 + (1/2)i, -i$ **31.** $(1/2)(\cos (-\pi/3) + i \sin (-\pi/3))$
33. $i, -\sqrt{3}/2 - i/2, \sqrt{3}/2 - i/2$
35. $z = \sqrt[4]{2}(-\sqrt{2 - \sqrt{2}}/2 + \sqrt{2 + \sqrt{2}}i/2)$ or
$z = \sqrt[4]{2}(\sqrt{2 - \sqrt{2}}/2 - \sqrt{2 + \sqrt{2}}i/2)$
Calculator Problem. $\sqrt[3]{3 + 4i} = 1.6289372 + 0.5201744i =$
$\sqrt[3]{5}(\text{cis } 0.3090984)$, $\sqrt[3]{3 + 4i} = -1.2649528 + 1.1506137i =$
$\sqrt[3]{5}(\text{cis } 2.4034935)$, $\sqrt[3]{3 + 4i} = -0.3639844 - 1.6707881i =$
$\sqrt[3]{5}(\text{cis } 4.4978885)$

CHAPTER 8

Section 8-2, page 190

1. $\pi/2$ **3.** $\pi/3$ **5.** $-\pi/4$ **7.** $3\pi/4$ **9.** $\pi/4$ **11.** $\pi/3$
13. 0   **15.** $-\pi/3$ **17.** $23.5°$ **19.** $16.9°$ **21.** $72.7°$
23-27. In the answers below, k has the set of integers as its
domain.   **23.** $3\pi/2 + 2\pi k$ **25.** $5\pi/6 + 2\pi k$ or $7\pi/6 + 2\pi k$
27. $187.1° + k \cdot 360°$ or $352.9° + k \cdot 360°$ **29.** $-\pi/4$
31. $-\pi/3$ **33.** Cos^{-1} would not be a function on this domain.
35. True.   **37.** True.   **39.** $t = \text{Cos } \theta$; all real numbers θ such
that $0 \leqslant \theta \leqslant \pi$ **41.** $x = \text{Cos } (4 - 3y)/2$ where $(4 - 2\pi)/3 \leqslant y$
$\leqslant 4/3$ **43.** $x = 1/2$
Calculator Problem. $\sin (\pi/5) = 0.9x - 1.3, x = 2.0975391$

Section 8-3, page 192

1. 1/2   **3.** 4/5   **5.** 1   **7.** cos $(\text{Sin}^{-1}t) = \sqrt{1-t^2}$ **9.** Let $\alpha = \text{Arcsin } x$ and $\beta = \text{Arcsin } y$. Then Sin $\alpha = x$, Sin $\beta = y$, Cos $\alpha = \sqrt{1-x^2}$, and Cos $\beta = \sqrt{1-y^2}$. $\sin(\text{Arcsin } x + \text{Arcsin } y) = \sin(\alpha + \beta) = \sin \alpha \cos \beta + \sin \beta \cos \alpha = x\sqrt{1-y^2} + y\sqrt{1-x^2}$.
11. Let $\alpha = \text{Arctan } 1/2$ and $\beta = \text{Arctan } 1/3$. Then Tan $\alpha = 1/2$ and Tan $\beta = 1/3$. Tan (Arctan $1/2$ + Arctan $1/3$) = Tan $(\alpha + \beta)$ = (Tan α + Tan β)/(1 − Tan α Tan β) = (1/2 + 1/3)/(1 − 1/2 · 1/3) = (5/6)/(5/6) = 1 = Tan $(\pi/4)$. Therefore, Arctan $1/2$ + Arctan $1/3 = \pi/4$.   **13.** Let $\alpha = \text{Tan}^{-1}1/5$ and $\beta = \text{Tan}^{-1}1/239$. Tan 4α = 120/119. Tan (4 $\text{Tan}^{-1}1/5$ − $\text{Tan}^{-1}1/239$) = Tan $(4\alpha - \beta)$ = (120/119 − 1/239)/(1 + 120/119 · 1/239) = (120 · 239 − 119)/(119 · 239 + 120) = 1. Tan (4 $\text{Tan}^{-1}1/5$ − $\text{Tan}^{-1}1/239$) = 1 → 4 $\text{Tan}^{-1}1/5$ + $\text{Tan}^{-1}1/239 = \pi/4$ **15.** Let $\alpha = \text{Arctan } 2/3$, then Tan $\alpha = 2/3$. $2\alpha = 2$ Arctan $2/3$ and Tan 2α = (2 · 2/3)/(1 − 4/9) = (4/3)/(5/9) = 12/5. Therefore, Arctan $12/5 = 2\alpha = 2$ Arctan $2/3$.
17. 24/7   **19.** 0   **21.** 836/845
23.

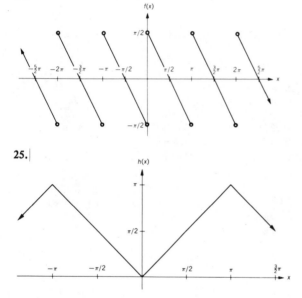

25.

Calculator Problem. α = 0.3009469 radians or 17.242991°

Section 8-4, page 195

1. $4\pi/3$ or $5\pi/3$ **3.** $3\pi/4$ or $7\pi/4$ **5.** $\pi/2$ **7.** 13.5° or 166.5°   **9.** 36.3° or 323.7°   **11.** 129.8° or 230.2°
13. $\pi/3, 5\pi/3$ **15.** $(-1 + \sqrt{5})/2 = 0.618 \mapsto \theta \doteq 38.17°$ or $\theta \doteq 141.8°$ **17.** $\pi/6$ or $5\pi/6$ **19.** $\pi/3, 5\pi/3$ **21.** $\pi/3$, $2\pi/3, 4\pi/3$, or $5\pi/3$ **23.** $\pi/4, 3\pi/4, 5\pi/4$, or $7\pi/4$
25-33. The letter k represents an integer in each statement.
25. $\pm\pi/3 + 2\pi k$ **27.** $(2k+1)\pi/3$ **29.** $\pi + 2\pi k$
31. $\pi/4 + k\pi/2$ **33.** $(2k+1)\pi/2$

35. cos $\theta = \theta$. Let $f(\theta) = \cos \theta$ and let $g(\theta) = \theta$. From the graph, we see that θ appears to be a little less than $\pi/4$. Using tables, we find $\theta = 42.4°$ approximately.

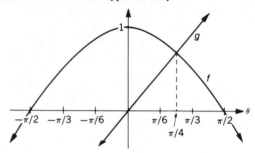

37. tan $\theta = 1 + \theta$. Let $f(\theta) = \tan \theta$ and $g(\theta) = 1 + \theta$. From the graph, it appears that the smallest positive value of θ satisfying tan $\theta = 1 + \theta$ is a little more than $\pi/3$. Using tables, we find $\theta \doteq 64.9°$.

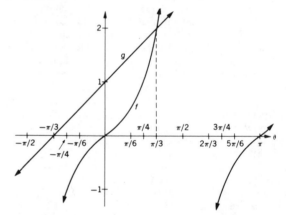

Calculator Problem.   When θ = 1.7142, cos θ = −0.1429126 and $(1/2)\theta - 1$ = −0.1429.

CHAPTER 9

Section 9-2, page 203

1. 1/2, 1, 3/2, 2, 5/2, 3   **3.** 2, 4, 6, 8, 10, 12   **5.** 1, 2, 4, 8, 16, 32   **7.** 2, 2/3, 2/9, 2/27, 2/81, 2/243   **9.** −1, 1/2, −1/3, 1/4, −1/5, 1/6   **11.** 5, 13/3, 11/3, 3, 7/3; A_{32} = (32/2)(2 · 5 + 31 · (−2/3)) = −512/3   **13.** Yes, the ninth term; no   **15.** G_n = $(1 - (2/3)^6)/(1 - 2/3)$ = 665/243   **17.** −22
19. 4   **21.** 710.5 m   **23.** 1 + 4 + 9 + 16 + 25   **25.** 1 + 2 + 3 + 4 + 5 + 6 + 7 + 8 + 9   **27.** −1 + 4 − 9 + 16 − 25 + 36
29. Arithmetic sequence   **31.** Neither   **33.** Neither
35. $A_n = n(n+1)/2$ **37.** $n(n+1)$ **39.** $\doteq \$10^{28}$
Calculator Problem.   **(a)** $S = a_{33} - 1 = \$35,245.77$
(b) a_{31}/a_{30} = 1,346,269/832,040 $\doteq$ 1.6180339; $(1 + \sqrt{5})/2 \doteq$ 1.6180339

Section 9-3, page 206

1. 1   **3.** 1/3   **5.** 1   **7.** 4/9   **9.** 342/11   **11.** 245/999
13. $-1/3$ **15.** 1/8   **17.** $5/(\sqrt{5}-1)$ **19.** $19h$ **21.** Let
G_n denote the sum of the first n terms of a geometric series.
Then, $G_n = a/(1-r) - [a/(1-r)] \cdot r^n$ and $|G_n - a/(1-r)| =$
$|a/(1-r)| \cdot |r|^n$. But, $|G_n| + |a/(1-r)| > |G_n - a/(1-r)|$ and
(i): $|G_n| > |a/(1-r)| \cdot |r|^n - |a/(1-r)|$. Let $f(x) = |r|^x$. For
$|r| > 1$, f is an increasing function which is not bounded above.
This implies that as n assumes larger and larger values, so does
$|r|^n$. Thus, the same can be said of the right hand side of (i).
Consequently, $\lim\limits_{n\to\infty} |G_n|$ and $\lim\limits_{n\to\infty} G_n$ do not exist.

Calculator Problem. $a = 1/4$, $r = 1/4$, $G = 1/4 \div (1 - 1/4) =$
$1/4 \div 3/4 = 1/3$. The sum of the first nine terms gives 0.333332.

Section 9-4, page 210

1-13. To show that P_k implies P_{k+1}:   **1.** add $2(k+1)$ to each
side of P_k.   **3.** add $5(k+1) - 3 = 5k + 2$ to each side of P_k.
5. add $(2k+1)^2$ to each side of P_k.   **7.** add $1/2^{k+1}$ to each
side of P_k.   **9.** observe that $2^{k+1} = 2 \cdot 2^k > 2 \cdot k$.   **11.** show
that $r^{k+1} = r^k \cdot r < s^k \cdot r$ and $s^k \cdot r < s^k \cdot s$.   **13.** observe that
$3^{2(k+1)} - 1 = 3^2(3^{2k} - 1) + (3^2 - 1)$.   **15.** Add $(a + kd)$ to
each side of P_k to show that P_k implies P_{k+1}.   **17.** Show that
$x^{k+1} - y^{k+1} = x(x^k - y^k) + y^k(x - y)$ is divisible by $x - y$.
19. Add $(k+1)(k+2)$ to each side of P_k.   **21. (a)** By definition of exponent.   **(b)** The Inductive Hypothesis implies the
conclusion by the way that the set S was selected.   Then: Part
(a); Associativity for multiplication; By the Inductive Hypothesis; By the definition of part (a); By the associativity for addition; P_k implies P_{k+1}.   **23.** Show that $(a^{k+1})^m = (a^k \cdot a)^m$
$= (a^k)^m \cdot a^m = a^{km} \cdot a^m = a^{km+m} = a^{(k+1)m}$.

Calculator Problem.   **(a)** $3^2 - 1 = 8 = 8 \cdot 1$ **(b)** $3^4 - 1 = 80$
$= 8 \cdot 10$ **(c)** $3^6 - 1 = 728 = 8 \cdot 91$ **(d)** $3^8 - 1 = 6561 =$
$8 \cdot 820$ **(e)** $3^{10} - 1 = 59{,}048 = 8 \cdot 7381$ **(f)** $3^{12} - 1 =$
$531{,}440 = 8 \cdot 66{,}430$ **(g)** $3^{14} - 1 = 4{,}782{,}968 = 8 \cdot 597{,}871$
(h) $3^{16} - 1 = 43{,}046{,}720 = 8 \cdot 5{,}380{,}840$

Section 9-5, page 214

1. 24   **3.** 120   **5.** 362,880   **7.** 362,880   **9.** 45   **11.** 2^8
13. (a) 720   **(b)** 1000   **15.** $(n+1)!/(n-1)! =$
$[(n+1)(n)(n-1)(n-2)\cdots(2)(1)]/[(n-1)(n-2)\cdots(2)(1)]$
$= (n+1)(n) = n^2 + n$ **17.** $P(n, r) = n!/(n-r)! =$
$[n!/(n-(r-1))!](n-(r-1)) = [n!/(n-(r-1))!](1 + (n-r))$
$= [n!/(n-(r-1))!] + [n!/(n-(r-1))!](n-r) = P(n, r-1)$
$+ (n-r)P(n, r-1)$.   **19.** 6^4 or 1296; 600

Calculator Problem. $\tan(\pi/2 - 0.0000001) = 9{,}998{,}797.7$;
$P(100.4) = 94{,}109{,}400$; $10^8 = 100{,}000{,}000$; $2^{30} =$
$1{,}073{,}741{,}800$; $P(13, 13) = 6{,}227{,}020{,}800$

Section 9-6, page 216

1. 35   **3.** 8   **5.** 28   **7.** 792   **9.** 4!/2!   **11.** 320; 20 less
13. $C(52, 13) \doteq 7 \cdot 10^{11}$ **15.** $C(n, n-r) =$
$n!/[(n-r)!(n-(n-r))!] = n!/(n-r)!r! = C(n, r)$ **17.** 210
19. (a) $2 \cdot 9!$ **(b)** $8 \cdot 9!$ **21.** Use an inductive proof similar
to those for Problems 21 and 23 of Section 9-4.
Calculator Problem.   **(a)** $16{,}777{,}216 = 8^8$ **(b)** $C(64, 8) =$
4.4262×10^9

Section 9-7, page 221

1. The eleventh row is 1, 10, 45, 120, 210, 252, 210, 120, 45,
10, 1   **3.** $a^5 - 5a^4b + 10a^3b^2 - 10a^2b^3 + 5ab^4 - b^5$
5. $a^{-3} + 3a^{-4} + 3a^{-5} + a^{-6}$ **7.** $2^8 + 21 \cdot 2^6 \cdot 3 +$
$35 \cdot 2^4 \cdot 3^2 + 7 \cdot 2^2 \cdot 3^3 = 10{,}084$ **9.** $1 - 7ab + 21a^2b^2 -$
$35a^3b^3 + 35a^4b^4 - 21a^5b^5 + 7a^6b^6 - a^7b^7$ **11.** $x^2 -$
$6(x^5y)^{1/3} + 15(x^4y^2)^{1/3} - 20xy + 15(x^2y^4)^{1/3} - 6(xy^5)^{1/3}$
$+ y^2$ **13.** $330a^7b^4$ **15.** $-37{,}500x^{-4}$ **17.** $-35x$
19. $\doteq 0.941480$ **21.** $(9!/5!4!)(x/2)^5y^4$ **23.** 326,592
25. 243   **27.** $-27b^3 + 54ab^2 - 36a^2b + 8a^3$

29. $0 = (1-1)^n = \dbinom{n}{0}1 + \dbinom{n}{1}(-1) + \dbinom{n}{2}(-1)^2 + \ldots +$

$(-1)^n\dbinom{n}{n} = \displaystyle\sum_{r=0}^{n}(-1)^r\dbinom{n}{r}$.   **31.** $(2n)!x^n/(n!)^2$

33. *Hint:* Show by adding the finite sequences,
$S = 0 \cdot C(n, 0) + 1 \cdot C(n, 1) + 2 \cdot C(n, 2) + \cdots +$
$n \cdot C(n, n)$ and $S = n \cdot C(n, n) + (n-1) \cdot C(n, n-1) +$
$(n-2) \cdot C(n, n-2) + \cdots + 0 \cdot C(n, 0)$, term by term and observing, $C(n, r) = C(n, n-r)$, that $2S = n[C(n, 0) + C(n, 1) +$
$C(n, 2) + \cdots + C(n, n)] = n \cdot 2^n$.
35. *Hint:* $(r+1)C(n, r+1)/C(n, r) = n - r$. Use this to show
that the given sum reduces to the sum of the first n natural
numbers.   **37.** $\doteq 1.0196$ **39.** $\doteq 1.117$ **41.** $(1+x)^{-1} =$
$1 + (-1)x + (-1)(-2)x^2/2! + (-1)(-2)(-3)x^3/3! + \cdots =$
$1 - x + x^2 - x^3 + \cdots$.
Calculator Problem.   **(a)** $2.05 \doteq 2.0493901$ **(b)** $4.01 \doteq$
4.0099875 **(c)** $2.0225 \doteq 2.0222515$ **(d)** $2.00625 \doteq$
2.0062113

Section 9-8, page 226

1. $|S_n - 3| = 2/n < \epsilon$, if $n \geqslant N$ and $N > 2/\epsilon$.   **3.** $|S_n - 1| =$
$1/(n+1) < \epsilon$, if $n \geqslant N$ and $N > 1/\epsilon$.   **5.** $|S_n - (1/2)| =$
$7/(2|2n-3|) < \epsilon$, if $n \geqslant N$ and $N > \text{Max}(3, 7/2\epsilon)$.
7. $|S_n - 2| = 2/(n^2 + 1) < 2/n^2 < \epsilon$, if $n > N$ and $N > \sqrt{2}/\epsilon$.
9. $|S_n - (7/3)| = 17/(3(3n+2)) < 17/n < \epsilon$, if $n \geqslant N$ and
$N > 17/\epsilon$.   **11.** $|S_n - (1/2)| < \epsilon$, if $n \geqslant N$ and $N > 1/\epsilon$.
13. $|S_n - x/(1-x)| < \epsilon$, if $n \geqslant N$ and $N + 1 >$
$\log \epsilon |1 - x|/\log |x|$.   **15.** $|S_n - a| = |\sin n|/n < \epsilon$, if $n \geqslant N$ and
$N > 1/\epsilon$.   **17.** $|S_n - 0| = n!/(2n)! < \epsilon$, if $n \geqslant N$ and $N > 1/\epsilon$.
19. $|S_n - (2x-1)/(1-x)| < \epsilon$, if $n \geqslant N$ and $N + 1 >$
$\log \epsilon |1 - x|/\log |2x - 1|$.
Calculator Problem. $k = 83$

CHAPTER 10

Section 10-2, page 233

1. $\sqrt{3}/3$ **3.** 1 **5.** -0.4942 **7.** 1/3 **9.** 8/9 **11.** 2/5
13. The line has slope $\sqrt{3}/3$ and passes through $(1, 2)$,
$(0, 2 - \sqrt{3}/3), (-2\sqrt{3} + 1, 0)$ **15.** The line passes through
$(1, -3)$ and is parallel to the x-axis.
17. $m = (y_1 - y_2)/(x_1 - x_2) = -(y_1 - y_2)/-(x_1 - x_2) =$
$(-y_1 + y_2)/(-x_1 + x_2) = (y_2 - y_1)/(x_2 - x_1)$
Calculator Problem. $\tan \theta = (0.96 + 3.18)/(-2.45 - 4.77)$,
$\theta = 2.6209562 = 150.16973°$

Calculator Problem. Estimate $m = 0$ at about $x = 0.7$.
By calculator, $x_0 = 0.6687403$.

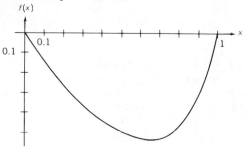

Section 10-3, page 237

1.

h	1	-1	0.5	-0.5	0.25	-0.25	0.1	-0.1
$f(1 + h)$	4	0	2.25	0.25	1.5625	0.5625	1.21	0.81
m	3	1	2.5	1.5	2.25	1.75	2.1	1.9

3. 2

5.

h	1	-1	$\frac{1}{2}$	$\frac{-1}{2}$	$\frac{1}{4}$	$\frac{-1}{4}$	0.1	-0.1	0.0001
$f(2 + h)$	$\frac{17}{2}$	$\frac{9}{2}$	$\frac{57}{8}$	$\frac{41}{8}$	$\frac{209}{32}$	$\frac{177}{32}$	6.205	5.805	6.000200005
m	$\frac{5}{2}$	$\frac{3}{2}$	$\frac{9}{4}$	$\frac{7}{4}$	$\frac{17}{8}$	$\frac{15}{8}$	2.05	1.95	2.00005

For values of h near zero, the secant lines approach the tangent line to the curve at $(2, 6)$.

7. $x_0 + (1/2)h$; x_0 **9. (a)** Yes; 3 **(b)** Yes; 3 **(c)** 3
11. $-1/2$ **13.** 1 **15.** 3/4 **17. (c)** 3/4 **(d)** $m = 3x_0{}^2 + 3x_0h + h^2$ **(e)** $3x_0{}^2$
19. (a), (b)

(c) The slope of the tangent line through $(1/2, -3/8)$ is $-1/4$.

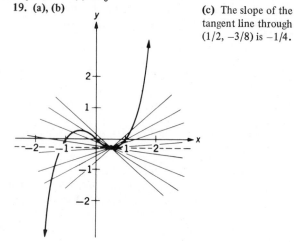

Section 10-4, page 242

1.

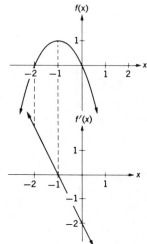

3.

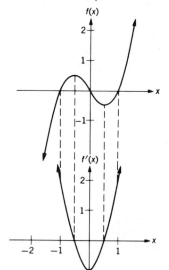

570

5.

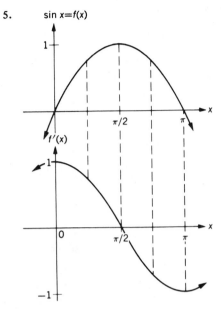

sin $x = f(x)$

7. $(1/2)x + (1/4)\Delta x$ **9.** 4 **11.** (7) $f'(x) = (1/2)x$
(8) $f'(x) = 2x - 4$ (9) $f'(x) = 4$ (10) $f'(x) = -1/x^2, x > 0$
13. (a), (b) The graph of g' is a line which has intercepts $(0, 1)$
and $(-2, 0)$. **(c)** $(1/2)x_0 + 1 + (1/4)h$ **(d)** $g'(x) = (1/2)x + 1$
(e) Suppose x_1 and x_2 are numbers in the domain of g such that
$-2 < x_1 < x_2$. Then, $g(x_2) - g(x_1) = (1/4)(x_2{}^2 - x_1{}^2) +$
$(x_2 - x_1)$, (1). Since $x_1 < x_2, x_2 - x_1 > 0$. Also, $-2 < x_1$ and
$-2 < x_2$. Therefore, $-4 < x_1 + x_2$, and $x_1 + x_2 + 4 > 0$. This
shows that (1) is positive and that $g(x_2) > g(x_1)$. Hence, for
$x > -2$, g is increasing. The result agrees with the graph of g, and
we can conclude from the graph of g' that the slope of the tangents to g is positive for $x > -2$. **15.** $h'(x) = f'(x) + g'(x)$
17. $f'(1) = 9, f'(0.1) = 0.144$ **19.** $1 < f(1) < 2$
Calculator Problem. $f'(1) = 1, f'(2) = 1/2, f'(3) = 1/3,$
$f'(4) = 1/4, \ldots.$

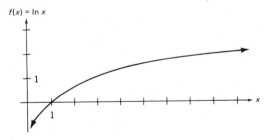

$f(x) = \ln x$

Section 10-5, page 247

1. -40 **3.** -46 **5.** -47.6 **7.** $8t_0 - 80 + 4\Delta t$
9. $8t_0 - 80$ **11.** 29.4 **13.** 44.1 **15.** 48.51 **17.** 49
19. 10.2 **21.** 17.55 **23.** $20 - 9.8t_0 + 4.9\Delta t$

25. $20 - 9.8t_0$ **27.** 2.04 m **29.** The instantaneous rate
of change is equal to $3x^2 - 2x + 1$ **31.** 1 **33.** -1.7
35. -2 **37.** $6t_0 - 2$ **39.** 10, 1 **41.** 6
Calculator Problem. **(a)** 0.2673923 **(b)** 0.3158649
(c) 0.3636012 **(d)** 0.410359 **(e)** 0.4559018
(f) 0.4956615 **(g)** 0.4995669 **(h)** 0.5000000 . . .

Section 10-6, page 251

1. Divide the interval $[0, a]$ into n congruent subintervals of
length a/n. Then the area under the graph of f for $0 \leqslant x \leqslant a$ is
the sum of the areas of n rectangles each of which has height c
and width a/n. Thus the area is equal to $a \cdot c$. **3.** By counting
squares we find that the area appears to be a little more than
5/16 square units. By formula, $A = a^3/3$, so when $a = 1$, $A =$
1/3. **5.** $A = 2a^3/3$ **7.** The area is equal to $a^3/3 + a$. The
area is the same as that under $y = x^2$ from 0 to a, plus the area
of a rectangle of length a and height of one unit.
9.

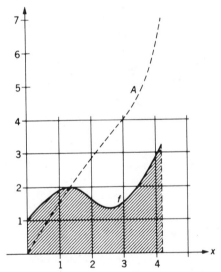

11. Divide the interval $[0, a]$ into
n congruent segments so that each
segment is of length a/n. $A(\overline{S}_n) =$
$(a/n) \cdot (a/n)^3 + (a/n) \cdot (2a/n)^3$
$+ \cdots + (a/n) \cdot (na/n)^3 =$
$(a^4/n^4)(1 + 2^3 + 3^3 + \cdots + n^3) =$
$(a^4/n^4)(n^2 \cdot (n + 1)^2/4) =$
$(a^4/4)(1 + (2/n) + (1/n^2))$. $A(\underline{S}_n)$
$= (a^4/4)(1 - (2/n) + (1/n^2))$. Now
as n becomes large, the areas of
both the upper and lower rectangles approach $a^4/4$ so that $A(S)$
$= a^4/4$.

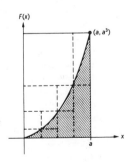

571

13. *Hint:* Find areas A_1, under the segment joining $(-1/2, 1/4)$ and $(2, 4)$; A_2, under $f(x) = x^2$ from $x = 0$ to $x = 2$; and A_3, under $f(x) = x^2$ from $x = -1/2$ to $x = 0$.

15. If the force F is constant and acts through a distance d, then work is equal to $F \cdot d$. If the force is not constant but varies with the distance, then F is a function of d and the work done is the area under the graph of this function. If F is proportional to the distance x, then $F = kx$, where k is a constant. Thus the work done would be $kx^2/2$.

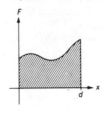

Calculator Problem. $0.9409459 \leqslant A(S) \leqslant 1.0660311$; exact area is 1.

Section 10-7, page 255

1. $A(x) = x$; $A'(x) = f(x) = 1$ **3.** $A(x) = x^3/3$; $A'(x) = x^2 = f(x)$ **5.** For the portion of the graph with $1 \leqslant f(x) \leqslant 2$, $A = (1/3)(1^2) = 1/3$. (See Problem 3.) The remaining portion has $A = 1 \times 1 = 1$. So the total area is $4/3$.
Calculator Problem. $1.6693643 < A < 2.2976828$; $A = 2$.

Section 10-8, page 260

1. $|(1/3)x + 1 - 3| = |(1/3)x - 2| < \epsilon$, if $|x - 6| < \delta$ and $\delta < 3$ **3.** We must show that given $\epsilon > 0$, there exists a $\delta > 0$ such that when $|x - 2| < \delta$, $|f(x) - 4| < \epsilon$. $|x^2 - 4| = |x - 2| \cdot |x + 2|$. If we let $|x - 2| < 1$, then $|x + 2| < 5$. If ϵ is given, then $|x^2 - 4| < \epsilon \rightarrow |x - 2| \cdot |x + 2| < \epsilon \rightarrow |x - 2| \cdot 5 < \epsilon \rightarrow |x - 2| < \epsilon/5$. Let δ be the minimum of 1 or $\epsilon/5$. Hence $f(x)$ is continuous at $x = 2$, because the limit exists. **7.** (a) Since $f(x) = 3x^3 - x + 1$ is continuous for all x, f is real-valued and continuous in the interval $[-1, 0]$. Now $f(-1) = -2$ and $f(0) = 1$, so $f(-1) < f(0)$. Since 0 is between $f(-1)$ and $f(0)$, there exists a c, $-1 < c < 0$, such that $0 = f(c)$ by the Intermediate Value Theorem.
(b) $x = -0.8$ **9.** The graph is $f(x) = x + 2$, $x \neq 2$, and $f(2) = 1$. f is not continuous at $x = 2$. **11.** $|(x + 1)/(x + 2) - (2/3)| = |(x - 1)/3(x + 2)| \leqslant (1/6)|x - 1|$, if $x \geqslant 0$. Then $|(x + 1)/(x + 2) - (2/3)| \leqslant (1/6)|x - 1| < \epsilon$, if $|x - 1| < \delta$ and δ is the minimum.
Calculator Problem. $h = 0.1 \rightarrow 0.8396036$, $h = 0.01 \rightarrow 0.863511$, $h = 0.001 \rightarrow 0.8657753$, $h = 0.0001 \rightarrow 0.86600$; $\cos(\pi/6) = 0.8660254$. As $h \rightarrow 0$, $[\sin(\pi/6 + h) - \sin(\pi/6)]/h \rightarrow \cos(\pi/6)$.

CHAPTER 11

Section 11-2, page 269

1. $2\sqrt{10}$ **3.** $(5\sqrt{2}/2, 5\sqrt{2}/2)$ or $(-5\sqrt{2}/2, -5\sqrt{2}/2)$; $(1 + 5\sqrt{2}/2, 1 + 5\sqrt{2}/2)$ or $(1 - 5\sqrt{2}/2, 1 - 5\sqrt{2}/2)$
5. $(6, 8)$ **7.** $(-3, -4)$ **9.** $(6, -8), (-6, 8), (-9, 12)$
Calculator Problem. (a) 26.29 km (b) 477.044 km

Section 11-3, page 275

1. $c_1 = 4/5, c_2 = 3/5$ **3.** $c_1 = \sqrt{3}/2, c_2 = 1/2$ **5.** $c_1 = 1$, $c_2 = 0$ **7.** $4/5, -3/5$; $\alpha \doteq 37°, \beta \doteq 143°$ **9.** $x = -2$
11. $x = 3d/5, y = 4d/5$ **13.** $x = 1 - d/\sqrt{2}, y = -2 - d/\sqrt{2}$
15. $x = -1 + 11d/5\sqrt{5}, y = 1 + 2d/5\sqrt{5}$ **17.** $(10, -5)$, $(2, -11), (6, -8), (-2, -14)$ **19.** $x = 2 + d, y = -3$; $x = 2$, $y = -3 + d$ **21.** (a) $(1/3)^2 + (-2\sqrt{2}/3)^2 = 1/9 + 8/9 = 1$
(b) Answers may vary. (c) $(0, 3 - 4\sqrt{2})$ (d) For example, $x = -2 - d/3, y = 3 + 2\sqrt{2}d/3$ or $x = d/3, y = (3 - 4\sqrt{2}) - 2\sqrt{2}d/3$ (e) The graph is a line with intercepts $(0, 3 - 4\sqrt{2})$ and $(-2 + (3\sqrt{2}/4), 0)$. **23.** A segment with endpoints $(-13/5, 19/5)$ and $(2/5, -1/5)$ **25.** *Hint:* Let $r = a/\sqrt{a^2 + b^2}$ and $s = b/\sqrt{a^2 + b^2}$. **27.** If d is a rational number, then $3 + \sqrt{3}d/2$ is irrational and $-d/2$ is rational. If $d = \sqrt{3}n$, where n is rational, then $3 + \sqrt{3}d/2$ is rational and $-d/2$ is irrational. Thus, only when $d = 0$ ($x = 3$ and $y = 0$) are both the x- and y-coordinates rational numbers.
Calculator Problem. y-intercept: $(0, 2.6252411)$ or $(0, 2.6)$; x-intercept: $(-8.0796639, 0)$ or $(-8.1, 0)$

Section 11-4, page 279

1. $3y - x = 2$ **3.** $5y - 3x = 11$ **5.** $y = 0$ **7.** $x + 2y = -3$
9. $y = -2x/5$ **11.** $y = -7/2$ **13-19.** Slope is given, then y-intercept. **13.** $3; -6$ **15.** $2; 2$ **17.** $-1/\pi; 2/\pi$
19. $-3/4; k/4$ **21.** $y = -2$ **23.** (a) For $(1, 0)$ and $(4, -12)$ slope $= -4$; for $(1, 0)$ and $(2, -4)$ slope $= -4$; for $(4, -12)$ and $(2, -4)$ slope $= -4$. (b) Any pair of the points determines the equation $4x + y = 4$. The third point satisfies this equation so that all three points are collinear. **25.** $y = \sqrt{3}x + 3\sqrt{3}$
27. $c_1 = (x - x_0)/d$ and $c_2 = (y - y_0)/d$. If $c_1 \neq 0$, then the ratio c_2/c_1 exists and $c_2/c_1 = (y - y_0)/(x - x_0) = m$. Conversely, if a line has slope, then $m = (y - y_0)/(x - x_0)$ exists and $x - x_0 \neq 0$. But this implies that $c_1 = (x - x_0)/d \neq 0$.
Calculator Problem. x-intercept: 5.30, y-intercept: 1.43, $m = -0.27$

Section 11-5, page 282

1-3. The graph is a line with intercepts: **1.** $(3, 0)$ and $(0, -2)$. **3.** $(\sqrt{7}, 0)$ and $(0, \sqrt{7})$. **5-7.** The graph is a line passing through the origin which contains the point: **5.** $(1, 3)$.

7. $(3, 1)$.   **9-11.** The graph is a line parallel to the: **9.** y-axis and $5/2$ units to the left of this axis.   **11.** y-axis and 2π units to the right of this axis.   **13-15.** The slope for each line is: **13.** -1.   **15.** -3.   **17.** $(1, -1)$ **19.** Parallel lines   **21.** $4x + y = -3$ **23.** $3x + (1 + 2\sqrt{2})y = 3 + 2\sqrt{2}$ **25.** $y = mx$ **27.** $(y - y_1)(x_2 - x_1) = (x - x_1)(y_2 - y_1)$ **29.** $A(2, 2), B(4, -2), C(0, 1)$. Use the Pythagorean Theorem and the Law of Cosines.   **31.** $(2, 3)$ **33.** The medians intersect at $(1, 1/3)$.
35.

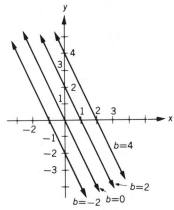

37. $x + y = 4$ **39.** Eliminate the parameter d from the parametric equations.   **41.** The medians intersect at $\left((1/3)(x_1 + x_2 + x_3), (1/3)(y_1 + y_2 + y_3)\right)$.
Calculator Problem. $x = 1.0112359, y = 1; x = 11.123595,$ $y = 10$

Section 11-6, page 287

1-11. Perpendicular lines: 1 and 3, 3 and 7, 9 and 10, 10 and 11, 1 and 12, 7 and 12. Parallel lines: 9 and 11, 3 and 12. Identical lines: 1 and 7   **13.** $x - 3y - 11 = 0$ **15.** The slope of the line containing $(29/4, 1)$ and $(1, -1)$ is $8/25$. The slope of the line containing $(-39/25, 7)$ and $(1, -1)$ is $-25/8$.
17. $(41/17, 1/17)$ **19.** $m_1 = -1/3, m_2 = 1/2$. Then $\tan\theta = (1/2 + 1/3)/(1 - 1/6) = (5/6)/(5/6) = 1$ and $\theta = \pi/4$.   **21.** $\pi/6$
23. Any line of the set of lines, $ax + by = k$, is perpendicular to any line of the set of lines, $bx - ay = k$.   **25.** Proof suggestion: The slope of l_1 is $-a_1/b_1$ and the slope of l_2 is $-a_2/b_2$. The two lines are parallel or identical if and only if they have the same slope. Show that $a_2/a_1 = b_2/b_1 = k$ and choose k such that $k = a_2/a_1$. For the case of perpendicularity, use the theorem which states that the slopes must be negative reciprocals of each other.
27. 8 square units   **29.** $|ax_1 + by_1 + c|/\sqrt{a^2 + b^2}$
Calculator Problem.   1.8692952 or $107.10272°$; 0.6287962 or $36.027373°$; 0.6435011 or $36.869897°$

CHAPTER 12

Section 12-2, page 294

7. (1) $\sqrt{17}$ (2) $\sqrt{74}$ (3) $\sqrt{2}$ (4) 10   (5) 13   (6) 9
9. The arrows will have the same length and the same direction as the given arrow.   **11.** $X = (11, 2)$ **13.** Yes.   **15.** The terminal point of the second arrow is $(6, 6)$.   **17.** $(P_1, P_2) = (P_3, P_4)$ if and only if $P_1 = P_3$ and $P_2 = P_4$. Equal arrows are certainly equivalent arrows, but equivalent arrows are not necessarily equal arrows.   **19.** Apply Theorem 12-1.
Calculator Problem. $(-0.39, 0.98)$

Section 12-3, page 296

1. 5   **3.** $\sqrt{2}$ **5.** 7   **7.** (1) $(-3, 4)$ (2) $(1, 0)$
(3) $(1, -1)$ (4) $(0, 9)$ (5) $(-7, 0)$ (6) $(40, 9)$
9. $\overrightarrow{XY} = \overrightarrow{OP}$ **11.** (P_1, P_2) is equivalent to (Q_1, Q_2).
13. The two vectors have the same direction. The magnitude of $\overrightarrow{AB}$ is twice the magnitude of $\overrightarrow{CD}$.   **15.** $|\overrightarrow{OP_1}| + |\overrightarrow{P_1P_2}| > |\overrightarrow{OP_2}|$ **17.** The points O, P_1, and P_2 must be collinear, and P_1 is between the other two points.
Calculator Problem.   All three vectors have the same direction. $\overrightarrow{P_3P_4}$ and $\overrightarrow{P_5P_6}$ also have the same magnitude, 4.8, so $\overrightarrow{P_3P_4} = \overrightarrow{P_5P_6}$.

Section 12-4, page 299

1. $\left((0, 0), (0, 4)\right)$; $\left((0, 0), (6, -2)\right)$ **3.** $\left((0, 0), (-6, 1)\right)$; $\left((0, 0), (2, 5)\right)$ **5.** Magnitude of the sum of the two vectors is 3, and the vector which is the sum is in the same direction as the vector whose magnitude is 5.   **7.** $(-9, 0)$ **9.** $(0, 0)$
11. $(-3, 2)$ **13.** (a) $(4, 6)$ (b) $(-10, -15)$ (c) $(2k, 3k)$
15. Yes; $-\mathbf{v}$ **17.** $\mathbf{s} = \mathbf{t} + (-\mathbf{r})$ **19.** (a) True   (b) False
(c) True   **21.** Show the existence of k. If $|\mathbf{a}| = r$ and $|\mathbf{b}| = s$, choose k so that $|k| = s/r$. Use Definition 12-6.
Calculator Problem. $\overrightarrow{OP}$ has end point $(\sqrt{5} - \sqrt{3} - \sqrt{2}, \sqrt{2} + \sqrt{7} - \sqrt{6}) = (-0.9101963, 1.6104751); |\overrightarrow{OP}| = 1.8498884$.

Section 12-5, page 303

1. $3\mathbf{i} + 4\mathbf{j}$ **3.** $-2\mathbf{i} + 2\mathbf{j}$ **5.** $(\sqrt{2} + 1)\mathbf{i} + (1 - 1/\sqrt{2})\mathbf{j}$
7. $\mathbf{i} + 6\mathbf{j}$ **9.** 0   **11.** $(5\sqrt{2}/2)\mathbf{i} + (7\sqrt{3}/2)\mathbf{j}$ **13.** $\sqrt{x^2 + y^2}$
15. $\sqrt{13}$ **17.** 1   **19.** 2   **21.** $x = -5$ and $y = -2$
23. $\mathbf{i} + 5\mathbf{j}, 7\mathbf{i} + 7\mathbf{j}, 8\mathbf{i} + 12\mathbf{j}$ **25.** $x = -6, y = -2$
27. $x = -3/2, y = -1/3$ **29.** $s = -4, t = 1$ **31.** Use Theorem 12-2.   **33.** Use the Pythagorean Theorem.
Calculator Problem. $\mathbf{v}_1 + \mathbf{v}_2 = 3.89\mathbf{i} + 3.11\mathbf{j}; |\mathbf{v}_1 + \mathbf{v}_2| = 4.9803815; \tan\theta = 3.11/3.89, \theta = 0.67442737$ or $38.641842°$

Section 12-6, page 305

1. $a + b = (7 - 3)i + (2 - 4)j = 4i - 2j$; $b + a = (-3 + 7)i + (-4 + 2)j = 4i - 2j$ **3.** Yes, by Assertion 4.   **5.** $6i + 6j$
7. $6i + 12j$ **9.** $3v$ **11.** $\sqrt{2}v$ **13.** $-3i$ **15.** $-2i + -3j$
17. $3i + -4j$ **19.** $r = a + (b + c)$ and $r = (a + b) + c$.
Assertion 3.   **21.** $2i + j$ **23.** $-i - 3j$
25.

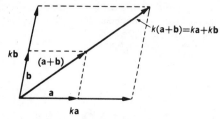

27. Using Definition 12-6 and assertion 8, it follows that,
$v + (-1)v = 1v + (-1)v = (1 + (-1))v = 0v = 0$
Calculator Problem. $v = -1.8710652i + 1.9326702j$

Section 12-7, page 309

1. $r = -2j + t(3i + 6j)$ **3.** $r = (-4i - j) + t(3i - j)$
5. $r = (-4i + 5j) + 11it$ **7-9.** Answers may vary.
7. $(0, -5), (4, -3)$; $r = -5j + t(4i + 2j)$ **9.** $(3, 0), (2, 2)$;
$r = 3i + t(-i + 2j)$ **11.** $(2, 3)$ **13.** $(-2, 6)$ **15.** $(0.8, 1.9)$
17. $(0, 0)$ **19.** $((a + b)/2, 0)$ **21.** $(3, 7/3)$ **23.** $r = (3 + t)i - (2 - 2t\sqrt{2})j$ **25. (a)** $(1/3, 5/3)$
(b) $(-13/3, 13/3)$ **(c)** No solution   **27.** Use the midpoint
formula and the result of Problem 24 above to show that the
coordinates of a point 2/3 the distance from a vertex to the
midpoint of the opposite side is
$((x_1 + x_2 + x_3)/3, (y_1 + y_2 + y_3)/3)$. Show that this point is
on all three medians.
Calculator Problem. $(-0.5839785, 1.2303165)$

CHAPTER 13

Section 13-2, page 317

1. $(0, 3, 0)$ **3.** $(0, 0, 1)$ **5.** $(-2, 0, 0)$ **7.** $(0, 0, 0)$ is the
origin; $(1, -1, 2)$ and $(-2, 2, 3)$ are in the fourth and sixth
octant, respectively; the pairs, $(0, 1, 2)$ and $(0, -1, 2)$, $(4, 0, 3)$
and $(4, 0, -3)$, $(\pi, \pi/2, 0)$ and $(-\sqrt{2}, \sqrt{2}, 0)$ are in the yz-, xz-
and xy-planes, respectively.   **9.** The first octant is the set of all
points which have all coordinates positive. The second octant
might be described as the set of points in space whose x-coordi-
nate is negative and whose y- and z-coordinates are positive.
Similar statements can be made for other octants. The first
octant could also be described as the set of points on the same
side of the xz-plane as the positive y-axis, on the same side of

the xy-plane as the positive z-axis, and on the same side of
the yz-plane as the positive x-axis. Similar statements can be
made for the other octants.   **11.** A plane parallel to the
yz-plane and intersecting the x-axis at -2; a line parallel to
the z-axis and containing the point $(1, -2, 0)$.   **13.** The
half-space which is the set of points on the same side of the
xz-plane as the negative y-axis.   **15.** All points in space
except those in the yz-plane.   **17.** Any point with
coordinates $(-1, -2, z)$, where z is any real number, will lie
on the line.   **19-21.** Portions of the planes are shown.
Horizontal shading represents a portion of the plane that
contains the segment and is parallel to the y-axis. Vertical
shading represents a portion of the plane containing the
segment and parallel to the z-axis.

19.

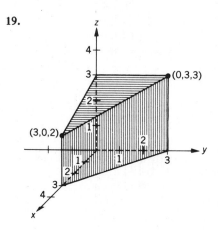

21.

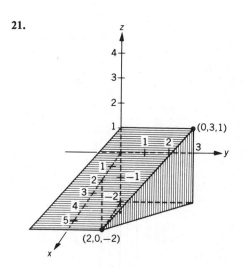

23. A plane parallel to the z-axis and intersecting the xy-plane in the line $2x + 3y = 6$. **25.** Two octants are needed since temperature can be either a positive or negative number. The graph shows that the internal energy, E, of a gas increases as the pressure, p, and temperature, T, increase.

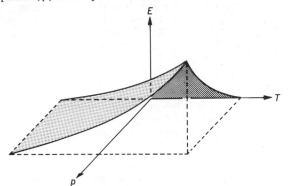

27. *Hint:* Use points $A_1(a_1, 0, 0)$, $A_2(0, a_2, 0)$, and $A_3(0, 0, a_3)$. Investigate the intersections of planes passing through these points.
Calculator Problem. $P = (2.466212, -5.7445626, 3.4820045)$. Hence the point with integer coordinates closest to P has coordinates $(2, -6, 3)$.

Section 13-3, page 319

1. 9 **3.** 7 **5.** 11 **7.** $5\sqrt{2}$ **9.** $\sqrt{d^2 + e^2 + f^2}$
11. $|\overline{XY}| = \sqrt{13}$, $|\overline{YZ}| = \sqrt{22}$, $|\overline{XZ}| = 3$ and $(\sqrt{13})^2 + 3^2 = (\sqrt{22})^2$, so the triangle is a right triangle. **13.** The distance between $(-2, 7, 2)$ and $(-4, 3, -3)$ is $3\sqrt{5}$. The distance between $(-4, 3, -3)$ and $(2, 6, -3)$ is also $3\sqrt{5}$. Therefore, the three points are vertices of an isosceles triangle. **15.** $x = 5$ or $x = -1$ **17.** Since r is the distance from (a, b, c) to $P(x, y, z)$, then by the distance formula, $r^2 = (x - a)^2 + (y - b)^2 + (z - c)^2$.
19. $y = 5$ or $y = -3$ **21.** *Hint:* Use the distance formula and the fact that $(a - b)^2 = (b - a)^2$.
Calculator Problem. $a = \sqrt{133} = 11.532562$; $b = \sqrt{210} = 14.491376$; $c = \sqrt{69} = 8.3066238$; $s = 17.165281$; $A = 47.856556$

Section 13-4, page 323

1. $-3/7, 2/7, 6/7$ **3.** $3/\sqrt{29}, -2/\sqrt{29}, 4/\sqrt{29}$
5. $a/\sqrt{a^2 + b^2 + c^2}, b/\sqrt{a^2 + b^2 + c^2}, c/\sqrt{a^2 + b^2 + c^2}$
9. $\cos \alpha = -3/\sqrt{10}, \cos \beta = 0, \cos \gamma = 1/\sqrt{10}$ **11.** If the line is directed upward the direction cosines are 0, 0, 1 and the direction angles are $\pi/2, \pi/2, 0$. If directed downward the direction cosines are 0, 0, -1 and the direction angles are $\pi/2, \pi/2, \pi$.
13. Yes; $(1/2)^2 + (1/\sqrt{2})^2 + (1/2)^2 = 1$. **15.** Same answer as Problem 5. Theorem 13-3. **17.** *Hint:* Use the fact that $0 \leqslant |a| \leqslant 1, 0 \leqslant |b| \leqslant 1$, and $0 \leqslant |c| \leqslant 1$. **19.** Use Theorem 13-2.
Calculator Problem. $c = \pm 1/\sqrt{3}$; $\alpha = \beta = \gamma = 54.73561°$ or $125.26438°$

Section 13-5, page 326

1. $x = (3/7)d, y = (2/7)d, z = (6/7)d$; $(6, 4, 12)$ is another point on the line. **3.** $x = 2 + 2d/3\sqrt{5}, y = 4 - 4d/3\sqrt{5}$, $z = 5d/3\sqrt{5}$; $(0, 8, -5)$ is another point on the line.
5. $x = 2 - d/\sqrt{3}, y = -1 + d/\sqrt{3}, z = 2 - d/\sqrt{3}$
7. $(3, -1, 3)$ **9.** $(4, -5/2, 4)$ **11.** xy-coordinate plane: $(0, 7/2, 0)$; yz-coordinate plane: $(0, 7/2, 0)$; xz-coordinate plane: $(7/3, 0, 7/3)$. **13.** The line is parallel to the yz-coordinate plane and contains the points $(5, 2, -2)$ and $(5, 0, 0)$.
15. The midpoint of $\overline{AB} = (4, 2, 1)$. The midpoint of $\overline{CD}$ is $(4, 2, 1)$. **17.** *Hint:* Show that both (x_0, y_0, z_0) and (x_1, y_1, z_1) belong to each line.
Calculator Problem. $x = 4 + 0.8090169d$; $y = 3 + 0.3090169d$; $z = 2 + 0.5d$; xy-plane $\rightarrow$ $(0.763932, 1.763932, 0)$, xz-plane $\rightarrow$ $(-3.8541019, 0, -2.8541019)$, yz-plane $\rightarrow$ $(0, 1.4721359, -0.4721359)$.

Section 13-6, page 331

1. Intercepts: $x = 3, y = -3, z = 3/2$; xy-trace: $x - y = 3$, $z = 0$; yz-trace: $2z - y = 3, x = 0$; xz-trace: $x + 2z = 3, y = 0$
3. Intercepts: $x = a, y = a, z = a$; xy-trace: $x + y = a, z = 0$; yz-trace: $y + z = a, x = 0$; xz-trace: $x + z = a, y = 0$
5. Intercepts: $x = -4, y = 2, z = 4$; xy-trace: $x - 2y = -4$, $z = 0$; yz-trace: $2y + z = 4, x = 0$; xz-trace: $x - z = -4, y = 0$
7. $x + y + z - 5 = 0$ **9.** Collinear points **11.** $3x - 12y + 4z = 12$ **13.** $4x + 3y - 3z = 12$ **15.** $6x - 15y + 10z = 30$
17. $(6/5, 12/5, 3)$ **19.** $(-1, 6, 2)$ **21.** Parallel planes
23. Let (x, y, z) be the set of points satisfying both equations. This set must lie on the line of intersection of the two planes. Now show that the desired equation is that of a plane, and that any point of the intersection of the two original equations satisfies the latter equation also; hence it is a plane containing the line of intersection of the two given planes.
25. $x + 2y + 2z - 5 = 0$
Calculator Problem. x-intercept: $0.59562842 \doteq 0.60$; y-intercept: $-0.26139089 \doteq -0.26$; z-intercept: $0.31918009 \doteq 0.32$

CHAPTER 14
Section 14-2, page 340

1. Magnitude, 6; $c_1 = 2/3, c_2 = 2/3, c_3 = 1/3$ **3.** Magnitude, $\sqrt{34}$; $c_1 = 3/\sqrt{34}, c_2 = 3/\sqrt{34}, c_3 = -4/\sqrt{34}$
5. $((0, 0, 0), (2, -5, -3))$ **7.** $(3, 6, 2)$ **9.** $(-1, 2, 3)$
11. $(-3, 2, -1)$ **13.** $(0, 0, 0)$ **15.** $(3, -2, 1)$ **17.** $P' = P(-6, 6, 2)$ **19.** $(0, 0, 0)$; that is $P = O$ and $\overrightarrow{OP}$ is the null vector. **21.** Yes; $s = t + (-r)$ **23.** Suppose that the position vector for $\mathbf{v}$ has endpoint $P = (x, y, z)$. Consider $\mathbf{v} + \mathbf{w}$ and use Theorem 14-2. **25.** $\mathbf{c} = \mathbf{a} - \mathbf{b}$
Calculator Problem. $\overrightarrow{OP} = (7.1, -9.0, -1.4)$; $|\overrightarrow{OP}| = \sqrt{133.37} = 11.548592$; $\cos \alpha = 0.6147935, \alpha = 0.9086722 \ (52.063082°)$, $\cos \beta = -0.7793157, \beta = 2.4643693 \ (141.19796°)$, $\cos \gamma = -0.1212268, \gamma = 1.6923221 \ (96.962915°)$

Section 14-3, page 342

1.

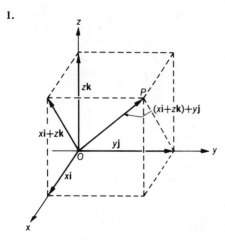

3. $2\mathbf{i} + 4\mathbf{j} + \mathbf{k}$ **5.** $3\mathbf{i} + 0\mathbf{j} - 2\mathbf{k}$ **7.** $(3\sqrt{3}/2)\mathbf{i} - 3\mathbf{j} + \sqrt{2}\,\mathbf{k}$
9. $(\sqrt{3}+1)\mathbf{i} + 2\mathbf{j} + (2\sqrt{2}-3)\mathbf{k}$ **11.** $((14+\sqrt{3})/2)\mathbf{i} + 24\mathbf{j} - \sqrt{2}\mathbf{k}$ **13.** $\sqrt{3}$ **15.** $\sqrt{26}$ **17.** $\sqrt{x^2+y^2+z^2}$
19. $x = 10/7, y = 11, z = -2$ **21.** $\mathbf{a} + (\mathbf{b}+\mathbf{c}) =$
$(2\mathbf{i}-(1/2)\mathbf{j}+5\mathbf{k}) + (2\mathbf{j}-3\mathbf{k}) = (2\mathbf{i}+(3/2)\mathbf{j}+2\mathbf{k})$. $(\mathbf{a}+\mathbf{b})+\mathbf{c} =$
$(3\mathbf{i}-(3/2)\mathbf{j}+3\mathbf{k}) + (-\mathbf{i}+3\mathbf{j}-\mathbf{k}) = (2\mathbf{i}+(3/2)\mathbf{j}+2\mathbf{k})$. **23.** Let
$\mathbf{a} = a_1\mathbf{i}+a_2\mathbf{j}+a_3\mathbf{k}$, $\mathbf{b} = b_1\mathbf{i}+b_2\mathbf{j}+b_3\mathbf{k}$, and $\mathbf{c} = c_1\mathbf{i}+c_2\mathbf{j}+c_3\mathbf{k}$.
Use Theorem 14-4, the associativity of real numbers and Theorem 14-3. **25.** Suppose $\mathbf{v} = x\mathbf{i}+y\mathbf{j}+z\mathbf{k}$. Find direction cosines of $\mathbf{v}$ and use part (4) of Theorem 14-5. **27.** The two
vectors with magnitudes 5 and 12 are perpendicular to each
other so that their sum is a vector of magnitude 13. The given
vector with magnitude 13 is directed oppositely to the sum of
the other two vectors so that the sum of the three vectors is the
zero vector. **29.** $|\overrightarrow{OP_1}|^2 = 17$, $|\overrightarrow{OP_2}|^2 = 42$, $|\overrightarrow{P_1P_2}|^2 = 59$.
Therefore, by the converse of the Pythagorean Theorem, P_1, O,
and P_2 are the vertices of a right triangle.
Calculator Problem. $\mathbf{c} = 0.3\mathbf{i} + 1.6\mathbf{j} - 4.4\mathbf{k}$; $|\mathbf{c}| = \sqrt{22.01} =$
4.6914816; $c_1 = 6.3945683 \times 10^{-2}, c_2 = 0.3410436$,
$c_3 = -0.937870$

Section 14-4, page 345

1. $\mathbf{r} = 3t\mathbf{i} + (1-t)\mathbf{j} + 2\mathbf{k}$ **3.** $\mathbf{r} = (4-7t)\mathbf{i} + (4-2t)\mathbf{j} + (-2+t)\mathbf{k}$ **5.** $\mathbf{r} = (a_1 + a_2 t - a_1 t)\mathbf{i} + (b_1 + b_2 t - b_1 t)\mathbf{j} + (c_1 + c_2 t - c_1 t)\mathbf{k}$ **7.** $(4, -1, -3)$ **9.** $(2, -2, -7)$
11. $(5, -1/2, -1)$ **13.** Find a vector equation of the line.
Then let $t = 1/2$. **15.** $(5/2, 7/2, 9/2)$ **17.** $(0, 0, 0)$
19. $(a/2, b/2, c/2)$ **21.** $(8, 8, 3)$
23. $((2x_1 + x_2)/3, (2y_1 + y_2)/3, (2z_1 + z_2)/3)$ and
$((x_1 + 2x_2)/3, (y_1 + 2y_2)/3, (z_1 + 2z_2)/3)$
25. $\mathbf{r} = t(2\mathbf{i} + 4\mathbf{j} + \sqrt{5}\,\mathbf{k})$. The speeds in the x-, y- and z-directions are 2, 4, and $\sqrt{5}$ units per second, respectively.
Calculator Problem. $(1.9724716, 13.949913, -0.9661977)$

Section 14-5, page 349

1. $(2, -1, 4)$ **3.** $(5, 1, 3)$ **5.** $(-1, -3, 5)$ **7.** $x = 1 - s - t$,
$y = s, z = t$ **9.** $x = t, y = 2s, z = 2t$ **11-15.** The required
graph is a plane: **11.** parallel to the yz-plane with intercept
$(3, 0, 0)$. **13.** perpendicular to the xy-plane with intercepts
$(2, 0, 0)$ and $(0, 2, 0)$. **15.** perpendicular to the xy-plane with
the trace, $x = 2y, z = 0$. **17.** $x + 5y + 2z = 19$ **19.** $\mathbf{r}_0 =$
$\overrightarrow{OP_0} = x_0\mathbf{i} + y_0\mathbf{j} + z_0\mathbf{k}$. $\overrightarrow{P_0P_1} = (x_1 - x_0)\mathbf{i} + (y_1 - y_0)\mathbf{j} + (z_1 - z_0)\mathbf{k}$. $\overrightarrow{P_0P_2} = (x_2 - x_0)\mathbf{i} + (y_2 - y_0)\mathbf{j} + (z_2 - z_0)\mathbf{k}$.
$\mathbf{r} = \overrightarrow{OP} = x\mathbf{i} + y\mathbf{j} + z\mathbf{k}$. Equation (2) is $\mathbf{r} = \mathbf{r}_0 + s\overrightarrow{P_0P_1} + t\overrightarrow{P_0P_2}$.
Considering the components of these vectors, we have
$x\mathbf{i} + y\mathbf{j} + z\mathbf{k} = (x_0\mathbf{i} + y_0\mathbf{j} + z_0\mathbf{k}) +$
$[s((x_1 - x_0)\mathbf{i} + (y_1 - y_0)\mathbf{j} + (z_1 - z_0)\mathbf{k})] +$
$[t((x_2 - x_0)\mathbf{i} + (y_2 - y_0)\mathbf{j} + (z_2 - z_0)\mathbf{k})]$. Then use associativity, commutativity, and distributivity, and Theorem 14-3.
21. (Answers may vary.) A vector equation of the line is
$\mathbf{r} = (2 - s + 2t)\mathbf{i} + (4 + s + 2t)\mathbf{j} + (-3 + 2s + 5t)\mathbf{k}$. A rectangular
equation is $x + 9y - 4z = 50$. **23.** $a = 3, b = -2, c = 2$
Calculator Problem. **(a)** $(2.2360679, -2.962496, 2.6348794)$
(b) $(5.7475489, -1.546428, 14.682655)$
(c) $(-35.891589, 24.828356, -21.620468)$

CHAPTER 15

Section 15-2, page 360

1. $-(3 + 2\sqrt{3})/12$ **3.** $2\sqrt{2}/3$ **5.** $7/9$ **7.** $-3/5\sqrt{5}$
9. -1 **11.** Use Corollary 3. **13.** $24/\sqrt{609}$ **15.** $-12/5\sqrt{6}$
17. $\theta = \text{Arccos}\,(19\sqrt{3}/105)$ **19.** Each angle is equal to
$\text{Arccos}\,\sqrt{3}/3$, for $c > 0$, or $\text{Arccos}\,(-\sqrt{3}/3)$, for $c < 0$.
21. Let $P_1 = P(1, 3, 5), P_2 = P(3, 0, 1), P_3 = P(1, 11, -1)$, and
$P_4 = P(-5, 3, 2)$. Then the cosine of the angle between the
vectors $\overrightarrow{P_1P_2}$ and $\overrightarrow{P_3P_4}$ is 0. Hence the measure of the angle
between the vectors is $\pi/2$ and, the lines containing the points
are perpendicular. **23.** If the nonzero vectors $\mathbf{a}$ and $\mathbf{b}$ are
perpendicular, then the measure of the angle θ between them is
$\pi/2$ and $\cos \theta = \cos \pi/2 = (a_1 b_1 + a_2 b_2 + a_3 b_3)/|\mathbf{a}|\,|\mathbf{b}| = 0$.
This implies that $a_1 b_1 + a_2 b_2 + a_3 b_3 = 0$. Conversely, if $\mathbf{a}$ and $\mathbf{b}$
are nonzero vectors with components (a_1, a_2, a_3) and
(b_1, b_2, b_3) respectively such that $a_1 b_1 + a_2 b_2 + a_3 b_3 = 0$,
then $(a_1 b_1 + a_2 b_2 + a_3 b_3)/|\mathbf{a}|\,|\mathbf{b}| = 0$. **25.** Let (x_1, y_1, z_1)
and (x_2, y_2, z_1) represent coordinates of two points on a line
parallel to the xy-plane. Use the definition of direction cosines
of a line.
Calculator Problem. **(a)** $|AB| = \sqrt{42}, |BC| = \sqrt{85}, |AC| = \sqrt{53}$
(b) $m(\angle A) = \text{Arccos}\,5/(\sqrt{42} \cdot \sqrt{53}) = 83.9166°, m(\angle B) =$
$\text{Arccos}\,37/(\sqrt{42} \cdot \sqrt{85}) = 51.738447°, m(\angle C) =$
$\text{Arccos}\,48/(\sqrt{53} \cdot \sqrt{85}) = 44.344952°$ **(c)** $28x + 29y + 24z = 94$

Section 15-3, page 364

1. -5 3. -11 5. 21 7. 9 9. $9\sqrt{2}/2$ 11. 0
13. -9 15. $\mathbf{u} \cdot \mathbf{i} = 1, \mathbf{u} \cdot \mathbf{j} = -2, \mathbf{u} \cdot \mathbf{k} = 2$ 17. 2
19. Component along the line of flight is $-75\sqrt{2}$. Speed of the plane will be $(900 - 75\sqrt{2})$ km/h   21. If $\mathbf{a}$ is any vector, there is no vector $\mathbf{b}$ such that $\mathbf{a} \cdot \mathbf{b} = \mathbf{a}$, because the dot product of two vectors is a real number, not a vector.   23. 8 25. *Hint:* Express $\mathbf{a}$, $\mathbf{b}$, and $\mathbf{c}$ in terms of their components and use Theorem 15-2, associativity, commutativity, and distributivity for real numbers.   27. Let $\mathbf{u} = u_1\mathbf{i} + u_2\mathbf{j} + u_3\mathbf{k}$ and $\mathbf{v} = v_1\mathbf{i} + v_2\mathbf{j} + v_3\mathbf{k}$ be any two vectors. $\mathbf{u} \cdot \mathbf{v} = u_1v_1 + u_2v_2 + u_3v_3 = v_1u_1 + v_2u_2 + v_3u_3 = \mathbf{v} \cdot \mathbf{u}$.   29. The domain is the set of all ordered pairs of vectors. The range is the set of real numbers. The dot product maps each ordered pair of vectors into a unique real number.
Calculator Problem. $\mathbf{a} \cdot \mathbf{c} = 0, \mathbf{a} \perp \mathbf{c}; \mathbf{a} \cdot \mathbf{d} = 0, \mathbf{a} \perp \mathbf{d}; \mathbf{c} \cdot \mathbf{d} = 0$, $\mathbf{c} \perp \mathbf{d}$. $\mathbf{a}$, $\mathbf{c}$, and $\mathbf{d}$ are mutually perpendicular.

Section 15-4, page 368

1. $(3/5)\mathbf{i} + (4/5)\mathbf{j}$ 3. $(-2/\sqrt{5})\mathbf{i} + (1/\sqrt{5})\mathbf{j}$ 5. $\sqrt{10}$
7. $4\sqrt{2}$ 9. $7\sqrt{5}/5$ 11. 0 13. $2/\sqrt{2}$ 15. $12/\sqrt{73}$
17. $14/\sqrt{17}$ 19. $2x - \sqrt{5}y - 9 = 0$
Calculator Problem. $p = |-18.44|/8.3944326 = 2.196694\ldots \doteq 2.20$

Section 15-5, page 371

1. $9/\sqrt{13}$ 3. $12/\sqrt{13}$ 5. $22/\sqrt{13}$ 7. 0 9. $\cos\theta = -2/\pm 2\sqrt{5}$, $\theta = 1.107$ or $63.4°$ 11. $\cos\theta = 1/\pm\sqrt{2}$, $\theta = \pi/4$ or $45°$ 13. $\cos\theta = -1/\pm\sqrt{10}$, $\theta = 1.249$ or $71.6°$
15. $d = 11/\sqrt{13}$. The origin is on the opposite side of the line from the point $(-2, 3)$.   17. $4x - 3y - 13 = 0$ and $4x - 3y + 17 = 0$ 19. Let α be the measure of the acute angle between the lines $7x - 4y + 3 = 0$ and $3x + 2y + 5 = 0$. Then $\cos\alpha = 1/\sqrt{5}$. Let β be the measure of the acute angle between the lines $3x + 2y + 5 = 0$ and $x - 8y + 45 = 0$. Then $\cos\beta = 1/\sqrt{5}$. Thus $\alpha = \beta$, so that a triangle is formed with two congruent angles, which implies that it is isosceles.   21. The lines $ax + by + c = 0$ and $bx - ay = k$ have unit normals $\mathbf{n} = a\mathbf{i}/\sqrt{a^2 + b^2} + b\mathbf{j}/\sqrt{a^2 + b^2}$ and $\mathbf{m} = b\mathbf{i}/\sqrt{a^2 + b^2} + -a\mathbf{j}/\sqrt{a^2 + b^2}$ respectively. The scalar product of their normals is 0. Thus $\mathbf{n} \cdot \mathbf{m} = ab/(a^2 + b^2) + -ab/(a^2 + b^2) = 0$
23. $x + 3y = 3$ 25. The cosines of the angles between the lines l_1 and l_2 are the same as the cosines of the angles between their unit normals, $\mathbf{n}_1$ and $\mathbf{n}_2$, respectively. Hence, by Theorems 15-1 and 15-2, $\mathbf{n}_1 \cdot \mathbf{n}_2 = \cos\theta = (a_1a_2 + b_1b_2)/\pm\sqrt{a_1^2 + b_1^2}\sqrt{a_2^2 + b_2^2}$.   27. $x + y - 6 = 0$
Calculator Problem. $\cos\theta = \pm 0.2760713$, $\theta = 73.974131°(1.2910921)$ or $106.02586°(1.8505005)$

Section 15-6, page 376

1. $d = \sqrt{3}$ 3. $d = 1/2$ 5. $d = 2\sqrt{2}$ 7. $d = 6/\sqrt{3}$
9. $26/9$ 11. 0 13. 0 15. $2/\sqrt{6}$. The point $(1, 1, 2)$ is on the opposite side of the plane from the origin.   17. $13/6$. The point $(-1, 2, 1)$ is on the same side of the plane as the origin.
19. $2/5$. The point $(2, 2, 2)$ is on the opposite side of the plane from the origin.   21. $-2/\sqrt{6}, 1/\sqrt{6}, 1/\sqrt{6}; 2/\sqrt{6}, -1/\sqrt{6}, -1/\sqrt{6}$ 23. No.   25. $x - 2y + 2z - 18 = 0$ and $x - 2y + 2z + 6 = 0$ 27. $13/\sqrt{26}$ 29. *Hint:* Use a unit normal to the plane.   31. $35.3°$ or $144.7°$ 33. $x - y + 3z = 3\sqrt{11} + 6$ or $x - y + 3z = -3\sqrt{11} + 6$
Calculator Problem. $d = 4.6710953$

Section 15-7, page 380

1.

×	i	j	k
i	0	k	−j
j	−k	0	i
k	j	−i	0

3. $6\mathbf{k}$ 5. $4\mathbf{i}$ 7. 0 9. $9\mathbf{k}$ 11. Yes, both are $6\mathbf{j}$.   13. No.
15. 12 17. *Hint:* Use parametric equations of the plane determined by position vectors of $\mathbf{a}$ and $\mathbf{b}$ and the origin.
Calculator Problem.   The angle θ between $\mathbf{a}$ and $\mathbf{b}$ is Arccos $11/10\sqrt{7}$. $|\mathbf{a} \times \mathbf{b}| = 10\sqrt{7}\sin\theta = \sqrt{579}$; $\mathbf{a} \times \mathbf{b} = 13\mathbf{i} - 11\mathbf{j} - 17\mathbf{k}$

Section 15-8, page 383

1. $-3\mathbf{j} - 3\mathbf{k}$ 3. $-\mathbf{i} - 2\mathbf{j} - 4\mathbf{k}$ 5. $-23\mathbf{i} + 5\mathbf{j} - 16\mathbf{k}$
7. (1) $3\sqrt{2}$ (2) $2\sqrt{14}$ (3) $\sqrt{21}$ (4) $7\sqrt{5}$ (5) $9\sqrt{10}$ (6) $4\sqrt{2}$ 9. $-3\mathbf{j} + 3\mathbf{k}$ 11. $3\mathbf{j} - 3\mathbf{k}$ 13. $-2\mathbf{i} - 16\mathbf{j} + 5\mathbf{k}$
15. $\mathbf{r} \times \mathbf{s} = -(\mathbf{s} \times \mathbf{r})$ 17. $\mathbf{a} \times (\mathbf{b} \times \mathbf{c}) = -10\mathbf{i} - 43\mathbf{j} - 63\mathbf{k} = (\mathbf{a} \cdot \mathbf{c})\mathbf{b} - (\mathbf{a} \cdot \mathbf{b})\mathbf{c}$ 19. $\mathbf{a} \times \mathbf{b} = (0 - 0)\mathbf{i} + (0 - 0)\mathbf{j} + (1 - 0)\mathbf{k} = \mathbf{k}$, which is correct since $\mathbf{i} \times \mathbf{j} = \mathbf{k}$.
Calculator Problem. $\mathbf{a} \times (\mathbf{b} + \mathbf{c}) = -28.03\mathbf{i} + 11.97\mathbf{j} + 32.97\mathbf{k}$

Section 15-9, page 386

1. $3\sqrt{2}/2$ square units   3. $\sqrt{61}$ square units
5. $(1/2)\left[((y_2 - y_1)(z_3 - z_1) - (y_3 - y_1)(z_2 - z_1))^2 + ((x_2 - x_1)(z_3 - z_1) - (x_3 - x_1)(z_2 - z_1))^2 + ((x_2 - x_1)(y_3 - y_1) - (x_3 - x_1)(y_2 - y_1))^2\right]^{1/2}$
9. $x - z = 0$ 11. 14 cubic units   13. $x - y = 1$
15. $3x + 11y + 12z = 26$ 17. $x + y + z = 5$ 19. The sum of the moments of $\mathbf{F}_1$ and $\mathbf{F}_2$ about O is $12\mathbf{k}$. The moment of the sum of the forces $\mathbf{F}_1$ and $\mathbf{F}_2$ is also $12\mathbf{k}$. This illustrates the distributive property of vector multiplication with respect to vector addition.

Calculator Problem.   area $(\triangle ABC) = (1/2)|\overrightarrow{BA} \times \overrightarrow{BC}| = 5.8843712$ square units

CHAPTER 16

Section 16-2, page 395

1. Unique solution   3. No solution   5. Unique solution
7. $x = 5, y = 1$ 9. $x = 2\sqrt{2}, y = -\sqrt{2}$ 11. $x = 3, y = 3$
13. $x = -4/13, y = -87/13$ 15. If a_1/b_1 is nearly equal to
a_2/b_2, then $|x|$ and $|y|$ become very large.   17. If $a_1b_2 - a_2b_1$
$= 0$, then $a_1b_2 = a_2b_1$ and $(b_2/b_1)a_1 = a_2$, so $a_2 = ka_1$ for
some real k. Also $b_2 = (a_2/a_1)b_1$ so $b_2 = kb_1$ for some real k.
19. As $a_1b_2 - a_2b_1$ approaches zero, $|x|$ and $|y|$ become very
large.
Calculator Problem.   (a) $x = -1, y = -1$ (b) $x = 2.5, y = 0.5$

Section 16-3, page 398

1. 1   3. 1.77   5. $ad - bc$ 7. $2x$ 9. $x = 6$ 11. $x = 3/2$
13. $x = -1, y = -4$ 15. $x = -1, y = 1$ 17. $x = 3, y = -2$
19. $x = 1, y = -1$ 21. $10x - 5(x - 2) < 0$; $5x + 10 < 0$ and
$x < -2$ 23. (1) Exchanging two rows (or two columns)
changes the sign of the determinant; (2) Interchanging each i-th
row with the i-th column does not alter the determinant.
Calculator Problem. $x \doteq -1.349, y \doteq -0.658$

Section 16-4, page 404

1. 15   3. 48   5. $x = 1/2, y = 1/3, z = 1/6$ 7. z is arbitrary,
$x = 6 - z, y = 7 - z$

9. $1\begin{vmatrix} 1 & -1 \\ -1 & 2 \end{vmatrix} - (-1)\begin{vmatrix} 2 & -1 \\ 1 & 2 \end{vmatrix} + 2\begin{vmatrix} 2 & 1 \\ 1 & -1 \end{vmatrix} = 0$

11. No solution   13. No solution   15. Infinitely many
solutions   17. $2x - 3y - 8 = 0$

19. (a) $\begin{vmatrix} 1 & 2 & 3 \\ 0 & -3 & -6 \\ 0 & -6 & -12 \end{vmatrix} = 0$

(b) $\begin{vmatrix} 0 & -1 & 1 \\ 1 & 3 & 2 \\ 3 & 2 & 3 \end{vmatrix} = \begin{vmatrix} 0 & 0 & 1 \\ 1 & 5 & 2 \\ 3 & 5 & 3 \end{vmatrix} = -10$

(c) $\begin{vmatrix} 3 & 0 & -1 \\ 2 & -1 & 1 \\ 4 & 1 & -2 \end{vmatrix} = \begin{vmatrix} 3 & 0 & -1 \\ 2 & -1 & 1 \\ 6 & 0 & -1 \end{vmatrix} = -3$

Calculator Problem. $x = -259.696/-45.844 \doteq 5.665$,
$y = 37.336/-45.844 \doteq -0.814, z = -59.908/-45.844 \doteq 1.307$

Section 16-5, page 406

1. 1   3. 64   5. $x = 1, y = -1, z = 2, w = -3$ 7. $x = -2$,
$w = -1, y = 0, z = 3$ 9. *Hint:* If the four equations have a
unique solution, then that solution may be found by applying
Cramer's Rule to the three equations of the system. Since the
solution must satisfy the fourth equation of the system, this
will imply that the determinant of the coefficients is zero.

11. $\begin{vmatrix} 1 & w & x + y + z & a \\ 0 & x - w & w - x & b - a \\ 0 & y - w & w - y & c - a \\ 0 & z - w & w - z & d - a \end{vmatrix}$

Calculator Problem. -74.994

Section 16-6, page 410

1. 3 rows and 4 columns   3. 4   5. $x = 1, y = 0$

7. $\begin{bmatrix} 7 & 8 \\ 1 & 2 \\ -1 & 1 \end{bmatrix}$ 9. $\begin{bmatrix} 5 & 1 & -1 \\ 2 & 1 & 7 \\ 4 & 3 & 4 \end{bmatrix}$ 11. $\begin{bmatrix} 1 & 0 & 1 \\ 0 & 0 & 0 \\ 0 & 6 & -2 \end{bmatrix}$ 13. $\begin{bmatrix} 28 \\ 0 \\ 4 \end{bmatrix}$

15. $\begin{bmatrix} 10 & -10 & 10 \end{bmatrix}$ 17. $\begin{bmatrix} 3 & 2 \\ 6 & 4 \end{bmatrix}$ 19. $\begin{bmatrix} -4 & -1 \\ -8 & -7 \end{bmatrix}$

21. $\begin{bmatrix} 2 & 1 \\ 2 & 2 \end{bmatrix}$ 23. $\begin{bmatrix} -7 & -3 \\ -4 & -5 \end{bmatrix}$ 25. $\begin{bmatrix} -6 & 2 \\ -5 & 3 \end{bmatrix}$ 27. $\begin{bmatrix} -1 & -1 \\ 1 & 0 \end{bmatrix}$

29. $x = 3, y = -3$ 31. $x = 7, y = 5$

33. $\begin{bmatrix} -3 & -1 \\ -6 & -5 \end{bmatrix}$ 35. $\begin{bmatrix} -5 & -3 \\ -12 & -8 \end{bmatrix}$

37. *Hint:* Use the definitions of matrix addition, scalar multiplication, and some properties of real numbers.   39. *Hint:* To
show that two $m \times n$ matrices are equal show that the elements
in the ith row and jth column of each matrix are equal.

Calculator Problem. $Y = \begin{bmatrix} 18.31 & 3.07 \\ 1.35 & -4.93 \end{bmatrix}$

Section 16-7, page 413

1. $\begin{bmatrix} 14 \\ 0 \end{bmatrix}$ 3. $\begin{bmatrix} 2 & -1 & -1 \end{bmatrix}$ 5. $\begin{bmatrix} 13 & 10 & 8 \\ 10 & 25 & 5 \\ 8 & 5 & 5 \end{bmatrix}$ 7. $\begin{bmatrix} -3 & -4 \\ 0 & 1 \end{bmatrix}$

9. Both products are zero. Two nonzero matrices can have a
product which is the zero matrix. In the set of real numbers, if
$x \cdot y = 0$, then $x = 0$ or $y = 0$.

11.
$$A(BC) = \begin{bmatrix} 1 & -1 \\ 2 & 3 \end{bmatrix}\begin{bmatrix} 0 & 4 \\ -12 & 18 \end{bmatrix} = \begin{bmatrix} 12 & -14 \\ -36 & 62 \end{bmatrix}$$

$$(AB)C = \begin{bmatrix} 3 & -4 \\ 1 & 12 \end{bmatrix}\begin{bmatrix} 0 & 2 \\ -3 & 5 \end{bmatrix} = \begin{bmatrix} 12 & -14 \\ -36 & 62 \end{bmatrix}$$

13. $\begin{bmatrix} 1 & 0 \\ -8 & 9 \end{bmatrix}$ **15.** $\begin{bmatrix} 3 & -2 \\ 1 & 7 \end{bmatrix}$ **17.** $\begin{bmatrix} -3 & -12 \\ 26 & 1 \end{bmatrix}$

19. This follows directly from the definition of matrix multiplication.

21. $\begin{bmatrix} 4 & 2 \\ 2 & 5 \end{bmatrix}$ **23.** $\begin{bmatrix} 5 & 6 \\ 6 & 8 \end{bmatrix}$ **25.** $\begin{bmatrix} 16 & 16 \\ 16 & 24 \end{bmatrix}$

Calculator Problem.

$$AB = \begin{bmatrix} 25.48 & -32.38 \\ -22.82 & 45.76 \end{bmatrix}; \quad BA = \begin{bmatrix} 25.4 & -4.88 & 19.79 \\ -5.78 & 5.98 & -9.59 \\ 40.16 & -15.92 & 39.86 \end{bmatrix}$$

Section 16-8, page 417

1. Has inverse **3.** No inverse

5. $\begin{bmatrix} 3 & -2 \\ -4 & 3 \end{bmatrix}$ **7.** $\begin{bmatrix} 1 & -2/3 \\ 1 & -1/2 \end{bmatrix}$ **9.** $\begin{bmatrix} -6 & 18 & -12 \\ 4 & 13 & -7 \\ 2 & -16 & 4 \end{bmatrix}$

11. $\begin{bmatrix} -3 & -2 & 3 \\ 7 & 4 & -6 \\ 1 & 1 & -1 \end{bmatrix}$ **13.** $\begin{bmatrix} -2/5 & 1/2 & -2/5 \\ 1/5 & 0 & 1/5 \\ -4/5 & 1/2 & 1/5 \end{bmatrix}$

15. $x = 14$ and $y = -19$ **17.** Assume that it is possible to define a matrix inverse, B, for the $n \times m$ matrix A. From Definition 16-11, $BA = I_n$ (1). Since BA is defined, (1) shows that B must be an $m \times n$ matrix, and that m must be equal to n. Hence, A must be a square matrix. **19.** Let A be a $n \times n$ matrix. Since the inverse of A, A^{-1}, is defined, it follows from Definition 16-11 that, $A^{-1}A = I_n$ and $AA^{-1} = I_n$. Again applying Definition 16-11, this means that $(A^{-1})^{-1} = A$.

21. $\begin{bmatrix} 4/13 & -6/13 & 4/13 & -5/13 \\ 8/13 & 1/13 & -5/13 & 3/13 \\ -6/13 & -4/13 & 7/13 & 1/13 \\ -7/13 & 4/13 & 6/13 & -1/13 \end{bmatrix}$

Calculator Problem.

$$A^{-1} = \begin{bmatrix} 0.625 & 16.25 & -13.958\overline{3} \\ 1.25 & 2.5 & -1.25 \\ -0.625 & 3.75 & -2.708\overline{3} \end{bmatrix}$$

Section 16-9, page 420

1. $\begin{bmatrix} 1 & -1 \\ 2 & 1 \end{bmatrix}\begin{bmatrix} x \\ y \end{bmatrix} = \begin{bmatrix} 2 \\ 4 \end{bmatrix}$ **3.** $\begin{bmatrix} 2 & -1 & 0 \\ 1 & 1 & 1 \\ 1 & 0 & -2 \end{bmatrix}\begin{bmatrix} x \\ y \\ z \end{bmatrix} = \begin{bmatrix} 3 \\ 4 \\ 1 \end{bmatrix}$

5. $2x + y - 2z = 2, x + 2y + 5z = 4, x + y + z = 2$ **7.** $x = 5$, $y = 1$ **9.** $x = -10, y = 5$ **11.** $x = 2, y = 1, z = -1$ **13.** $x = 3, y = -4$ **15.** $x = -9, y = 7, z = 4$

17. $\begin{bmatrix} 1 & -1 \\ -2 & 3 \end{bmatrix}$ **19.** The proof of Theorem 16-12 follows from the definition of matrix multiplication and matrix equality.

Calculator Problem. $x \doteq -27.831323, y \doteq -24.251705$

CHAPTER 17

Section 17-2, page 428

1. $x^2 + y^2 + 2x - 4y + 3 = 0$ **3.** $x^2 + y^2 + 2\pi x - 6y + \pi^2 = 0$
5. $x^2 + y^2 = a^2$ **7.** $(x - 1)^2 + (y + 4)^2 = 1$; $(1, -4)$, 1
9. $(x + 5/2)^2 + y^2 = 35/4$; $(-5/2, 0), \sqrt{35}/2$ **11.** $(x - 5/2)^2 + (y - 7/2)^2 = -3/2$. (There is no graph.) **13.** $(0, 1)$; 5
15. $(0, 5)$; 5 **17.** $(2\sqrt{2}, -2\sqrt{2})$ or $(-2\sqrt{2}, 2\sqrt{2})$; 4
19. $(x + 2)^2 + (y + 3)^2 = 25$ **21.** $2x - y - 9 = 0$
23. $(1, -1)$ is the only point of intersection. **25.** If $P(x, y)$ is a point of the intersection of the given circles, then $x^2 + y^2 - 6x + 4 = x^2 + y^2 - 3x + 3y + 1$ or $x + y = 1$. **27.** The graph is that part of the circle which has center at $(-2, 1)$ and radius 3 and lies in quadrant I. **29.** *Hint:* If $P_1 = P(x_1, y_1)$ belongs to the intersection of the two circles, then $x_1^2 + y_1^2 + ax_1 + by_1 + c = 0$ and $x_1^2 + y_1^2 + Ax_1 + By_1 + C = 0$. Subtract these two equations and show that the coordinates of P_1 satisfy a linear equation. **31.** *Hint:* The result follows immediately from the Pythagorean Theorem and the distance formula.
33. $k = \pm 2\sqrt{5}$ **35.** The circle with center at the origin and radius 4. **37.** A circle through the points of intersection of the circles of Problems 34 and 35.
Calculator Problem. The center is $(0.5850182, -0.8827941)$. The radius is 6.2191305 units.

Section 17-3, page 432

1.

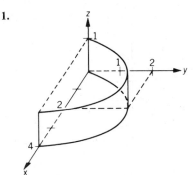

3.

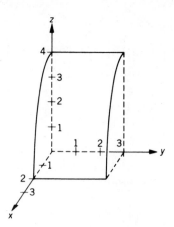

9.

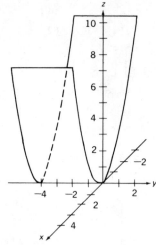

5.

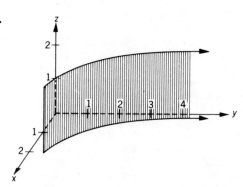

11.

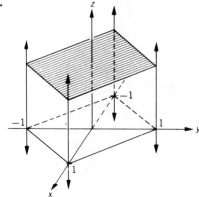

7. $(x - 2)^2 + (y - 4)^2 = 4$

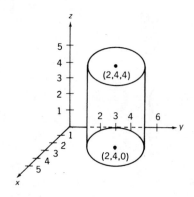

13.

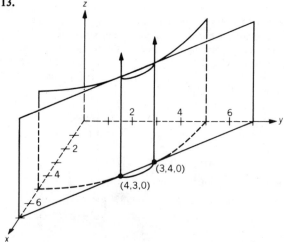

15.

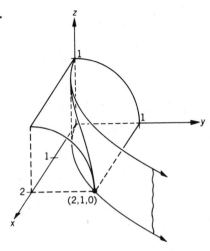

15. An equation of the cylinder is $x^2 + (z-1)^2 = 7$.

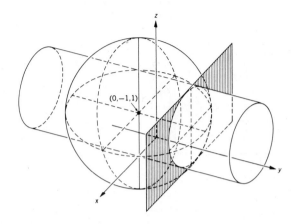

17. $(1 + \sqrt{2}, -1 - \sqrt{2}, -2)$ **19.** $(1, 0, 2)$
Calculator Problem. $(4, 36/5, 27/5)$

17.

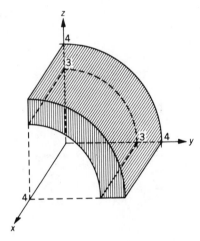

Calculator Problem. $\sqrt{4\pi^2 + 8^2} = \sqrt{103.4781} = 10.172434$

CHAPTER 18

Section 18-2, page 441

1. $e = 1$; parabola   **3.** $e = 5/2$; hyperbola
5. $e = 1$; parabola
7.

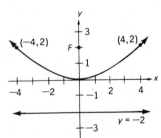

9. $M = (4, -2)$; $|PM| = 4$, $|PF| = 4$ **11.** $M = (2\sqrt{2}, -2)$;
$|PM| = 3$, $|PF| = \sqrt{(2\sqrt{2})^2 + (-1)^2} = 3$ **13.** $M = (2, -2)$;
$|PM| = 5/2$, $|PF| = 5/2$ **15.** $M = (\pm a, -2)$; $|PM| = $
$(a^2 + 16)/8$, $|PF| = (a^2 + 16)/8$

Section 17-4, page 435

1. $x^2 + y^2 + z^2 - 4x - 2y + 1 = 0$ **3.** $x^2 + y^2 + z^2 + 8x - 4y + 6z + 4 = 0$ **5.** $x^2 + y^2 + z^2 + 2x - 4y + 4z = 0$
7. $(1/2, 1/2, 1/2)$; $\sqrt{3}$ **9.** $(10, 10, 0)$; 1 **11.** Empty
13. A point

17.

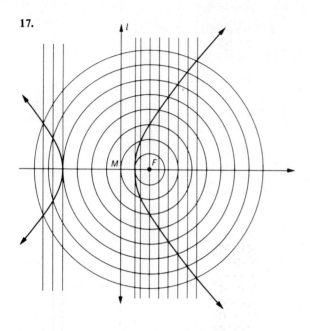

19. $(a^2 + b^2)(x^2 + y^2 - 2xh - 2yk + h^2 + k^2) = e^2(ax + by + c)^2$

Calculator Problem. $|FP| = 7.7984934$, $|PM| = 12.450273$, $|FP|/|PM| = 0.6263712$. The conic is an ellipse since $e < 1$.

Section 18-3, page 445

1.

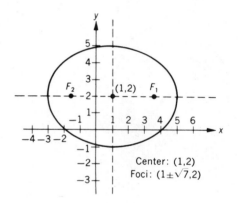

3. Vertex: $(0, 0)$; Focus: $(-3/2, 0)$; Directrix: $x = 3/2$
5. Vertex: $(0, 0)$; Focus: $(0, -1/2)$; Directrix: $y = 1/2$

7. Vertex: $(-1, -2)$; Focus: $(0, -2)$; Directrix: $x = -2$
9. Vertex: $(0, 3)$; Focus: $(0, 8/3)$; Directrix: $y = 10/3$
11. $(y - 3)^2 = 12(x - 1)$ **13.** $(y + 2)^2 = -12(x + 1)$
15. Points of intersection: $(-4, -1)$, $(2, 2)$. The graphs are a parabola (Vertex: $(9/4, 3/2)$; Focus: $(2, 3/2)$; Directrix: $x = 5/2$) and a line (Intercepts: $(-2, 0)$, $(0, 1)$).   **17.** Points of intersection: $(0, -1)$, $(1, 2)$. The graphs are parabolas. (Vertex: $(4/3, 1)$; Focus: $(7/12, 1)$; Directrix: $x = 25/12$; Vertex: $(-1/3, 0)$; Focus: $(5/12, 0)$; Directrix: $x = -13/12$).
19. $x_0/2c$ **21.** $2cx + x_0y - x_0y_0 - 2cx_0 = 0$ **23.** *Hint:* Use Theorem 15-8.
Calculator Problem. $m(\angle 1) = m(\angle 2) = \pi/4$

Section 18-4, page 451

1. $e = \sqrt{5}/3$; Foci: $(\pm\sqrt{5}, 0)$; Equations of directrices: $x = \pm 9\sqrt{5}/5$ **3.** $e = \sqrt{3}/2$; Foci: $(\pm 5\sqrt{3}/2, 0)$; Equations of directrices: $x = \pm 10\sqrt{3}/3$ **5.** $e = 0$; the foci coincide with the center of the circle. There are no directrices.
7. $(x - 1)^2/16 + (y - 2)^2/9 = 1$

Center: (1,2)
Foci: $(1 \pm \sqrt{7}, 2)$

9. $(x + 3)^2/9 + (y + 1)^2/25 = 1$; Center: $(-3, -1)$; Foci: $(-3, 3)$ and $(-3, -5)$ **11.** $(x + 3)^2/11 + (y + 2)^2/22 = 1$; Center: $(-3, -2)$; Foci: $(-3, -2 \pm \sqrt{11})$ **13.** $x^2/6 + y^2/3 = 1$
15. $x^2/4 + y^2/8 = 1$ **17.** $(x - 3)^2/16 + (y - 2)^2/7 = 1$
19. $(x - 1)^2/45 + (y - 1)^2/25 = 1$ **21.** $(x - 1)^2/21 + (y - 2)^2/25 = 1$ **23.** $x^2/36 + y^2/16 = 1$ **25.** Points of intersection are $\left((1 + \sqrt{21})/4, (1 - 3\sqrt{21})/4\right)$ and $\left((1 - \sqrt{21})/4, (1 + 3\sqrt{21})/4\right)$. The graph of $3x^2 + y^2 = 16$ is an ellipse with center $(0, 0)$ and intercepts $(0, \pm 4)$ and $(\pm\sqrt{16/3}, 0)$. The graph of $3x + y = 1$ is a line with intercepts $(1/3, 0)$ and $(0, 1)$.   **27.** Points of intersection are $(1, 2)$ and $(1, -2)$. The graph of $x^2 + 2y^2 = 9$ is an ellipse with center $(0, 0)$ and intercepts $(\pm 3, 0)$ and $(0, \pm\sqrt{9/2})$. The graph of $x^2 + y^2 - 4x = 1$ is a circle with center at $(2, 0)$ and radius $\sqrt{5}$.
29. The equation is satisfied only by the ordered pair $(0, 0)$.

31. Completing the squares, we get $4(x - 2)^2 + (y - 1)^2 = -1$. Since the sum of the squares of real numbers is never negative, the graph of this equation is the empty set. **33.** The points of intersection are $(-2, 0)$ and $(5/3, 11)$. The graph of $y - 3x = 6$ is a line with intercepts $(-2, 0)$ and $(0, 6)$. The graph of the quadratic is an ellipse which contains the points $(1 + \sqrt{85}/3, 0)$ and $(0, 2 + \sqrt{85})$, and has its center at $(1, 2)$.
35.

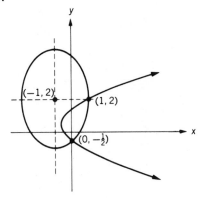

37. The point of intersection is $(1, 1)$. $x^2 + y^2 - 6x + 4 = 0$ is the equation of a circle with center $(3, 0)$ and radius $\sqrt{5}$. $2x - y = 1$ is the equation of a line with intercepts $(0, -1)$ and $(1/2, 0)$. **39.** $(2 + 2\sqrt{2}, 2)$ and $(2 - 2\sqrt{2}, 2)$ are the points of intersection. Both given equations represent parabolas. The first has its vertex at $(2, 1)$, focus at $(2, 3)$ and its axis parallel to the x-axis. The second has its vertex at $(2, 3)$, focus at $(2, 1)$ and its axis parallel to the x-axis. **41.** *Hint:* $|PF_1| = \sqrt{(x - c)^2 + y^2}$ and $|PF_2| = \sqrt{(x + c)^2 + y^2}$. Use the equation $b^2x^2 + a^2y^2 = a^2b^2$ and the relation $b^2 = a^2 - c^2$ to show that $|PF_1| = a - cx/a$ and $|PF_2| = a + cx/a$.
Calculator Problem. $|PF_1| = 7.981423$, $|PF_2| = 2.018576$, $|PF_1| + |PF_2| = 9.999999 \doteq 10 = 2a$

Section 18-5, page 457

1. $5/3$, $(\pm 5, 0)$, $y = \pm 4x/3$ **3.** $\sqrt{3}$, $(\pm 2\sqrt{3}, 0)$, $y = \pm\sqrt{2}x$
5-9. The center, foci, eccentricity and equations of the asymptotes are: **5.** $(1, -2)$; $(1, 1/2)$ and $(1, -9/2)$; $5/3$; $y + 2 = \pm(3/4)(x - 1)$. **7.** $(-3, 1)$; $(-3 \pm \sqrt{34}, 1)$; $\sqrt{34}/3$; $y - 1 = \pm(5/3)(x + 3)$. **9.** $(3, -2)$; $(3 \pm 3\sqrt{3}, -2)$; $\sqrt{3}$; $y + 2 = \pm\sqrt{2}(x - 3)$. **11.** $x^2 - 2y^2 = 2$ **13.** $x^2 - 9y^2 = 9$ **15.** $(x + 2)^2/(4/25) - (y - 3)^2 = 1$ **17.** $9x^2 - 16y^2 - 54x + 64y - 127 = 0$ **19.** $5x^2 - 4y^2 - 10x + 8y - 99 = 0$

21. The points of intersection are $(\sqrt{2}, 1), (\sqrt{2}, -1), (-\sqrt{2}, 1)$ and $(-\sqrt{2}, -1)$.

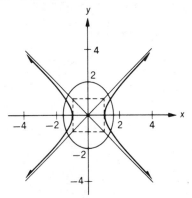

23. The points of intersection are $\left(1 + \sqrt{3}, \pm\sqrt{1 + \sqrt{3}}\right)$.

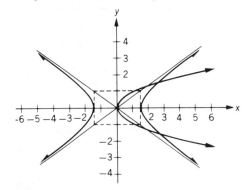

25. The points of intersection are $(8 + 2\sqrt{23}, 1), (8 - 2\sqrt{23}, 1)$, $(8 + 2\sqrt{13}, -1), (8 - 2\sqrt{13}, -1)$. **27.** $|F_2P| = \sqrt{(x + c)^2 + y^2}$ and $|F_1P| = \sqrt{(x - c)^2 + y^2}$. $|F_2P| - |F_1P| =$
$\sqrt{(x + c)^2 + (b^2x^2 - a^2b^2)/a^2} - \sqrt{(x - c)^2 + (b^2x^2 - a^2b^2)/a^2} =$
$\left(\sqrt{a^2(x + c)^2 + b^2x^2 - a^2b^2} - \sqrt{a^2(x - c)^2 + b^2x^2 - a^2b^2}\right)/a =$
$\left(\sqrt{(a^2 + b^2)x^2 + 2cxa^2 + a^4} - \sqrt{(a^2 + b^2)x^2 - 2cxa^2 + a^4}\right)/a =$
$\left(\sqrt{(cx + a^2)^2} - \sqrt{(cx - a^2)^2}\right)/a = ((cx + a^2) - (cx - a^2))/a =$
$2a^2/a = 2a$
Calculator Problem. $F_1 = (5 + \sqrt{10}, 3)$, $F_2 = (5 - \sqrt{10}, 3)$. $|F_2P| = \sqrt{30\sqrt{2} + 59} = 10.071067$, $|F_1P| = \sqrt{59 - 30\sqrt{2}} = 4.071067$, $|F_2P| - |F_1P| = 6.000000 = 2 \cdot 3 = 2a$

Section 18-6, page 461

1. $x = y$ and $x = -y$, intersecting at $(0, 0)$ **3.** The equation is equivalent to $x^2 + 2y^2 = -1$. But the sum of the squares of two real numbers cannot be negative, so the equation has no real solutions and thus an empty graph. **5.** The single point $(0, 0)$

7. The graph is the union of the two lines $x - 2y = 0$ and $x + 2y = 0$. **9.** The graph is the union of the pair of lines with equations $\sqrt{2}x - \sqrt{3}y + \sqrt{3}/2 = 0$ and $\sqrt{2}x + \sqrt{3}y - \sqrt{3}/2 = 0$. **11.** The graph is the union of the lines $y = 0$ and $y - 2x = 0$. **13.** The graph is the union of the lines $x + y = 0$ and $x + y + 1 = 0$.
Calculator Problem. $y^2 = 55.88x$; $x = 6.4516/55.88 = 0.1154545$ m or 11.54545 cm

Section 18-7, page 464

1. $B^2 - 4AC = -3$, ellipse   **3.** $B^2 - 4AC = 0$, parabola
5. $B^2 - 4AC = 1$, hyperbola
7.

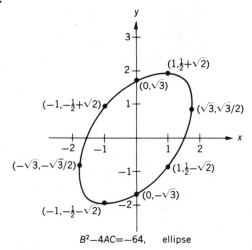

$B^2 - 4AC = -64$,   ellipse

9.

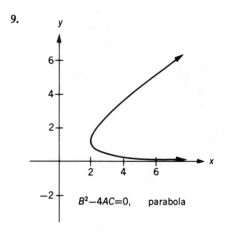

$B^2 - 4AC = 0$,   parabola

11. *Hint:* If $P(x, y)$ is any point on the conic, then the ratio of the distance from P to the focus to the distance from P to the directrix must equal the eccentricity, $\sqrt{2}$. Show that this ratio implies the second-degree equation $2xy + 4x + 4y - 1 = 0$ and that this conic is a hyperbola.

Calculator Problem. $y = \left(3x \pm \sqrt{25x^2 - 48}\right)/2$; x is such that $25x^2 - 48 \geqslant 0$ or $|x| \geqslant \sqrt{48/25}$. Thus $x \geqslant \sqrt{48/25}$ or $x \leqslant -\sqrt{48/25}$. The graph is a hyperbola.

Section 18-8, page 466

1.   **3.**

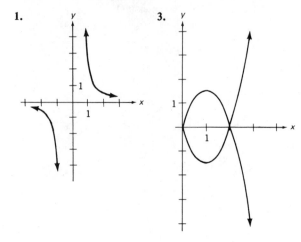

5.

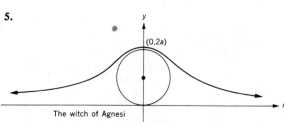

The witch of Agnesi

7.

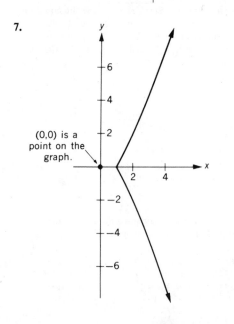

$(0,0)$ is a point on the graph.

9.

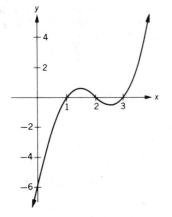

11.

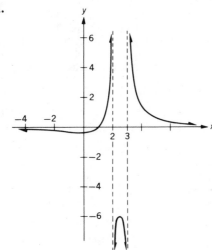

13.

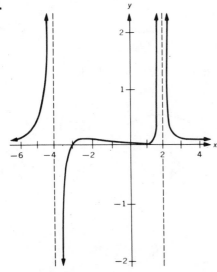

15.

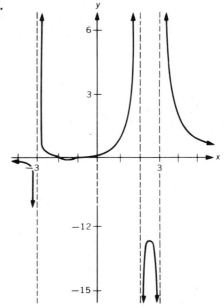

17.

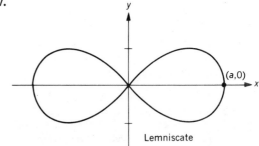

Lemniscate

Calculator Problem. (a) $e = c/a = 1.6714671 \times 10^{-2} \doteq 0.0167$
(b) $a + c = 152,105,090$ km   (c) $a - c = 147,103,910$ km

Section 18-9, page 470

1-9. The sketches referred to are those given in Section 18-9 of
the text.   **1.** Ellipsoid with center $(0, 0, 0)$ and intercepts
$(\pm\sqrt{6}, 0, 0)$, $(0, \pm\sqrt{3}, 0)$ and $(0, 0, \pm\sqrt{2})$.   **3.** Hyperboloid of
two sheets. The sketch is similar to sketch (c) rotated about the
x-axis through an angle of $90°$.   **5.** Paraboloid. The sketch is
similar to sketch (d) rotated about the x-axis through an angle
of $-90°$.   **7.** The two intersecting planes $x + z = 1$ and $x = y$.
9. Parabolic cylinder. The sketch is similar to sketch (g).
11. $(x - 1)^2 + 2(y - 2)^2 + 3z^2 = 6$. This is an equation of an
ellipsoid with center at $(1, 2, 0)$.   **13.** The equation $y^2 + 4x$
$- 4y + 8 = 0$ is equivalent to $(y - 2)^2 = -4(x + 1)$. This is an
equation of a parabolic cylinder.   **15.** The given equation is

585

equivalent to $(x + 1)^2/2 + (y + 1)^2/3 = z + 1$. This is an equation of a paraboloid. **17.** The trace of equation (1) in the xy-plane is found by setting $z = 0$. We get $Ax^2 + By^2 + Dxy + Gx + Hy + J = 0$. This equation has one of the conic sections as its graph if it is not degenerate. In planes parallel to the xy-plane, we simply get new constant terms in the above equation. Similar statements can be made for the other coordinate planes.
Calculator Problem. **(a)** \$1.68 **(b)** \$354,813.44 **(c)** \$517,384.83 **(d)** $\doteq 35$ years **(e)** $\doteq 9$ years **(f)** $\doteq 7$ years **(g)** $\doteq 4$ years

CHAPTER 19

Section 19-2, page 477

1. $(6, -1)$ **3.** $(2, -3)$ **5.** $(5, -3)$ **7.** $x = y$
9. $4x'^2 - 9y'^2 = 25$ **11.** $(h, k) = (3, -2)$; $4x'^2 + y'^2 = 16$.
If we complete squares, we get the equation $4(x - 3)^2 + (y + 2)^2 = 16$. **13.** *Hint:* Use the definition of slope, $m = (y_2 - y_1)/(x_2 - x_1)$, and the transformation equations, $x_1 = x_1' + h, y_1 = y_1' + k, x_2 = x_2' + h, y_2 = y_2' + k$.
Calculator Problem. $(h, k) = (1.85, -3.95)$; $x'^2 + y'^2 = 19.155$

Section 19-3, page 481

1. $\theta = \pi/4, x'^2 - y'^2 = 8$ **3.** $\theta = \text{Arcsin}(3/5)$, $(2y' - x')(2y' + x') = 0$ **5.** $\theta = \text{Arccos}(2/\sqrt{5}), x'^2/1 + y'^2/4 = 1$ **7.** (1) $B^2 - 4AC = 1 - 4(0)(0) = 1$; $B'^2 - 4A'C' = 0 - 4(1/2)(-1/2) = 1$ (2) $B^2 - 4AC = (-4)^2 - 4(3)(0) = 16$; $B'^2 - 4A'C' = 0 - 4(-1)(4) = 16$ (3) $B^2 - 4AC = (-24)^2 - 4(4)(11) = 400$; $B'^2 - 4A'C' = 0 - 4(-5)(20) = 400$ (4) $B^2 - 4AC = (-2)^2 - 4(1)(1) = 0$; $B'^2 - 4A'C' = 0 - 4(0)(2) = 0$ (5) $B^2 - 4AC = (12)^2 - 4(17)(8) = -400$; $B'^2 - 4A'C' = 0 - 4(20)(5) = -400$ (6) $B^2 - 4AC = (10\sqrt{3})^2 - 4(21)(31) = -2304$; $B'^2 - 4A'C' = 0 - 4(36)(16) = -2304$
9. $x' = y \sin \theta + x \cos \theta, y' = y \cos \theta - x \sin \theta$. *Hint:* Using the notation given at the beginning of Section 19-3, observe that $x' = \mathbf{i}' \cdot (x\mathbf{i} + y\mathbf{j}) = x \cos \theta + y \cos (\pi/2 - \theta)$ and $y' = \mathbf{j}' \cdot (x\mathbf{i} + y\mathbf{j}) = x \cos (\pi/2 + \theta) + y \cos \theta$. **11.** $B' = (C - A) \sin 2\theta + B \cos 2\theta$; $A' = A \cos^2\theta + B \sin \theta \cos \theta + C \sin^2\theta$; $C' = A \sin^2\theta - B \sin \theta \cos \theta + C \cos^2\theta$. Find expressions for $A' - C'$ and $A' + C'$ and use the fact that $B'^2 - 4A'C' = B'^2 + (A' - C')^2 - (A' + C')^2$. **13.** No. By Theorem 19-1 such a rotation would imply $B = 0$. **15.** Let $d = \sqrt{(x_1 - x_2)^2 + (y_1 - y_2)^2}$ and $d' = \sqrt{(x_1' - x_2')^2 + (y_1' - y_2')^2}$, (1).
Then, $(x_1 - x_2) = (x_1' - x_2') \cos \theta - (y_1' - y_2') \sin \theta = d'[((x_1' - x_2')/d') \cos \theta - ((y_1' - y_2')/d') \sin \theta] = d' \sin (\beta - \theta)$, (2), where $\sin \beta = (x_1' - x_2')/d'$ and

$\cos \beta = (y_1' - y_2')/d'$. Similarly it can be shown that $(y_1 - y_2) = d' \cos (\beta - \theta)$, (3). Substituting (2) and (3) into (1), it follows that, $d = \sqrt{(d')^2 \sin^2 (\beta - \theta) + (d')^2 \cos^2 (\beta - \theta)} = \sqrt{(d')^2} = d'$.
Calculator Problem. $2x'^2 + \sqrt{2}x' + 5\sqrt{2}y' - 8 = 0$
$(x'' + \sqrt{2}/4)^2 = (-5\sqrt{2}/2)(y'' - 33/(20\sqrt{2}))$

Section 19-4, page 484

1. The same point is represented by $(4, \pi/3)$, $(-4, 4\pi/3)$ and $(-4, -2\pi/3)$. Similarly for $(-4, \pi/3)$ and $(4, -2\pi/3)$. **3.** The same point is represented by $(2, 1), (-2, \pi + 1)$ and $(-2, 1 - \pi)$. Similarly for $(-2, 1)$ and $(2, 1 - \pi)$. **5.** $(3, \pi/3)$ is the same point as $(3, 7\pi/3)$, $(-3, 4\pi/3)$, and $(-3, -2\pi/3)$.
7. $(-1, -\pi/4)$ is the same point as $(1, 3\pi/4)$, $(1, -5\pi/4)$, and $(-1, 7\pi/4)$. **9.** $(-1, \pi/2)$ is the same point as $(1, -\pi/2)$, $(1, 3\pi/2)$, and $(-1, -3\pi/2)$. **11.** A line passing through $(0, 0°)$ and $W(\pi/4)$ **13.** The polar equation of a circle with center at 0 and radius equal to 3 **15.** A line which is inclined $150°$ to the polar axis **17.** A line which has the rectangular equation $x = 1$
Calculator Problem.

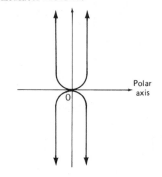

Section 19-5, page 489

1. A circle with center $(3/2, \pi/2)$ and radius $3/2$
3.

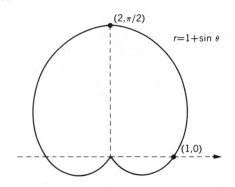

$(2, \pi/2)$

$r = 1 + \sin \theta$

$(1, 0)$

5.

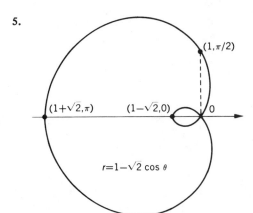

$(1,\pi/2)$

$(1+\sqrt{2},\pi)$ $(1-\sqrt{2},0)$ 0

$r=1-\sqrt{2}\cos\theta$

7. A line parallel to the polar axis and containing the point $(0,\pi/2)$ **9.** A four-leaved rose similar to (1) of the text with $(a,\pi/4)$ a maximum **11.** An eight-leaved rose with $(-a,5\pi/4)$ and $(a,0)$ as maximums **13.** A lemniscate similar to (1) of the text with $(a,\pi/4)$ as a maximum

15.

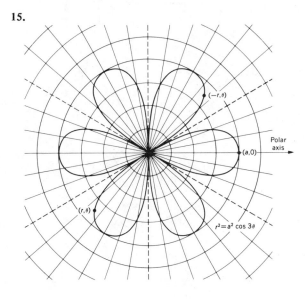

Polar axis

$(a,0)$

$(-r,\theta)$

(r,θ)

$r^2=a^2\cos 3\theta$

17. A circle with center $(0,0°)$ and radius 1 **19. (a)** $\overline{AO}$ and $\overline{AB}$ are radii of the unit circle $r=2\cos\theta$, which has center at A. Therefore, the angles opposite these segments are congruent angles (namely, $\angle AOB \cong \angle OBA$) and both angles have measure of θ. **(b)** $\angle BAD$ is the supplement of $\angle OAB$, and $m(\angle OAB) = \pi - 2\theta$. Therefore $m(\angle BAD) = \alpha + \beta = \pi - (\pi - 2\theta) = 2\theta$. **(c)** O, B, and C are collinear points, and B is between O and C. $|OB| = 2\cos\theta$ and $|OC| = 1 + 2\cos\theta$. $|BC| = |OC| - |OB| = (1 + 2\cos\theta) - (2\cos\theta) = 1$. **(d)** $\overline{BC}$ and $\overline{AB}$ are congruent

segments because both are one unit in length from parts (a) and (c). Therefore, in $\triangle ABC$ we have $\angle BAC \cong \angle BCA$ and both angles have measure β. **(e)** $\angle OBA$ is an exterior angle of $\triangle ABC$ and, by a theorem of plane geometry, $m(\angle OBA) = m(\angle BAC) + m(\angle BCA)$ or $\theta = \beta + \beta = 2\beta$. **(f)** Using the results of parts (b) and (e) above, we have $\alpha + \beta = 2\theta$ and $\theta = 2\beta$, so that $\alpha + \beta = 2(2\beta) = 4\beta$ and $\alpha = 3\beta$. Referring to the figure, we find that $m(\angle BAC) = (1/3)m(\angle CAD)$, so $\angle BAC$ is the desired trisection of $\angle CAD$.
Calculator Problem. $x^2/16 + y^2/9 = 1$

Section 19-6, page 492

1. $(3\sqrt{3}/2, 3/2)$ **3.** $(2\sqrt{2}, -2\sqrt{2})$ **5.** $(\sqrt{3}/2, -3/2)$
7. $(5\sqrt{2}, \pi/4)$ **9.** $(2\sqrt{2}, 5\pi/4)$ **11.** $(1, 53.1°)$ **13.** $r = a$
15. $r = 2/(\cos\theta + \sin\theta)$ **17.** $r^2 = a^2\cos 2\theta$. The graph is a lemniscate. **19.** $x^2 + y^2 = ay$ **21.** $2(x + 1/2)$
23.

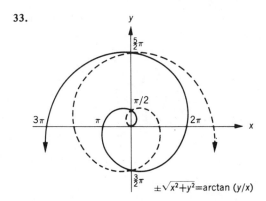

$x^2(x^2+y^2)=y^2$

25. $r^2 = a^2\cos^2 2\theta$. The graph is a four-leaved rose.
27. $r = p/\cos(\theta - \gamma)$. The graph is a line with rectangular intercepts $(p/\cos\gamma, 0)$ and $(0, p/\sin\gamma)$.
29. $r\cos\theta = \tan^2\theta$, $\theta \neq (2k + 1)\pi/2$, k an integer. The graph is a semi-cubical parabola.
31. $(x^2 + y^2)^3 = 4a^2x^2y^2$. The graph is a four-leaved rose.

33.

$\pm\sqrt{x^2+y^2}=\arctan(y/x)$

35. *Hint:* Use the Law of Cosines. **37.** $y + 2x = 4$

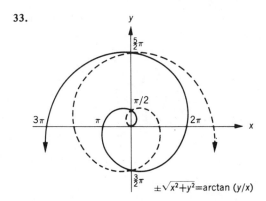

587

Calculator Problem.   (a) $\theta_1 = \pi/2$, $\theta_2 = -\pi/4$;
$d = \sqrt{4^2 + (4\sqrt{2})^2 - 2\cdot 4\cdot 4\sqrt{2}\cos(3\pi/4)} = \sqrt{80}$
(b) $P_1 = (0, 4)$, $P_2 = (4, -4)$; $d = \sqrt{4^2 + 8^2} = \sqrt{80}$

Section 19-7, page 493

1.

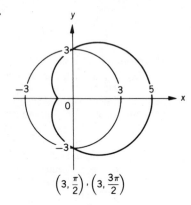

$$\left(3, \frac{\pi}{2}\right)\cdot\left(3, \frac{3\pi}{2}\right)$$

3.

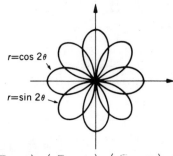

$$(0,0), \left(\frac{1}{2}, \frac{\pi}{6}\right)\cdot\left(\frac{1}{2}, \frac{5\pi}{6}\right)\cdot\left(1, \frac{\pi}{2}\right)$$

5.

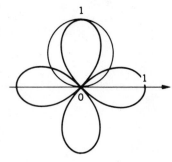

$r = \cos 2\theta$
$r = \sin 2\theta$

$$(0,0), \left(\frac{\sqrt{2}}{2}, \pm\frac{\pi}{8}\right)\cdot\left(\frac{\sqrt{2}}{2}, \pm\frac{3\pi}{8}\right)\cdot\left(\frac{\sqrt{2}}{2}, \pm\frac{5\pi}{8}\right)\cdot\left(\frac{\sqrt{2}}{2}, \pm\frac{7\pi}{8}\right)$$

7.

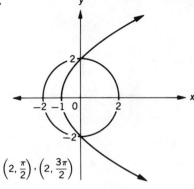

$$\left(2, \frac{\pi}{2}\right)\cdot\left(2, \frac{3\pi}{2}\right)$$

9.

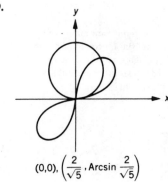

$$(0,0), \left(\frac{2}{\sqrt{5}}, \text{Arcsin}\frac{2}{\sqrt{5}}\right)$$

11.

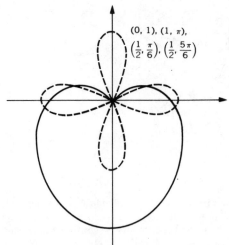

$(0, 1), (1, \pi),$
$\left(\frac{1}{2}, \frac{\pi}{6}\right)\cdot\left(\frac{1}{2}, \frac{5\pi}{6}\right)$

13. $(-1, 0°)$ **15.** For example, $r = \cos\theta/2$. If (r_0, θ_0) satisfies this equation, then $r_0 = \cos\theta_0/2$. But, $\cos(\theta_0 + 2(2k-1)\pi)/2 = -\cos\theta_0/2 = -r_0$, and $|\cos(\theta_0 + (2k-1)\pi)/2| = |\sin\theta_0/2|$.

Calculator Problem.

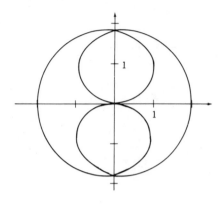

Section 19-8, page 495

1.

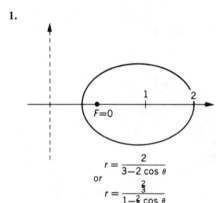

$$r = \frac{2}{3 - 2 \cos \theta}$$

or

$$r = \frac{\frac{2}{3}}{1 - \frac{2}{3} \cos \theta}$$

3.

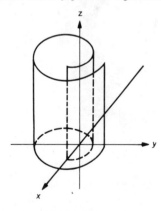

$$r = \frac{4}{1 - 2 \cos \theta}$$

5. $r = pe/(1 + e \cos \theta)$ **7.** If $r = 2p \sec^2 \theta/2$, then $r = 2p/\cos^2 \theta/2 = 2p/(1 + \cos \theta)/2$ or $r = 4p/(1 + \cos \theta)$. Comparing this equation with the standard polar equation for conics, we see that $r = 4p/(1 + \cos \theta)$ is an equation of a parabola ($e = 1$).
9. $r = ep/(1 + e \cos (\theta - \alpha))$
Calculator Problem. $(\pi, 0.4705882)$

Section 19-9, page 498

1. $\theta = \pi/6 \rightarrow x - \sqrt{3} y = 1$. The graph is a plane perpendicular to the xy-plane whose trace in the xy-plane makes an angle of $30°$ with the positive x-axis. **3.** $r = z \rightarrow x^2 + y^2 - z^2 = 0$. The graph is a quadric cone with vertex $(0, 0, 0)$ and circular cross sections parallel to the xy-plane.
5. The graph is a parabolic cylinder.

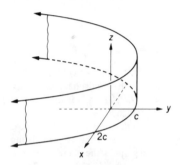

7. $r = 2 \rightarrow x^2 + y^2 = 4$. The graph is a right circular cylinder whose trace in the xy-plane is the circle $x^2 + y^2 = 4$.
9. $r = \sin \theta - \cos \theta \rightarrow (x + 1/2)^2 + (y - 1/2)^2 = 1/2$. The surface is the right circular cylinder of radius $\sqrt{2}/2$ with its axis along the line through $(-1/2, 1/2)$ and perpendicular to the xy-plane.
11. The graph is a cylinder whose cross sections in planes parallel to the xy-plane are logarithmic spirals.

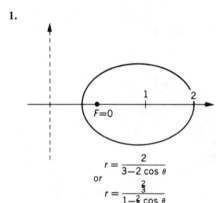

13. $8\theta^2 - 6\pi\theta + \pi^2 = 0$. The graph consists of two planes. One is the yz-plane, containing the z-axis, and the other is a plane perpendicular to the xy-plane whose trace in the xy-plane makes an angle of $45°$ with the positive x-axis.

15. $|P_1P_2| = \sqrt{r_1^2 + r_2^2 - 2r_1r_2 \cos(\theta_1 - \theta_2) + (z_1 - z_2)^2}$.
17. $r = c \sec^2(1/2)\theta = c/\cos^2(1/2)\theta = c/((1 + \cos\theta)/2) = 2c/(1 + \cos\theta)$. This is equivalent to $y^2 = -4c(x - c)$, which is a parabolic cylinder.
Calculator Problem.

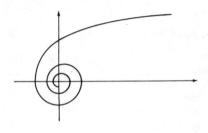

Calculator Problem.

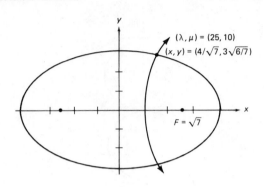

Section 19-10, page 500

1. $(0, 3, 0)$ **3.** $(1/2, 1/2, \sqrt{2}/2)$ **5.** $(-5\sqrt{3}/2, -5/2, 0)$
7. The graph is the lower part of the hemisphere which has center $(0, 0, 0)$ and radius 4. **9.** The graph is the upper portion of the right circular cone which has vertex $(0, 0, 0)$ and circular cross sections parallel to the xy-plane. **11.** The graph is a right circular cylinder whose trace in the xy-plane is the circle $x^2 + y^2 = a^2$. **13.** The graph is the plane $z = a$.
15. $r \cos\theta = a$ **17.** $\theta = \pi/4$ **19.** $(4, -2, \sqrt{5})$ **21.** $d =$
$\sqrt{\rho_1^2 + \rho_2^2 - 2\rho_1\rho_2(\cos\varphi_1 \cos\varphi_2 + \sin\varphi_1 \sin\varphi_2 \cos(\theta_1 - \theta_2))}$
Calculator Problem. 5.4965131; 6.0595259

CHAPTER 20

Section 20-2, page 511

1.

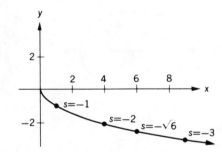

Section 19-11, page 502

1. $(0, 2)$ **3.** $(-1, 2\sqrt{2})$ **5.** $(\sqrt{2} - 1, \sqrt{2} + 1)$
7. $((\sqrt{13} + 3)/2, (\sqrt{13} - 3)/2)$
9.

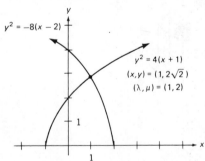

3.

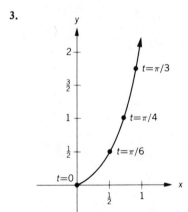

11. Compare the equations of the given families with the standard equation of a parabola. Show that the λ-family of parabolas have vertices at $(-\lambda, 0)$ and that the μ-family of parabolas have vertices at $(\mu, 0)$.

5.

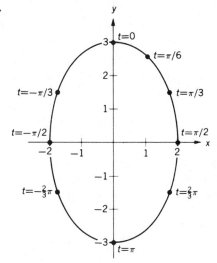

7.

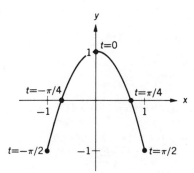

9. The graph is a line segment in the plane $z = 1$.

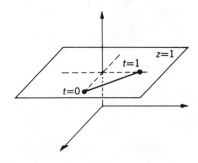

11. The graph is a circle in the plane $z = 1$ with center at $(0, 0, 1)$ and radius 1.

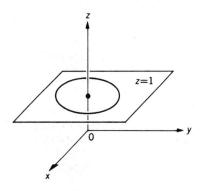

13. The parameter t is proportional to the directed distance from the point $(2, -2, 0)$.

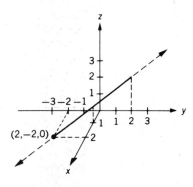

15. *Hint:* Show that for every s in $[c, d]$, there is a unique point (x, y) on the curve.
Calculator Problem. An ellipse with semi-axes $4\sqrt{2}$ and 4 inclined at $\pi/4$ with the xz-plane.

Section 20-3, page 513

1. The graph is a circle with center $(2, 0)$ and radius 1.
3. The graph is the set of points on the ray from $(1, 1)$ passing through $(0, 2)$. **5.** The graph is the ellipse $(x + 1)^2/9 + (y - 1)^2/4 = 1$. **7.** The graph is the parabola $x^2 = y - 1$.
9. For any real number θ, $-1 \leqslant \cos \theta \leqslant 1$ so that x varies between 0 and -1 while y varies between 0 and -2. The graph is a portion of the parabola whose equation in rectangular form is $(y + 1)^2 = (x + 1)$. **11.** $x^2 + y^2 = A^2(\cos^2 t + \sin^2 t) + B^2(\sin^2 t + \cos^2 t) = A^2 + B^2$. This is the rectangular equation of a circle with center at the origin and radius $\sqrt{A^2 + B^2}$. As t increases a point "moves" counterclockwise on the circle.
13. Since $\sin^2 \theta + \cos^2 \theta = 1$, $(x - h)^2/a^2 + (y - k)^2/b^2 = 1$.

15. (a) See Section 18-8, Problem 18. **(b)** From the parametric equations, $x = yt$. Substituting $t = x/y$ in the first equation, we have $x = 3x^2/y^2/(1 + x^3/y^3)$. This equation can be simplified to $x^3 + y^3 - 3xy = 0$. **(c)** $x + y + 1 = 3t^2/(1 + t^3)$ $+ 3t/(1 + t^3) + 1 = (1 + t)^2/(1 - t + t^2)$. Thus when t is near -1, $(1 + t)^2/(1 - t + t^2)$ is near 0, so that $x + y + 1$ is near 0. This means that when t is near -1 the point (x, y) on the curve is very near to the line $x + y + 1 = 0$, so that the line is an asymptote of the curve.
Calculator Problem.
(a)

t	0	0.5	1	1.5	2	2.5	3
x	0	20	40	60	80	100	120
y	0	6.275	10.1	11.475	10.4	6.875	0.9

(b) Yes **(c)** When $y = 0$, $t = 0$, or $t = 15/4.9 = 3.06 \ldots$
(d) $x = 40 \times 3.06 \ldots = 122.44897$ m **(e)** When $t = (1/2)(15/4.9)$, $y = 11.47959$. **(f)** When $x = 100$, $y = 6.87$. The ball cleared the wall by 3.875 m.

Section 20-4, page 517

1. $x = (1/2)t$, $y = 4 - t$ **3.** $x = 10^t$, $y = 2/t$
5. $x = (1/3) \cos t$, $y = \sin t$ **7.** $x = t$, $y = f(t)$
9. $x = -2 + 4 \sin t$, $y = 3 + 2 \cos t$ **11.** $x = 1 + 2 \cos t$
13. $y = 2t/(1 + t^2)$ **15.** $x = -b/2m$, $y = -b/2$, $m \neq 0$
17. *Hint:* Let $m = p/q$, where p and q are relatively prime integers, and $p < q$. Use the parametric equations to show that $x = (q^2 - p^2)/(q^2 + p^2)$ and $y = (2pq)/(q^2 + p^2)$. But (x, y) is a point on the unit circle with center at the origin, so $x^2 + y^2 = 1$. This implies that $(q^2 - p^2)$, $2pq$, and $(q^2 + p^2)$ are Pythagorean triples. **19.** Divide the interval $[0, 1]$ into thirds and map successive thirds into C as follows. If $0 \leqslant t \leqslant 1/3$, $x = 1 - 3t$, $y = 0$. If $1/3 \leqslant t \leqslant 2/3$, $x = 3t - 1$, $y = 3t - 1$. If $2/3 \leqslant t \leqslant 1$, $x = 3 - 3t$, $y = 1$. **21.** $x = a \cot \theta$ and $y = a \sin^2 \theta$. A rectangular equation of the set of all points P is $y = a^3/(a^2 + x^2)$.
23. $x = a(\arccos(1 - y/a)) - \sqrt{y(2a - y)}$ **25.** $m(\overset{\frown}{AP}) = b\theta$ $= a$, $a = 4b$ so that $\theta = 4\varphi$ or $\varphi = (1/4)\theta$. $m(\angle PCB) = (3\varphi - \pi/2)$. Then $\overrightarrow{OP} = \overrightarrow{OC} + \overrightarrow{CP}$, $\overrightarrow{CP} = \overrightarrow{CB} + \overrightarrow{BP}$, $\overrightarrow{OC} = (3b \cos \varphi)\mathbf{i} + (3b \sin \varphi)\mathbf{j}$, $\overrightarrow{CB} = (b \cos 3\varphi)\mathbf{i} + (-b \sin 3\varphi)\mathbf{j}$. From the trigonometric identities we have $\cos 3\varphi = 4 \cos^3 \varphi - 3 \cos \varphi$ and $\sin 3\varphi = 3 \sin \varphi - 4 \sin^3 \varphi$. So $\overrightarrow{OP} = (4b \cos^3 \varphi)\mathbf{i} + (4b \sin^3 \varphi)\mathbf{j}$ and, since $a = 4b$, $\overrightarrow{OP} = (a \cos^3 \varphi)\mathbf{i} + (a \sin^3 \varphi)\mathbf{j}$. If the components of $\overrightarrow{OP}$ are x and y, then $x = a \cos^3 \varphi$ and $y = a \sin^3 \varphi$. **27.** The tracing point P of the prolate cycloid is at

$(0, a - b)$ when $\theta = 0$. By addition of vectors, $\overrightarrow{OP} = \overrightarrow{OA} + \overrightarrow{AC} + \overrightarrow{CP}$, $\overrightarrow{OA} = a\theta\mathbf{i}$, $\overrightarrow{AC} = a\mathbf{j}$, $\overrightarrow{CP} = (-b \sin \theta)\mathbf{i} + (-b \cos \theta)\mathbf{j}$. Therefore, $\overrightarrow{OP} = (a\theta - b \sin \theta)\mathbf{i} + (a - b \cos \theta)\mathbf{j}$. If x and y are the components of $\overrightarrow{OP}$, then $x = a\theta - b \sin \theta$ and $y = a - b \cos \theta$.
29. From the definition of the epicycloids, $a\varphi = b\theta$ so that $\theta = a\varphi/b$. If $P = P(x, y)$ is the tracing point of the epicycloid, then, $\overrightarrow{OP} = \overrightarrow{OC} + \overrightarrow{CP}$. $\overrightarrow{OC} = ((a + b) \cos \varphi)\mathbf{i} + ((a + b) \sin \varphi)\mathbf{j}$. From the figure $m(\angle BCP) = ((a + b)/b)\varphi - \pi/2$. Therefore, $\overrightarrow{CP} = [-b \cos (a + b)\varphi/b]\mathbf{i} + [-b \sin (a + b)\varphi/b]\mathbf{j}$. $\overrightarrow{OC} + \overrightarrow{CP} = \overrightarrow{OP} = [(a + b) \cos \varphi - b \cos (a + b)\varphi/b]\mathbf{i} + [(a + b) \sin \varphi - b \sin (a + b)\varphi/b]\mathbf{j}$. If x and y are the components of $\overrightarrow{OP}$, then $x = (a + b) \cos \varphi - b \cos (a + b)\varphi/b$ and $y = (a + b) \sin \varphi - b \sin (a + b)\varphi/b$.
31.

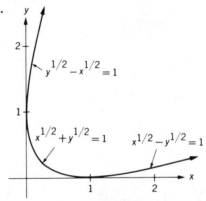

33. Parametric equations: $x = b \tan \theta + a \sin \theta$, $y = a \cos \theta$. Rectangular equation: $x^2y^2 = (a^2 - y^2)(b + y)^2$.
Calculator Problem. The graph is the square $ABCD$ with $A = (-1, 0)$, $B = (0, 1)$, $C = (1, 0)$, $D = (0, -1)$.

Section 20-5, page 522

1. $x - 3y + z = 6$ **3.** The equations are equivalent to $x - 2 = 4 \sin \varphi \cos \theta$, $y - 3 = 4 \sin \varphi \cos \theta$, $z - 4 = 4 \cos \varphi$. So (see Example 3) these are equations of a sphere with radius 4 and center $(2, 3, 4)$. **5.** $x = a \cos u$, $y = a \sin u$, and $z = v$. The region R is the set of points in the uv-plane such that $0 \leqslant u \leqslant 2\pi$ and $-\infty < v < \infty$. **7.** $z = \rho$, $x = \rho \cos \theta$ and $y = \rho \sin \theta$. Then $x^2 + y^2 = \rho^2 \cos^2 \theta + \rho^2 \sin^2 \theta = \rho^2 = z^2$. **9.** If all functions are constant, the surface degenerates to a point. If two of the functions are constant, the surface becomes part of a straight line. If only one function is constant, the surface simply lies in a plane.
Calculator Problem. 5607 when inverted is LOGS

APPENDIX

Section A-1, page 527

1. $10^{-1} \cdot 2$; characteristic is -1 3. $10^2 \cdot 2$; 2
5. $10^{-17} \cdot 1$; -17 7. $10^2 \cdot 1.57$; 2,   9. $10^{-1} \cdot 1.005$; -1
11. $10^0 \cdot 6.91$; 0   13. 2.0212   15. $7.9410 - 10$
17. 1.6599   19. $3.8451 - 10$ 21. 4.8370
23. $6.3118 - 10$ 25. 0.883   27. 0.00447   29. 166
31. 0.00000000498   33. 0.00381   35. 0.000000956
37. 6.3856   39. $7.9090 - 10$ 41. $6.0531 - 10$

Section A-2, page 529

1. 2.6834   3. $7.9406 - 10$ 5. 4.7721   7. 5.1316
9. 3.3017   11. $9.9944 - 10$ 13. $9.7808 - 10$
15. 0.1000   17. 0.5452   19. 6.838   21. 2863
23. 787.8   25. $10^4(9.535)$ 27. $10^{-1}(6.338)$ 29. 8.922
31. 936   33. 20.1   35. 29.5   37. 7728   39. 122,400
41. 0.0603   43. 12.6   45. 4691   47. 1347
49. 147,600   51. 0.5057   53. 0.8953   55. 0.8029
57. -7.044 59. -0.5348 61. -1.1716 63. $51.05°$
65. $47.73°$ 67. $7.15°$ 69. $2.29°$ 71. $5.16°$
73. $55.18°$